The Apostolate's Family Catechism™

Volume 1, Questions 1–189

Apostolate for Family Consecration®

Fourth Edition, Revised and Expanded

Contributors and Editors:
Rev. Burns K. Seeley, Ph.D.
Dr. Regis Martin, S.T.D., Professor of Theology, Franciscan University of Steubenville
Rev. Bernard Geiger, O.F.M. Conv.
Hugh Owen

Theological Illustrations by Charles Jaskiewicz and Timothy Boudreaux.

The Apostolate's Family Catechism™

by Rev. Lawrence G. Lovasik, S.V.D.

Initiated and structured by Jerome and Gwen Coniker

Volume 1
Questions 1–189

Also available in Spanish, Chinese and Filipino.

For an explanation of the Holy Family of Fatima image on the front cover, please see pages 778-779 in Volume 2.

The Ad Hoc Committee to Oversee the Use of the Catechism, United States Conference of Catholic Bishops, has found *The Apostolate's Family Catechism*, copyright 2008, to be in conformity with the *Catechism of the Catholic Church*.

Third and Fourth Editions:

Nihil Obstat: Reverend James M. Dunfee
Censor Liborum
September 14, 2000

Imprimatur: Gilbert I. Sheldon
Bishop of Steubenville
June 15, 2001

Second Edition:
Nihil Obstat: Msgr. Jose C. Abriol, P.A..
Vicar General, Archdiocese of Manila
Imprimatur: Jaime L. Cardinal Sin
Archbishop of Manila, June 30, 1994

First Edition:
Nihil Obstat: Reverend John A. Hardon, S.J.
Censor Deputatus
Imprimatur: Rev. Msgr. John F. Donoghue
Vicar General, Archdiocese of
Washington, D.C., October 1, 1974

APOSTOLATE FOR FAMILY CONSECRATION®
Catholic Familyland® & Familyland® Television Network
3375 County Road 36
Bloomingdale, Ohio 43910-7903 U.S.A.
(740) 765-5500 1-800-77-FAMILY FAX: (740) 765-5561
www.familyland.org usa@familyland.org

In Asia:
St. Joseph Center for Asia
BF Vista Grande, P.O. Box 0026
Las Piñas City, PHILIPPINES
Tel: (632) 871-4440 or 871-4439
FAX: (632) 875-3506 asia@familyland.org

Other International Centers:
latinoamerica@familyland.org
europe@familyland.org
africa@familyland.org
russia@familyland.org

Published 1993. Fourth Edition 2008. Printed in the United States of America.
Scripture quotations are taken from the Revised Standard Version of the Bible, © 1946, 1952, 1971 by the Division of Christian Education of the National Council of the Churches of Christ in the USA. Used by permission. Excerpts of the Second Vatican Council Documents from *Vatican Council II*, edited by Rev. Austin Flannery, O.P., are used with the permission of Costello Publishing Co., Northport, NY. Excerpts from the Catechism of the Catholic Church, second edition, copyright © 2000, Libreria Editrice Vaticana-United States Conference of Catholic Bishops, Washington, D.C. Used with permission. All rights reserved. Basic Prayers and Teachings in Appendix C taken from the "Preparation for Total Consecration" book, Imprimatur by Archbishop Gaudencio Rosales © 2006, and the "Consecration in Truth" catechetical series, Imprimatur by Bishop Gilbert Sheldon, © 2001.

The prayers found throughout the catechism are, in part, composed by the author and, in part, based upon prayers found in the Church's liturgy and in manuals of prayer.

ISBN: 9780932406705
Library of Congress Control Number: 2007934557

Contents

Section 1: God, the Holy Trinity, Creation, and the Fall

Part 2: The Revelation of God: The Holy Trinity

Part 3: Creation: Material and Spiritual

Part 4: The Creation of Man

Section 2: Jesus Christ, Son of God, Savior

Part 1: The Incarnation

Part 2: Jesus Is True Man and Our Redeemer

Section 3: The Holy Spirit

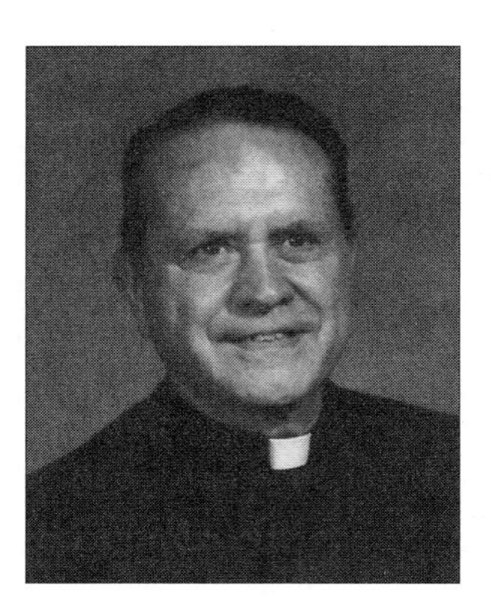

About the Author

Father Lawrence Lovasik, S.V.D., a Divine Word Missionary, was born on June 22, 1913, and ordained a priest on August 14, 1938. For over forty years he preached at parish missions and conducted retreats throughout the world.

Fr. Lovasik has written more than thirty books and over 100 articles; these include catechisms, Bible stories for children, lives of the saints, prayer books, and homilies for priests. His works have passed the test of time, since he had a rare gift of being able to write for children and adults alike.

In 1954, Fr. Lovasik founded the Congregation of the Sisters of the Divine Spirit, and in 1967, he founded the Family Service Corps, a secular institute devoted to charitable work for the needy, the sick and the elderly.

Father was a close friend of the Apostolate for Family Consecration, serving on its Advisory Council and writing several books for it, the largest being this seven-section family catechism.

A dedicated priest, he had an immense love for the Holy Eucharist, often spending hours at a time in Its Presence. Providentially, he died as he lived, in the Eucharistic Presence of our Lord on June 9, 1986.

May his catechetical teachings penetrate deeply into this Third Millennium and prepare the People of God for the Second Coming. *"Christ has died, Christ has risen, Christ will come again!"*

Preface

There is no better way of absorbing the truths of our Catholic Faith and living them than through prayerful study. The use of this handbook of catechetical meditations will strengthen your faith by encouraging you to make at least a brief meditation consisting of instruction and prayer.

The instruction will provide you with basic information on the teaching of the Catholic Church, while the prayers, centered on the doctrine explained, will be the best means of obtaining God's grace not only to understand your Faith, but also to practice and share it. Faithfulness to the practice of daily meditation will surely have a lasting impact on your spiritual life.

The catechetical material is according to the "Basic Teachings for Catholic Education" contained in the National Catechetical Directory for Catholics of the United States approved by the Sacred Congregation for the Clergy, Vatican II documents and Sacred Scripture. The sixteen documents of Vatican II constitute the most remarkable message that God has sent, through His Church, to modern man. Echoing the preaching of the Prophets, the Apostles, the Fathers and Doctors of the East and West, the Council has proclaimed to the whole world the faith of the entire Church. It is the solemn proclamation of the Gospel, which is handed down in history as God's supreme command. Pope Paul VI wrote: "We must give thanks to God and have confidence in the future of the Church when we think of the Council: it will be the great catechism of our times."

Passages from the sixteen documents of Vatican II have been chosen to explain the meaning of revealed truths taught by the Church. It is very important that the thought of the Council be consulted on the essential question which man asks of the Church of Christ today. [Editor's note: All of the questions are also cross-referenced with the *Catechism of the Catholic Church* and many papal documents.]

Prayer is a very important part of this catechism because it is a means by which we communicate with God. It is also a means of grace, as God is the source of all grace. Without prayer, it is impossible to lead a Christian life. Jesus said, "Without me you can do nothing" (John 15:5). The prayers used in this catechism have their source in the Liturgy of the Church. By using them devoutly, we can obtain the actual grace we need to make the use of this catechism fruitful: we shall receive the light we need to understand God's truth, and the strength to keep His commandments and lead a holy life.

I entrust this work to the loving care of the Blessed Virgin Mary, the Mother of God and the Mother of the Church.

Father Lawrence Lovasik, S.V.D.
Divine Word Missionary

Acknowledgments

The publisher is deeply grateful to Fr. Lawrence Lovasik for his timeless work in writing this catechism and to all who have given their generous assistance in making *The Apostolate's Family Catechism* a reality. We thank Fr. Burns K. Seeley, Ph.D., for his countless hours of gathering cross-references with the *Catechism of the Catholic Church*, papal documents, and other catechetical and theological books, for helping to theologically edit the first edition, and for writing the "Thought Provokers", which can be used by parents and teachers. Montserrat Friedrich's part was indispensable in developing not only this English edition but also in working with Fr. Charles Ferrer for the translation into the Spanish edition. We especially thank her for the countless hours spent prayerfully designing and working with the artist to create the hundreds of theological illustrations. The additional theological editing and writing by Dr. Regis Martin and Fr. Bernard Geiger, OFM Conv., Fr. Kevin Barrett, and the conformity review by the United States Conference of Catholic Bishops were also indispensable in developing this catechism for use in schools and parishes. We also thank Bishop R. Daniel Conlon and the diocese of Steubenville for reviewing the text for his *Imprimatur*. A very special thanks to Charles Jaskiewicz who poured into this work for families, not only his great talent, but also his heart and soul, as he drew the over 700 beautiful theological illustrations that truly inspire meditation on the truths of our Faith and touch the hearts of all ages, and to Timothy Boudreaux, of the Apostolate's Catholic Corps, for the charcoal renderings of some of the catechetical diagrams that Fr. Lovasik designed. The "Doctrine, Moral, Worship Exercises" developed by Hugh Owen and Lettie Taberdo are very helpful in putting into practice and applying the basic truths of our Faith to our everyday lives. We also thank the staff and Catholic Corps of the Apostolate for Family Consecration who perseveringly labored to edit, format, proof and prepare this edition of the catechism for printing, including: Mary Sue, Jomelia Brondial, Renee Scheu, Roseanna Tamayo, Adrianna Sarlo, Diane Boston, Carolyn Stegmann, Maggie Zbiegien, Zennel Sy, Julie Margo and Christie Kolar. We wish to express a deep appreciation to all those who reviewed and endorsed the catechism for use in homes, schools and parishes, including: Mario Luigi Cardinal Ciappi, Edouard Cardinal Gagnon, William Cardinal Baum, Silvio Cardinal Oddi, Alfonso Cardinal Lopez Trujillo, Anthony Cardinal Bevilacqua, Jaime Cardinal Sin, Archbishop John J. Myers, Archbishop Timothy M. Dolan, and Blessed Teresa of Calcutta. And in particular, we would like to thank Roman Curia Cardinal Francis Arinze for his powerful teachings on this Family Catechism on CD and DVD, and for his numerous teachings on Scripture, Vatican Council II documents, and papal documents, which are cross-referenced with this Catechism and are available online at www.familyland.org.

Introduction

by Jerome F. Coniker

Jerry Coniker and his late wife Gwen are the founders of the Apostolate for Family Consecration, an international association of Christ's faithful dedicated to consecrating families, parishes and movements in the truths of the Catholic faith through the modern means of communications, in the spirit of Pope John Paul II.

This Catechism has been a labor of love. As parents of 13 children (one with the Lord) and 65 grandchildren, Gwen and I were often faced with the dilemma of how to teach our children the Faith in an organized way in our fast moving society. The greatest problem was finding a catechism that would suit the whole family—most catechisms are written only for particular age brackets or adults.

We asked Fr. Lawrence Lovasik, S.V.D., to write a catechism that every family and school could use. It needed to be simple enough for children to understand, yet with a spiritual depth to challenge parents and teachers. Fr. Lovasik was one of those rare authors who could write for all ages. His works include best selling Bible stories and stories of saints for children, prayer books for adults and homilies for priests.

This Catechism is not intended to be used as a rote type of formation program where one just memorizes the answer and then goes on; but a catechism with which one learns the Faith and is inspired to live and share it with zeal and joy.

Pope John Paul II's theologian, Cardinal Mario Luigi Ciappi, reminded us what Our Blessed Mother taught at Fatima, Portugal, that consecration would save the world and bring an "era of peace." Our Lord describes consecration in John 17:17, "Consecrate them in truth. Your word is Truth." By being introduced to the *Catechism of the Catholic Church* through *The Apostolate's Family Catechism*, families, students and teachers will be immersed in the truth which will make them free (cf. Jn 8:32). They will then be able to help bring about the civilization of love that Pope John Paul II worked so hard to bring about. In fact this catechism was endorsed by Cardinal Joseph Ratzinger (now Pope Benedict XVI) while he was Prefect of the Sacred Congregation for the Doctrine of the Faith.

The Apostolate's Family Catechism is a living catechism because additional cross-references (called the "Family Wisdom Library") are continually being added as new papal documents and dependable resources are issued. This enables families, teachers and students to be brought up-to-date with the latest teachings of the Church on particular issues. For references added after this publication, please see our website at familyland.org.

I recommend that parents use the catechetical summary prayers in the Catechism at meal times to call down the Holy Spirit on their family as they discuss specific catechetical references that their children are studying.

I pray your use of *The Apostolate's Family Catechism* and accompanying resources, especially Cardinal Francis Arinze's teachings on each question in the catechism on video and audio (available free online at familyland.org), will truly bring about the unity of the truth that Our Lord talks about in John 17: "...protect them from the evil one...Consecrate them in Truth."

Jerry Coniker

Features of
The Apostolate's Family Catechism™

1. Question-and-Answer format

- Explains the truths of the Faith, covering the Creed, Ten Commandments, Sacraments and Prayer
- Simple yet profound
- Complete and faithful presentation of doctrine
- Makes it easy to find the answers to common questions about the Faith

Q. 70. What is temptation?

Temptation is an invitation to sin that comes from either within us or from outside us.

Temptations are not sins. Sin occurs only when we consent to a temptation. With God's help we can resist them.

2. Quotes from Scripture and Vatican II documents
after each Question and Answer

- *Scripture quotations* enable families to understand and defend their Faith
- *Vatican II quotations* bring Tradition alive and present extensive Scriptural references

Q. 250. What is Holy Communion?

Sacred Scripture

For my flesh is food indeed, and my blood is drink indeed. He who eats my flesh and drinks my blood abides in me, and I in him. *John 6:55–56*

Vatican Council II

Really sharing in the body of the Lord in the breaking of the eucharistic bread, we are taken up into communion with him and with one another. "Because the bread is one, we, though many, are one body, all of us who partake of the one bread" (1 Cor. 10:17). In this way all of us are made members of his body (cf. 1 Cor. 12:27), "but severally members one of another" (Romans 12:4). *Lumen Gentium,7*

3. Quotes from the *Catechism of the Catholic Church* and Papal Documents *after each Question and Answer*

- Substantial quotations from the *Catechism of the Catholic Church* lead families deeper into the ocean of Truth and shows them the richness of our Faith
- Supports the answers on each aspect of the Faith
- Deepens understanding of Church teachings and helps answer issues and questions of our time
- Connects Church teachings with Scripture and Tradition, the basis of our Faith
- Keeps you in the heart of the Church through its cross references with current papal documents

Catechism of the Catholic Church

1359 The Eucharist, the sacrament of our salvation accomplished by Christ on the cross, is also a sacrifice of praise in thanksgiving for the work of creation. In the Eucharistic sacrifice the whole of creation loved by God is presented to the Father through the death and the Resurrection of Christ. Through Christ the Church can offer the sacrifice of praise in thanksgiving for all that God has made good, beautiful, and just in creation and in humanity.

4. Theological Illustrations

- Provides visual representation of doctrines
- Makes the Faith come alive for all ages
- Inspires meditation and vibrant discussion

5. Doctrine–Moral–Worship Exercises

within each Chapter, with answers in Appendix A

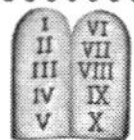

Doctrine • Moral • Worship Exercise

(See Appendix A for answer key, questions 57-58.)

1. Why do we say that to sin is a personal decision to say "no" to God?
2. Recall the last instance in which you chose to do your will rather than God's will. How did this affect you?
3. In what concrete ways can you cooperate with the will of God?

- Reviews key doctrines
- Helps apply doctrines to our daily lives
- Facilitates meaningful participation in personal and public worship
- Inspires an ongoing and lifelong faith journey
- Inspires lively discussions

6. Prayers *within each Chapter*

Summary Prayer (Question 58)

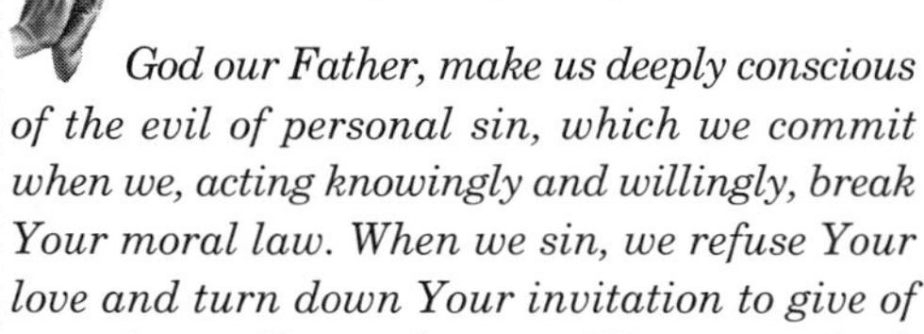

God our Father, make us deeply conscious of the evil of personal sin, which we commit when we, acting knowingly and willingly, break Your moral law. When we sin, we refuse Your love and turn down Your invitation to give of ourselves to You and to our fellow men. Such personal acts of selfishness cause harm to us and to others. For these, we beg Your forgiveness and help, through Jesus Christ our Lord. Amen.

- Summarizes and transforms key doctrines into prayer and inspires discussions in school and at meals.
- Brings doctrine from the mind to the heart
- Helps develop and deepen our personal relationship with the Holy Trinity

7. Thought Provokers *at the end of each Chapter, with answers in Appendix B*

- Facilitates further discussion on various aspects of the Faith
- Expounds Church teachings in an interesting way

Thought Provokers

Please see Appendix B for the answers.

Q. 94: Jesus suffered with extreme intensity on the Cross, but did He experience it in His divine nature?

Q. 95: Quoting Psalm 22, Jesus cried out from the Cross, "My God, my God, why hast thou forsaken me?" Doesn't this suggest that Jesus believed He has been abandoned by His Father?

8. By Heart Catechism and Scripture Review™ *at the end of each Part*

By Heart Catechism and Scripture Review™

Q. 59. What is mortal sin? Mortal sin is choosing to disobey God in a serious matter. Mortal sin destroys God's life in our soul.

SR 59 Romans 6:23

For the wages of sin is death, but the free gift of God is eternal life in Christ Jesus our Lord.

- Provides shortened Questions-and-Answers and Scripture references for key doctrine
- Facilitates easy memorization of the basics of the Faith
- Helps one defend the Faith from a Scriptural standpoint and draws people back into the Church

9. *Internet-based* Family Wisdom Library™ *at the end of each Section*

- Provides additional cross-references with Church documents and other resources, including the *Compendium of the Catechism of the Catholic Church*, the *United States Catholic Catechism for Adults, God is Love, Sacrament of Charity* and many other documents
- Opens the window to the vast resources of Church teachings
- Makes this Family Catechism a living catechism in harmony with the latest hierarchical teachings of the Church as new papal documents are cross-referenced online
- Integrates the Family Apostolate's vast *video library* that features over 500 prominent teachers on more than 15,000 video programs, including 1900 programs of Francis Cardinal Arinze's captivating teachings

Family Wisdom Library™

Papal documents listed below can be viewed at www.vatican.va.
For new cross-references, visit www.familyland.org.

Q. 73. What does the Incarnation mean?

Church Documents

Compendium of the Catechism of the Catholic Church, sect. 86
Gaudium et Spes (Pastoral Constitution on the Church in the Modern World), Vatican II, sect. 22, 58, 78
God is Love, Benedict XVI, sect. 41-42
Mother of the Redeemer, John Paul II, sect. 1, 9
On the Dignity and Vocation of Women, John Paul II, sect. 3-4
On the Holy Spirit in the Life of the Church and the World, John Paul II, sect. 49-50
The Relationship Between Faith and Reason, John Paul II, sect. 80, 93
Sacrament of Charity, Benedict XVI, sect. 7-8
U. S. Catholic Catechism for Adults, [2006] pp. 83, 86-87

Recommended Uses of *The Apostolate's Family Catechism*™

Family catechesis precedes, accompanies and enriches all other forms of catechesis.
(Catechesi Tradendae, Pope John Paul II, 68)

- **At Home**. It is important that parents set aside time regularly to teach their children the Faith. Families may read aloud and discuss each question-and-answer in the Family Catechism, during dinner or at any convenient time during the day or the week. They may read the questions sequentially, or select certain questions that are of special interest or that pertain to the particular liturgical season

  Parents can make use of the theological illustrations to help explain each question and answer to their children, especially the young ones. Some of the quotes from Scripture, Vatican II, or the *Catechism of the Catholic Church* may also be read aloud by the family in order to deepen their understanding of the topic. To help relate the teachings to their daily life, parents can use the "Doctrine–Moral–Worship Exercises" with their children.

  Family Catechesis Discussion Guides are available for a systematic 3-year study of *The Apostolate's Family Catechism*. The Discussion Guides also recommend particular segments from the Family Catechism Commentaries that feature Francis Cardinal Arinze. Each year, the family studies more deeply the Creed, the Sacraments, Prayer and the Ten Commandments. The Discussion Guides and commentaries are available for free at www.familyland.org.

  At the end of the learning and sharing time, it is recommended that the family pray together using the prayers within the particular questions that were read, in order to assimilate the teaching from the mind to the heart and to develop their communication with God. For further learning, the family can utilize the "Thought Provokers" and "Family Wisdom Library," which provide additional teachings and cross-references.

  Through The Apostolate's Family Catechism, *parents will find it easier to fulfill their role as the primary educators of the faith to their children.*

- **In School, Parish and/or Home School Religious Education.**
  The Apostolate's Family Catechism is the main textbook in the *Consecration in Truth* Multimedia Catechetical Series for Levels 1-12. Teaching Guides and Student Workbooks for each grade level present and elaborate on the concepts found in *The Apostolate's Family Catechism* in a systematic and age-appropriate way. Students cover the four pillars of the *Catechism of the Catholic Church* (the Creed, Ten Commandments, Sacraments and Prayer) in a deeper and varied way each year. (See pages 744-746 in Volume 2 for more information).

The *Consecration in Truth* Catechetical Series has a unique approach that gets the parents involved in the religious education of their children, in order to truly unite the family with the school and parish.

- **RCIA and Continuous Adult Formation.** *The Apostolate's Family Catechism* can be used to help teach the faith to adults who are about to enter the Catholic Church. It provides a simple yet comprehensive and systematic way of learning the faith. The Family Catechism can also be used by other adults who desire to learn more about their faith. They may use the Family Catechism as their main material for discussion and sharing in their formation meetings.

  The simplicity of the Family Catechism makes it easy to use by the average lay person. References to Sacred Scripture, Vatican II documents, the *Catechism of the Catholic Church*, and other papal and Church documents and resources provide opportunities for lay people to go deeper into each aspect of the faith without having to spend a lot of research time. The "Doctrine–Moral–Worship Exercises" and "Thought Provokers" also provide a springboard for further discussion on the teachings and on how to practically apply these teachings to life.

  The Family Catechesis 3-year Discussion Guides used by families can also be used for RCIA or adult formation. For those in RCIA, the first year provides the foundational knowledge of the faith while the succeeding two years serve to reinforce and expand the understanding of the faith. The Discussion Guides are available at www.familyland.org for free.

- **Evangelization Resource.** The *Apostolate's Family Catechism* may be used as an evangelization tool in the parish, as well as the accompanying commentaries by expert and solid teachers (on DVD and CD). These resources help the laity to fulfill their basic duty of sharing the truths of the Faith with others and make it easy for the average lay person to carry out their task of evangelization. (See pages 753-755 in Volume 2 for more information).

The Apostolate's Family Catechism Commentaries on audio and video feature Francis Cardinal Arinze and Sr. John Vianney in English for children, Fr. Pablo Straub, C.Ss.R, in Spanish, and Bishop Ramon Arguelles and Bishop Socrates Villegas in Filipino. These commentaries are strongly recommended to aid and complement the use of *The Apostolate's Family Catechism* in all of the above settings. The Family Catechism Commentaries cover the questions and answers in *The Apostolate's Family Catechism*. They provide clear and concise explanations to help parents, teachers, students, catechists and other laity. **These commentaries can be downloaded for free at www.familyland.org (see page iv). They are also available on DVD and CD.**

Abbreviations for the Vatican Council II documents referenced

Bishops	Decree on the Pastoral Office of Bishops in the Church
Christian Education	Declaration on Christian Education
Dei Verbum	Dogmatic Constitution on Divine Revelation
Eastern Churches	Decree on the Catholic Eastern Churches
Ecumenism	Decree on Ecumenism
Gaudium et Spes	Pastoral Constitution on the Church in the Modern World
Lay People	Decree on the Apostolate of Lay People
Lumen Gentium	Dogmatic Constitution on the Church
Liberty	Declaration on Religious Liberty
Missionary Activity	Decree on the Church's Missionary Activity
Non-Christian Religions	Declaration on the Relation of the Church to Non-Christian Religions
Priests	Decree on the Ministry and Life of Priests
Religious Life	Decree on the Up-to-date Renewal of Religious Life
Sacrosanctum Concilium	The Constitution on the Sacred Liturgy
Social Communications	Decree on the Means of Social Communication

Abbreviations for the Old Testament

Gen	Genesis
Ex	Exodus
Lev	Leviticus
Num	Numbers
Deut	Deuteronomy
Josh	Joshua
Judg	Judges
Ruth	Ruth
1 Sam	1 Samuel
2 Sam	2 Samuel
1 Kings	1 Kings
2 Kings	2 Kings
1 Chron	1 Chronicles
2 Chron	2 Chronicles
Ezra	Ezra
Neh	Nehemiah
Tob	Tobit
Jud	Judith
Esther	Esther
Job	Job
Ps	Psalms
Prov	Proverbs
Eccles	Ecclesiastes
Song	Song of Solomon
Wis	Wisdom
Sir	Sirach (Ecclesiasticus)
Is	Isaiah
Jer	Jeremiah
Lam	Lamentations
Bar	Baruch
Ezek	Ezekiel
Dan	Daniel
Hos	Hosea
Joel	Joel
Amos	Amos
Obad	Obadiah
Jon	Jonah
Mic	Micah
Nahum	Nahum
Hab	Habakkuk
Zeph	Zephaniah
Hag	Haggai
Zech	Zechariah
Mal	Malachi
1 Mac	1 Maccabees
2 Mac	2 Maccabees

Abbreviations for the New Testament

Mt	Matthew
Mk	Mark
Lk	Luke
Jn	John
Acts	Acts of the Apostles
Rom	Romans
1 Cor	1 Corinthians
2 Cor	2 Corinthians
Gal	Galatians
Eph	Ephesians
Phil	Philippians
Col	Colossians
1 Thess	1 Thessalonians
2 Thess	2 Thessalonians
1 Tim	1 Timothy
2 Tim	2 Timothy
Tit	Titus
Philem	Philemon
Heb	Hebrews
Jas	James
1 Pet	1 Peter
2 Pet	2 Peter
1 Jn	1 John
2 Jn	2 John
3 Jn	3 John
Jude	Jude
Rev	Revelation (Apocalypse)

#J2-363

Endorsements

Letter by Pope John Paul II, read by his ambassador to the United States, Archbishop Agostino Cacciavillan, at the Apostolate for Family Consecration's first annual Totus Tuus Consecrate Them in Truth Family Conference.

I have learned with pleasure that on October 22–24, the Apostolate for Family Consecration will sponsor a Conference...on the theme "Consecrate Them in Truth." I would ask you kindly to convey to all associated with this worthy initiative my greetings and the assurance of my closeness in prayer.

Since the Conference aims to support and implement the message of the recent World Youth Day, I renew the invitation which I made in Denver: "I ask you to have the courage to commit yourselves to the truth. Have the courage to believe the Good News about Life which Jesus teaches in the Gospel. Open your minds and hearts to the beauty of all that God has made and to his special, personal love for each of you" (Vigil, Aug. 14, 1993, No. 4).

It is my hope that the Conference will inspire many Christian families to become ever more authentic "domestic Churches," in which the word of God is received with joy, bears fruit in lives of holiness and love, and shines forth with new brilliance as a beacon of hope for all to see. The faith-filled witness of Christian families is an essential element in the new evangelization to which the Holy Spirit is calling the Church in our time.

I am pleased that the Conference will seek to develop effective means of passing on to families and parishes the rich deposit of the Church's faith as presented in the *Catechism of the Catholic Church.* **Because "family catechesis precedes, accompanies and enriches all other forms of catechesis" (*Catechesi Tradendae*, 68), I encourage the Apostolate for Family Consecration in its efforts to promote an effective catechesis in homes and parishes.**

With these sentiments, I commend the work of the Conference to the intercession of Mary, Mother of the Church. To the organizers, speakers and participants, I cordially impart my Apostolic Blessing, which I willingly extend to all the members of their families.

From the Vatican, October 10, 1993

Joannes Paulus PP. II

John Paul II

Pope John Paul II blesses the Coniker family, and the entire work of the Apostolate for Family Consecration, as Jerry, Gwen, and Joe Coniker present *The Apostolate's Family Catechism* to His Holiness.

Blessed Teresa of Calcutta embraces Gwen Coniker.

Blessed Teresa wrote:

"*The Apostolate's Family Catechism*" will now enable parents to fulfill their primary obligation in teaching their children. I pray that every parent will join the Apostolate for Family Consecration and use the Apostolate's catechetical program in their neighborhood." Blessed Teresa had joined the Apostolate for Family Consecration's advisory council on May 1, 1976 and has been videotaped several times by our founders, including her last taped interview before she died.

COMMISSIONE INTERDICASTERIALE
PER IL
CATECHISMO DELLA CHIESA CATTOLICA

Il Presidente

Prot. N. XII/91 C
(Si prega citare il numero nella risposta)

00193 Roma
March 4, 1994

Piazza del S. Uffizio. 11

now Pope Benedict XVI

Dear Mr. Coniker:

Thank you for your courtesy in sending a copy of The Apostolate's Family Catechism published by the Apostolate for Family Consecration. The work's publication in this year of the family could not be more timely. It anticipates many of the themes of His Holiness Pope John Paul's Letter to Families of February 2, 1994. The cross-references provided to the Catechism of the Catholic Church will make it an especially helpful instrument to parents and teachers.

With prayerful best wishes for the success of your vital apostolate, I remain

Sincerely yours in Christ,

† Joseph Card. Ratzinger

Joseph Cardinal Ratzinger, President
Interdicasterial Commission for the
Catechism of the Catholic Church

Mr. Jerome F. CONIKER
President
Apostolate for Family Consecration
Route 2, Box 700
Bloomingdale, OH 43910
U.S.A

Rome, 9 September 1993

Jerome F. Coniker
President
Apostolate for Family Consecration
John Paul II Holy Family Center
Seminary Road, Route 2, Box 700
Bloomingdale, OH 43910

Subject: The Apostolate's Family Catechism

Dear Mr. Coniker:

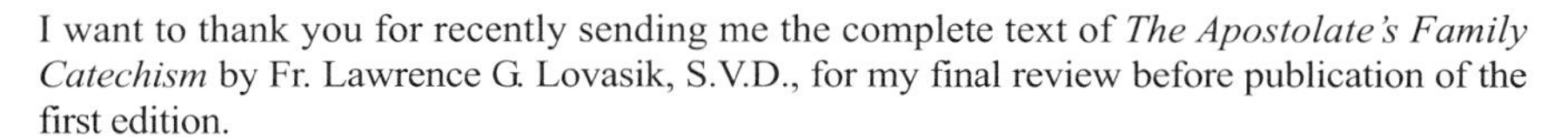

I want to thank you for recently sending me the complete text of *The Apostolate's Family Catechism* by Fr. Lawrence G. Lovasik, S.V.D., for my final review before publication of the first edition.

It is indeed providential that you are publishing your family catechism at this time so that it can serve the new *Catechism of the Catholic Church*, promulgated by Pope John Paul II. Your methodical cross-references from the *Catechism of the Catholic Church* into *The Apostolate's Family Catechism* are a major service to the Church and to family life. This is because your family catechism will make it extremely easy for parents and teachers to confidently teach their children and students the Faith, and have easy access to the new *Catechism of the Catholic Church* which is a vital resource for every Catholic family and school. I am also extremely pleased to learn that the Apostolate for Family Consecration is a co-publisher of the English edition of the new *Catechism of the Catholic Church*.

Francis Cardinal Arinze's audio and video taped reviews and commentaries on The *Apostolate's Family Catechism* adds a priceless dimension to your entire catechetical program, since the Holy Father has so clearly stated that we are living in a "media culture" and that audio and video cassettes should be used to evangelize this generation.

I understand that your staff theologian, Burns K. Seeley, Ph.D., has thoroughly reviewed and edited the manuscript since my last review and approval while I was the Pro-theologian of the Supreme Pontiff.

I am happy to approve the edited and cross-referenced version of *The Apostolate's Family Catechism* and highly recommend it to families and schools as a sure source for authentic Catholic doctrine.

May God continue to bless you, your family, and your apostolate.

Yours in the Hearts of Jesus and Mary,

Mario Luigi Card. Ciappi, O.P.

Mario Luigi Cardinal Ciappi
Pro-theologian Emeritus

After the printing of the first edition, the Family Apostolate's founder wrote Cardinal Ciappi and asked him if he would take the time to slowly review the catechism again and make any suggestions for the second edition. His Eminence responded on December 2, 1994, and wrote: "I did review it again; I have nothing to suggest for the second edition."

PONTIFICIUM CONSILIUM
PRO FAMILIA

Prot N. 206/ 96

Vatican City State
September 17, 1997

Mr. Jerome F. Coniker
President
The Apostolate for Family Consecration
Seminary Rd.
Bloomingdale, Ohio 43910
United States of America

Dear Mr. Coniker,

The Apostolate's Family Catechism is an impressive and beautifully presented work. The systematic method, the art, the cross references leading into the *Catechism of the Catholic Church,* all assist the family to become the first school of faith and the virtues. As the Holy Father has pointed out: "Family catechetics precedes, accompanies and enriches all other forms of catechesis (*Catechesi Tradendae*, 68).

However, this Catechism is not simply an instrument for the formation in faith of the children. It can become the key to a deepening of the faith of the members of the family. Through the use of this Catechism and the media resources provided by the Apostolate, families may be equipped for their special mission of evangelization that has been proclaimed by the Holy Father Pope John Paul II.

This significant project is surely to be commended.

With every prayerful wish for your work, I remain

Sincerely yours in Christ

A. Card. López Trujillo

Alfonso Cardinal Lopez Trujillo
President
Pontifical Council for the Family

Cardinal Silvio Oddi, while Prefect of the Sacred Congregation of the Clergy, wrote the following:

"We are happy to notice that 'The Apostolate's Family Catechism' gives the parents a complete tool to fulfill their obligations as being the primary teachers of the Faith to their children, and, at the same time, gives parents a good refresher course in the Faith."

Cardinal William Baum, one of the three Roman Curia Cardinals on the Commission for the papally-promulgated *Catechism of the Catholic Church*, and Prefect *Emeritus* of the Congregation for Education, wrote:

"We believe that *The Apostolate's Family Catechism*, with which the Catechism for the Universal Church is cross-referenced, will truly be a break through for family formation and for parents, who indeed are the primary educators of their children. This integrated program of teaching the catechism in the home, and then gathering together once a week with other families to hear Cardinal Arinze and others teach on your "Be Not Afraid Family Hours" in churches, can be very effective in rebuilding both the domestic church and the parish community.

Jaime Cardinal Sin, while Archbishop of the Manila Diocese, wrote to the Philippine Women's University:

"You have received a copy of a catechism which is the approved Family Catechism of the Archdiocese of Manila, and it is now also your religion text book at the Philippine Women's University. Cherish it next to the Bible. It is a treasury of fundamental truths and prayers that will help you cope with the challenges you will face in this life...As you study this Catechism, you will learn how to be Pro-God, Pro-Life, and Pro-Family. Learning more about the Truth prepares you to love God above all things (see Mt. 22:37-39) and to love others as God loves them (Jn 13:34). When you learn to give yourself to God and to others out of love for God, then you will know that your study of the Catechism is bearing fruit. At the very least, you should know and obey God's laws because, as Jesus said, 'If you love me, you will keep my commandments' (Jn 14:15); 'for this is the love of God, that we keep his commandments' (1 Jn 5:3)."

Family Apostolate co-founder, Jerry Coniker, with Jaime Cardinal Sin, Manila, Philippines

This illustration depicts three great papal theologians who have made valuable contributions to the Church. The first papal theologian was St. Dominic, founder of the Dominican order. St. Thomas Aquinas, the Angelic Doctor, was the fourth papal theologian. The late Mario Luigi Cardinal Ciappi, O.P. (foreground), the eighty-fourth successor of St. Dominic as papal theologian, was also the primary theological director for the Apostolate for Family Consecration from 1979–1996. He is one of the greatest theologians and mariologists of our time.

Please read the following letters by Cardinal Ciappi. For his letter endorsing *The Apostolate's Family Catechism*, page xxix.

For the first time in our age, we now have the multimedia resources to fully implement the Marian Multiplier Formula which Cardinal Ciappi describes in the following letter:

00120 Citta del Vaticano
Vatican City

August 24, 1989

Mr. and Mrs. Jerome F. Coniker
Apostolate for Family Consecration
6305 Third Ave.
Kenosha, WI
U.S.A.

Dear Jerry and Gwen Coniker and all the families of The Apostolate,

I wish to encourage your continued stress on total consecration to Jesus through Mary.

Paragraph 4 of Pope Paul VI's Apostolic Constitution on the Revision of Indulgences states:

"By the hidden and kindly mystery of God's will, a supernatural solidarity reigns among men. A consequence of this is that the sin of one person harms other people just as one person's holiness helps others."

If this is true, how true it is that when we give all our merits to Mary, she multiplies them by Her own incalculable merits. This puts into motion positive spiritual forces to repair the damage due to sin and significantly change the course of history, if enough make this commitment.

Mary's merits can multiply the effects of one person's holiness and help countless souls. Only Heaven knows the depth of holiness a soul must achieve to tip the scales for world peace.

I agree that this apostolate of family consecration is the best way to defeat the scourge of abortion and renew family life.

The spiritual offensive must always be in the vanguard, presupposing all other activities.

The "Marian Era of Evangelization Campaign" can put into motion a chain of events to bring about that era of peace promised at Fatima. With His Holiness Pope John Paul, we look expectantly and prayerfully for this era to begin with the dawn of the third millennium, the year 2001.

Praying for the success of your most needed apostolate, I remain,

Yours in the Hearts of Jesus and Mary,

Mario Luigi Card. Ciappi, O.P.

Mario Luigi Cardinal Ciappi, O.P.
Pro-theologian of the Pontifical Household

00120 Citta del Vaticano
Vatican City

October 9, 1994

Dear Jerry and Gwen:

Once again, your Totus Tuus "Consecrate Them in Truth" Conference will be serving the Church in a very timely way.

I want to thank everyone who will be attending the Conference this November in Philadelphia, which is focused on the priorities and spirituality of Pope John Paul II. It will truly give families a strong motivation to deepen their knowledge of the Faith and to share it with others in their neighborhoods.

Your use of the social communications and the way in which you are using audio and video tape is a "fail-safe method" of teaching and will allow families of today's media culture, which the Holy Father frequently mentions, to become powerful instruments of the Immaculata to bring about the era of peace she promised at Fatima.

Yes, a miracle was promised at Fatima, the greatest miracle in the history of the world, second only to the Resurrection. And that miracle will be an era of peace which has never really been granted before to the world.

I believe that this peace will begin in the domestic church, the family, and go out to the parishes and into the diocese, the country, and the world. This lasting peace will be the fruit of a life of service and of evangelizing one's family and neighbors with the truth that will set them free!

Our Blessed Mother promised us this era of peace if we say the daily Rosary, practice the First Saturday Communion of Reparation, and live lives consecrated in the truth. This consecration includes giving all of our possessions, both interior and exterior, to Jesus through the Immaculate Heart of Mary, and, as you know, in the Apostolate for Family Consecration, we like to add, "in union with St. Joseph."

As the primary theological advisor to The Apostolate for Family Consecration since 1979, I have reminded its members frequently that consecration is not just a prayer or a devotion but a commitment to a way of life which must be nourished through continuous formation in the eternal truths of our faith.

Yours in the Hearts of Jesus and Mary,

Mario Luigi Card. Ciappi, O.P.

Mario Luigi Cardinal Ciappi, O.P.
Papal Theologian Emeritus for Popes Pius XII,
John XXIII, Paul VI, John Paul I, and John Paul II

ARCHDIOCESE OF CHICAGO

Office of the Archbishop

Post Office Box 1979
Chicago, Illinois 60690-1979

September 17, 2004

Jerome F. Coniker, President
Apostolate for Family Consecration
3375 County Road 36
Bloomingdale, Ohio 43910

Dear Mr. Coniker,

I understand that Francis Cardinal Arinze, Prefect of the Congregation for Divine Worship and Discipline of the Sacraments, Fr. Pablo Straub, Redemptorist priest, and Sr. John Vianney are your primary teachers on audio (for use in the home) and on video and DVD (for use in schools and religious education programs). Cardinal Arinze teaches the older children and teens (levels 5-12) and adults and Sr. John Vianney speaks to the children K-4 with stories and illustrations. Fr. Pablo's teachings in Spanish make the Faith come alive for both children and parents. These resources make your catechetical programs for levels K-12 valuable tools for teaching the Faith to our media generation.

I am pleased that the two-volume edition of "The Apostolate's Family Catechism" has been approved by Cardinal Joseph Ratzinger and that the Apostolate's complete "Consecration in Truth Catechetical Program" for levels 1-12, which includes your unabridged and fully illustrated catechism, your two-volume catechism, teaching guides and student workbooks, has been found to be in conformity with the "Catechism of the Catholic Church" by the Ad Hoc Committee to Oversee the Use of the Catechism, United States Conference of Catholic Bishops.

I understand that this multi-media approach will simultaneously teach children and parents the "Catechism of the Catholic Church," Scripture, Vatican II, and major documents of Pope John Paul II, with emphasis on Veritatis Splendor, using the modern means of communications. Particularly important are the Teacher Prep CD's for each lesson.

It would be good for our parishes, schools and religious education programs in the Archdiocese of Chicago to consider using your complete "Consecration in Truth" Catechetical program, that includes the two-volume family Catechism and its related audio and videos for levels K-12.

May God bless you and all those who participate in this program.

Sincerely yours in Christ,

Francis Cardinal George

Francis Cardinal George, O.M.I.
Archbishop of Chicago

(Similar letters of endorsement were also written by Archbishop Timothy M. Dolan, Milwaukee Archdiocese, and Archbishop John J. Myers, Newark Archdiocese.)

#M3-350

God, the Holy Trinity, Creation, and the Fall

"We believe in one God, the Father, the Almighty, Maker of Heaven and earth, of all that is, seen and unseen."

#T3-37-2

God and His Perfections

#F3-42-2

Hear, O Israel: The Lord our God is one Lord. *(Deuteronomy 6:4)*

CHAPTER ONE

God Is the Supreme Being

Q. 1. Who is God?

God is the Supreme Being. The word supreme means above all others. God is the source of all being. He is above all that exists.

#F3-19-2

God is the source of all being. He is above all that exists.

Sacred Scripture
Q. 1. Ps 147:5; Sir 18:1-6.

Catechism of the Catholic Church
Q. 1. Paragraphs 1, 14, 27-30, 32; **34**-37, **41-43**, 47-48, 64, 200, **203-279.**

For cross-references with Vatican II, Papal documents & other resources, see Family Wisdom Library on page 196.
For commentaries on each question with Cardinal Arinze, Sr. John Vianney and Fr. Straub (in Spanish), see Appendix C.

Sacred Scripture

The God who made the world and everything in it, being Lord of heaven and earth, does not live in shrines made by man, nor is he served by human hands, as though he needed anything, since he himself gives to all men life and breath and everything. *Acts 17:24-25*

Catechism of the Catholic Church

300 God is infinitely greater than all his works: "You have set your glory above the heavens."[1] Indeed, God's "greatness is unsearchable."[2] But because he is the free and sovereign Creator, the first cause of all that exists, God is present to his creatures' inmost being: "In him we live and move and have our being."[3] In the words of St. Augustine, God is "higher than my highest and more inward than my innermost self."[4]

Q. 2. Who made God?

No one made God. He always was, and He always will be.

Sacred Scripture

Then Moses said to God, "If I come to the people of Israel and say to them, 'The God of your fathers has sent me to you,' and they ask me, 'What is his name?' what shall I say to them?" God said to Moses, "I AM WHO I AM." *Exodus 3:13-14*

#F3-21-S

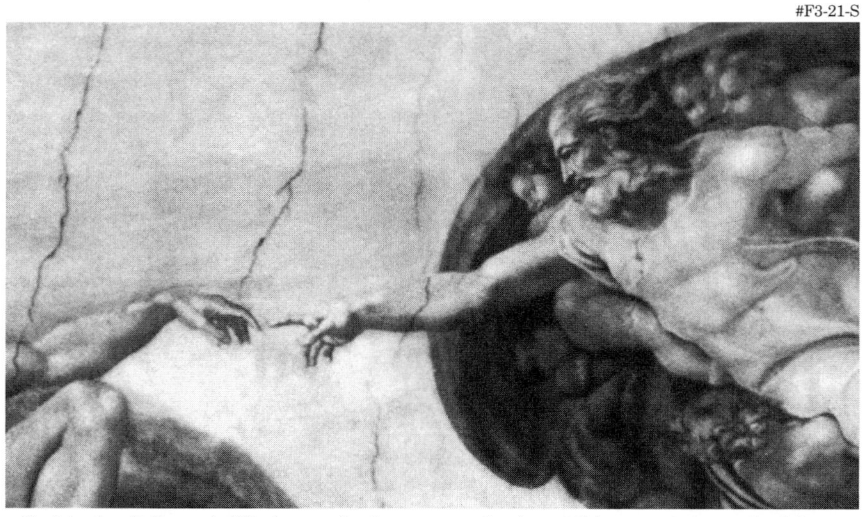

God is the fullness of Being and of every perfection, without origin and without end. All creatures receive all that they are and have from him.
(Catechism of the Catholic Church, 213)

Sacred Scripture
Q. 2. Job 36:26; Jn 1:1-4.

For cross-references with Vatican II, Papal documents & other resources, see Family Wisdom Library on page 196.
For commentaries on each question with Cardinal Arinze, Sr. John Vianney and Fr. Straub (in Spanish), see Appendix C.

Catechism of the Catholic Church

213 The revelation of the ineffable name "I Am who Am" contains then the truth that God alone IS. The Greek Septuagint translation of the Hebrew Scriptures, and following it the Church's Tradition, understood the divine name in this sense: God is the fullness of Being and of every perfection, without origin and without end. All creatures receive all that they are and have from him; but he alone *is* his very being, and he is of himself everything that he is.

Vatican Council II

Throughout history even to the present day, there is found among different peoples a certain awareness of a hidden power, which lies behind the course of nature and the events of human life. At times there is present even a recognition of a supreme being, or still more of a Father. This awareness and recognition results in a way of life that is imbued with a deep religious sense. *Non-Christian Religions, 2*

Summary Prayer

O God, we believe that You are the Supreme Being. No one made You. You always were, and You always will be. You alone are God; nothing happens without You. To You be all honor and glory, now and forever. Amen.

Q. 3. Can there be more than one God?

There cannot be more than one God because there cannot be two supreme beings. To say otherwise would be a contradiction.

Sacred Scripture

Hear, O Israel: The Lord our God is one Lord. *Deuteronomy 6:4*

Remember the former things of old; for I am God, and there is no other; I am God, and there is none like me. *Isaiah 46:9*

For although there may be so-called gods in heaven or on earth—as indeed there are many "gods" and many "lords"—yet for us there is one God, the Father, from whom are all things and for whom we exist. *1 Corinthians 8:5-6*

Catechism of the Catholic Church

229 Faith in God leads us to turn to him alone as our first origin and our ultimate goal, and neither to prefer anything to him nor to substitute anything for him.

Sacred Scripture
Q. 3. Ps 86:8–10; Mk 12:28-30; 1 Tim 1:17.

Catechism of the Catholic Church
Q. 3. Paragraphs 27–28, 46, **200**, 222–231, 268, 2096.

For cross-references with Vatican II, Papal documents & other resources, see Family Wisdom Library on page 196.
For commentaries on each question with Cardinal Arinze, Sr. John Vianney and Fr. Straub (in Spanish), see Appendix C.

Q. 4. Why must there be a God?

There must be a God because nothing happens in the universe unless someone intelligent ultimately makes it happen. When scientists study how the world developed, they come to a point where they have to ask, "Who started it all?" There must be someone who was not made by anyone else, someone who never had a beginning. That someone is God.

#F3-66-2

There must be a God because nothing happens in the universe unless someone intelligent ultimately makes it happen.

Sacred Scripture

Ever since the creation of the world his invisible nature, namely, his eternal power and deity, has been clearly perceived in the things that have been made. *Romans 1:20*

Catechism of the Catholic Church

34 The world, and man, attest that they contain within themselves neither their first principle nor their final end, but rather that they participate in Being itself, which alone is without origin or end. Thus, in different ways, man can come to know that there exists a reality which is the first cause and final end of all things, a reality "that everyone calls 'God.'"[1]

Sacred Scripture
Q. 4. Wis 13:1-9; Ps 19:1-4.

Catechism of the Catholic Church
Q. 4. Paragraphs **36**, 37, 46, 282–289.

For cross-references with Vatican II, Papal documents & other resources, see Family Wisdom Library on page 196.
For commentaries on each question with Cardinal Arinze, Sr. John Vianney and Fr. Straub (in Spanish), see Appendix C.

Summary Prayer

Most loving Father, we worship You as our first beginning. We long for You as our last end, we praise You as our constant helper, and call on You as our loving protector, through our Lord Jesus Christ, in unity with the Holy Spirit. Amen.

Q. 5. Why is God an infinitely perfect being?

God is an infinitely perfect being because in Him there is no limitation of any kind. God is an infinitely perfect spiritual being, without beginning or end. He knows and loves without limit.

Angels and men are also spiritual beings, but being creatures, they are limited or finite. Consequently, their perfections are limited.

Angels are pure spirits, meaning that they have no bodies. Men are both spiritual and material. They have material bodies and spiritual souls. Being spiritual, angels and men have minds and wills. They can know and love, but only to a limited degree. God alone is the infinitely perfect being. He is the infinitely perfect Spirit.

Sacred Scripture

This God—his way is perfect; the promise of the Lord proves true; he is a shield for all those who take refuge in him. *2 Samuel 22:31*

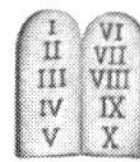

Doctrine • Moral • Worship Exercise

(See Appendix A for answer key, questions 1-5.)

1. What does "God is the Supreme Being" mean?
2. How can you show your friends and family each day that God is the Supreme Being of your life?
3. Since God is the Supreme Being, He deserves all of our adoration and worship. How can you give God the adoration and worship He deserves?

Sacred Scripture
Q. 5. Mt 5:46-48.

Catechism of the Catholic Church
Q. 5. Paragraphs 1, 41, **42**, 43, 48, **206**, 251, 385, 393, 1064, 2086, 2096.

For cross-references with Vatican II, Papal documents & other resources, see Family Wisdom Library on page 196.
For commentaries on each question with Cardinal Arinze, Sr. John Vianney and Fr. Straub (in Spanish), see Appendix C.

Chapter Summary Prayer

My God, we believe that You are the infinitely perfect Spirit. You can know and love. Your knowledge and love have no limit. Lord, we believe in You; increase our faith. We trust in You; strengthen our trust. We love You; may we love You more and more.

Almighty God, increase our strength of will for doing good that Christ may find an eager welcome in our hearts and call us to His side in the Kingdom of Heaven. We ask this through the same Christ our Lord. Amen.

Thought Provokers

Please see Appendix B for the answers.

Q. 1: A. Where in the Bible is it taught that God is the supreme Being?

B. By the use of reason alone, how can we conclude that God is the Supreme Being in the universe?

Q. 2: A. Where in Sacred Scriptures can we learn that God is uncreated?

B. How can reason alone demonstrate that God is uncreated?

Q. 3: A. Where in the Bible does it say that there is only one God?

B. Is it reasonable to say that there is only one God?

Q. 4: How can you explain that there must be a God who "started it all"?

Q. 5: What is a spirit?

CHAPTER TWO

God's Perfections

Q. 6. What are God's perfections?

The attributes of God are His perfections; that is, things such as infinite goodness, eternal, all-knowing, all-present, almighty.

Catechism of the Catholic Church

41 All creatures bear a certain resemblance to God, most especially man, created in the image and likeness of God. The manifold perfections of creatures—their truth, their goodness, their beauty—all reflect the infinite perfection of God. Consequently we can name God by taking his creatures' perfections as our starting point, "for from the greatness and beauty of created things comes a corresponding perception of their Creator."[1]

#F3-41-2

The manifold perfections of creatures—their truth, their goodness, their beauty —all reflect the infinite perfection of God. *(Catechism of the Catholic Church, 41)*

Catechism of the Catholic Church
Q. 6. Paragraphs 1, 30, 42, 212–**221**, 268–276, 1429, 2086.

For cross-references with Vatican II, Papal documents & other resources, see Family Wisdom Library on page 196.
For commentaries on each question with Cardinal Arinze, Sr. John Vianney and Fr. Straub (in Spanish), see Appendix C.

Q. 7. Is God infinitely good?

God is infinitely good. His goodness is limitless, as are all of His perfections.

#F1-56-2

God in his great and merciful kindness freely creates us and moreover, graciously calls us to share in his life and glory. He generously pours out, and never ceases to pour out, his divine goodness. *(Missionary Activity, 2)*

Sacred Scripture

No one is good but God alone. *Luke 18:19*

A God of faithfulness and without iniquity, just and right is he. *Deuteronomy 32:4*

Catechism of the Catholic Church

221 But St. John goes even further when he affirms that "God is love":[1] God's very being is love. By sending his only Son and the Spirit of Love in the fullness of time, God has revealed his innermost secret:[2] God himself is an eternal exchange of love, Father, Son, and Holy Spirit, and he has destined us to share in that exchange.

Splendor of Truth

To ask about the good, in fact, ultimately means to turn towards God, the fullness of goodness... God alone is worthy of being loved "with all one's heart, and with all one's soul, and with all one's mind" (Mt 22:37). He is the source of man's happiness. Jesus brings the question about morally good action back to its religious foundations, to the acknowledgment of God, who alone is goodness, fullness of life, the final end of human activity, and perfect happiness. *(section 9)*

Catechism of the Catholic Church
Q. 7. Paragraphs 1, 9, 11, **214**, **310**, 339.

For cross-references with Vatican II, Papal documents & other resources, see Family Wisdom Library on page 196.
For commentaries on each question with Cardinal Arinze, Sr. John Vianney and Fr. Straub (in Spanish), see Appendix C.

Vatican Council II

God in his great and merciful kindness freely creates us and moreover, graciously calls us to share in his life and glory. He generously pours out, and never ceases to pour out, his divine goodness. *Missionary Activity, 2*

Summary Prayer

O God, we believe that You are infinitely perfect and infinitely good. Gifts without measure flow from Your goodness to bring us Your peace.

Our lives are Your gift. Guide us on our journey, for only Your love makes us whole. Keep us strong in Your love. From Your goodness we have received all that is good. Direct our steps in our everyday efforts. May the changing moods of the human heart and the limits which our failings impose on our hope never blind us to You, source of every good, forever and ever. Amen.

Q. 8. Is God eternal?

God is eternal. This is true because He always was, is now, and always will be.

#E4-13-2

God reveals himself as the God who is always there, present to his people in order to save them. *(Catechism of the Catholic Church, 207)*

Sacred Scripture
Q. 8. Ps 45:6; Jn 17:5.

Catechism of the Catholic Church
Q. 8. Paragraphs 34, 101,108, 212-213, 220, 240, 243, 262, 276.

For cross-references with Vatican II, Papal documents & other resources, see Family Wisdom Library on page 196.
For commentaries on each question with Cardinal Arinze, Sr. John Vianney and Fr. Straub (in Spanish), see Appendix C.

Sacred Scripture

Before the mountains were brought forth, or ever thou hadst formed the earth and the world, from everlasting to everlasting thou art God. *Psalm 90:2*

For the mountains may depart and the hills be removed, but my steadfast love shall not depart from you, and my covenant of peace shall not be removed, says the Lord, who has compassion on you. *Isaiah 54:10*

Catechism of the Catholic Church

207 By revealing his name God at the same time reveals his faithfulness which is from everlasting to everlasting, valid for the past ("I am the God of your fathers"), as for the future ("I will be with you").[1] God, who reveals his name as "I AM," reveals himself as the God who is always there, present to his people in order to save them.

Q. 9. Why is God all-knowing?

God is all-knowing because He knows all things in the past, present, and future, as well as all potential things. God knows all things that are or ever could be. Everything is like one thought in the mind of God. Therefore, we say God is all-knowing.

Sacred Scripture

Thou hast knowledge of all things. *Esther 14:15*

#F3-44-2

God is all-knowing because He knows all things in the past, present, and future, as well as all potential things.

Sacred Scripture
Q. 9. Ps 139:1-6; 1 Jn 3:19-20.

Catechism of the Catholic Church
Q. 9. Paragraphs 207, **208**, 209, 217, 291, **300-303**, 310-312, 599.

For cross-references with Vatican II, Papal documents & other resources, see Family Wisdom Library on page 196.
For commentaries on each question with Cardinal Arinze, Sr. John Vianney and Fr. Straub (in Spanish), see Appendix C.

Catechism of the Catholic Church

216 God's truth is his wisdom, which commands the whole created order and governs the world.[1] God, who alone made heaven and earth, can alone impart true knowledge of every created thing in relation to himself.[2]

Catechism by Diagram

#F3-15

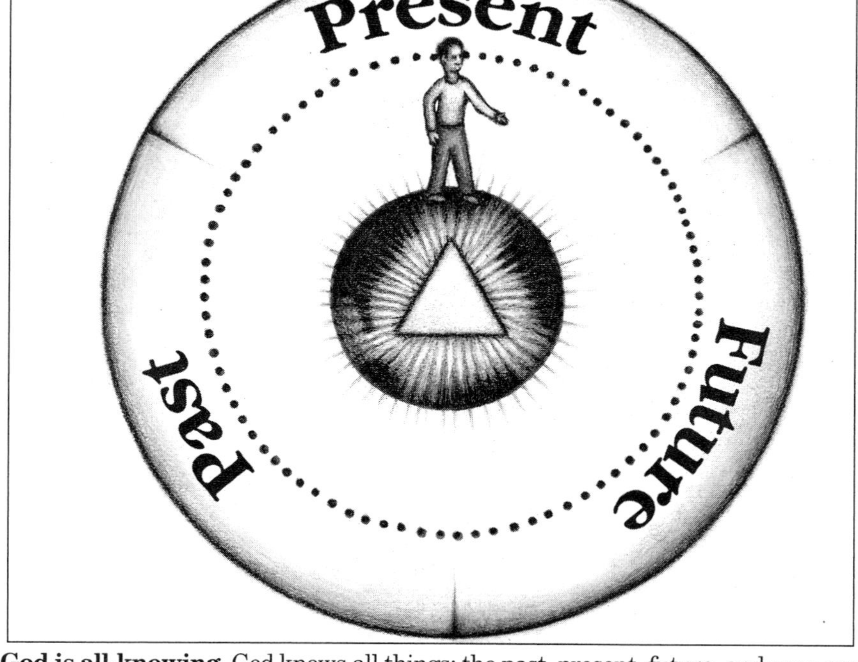

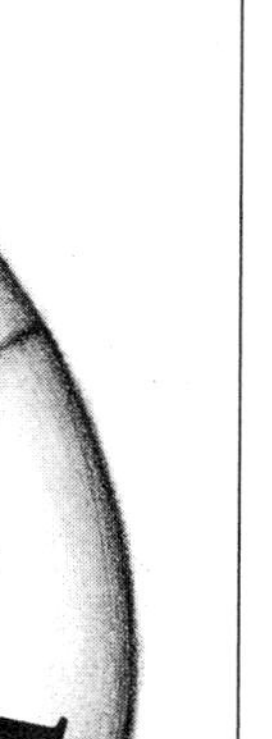

God is all-knowing. God knows all things: the past, present, future, and even our most secret thoughts, words, and actions. Nothing can be hidden from Him. The triangle stands for God. The solid circle shows that there is no end to His knowledge, just as a circle has no beginning and no end. The dotted circle around man shows that there is a limit to what man knows. He remembers only some of the past. He knows little of the present, and knows nothing of the future.

Summary Prayer

O God, we believe that You are eternal, because You always were, are now, and always will be. We believe that You are all-knowing, because You know the past, present, and all that ever will or can be. Teach us to realize that this world is passing, that our true future is the happiness of Heaven, that life on earth is short, and that the life to come is eternal. Help us to follow Christ with love and to gain eternal life with You. Amen.

Q. 10. Is God present everywhere?

God is present everywhere, all the time. There is no place where God is not.

Sacred Scripture

Whither shall I go from thy Spirit? Or wither shall I flee from thy presence? If I ascend to heaven, thou are there! If I make my bed in Sheol, thou art there! If I take the wings of the morning and dwell in the uttermost parts of the sea, even there thy hand shall lead me, and thy right hand shall hold me. If I say, "Let only darkness cover me, and the light about me be night," even the darkness is not dark to thee, the night is bright as the day; for darkness is as light with thee. *Psalms 139:7–12*

Q. 11. Is God almighty?

God is almighty because He can do and make anything which is good and non-contradictory. Thus, God cannot commit sin because He cannot contradict His infinite goodness. Nor can He violate the principle of non-contradiction, which states that a thing cannot both be and not be at the same time.

#F3-13-S

God is almighty because He can do and make anything which is good and non-contradictory.

Sacred Scripture	**Catechism of the Catholic Church**
Q. 10. 1 Kings 8:27; Prov 15:3.	Q. 10. Paragraphs **207**, 301, 2671.
Q. 11. 1 Chron 29:11; Job 42:2.	Q. 11. Paragraphs **269–278.**

For cross-references with Vatican II, Papal documents & other resources, see Family Wisdom Library on page 196.
For commentaries on each question with Cardinal Arinze, Sr. John Vianney and Fr. Straub (in Spanish), see Appendix C.

Sacred Scripture

With God all things are possible. *Matthew 19:26*

Catechism of the Catholic Church

268 Of all the divine attributes, only God's omnipotence is named in the Creed: to confess this power has great bearing on our lives. We believe that his might is *universal*, for God who created everything also rules everything and can do everything. God's power is *loving*, for he is our Father, and *mysterious*, for only faith can discern it when it "is made perfect in weakness."[1]

Catechism by Diagram

#F3-16.2

God is almighty. God can do all things. He controls the powers of nature: the sea, wind, rain, clouds, lightning, thunder. The man in the boat has no power to control these things.

Summary Prayer

Eternal Father, You are almighty, reaching from end to end of the universe, and ordering all things with Your mighty arm. For You, time is the unfolding of truth that already is and the unveiling of beauty that is yet to be.

Guide us by Your wisdom, correct us with Your justice, comfort us with Your mercy, and protect us with Your power, through our Lord Jesus Christ. Amen.

Doctrine • Moral • Worship Exercise

(See Appendix A for answer key, questions 6-11.)

1. God is the Supreme Being. He possesses many qualities. List six of these qualities.
2. In what ways have you experienced God's goodness? His truthfulness? His justice?
3. How can you recognize God's presence wherever go?

Chapter Summary Prayer

Father of everlasting goodness, our origin and guide, be close to us and hear our prayers which we offer to praise You. Our faith gives us the promise of peace and makes known the demands of love. Remove our selfishness, which blurs the vision of the virtue of faith.

Let our spiritual sacrifice, offered with Your Son in the Mass, make us an everlasting gift to You. Give us the strength of new life by the gift of the Eucharist. Protect us with Your love and prepare us for eternal life. Grant us, in this life, the good things which lead to the everlasting life You have prepared for us.

Merciful Father, fill our hearts with Your love and keep us faithful to the Gospel of Christ. Give us the grace to rise above our human weaknesses. Fill our hearts with the light of Your Gospel, that our thoughts may please You and our love may be sincere. We ask this through Jesus Christ our Lord. Amen.

Thought Provokers

Please see Appendix B for the answers.

Q. 6: What do we mean when we speak of God's perfections?

Q. 7: God is infinitely good. Based upon your own experience, and from the use of your reason, note instances of God's goodness shown in your own life, in the lives of others, and in the world.

Q. 8: A. What is the difference between God's eternity and His infinity?

B. Our own experience tells us that every creature has a beginning. But if God were to have a beginning (which He does not have), what else would that tell us about Him which would be contrary to the Catholic Faith?

Q. 9: What does God know?

Q. 10: Where is God present?

Q. 11: If God is almighty, is there anything that He cannot do?

CHAPTER THREE

More of God's Perfections

Q. 12. Is God all-wise?

Yes, God alone, the Creator of all things, is all-wise. He knows what is best for all of His creatures.

Catechism by Diagram

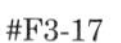

God is all-wise. We know about the wisdom of God from the order in the universe: the sun, moon, stars, and planets. The earth moves around the sun. The moon moves around the earth. God knows best how to use the things He has created.

Sacred Scripture

His understanding is beyond measure. *Psalm 147:5*

Catechism of the Catholic Church

295 We believe that God created the world according to his wisdom.[1] It is not the product of any necessity whatever, nor of blind fate or chance. We believe that it proceeds from God's free will; he wanted to make his creatures share in

Sacred Scripture
Q. 12. Rom 16:27.

Catechism of the Catholic Church
Q. 12. Paragraphs 310, **339**, 2500.

For cross-references with Vatican II, Papal documents & other resources, see Family Wisdom Library on page 196.
For commentaries on each question with Cardinal Arinze, Sr. John Vianney and Fr. Straub (in Spanish), see Appendix C.

his being, wisdom, and goodness: "For you created all things, and by your will they existed and were created."[2] Therefore the Psalmist exclaims: "O Lord, how manifold are your works! In wisdom you have made them all"; and "The Lord is good to all, and his compassion is over all that he has made."[3]

Summary Prayer

O God, we believe that You are all-wise, for You know best the things which You have created. We abandon ourselves to Your loving care, and we cheerfully accept all that You send us. All glory and praise be to the Father, the Son, and the Holy Spirit. Amen.

Q. 13. Why is God all-holy?

God is all-holy because He is infinitely full of all that is good and lovable.

#F3-45-2

Holy, holy, holy is the Lord of hosts. *(Isaiah 6:3)*

Sacred Scripture

And the Lord said to Moses, "This very thing that you have spoken I will do; for you have found favor in my sight, and I know you by name." Moses said, "I pray thee, show me thy glory." And he said, "I will make all my goodness pass before you, and will proclaim before you my name 'The Lord'; and I will be gracious to whom I will be gracious, and I will show mercy on whom I will show mercy." *Exodus 33:17-19*

Holy, holy, holy is the Lord of hosts; the whole earth is full of his glory. *Isaiah 6:3*

Sacred Scripture
Q. 13. 1 Sam 2:2; Ps 111; Lk 1:49-55.

Catechism of the Catholic Church
Q. 13. Paragraphs **208**, 826, 2809-2810.

For cross-references with Vatican II, Papal documents & other resources, see Family Wisdom Library on page 196.
For commentaries on each question with Cardinal Arinze, Sr. John Vianney and Fr. Straub (in Spanish), see Appendix C.

Summary Prayer

O God, we believe You are all-holy. All creation rightly gives You praise; for all life and all holiness comes from You. In the plan of Your wisdom, she who bore the Christ in her womb was raised in glory to be with Him in Heaven. May we follow her example in reflecting Your holiness and join in her hymn of endless love and praise, through the same Christ our Lord. Amen.

Q. 14. Why is God all-merciful?

God is all-merciful because there is no end to His mercy. As often as we are sorry for our sins and confess them, so often will God forgive us.

#C17-3-2

As often as we are sorry for our sins and confess them, so often will God forgive us.

Sacred Scripture

But God, who is rich in mercy, out of the great love with which he loved us, even when we were dead through our trespasses, made us alive together with Christ (by grace you have been saved), and raised us up with him, and made us sit with him in the heavenly places in Christ Jesus, that in the coming ages he might show the immeasurable riches of his grace in kindness toward us in Christ Jesus. *Ephesians 2:4-7*

Sacred Scripture
Q. 14. 2 Chron 30:6-9; Lk 15:11-32.

Catechism of the Catholic Church
Q. 14. Paragraphs 211, **270**, 1261, 1429, 1489.

For cross-references with Vatican II, Papal documents & other resources, see Family Wisdom Library on page 196.
For commentaries on each question with Cardinal Arinze, Sr. John Vianney and Fr. Straub (in Spanish), see Appendix C.

Catechism of the Catholic Church

1608 Nevertheless, the order of creation persists, though seriously disturbed. To heal the wounds of sin, man and woman need the help of the grace that God in his infinite mercy never refuses them.[1] Without his help man and woman cannot achieve the union of their lives for which God created them "in the beginning."

Splendor of Truth

No human sin can erase the mercy of God, or prevent him from unleashing all his triumphant power, if we only call upon him. Indeed, sin itself makes even more radiant the love of the Father who, in order to ransom a slave, sacrificed his Son: his mercy towards us is Redemption. *(section 118)*

Vatican Council II

We know neither the moment of the consummation of the earth and of man nor the way the universe will be transformed. The form of this world, distorted by sin, is passing away and we are taught that God is preparing a new dwelling and a new earth in which righteousness dwells, whose happiness will fill and surpass all the desires of peace arising in the hearts of men. *Gaudium et Spes, 39*

Q. 15. Why is God all-just?

God is all-just because He is completely honest and fair with everybody.

He promises to reward us for our good deeds and to punish us for our evil deeds. Yet, He is always merciful to those who turn to Him. (See Q. 14.)

Sacred Scripture

And he judges the world with righteousness, he judges the peoples with equity. The Lord is a stronghold for the oppressed, a stronghold in times of trouble. *Psalm 9:8-9*

Catechism of the Catholic Church

1040 The Last Judgment will come when Christ returns in glory. Only the Father knows the day and the hour; only he determines the moment of its coming. Then through his Son Jesus Christ he will pronounce the final word on all history. We shall know the ultimate meaning of the whole work of creation and of the entire economy of salvation and understand the marvellous ways by which his Providence led everything towards its final end. The Last Judgment will reveal that God's justice triumphs over all the injustices committed by his creatures and that God's love is stronger than death.[1]

Sacred Scripture
Q. 15. Deut 32:4; Lk 18:9-14.

Catechism of the Catholic Church
Q. 15. Paragraphs 271, 1991-94, 2009, 2091.

For cross-references with Vatican II, Papal documents & other resources, see Family Wisdom Library on page 196.
For commentaries on each question with Cardinal Arinze, Sr. John Vianney and Fr. Straub (in Spanish), see Appendix C.

Catechism by Diagram

#F3-18

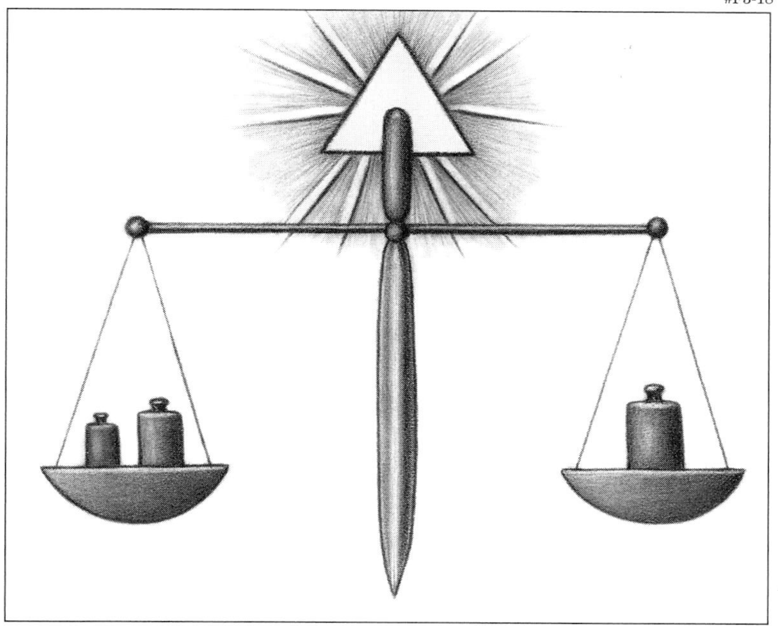

God is all-just. God is honest and fair with everybody. Just as a scale balances weights, so God (triangle) is fair in judging the actions of people. He will reward the good and punish the wicked.

Splendor of Truth

It is quite human for a sinner to acknowledge his weakness and to ask mercy for his failings; what is unacceptable is the attitude of one who makes his own weakness the criterion of the truth about the good, so that he can feel self-justified, without even the need to have recourse to God and his mercy.

Instead, we should take to heart the message of the Gospel parable of the Pharisee and the tax collector (cf. Lk 18:9-14). The tax collector might possibly have had some justification for the sins he committed, such as to diminish his responsibility. But his prayer does not dwell on such justifications, but rather on his own unworthiness before God's infinite holiness... The Pharisee, on the other hand, is self-justified, finding some excuse for each of his failings. *(section 104)*

Doctrine • Moral • Worship Exercise

(See Appendix A for answer key, questions 12-15.)

1. In what ways has God shown His mercy to you?
2. We also possess God's justice and mercy. Think of some experiences in your life when you have been merciful and just to others.
3. In your daily life, what are some ways that you can imitate God's mercy?

Chapter Summary Prayer

Source of all holiness, the work of Your hands is reflected in Your saints. The beauty of Your truth is reflected in the faith they had on earth. May we who aspire to have a part in their joy be filled with the Spirit that blessed their lives, so that having shared their faith on earth, we may also know their peace in Your Kingdom.

We believe You are all-just and all-merciful. In You, justice and mercy meet. With unparalleled love, You have saved us from death and have drawn us into the circle of Your life. Open our eyes to the wonders this life sets before us, so that we may serve You free from fear and address You as God, our merciful Father. O God, make us steadfast in faith, joyful in hope, and untiring in love all the days of our lives. We ask this through Jesus Christ our Lord, to Whom, with You and the Holy Spirit, be all honor and glory. Amen.

Thought Provokers

Please see Appendix B for the answers.

Q. 12: In what is God's wisdom especially seen?

Q. 13: A. Can man become holy?

B. How do we cease to be holy?

Q. 14: If God were not merciful, we sinners could never receive His forgiveness and sanctifying grace. We could not become just or righteous in the eyes of God. In addition to avoiding divine punishment, why should we be merciful towards those who have wronged us?

Q. 15: God, being holy, is necessarily just (or righteous) as well. Moreover, we humans, created in God's image and likeness, are expected to be just (or righteous) also. But the fact that we sin clearly shows that we are not always just. What, if anything, can be done to remedy this situation?

CHAPTER FOUR

Worship of God

Q. 16. In what ways has God shown His love for us?

God has shown His love for us by: (1) making firm promises to men; (2) freeing and saving us; and (3) loving each of us with the love of a father and always caring for us.

#J2-305-2

For God so loved the world that he gave his only Son, that whoever believes in him should not perish but have eternal life. *(John 3:16)*

1. God made firm promises to men.

After our first parents, Adam and Eve, sinned, God made a promise to redeem all men. He kept His promise by choosing Abraham's descendants (the people of Israel) to be His own special people. He then established the Mosaic Covenant (Old Law), within which were contained the Ten Commandments. The Old Law was the first stage of revealed law and a preparation for the Gospel.

Even though Israel did not live up to the Covenant, God remained faithful to His people. At last, He came among them in the Person

Sacred Scripture
Q. 16. Rom 5:6-8; Heb 2:14-18.

Catechism of the Catholic Church
Q. 16. Paragraphs 55-56, 62, **64-68**, 72-75, 122, 128, 211-212, 215, **422**, 426, 497, **638**, 652, 822.

For cross-references with Vatican II, Papal documents & other resources, see Family Wisdom Library on page 196.
For commentaries on each question with Cardinal Arinze, Sr. John Vianney and Fr. Straub (in Spanish), see Appendix C.

of His Son, Jesus, Who made a New Covenant in His Blood by His Death on the Cross.

2. God freed us and saved us.

Through Jesus Christ, God freed us (both Jews and Gentiles) from the power of eternal death and the domination of sin. Through the suffering, Death, and Resurrection of Jesus, we have received grace and God's own life, and a sharing in His nature. Through Him, we have the hope of complete freedom from sin and the hope of eternal life with God in Heaven.

3. God truly loves each of us and takes care of us as a loving father.

In His love, God has made us His children through Baptism and has prepared for us our eternal home in His heavenly Kingdom.

Sacred Scripture

For God so loved the world that he gave his only Son, that whoever believes in him should not perish but have eternal life. *John 3:16*

Catechism of the Catholic Church

609 By embracing in his human heart the Father's love for men, Jesus "loved them to the end," for "greater love has no man than this, that a man lay down his life for his friends."[1] In suffering and death his humanity became the free and perfect instrument of his divine love which desires the salvation of men.[2] Indeed, out of love for his Father and for men, whom the Father wants to save, Jesus freely accepted his Passion and death: "No one takes [my life] from me, but I lay it down of my own accord."[3] Hence the sovereign freedom of God's Son as he went out to his death.[4]

Vatican Council II

It pleased God, in his goodness and wisdom, to reveal himself and to make known the mystery of his will (cf. Eph. 1:9). His will was that men should have access to the Father, through Christ, the Word made flesh, in the Holy Spirit, and thus become sharers in the divine nature (cf. Eph. 2:18; 2 Pet. 1:4). By this revelation, then, the invisible God (cf. Col. 1:15; 1 Tim. 1:17), from the fullness of his love, addresses men as his friends (cf. Ex. 33:11; Jn. 15:14-15), and moves among them (Bar. 3:38), in order to invite and receive them into his own company. *Dei Verbum, 2*

Summary Prayer

Almighty God, Father of the world to come, Your goodness is beyond what our spirit can touch. Your strength is more than the mind can bear.

You draw people to Yourself by making firm promises to free and save us. You love each of us with the love of a father who always cares for us, through Jesus Christ our Lord. Amen.

#T3-23-2

God truly loves each of us and takes care of us as a loving father.

Q. 17. How should we respond to God's goodness?

We should respond to God's goodness by (1) finding joy in Him since He gives us eternal hope, and (2) worshiping Him and serving Him.

#P26-4-2

We owe God our worship and loving service.

1. We should find joy in God.

We belong to God. He loves us and wants us to love Him, so that we might be with Him in Heaven for all eternity. Through fervent prayer and the proper reception of the sacraments, God gives us the grace to love Him and to find our joy in Him.

2. We are to worship and serve our God and Creator.

We owe God our worship and loving service. We worship Him by loving Him and adoring Him. We show loving service to God by obedience to His will.

Sacred Scripture

Blessed be the God and Father of our Lord Jesus Christ! By his great mercy we have been born anew to a living hope through the resurrection of Jesus Christ from the dead, and to an inheritance which is imperishable, undefiled, and unfading, kept in heaven for you. *1 Peter 1:3-4*

Sacred Scripture
Q. 17. Mk 12:28-30; Jn 15:12-17; Rom 5:1-5.

Catechism of the Catholic Church
Q. 17. Paragraphs 30, 346-347, **425**, 736, **901**, 1070, 1089, 1121, **1697.**

For cross-references with Vatican II, Papal documents & other resources, see Family Wisdom Library on page 196.
For commentaries on each question with Cardinal Arinze, Sr. John Vianney and Fr. Straub (in Spanish), see Appendix C.

Catechism of the Catholic Church

301 With creation, God does not abandon his creatures to themselves. He not only gives them being and existence, but also, and at every moment, upholds and sustains them in being, enables them to act and brings them to their final end. Recognizing this utter dependence with respect to the Creator is a source of wisdom and freedom, of joy and confidence.

Splendor of Truth

Man always has before him the spiritual horizon of hope, thanks to the help of divine grace and with the cooperation of human freedom.

It is in the saving Cross of Jesus, in the gift of the Holy Spirit, in the sacraments which flow forth from the pierced side of the Redeemer (cf. Jn 19:34), that believers find the grace and the strength always to keep God's holy law, even amid the gravest of hardships. *(section 103)*

Summary Prayer

Almighty God and Father, may the thought of Your goodness make us find joy in You and prompt us to worship You. We worship You by offering ourselves to You through Jesus Christ Your Son. We are determined to do Your will in all our actions, and to use well the talents You have given us. From Your goodness we hope to receive the grace to live a life of love for You, and to be able to love and help the people around us, through Jesus Christ Your Son. Amen.

Q. 18. In what ways do we worship God?

We worship God when we participate in the sacred liturgy, and in a special way when we adore Him in the Holy Sacrifice of the Mass. In the Mass, we offer ourselves to the Father together with Jesus' offering of Himself. We worship God, as well, when we pray to Him by ourselves or with others.

We also worship God when we keep His commandments as obedient children.

We worship God by using well the talents He has given us. He created us so that we may know, love, and serve Him, and we should use our talents in His service.

Sacred Scripture
Q. 18. 1 Chron 16:28-34; Col 3:15-17.

Catechism of the Catholic Church
Q. 18. Paragraphs **901**, **1388**, 2041-2042, 2192, 2558-2865.

For cross-references with Vatican II, Papal documents & other resources, see Family Wisdom Library on page 196.
For commentaries on each question with Cardinal Arinze, Sr. John Vianney and Fr. Straub (in Spanish), see Appendix C.

#L3-8-2

We worship God when we participate in the Holy Sacrifice of the Mass and offer ourselves to the Father together with Jesus' offering of Himself.

Sacred Scripture

I appeal to you therefore, brethren, by the mercies of God, to present your bodies as a living sacrifice, holy and acceptable to God, which is your spiritual worship. *Romans 12:1*

Through him then let us continually offer up a sacrifice of praise to God, that is, the fruit of lips that acknowledge his name. Do not neglect to do good and to share what you have, for such sacrifices are pleasing to God. *Hebrews 13:15-16*

Catechism of the Catholic Church

1378 *Worship of the Eucharist.* In the liturgy of the Mass we express our faith in the real presence of Christ under the species of bread and wine by, among other ways, genuflecting or bowing deeply as a sign of adoration of the Lord. "The Catholic Church has always offered and still offers to the sacrament of the Eucharist the cult of adoration, not only during Mass, but also outside of it, reserving the consecrated hosts with the utmost care, exposing them to the solemn veneration of the faithful, and carrying them in procession."[1]

Splendor of Truth

Christ reveals, first and foremost, that the frank and open acceptance of truth is the condition for authentic freedom: "You will know the truth, and the truth will set you free" (Jn 8:32)... The true worshippers of God must thus worship Him "in spirit and truth" (Jn 4:23): in this worship they become free. Worship of God and a relationship with truth are revealed in Jesus Christ as the deepest foundation of freedom. *(section 87)*

Vatican Council II

The spiritual life, however, is not limited solely to participation in the liturgy. The Christian is indeed called to pray with others, but he must also enter into his bedroom to pray to his Father in secret; furthermore, according to the teaching of the apostle, he must pray without ceasing. *Sacrosanctum Concilium, 12*

Through the ministry of priests the spiritual sacrifice of the faithful is completed in union with the sacrifice of Christ the only mediator, which in the Eucharist is offered through the priests' hands in the name of the whole Church in an unbloody and sacramental manner until the Lord himself come (cf. 1 Cor. 11:26). *Priests, 2*

#C11-105-2

We worship God when we use our talents in His service.

Summary Prayer

Lord, may the sacrifice of Your Son in the Mass and our sacrifice of praise purify us in mind and heart and make us always eager to serve You. You give us the Body and Blood of Your Son to renew Your life within us. In Your mercy, assure our redemption and bring us to the eternal life we celebrate in the Eucharist through Christ our Lord. Amen.

Q. 19. What should we hope to receive from the goodness of God?

From God's goodness we should hope to receive the graces we need to live a life of sacrificial love, both for God and for our neighbor.

Our lives can be very happy, if we respond generously to these graces everyday to love God and our neighbor and to help those whom God brings into our lives.

#P26-74

Our lives can be very happy, if we respond generously to the graces God gives us everyday.

Sacred Scripture

I give thanks to God always for you because of the grace of God which was given you in Christ Jesus, that in every way you were enriched in him with all speech and all knowledge—even as the testimony to Christ was confirmed among you—so that you are not lacking in any spiritual gift, as you wait for the revealing of our Lord Jesus Christ; who will sustain you to the end, guiltless in the day of our Lord Jesus Christ. God is faithful, by whom you were called into the fellowship of his Son, Jesus Christ our Lord. *1 Corinthians 1:4-9*

Rather, speaking the truth in love, we are to grow up in every way into him who is the head, into Christ. *Ephesians 4:15*

Splendor of Truth

Jesus reveals by his whole life, and not only by his words, that freedom is acquired in love, that is, in the gift of self. The one who says: "Greater love has no man than this, that a man lay down his life for his friends" (Jn 15:13), freely

Sacred Scripture
Q. 19. 2 Cor 9:6-15; Phil 4:13; Heb 4:16; 1 Pet 5:10; 2 Pet 1:2-4.

Catechism of the Catholic Church
Q. 19. Paragraphs 274, **301**, 304, **305**, 313, **2086**, 2836-2837.

For cross-references with Vatican II, Papal documents & other resources, see Family Wisdom Library on page 196.
For commentaries on each question with Cardinal Arinze, Sr. John Vianney and Fr. Straub (in Spanish), see Appendix C.

goes out to meet his Passion (cf. Mt 26:46), and in obedience to the Father gives his life on the Cross for all men (cf. Phil 2:6-11). Contemplation of Jesus Crucified is thus the highroad which the Church must tread every day if she wishes to understand the full meaning of freedom: the gift of self in service to God and one's brethren. *(section 87)*

Vatican Council II

For if man exists it is because God has created him through love, and through love continues to hold him in existence. He cannot live fully according to truth unless he freely acknowledges that love and entrusts himself to his creator. *Gaudium et Spes, 19*

Q. 20. Why is it that so few people pay attention to God?

So few people pay attention to God because their lives are occupied mainly with the affairs of men rather than with God.

#L3-2-2

So few people pay attention to God because their lives are occupied mainly with the affairs of men rather than with God.

While God is always good to us, there are many people who care very little for Him. They purposely break God's commandments and are more interested in their own pleasures and in the things of this world than in doing the will of God.

We must not follow those who do not believe in God. We should accept God's Word with deep faith and trust in His infinite love for us, for He is faithful to His covenant, His promises.

Sacred Scripture
Q. 20. Deut. 8:11-20; Job 8:11-19.

Catechism of the Catholic Church
Q. 20. Paragraphs 324, 2113, 2123-2125, 2127-2128, **2514-2516**.

For cross-references with Vatican II, Papal documents & other resources, see Family Wisdom Library on page 196.
For commentaries on each question with Cardinal Arinze, Sr. John Vianney and Fr. Straub (in Spanish), see Appendix C.

#L3-10-2

For the gate is wide and the way is easy, that leads to destruction, and those who enter by it are many. For the gate is narrow and the way is hard, that leads to life, and those who find it are few. *(Matthew 7:14)*

Sacred Scripture

"Take heed lest you forget the Lord your God, by not keeping his commandments and his ordinances and his statutes, which I command you this day... Beware lest you say in your heart, 'My power and the might of my hand have gotten me this wealth.' You shall remember the Lord your God, for it is he who gives you power to get wealth; that he may confirm his covenant which he swore to your fathers, as at this day. And if you forget the Lord your God and go after other gods and serve them and worship them, I solemnly warn you this day that you shall surely perish." *Deuteronomy 8:11, 17-19*

Enter by the narrow gate; for the gate is wide and the way is easy, that leads to destruction, and those who enter by it are many. For the gate is narrow and the way is hard, that leads to life, and those who find it are few. *Matthew 7:13-14*

Catechism of the Catholic Church

2113 Idolatry not only refers to false pagan worship. It remains a constant temptation to faith. Idolatry consists in divinizing what is not God. Man commits idolatry whenever he honors and reveres a creature in place of God, whether this be gods or demons (for example, satanism), power, pleasure, race, ancestors, the state, money, etc. Jesus says, "You cannot serve God and mammon."[1] Many martyrs died for not adoring "the Beast"[2] refusing even to simulate such worship. Idolatry rejects the unique Lordship of God; it is therefore incompatible with communion with God.[3]

Vatican Council II

Man therefore is divided in himself. As a result, the whole life of men, both individual and social, shows itself to be a struggle, and a dramatic one, between good and evil, between light and darkness. Man finds that he is unable of himself to overcome the assaults of evil successfully, so that everyone feels as though bound by chains. *Gaudium et Spes, 13*

Q. 21. Does every man have some desire for God?

Yes, every man has some desire for God, no matter how hidden it may be. As St. Augustine has said, "You have made us for yourself, O Lord, and our hearts are restless until they rest in You."

Even if we do not acknowledge it, there is a secret desire in our hearts for God. To the degree that God has helped us to know Him more than many others do, He expects us to love Him more and to serve Him better. Our life will be blessed if we do so, and we can look forward to being with God forever in Heaven.

#P25-7-2

Every man has some desire for God, no matter how hidden it may be.

Sacred Scripture

O God, thou art my God, I seek thee, my soul thirsts for thee; my flesh faints for thee, as in a dry and weary land where no water is. *Psalm 63:1*

Catechism of the Catholic Church

27 The desire for God is written in the human heart, because man is created by God and for God; and God never ceases to draw man to himself. Only in God will he find the truth and happiness he never stops searching for: "The dignity of man rests above all on the fact that he is called to communion with God. This invitation to converse with God is addressed to man as soon as he comes into being. For if man exists, it is because God has created him through love, and through love continues to hold him in existence. He cannot live fully according to truth unless he freely acknowledges that love and entrusts himself to his creator."[1]

Sacred Scripture	**Catechism of the Catholic Church**
Q. 21. Ps 119:20.	Q. 21. Paragraphs 28-30.

For cross-references with Vatican II, Papal documents & other resources, see Family Wisdom Library on page 196.
For commentaries on each question with Cardinal Arinze, Sr. John Vianney and Fr. Straub (in Spanish), see Appendix C.

Splendor of Truth

As a result of that mysterious original sin, committed at the prompting of Satan, the one who is "a liar and the father of lies" (Jn 8:44), man is constantly tempted to turn his gaze away from the living and true God in order to direct it towards idols (cf. 1 Thes 1:9), exchanging "the truth about God for a lie" (Rom 1:25). Man's capacity to know the truth is also darkened, and his will to submit to it is weakened. Thus, giving himself over to relativism and skepticism (cf. Jn 18:38), he goes off in search of an illusory freedom apart from truth itself.

But no darkness of error or of sin can totally take away from man the light of God the Creator. In the depths of his heart there always remains a yearning for absolute truth and a thirst to attain full knowledge of it. *(section 1)*

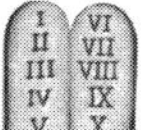

Doctrine • Moral • Worship Exercise

(See Appendix A for answer key, questions 16-21.)

1. How did God prove His love for man despite Adam and Eve's sin?
2. When we look at the world around us and see poverty, wars, natural disasters, abuse, etc., how can we be sure that God really loves us? How does God show that He keeps His promises?
3. What can you do to show that you love and worship God, even amidst the challenges and trials of daily life?

Chapter Summary Prayer

Lord, may we know and cherish the heavenly gifts You have given us. Your love never fails. The hand of Your loving kindness powerfully, yet gently, guides all the moments of our day. In You we live and move and have our being. Each day You show us a father's love. Your Holy Spirit, dwelling within us, gives us on earth the hope of unending joy. Your gift of the Spirit is the foretaste and promise of the Paschal feast of Heaven. With thankful praise, in company with the angels, we glorify the wonders of Your power.

Father in Heaven, be with us in our pilgrimage of life, anticipate our needs, and prevent our falling. Send Your Spirit to unite us in faith, that sharing in Your service, we may rejoice in Your presence. Increase our faith in You and bring our trust to its promised fulfillment in the joy of Your Kingdom.

God of the universe, we worship You as Lord. We rejoice to call You Father. In the midst of this world's uncertainty, we look to Your Covenant. Keep us in Your peace and secure in Your love. Grant us an unfailing respect for Your Name, and keep us always in Your love, through Jesus Christ our Savior. Amen.

Thought Provokers

Please see Appendix B for the answers.

Q. 16: Reflect on the following words of St. Paul: "Why, one will hardly die for a righteous man—though perhaps for a good man one will dare even to die. But God shows his love for us in that while we were yet sinners Christ died for us" (Romans 5:7–8).

Q. 17: A. When we reflect on the great goodness of God, especially as experienced in our own lives, it is only right and just that we should thank Him. What is the best way to thank God?

B. In addition to thanksgiving, what should the thought of God's goodness lead us to think or do?

Q. 18: We worship God when we surrender to Him our entire selves, everything we are and have, to use as He wishes. Why is full participation in the celebration of the Holy Eucharist the most perfect form of worship we can offer God during our stay on earth?

Q. 19: What is the basis of people's hope for the grace necessary to do God's will and to obtain eternal happiness in Heaven?

Q. 20: When men do not place God and His will for them first in their lives, what ultimately becomes their chief concern?

Q. 21: By using your reason, can you demonstrate the truth that every person has some desire for God in his heart?

By Heart Catechism and Scripture Review™

The "By Heart Catechism and Scripture Review" lists a selected number of questions and Scripture references from "The Apostolate's Family Catechism" to make memorization easier. Q = Question, SR = Scripture Reference

Q. 1. Who is God? God is the Supreme Being. God is the being above all beings. He is above all that exists.

Q. 2. Who made God? No one made God. He always was, and He always will be.

Q. 3. Can there be more than one God? No, there cannot be more than one God because there cannot be two supreme beings.

Q. 4. Why must there be a God? There must be a God because nothing happens unless someone makes it happen. There must be someone who started it all and who was not made by anyone else.

Q. 5. Why is God an endlessly perfect Being? God is an endlessly or infinitely perfect being, because He has no limits of any kind.

Q. 6. What are God's perfections? God's perfections are His qualities like infinite goodness, eternal, all-knowing, all-present and almighty.

Q. 8. Is God eternal? Yes, God is eternal because He always was, He is now, and He always will be.

SR 8 Psalm 90:2

Before the mountains were brought forth, or ever thou had formed the earth and the world, from everlasting to everlasting thou art God.

Q. 9. Why is God all-knowing? God is all-knowing because He knows all things in the past, in the present, and in the future, as well as everything that could be.

Q. 10. Is God present everywhere? Yes, God is present everywhere, all of the time.

Q. 11. Is God almighty? Yes, God is almighty because He can do every good thing.

By Heart Catechism and Scripture Review™

The "By Heart Catechism and Scripture Review" lists a selected number of questions and Scripture references from "The Apostolate's Family Catechism" to make memorization easier. Q = Question, SR = Scripture Reference

SR 11 Matthew 19:26

With God all things are possible.

SR 13 Isaiah 6:3

Holy, holy, holy is the Lord of hosts; the whole earth is full of his glory.

Q. 14. Why is God all-merciful? God is all-merciful because there is no end to His mercy. As often as we are sorry for our sins and confess them, so often will God forgive us.

Q. 15. Why is God all-just? God is all-just because He is completely honest and fair with everyone.

Q. 16. In what ways has God shown His love for us? God has shown His love for us by sending His Son in fulfillment of His promise to save mankind from the power of sin and death. Through Jesus, God has made us His children and cares for us as a loving father.

SR 16 John 3:16

For God so loved the world that he gave his only Son, that whoever believes in him should not perish but have eternal life.

Q. 17. How should we respond to God's goodness? We should respond to God's goodness by: (1) finding joy in God, and (2) worshiping and serving Him.

Q. 18. In what ways do we worship God? We worship God in the liturgy, especially in the Holy Sacrifice of the Mass, and when we pray by ourselves or with our families. We also worship God by serving Him in all that we do.

#T3-55

It was the Son's task to accomplish the Father's plan of salvation in the fullness of time. *(Catechism of the Catholic Church, 763)*

The Revelation of God: The Holy Trinity

#O8-21-2

God made a promise to redeem all men. He kept His promise by choosing Abraham's descendants (the people of Israel) to be His own special people.

CHAPTER FIVE

God Reveals Himself

Q. 22. What is the History of Salvation?

The History of Salvation is the account of God's dealings with mankind and how He saved us.

Throughout Salvation History, God the Father, God the Son, and God the Holy Spirit made Themselves known to man, made peace with him by means of the Crucifixion and Death of Jesus, and united Themselves with those who turned away from sin.

#H9-3-2

The History of Salvation is the account of God's dealings with mankind and how He saved us.

Sacred Scripture

Therefore, since we are justified by faith, we have peace with God through our Lord Jesus Christ. Through him we have obtained access to this grace in which we stand, and we rejoice in our hope of sharing the glory of God. *Romans 5:1-2*

For if while we were enemies we were reconciled to God by the death of his Son, much more, now that we are reconciled, shall we be saved by his life. Not only so, but we also rejoice in God through our Lord Jesus Christ, through whom we have now received our reconciliation. *Romans 5:10-11*

Sacred Scripture
Q. 22. Lk 24:13-27; Eph 1:3-10.

Catechism of the Catholic Church
Q. 22. Paragraphs **431-432**, 586, **758-769**, 1040, 1066, 1080, 1095, 1217, 2591, 2606, 2738.

For cross-references with Vatican II, Papal documents & other resources, see Family Wisdom Library on page 196.
For commentaries on each question with Cardinal Arinze, Sr. John Vianney and Fr. Straub (in Spanish), see Appendix C.

Catechism of the Catholic Church

763 It was the Son's task to accomplish the Father's plan of salvation in the fullness of time. Its accomplishment was the reason for his being sent.[1] "The Lord Jesus inaugurated his Church by preaching the Good News, that is, the coming of the Reign of God, promised over the ages in the scriptures."[2] To fulfill the Father's will, Christ ushered in the Kingdom of heaven on earth. The Church "is the Reign of Christ already present in mystery."[3]

Splendor of Truth

Jesus Christ, the "light of the nations," shines upon the face of his Church, which he sends forth to the whole world to proclaim the Gospel to every creature (cf. Mk 16:15). *(section 2)*

#R19.4-2

The Lord Jesus inaugurated his Church by preaching the Good News, that is, the coming of the Reign of God, promised over the ages in the scriptures. *(Catechism of the Catholic Church, 763)*

Vatican Council II

The eternal Father, in accordance with the utterly gratuitous and mysterious design of his wisdom and goodness, created the whole universe, and chose to raise up men to share in his own divine life; and when they had fallen in Adam, he did not abandon them, but at all times held out to them the means of salvation, bestowed in consideration of Christ, the Redeemer, "who is the image of the invisible God, the firstborn of every creature" (Col. 1:15). All the elect, before time began, the Father foreknew and also predestined "to become conformed to the image of his Son, that he should be the firstborn among many brethren" (Romans 8:29). He determined to call together in a holy Church those who should believe in Christ. *Lumen Gentium, 2*

This economy of Revelation is realized by deeds and words, which are intrinsically bound up with each other. As a result, the works performed by God in the history of salvation show forth and bear out the doctrine and realities signified by the words; the words, for their part, proclaim the works, and bring to light the mystery they contain. *Dei Verbum, 2*

By divine Revelation God wished to manifest and communicate both himself and the eternal decrees of his will concerning the salvation of mankind. He wished, in other words, "to share with us divine benefits which entirely surpass the powers of the human mind to understand" (First Vatican Council, Dogm. Const. on Cath. Faith, 2)." *Dei Verbum, 6*

Summary Prayer

Almighty God, the History of Salvation tells us how You saved us; You revealed Yourself to men, and made peace by Christ's Death on the Cross. You united with Yourself those who turned away from sin.

You revealed Yourself as an all-powerful Being existing above and beyond man and his world. You became real for us when You willed to let us know You personally through divine Revelation. We thank You for giving Yourself to us and showing us Your will for the Salvation of mankind, through Christ our Lord. Amen.

Q. 23. How did God deal with mankind?

God dealt with mankind by fully revealing Himself and His plan for our Salvation through Jesus Christ and the Holy Spirit.

God showing something of Himself to us is known as revelation. Sacred Scripture—the Bible—is the written account of God's Revelation to us and describes God's actions in the world. We know that Sacred Scripture is true because it is God's own Word, which He made known to its writers.

God made Himself known to us in order to save us from sin. Sin caused us to lose God's life within our very being and made us slaves to sin and subject to death. God sent His only Son, Jesus Christ, to save us from sin and death and to give us His life of grace. Because of Jesus, we can now receive God's forgiveness for our sins, if we are really sorry and if we resolve to try not to offend Him again.

Sacred Scripture
Q. 23. Is 45:17; Jn 3:16.

Catechism of the Catholic Church
Q. 23. Paragraphs 35, **51-141**, 161, 169, 183, 289.

For cross-references with Vatican II, Papal documents & other resources, see Family Wisdom Library on page 196.
For commentaries on each question with Cardinal Arinze, Sr. John Vianney and Fr. Straub (in Spanish), see Appendix C.

Sacred Scripture

He was in the world, and the world was made through him, yet the world knew him not. He came to his own home, and his own people received him not. But to all who received him, who believed in his name, he gave power to become children of God. *John 1:10-12*

While we were yet helpless, at the right time Christ died for the ungodly. Why, one will hardly die for a righteous man—though perhaps for a good man one will dare even to die. But God shows his love for us in that while we were yet sinners Christ died for us. *Romans 5:6-8*

Catechism of the Catholic Church

50 By natural reason man can know God with certainty, on the basis of his works. But there is another order of knowledge, which man cannot possibly arrive at by his own powers: the order of divine Revelation.[1] Through an utterly free decision, God has revealed himself and given himself to man. This he does by revealing the mystery, his plan of loving goodness, formed from all eternity in Christ, for the benefit of all men. God has fully revealed this plan by sending us his beloved Son, our Lord Jesus Christ, and the Holy Spirit.

#J2-342-2

God dealt with mankind by fully revealing Himself and His plan for our Salvation through Jesus Christ and the Holy Spirit.

Vatican Council II

After the era of the patriarchs, he taught this nation [Israel], by Moses and the prophets, to recognize him as the only living and true God, as a provident Father and just judge. He taught them, too, to look for the promised Saviour. And so, throughout the ages, he prepared the way for the Gospel. *Dei Verbum, 3*

#A18-18-2

We know that Sacred Scripture is true because it is God's own Word, which He made known to its writers.

Summary Prayer

Most loving Father, through the Death and Resurrection of Your Son Jesus Christ, You, in fact, redeemed man. But we must now successfully complete our pilgrimage in the wilderness of this life in order to gain eternal happiness in Heaven.

Grant us living water from the rock and Bread from Heaven, that we may survive our desert pilgrimage and thank You eternally for Your kindness, through Your only begotten Son, Jesus Christ. Amen.

Q. 24. How did God choose to show Himself to the people of the Old Testament?

God chose to show Himself to the people of the Old Testament as the one, true, and personal God. Noah, Abraham, Joseph, David, Daniel, and all of the people of the Old Testament learned that God was real, that He was faithful and true in all His words and actions, that He loved them as a father loves his son, and that His love is everlasting.

Sacred Scripture
Q. 24. Gen 9:8-13.

Catechism of the Catholic Church
Q. 24. Paragraphs **54-64**, **77-78**, 121-123, 128, 200, 204, 238-239, 286-288.

For cross-references with Vatican II, Papal documents & other resources, see Family Wisdom Library on page 196.
For commentaries on each question with Cardinal Arinze, Sr. John Vianney and Fr. Straub (in Spanish), see Appendix C.

Thus we read, for example: "For thou, O Lord, art good and forgiving, abounding in steadfast love to all who call on thee" (Psalm 86:5), and "As a father pities his children, so the Lord pities those who fear him" (Psalm 103:13). The mystery of the Holy Trinity would not be revealed until the New Testament.

God is the one, all-powerful Being, existing above and beyond man and his world. The true God is real. He becomes real for us when we come to know Him. To know God personally, we have to be very attentive to whatever He shows us of Himself. By making Himself known to us through Revelation, God gave Himself to us and showed us His will for the Salvation of all mankind.

#C16-2-2

God revealed Himself in the Old Testament as the one God, true and personal.

God shows Himself in all of creation and history, but the Catholic Church is interested in the personal way in which God showed and continues to show Himself to His beloved human beings made in His image and likeness. This revelation is found in the Bible and in Sacred Tradition, and from it we learn what our life really is and how we must live it.

Sacred Scripture

When Abram was ninety-nine years old the Lord appeared to Abram, and said to him, "I am God Almighty; walk before me, and be blameless... And I will establish my covenant between me and you and your descendants after you throughout their generations for an everlasting covenant, to be God to you and to your descendants after you." *Genesis 17:1, 7*

Catechism of the Catholic Church

201 To Israel, his chosen, God revealed himself as the only One: "Hear, O Israel: The Lord our God is one Lord; and you shall love the Lord your God with all your heart, and with all your soul, and with all your might."[1] Through the prophets, God calls Israel and all nations to turn to him, the one and only God: "Turn to me and be saved, all the ends of the earth! For I am God, and there is no other.... To me every knee shall bow, every tongue shall swear. 'Only in the Lord, it shall be said of me, are righteousness and strength.'"[2]

Splendor of Truth

Within the unity of the Church, promoting and preserving the faith and the moral life is the task entrusted by Jesus to the Apostles (cf. Mt 28:19-20), a task which continues in the ministry of their successors. This is apparent from the living Tradition, whereby—as the Second Vatican Council teaches—"the Church, in her teaching, life and worship, perpetuates and hands on to every generation all that she is and all that she believes. This tradition which comes from the Apostles, progresses in the Church under the assistance of the Holy Spirit." *(section 27)*

Vatican Council II

And furthermore, wishing to open up the way to heavenly salvation, he [God] manifested himself to our first parents from the very beginning. After the fall, he buoyed them up with the hope of salvation, by promising redemption (cf. Gen. 3:15); and he has never ceased to take care of the human race. For he wishes to give eternal life to all those who seek salvation by patience in well-doing (cf. Rom. 2:6-7). In his own time God called Abraham, and made him into a great nation (cf. Gen. 12:2). *Dei Verbum, 3*

Summary Prayer

Heavenly Father, You revealed Yourself in the Old Testament as the one, true, personal God. Abraham, Joseph, and Moses prefigured Your plan, Father, to redeem mankind from slavery and to lead them into the land of promise.

Through the Death and Resurrection of Your Son, You redeemed man. But we must now successfully complete our pilgrimage in the wilderness of this life in order to gain eternal happiness in Heaven. Grant that we may grow to know You in a more personal way, especially as we meditate on Your Word in Sacred Scripture and in Sacred Tradition. We ask this through Jesus Christ our Redeemer and Lord. Amen.

Doctrine • Moral • Worship Exercise

(See Appendix A for answer key, questions 22-24.)

1. What distinct quality of God is revealed in the History of Salvation?
2. Cite instances in your life when you have experienced God as a saving God.
3. How can you respond to what God has revealed?

Chapter Summary Prayer

Lord, You established peace within the borders of Jerusalem. Give the fullness of peace to Your faithful people. May peace rule us in this life and possess us in eternal life. You fill us with the best of wheat, the Bread of Life, in the Eucharist. Grant that what we see dimly now as in a mirror, we may come to perceive clearly in the brightness of Your truth.

Almighty God, every good thing comes from You. Fill our hearts with love for You. Increase our faith, and by Your constant care, protect the good You have given us. May the Holy Sacrifice of the Mass bring us Your blessing and accomplish within us its promise of Salvation.

Father of our Lord Jesus Christ, faith in Your Word is the way to wisdom, and to ponder Your divine plan is to grow in the truth. Open our eyes that we may do Your will, and our ears to hear the sound of Your call, so that our every action may increase our sharing in the life You have offered us, through Christ our Lord. Amen.

Thought Provokers

Please see Appendix B for the answers.

Q. 22: Can you trace, in outline form, the history of man's Salvation, beginning with the period immediately after the Fall and continuing up to our own day?

Q. 23: Jesus is the Savior of all mankind. Therefore, He must also be the Savior of those who lived before He became our Savior; for example, Moses, Abraham, Sarah, Miriam, David, etc. How can this be possible?

Q. 24: A. In the Old Testament, God is clearly revealed as being the one and only true God. Find passages in the Old Testament that are capable of being interpreted as referring not only to God the Father, but also to God the Holy Spirit and God the Son.

B. How is it possible for something to be both one and three at the same time?

T3-54

The Trinity is One. We do not confess three Gods, but one God in three persons, the "consubstantial Trinity." *(Catechism of the Catholic Church, 253)*

CHAPTER SIX

The Mystery of the Holy Trinity

Q. 25. What is the mystery of the Holy Trinity?

The mystery of the Holy Trinity is that there is in the one, true God only one divine substance, yet three divine Persons: God the Father, God the Son, and God the Holy Spirit. The Trinity is called a mystery of faith because it is a truth that cannot be known unless it is revealed by God, and it is a truth that we will not be able to fully understand.

Jesus Christ made known to us the secrets of the Kingdom of Heaven. The greatest of these is the secret of God Himself. Jesus taught us of the life of God. He said that there are three Persons in the one God and that each of these Persons are equal to the other. He also revealed the names of these three divine Persons: the Father, the Son, and the Holy Spirit.

The Holy Trinity is the central mystery of Christian faith and life.

#T3-27-2

The mystery of the Holy Trinity is that there is in the one, true God only one divine substance, yet three divine Persons.

Sacred Scripture
Q. 25. Mt 28:19; Jn 14:8-17.

Catechism of the Catholic Church
Q. 25. Paragraphs 232-237, 253-256.

For cross-references with Vatican II, Papal documents & other resources, see Family Wisdom Library on page 196.
For commentaries on each question with Cardinal Arinze, Sr. John Vianney and Fr. Straub (in Spanish), see Appendix C.

Catechism by Diagram

#T3-15

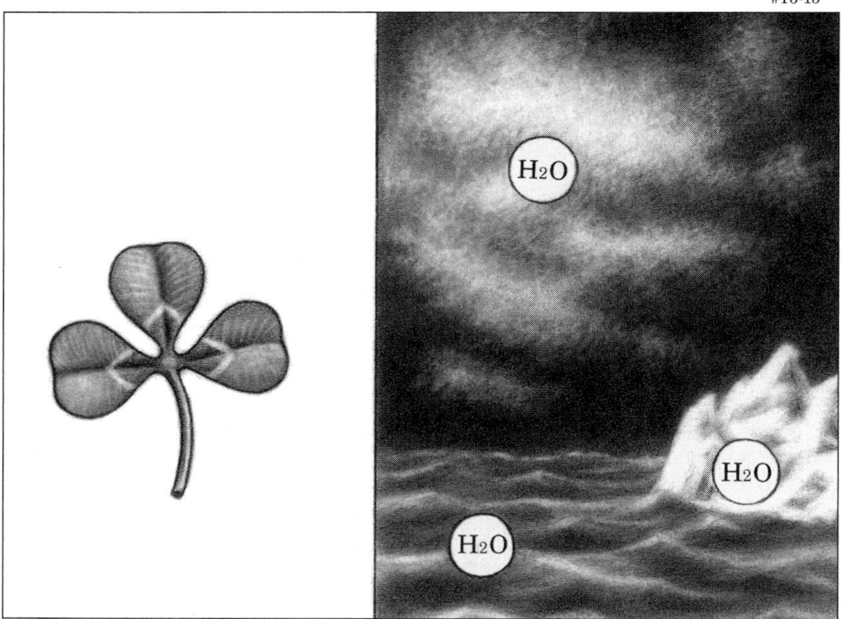

Three in One. The clover has three parts, but it is only one clover. Water, which contains hydrogen and oxygen, appears in three different states: liquid (water), steam (gas), and solid (ice). So in the Trinity there is only one God, but there are three Persons, all having the same divine substance.

Sacred Scripture

And when Jesus was baptized, he went up immediately from the water, and behold, the heavens were opened and he saw the Spirit of God descending like a dove, and alighting on him. *Matthew 3:16*

Catechism of the Catholic Church

253 *The Trinity is One.* We do not confess three Gods, but one God in three persons, the "consubstantial Trinity."[1] The divine persons do not share the one divinity among themselves but each of them is God whole and entire: "The Father is that which the Son is, the Son that which the Father is, the Father and the Son that which the Holy Spirit is, i.e., by nature one God." In the words of the Fourth Lateran Council (1215): "Each of the persons is that supreme reality, viz., the divine substance, essence or nature."[2]

Vatican Council II

By divine revelation God wished to manifest and communicate both himself and the eternal decrees of his will concerning the salvation of mankind. He wished, in other words, "to share with us divine benefits which entirely surpass the power of the human mind to understand." *Dei Verbum, 6*

The highest exemplar and source of this mystery [that is, the unity of the church] is the unity, in the Trinity of Persons, of one God, the Father and the Son in the Holy Spirit. *Ecumenism, 2*

Q. 26. Why do we believe in the mystery of the Holy Trinity?

We believe in the mystery of the Holy Trinity because God revealed it; He is all-wise and all-truthful.

To better understand, as best we can, the mystery of the Holy Trinity, we must await God's unveiling of Himself in Heaven.

Sacred Scripture

But the Counselor, the Holy Spirit, whom the Father will send in my name, he will teach you all things, and bring to your remembrance all that I have said to you. *John 14:26*

Catechism of the Catholic Church

234 The mystery of the Most Holy Trinity is the central mystery of Christian faith and life. It is the mystery of God in himself. It is therefore the source of all the other mysteries of faith, the light that enlightens them. It is the most fundamental and essential teaching in the "hierarchy of the truths of faith."[1] The whole history of salvation is identical with the history of the way and the means by which the one true God, Father, Son, and Holy Spirit, reveals himself to men "and reconciles and unites with himself those who turn away from sin."[2]

#R4.2-10

The mystery of the Most Holy Trinity is the central mystery of Christian faith and life. *(Catechism of the Catholic Church, 234)*

Catechism of the Catholic Church
Q. 26. Paragraphs **244-245**, 267.

For cross-references with Vatican II, Papal documents & other resources, see Family Wisdom Library on page 196.
For commentaries on each question with Cardinal Arinze, Sr. John Vianney and Fr. Straub (in Spanish), see Appendix C.

Q. 27. How is the mystery of the Holy Trinity revealed in the New Testament?

In the New Testament, the mystery of the Holy Trinity is revealed through the Person, words, and actions of Jesus Christ.

God revealed this mystery to us because He wants us to know Him as He is, so that we might love Him more in return for His boundless love for us.

#T3-32-2

In the New Testament, the mystery of the Holy Trinity is revealed through the Person, words, and actions of Jesus Christ.

Sacred Scripture
Q. 27. Eph 2:17-22; Heb 1:1-2.

Catechism of the Catholic Church
Q. 27. Paragraph 244.

For cross-references with Vatican II, Papal documents & other resources, see Family Wisdom Library on page 196.
For commentaries on each question with Cardinal Arinze, Sr. John Vianney and Fr. Straub (in Spanish), see Appendix C.

Sacred Scripture

And I will pray the Father, and he will give you another Counselor, to be with you for ever, even the Spirit of truth, whom the world cannot receive, because it neither sees him nor knows him; you know him, for he dwells with you, and will be in you. *John 14:16-17*

Catechism of the Catholic Church

243 Before his Passover, Jesus announced the sending of "another Paraclete" (Advocate), the Holy Spirit. At work since creation, having previously "spoken through the prophets," the Spirit will now be with and in the disciples, to teach them and guide them "into all the truth."[1] The Holy Spirit is thus revealed as another divine person with Jesus and the Father.

Vatican Council II

After God had spoken many times and in various ways through the prophets, "in these last days he has spoken to us by a Son" (Heb. 1:1-2). For he sent his Son, the eternal Word who enlightens all men, to dwell among men and to tell them about the inner life of God. Hence, Jesus Christ, sent as "a man among men," "speaks the words of God" (Jn. 3:34), and accomplishes the saving work which the Father gave him to do (cf. Jn. 5:36; 17:4). As a result, he himself—to see whom is to see the Father (cf. Jn. 14:9)—completed and perfected Revelation and confirmed it with divine guarantees. He did this by the total fact of his presence and self-manifestation—by words and works, signs and miracles, but above all by his death and glorious resurrection from the dead, and finally by sending the Spirit of truth. He revealed that God was with us, to deliver us from the darkness of sin and death, and to raise us up to eternal life. *Dei Verbum, 4*

#L3-5-2

Jesus revealed that God was with us, to deliver us from the darkness of sin and death, and to raise us up to eternal life. *(Dei Verbum, 4)*

Jesus Reveals Himself

Q. 28. What did Jesus reveal about Himself?

Jesus revealed Himself as the second Person of the Holy Trinity, the eternal and divine Son of God.

#T3-26-2

Jesus revealed Himself as the Second Person of the Holy Trinity, the eternal and divine Son of God.

Sacred Scripture

For God so loved the world that he gave his only Son, that whoever believes in him should not perish but have eternal life. *John 3:16*

I and the Father are one. *John 10:30*

All that the Father has is mine. *John 16:15*

And now, Father, glorify thou me in thy own presence with the glory which I had with thee before the world was made. *John 17:5*

Catechism of the Catholic Church

443 Peter could recognize the transcendent character of the Messiah's divine sonship because Jesus had clearly allowed it to be so understood. To his accusers' question before the Sanhedrin, "Are you the Son of God, then?" Jesus answered, "You say that I am."[1] Well before this, Jesus referred to himself as "the Son" who knows the Father, as distinct from the "servants" God had earlier sent to his people; he is superior even to the angels.[2] He distinguished his sonship from that of his disciples by never saying "our Father," except to command them: "You, then, pray like this: 'Our Father,'" and he emphasized this distinction, saying "my Father and your Father."[3]

Sacred Scripture
Q. 28. Jn 4:23-26, 6:35-40.

Catechism of the Catholic Church
Q. 28. Paragraphs **444**-445.

For cross-references with Vatican II, Papal documents & other resources, see Family Wisdom Library on page 196.
For commentaries on each question with Cardinal Arinze, Sr. John Vianney and Fr. Straub (in Spanish), see Appendix C.

Vatican Council II

Christ established on earth the kingdom of God, revealed his Father and himself by deeds and words; and by his death, resurrection and glorious ascension, as well as by sending the Holy Spirit, completed his work. *Dei Verbum, 17*

Jesus Reveals the Father

Q. 29. How was God the Father revealed by Jesus?

Jesus revealed the Father by calling Him by that name.

When Jesus drove the money changers from the temple, He said, "You shall not make my Father's house a house of trade" (John 2:16).

#J2-314-2

Jesus taught us to love the Father because the Father loves us and wants to help us in all our needs.

He said to His disciples, "By this my Father is glorified; that you bear much fruit, and so prove to be my disciples. As the Father has loved me, so have I loved you; abide in my love" (John 15:8-9).

Jesus taught us to love the Father because the Father loves us and wants to help us in all our needs. And when our earthly lives come to an end, He wants to bring us to His dwelling in Heaven.

Sacred Scripture
Q. 29. Mt 6:7-15; Jn 14:1-11.

Catechism of the Catholic Church
Q. 29. Paragraphs **238-242**, 2780.

For cross-references with Vatican II, Papal documents & other resources, see Family Wisdom Library on page 196.
For commentaries on each question with Cardinal Arinze, Sr. John Vianney and Fr. Straub (in Spanish), see Appendix C.

Sacred Scripture

He who has seen me has seen the Father... Do you not believe that I am in the Father and the Father in me? The words that I say to you I do not speak on my own authority; but the Father who dwells in me does his works. *John 14:9-10*

Catechism of the Catholic Church

240 Jesus revealed that God is Father in an unheard-of sense: he is Father not only in being Creator; he is eternally Father in his relation to his only Son, who is eternally Son only in relation to his Father: "No one knows the Son except the Father, and no one knows the Father except the Son and any one to whom the Son chooses to reveal him."[1]

Jesus Reveals the Holy Spirit

Q. 30. How did Jesus reveal the Holy Spirit?

Jesus revealed God the Holy Spirit as the Third Divine Person of the Holy Trinity Whom He and the Father would send to His Church to teach, guide and strengthen it.

#J2-367-2

At the Last Supper, Jesus told the Apostles, "But when the Counselor comes, whom I shall send to you from the Father, even the Spirit of truth, who proceeds from the Father, he will bear witness to me" *(John 15:26).*

Sacred Scripture
Q. 30. Acts 1:1-9.

Catechism of the Catholic Church
Q. 30. Paragraphs: **238-244**, 687, 727-730.

For cross-references with Vatican II, Papal documents & other resources, see Family Wisdom Library on page 196.
For commentaries on each question with Cardinal Arinze, Sr. John Vianney and Fr. Straub (in Spanish), see Appendix C.

Jesus taught that God the Holy Spirit was the equal of Himself and the Father. At the Last Supper Jesus told the Apostles: "But when the Counselor comes, whom I shall send to you from the Father, even the Spirit of truth, who proceeds from the Father, he will bear witness to me" (John 15:26).

Sacred Scripture

And when they bring you before the synagogues and the rulers and the authorities, do not be anxious how or what you are to answer or what you are to say; for the Holy Spirit will teach you in that very hour what you ought to say. *Luke 12:11-12*

Catechism of the Catholic Church

728 Jesus does not reveal the Holy Spirit fully, until he himself has been glorified through his Death and Resurrection. Nevertheless, little by little he alludes to him even in his teaching of the multitudes, as when he reveals that his own flesh will be food for the life of the world.[1] He also alludes to the Spirit in speaking to Nicodemus,[2] to the Samaritan woman,[3] and to those who take part in the feast of Tabernacles.[4] To his disciples he speaks openly of the Spirit in connection with prayer[5] and with the witness they will have to bear.[6]

Doctrine • Moral • Worship Exercise

(See Appendix A for answer key, questions 25-30.)

1. Describe the mystery of the Holy Trinity in your own words.
2. In your daily life, how can you show to those around you that you believe in the Holy Trinity?
3. Look for ways to help others to know and love the Holy Trinity.

Chapter Summary Prayer

Father, all-powerful and ever-living God, when Your children sinned and wandered from Your friendship, You reunited them with Yourself through the blood of Your Son and the power of the Holy Spirit. You gather them into Your Church to be one as You, Father, are one with Your Son and the Holy Spirit. You call them to be Your people, to praise Your wisdom in all Your works. You make them the Body of Christ and the dwelling-place of the Holy Spirit.

Father, all-powerful and ever-living God, we joyfully proclaim our faith in the mystery of Your Godhead. You have revealed Your glory as well as the glory of Your Son and of the Holy Spirit: three Persons equal in majesty, undivided in splendor, yet one Lord, one God, ever to be adored in Your everlasting glory. With all the choirs of angels in Heaven we proclaim Your glory, through Jesus Christ our Savior to Whom, with You and the Holy Spirit, be all honor and glory. Amen.

Thought Provokers

Please see Appendix B for the answers.

Q. 25: How can the mystery of the Holy Trinity be explained in understandable (yet incomplete) terms to a child?

Q. 26: Find passages in the New Testament that demonstrate the teaching of the divinity of the Father, the Son, and the Holy Spirit, and that God is one.

Q. 27: The word "Trinity" is not a biblical term. Nevertheless, it appropriately describes God as revealed in the New Testament. Why?

Q. 28: Who did Jesus say He was?

Q. 29: How would you explain that Jesus speaks of the Father as other than Himself, yet at the same time says that He and the Father are one?

Q. 30: Recall at least one passage from the New Testament which shows that Jesus refers at least indirectly to the divinity of the Holy Spirit.

CHAPTER SEVEN

The Holy Trinity: Father, Son and Holy Spirit

Q. 31. What did Jesus teach His disciples about God the Father, God the Son, and God the Holy Spirit?

Jesus, the Divine Teacher, taught His disciples about the true God. He told them that He, the Son, is the way to the Father and that by getting to know Him, they would get to know the Father also. Moreover, they would also be able to see the love of the Father in the actions of the Son, because Jesus said that He and His Father are one.

#J2-294-2

Jesus taught His disciples that He, the Son, is the way to the Father and that by getting to know Him, they would get to know the Father also.

Jesus taught His disciples about becoming sons of God through the gift of the Spirit. Jesus calls us as well to become sons (or children) of God. We do this through a new life which He gives us. This new life is God's own life, given to us by the Holy Spirit. This is called "grace" or "sanctifying grace" or "habitual grace." Because Jesus is

Sacred Scripture
Q. 31. Lk 11:13.

Catechism of the Catholic Church
Q. 31. Paragraphs 243, 423, 443.

For cross-references with Vatican II, Papal documents & other resources, see Family Wisdom Library on page 196.
For commentaries on each question with Cardinal Arinze, Sr. John Vianney and Fr. Straub (in Spanish), see Appendix C.

the Son of God, He is able to give us a share of God's life and to make us children of God.*

Sacred Scripture

But to all who received him, who believed in his name, he gave power to become children of God. *John 1:12*

#H9-2-2

Because Jesus is the Son of God, He is able to give us a share of God's life and to make us children of God.

Jesus said to him, "I am the way, and the truth, and the life; no one comes to the Father, but by me. If you had known me, you would have known my Father also; henceforth you know him and have seen him."

Philip said to him, "Lord, show us the Father, and we shall be satisfied." Jesus said to him, "Have I been with you so long, and yet you do not know me, Philip? He who has seen me has seen the Father; how can you say, 'Show us the Father'? Do you not believe that I am in the Father and the Father in me? The words that I say to you I do not speak on my own authority; but the Father who dwells in me does his works. Believe me that I am in the Father and the Father in me; or else believe me for the sake of the works themselves.

"Truly, truly, I say to you, he who believes in me will also do the works that I do; and greater works than these will he do, because I go to the Father. Whatever you ask in my name, I will do it, that the Father may be glorified in the Son; if you ask anything in my name, I will do it.

"If you love me, you will keep my commandments. And I will pray the Father, and he will give you another Counselor, to be with you for ever, even the Spirit of truth, whom the world cannot receive, because it neither sees him nor knows him; you know him, for he dwells with you, and will be in you." *John 14:6-17*

*[*Note: When the word "God" by itself is used in Scripture or in the Church's liturgy, it usually refers solely to God the Father.*]

Splendor of Truth

People today need to turn to Christ once again in order to receive from him the answer to their questions about what is good and what is evil. Christ is the Teacher, the Risen One who has life in himself and who is always present in his Church and in the world. It is he who opens up to the faithful the book of Scriptures and, by fully revealing the Father's will, teaches the truth about moral action. At the source and summit of the economy of salvation, as the Alpha and the Omega of human history (cf. Rev 1:8; 21:6; 22:13), Christ sheds light on man's condition and his integral vocation. *(section 8)*

Vatican Council II

When the work which the Father gave the Son to do on earth (cf. Jn. 17:4) was accomplished, the Holy Spirit was sent on the day of Pentecost in order that he might continually sanctify the Church, and that, consequently, those who believe might have access through Christ in one Spirit to the Father (cf. Eph. 2:18). He is the Spirit of life, the fountain of water springing up to eternal life. *Lumen Gentium, 4*

Summary Prayer

Most Merciful Father, in loving gratitude for all that You have accomplished for our Salvation through Jesus Christ our Lord, we pray for the fullness of the Gifts of the Holy Spirit, that we may praise You as we ought, as we await the full outcome of Your divine purposes; for You indeed are our God together with God the Son and God the Holy Spirit. To You, Triune God, be all honor and glory, now and forever. Amen.

#T3-31-2

Most Merciful Father, in loving gratitude for all that You have accomplished for our Salvation through Jesus Christ our Lord, we pray for the fullness of the Gifts of the Holy Spirit.

Q. 32. Who is God the Father?

God the Father is the First Person of the Holy Trinity, Who eternally begets or generates God the Son.

This begetting is similar to a person who begets an idea or work in his mind.

#R4.2-8

God the Father is the First Person of the Holy Trinity, Who eternally begets or generates God the Son.

Sacred Scripture

No one has ever seen God; the only Son, who is in the bosom of the Father, he has made him known. *John 1:18*

Catechism of the Catholic Church

270 God is the *Father* Almighty, whose fatherhood and power shed light on one another: God reveals his fatherly omnipotence by the way he takes care of our needs; by the filial adoption that he gives us ("I will be a father to you, and you shall be my sons and daughters, says the Lord Almighty."):[1] finally by his infinite mercy, for he displays his power at its height by freely forgiving sins.

Splendor of Truth

What man is and what he must do becomes clear as soon as God reveals himself. *(section 10)*

Sacred Scripture
Q. 32. 2 Cor 6:18.

Catechism of the Catholic Church
Q. 32. Paragraphs **238-248**, 279.

For cross-references with Vatican II, Papal documents & other resources, see Family Wisdom Library on page 196.
For commentaries on each question with Cardinal Arinze, Sr. John Vianney and Fr. Straub (in Spanish), see Appendix C.

Vatican Council II

This plan flows from "fountain-like love," the love of God the Father. As the principle without principle from whom the Son is generated and from whom the Holy Spirit proceeds through the Son, God in his great and merciful kindness freely creates us and moreover, graciously calls us to share in his life and glory. *Missionary Activity, 2*

Q. 33. Who is God the Son?

God the Son is the Second Person of the Holy Trinity, because from all eternity He is begotten in the mind of the Father.

He is called the Divine Word because He is the mental word in which God the Father expresses the thought of Himself; this thought or Word is the perfect and eternal image of the Father.

Sacred Scripture

In the beginning was the Word, and the Word was with God, and the Word was God. He was in the beginning with God; all things were made through him, and without him was not anything made that was made... And the Word became flesh and dwelt among us, full of grace and truth; we have beheld his glory, glory as of the only Son from the Father. *John 1:1-3, 14*

He is the image of the invisible God, the first-born of all creation. *Colossians 1:15*

#R19.1-5

The Gospels report that at two solemn moments, the Baptism and the Transfiguration of Christ, the voice of the Father designates Jesus his "beloved Son." *(Catechism of the Catholic Church, 444)*

Sacred Scripture
Q. 33. Mt 3:16-17; Jn 14:6-7.

Catechism of the Catholic Church
Q. 33. Paragraphs **422-483**.

For cross-references with Vatican II, Papal documents & other resources, see Family Wisdom Library on page 196.
For commentaries on each question with Cardinal Arinze, Sr. John Vianney and Fr. Straub (in Spanish), see Appendix

Catechism of the Catholic Church

444 The Gospels report that at two solemn moments, the Baptism and the Transfiguration of Christ, the voice of the Father designates Jesus his "beloved Son."[1] Jesus calls himself the "only Son of God," and by this title affirms his eternal preexistence.[2] He asks for faith in "the name of the only Son of God."[3] In the centurion's exclamation before the crucified Christ, "Truly this man was the Son of God,"[4] that Christian confession is already heard. Only in the Paschal mystery can the believer give the title "Son of God" its full meaning.

Q. 34. Who is God the Holy Spirit?

God the Holy Spirit is the Third Person of the Holy Trinity. He is infinitely perfect, living Love which flows or proceeds eternally from the Father and the Son as love personified. He is the love of the Trinity.

Sacred Scripture

God's love has been poured into our hearts through the Holy Spirit who has been given to us. *Romans 5:5*

#T3-29-2

God the Holy Spirit is the Third Person of the Holy Trinity Who proceeds eternally from the Father and the Son. He is the love of the Trinity.

Sacred Scripture
Q. 34. 2 Cor 3:17-18.

Catechism of the Catholic Church
Q. 34. Paragraphs 243-248, **683-701**, 737-741.

For cross-references with Vatican II, Papal documents & other resources, see Family Wisdom Library on page 196.
For commentaries on each question with Cardinal Arinze, Sr. John Vianney and Fr. Straub (in Spanish), see Appendix C.

Catechism of the Catholic Church

689 The One whom the Father has sent into our hearts, the Spirit of his Son, is truly God.[1] Consubstantial with the Father and the Son, the Spirit is inseparable from them, in both the inner life of the Trinity and his gift of love for the world. In adoring the Holy Trinity, life-giving, consubstantial, and indivisible, the Church's faith also professes the distinction of persons. When the Father sends his Word, he always sends his Breath. In their joint mission, the Son and the Holy Spirit are distinct but inseparable. To be sure, it is Christ who is seen, the visible image of the invisible God, but it is the Spirit who reveals him.

Q. 35. In what ways can we honor the Holy Trinity?

We honor the Holy Trinity by trying to understand, as much as we can by faith, that by Baptism we are called to a close union of love with the three divine Persons. God the Father is our Father and Author of Life; God the Son is our Lord and Savior; and God the Holy Spirit is our Teacher and Guide.

#F1-46-2

We honor the Holy Trinity by trying to understand, as much as we can by faith, that by Baptism we are called to a close union of love with the three divine Persons.

God, the Holy Trinity, Who is closer to us than we are to ourselves, lives in our souls by grace. We honor Him when we remember His presence in our souls—the presence of the Father, the Son and the Holy Spirit.

Sacred Scripture
Q. 35. Col 3:17.

Catechism of the Catholic Church
Q. 35. Paragraphs 257-260, 265-266, 1239, **2655**, 2662-**2789**.

For cross-references with Vatican II, Papal documents & other resources, see Family Wisdom Library on page 196.
For commentaries on each question with Cardinal Arinze, Sr. John Vianney and Fr. Straub (in Spanish), see Appendix C.

Jesus said, "If a man loves me, he will keep my word, and my Father will love him, and we will come to him and make our home with him." (John 14:23), and "I will pray the Father, and he will give you another Counselor, to be with you for ever" (John 14:16).

We show our love for the Holy Trinity when we pray. We may pray simply as the Church does most often—to the Father, through the Son, in union with the Holy Spirit.

Sacred Scripture

The grace of the Lord Jesus Christ and the love of God and the fellowship of the Holy Spirit be with you all. *2 Corinthians 13:14*

Catechism of the Catholic Church

1082 In the Church's liturgy the divine blessing is fully revealed and communicated. The Father is acknowledged and adored as the source and the end of all the blessings of creation and salvation. In his Word who became incarnate, died, and rose for us, he fills us with his blessings. Through his Word, he pours into our hearts the Gift that contains all gifts, the Holy Spirit.

Vatican Council II

Thus by Baptism men are grafted into the paschal mystery of Christ; they die with him, are buried with him, and rise with him. They receive the spirit of adoption as sons "in which we cry, Abba, Father" (Rom. 8:15) and thus become true adorers such as the Father seeks. *Sacrosanctum Concilium, 6*

Summary Prayer

Most Holy Trinity, one true God in three divine Persons, help us to honor You by trying to remember Your presence in our souls. Help us to show our love for You, Father, Son, and Holy Spirit, by frequent prayer. Help us to show our love for You by trying to understand, as much as we can through faith, that through Baptism we are called to a close union of love with You, for You live in our souls by grace.

God, You are our Father. Jesus Christ, You are our Lord and Savior. Holy Spirit, You are our Teacher and Guide.

Father, Son, and Holy Spirit, Holy Trinity, merciful friends of mankind, grant that we may stand before You in purity and holiness and reverently serve You as our God, to Whom worship is due from all, now and forever. Amen.

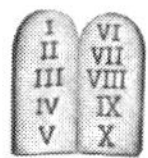

Doctrine • Moral • Worship Exercise

(See Appendix A for answer key, questions 31-35.)

1. Describe the distinct roles of the Father, the Son, and the Holy Spirit.
2. In what way can you honor the presence of the Trinity in every person you meet each day (i.e., parents, friends, teachers, and others)?
3. Write a prayer asking the Holy Trinity to help your family to become a more perfect model of Their unity.

Chapter Summary Prayer

Father, You revealed Your Son to the nations by the guidance of a star. Lead us to Your glory in Heaven by the light of faith. Father of light, unchanging God, You revealed to men of faith the resplendent fact of the Word made flesh. Your light is strong, Your love is near; draw us beyond the limits which this world imposes to the life where Your Spirit makes all life complete.

Almighty Father, eternal God, when the Spirit descended upon Jesus at His baptism in the Jordan River, You revealed Him as Your own beloved Son. Keep us, Your children born of water and the Spirit, faithful to our calling. May all who share in the sonship of Christ follow in His path of service to man, and reflect the glory of His Kingdom even to the ends of the earth.

Accept the prayers of Your servants, Lord, and prepare our hearts to praise Your holy Name. Come to our aid in times of trouble, and make us worthy to praise Your holy Name.

Father, You sent Your Word to bring us truth and Your Spirit to make us holy. Through Them we come to know the mystery of Your life. Help us to worship You, one God in three Persons, by proclaiming and living our faith in You.

God, we praise You: Father all-powerful; Christ, Lord and Savior; and Spirit of love. You reveal Yourself in the depths of our being, drawing us to share in Your life and Your love. One God, three Persons, be near to the people formed in Your image, close to the world Your love brings to life.

We worship You, O Trinity of Persons, one eternal God. May our faith and the Sacrament of the Eucharist we receive bring us health of mind and body, now and forever. Amen.

Thought Provokers

Please see Appendix B for the answers.

Q. 31: Note the simple language Jesus used to teach us about the Most Holy Trinity, the greatest of all mysteries. What can parents and other teachers learn from this approach to teaching?

Q. 32: A. God the Father begot God the Son, but He did not create Him. What is the difference between begetting and creating?

B. If, contrary to fact, the Father created the Son, would the Son be divine?

Q. 33: With respect to mankind, what did God the Son do that was not done by either God the Father or God the Holy Spirit?

Q. 34: We should refer to God the Holy Spirit as "He" and not "it." Why?

Q. 35: Think of three or four ways in which we can honor the Holy Trinity.

By Heart Catechism and Scripture Review™

The "By Heart Catechism and Scripture Review" lists a selected number of questions and Scripture references from "The Apostolate's Family Catechism" to make memorization easier. Q = Question, SR = Scripture Reference

Q. 22. What is the History of Salvation? The History of Salvation is the account of God's dealings with mankind and how He saved us.

Q. 23. How did God deal with mankind? God dealt with mankind by fully revealing Himself and His plan for our Salvation through Jesus Christ and the Holy Spirit.

Q. 25. What is the mystery of the Holy Trinity? The mystery of the Holy Trinity is the truth that there is one God in three Persons: the Father, the Son, and the Holy Spirit.

Q. 26. Why do we believe in the mystery of the Holy Trinity? We believe in the mystery of the Holy Trinity because God revealed it to us. He is all-wise and all-truthful.

Q. 27. How is the mystery of the Holy Trinity revealed in the New Testament? The mystery of the Holy Trinity is revealed in the Person, words, and deeds of Jesus Christ Our Lord.

Q. 32. Who is God the Father? God the Father is the First Person of the Holy Trinity, Who eternally begets or brings forth God the Son.

Q. 33. Who is God the Son? God the Son is the Second Person of the Holy Trinity, because from all eternity He is begotten in the mind of the Father.

Q. 34. Who is God the Holy Spirit? God the Holy Spirit is the Third Person of the Holy Trinity. He is the endless, living Love which always flows from the Father and the Son.

Q. 35. In what ways do we honor the Holy Trinity? We honor the Holy Trinity by: (1) trying to understand that Baptism calls us to a close union of love with the three divine Persons, (2) remembering the presence of the Trinity in our souls, (3) doing God's will, and (4) praying.

#N1.4-55-2

Creation: Material and Spiritual

#F3-33-2

I beseech you, my child, to look at the heaven and the earth and see everything that is in them, and recognize that God did not make them out of things that existed.
(2 Maccabees 7:28)

CHAPTER EIGHT

Creation

Q. 36. What is Creation?

Creation means that God brought all things in the universe into existence out of nothing and that He keeps them in existence. Only God, Whose power is without limit, can do that. We owe everything we have to God.

In the beginning God said, "'Let there be light'; and there was light... 'Let there be a firmament in the midst of the waters, and let it separate the waters from the waters,'" and so it happened (Genesis 1:3, 6).

#F3-11-2

Creation means that God brought all things in the universe into existence out of nothing and that He keeps them in existence.

Sacred Scripture

I beseech you, my child, to look at the heaven and the earth and see everything that is in them, and recognize that God did not make them out of things that existed. Thus also mankind comes into being. *2 Maccabees 7:28*

Catechism of the Catholic Church

316 Though the work of creation is attributed to the Father in particular, it is equally a truth of faith that the Father, Son, and Holy Spirit together are the one, indivisible principle of creation.

Sacred Scripture
Q. 36. Job 38:1-18, Ps 33:6-9.

Catechism of the Catholic Church
Q. 36. Paragraphs 279-301, 338, 2415.

For cross-references with Vatican II, Papal documents & other resources, see Family Wisdom Library on page 196.
For commentaries on each question with Cardinal Arinze, Sr. John Vianney and Fr. Straub (in Spanish), see Appendix C.

320 God created the universe and keeps it in existence by his Word, the Son "upholding the universe by his word of power"[1] and by his Creator Spirit, the giver of life.

Vatican Council II

The eternal Father, in accordance with the utterly gratuitous and mysterious design of his wisdom and goodness, created the whole universe, and chose to raise up men to share in his own divine life. *Lumen Gentium, 2*

Catechism by Diagram

#F3-26

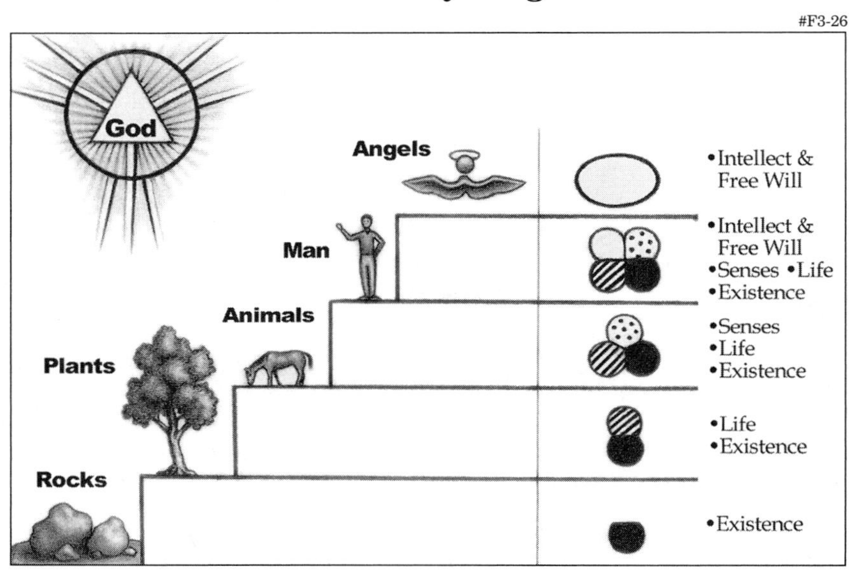

God's Creatures. Material things (rocks) have physical existence (black circle). Plants have a plant life and existence. Animals have feeling, life, and existence. Man has a human soul—mind and will—life, feeling, and existence. An angel is a spirit with a mind and a will, without need for a body, greater than a human being, but still created. But God is the Supreme Spirit Who was never created.

Summary Prayer

Heavenly Father, Creation is the way You gave both life and the world to man. All that we see around us and all that we have are from You. You are the Lord of life and of the universe.

Not only do You bring all things into existence, but You keep them in existence. If You should withdraw from any of Your creatures, they would fall back into the nothingness from which they came. For our creation and continued existence, we give You thanks through our Lord Jesus Christ, to Whom with You and the Holy Spirit be all honor and glory, forever and ever. Amen.

Q. 37. Can we know God through created things?

Yes, among other ways, God makes Himself known to us through the things that He has made.

Sacred Scripture teaches us that man can come to know God through created things.

The Church also teaches that, from the natural light of human reason, man can come to know God as the beginning and end of all that is, and that created things around us help us to see that the one who made them is God. If we really love God, we will try to learn as much as we can about Him, including learning about Him from the things He has made.

#N1.6-17-2

Created things around us help us to see that the one who made them is God.

Sacred Scripture

The heavens are telling the glory of God; and the firmament proclaims his handiwork. Day to day pours forth speech, and night to night declares knowledge. *Psalm 19:1, 2*

Ever since the creation of the world his invisible nature, namely, his eternal power and deity, has been clearly perceived in the things that have been made. *Romans 1:20*

For all men who were ignorant of God were foolish by nature; and they were unable from the good things that are seen to know him who exists, nor did they recognize the craftsman while paying heed to his works; but they supposed that

---

Catechism of the Catholic Church
Q. 37. Paragraphs **31-35**, 54, 337, 341.

For cross-references with Vatican II, Papal documents & other resources, see Family Wisdom Library on page 196.
For commentaries on each question with Cardinal Arinze, Sr. John Vianney and Fr. Straub (in Spanish), see Appendix C.

either fire or wind or swift air, or the circle of the stars, or turbulent water, or the luminaries of heaven were the gods that rule the world.

If through delight in the beauty of these things men assumed them to be gods, let them know how much better than these is their Lord, for the author of beauty created them.

And if men were amazed at their power and working, let them perceive from them how much more powerful is he who formed them.

For from the greatness and beauty of created things comes a corresponding perception of their Creator.

Yet these men are little to be blamed, for perhaps they go astray while seeking God and desiring to find him. For as they live among his works they keep searching, and they trust in what they see, because the things that are seen are beautiful.

Yet again, not even they are to be excused; for if they had the power to know so much that they could investigate the world, how did they fail to find sooner the Lord of these things? *Wisdom 13:1-9*

#N1.6-16-2

If we really love God, we will try to learn as much as we can about Him, including learning about Him from the things He has made.

Catechism of the Catholic Church

32 The *world*: starting from movement, becoming, contingency, and the world's order and beauty, one can come to a knowledge of God as the origin and the end of the universe.

Vatican Council II

The sacred Synod professes that "God, the first principle and last end of all things, can be known with certainty from the created world, by the natural light of human reason" (cf. Rom. 1:20). It teaches that it is to his Revelation that we must attribute the fact "that those things, which in themselves are not beyond the grasp of human reason, can, in the present condition of the human race, be known by all men with ease, with firm certainty, and without the contamination of error" (First Vatican Council, Dogm. Const. on Cath. Faith, 2). *Dei Verbum, 6*

#F3-29-2

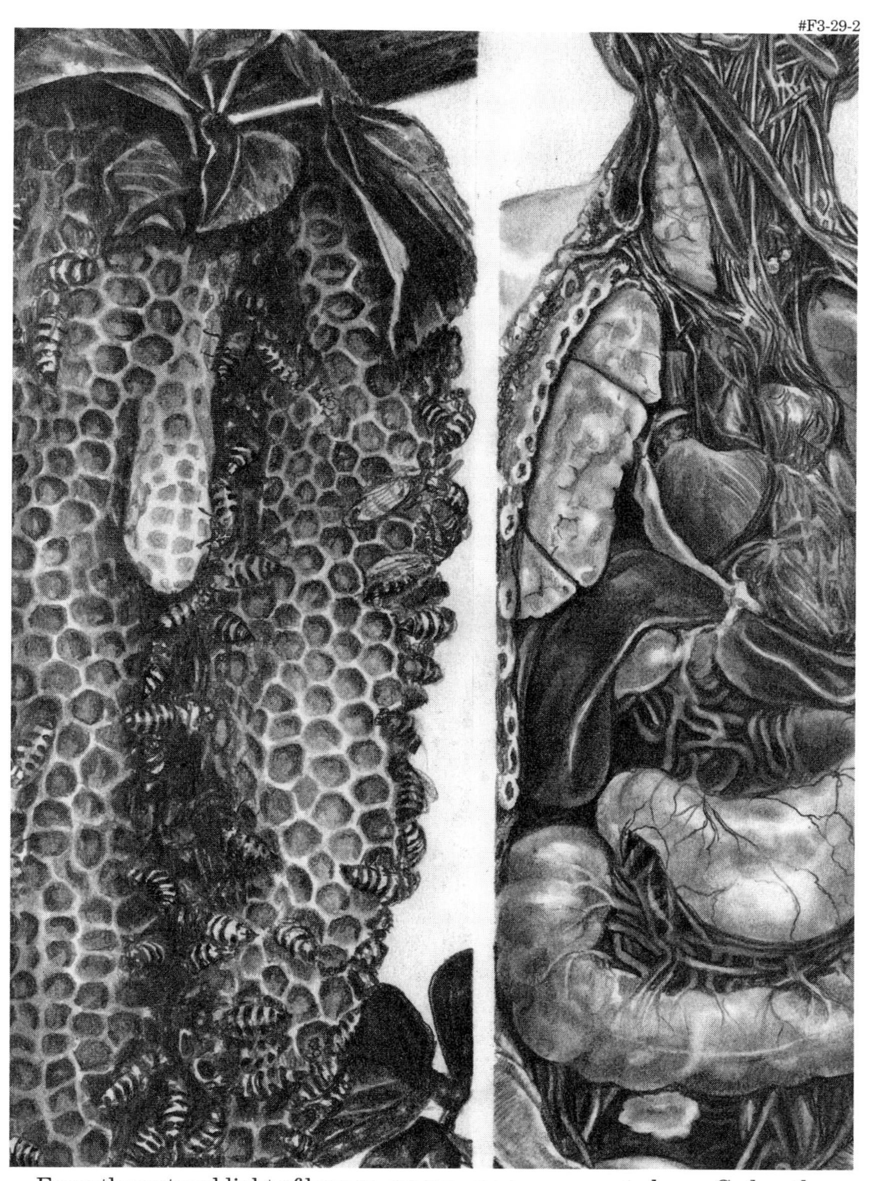

From the natural light of human reason, man can come to know God as the beginning and end of all that is.

Summary Prayer

Almighty God and Father, we believe that by thinking about the things You have created, we can come to know You as the beginning and end of all that exists. You love us by making Yourself known to us in Creation. Created things around us help us to see that You are God and that You can do all things. We love You, our Creator, and we want to try to learn as much as we can about You, even from the things You made. Enrich us all from the fullness of Your eternal wisdom and power, through Jesus Christ our Lord. Amen.

Doctrine • Moral • Worship Exercise

(See Appendix A for answer key, questions 36-37.)

1. What does Creation tell us about our God?
2. How can you help our society to preserve God's Creation?
3. Read Psalm 8 and express your heartfelt gratitude to our Creator.

Chapter Summary Prayer

Father, all powerful and ever-living God, all things are of Your making. All times and seasons obey Your laws. You know the number of the stars and call each of them by name.

We believe that You made the whole universe out of nothing, for Your power is without limit. You created all things in wonderful beauty and order.

You have placed all the powers of nature under the control of man and his work. May we reflect You in all our efforts and work with our brothers and sisters at our common tasks, establishing Your love and guiding Your Creation to perfect fulfillment.

By the human labor we offer You, join us to the saving work of Christ, who is Lord forever. Guide and govern us by Your help in this life as You have renewed us by the mystery of eternal life, through the same Christ our Lord. Amen.

Thought Provokers

Please see Appendix B for the answers.

Q. 36: God has created all things, visible and invisible; seen and unseen. This being true, in what sense can we say that God creates a baby or a giraffe or an oak tree?

Q.37: When we see the beautiful order and harmony in creation, we naturally see reflected in it something of the mind of the Maker. On the other hand, we are accustomed to hearing today that such and such a thing is a product of evolution. Doesn't this explanation simply by-pass the question of who made the process of evolution, assuming that there may well be elements of truth in some of the various evolutionary theories?

#H7-2

To share in His happiness for all eternity is the end for which mankind and the angels were first created. God's plan for our Salvation was at work in the universe from the first moment of its creation.

CHAPTER NINE

Angelic Creation and the Fall of the Bad Angels

Q. 38. When did the mystery of Salvation begin?

The mystery of Salvation began with the creation of angels and of the world.

We fallen creatures quite often think of Salvation only in terms of being saved *from* sin and Hell. But more importantly, we are saved *for* God, to share in His happiness for all eternity. This is the end for which mankind and the angels were first created. God's plan for our Salvation was at work in the universe from the first moment of its creation. Creation itself, for instance, points to God, its Maker. This fact, known by God from all eternity, would later help many fallen humans to recognize the One to Whom they owe their primary allegiance (cf. Romans 1:18-20).

Sacred Scripture

Then the King will say to those at his right hand, "Come, O blessed of my Father, inherit the kingdom prepared for you from the foundation of the world." *Matthew 25:34*

For he has made known to us in all wisdom and insight the mystery of his will, according to his purpose which he set forth in Christ as a plan for the fullness of time, to unite all things in him, things in heaven and things on earth. *Ephesians 1:9-10*

Catechism of the Catholic Church

288 Thus the revelation of creation is inseparable from the revelation and forging of the covenant of the one God with his People. Creation is revealed as the first step toward this covenant, the first and universal witness to God's all-powerful love.[1] And so, the truth of creation is also expressed with growing vigor in the message of the prophets, the prayer of the psalms and the liturgy, and in the wisdom sayings of the Chosen People.

Sacred Scripture
Q. 38. Jn 17:24; Eph 1:3-6; 1 Pet 1:18-21.

Catechism of the Catholic Church
Q. 38. Paragraphs 27, 198, 280, 287-**289**, **332**, 342.

For cross-references with Vatican II, Papal documents & other resources, see Family Wisdom Library on page 196.
For commentaries on each question with Cardinal Arinze, Sr. John Vianney and Fr. Straub (in Spanish), see Appendix C.

Q. 39. Who are the angels?

Angels are pure spirits, that is, beings with intellect and free will, but without bodies. Angels are complete persons without bodies or the need for bodies, far superior to human beings.

#F3-20-2

Angels are pure spirits, far superior to human beings. God gave them brilliant minds to understand His beauty and goodness, and He gave them free will to praise and love Him.

God created the angels long before He created man. Angels are immortal. They were given brilliant minds to understand God's beauty and goodness, and they had free will to praise and love Him.

Sacred Scripture
Q. 39. Mt 18:10.

Catechism of the Catholic Church
Q. 39. Paragraphs 328-335.

For cross-references with Vatican II, Papal documents & other resources, see Family Wisdom Library on page 196.
For commentaries on each question with Cardinal Arinze, Sr. John Vianney and Fr. Straub (in Spanish), see Appendix C.

God created the angels with free will so that they might be able to make acts of love for God, freely choosing to serve Him. Only after they had done so would they see God face to face and enter into that everlasting union with God which we call Heaven.

The Bible tells us that the number of angels is very great. It says, "A thousand thousands served him, and ten thousand times ten thousand stood before him" (Daniel 7:10).

The Bible mentions four important angels by name: (1) Gabriel, who announced to Mary that she was to be the Mother of God; (2) Raphael, who accompanied Tobias on his journey to Media and brought him home safely with a new bride; (3) Michael, who drove the rebellious angels into Hell and who is the special protector of the Catholic Church; and (4) Satan, who is the principal fallen angel that led the rebellion against God.

#A33-19-2

From its beginning until death, human life is surrounded by their [guardian angels] watchful care and intercession.
(Catechism of the Catholic Church, 336)

Sacred Scripture

Are they not all ministering spirits sent forth to serve, for the sake of those who are to obtain salvation? *Hebrews 1:14*

Then I looked, and I heard around the throne and the living creatures and the elders the voice of many angels, numbering myriads of myriads and thousands of thousands, saying with a loud voice, "Worthy is the Lamb who was slain, to receive power and wealth and wisdom and might and honor and glory and blessing!" *Revelation 5:11-12*

Catechism of the Catholic Church

336 From its beginning until death, human life is surrounded by their watchful care and intercession.[1] "Beside each believer stands an angel as protector and shepherd leading him to life."[2] Already here on earth the Christian life shares by faith in the blessed company of angels and men united in God.

Q. 40. Who are the devils?

The devils are fallen angels, enemies of mankind. Their efforts are directed toward leading people into their own rebellion against God.

God has not made known to us the test to which the angels were put prior to the fall of the devils. Some Church Fathers and theologians have speculated that God the Father gave the angels a preview of Jesus Christ, the Redeemer of the human race, and commanded that they adore Him. They, perhaps, could not bring themselves to make an act of adoration toward Jesus Christ, and so they rebelled against the Father's plan of Salvation.

Led by one of the most gifted of all the angels, Satan (or Lucifer, that is, Lightbearer), many of the angels turned away from God. Satan cried out, "I will not serve!" Then the Archangel Michael took up the battle cry: "Who is like God?" Michael and the good angels cast the rebellious angels out from Heaven. "Now war arose in heaven, Michael and his angels fighting against the dragon; and the dragon and his angels fought, but they were defeated and there was no longer any place for them in heaven. And the great dragon was thrown down, that ancient serpent, who is called the Devil and Satan, the deceiver of the whole world—he was thrown down to the earth, and his angels were thrown down with him" (Revelation 12:7-9).

Sacred Scripture
Q. 40. Lk 8:26-33.

Catechism of the Catholic Church
Q. 40. Paragraphs 392-395.

For cross-references with Vatican II, Papal documents & other resources, see Family Wisdom Library on page 196.
For commentaries on each question with Cardinal Arinze, Sr. John Vianney and Fr. Straub (in Spanish), see Appendix C.

There was no second chance for the sinning angels. By their willful rejection of God, their wills were fixed against Him forever. They did not and do not want to turn back. There burns in them an everlasting hatred for God and for all His works.

The devils tempt us to commit sin, but they can never force us to do so. They cannot get inside the human soul and use it to suit themselves. They cannot destroy our freedom of choice, but they are enemies to be feared. They still have great intelligence and power.

Catechism by Diagram

#H8-1

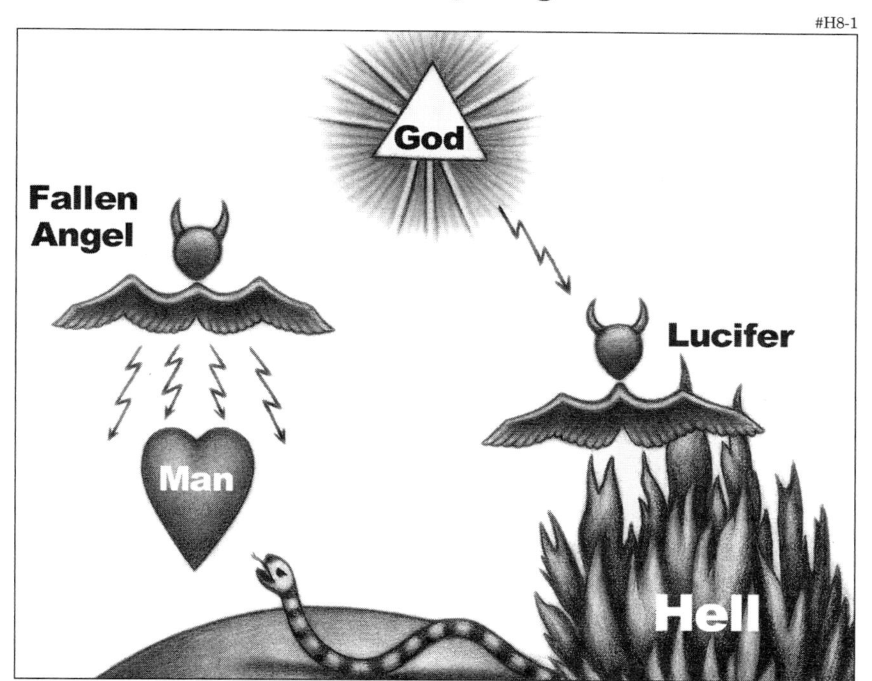

The Fall of the Angels. Hell began when Lucifer, the leader of the proud angels, rebelled against God and was cast, together with the other rebellious angels, into eternal punishment. The efforts of the fallen angels are directed toward leading people into their own rebellion against God.

Sacred Scripture

How you are fallen from heaven, O Day Star, son of Dawn! How you are cut down to the ground, you who laid the nations low! You said in your heart, "I will ascend to heaven; above the stars of God I will set my throne on high; I will sit on the mount of assembly in the far north; I will ascend above the heights of the clouds, I will make myself like the Most High." *Isaiah 14:12-14*

Finally, be strong in the Lord and in the strength of his might. Put on the whole armor of God, that you may be able to stand against the wiles of the devil. For we are not contending against flesh and blood, but against the principalities, against the powers, against the world rulers of this present darkness, against the spiritual hosts of wickedness in the heavenly places. *Ephesians 6:10-12*

Be sober, be watchful. Your adversary the devil prowls around like a roaring lion, seeking someone to devour. Resist him, firm in your faith, knowing that the same experience of suffering is required of your brotherhood throughout the world. *1 Peter 5:8-9*

Catechism of the Catholic Church

391 Behind the disobedient choice of our first parents lurks a seductive voice, opposed to God, which makes them fall into death out of envy.[1] Scripture and the Church's Tradition see in this being a fallen angel, called "Satan" or the "devil."[2] The Church teaches that Satan was at first a good angel, made by God: "The devil and the other demons were indeed created naturally good by God, but they became evil by their own doing."[3]

Splendor of Truth

Reason and experience not only confirm the weakness of human freedom, they also confirm its tragic aspects. Man comes to realize that his freedom is in some mysterious way inclined to betray this openness to the True and the Good, and that all too often he actually prefers to choose finite, limited and ephemeral goods. What is more, within his errors and negative decisions, man glimpses the source of a deep rebellion, which leads him to reject the Truth and the Good in order to set himself up as an absolute principle unto himself: "You will be like God" (Gen 3:5). Consequently, freedom itself needs to be set free. It is Christ who sets it free: he "has set us free for freedom" (cf. Gal 5:1). *(section 86)*

Vatican Council II

Although set by God in a state of rectitude, man, enticed by the evil one, abused his freedom at the very start of history. *Gaudium et Spes, 13*

Summary Prayer

Heavenly Father, some of the angels rebelled against You because of their pride. Your good angels cast them out of Your presence, and now the fallen angels are separated from You forever. Their efforts are directed toward leading us into our own rebellion against You. Give us the strength we need to resist their temptations, through our only Lord and Savior, Jesus Christ. Amen.

#A33-29

Satan cried out, "I will not serve!" Then the Archangel Michael took up the battle cry: "Who is like God?" Michael and the good angels cast the rebellious angels out from Heaven.

Q. 41. Where are the angels who remained faithful to God?

The angels who remained faithful to God are now with Him in Heaven, engaged in the eternal love and adoration of God which one day will be our joy. Their will always conforms to God's will. The angels are messengers of God. They pray for us and use their power to aid those who want and will accept their help.

#A33-17-2

The angels who remained faithful to God are now with Him in Heaven, engaged in the eternal love and adoration of God which one day will be our joy.

"See that you do not despise one of these little ones; for I tell you that in heaven their angels always behold the face of my Father who is in heaven" (Matthew 18:10).

Many of our temptations come from the devil, who tries to lead us into eternal damnation. God's good angels help us to overcome these temptations, especially by aiding us to secure God's grace through regular confession and frequent Holy Communion, prayer, and good works.

We believe that each of us has an individual guardian angel. We should often ask for his help. As we honor God by our devotion to His friends, the saints, we should also honor and invoke the angels, His first masterpieces. We need the help of the angels to reach the heavenly Kingdom. They are gifts of God for us.

Sacred Scripture
Q. 41. Mk 13:32; 2 Thess 1:5-8.

Catechism of the Catholic Church
Q. 41. Paragraphs **326**, 331, 1024.

For cross-references with Vatican II, Papal documents & other resources, see Family Wisdom Library on page 196.
For commentaries on each question with Cardinal Arinze, Sr. John Vianney and Fr. Straub (in Spanish), see Appendix C.

#A33.1-1

We believe that each of us has an individual guardian angel. We should often ask for his help.

Sacred Scripture

And all the angels stood round the throne and round the elders and the four living creatures, and they fell on their faces before the throne and worshiped God saying, "Amen! Blessing and glory and wisdom and thanksgiving and honor and power and might be to our God for ever and ever! Amen." *Revelation 7:11–12*

Catechism of the Catholic Church

329 St. Augustine says: "'Angel' is the name of their office, not of their nature. If you seek the name of their nature, it is 'spirit'; if you seek the name of their office, it is 'angel': from what they are, 'spirit,' from what they do, 'angel.'"[1] With their whole beings the angels are *servants* and messengers of God. Because they "always behold the face of my Father who is in heaven" they are the "mighty ones who do his word, hearkening to the voice of his word."[2]

Catechism by Diagram

#H8-2

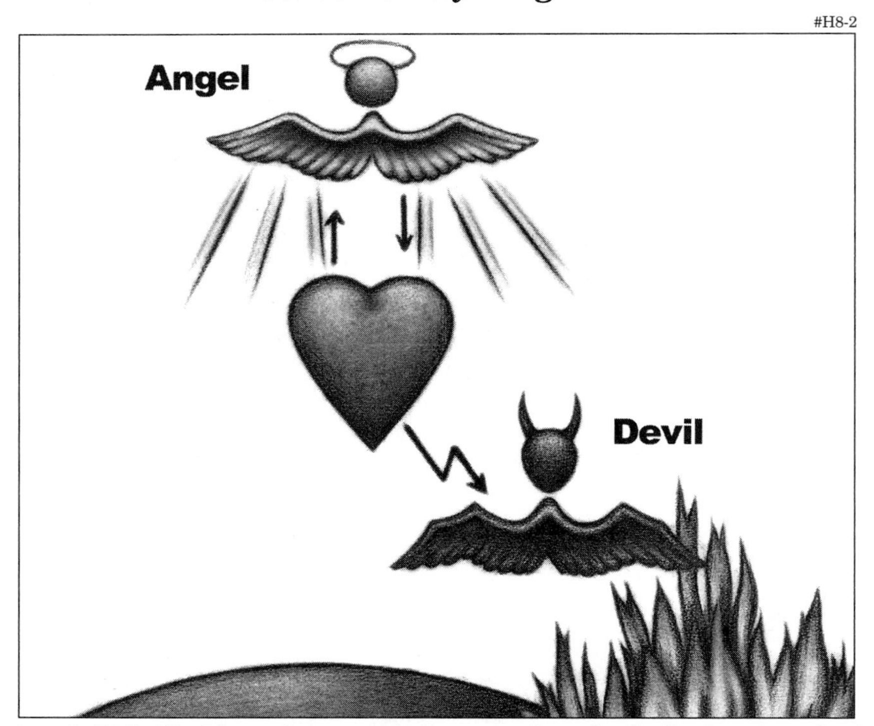

Angels Help Us. Many of our temptations come from the devil, who tries to lead us into eternal damnation (fire). God's angels help us (heart) to overcome these temptations, especially by aiding us to secure God's grace through regular confession and frequent Holy Communion, prayer and good works. They also help us on earth to avoid occasions of sin.

#F1-52-2

Many of our temptations come from the devil; God's good angels help us to overcome these temptations.

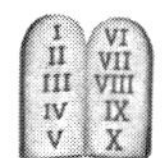

Doctrine • Moral • Worship Exercise

(See Appendix A for answer key, questions 38-41.)

1. What characteristics of angels can we also find in human beings?
2. Think of instances in your life in which your guardian angel can help you.
3. Write a prayer to your guardian angel, asking him to help you to overcome the devil's temptations in your daily life.

Chapter Summary Prayer

God our Father, in a wonderful way, You guide and govern the work of angels and men. May those who serve You constantly in Heaven keep our lives safe and sure on earth. With the care of the angels, especially our guardian angels, may we make progress in the way of Salvation.

In praising Your faithful angels and archangels, we also praise Your glory, for in honoring them, we honor You, their Creator. Their splendor shows us Your greatness, which surpasses in goodness the whole of Creation.

Through Christ our Lord, the great army of angels rejoices in Your glory. In adoration and joy, we make their hymn of praise our own. "Holy, holy, holy, Lord, God of power and might. Heaven and earth are full of Your glory. Hosanna in the highest!" Amen.

Thought Provokers

Please see Appendix B for the answers.

Q. 38: We fallen creatures quite often think of Salvation only in terms of being saved from sin and Hell; more importantly, we are saved for something. What?

Q. 39: A. Angels, since they can't be seen, are often said not to exist. Does the mere fact that something can't be seen mean that it does not exist?

B. What are some invisible things which scientists say exist

C. Can scientists, using scientific methods, demonstrate the existence of the human will and the human intellect?

D. Could scientists prove that angels exist?

Q. 40: A. What advantages and gifts do the good angels have which are not present in the evil angels?

B. What advantages are there in establishing a friendship with your God-given guardian angel?

Q. 41: Can you think of any reason or reasons why Jesus is not the Savior of the good angels?

By Heart Catechism and Scripture Review™

The "By Heart Catechism and Scripture Review" lists a selected number of questions and Scripture references from "The Apostolate's Family Catechism" to make memorization easier. Q = Question, SR = Scripture Reference

Q. 36. What is Creation? Creation is the whole universe which God made out of nothing.

SR 36 2 Maccabees 7:28
I beseech you, my child, to look at the heaven and the earth and see everything that is in them, and recognize that God did not make them out of things that existed. Thus also mankind comes into being.

Q. 37. Can we know God through created things? Yes, we can know God through created things by the natural light of human reason.

Q. 39. Who are the angels? The angels are pure spirits created by God. They are immortal and have intellect and free will.

Q. 40. Who are the devils? The devils are fallen angels who try to lead people into rebellion against God.

Q. 41. Where are the angels who obeyed God? The angels who obeyed God are in Heaven. They are messengers of God, and they pray for us and use their powers to help us. Every person has a Guardian Angel who helps him to do God's Will.

SR 41 Matthew 18:10
See that you do not despise one of these little ones; for I tell you that in heaven their angels always behold the face of my Father who is in heaven.

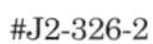
#J2-326-2

The Creation of Man

#A19-20

"Then God said, 'Let us make man in our image, after our likeness'" *(Genesis 1:26)*. He then breathed life into the body, creating a soul that would never die.

CHAPTER TEN

The Creation of Man

Q. 42. How was man created?

After creating the universe, God formed a man's body out of the dust of the earth. He then breathed life into the body, creating a soul that would never die. Together, that soul and body formed the first human being, which God called "Adam."

The story of the Creation of the world and man is told in the Book of Genesis. Scripture says that on the sixth day God made all the animals. "Then God said, 'Let us make man in our image, after our likeness; and let them have dominion over the fish of the sea, and over the birds of the air, and over the cattle, and over all the earth, and over every creeping thing that creeps upon the earth'" (Genesis 1:26).

God gave man a body and a soul. Like the animals, man has a body. And like the spiritual angels, man has a spiritual mind to know his Creator, and a spiritual will to love Him.

Sacred Scripture

Thou hast given him dominion over the works of thy hands; thou hast put all things under his feet. *Psalm 8:6*

Catechism of the Catholic Church

364 The human body shares in the dignity of "the image of God": it is a human body precisely because it is animated by a spiritual soul, and it is the whole human person that is intended to become, in the body of Christ, a temple of the Spirit.[1]

Summary Prayer

Lord our God, we believe that after creating the universe You formed man out of the dust of the earth, and then breathed into him a soul that would never die. The spirit that gives us life is an image of You, the infinitely perfect Spirit. Help us to use our minds to know You and our free wills to love You, through our Lord Jesus Christ, to Whom with You and the Holy Spirit be all honor and glory. Amen.

Sacred Scripture
Q. 42. Gen 2:21-23.

Catechism of the Catholic Church
Q. 42. Paragraphs 355-365.

For cross-references with Vatican II, Papal documents & other resources, see Family Wisdom Library on page 196.
For commentaries on each question with Cardinal Arinze, Sr. John Vianney and Fr. Straub (in Spanish), see Appendix C.

Q. 43. In what way was man created in the image and likeness of God?

Man is created in the image and likeness of God in that God gave man an immortal soul. Man's soul, like God, has the faculties of consciousness, intellect, and free will. Man's body shares in the dignity of the image of God: "it is a human body precisely because it is animated by a spiritual soul" (*Catechism of the Catholic Church*, 364). Moreover, our bodies remind us of the power, wisdom, and greatness of God in the perfection of their intricate organization and unity.

#F3-47-2

Man's soul, like God, has the faculties of consciousness, intellect, and free will. Man's body shares in the dignity of the image of God.

The body's higher faculties of physical consciousness, memory, imagination, and emotions combine with the faculties of the soul, especially free will, to produce authentically human acts. Man is able to be conscious and to truly know, understand, and remember truth. He is thus free to voluntarily and responsibly choose to do good and avoid evil.

God created man to live in society with his fellow men. Living in society, man resembles the union of the Trinity of divine persons. In order to fulfill its purpose, society must foster the exercise of virtue in its members. It must remove, as much as possible, obstacles to this exercise. Such a society must avoid whatever blocks or undermines virtue.

Catechism of the Catholic Church
Q. 43. Paragraphs 355, 357, 362, **363-364.**

For cross-references with Vatican II, Papal documents & other resources, see Family Wisdom Library on page 196.
For commentaries on each question with Cardinal Arinze, Sr. John Vianney and Fr. Straub (in Spanish), see Appendix C.

#L3-6-2

Of all visible creatures only man is "able to know and love his creator." He is "the only creature on earth that God has willed for its own sake." *(Catechism of the Catholic Church, 356)*

Sacred Scripture

The Lord created man out of earth; and turned him back to it again. He gave to men few days, a limited time, but granted them authority over the things upon the earth. He endowed them with strength like his own, and made them in his own image. He placed the fear of them in all living beings, and granted them dominion over beasts and birds. *Sirach 17:1-4*

Catechism of the Catholic Church

356 Of all visible creatures only man is "able to know and love his creator."[1] He is "the only creature on earth that God has willed for its own sake,"[2] and he alone is called to share, by knowledge and love, in God's own life. It was for this end that he was created, and this is the fundamental reason for his dignity.

Splendor of Truth

The spiritual and immortal soul is the principle unity of the human being, whereby it exists as a whole...as a person. These definitions not only point out that the body, which has been promised the resurrection, will also share in glory. They also remind us that reason and free will are linked with all the bodily and sense faculties. The person, including the body, is completely entrusted to himself, and it is in the unity of body and soul that the person is the subject of his own moral acts. *(section 48)*

Vatican Council II

Man, though made of body and soul, is a unity. Through his very bodily condition he sums up in himself the elements of the material world. Through him they are thus brought to their highest perfection and can raise their voice in praise freely given to the creator. For this reason man may not despise his bodily life. Rather he is obliged to regard his body as good and to hold it in honor since God has created it and will raise it up on the last day. Nevertheless man has been wounded by sin. He finds by experience that his body is in revolt. His very dignity therefore requires that he should glorify God in his body, and not allow it to serve the evil inclinations of his heart. *Gaudium et Spes, 14*

When he is drawn to think about his real self he turns to those deep recesses of his being where God who probes the heart awaits him, and where he himself decides his own destiny in the sight of God. So when he recognizes in himself a spiritual and immortal soul, he is not being led astray by false imaginings that are due to merely physical or social causes. On the contrary, he grasps what is profoundly true in this matter. *Gaudium et Spes, 14*

#E5-6

God created man to live in society with his fellow men. Living in society, man resembles the union of the Trinity of divine persons.

Summary Prayer

Father of everlasting goodness, You have made us into Your own image and likeness. Our bodies remind us of Your power and wisdom and greatness; our souls especially are portraits of You, our Maker. May we praise You forever, through Jesus Christ our Lord. Amen.

#C11-104-2

Man, though made of body and soul, is a unity. Through him they are thus brought to their highest perfection and can raise their voice in praise freely given to the creator. *(Gaudium et Spes, 14)*

Q. 44. Is the soul directly created by God?

Yes, God personally and directly creates each soul and infuses it into the body.

We must believe that the human race is descended from Adam and Eve, our first parents, and that Adam's and Eve's souls were directly created by God.

Husbands and wives cooperate with God in the formation of the human body. But the soul, which makes that body a human being, is directly created by God and is given at the moment of conception within the mother's womb.

#H19-2

God personally and directly creates each soul and infuses it into the body.

Sacred Scripture

For when a potter kneads the soft earth and laboriously molds each vessel for our service, he fashions out of the same clay both the vessels that serve clean uses and those for contrary uses, making all in like manner; but which shall be the use of each of these the worker in clay decides.

With misspent toil, he forms a futile god from the same clay—this man who was made of earth a short time before and after a little while goes to the earth from which he was taken, when he is required to return the soul that was lent him. But he is not concerned that he is destined to die or that his life is brief, but he competes with workers in gold and silver, and imitates workers in copper; and he counts it his glory that he molds counterfeit gods.

Sacred Scripture
Q. 44. Gen 2:7.

Catechism of the Catholic Church
Q. 44. Paragraphs 363-368.

For cross-references with Vatican II, Papal documents & other resources, see Family Wisdom Library on page 196.
For commentaries on each question with Cardinal Arinze, Sr. John Vianney and Fr. Straub (in Spanish), see Appendix C.

His heart is ashes, his hope is cheaper than dirt, and his life is of less worth than clay, because he failed to know the one who formed him and inspired him with an active soul and breathed into him a living spirit. *Wisdom 15:7-11*

Catechism of the Catholic Church

366 The Church teaches that every spiritual soul is created immediately by God — it is not "produced" by the parents — and also that it is immortal: it does not perish when it separates from the body at death, and it will be reunited with the body at the final Resurrection.[1]

1703 Endowed with "a spiritual and immortal" soul,[1] the human person is "the only creature on earth that God has willed for its own sake."[2] From his conception, he is destined for eternal beatitude.

2270 Human life must be respected and protected absolutely from the moment of conception. From the first moment of his existence, a human being must be recognized as having the rights of a person – among which is the inviolable right of every innocent being to life.[1]...

#F1.9-1

Husbands and wives cooperate with God in the formation of the human body. But the soul, which makes that body a human being, is directly created by God and is given at the moment of conception within the mother's womb.

Summary Prayer

Lord of Heaven and earth, in Your love You created man. Through Your beloved Son You created our human family. Through Him You restore us to Your likeness. Therefore, it is Your right to receive the obedience of all Creation, the praise of the Church on earth, and the thanksgiving of Your saints in Heaven, through the same Christ our Lord. Amen.

#F1-152

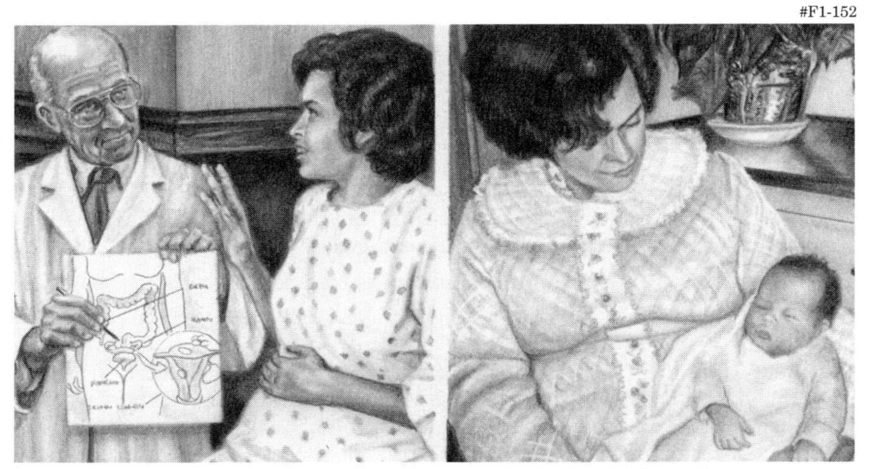

Human life must be respected and protected absolutely from the moment of conception. From the first moment of his existence, a human being must be recognized as having the rights of a person.
(Catechism of the Catholic Church, 2270)

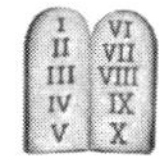

Doctrine • Moral • Worship Exercise

(See Appendix A for answer key, questions 42-44.)

1. How can your choices and decisions in life exemplify or mirror your dignity as God's greatest creation?
2. Which particular attribute of God can you see in each of the members of your family?
3. Look for ways to respect the image of God in those with whom you live and interact.

Chapter Summary Prayer

Creator and Ruler of Heaven and earth, You made man in Your likeness to subdue the earth and master it, and to recognize the work of Your hands in created beauty. Grant that Your children, thus surrounded on all sides by signs of Your presence, may live continually in Christ, praising You through Him and with Him.

God, devoted to us as a Father, You created us as a sign of Your power and elected us, Your people, to show Your goodness. Accept the thanks Your children offer, that all men may enter Your courts, praising You in song.

We thank You for Your blessings in the past and for all that, with Your help, we must yet achieve, through Christ our Lord. Amen.

Thought Provokers

Please see Appendix B for the answers.

Q. 42: A. Compare the two creation accounts found in the first two chapters of Genesis. With respect to the creation of man, how are the two accounts similar and how do they differ?

B. Even though these two accounts seem to contradict one another from a strictly scientific point of view, they both teach basic truths about God and man. What are some of the more important truths?

C. Stories such as *Moby Dick* and *Tom Sawyer* are labeled as fiction, yet they contain basic truths about human nature. How do Jesus' parables compare to these stories?

D. Can there possibly be a similarity between the two Genesis creation accounts and Jesus' parables? If so, what do you think it might be?

Q. 43: A. In what ways can our bodily acts reflect the image and likeness of God?

B. In what ways can our bodily acts reflect Satan?

Q. 44: A. What are some of the principal differences between the soul and the body in human beings?

B. How are humans radically different from all other animals in terms of what we can do?

#F1-153

The Church teaches that every spiritual soul is created immediately by God...and also that it is immortal. *(Catechism of the Catholic Church, 366)*

#A19-16-2

God gave Adam and Eve strength of will and control of their senses and emotions, as well as freedom from suffering and death.

CHAPTER ELEVEN

Our First Parents: Adam and Eve

Q. 45. What special gifts did God give to Adam and Eve?

One special gift God gave Adam and Eve at their creation was original holiness and justice. Original justice consisted in the basic supernatural gifts of sanctifying grace, the seven Gifts of the Holy Spirit, and the infused virtues, especially the theological and cardinal virtues.

God also gave Adam and Eve the preternatural gifts, namely capacities and powers above and beyond the powers of created human nature, but not beyond the powers of angelic nature. The preternatural gifts include infused knowledge, freedom from concupiscence (the tendency toward sin and the disorder of our emotions as a result of original sin), and bodily immortality. These gifts gave Adam and Eve strength of will and control of their senses and emotions, as well as freedom from suffering and death.

In His plan, God established His original covenant with Adam and Eve. If they would obey His command to increase and multiply, to fill the earth and subdue it, and especially His command forbidding them to eat of the tree of knowledge of good and evil, they would never die. After their life on earth had ended, they would receive a new kind of life because of their union with God. God's love would flow into their souls through sanctifying grace, and they would know God as He is, face to face.

Catechism of the Catholic Church

374 The first man was not only created good, but was also established in friendship with his Creator and in harmony with himself and with the creation around him, in a state that would be surpassed only by the glory of the new creation in Christ.

Vatican Council II

While the mind is at a loss before the mystery of death, the Church, taught by divine Revelation, declares that God has created man in view of a blessed destiny that lies beyond the limits of his sad state on earth. Moreover, the

Catechism of the Catholic Church
Q. 45. Paragraphs **54**, 356-361, 369-370, **374-379**, 380-384.

For cross-references with Vatican II, Papal documents & other resources, see Family Wisdom Library on page 196.
For commentaries on each question with Cardinal Arinze, Sr. John Vianney and Fr. Straub (in Spanish), see Appendix C.

Christian faith teaches that bodily death, from which man would have been immune had he not sinned, will be overcome when that wholeness which he lost through his own fault will be given once again to him by the almighty and merciful Savior. *Gaudium et Spes, 18*

#F3-54-2

The first man was not only created good, but was also established in friendship with his Creator and in harmony with himself and with the creation around him, in a state that would be surpassed only by the glory of the new creation in Christ. *(Catechism of the Catholic Church, 374)*

Summary Prayer

Father of everlasting goodness, our origin and guide, You created Adam and Eve as a sign of Your power and to show Your goodness. We thank You for the special gifts You bestowed upon our first parents: wisdom, strength of will, freedom from suffering and death, and sanctifying grace. It was Your will that all of their children should enjoy these blessings. You made all human beings that they might give glory to You by their love for You. But Adam failed to give his love to You. He failed the test of obedience and committed the first sin. Thankfully, however, You, Father, have redeemed us through Your Incarnate Son, Who is the New Adam, in cooperation with Mary, the New Eve. May all glory, honor and praise be to You, to Jesus, and the Holy Spirit, now and forever. Amen.

Catechism by Diagram

#F3-27

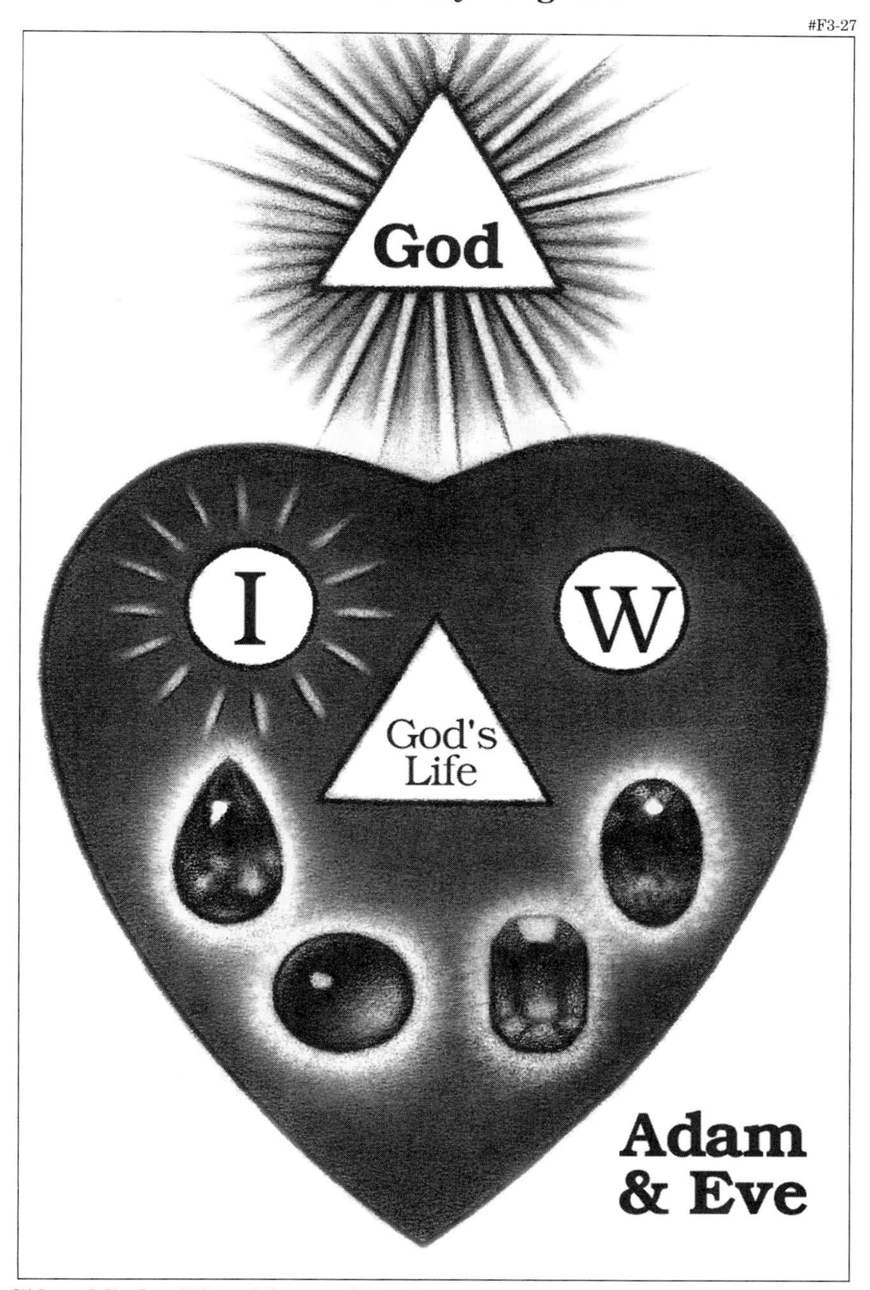

Gifts of God to Man. Adam and Eve (heart) received from God the supernatural gift of sanctifying grace—a sharing in God's life. They received very special gifts (gems): freedom from suffering and death, a keen intellect (I), and a strong will (W).

Q. 46. What commandment did God give Adam and Eve?

God gave Adam and Eve a commandment to worship Him by an act of sacrifice: they were not to eat the fruit which grew on the tree of the knowledge of good and evil.

#A19-17-2

Adam and Eve failed the test of obedience and trust in God. In this life, we prove our love for God by doing His will.

But Adam and Eve failed this test of obedience and trust in God by eating the forbidden fruit. They committed the first sin—the original sin. In this life, we prove our love for God by doing His will—being obedient to Him—and by keeping our covenant with Him—the New Covenant with man in Jesus Christ.

Sacred Scripture

Therefore as sin came into the world through one man and death through sin, and so death spread to all men. *Romans 5:12*

Catechism of the Catholic Church

396 God created man in his image and established him in his friendship. A spiritual creature, man can live this friendship only in free submission to God. The prohibition against eating "of the tree of the knowledge of good and evil" spells this out: "for in the day that you eat of it, you shall die."[1] The "tree of the

Sacred Scripture
Q. 46. Gen 2:8-17.

Catechism of the Catholic Church
Q. 46. Paragraphs 397-409.

For cross-references with Vatican II, Papal documents & other resources, see Family Wisdom Library on page 196.
For commentaries on each question with Cardinal Arinze, Sr. John Vianney and Fr. Straub (in Spanish), see Appendix C.

knowledge of good and evil"[2] symbolically evokes the insurmountable limits that man, being a creature, must freely recognize and respect with trust. Man is dependent on his Creator and subject to the laws of creation and to the moral norms that govern the use of freedom.

Splendor of Truth

Called to salvation through faith in Jesus Christ, "the true light that enlightens everyone" (Jn 1:9), people become "light in the Lord" and "children of light" (Eph 5:8), and are made holy by "obedience to the truth" (1 Pet 1:22). *(section 1)*

Summary Prayer

Heavenly Father, teach us that in this life we must prove our love for You by doing Your will and by being obedient to Your commandments.

You have taught us that to have faith in Your word is the way to wisdom, and to ponder Your divine plan is to grow in the truth. Open our eyes to Your deeds, and our hearts to the sound of Your call, so that our every act may increase our sharing in the life You have offered us. Heal hearts that are broken; gather together those who have been scattered, and enrich us all from the fullness of Your wisdom. It is Your right to receive the obedience of all Creation, the praise of all those You have made in Your own image and likeness.

You made man in Your own image and set him over all Creation. We praise You as the God of Creation, as the Father of Jesus, the Savior of mankind, in Whose image we seek to live. We thank You for the blessings You have bestowed on mankind, through the same Jesus our Lord. Amen.

Doctrine • Moral • Worship Exercise

(See Appendix A for answer key, questions 45-46.)

1. What benefits do we receive if we are obedient to God?
2. Explain how your obedience to those in authority shows your love for God.
3. Make at least three resolutions that will help you to do God's will.

Q. 47. What was God's first gift leading us to Christ?

God's first gift leading us to Christ was the creation of man.

If God had not created our first parents, there would have been no need for God to become man in order to save us. Why not?... Because there would have been no humans to be saved from sin and eternal death, and there would have been no humans to whom God could reveal the fullness of divine love.

Jesus Christ is the one whom God the Father sent to lead His people to Him. It is only through Jesus that we can be saved. That is why we can say that God's first gift leading us to Christ was His creation of man.

#F3-24-2

God's first gift leading us to Christ was His creation of man.

Sacred Scripture

For as by a man came death, by a man has come also the resurrection of the dead. For as in Adam all die, so also in Christ shall all be made alive. *1 Corinthians 15:21-22*

[Jesus Christ] is the [visible] image of the invisible God, the first-born of all creation; for in him all things were created, in heaven and on earth, visible and invisible, whether thrones or dominions or principalities or authorities—all things were created through and for him." *Colossians 1:15-16*

Sacred Scripture
Q. 47. Acts 4:12.

Catechism of the Catholic Church
Q. 47. Paragraphs 55, **356**-360.

For cross-references with Vatican II, Papal documents & other resources, see Family Wisdom Library on page 196.
For commentaries on each question with Cardinal Arinze, Sr. John Vianney and Fr. Straub (in Spanish), see Appendix C.

Catechism by Diagram

#F3-28

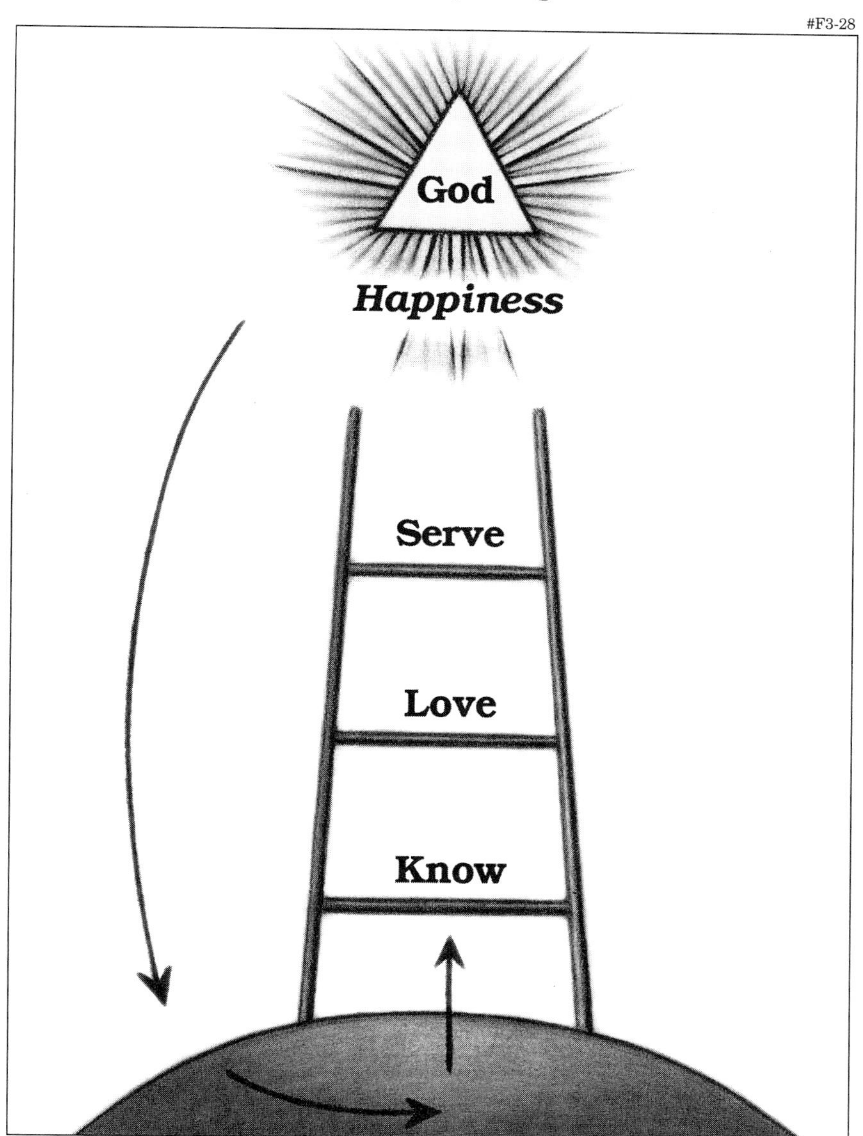

The Ladder to Heaven. God made us. He made the earth, and everything on the earth, for our own use and pleasure. All that He asks of us is that we learn to know Him, and in knowing Him, that we love and serve Him. To gain happiness in Heaven, we must do this, with God's grace. We came from God our Creator (arrow pointing to earth). After our life on earth, we shall, through God's grace, return to Heaven (arrow up to God) by taking the three steps on the ladder.

#J2-556-2

God,... in a plan of sheer goodness freely created man to make him share in his own blessed life... When the fullness of time had come, God sent his Son as Redeemer and Savior. *(Catechism of the Catholic Church, 1)*

Catechism of the Catholic Church

1 God, infinitely perfect and blessed in himself, in a plan of sheer goodness freely created man to make him share in his own blessed life. For this reason, at every time and in every place, God draws close to man. He calls man to seek him, to know him, to love him with all his strength. He calls together all men, scattered and divided by sin, into the unity of his family, the Church. To accomplish this, when the fullness of time had come, God sent his Son as Redeemer and Savior. In his Son and through him, he invites men to become, in the Holy Spirit, his adopted children and thus heirs of his blessed life.

Vatican Council II

For sacred Scripture teaches that man was created "to the image of God," as able to know and love his creator, and as set by him over all earthly creatures that he might rule them, and make use of them, while glorifying God. "What is man that thou are mindful of him, and the son of man that thou dost care for him? Yet thou hast made him little less than God, and dost crown him with glory and honor. Thou hast given him dominion over the works of thy hands; thou hast put all things under his feet" (Ps. 8:5-8). *Gaudium et Spes, 12*

Although set by God in a state of rectitude, man, enticed by the evil one, abused his freedom at the very start of history. He lifted himself up against God, and sought to attain his goal apart from him. Although they had known God, they did not glorify him as God, but their senseless hearts were darkened, and they served the creature rather than the creator. What Revelation makes known to us is confirmed by our own experience. For when

man looks into his own heart he finds that he is drawn towards what is wrong and sunk in many evils which cannot come from his good creator. Often refusing to acknowledge God as his source, man has also upset the relationship which should link him to his last end; and at the same time he has broken the right order that should reign within himself as well as between himself and other men and all creatures.

Man therefore is divided in himself. As a result, the whole life of men, both individual and social, shows itself to be a struggle, and a dramatic one, between good and evil, between light and darkness. Man finds that he is unable of himself to overcome the assaults of evil successfully, so that everyone feels as though bound by chains. But the Lord himself came to free and strengthen man, renewing him inwardly and casting out the "prince of this world" (Jn. 12:31), who held him in bondage of sin. For sin brought man to a lower state, forcing him away from the completeness that is his to attain.

Both the high calling and the deep misery which men experience find their final explanation in the light of this Revelation. *Gaudium et Spes, 13*

While the mind is at a loss before the mystery of death, the Church, taught by divine Revelation, declares that God has created man in view of a blessed destiny that lies beyond the limits of his sad state on earth.

Moreover, the Christian faith teaches that bodily death, from which man would have been immune had he not sinned, will be overcome when that wholeness which he lost through his own fault will be given once again to him by the almighty and merciful Savior. For God has called man, and still calls him, to cleave with all his being to him in sharing forever a life that is divine and free from all decay. Christ won this victory when he rose to life, for by his death he freed man from death. Faith, therefore, with its solidly based teaching, provides every thoughtful man with an answer to his anxious queries about his future lot. At the same time it makes him able to be united in Christ with his loved ones who have already died, and gives hope that they have found true life with God. *Gaudium et Spes, 18*

Doctrine • Moral • Worship Exercise

(See Appendix A for answer key, question 47.)

1. What was God's response to the disobedience of our first parents and our own disobedience?
2. In your daily life, how do you show, in word and in deed, that Jesus Christ is your Savior?
3. Think of instances from the past week in which Jesus strengthened you in times of temptations and saved you from sinful situations. Thank Jesus for those saving actions.

#D2-22

The Christian faith teaches that bodily death, from which man would have been immune had he not sinned, will be overcome when that wholeness which he lost through his own fault will be given once again to him by the almighty and merciful Savior. *(Gaudium et Spes, 18)*

Chapter Summary Prayer

Lord God, we praise You for creating us human beings, and still more for restoring us in Christ. Through Your Catholic Church, You always work to save us, and now we rejoice in the great love You give us, Your chosen people. Protect all who have become Your children, and continue to bless those who are baptized.

In the Sacrament of Baptism, You restore us to life. Forgive our sins and fulfill our hopes and desires. We thank You for calling us to share in Your divine life. Father in Heaven, You prepared the Virgin Mary to be the worthy mother of Your Son. You let her share beforehand in the Salvation Christ would bring by His Death, and kept her sinless from the first moment of her conception. Help us by her prayers to live in Your presence without sin. Father, help us to be like Christ, Your Son, Who loved the world, and died for our Salvation. Inspire us by His love and guide us by His example. The love of Your Son led Him to accept the suffering of the Cross so that His brothers might glory in new life. All glory be to the Father, to the Son, and to the Holy Spirit. Amen.

Thought Provokers

Please see Appendix B for the answers.

Q. 45: What effects do the loss of the special gifts given to our First Parents have on our everyday lives (i.e., the loss of the gifts of integrity, infused knowledge, and bodily immortality)?

Q. 46: How do you think temptations to sin affected the minds and wills of our First Parents before they fell from grace, as opposed to afterwards? Or put another way, how do you think temptations would affect us if we had not been conceived in the state of original sin and had not fallen?

Q. 47: How would you explain that the creation of man is the first gift of God that leads to Christ?

#O8-14-2

By Moses and the prophets, in the Old Testament, God taught His people "to recognize him as the only living and true God, as a provident Father and just judge. He taught them, too, to look for the promised Savior" *(Dei Verbum, 3).*

CHAPTER TWELVE

God's Presence in Created History

Q. 48. What did God's action in the Old Testament reveal and prove to us?

God's action in the Old Testament revealed His omnipotence—His divine power—and proved that He is always faithful to His people.

#F3-40

In the Old Testament, God's people learned the truth of His almighty power in Creation.

In the Old Testament, God's people learned the truth of His almighty power in Creation.

This reminded the people that God always remains with His people to protect and help them. His powerful and victorious deeds show that He keeps His promises and that He loves His people.

After speaking through the Old Testament prophets, God the Father sent our Savior, Jesus Christ, Who is God the Son made

Sacred Scripture
Q. 48. Gen 17:1-8; Ex 14; Dan 6:26-27.

Catechism of the Catholic Church
Q. 48. Paragraphs 56-61, **64**, 70-72, 761-762.

For cross-references with Vatican II, Papal documents & other resources, see Family Wisdom Library on page 196.
For commentaries on each question with Cardinal Arinze, Sr. John Vianney and Fr. Straub (in Spanish), see Appendix C.

man. Being both God and man, Jesus gave us the "Good News" of Salvation. This message is found in the New Testament. By His words and actions, Jesus made known the deepest truths about God. The Blessed Trinity (Father, Son, and Holy Spirit) is the deepest of all these truths.

Sacred Scripture

Why do you say, O Jacob, and speak, O Israel, "My way is hid from the Lord, and my right is disregarded by my God?" Have you not known? Have you not heard? The Lord is the everlasting God, the Creator of the ends of the earth. He does not faint or grow weary, his understanding is unsearchable. He gives power to the faint, and to him who has no might he increases strength. *Isaiah 40:27-29*

"I, I am he that comforts you; who are you that you are afraid of man who dies, of the son of man who is made like grass, and have forgotten the Lord, your Maker, who stretched out the heavens and laid the foundations of the earth?" *Isaiah 51:12, 13*

Catechism of the Catholic Church

62 After the patriarchs, God formed Israel as his people by freeing them from slavery in Egypt. He established with them the covenant of Mount Sinai and, through Moses, gave them his law so that they would recognize him and serve him as the one living and true God, the provident Father and just judge, and so that they would look for the promised Savior.[1]

Vatican Council II

God, who creates and conserves all things by his Word (cf. Jn. 1:3), provides men with constant evidence of himself in created realities (cf. Rom. 1:19-20). And furthermore, wishing to open up the way to heavenly salvation, he manifested himself to our first parents from the very beginning. After the fall, he buoyed them up with the hope of salvation, by promising redemption (cf. Gen. 3:15); and he has never ceased to take care of the human race. For he wishes to give eternal life to all those who seek salvation by patience in well-doing (cf. Rom. 2:6-7). In his own time God called Abraham, and made him into a great nation (cf. Gen. 12:2). After the era of the patriarchs, he taught this nation, by Moses and the prophets, to recognize him as the only living and true God, as a provident Father and just judge. He taught them, too, to look for the promised Savior. And so, throughout the ages, he prepared the way for the Gospel. *Dei Verbum, 3*

In his fatherly care for all of us, God desired that all men should form one family and deal with each other in a spirit of brotherhood. All, in fact, are destined to the very same end, namely God himself, since they have been created in the likeness of God who "made from one every nation of men who live on all the face of the earth" (Acts 17:26). *Gaudium et Spes, 24*

#O8-34

God always remains with His people to protect and help them. His powerful and victorious deeds show that He keeps His promises and that He loves His people.

Summary Prayer

Almighty Father, Your power in Creation reminds Your people that You remain always with them to protect and help them. Your wonderful deeds of power show that You keep Your promises and that You love Your people.

But Your all-powerful action for our Salvation is especially seen in the coming of Your Son, Jesus Christ, Who told us about our hope of Salvation. He made known the deepest truths about You, especially about the Blessed Trinity. May all glory and honor be given to You, Father, Son, and Holy Spirit, now and forever. Amen.

Q. 49. In what event is God's all-powerful action for our Salvation especially seen?

God's all-powerful action for our Salvation is seen especially in Christ's Resurrection from the dead.

Though man was made by God in a state of holiness, he rebelled against God of his own free will, being tempted to do so by the devil. In order to free man from the slavery of sin and to make him holy once more, God sent His Son to earth to take on human flesh, to suffer and die on the Cross, and to rise gloriously from the dead. Thus it was by means of the Resurrection that God showed His all-powerful action for our Salvation.

Sacred Scripture

Blessed be the God and Father of our Lord Jesus Christ! By his great mercy we have been born anew to a living hope through the resurrection of Jesus Christ from the dead, and to an inheritance which is imperishable, undefiled, and unfading, kept in heaven for you, who by God's power are guarded through faith for a salvation ready to be revealed in the last time. *1 Peter 1:3-5*

Catechism of the Catholic Church

648 Christ's Resurrection is an object of faith in that it is a transcendent intervention of God himself in creation and history. In it the three divine persons act together as one, and manifest their own proper characteristics. The Father's power "raised up" Christ his Son and by doing so perfectly introduced his Son's humanity, including his body, into the Trinity. Jesus is conclusively revealed as "Son of God in power according to the Spirit of holiness by his Resurrection from the dead."[1] St. Paul insists on the manifestation of God's power[2] through the working of the Spirit who gave life to Jesus' dead humanity and called it to the glorious state of Lordship.

Sacred Scripture
Q. 49. Mt 28; Mk 16; Lk 24; Jn 20; Acts 13:30-33; 1 Cor 15:3-22.

Catechism of the Catholic Church
Q. 49. Paragraphs **638**-658.

For cross-references with Vatican II, Papal documents & other resources, see Family Wisdom Library on page 196.
For commentaries on each question with Cardinal Arinze, Sr. John Vianney and Fr. Straub (in Spanish), see Appendix C.

#R4.1-22

In order to free man from the slavery of sin and to make him holy once more, God sent His Son to earth to take on human flesh, to suffer and die on the Cross, and to rise gloriously from the dead.

Splendor of Truth

Communion with the Crucified and Risen Lord is the never-ending source from which the Church draws unceasingly in order to live in freedom, to give of herself and to serve. *(section 87)*

Vatican Council II

The wonderful works of God among the people of the Old Testament were but a prelude to the work of Christ our Lord in redeeming mankind and giving perfect glory to God. He achieved his task principally by the paschal mystery of his blessed passion, resurrection from the dead, and glorious ascension, whereby "dying, he destroyed our death, and rising, restored our life." *Sacrosanctum Concilium, 5*

Q. 50. How should we regard Creation?

We should regard Creation as the continuing action of God, from the beginning till the end of time, as He brings about the Salvation of men and their destiny.

When we think about the creation of the angels, the universe, and mankind, we should see it as a part of God's all-powerful action at work in the Salvation of mankind. His great love for man led Him

Sacred Scripture
Q. 50. Is 45:5-13; 2 Pet 3:1-9.

Catechism of the Catholic Church
Q. 50. Paragraphs 302-324.

For cross-references with Vatican II, Papal documents & other resources, see Family Wisdom Library on page 196.
For commentaries on each question with Cardinal Arinze, Sr. John Vianney and Fr. Straub (in Spanish), see Appendix C.

to create and save him. The entire work of Salvation finds its fundamental meaning in Jesus Christ, the Incarnate Word. That work, beginning with the Creation of the world, revealed itself in Christ's Incarnation, in His earthly life, and in His Death and Resurrection.

The work of Salvation will be seen at the time of Christ's second coming in power on the Day of the Lord, when He defeats Satan and his forces, casts the Antichrist and his prophet into Hell, and purges the world of those who bear the mark of the Antichrist.

It will especially be seen at Christ's final coming in glory at the end of time. This event will finish God's work of Creation and the Salvation of man.

#H1-233-2

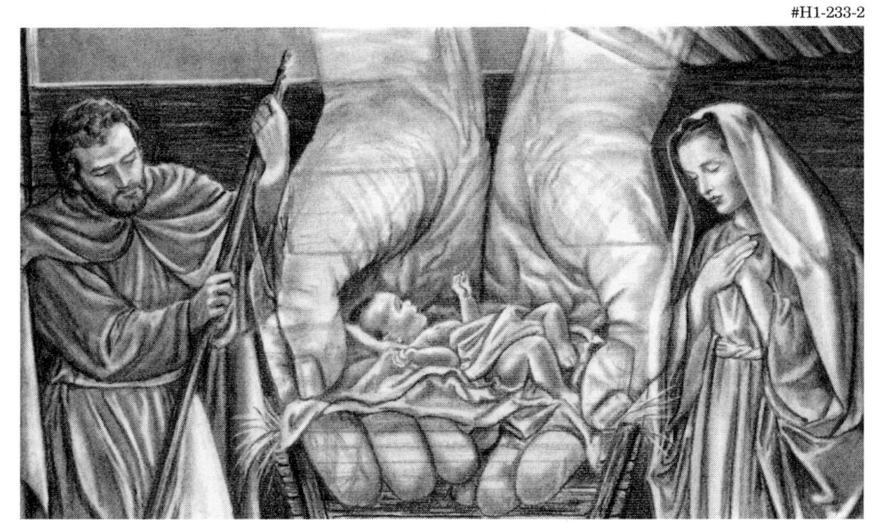

Creation is the foundation of "all God's saving plans," the "beginning of the history of salvation" that culminates in Christ.
(Catechism of the Catholic Church, 280)

Sacred Scripture

I consider that the sufferings of this present time are not worth comparing with the glory that is to be revealed to us. For the creation waits with eager longing for the revealing of the sons of God; for the creation was subjected to futility, not of its own will but by the will of him who subjected it in hope; because the creation itself will be set free from its bondage to decay and obtain the glorious liberty of the children of God. We know that the whole creation has been groaning in travail together until now; and not only the creation, but we ourselves who have the first fruits of the Spirit groan inwardly as we wait for adoption as sons, the redemption of our bodies. *Romans 8:18-23*

#T3-24-2

God has created man in view of a blessed destiny that lies beyond the limits of his sad state on earth. *(Gaudium et Spes, 18)*

[Jesus] is the image of the invisible God, the first-born of all creation; for in him all things were created, in heaven and on earth, visible and invisible, whether thrones or dominions or principalities or authorities—all things were created through him and for him. He is before all things, and in him all things hold together. He is the head of the body, the church; he is the beginning, the firstborn from the dead, that in everything he might be pre-eminent. For in him all the fullness of God was pleased to dwell, and through him to reconcile to himself all things, whether on earth or in heaven, making peace by the blood of his cross. *Colossians 1:15-20*

Catechism of the Catholic Church

280 Creation is the foundation of "all God's saving plans," the "beginning of the history of salvation"[1] that culminates in Christ. Conversely, the mystery of Christ casts conclusive light on the mystery of creation and reveals the end for which "in the beginning God created the heavens and the earth": from the beginning, God envisaged the glory of the new creation in Christ.[2]

Vatican Council II

God, who creates and conserves all things by his word (cf. Jn. 1:3), provides men with constant evidence of himself in created realities (cf. Rom. 1:19-20). *Dei Verbum, 3*

The Church, taught by divine Revelation, declares that God has created man in view of a blessed destiny that lies beyond the limits of his sad state on earth. *Gaudium et Spes, 18*

Q. 51. How was God especially present in the history of man?

God's saving deeds are seen in the history of man and of the world, especially in the life, Death, and Resurrection of Jesus, His Incarnate Son.

#O8-1-2

The New Covenant in Christ Jesus builds on and fulfills all the previous covenants God made with mankind. It is the Covenant foretold and promised through the prophets.

God was present in ancient Israel through the covenants He made with man. These covenants included the original covenant God made with Adam and Eve in the Garden of Eden (Gen 2:7 8, 15-17), the covenant with Noah after the Great Flood (Gen 6:18-22; 9:1-17), the covenant with Abraham (Gen 15:1ff; 17:1ff), the covenant of Mt. Sinai (Ex 19:1ff; 24:8), and the covenant with David (2 Sam 7:1ff; Ps 89:27-38).

The New Covenant in Christ Jesus builds on and fulfills all the previous covenants God made with mankind. It is the Covenant foretold and promised through the prophets (Hosea 2:1ff; Is 42:6; Jer 3:31-34; 32:40-44, Ez 37:26-28; Zec 9:9-17). The New Covenant provides for the fulfillment of God's universal plan for man. It, once and forever, establishes the eternal, spousal relationship God desires to have with all mankind, collectively and individually.

Sacred Scripture
Q. 51. Ps 105; Jer 31:31-34; Acts 7, 13:16-23.

Catechism of the Catholic Church
Q. 51. Paragraphs **62-65,** 218, **518.**

For cross-references with Vatican II, Papal documents & other resources, see Family Wisdom Library on page 196.
For commentaries on each question with Cardinal Arinze, Sr. John Vianney and Fr. Straub (in Spanish), see Appendix C.

Sacred Scripture

O sing to the Lord a new song, for he has done marvelous things! His right hand and his holy arm have gotten him victory. The Lord has made known his victory, he has revealed his vindication in the sight of the nations. He has remembered his steadfast love and faithfulness to the house of Israel. All the ends of the earth have seen the victory of our God. *Psalm 98:1-3*

The next day he saw Jesus coming toward him, and said, "Behold, the Lamb of God, who takes away the sin of the world! This is he of whom I said, 'After me comes a man who ranks before me, for he was before me.' I myself did not know him; but for this I came baptizing with water, that he might be revealed to Israel." *John 1:29-31*

"Let all the house of Israel therefore know assuredly that God has made him both Lord and Christ, this Jesus whom you crucified." *Acts 2:36*

Catechism of the Catholic Church

219 God's love for Israel is compared to a father's love for his son. His love for his people is stronger than a mother's for her children. God loves his people more than a bridegroom his beloved; his love will be victorious over even the worst infidelities and will extend to his most precious gift: "God so loved the world that he gave his only Son."[1]

Vatican Council II

The Word of God, through whom all things were made, became man and dwelt among men: a perfect man, he entered world history, taking that history into himself and recapitulating it. He reveals to us that "God is love" (1 Jn. 4:8) and at the same time teaches that the fundamental law of human perfection, and consequently of the transformation of the world, is the new commandment of love. *Gaudium et Spes, 38*

Q. 52. How is God present to us in our own day?

God continues to be present to us in our day through His New Covenant with man, and by using His unlimited power to help us. His saving work will be finished only at the end of the world.

The most important events in the history of the world are the life, Death, and Resurrection of Jesus. It is through these events that God has especially revealed Himself, His love for man, and His New Covenant with him. He also revealed Himself in other events found in Sacred Scripture and in the life of the Church. Moreover, God will always remain with us, continually revealing His power and love as we struggle to overcome sin and to keep our New Covenant with Him.

Sacred Scripture
Q. 52. Mt 16:18-19, 28:18-19; Heb 13:5-8.

Catechism of the Catholic Church
Q. 52. Paragraphs 62-64, **218**, 518.

For cross-references with Vatican II, Papal documents & other resources, see Family Wisdom Library on page 196.
For commentaries on each question with Cardinal Arinze, Sr. John Vianney and Fr. Straub (in Spanish), see Appendix C.

#F1-48-2

God will always remain with us, continually revealing His power and love as we struggle to overcome sin and to keep our New Covenant with Him.

Sacred Scripture

The steadfast love of the Lord never ceases, his mercies never come to an end; they are new every morning; great is thy faithfulness. *Lamentations 3:22, 23*

But when the time had fully come, God sent forth his Son, born of woman, born under the law, to redeem those who were under the law, so that we might receive adoption as sons. And because you are sons, God has sent the Spirit of his Son into our hearts, crying "Abba! Father!" So through God you are no longer a slave but a son, and if a son then an heir. *Galatians 4:4-7*

Catechism of the Catholic Church

769 "The Church... will receive its perfection only in the glory of heaven,"[1] at the time of Christ's glorious return. Until that day, "the Church progresses on her pilgrimage amidst this world's persecutions and God's consolations."[2] Here below she knows that she is in exile far from the Lord, and longs for the full coming of the Kingdom, when she will "be united in glory with her king."[3] The Church, and through her the world, will not be perfected in glory without great trials. Only then will "all the just from the time of Adam, 'from Abel, the just one, to the last of the elect,'... be gathered together in the universal Church in the Father's presence."[4]

Vatican Council II

Therefore, the world which the Council has in mind is the whole human family..., the world, which in the Christian vision has been created and is sustained by the love of its maker, which has been freed from the slavery of sin by Christ, who was crucified and rose again in order to break the stranglehold of the evil one, so that it might be fashioned anew according to God's design and brought to its fulfillment. *Gaudium et Spes, 2*

The Church holds that to acknowledge God is in no way to oppose the dignity of man, since such dignity is grounded and brought to perfection in God. Man has in fact been placed in society by God, who created him as an intelligent and free being; but over and above this he is called as a son to intimacy with God and to share in his happiness. *Gaudium et Spes, 21*

Doctrine • Moral • Worship Exercise

(See Appendix A for answer key, questions 48-52.)

1. In what event in history did God's all-powerful action free man from the slavery of sin?
2. God is present among us in many ways. Think of instances from the past month in which you experienced God's presence.
3. How can you be an instrument of God's presence to the people around you?

Chapter Summary Prayer

God and Father of all who believe in You, You promised Abraham that he would become the father of many nations; through the Death and Resurrection of Christ, You fulfill that promise. Everywhere throughout the world You increase Your Chosen People. May we respond to Your call by joyfully accepting Your invitation to the new life of grace.

Jesus freed us from the slavery of sin and made it possible for us to be holy again through His sufferings and Death, and through His glorious Resurrection. We see Creation as Your continuing action as You work out the Salvation of mankind.

You are now present in human history using Your limitless power to help us. Save us from our sins. Protect us from all dangers and lead us to Salvation. Teach us to live by Your wisdom and to love the things of Heaven by our sharing in the mystery of the Eucharist. We ask this through Jesus Christ our Lord. Amen.

Thought Provokers

Please see Appendix B for the answers.

Q. 48: The Church teaches that God is providential. He, foreseeing our needs, provides for them. What are some of the ways that God, taking into account our capabilities and circumstances, provides for our needs (not necessarily our desires or wants)?

Q. 49: It is comforting to know that very reliable historical evidence supports the Christian belief in the bodily Resurrection of Jesus from the dead. In spite of this, however, there are those who deny it. What would be some of the implications for Christianity, if contrary to fact, those who deny the Resurrection were correct?

Q. 50: Think for a few moments of several ways in which God continuously cares and provides for His creation directly, especially for each of us humans!

Q. 51: God, being providential, is constantly acting in human history. How does history viewed in this manner differ from the histories presented in so many contemporary textbooks?

Q. 52: While God is always present in the physical universe; beginning with the descent of the Holy Spirit on the first Christians at Pentecost, He has been present in the world in a special way through His Catholic Church. What are some of the advantages for mankind in having this particular presence of God in the world?

By Heart Catechism and Scripture Review™

The "By Heart Catechism and Scripture Review" lists a selected number of questions and Scripture references from "The Apostolate's Family Catechism" to make memorization easier. Q = Question, SR = Scripture Reference

Q. 42. How was man created? God formed man's body out of the dust of the earth. Then God breathed life into the body, creating a soul that would never die.

SR 42 Psalm 8:5-6

Yet thou has made him little less than God, and does crown him with glory and honor. Thou has given him dominion over the works of thy hands.

Q. 43. In what way is man created in the image and likeness of God? Man is created in the image and likeness of God in that God gave man an immortal soul that has an intellect and free will.

Q. 44. Is the soul directly created by God? Yes, God creates each soul and infuses it into the body.

Q. 45. What special gifts did God give to Adam and Eve? God gave Adam and Eve the special gifts of original holiness and justice, wisdom, strength of will, and freedom from suffering and death.

Q. 46. What commandment did God give Adam and Eve? God told Adam and Eve not to eat the fruit of the Tree of the Knowledge of Good and Evil.

SR 46 Romans 5:12

Therefore as sin came into the world through one man and death through sin, and so death spread to all men because all men sinned.

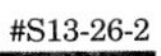
#S13-26-2

The Sins of Man: Original Sin and Personal Sin

#A19-12-2

God created man in a state of holiness, but man abused his freedom as a result of Satan's temptation. He defied God and sought happiness apart from Him.

CHAPTER THIRTEEN

The Fall of Man and Original Sin

Q. 53. What was the Original Sin?

Adam, the first man, abused his freedom by disobeying and rejecting God's care. He wanted to search for happiness in his own way. This, coupled with the sin of Eve, was the Original Sin.

God created man in a state of holiness, but man abused his freedom as a result of Satan's temptation. He defied God and sought happiness apart from Him.

Man was the highest achievement of God's visible creation. Of all God's creatures on earth, man alone could return to God the love which God first gave him. God wanted man to be a part of His family. He wanted man to be united in love to Himself and to one another. God wanted nothing to harm this family—no sickness, death, ignorance, or weakness.

Sacred Scripture

And to Adam he said, "Because you have listened to the voice of your wife, and have eaten of the tree of which I commanded you, 'You shall not eat of it,' cursed is the ground because of you; in toil you shall eat of it all the days of your life... In the sweat of your face you shall eat bread till you return to the ground, for out of it you were taken; you are dust, and to dust you shall return." Genesis 3:17, 19

Catechism of the Catholic Church

397 Man, tempted by the devil, let his trust in his Creator die in his heart and, abusing his freedom, disobeyed God's command. This is what man's first sin consisted of.[1] All subsequent sin would be disobedience toward God and lack of trust in his goodness.

Splendor of Truth

Human freedom belongs to us as creatures; it is a freedom which is given as a gift, one to be received like a seed and to be cultivated responsibly. It is an essential part of that creaturely image which is the basis of the dignity of the person. *(section 86)*

Sacred Scripture
Q. 53. Gen 3.

Catechism of the Catholic Church
Q. 53. Paragraphs 396-401.

For cross-references with Vatican II, Papal documents & other resources, see Family Wisdom Library on page 196.
For commentaries on each question with Cardinal Arinze, Sr. John Vianney and Fr. Straub (in Spanish), see Appendix C.

Vatican Council II

Although set by God in a state of rectitude, man, enticed by the evil one, abused his freedom at the very start of history. He lifted himself up against God, and sought to attain his goal apart from him. Although they had known God, they did not glorify him as God, but their senseless hearts were darkened, and they served the creature rather than the Creator. *Gaudium et Spes, 13*

Catechism by Diagram

#A19-7

The Fall of Man. Top diagram: Adam and Eve enjoyed the grace of God and were united by love for each other and for God. The serpent told them to eat of the forbidden fruit. Bottom diagram: Adam and Eve disobeyed God and lost His grace (broken arrow and Holy Spirit leaving). God sent them out of paradise (line pointing out).

Q. 54. Why are all men conceived and born in Original Sin?

When Adam sinned, he lost original holiness and justice. He cut himself off from God, and his human nature was harmed in its natural powers, and sickness and death entered his life. In losing these gifts, he could not pass them on to his descendants.

As a result, people are born into this world separated from their loving Father and subject to death. The main sign of sin in the world is man's rejection of God. Other signs are war, poverty, starvation, hatred of people, violence, and other injustices.

Jesus Christ, our Lord and Savior, restored the supernatural gifts to us through His Passion, Death, and Resurrection, and through the Church He founded.

#J2-440

Jesus Christ, our Lord and Savior, restored the supernatural gifts to us through His Passion, Death, and Resurrection, and through the Church He founded.

Catechism of the Catholic Church
Q. 54. Paragraphs **402**-409.

For cross-references with Vatican II, Papal documents & other resources, see Family Wisdom Library on page 196.
For commentaries on each question with Cardinal Arinze, Sr. John Vianney and Fr. Straub (in Spanish), see Appendix C.

#A19-19

When Adam sinned, he lost original holiness and justice. He cut himself off from God. In losing these gifts, he could not pass them on to his descendants.

Sacred Scripture

What then? Are we Jews any better off? No, not at all; for I have already charged that all men, both Jews and Greeks, are under the power of sin, as it is written: "None is righteous, no, not one; no one understands, no one seeks for God. All have turned aside, together they have gone wrong; no one does good, not even one." *Romans 3:9-12*

Therefore as sin came into the world through one man and death through sin, and so death spread to all men because all men sinned. *Romans 5:12*

Catechism of the Catholic Church

404 How did the sin of Adam become the sin of all his descendants? The whole human race is in Adam "as one body of one man."[1] By this "unity of the human race" all men are implicated in Adam's sin, as all are implicated in Christ's justice. Still, the transmission of original sin is a mystery that we cannot fully understand. But we do know by Revelation that Adam had received original holiness and justice not for himself alone, but for all human nature. By yielding to the tempter, Adam and Eve committed a *personal sin*, but this sin affected *the human nature* that they would then transmit *in a fallen state*.[2] It is a sin which will be transmitted by propagation to all mankind, that is, by the transmission of a human nature deprived of original holiness and justice. And that is why original sin is called "sin" only in an analogical sense: it is a sin "contracted" and not "committed"—a state and not an act.

Splendor of Truth

As a result of that mysterious original sin, committed at the prompting of Satan, the one who is "a liar and the father of lies" (Jn 8:44), man is constantly tempted to turn his gaze away from the living and true God in order to direct it towards idols (cf. 1 Thes 1:9), exchanging "the truth about God for a lie" (Rom 1:25). Man's capacity to know the truth is also darkened, and his will to submit to it is weakened. Thus, giving himself over to relativism and skepticism (cf. Jn 18:38), he goes off in search of an illusory freedom apart from truth itself.

But no darkness of error or of sin can totally take away from man the light of God the Creator. In the depths of his heart there always remains a yearning for absolute truth and a thirst to attain full knowledge of it. *(section 1)*

Vatican Council II

In the course of history the use of temporal things has been tarnished by serious defects. Under the influence of original sin men have often fallen into very many errors about the true God, human nature and the principles of morality. As a consequence human conduct and institutions became corrupted, the human person itself held in contempt. *Lay People, 7*

What Revelation makes known to us is confirmed by our own experience. For when man looks into his own heart he finds that he is drawn towards what is wrong and sunk in many evils which cannot come from his good Creator. Often refusing to acknowledge God as his source, man has also upset the relationship which should link him to his last end; and at the same time he has broken the right order that should reign within himself as well as between himself and other men and all creatures. *Gaudium et Spes, 13*

Q. 55. What happens in Baptism?

In Baptism, God unites our soul to Himself. God's love, the Holy Spirit, is poured into our soul. Our soul is lifted to a new kind of life which is a sharing in God's own life.

Although Baptism gives us the supernatural gift of sanctifying grace, it does not bring us some special gifts which Adam and Eve alone received, such as freedom from suffering and death. But God has restored to us the really important gift of the supernatural life of grace. This gift was given to us through the sufferings and Death of His Son.

#B6-2-2

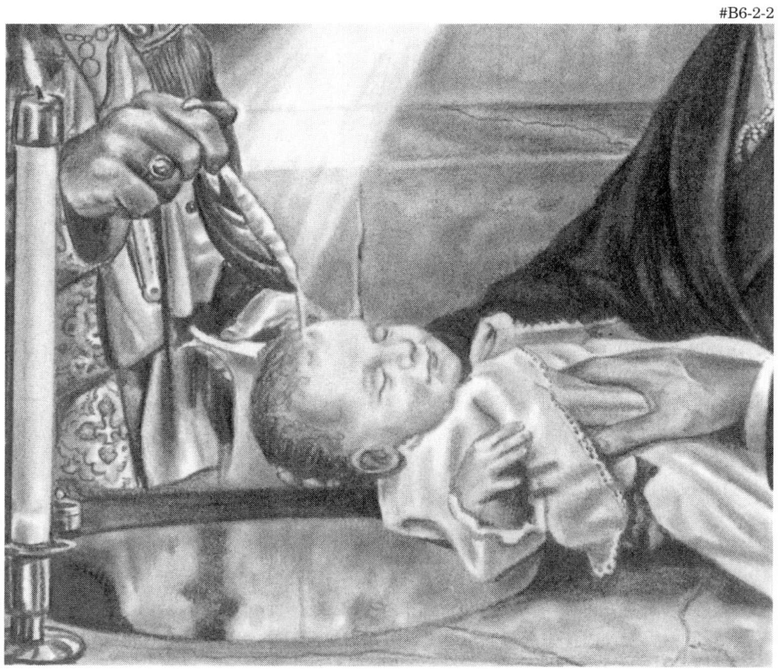

Baptism restores the gift of the supernatural life of grace that was lost through Original Sin.

Sacred Scripture

And Peter said to them, "Repent, and be baptized every one of you in the name of Jesus Christ for the forgiveness of your sins; and you shall receive the gift of the Holy Spirit." *Acts 2:38*

For as many of you as were baptized into Christ have put on Christ. *Galatians 3:27*

Sacred Scripture
Q. 55. Jn 3:3-5; Rom 6:3-4; 2 Cor 5:17.

Catechism of the Catholic Church
Q. 55. Paragraphs 1226-1228, 1262-**1284**.

For cross-references with Vatican II, Papal documents & other resources, see Family Wisdom Library on page 196.
For commentaries on each question with Cardinal Arinze, Sr. John Vianney and Fr. Straub (in Spanish), see Appendix C.

Catechism of the Catholic Church

1263 By Baptism *all sins* are forgiven, original sin and all personal sins, as well as all punishment for sin.[1] In those who have been reborn nothing remains that would impede their entry into the Kingdom of God, neither Adam's sin, nor personal sin, nor the consequences of sin, the gravest of which is separation from God.

Q. 56. Was anyone exempt from Original Sin?

The Blessed Virgin Mary was chosen to be the Mother of the Son of God, and thus she was preserved, from the very first moment of her conception, from the spiritual darkness of Original Sin.

She was always united with God; her soul was flooded with His love. We call this privilege her Immaculate Conception. The Church celebrates this great feast on December 8th.

Sacred Scripture

"I will put enmity between you and the woman, and between your seed and her seed; he shall bruise your head, and you shall bruise his heel." *Genesis 3:15*

"Hail, full of grace, the Lord is with you!" *Luke 1:28*

Catechism of the Catholic Church

491 Through the centuries the Church has become ever more aware that Mary, "full of grace" through God,[1] was redeemed from the moment of her conception. That is what the dogma of the Immaculate Conception confesses, as Pope Pius IX proclaimed in 1854: "The most Blessed Virgin Mary was, from the first moment of her conception, by a singular grace and privilege of almighty God and by virtue of the merits of Jesus Christ, Savior of the human race, preserved immune from all stain of original sin."

Doctrine • Moral • Worship Exercise

(See Appendix A for answer key, questions 53-56.)

1. What are some of the effects of original sin on all mankind?
2. What graces do we receive at Baptism which enable us to live as God's own children?
3. Think of ways in which you can imitate the Blessed Virgin Mary in her faithfulness to God.

Sacred Scripture
Q. 56. Lk 1:42-49.

Catechism of the Catholic Church
Q. 56. Paragraphs 490, **492**, 493.

For cross-references with Vatican II, Papal documents & other resources, see Family Wisdom Library on page 196.
For commentaries on each question with Cardinal Arinze, Sr. John Vianney and Fr. Straub (in Spanish), see Appendix C.

#M3-246-2

The Blessed Virgin Mary was preserved, from the very first moment of her conception, from the spiritual darkness of Original Sin.

Chapter Summary Prayer

Loving Creator, in Your infinite goodness You made man in a state of holiness. Man was the crown of Your visible Creation, for he alone could give back to You the love which You first gave him. It was Your will that people should live as Your family, united to each other and to You in love.

But Adam sinned. He cut himself off from You, the source of all that is good. He was stripped of the grace You had given him. His human nature was harmed in its natural powers. Sickness and death entered his life as well. Thus, we are born into this world separated from You and subject to death.

Jesus, you came among us as a man, to lead mankind from darkness into the light of faith. Through Adam's fall we were born as slaves of sin, but now through Baptism in You we are reborn as Your adopted children.

Lord God, we praise You for creating man, and still more for restoring him in Christ. Your Son shared our weakness; may we share His glory now and forever. Amen.

Thought Provokers

Please see Appendix B for the answers.

Q. 53: A. What similarities exist between the Original Sin committed by our First Parents and the sins we commit?

B. Can you think of any dissimilarities?

Q. 54: What is meant by the term "fallen" when applied to the human race? That is, from what has mankind fallen?

Q. 55: Why is water an especially appropriate outward sign for the Sacrament of Baptism?

Q. 56: What similarities can be found between the Blessed Virgin Mary and Eve (i.e., Eve prior to her falling from divine grace)?

#O8-18-2

A sin must be a conscious and deliberate violation of the moral law.

CHAPTER FOURTEEN

Personal Sin

Q. 57. What is actual or personal sin?

Actual or personal sin is an offense against God. Personal sin, as opposed to Original Sin, is the willful disobedience to God's will.

This disobedience may be an action, a thought, a desire, or an intention. A sin must be a conscious and deliberate violation of the moral law. Thus, to sin is to actually say "no" to God. We sin when we refuse God's love and turn down His invitation to give of ourselves to God and to our fellow men. Furthermore, we sin through personal acts of selfishness which cause harm to others or ourselves.

#F1-65

Personal sin is the willful disobedience to God's will. We sin through personal acts of selfishness which cause harm to others or ourselves.

Sacred Scripture

Let not sin therefore reign in your mortal bodies, to make you obey their passions. Do not yield your members to sin as instruments of wickedness, but yield yourselves to God as men who have been brought from death to life, and your members to God as instruments of righteousness. For sin will have no dominion over you, since you are not under law but under grace. *Romans 6:12-13*

Sacred Scripture
Q. 57. Rom 1:28-32.

Catechism of the Catholic Church
Q. 57. Paragraphs 404, **1849**-1876.

For cross-references with Vatican II, Papal documents & other resources, see Family Wisdom Library on page 196.
For commentaries on each question with Cardinal Arinze, Sr. John Vianney and Fr. Straub (in Spanish), see Appendix C.

#R19.3-11-2

Sin is an offense against God: "Against thee, thee only, have I sinned, and done that which is evil in thy sight" *(Psalms 51:4)*. Sin sets itself against God's love for us and turns our hearts away from it. *(Catechism of the Catholic Church, 1850)*

Catechism of the Catholic Church

1850 Sin is an offense against God: "Against you, you alone, have I sinned, and done that which is evil in your sight."[1] Sin sets itself against God's love for us and turns our hearts away from it. Like the first sin, it is disobedience, a revolt against God through the will to become "like gods,"[2] knowing and determining good and evil. Sin is thus "love of oneself even to contempt of God."[3] In this proud self-exaltation, sin is diametrically opposed to the obedience of Jesus, which achieves our salvation.[4]

Splendor of Truth

We are in a certain way our own parents, creating ourselves as we will, by our decisions. *(section 71)*

If the object of the concrete action is not in harmony with the true good of the person, the choice of that action makes our will and ourselves morally evil, thus putting us in conflict with our ultimate end, the supreme good, God himself. *(section 72)*

In Jesus Christ and in his Spirit, the Christian is a "new creation," a child of God; by his actions he shows his likeness or unlikeness to the image of the Son who is the first-born among many brethren (cf. Rom 8:29), he lives out his fidelity or infidelity to the gift of the Spirit, and he opens or closes himself to eternal life. *(section 73)*

Q. 58. When someone commits a personal sin, what happens?

When someone commits a personal sin, he: (1) fails to love God; (2) turns away from pursuing his lifetime goal of doing the will of God; and (3) by means of a serious offense (mortal sin), ruptures his relationship with the Father, the Son, and the Holy Spirit.

To sin is to refuse to let God have His way in our life. We turn away from God because we want to live without regard for His will. When we sin, we choose whatever we think will make us happy, even though it does not fit into God's plan for our eternal happiness. We fail to trust God completely when we sin. Serious sin makes us unhappy and sometimes even enslaves us to sin. Jesus said, "Truly, truly, I say to you, every one who commits sin is a slave to sin" (John 8:34).

#S13-34-2

To sin is to refuse to let God have His way in our life. We turn away from God because we want to live without regard for His will.

Sacred Scripture

Do you not know that if you yield yourselves to any one as obedient slaves, you are slaves of the one whom you obey, either of sin, which leads to death, or of obedience, which leads to righteousness?... What return did you get from the things of which you are now ashamed? The end of those things is death. But now that you have been set free from sin and have become slaves of God, the return you get is sanctification and its end, eternal life. *Romans 6:16, 21-22*

Sacred Scripture
Q. 58. Eph 5:5-6.

Catechism of the Catholic Church
Q. 58. Paragraphs 311, 1440, **1849-1856**.

For cross-references with Vatican II, Papal documents & other resources, see Family Wisdom Library on page 196.
For commentaries on each question with Cardinal Arinze, Sr. John Vianney and Fr. Straub (in Spanish), see Appendix C.

#P42-5

A supernatural solidarity reigns among men. A consequence of this is that the sin of one person harms other people just as one person's holiness helps others.
(Pope Paul VI, Revision of Indulgences, 4)

Catechism of the Catholic Church

1440 Sin is before all else an offense against God, a rupture of communion with him. At the same time it damages communion with the Church. For this reason conversion entails both God's forgiveness and reconciliation with the Church, which are expressed and accomplished liturgically by the sacrament of Penance and Reconciliation.[1]

Papal Documents

Throughout history Christians have always believed that sin is not only a breaking of God's law but that it shows contempt for or disregard of the friendship between God and man. The latter is not always directly evident. Further, they have believed that sin is a real offense against God, the effect of which cannot be estimated. Again, it is a display of ingratitude, a rejection of the love God has shown us through Jesus Christ. *Pope Paul VI, Revision of Indulgences, 2*

The very facts that punishment for sin exists and that it is so severe make it possible for us to understand how foolish and malicious sin is and how harmful its consequences are. *Pope Paul VI, Revision of Indulgences, 3*

By the hidden and kindly mystery of God's will a supernatural solidarity reigns among men. A consequence of this is that the sin of one person harms other people just as one person's holiness helps others. *Pope Paul VI, Revision of Indulgences, 4*

To speak of social sin means in the first place to recognize that, by virtue of human solidarity which is as mysterious and intangible as it is real and concrete, each individual's sin in some way affects others. This is the other aspect of that solidarity which on the religious level is developed in the profound

and magnificent mystery of the Communion of Saints, thanks to which it has been possible to say that "every soul that rises above itself, raises up the world." To this law of ascent there unfortunately corresponds the law of descent.

Consequently one can speak of a communion of sin, whereby a soul that lowers itself through sin drags down with itself the Church and, in some way, the whole world. In other words, there is no sin, not even the most intimate and secret one, the most strictly individual one, that exclusively concerns the person committing it. With greater or lesser violence, with greater or lesser harm, every sin has repercussions on the entire ecclesial body and the whole human family. According to this first meaning of the term, every sin can undoubtedly be considered as social sin. *Pope John Paul II, Apostolic Letter, Reconciliation and Penance, 16*

Catechism by Diagram

#S13-7

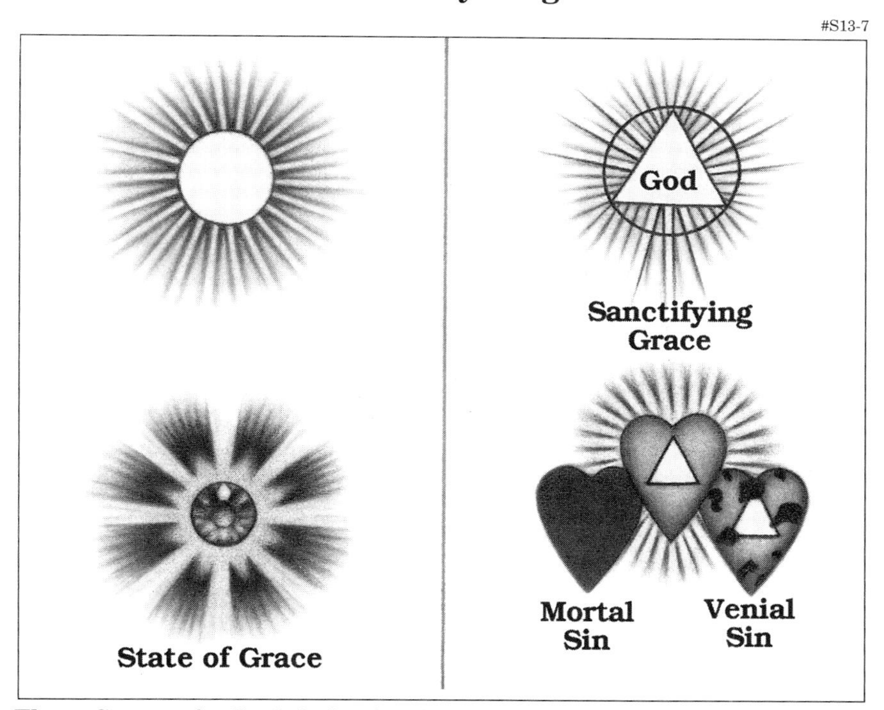

Three States of a Soul. Left side: The soul in the state of grace is filled with divine brightness, like a diamond reflecting the brightness of the sun. Right side: The three hearts represent the different states in which the soul can be: (1) a soul in sanctifying grace reflects God's beauty; (2) a soul in mortal sin (heart filled with blackness); and (3) a soul in venial sin (heart with spots). Sanctifying grace is a sharing of God's life. Venial sin weakens the life of God in a person's soul. Mortal sin destroys the life of God in the soul.

Summary Prayer

God our Father, make us deeply conscious of the evil of personal sin, which we commit when we, acting knowingly and willingly, break Your moral law. When we sin, we refuse Your love and turn down Your invitation to give of ourselves to You and to our fellow men. Such personal acts of selfishness cause harm to us and to others. For these, we beg Your forgiveness and help, through Jesus Christ our Lord. Amen.

#S13-19-2

Throughout history Christians have always believed that sin is not only a breaking of God's law but that it shows contempt for or disregard of the friendship between God and man. *(Pope Paul VI, Revision of Indulgences, 2)*

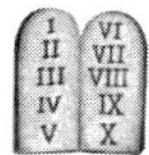

Doctrine • Moral • Worship Exercise

(See Appendix A for answer key, questions 57-58.)

1. Why do we say that to sin is a personal decision to say "no" to God?
2. Recall the last instance in which you chose to do your will rather than God's will. How did this affect you?
3. In what concrete ways can you cooperate with the will of God?

Chapter Summary Prayer

God our Father, help us to realize that when we sin we fail in loving You. In fact, we turn away from You by refusing to do Your will. A serious or grave sin breaks our relationship with You.

Lord, God of power, You rescued Your Son from the grasp of evil men. Deliver us from evil and confirm our trust in You, so that in our rising we may sing of Your power, and exult in Your mercy.

Make our lives blameless, Lord. Help us to do what is right, and to speak what is true, that we may dwell in Your presence and find rest in Your heavenly home, through Christ our Lord. Amen.

Thought Provokers

Please see Appendix B for the answers.

Q. 57: What are some of the basic reasons for the sins we commit?

Q. 58: When we commit one or more sins, what happens to us as far as our relationship with God is concerned and how should we react to the fact that we have sinned?

#T16-2

Mortal sin is a serious or grave violation of the law of God. The result of committing a mortal sin is the destruction of the life of God in the soul.

CHAPTER FIFTEEN

Mortal and Venial Sin

Q. 59. What is mortal sin?

Mortal sin is a serious or grave violation of the law of God. It is the fully deliberate choice of a person who knows that what he chooses is gravely forbidden by God. The result of committing a mortal sin is the destruction of the life of God in the soul.

By committing a mortal sin, we lose God's life regained for us by our Redeemer, Jesus Christ.

Sacred Scripture

For the wages of sin is death, but the free gift of God is eternal life in Christ Jesus our Lord. *Romans 6:23*

Splendor of Truth

With the whole tradition of the Church, we call mortal sin the act by which man freely and consciously rejects God, his law, the covenant of love that God offers, preferring to turn in on himself or to some created and finite reality, something contrary to the divine will (conversio ad creaturam). This can occur in a direct and formal way, in the sins of idolatry, apostasy and atheism; or in an equivalent way, as in every act of disobedience to God's commandments in a grave matter. *(section 70)*

Summary Prayer

Our Heavenly Father, preserve us from mortal sin, which is the loss of Your life in our souls. It destroys the life that You share with us, Your creatures. Keep us from all sin, but especially from a serious violation of Your law, so that we may never be separated from You. Keep us from even venial sin, which weakens our love for You and harms us and other people. We ask this through Jesus Christ our Lord, to Whom, with You and the Holy Spirit, be all honor and glory. Amen.

Catechism of the Catholic Church
Q. 59. Paragraphs **1855-1861**.

For cross-references with Vatican II, Papal documents & other resources, see Family Wisdom Library on page 196.
For commentaries on each question with Cardinal Arinze, Sr. John Vianney and Fr. Straub (in Spanish), see Appendix C.

Q. 60. What are the effects of mortal sin?

As explained before, the effects of mortal sin are separation from God and damage to ourselves and others.

If we do not wish to change and if we always refuse to do what God wants us to do, the separation from God is permanent. The permanent separation from God after death takes place in Hell.

#S13-22-2

The effects of mortal sin are separation from God and damage to ourselves and others.

Sacred Scripture

But your iniquities have made a separation between you and your God, and your sins have hid his face from you so that he does not hear. *Isaiah 59:2*

The way of sinners is smoothly paved with stones, but at its end is the pit of Hades. *Sirach 21:10*

Then he will say to those at his left hand, "Depart from me, you cursed, into the eternal fire prepared for the devil and his angels." *Matthew 25:41*

Catechism of the Catholic Church

1861 Mortal sin is a radical possibility of human freedom, as is love itself. It results in the loss of charity and the privation of sanctifying grace, that is, of the state of grace. If it is not redeemed by repentance and God's forgiveness, it causes exclusion from Christ's kingdom and the eternal death of hell, for our freedom has the power to make choices for ever, with no turning back. However, although we can judge that an act is in itself a grave offense, we must entrust judgment of persons to the justice and mercy of God.

Sacred Scripture
Q. 60. Is 13:9-11; 1 Cor 6:9; Gal 5:19-21.

Catechism of the Catholic Church
Q. 60. Paragraphs 1446, **1856**, 1861.

For cross-references with Vatican II, Papal documents & other resources, see Family Wisdom Library on page 196.
For commentaries on each question with Cardinal Arinze, Sr. John Vianney and Fr. Straub (in Spanish), see Appendix C.

Splendor of Truth

With every freely committed mortal sin, he (man) offends God as the giver of the law and as a result becomes guilty with regard to the entire law (cf. Jas 2:8-11); even if he perseveres in faith, he loses "sanctifying grace," "charity" and "eternal happiness." *(section 68)*

Catechism by Diagram

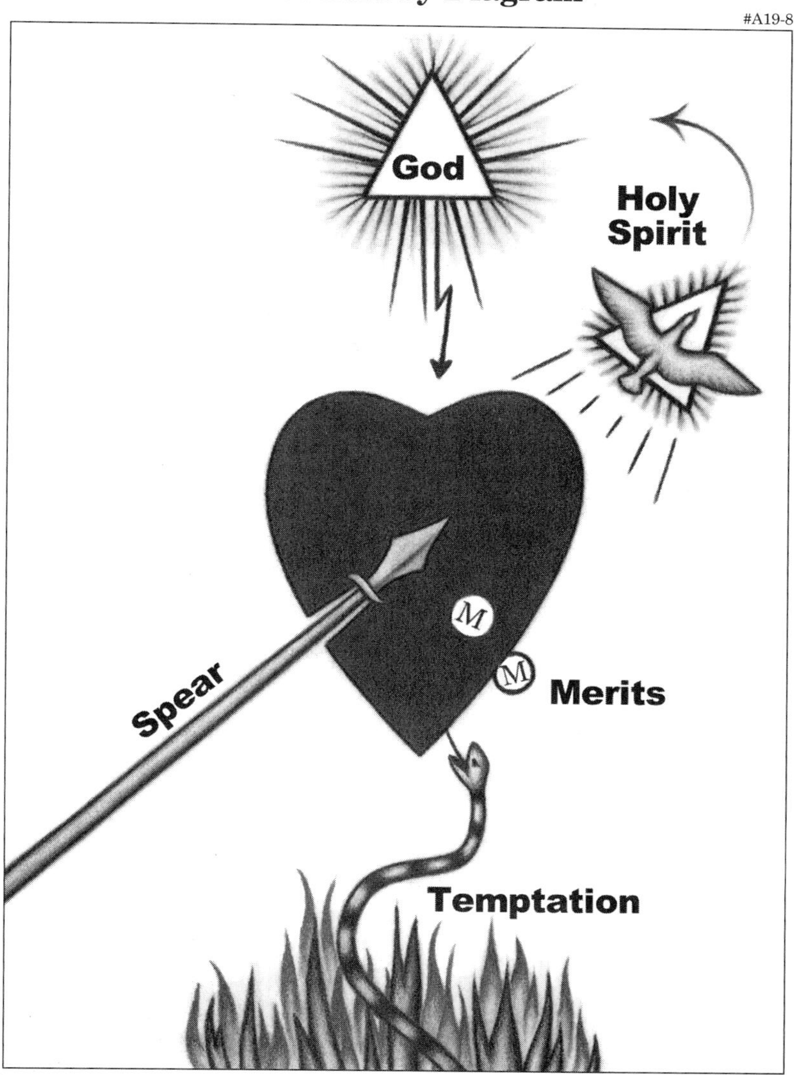

Effects of Mortal Sin. Mortal sin destroys the supernatural life of the soul, sanctifying grace. It is a death-dealing sin (spear). Mortal sin weakens the power of the sinner to fight against temptation (serpent), and makes him lose the merits (circle with M) of his deeds. A mortal sin puts the sinner in danger of being lost forever in Hell.

Q. 61. What is a venial sin?

Venial sin is a minor violation of the law of God. It does not take away God's life from the soul or break God's friendship, but it weakens our love for God. It also harms us and other people.

#F1-90

Venial sin weakens our love for God and harms us and other people.

Sacred Scripture

He who despises small things will fail little by little. *Sirach 19:1*

He who is faithful in a very little is faithful also in much; and he who is dishonest in a very little is dishonest also in much. *Luke 16:10*

Catechism of the Catholic Church

1862 One commits venial sin when, in a less serious matter, he does not observe the standard prescribed by the moral law, or when he disobeys the moral law in a grave matter, but without full knowledge or without complete consent.

Sacred Scripture
Q. 61. 1 Jn 5:16-17.

Catechism of the Catholic Church
Q. 61. Paragraphs 1855, **1863**, 1875.

For cross-references with Vatican II, Papal documents & other resources, see Family Wisdom Library on page 196.
For commentaries on each question with Cardinal Arinze, Sr. John Vianney and Fr. Straub (in Spanish), see Appendix C.

Catechism by Diagram

#S13-8

Venial Sin. Venial sin is a lesser refusal by which man fails to do what God asks of him. It does not take away God's life from the soul (heart with triangle), but it weakens its love for God (spots in the heart). "Deliberate and unrepented venial sin disposes us little by little to commit mortal sin (arrows to fire)" (*Catechism of the Catholic Church*, #1863).

Summary Prayer

God of wisdom and love, source of all goodness, send Your Spirit to teach us the truth about sin, and guide our actions in Your way of peace. May Your healing love turn us from every sin and keep us on the way that leads to You. Help us always to overcome evil with good, that we may rejoice in Your triumph forever.

God our Savior, bring us back to You, and fill our minds with Your wisdom concerning the evil of sin. May we be enriched by the Sacraments of the Eucharist and Reconciliation, and by earnest prayer, so that the offering of our love may be acceptable to You.

May Your grace transform our lives and bring us Your mercy. May we rejoice in Your healing power and experience Your saving love in mind and body. Make us grow in our desire for You that we may be protected from the sins which would separate us from You. We ask this through Jesus Christ our only Savior. Amen.

Q. 62. Under what conditions does a Christian commit a mortal sin?

To commit a mortal sin the Christian must: (1) have committed a grave sin; (2) have known its gravity; and (3) have been free to avoid offending God.

#S13-44-2

The person who commits the sin must know what he is doing, and that what he is doing is a serious offense against God.

Sacred Scripture
Q. 62. Jn 9:41; 2 Thess 2:9-12.

Catechism of the Catholic Church
Q. 62. Paragraphs **1857**-1861.

For cross-references with Vatican II, Papal documents & other resources, see Family Wisdom Library on page 196.
For commentaries on each question with Cardinal Arinze, Sr. John Vianney and Fr. Straub (in Spanish), see Appendix C.

1. The offense in itself must be serious or grave, that is, something that has been forbidden by God under pain of losing His friendship.

2. The person who commits the sin must know what he is doing, and that what he is doing is a serious offense against God. (If, on the other hand, he does not know this but deliberately kept himself in ignorance about the matter, his ignorance is not excusable.)

3. There must be full consent of the will. A person who acts under any circumstance which would deprive him of the full exercise of his will would not be guilty of mortal sin.

#M5-8

To commit a mortal sin the Christian must have committed a grave sin, that is, something that has been forbidden by God under pain of losing His friendship.

Catechism of the Catholic Church

1858 *Grave matter* is specified by the Ten Commandments, corresponding to the answer of Jesus to the rich young man: "Do not kill, Do not commit adultery, Do not steal, Do not bear false witness, Do not defraud, Honor your father and your mother."[1] The gravity of sins is more or less great: murder is graver than theft. One must also take into account who is wronged: violence against parents is in itself graver than violence against a stranger.

Splendor of Truth

It is always from the truth that the dignity of conscience derives... Conscience, as the ultimate concrete judgment, compromises its dignity when it is culpably erroneous, that is to say, "when man shows little concern for seeking what is true and good, and conscience gradually becomes almost blind from being accustomed to sin." *(section 63)*

Roman Curia Document

Nor should one fail to mention the doctrine of the nature and effects of personal sin, by which a person knowingly and deliberately transgresses the moral law and offends God gravely in a grave manner. *General Catechetical Directory, 62 [1971]*

Catechism by Diagram

#S13-9

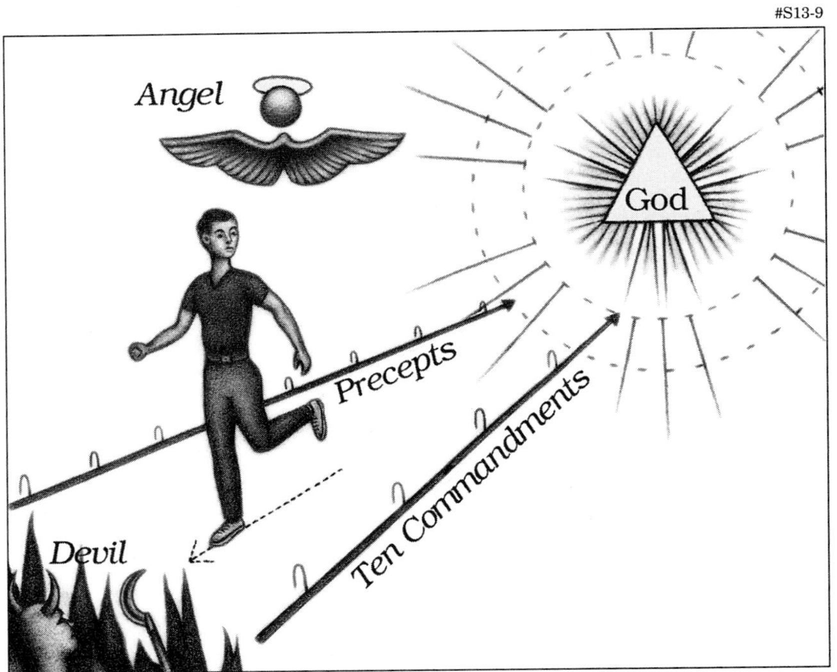

Mortal Sin. For a sin to be a mortal sin, three conditions must be met. If any of the three conditions are missing, it is not a mortal sin. First, the matter must be serious, whether it be a thought, word, action, or intended action (Ten Commandments, Precepts of the Church). Second, the person must have full knowledge that the thing he is doing is seriously wrong. Third, the person must freely consent to the action which God has forbidden (man chooses to walk away from God, dotted arrow toward devil).

Summary Prayer

Father in Heaven, help us to understand that we cannot offend You by committing a mortal sin unless we have a clear knowledge that a given thought, word, deed, or intention is gravely sinful, and we are free to avoid offending You. Give us the wisdom to choose only those right actions which You want us to do, and to avoid those actions which You do not want us to do. Give us the strength of Your grace to do Your will in all things. We ask this in Jesus' name. Amen.

Q. 63. When is an act right or wrong?

An act is right when it corresponds to the truth of the moral order—God's law. In other words, it is something God wants us to do. An act is wrong if it breaks God's law and, therefore, is not something God wants us to do. Freedom makes us responsible for our voluntary actions. We sin not only by freely choosing to do what God has forbidden, but also by failing to do what God has commanded.

#F1-149

An act is right when it is something God wants us to do. An act is wrong if it breaks God's law.

Sacred Scripture

The law of the Lord is perfect, reviving the soul; the testimony of the Lord is sure, making wise the simple; the precepts of the Lord are right, rejoicing the heart; the commandment of the Lord is pure, enlightening the eyes;... Moreover by them is thy servant warned; in keeping them there is great reward. *Psalm 19: 7-8, 11*

Whoever knows what is right to do and fails to do it, for him it is sin. *James 4:17*

Catechism of the Catholic Church

1755 A morally good act requires the goodness of the object, of the end, and of the circumstances together. An evil end corrupts the action, even if the object is good in itself (such as praying and fasting "in order to be seen by men"). The object of the choice can by itself vitiate an act in its entirety. There are some concrete acts—such as fornication—that it is always wrong to choose, because choosing them entails a disorder of the will, that is, a moral evil.

Sacred Scripture
Q. 63. Ex. 20:1-17; Mt 5:17-48.

Catechism of the Catholic Church
Q. 63. Paragraphs **1749-1760.**

For cross-references with Vatican II, Papal documents & other resources, see Family Wisdom Library on page 196.
For commentaries on each question with Cardinal Arinze, Sr. John Vianney and Fr. Straub (in Spanish), see Appendix C.

1761 There are concrete acts that it is always wrong to choose, because their choice entails a disorder of the will, i.e., a moral evil. One may not do evil so that good may result from it.

Veritatis Splendor

If acts are intrinsically evil, a good intention or particular circumstances can diminish their evil, but they cannot remove it. They remain "irremediably" evil acts; per se and in themselves they are not capable of being ordered to God and to the good of the person.... Circumstances or intentions can never transform an act intrinsically evil by virtue of its object into an act "subjectively" good or defensible as a choice. *(section 81)*

#S13-33-2

We sin not only by freely choosing to do what God has forbidden, but also by failing to do what God has commanded.

Papal Document

During the Synod Assembly some Fathers proposed a threefold distinction of sins, classifying them as venial, grave and mortal. This threefold distinction might illustrate the fact that there is a scale of seriousness among grave sins. But it still remains true that the essential and decisive distinction is between sin which destroys charity and sin which does not kill the supernatural life: there is no middle way between life and death.

Likewise, care will have to be taken not to reduce mortal sin to an act of "fundamental option"—as is commonly said today—against God, intending thereby an explicit and formal contempt for God or neighbor. For mortal sin exists also when a person knowingly and willingly, for whatever reason, chooses something gravely disordered. In fact, such a choice already includes contempt for the divine law, a rejection of God's love for humanity and the whole of creation; the person turns away from God and loses charity. Thus the fundamental orientation can be radically changed by individual acts. Clearly there can occur situations which are very complex and obscure from a psychological viewpoint and which have an influence on the sinner's subjective culpability. But from a consideration of the psychological sphere one cannot proceed to the construction of a theological category, which is what the 'fundamental option' precisely is, understanding it in such a way that it objectively changes or casts doubt upon the traditional concept of mortal sin.

"While every sincere and prudent attempt to clarify the psychological and theological mystery of sin is to be valued, the Church nevertheless has a duty to remind all scholars in this field of the need to be faithful to the word of God that teaches us also about sin. She likewise has to remind them of the risk of contributing to a further weakening of the sense of sin in the modern world."
Pope John Paul II, Apostolic Letter, Reconciliation and Penance, 17

#S13-49

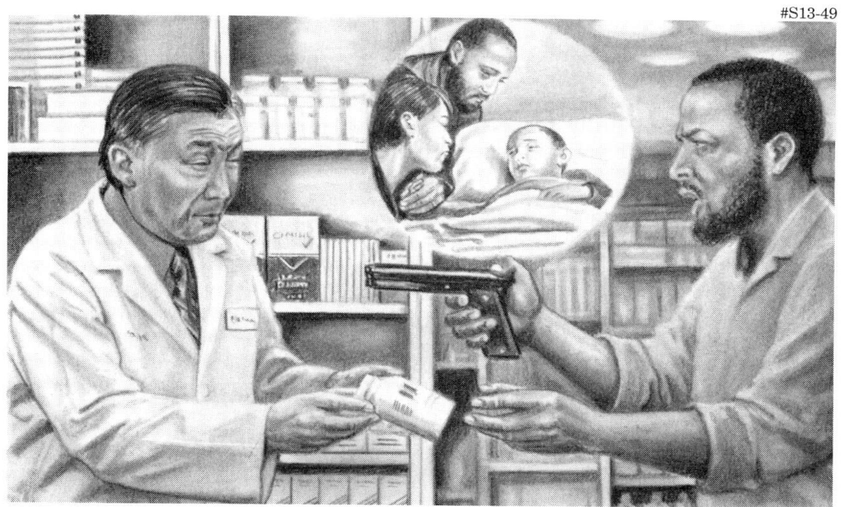

There are concrete acts that it is always wrong to choose... One may not do evil so that good may result from it. *(Catechism of the Catholic Church, 1761)*

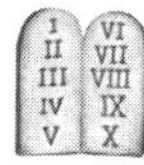

Doctrine • Moral • Worship Exercise

(See Appendix A for answer key, questions 59-63.)

1. Explain why committing both mortal and venial sins are ways of saying "no" to God.
2. What are the effects of mortal sin and venial sin?
3. Schedule a nightly examination of conscience. If you have committed a mortal sin, how can the Sacrament of Penance restore your relationship with God?

Chapter Summary Prayer

Father, without You we can do nothing to please You. By Your Spirit, help us to know what is right and to be eager to do Your will.

Guide us in Your gentle mercy, for left to ourselves, we cannot do Your will. Make our hearts obedient to Your will. May the power of Your holy sacraments free us from sin, and help us to please You in our daily life. Father of love, hear our prayer. Help us to know Your will and to do it with courage and faith. Make us grow in holiness. Through the Mass, may our whole life be a sacrifice pleasing to You. We ask this through Your Son, Our Lord and Savior Jesus Christ. Amen.

Thought Provokers

Please see Appendix B for the answers.

Q. 59: Mortal sin is rightly said to result in the "death of the soul." What does this mean, especially when one considers the fact that the soul is immortal by nature?

Q. 60: What concrete steps can be taken in our lives to avoid committing mortal sins?

Q. 61: If venial sins do not separate us from the state of grace, why should we be concerned about avoiding them and confessing them?

Q. 62: A. What effects do our mortal sins have on us?

B. In what ways can our mortal sins affect others?

Q. 63: Where is the ultimate, unchangeable, and eternal norm or standard for morally good acts to be found?

CHAPTER SIXTEEN

Knowing God's Will and His Merciful Forgiveness

Q. 64. How do we know God's will?

We know God's will through our reason, through the Bible, through Sacred Tradition, and through the teaching office or Magisterium of the Church, which is God's living voice.

Sacred Scripture

Do not be conformed to this world but be transformed by the renewal of your mind, that you may prove what is the will of God, what is good and acceptable and perfect. *Romans 12:2*

#F1-68

We know God's will through our reason, through the Bible, through Sacred Tradition, and through the teaching office or Magisterium of the Church.

Catechism of the Catholic Church

1954 Man participates in the wisdom and goodness of the Creator who gives him mastery over his acts and the ability to govern himself with a view to the true and the good. The natural law expresses the original moral sense which enables man to discern by reason the good and the evil, the truth and the lie.

Splendor of Truth

In order to make this "encounter" with Christ possible, God willed his Church. Indeed, the Church "wishes to serve this single end: that each person may be able to find Christ, in order that Christ may walk with each person the path of life." *(section 7)*

Sacred Scripture
Q. 64. Jer 7:23; Ps 1:1-3; 1 Cor 11:1-2; 2 Thess 2:14-15; 2 Tim 3-16.

Catechism of the Catholic Church
Q. 64. Paragraphs 1951, 1961-1962, 1965, **2032-2037**, 2057.

For cross-references with Vatican II, Papal documents & other resources, see Family Wisdom Library on page 196.
For commentaries on each question with Cardinal Arinze, Sr. John Vianney and Fr. Straub (in Spanish), see Appendix C.

A close connection is made between eternal life and obedience to God's commandments: God's commandments show man the path of life and they lead to it... Jesus himself definitively confirms them and proposes them to us as the way and condition of salvation. *(section 12)*

Reason draws its own truth and authority from the eternal law, which is none other than divine wisdom itself... The moral law has its origin in God and always finds its source in him: at the same time, by virtue of natural reason, which derives from divine wisdom, it is a properly human law. Indeed, as we have seen, the natural law "is nothing other than the light of understanding infused in us by God, whereby we understand what must be done and what must be avoided. God gave this light and this law to man at creation"... Man possesses in himself his own law, received from the Creator. *(section 40)*

Summary Prayer

Almighty God, we thank You for Your infinite mercy and love. We proclaim Your mighty works, for You have called us out of darkness into Your own wonderful light.

Heavenly Father, teach us to know Your will. Give us a better understanding of the Bible, of Sacred Tradition, and of the teaching office of Your Church—Your living voice on earth. Give us especially a better understanding of the Ten Commandments and of the Precepts of the Church. We ask this through Jesus Christ our Lord. Amen.

Q. 65. Does God forgive our sins?

Yes, if we are truly sorry, acknowledging our sins and seeking His pardon, God will forgive them because He is all merciful. By the power of His grace, God offers Salvation to all men. We especially encounter God's merciful forgiveness in the Sacrament of Penance.

Jesus, our Savior, was sent by the Father to suffer, die, and rise from the dead in order to save us from sin. He is our Redeemer because He paid the price for our sins, and thus freed us from slavery to sin and death.

God will pardon us if we are truly sorry for our sins and want to change our sinful ways. We can always look to God for merciful forgiveness.

Sacred Scripture
Q. 65. 2 Chron 6:36-39; Ps 32:5; Is 55:6-7; Lk 15:11-24.

Catechism of the Catholic Church
Q. 65. Paragraphs 210, **218**, 270, 393,1428, 1448-**1449**.

For cross-references with Vatican II, Papal documents & other resources, see Family Wisdom Library on page 196.
For commentaries on each question with Cardinal Arinze, Sr. John Vianney and Fr. Straub (in Spanish), see Appendix C.

#C17-22

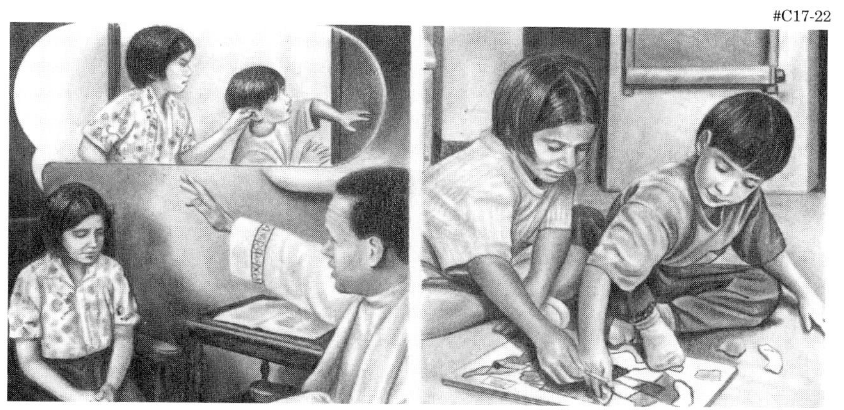

God will pardon us if we are truly sorry for our sins and want to change our sinful ways.

Sacred Scripture

He who conceals his transgressions will not prosper, but he who confesses and forsakes them will obtain mercy. *Proverbs 28:13*

He has delivered us from the dominion of darkness and transferred us to the kingdom of his beloved Son, in whom we have redemption, the forgiveness of sins. *Colossians 1:13-14*

Catechism of the Catholic Church

208 Faced with God's fascinating and mysterious presence, man discovers his own insignificance. Before the burning bush, Moses takes off his sandals and veils his face in the presence of God's holiness.[1] Before the glory of the thrice-holy God, Isaiah cries out: "Woe is me! I am lost; for I am a man of unclean lips."[2] Before the divine signs wrought by Jesus, Peter exclaims: "Depart from me, for I am a sinful man, O Lord."[3] But because God is holy, he can forgive the man who realizes that he is a sinner before him: "I will not execute my fierce anger… for I am God and not man, the Holy One in your midst."[4] The apostle John says likewise: "We shall… reassure our hearts before him whenever our hearts condemn us; for God is greater than our hearts, and he knows everything."[5]

Splendor of Truth

Christ has redeemed us! This means that he has given us the possibility of realizing the entire truth of our being; he has set our freedom free from the domination of concupiscence. And if redeemed man still sins, this is not due to an imperfection of Christ's redemptive act, but to man's will not to avail himself of the grace which flows from that act. *(section 103)*

Summary Prayer

God of mercy, we believe that You are merciful, and that You will pardon the sinner who is truly sorry. For this we give You thanks and praise through Jesus Christ our Lord. Amen.

#J2-441

But because God is holy, he can forgive the man who realizes that he is a sinner before him. *(Catechism of the Catholic Church, 208)*

Q. 66. How does God draw the sinner to Salvation?

The power of God's graces draws the sinner to Salvation.

In the Sacrament of Penance or Reconciliation, through the priest, Christ meets the sinner, forgives his sins, and gives him again the peace which belongs to God's children. He also gives the sinner the added power of grace to overcome sin in the future and the strength to be faithful to God's law of love.

Furthermore, He gives the sinner grace to love God with all his heart and to love his neighbor as himself for the love of God. Jesus also gives the sinner the help he needs to forgive his brothers and sisters just as God has forgiven him, to purge grudges from his life, and to work in harmony with others in God's family.

#C17.2-1

As the Good Shepherd, Christ knows His sheep. When one strays, He goes out in search of it. Finding it, He returns rejoicing to the fold. This shows the joy which Christ feels when a sinner has a change of heart.

Sacred Scripture
Q. 66. Lk 15:3-7; 2 Cor 5:18-20.

Catechism of the Catholic Church
Q. 66. Paragraphs 504, 545, 588-589, **827**, **1424**, 1444, **1446**.

For cross-references with Vatican II, Papal documents & other resources, see Family Wisdom Library on page 196.
For commentaries on each question with Cardinal Arinze, Sr. John Vianney and Fr. Straub (in Spanish), see Appendix C.

#C17-1-2

In the Sacrament of Reconciliation, Christ, through His Church and through the ministry of His priest, comes to us with pardon and peace.

As the Good Shepherd, Christ knows His sheep. When one strays, He goes out in search of it. Finding it, He places it on His shoulders and returns rejoicing to the fold. This shows the joy which Christ feels when a sinner has a change of heart.

In the Sacrament of Reconciliation, Christ, through His Church and through the ministry of His priest, comes to us with pardon and peace. In the name of Christ and by the power given to him at ordination, the priest absolves the sinner saying, "I absolve you in the name of the Father, and of the Son, and of the Holy Spirit."

Christ and the Holy Spirit require us to be sorry for our sins and to have a change of heart. When we encounter Christ in this sacrament, we pledge to reverse our sinful ways. Furthermore, we promise to make genuine moral improvements in our lives. A continual conversion to Christ and His Church is required of us. We must continue to fight our sinful desires and refrain from whatever caused us to hurt God and His family.

Sacred Scripture

Let us then with confidence draw near to the throne of grace, that we may receive mercy and find grace to help in time of need. *Hebrews 4:16*

Catechism of the Catholic Church

605 At the end of the parable of the lost sheep Jesus recalled that God's love excludes no one: "So it is not the will of your Father who is in heaven that one of these little ones should perish."[1] He affirms that he came "to give his life as

a ransom for many"; this last term is not restrictive, but contrasts the whole of humanity with the unique person of the redeemer who hands himself over to save us.[2] The Church, following the apostles, teaches that Christ died for all men without exception: "There is not, never has been, and never will be a single human being for whom Christ did not suffer."[3]

Splendor of Truth

All people must take great care not to allow themselves to be tainted by the attitude of the Pharisee, which would seek to eliminate awareness of one's own limits and of one's own sin. In our own day this attitude is expressed particularly in the attempt to adapt the moral norm to one's own capacities and personal interests, and even in the rejection of the very idea of a norm. Accepting, on the other hand, the "disproportion" between the law and human ability kindles the desire for grace and prepares one to receive it. *(section 105)*

Vatican Council II

No one is freed from sin by himself or by his own efforts, no one is raised above himself or completely delivered from his own weakness, solitude or slavery; all have need of Christ who is the model, master, liberator, saviour, and giver of life. *Missionary Activity, 8*

#S13-20-2

No one is freed from sin by himself or by his own efforts...all have need of Christ who is the model, master, liberator, saviour, and giver of life.
(Missionary Activity, 8)

Summary Prayer

Heavenly Father, we believe that You love us so much that, when we have sinned, You are ready to draw us to Salvation by the power of Your grace. We thank You for giving us the Sacrament of Reconciliation, where Your loving Son

meets the sinner, forgives his sins, and gives him again the peace which belongs to Your children. He also gives the sinner the power of grace to overcome sin in the future. He is the Good Shepherd who goes out in search of the sheep that has strayed. We thank You for this merciful love, through Jesus Christ our Lord. Amen.

Q. 67. How are venial sins forgiven?

Venial sins are forgiven by God even without the Sacrament of Reconciliation. A sincere act of contrition and the will to amend our lives is enough to obtain forgiveness. Nonetheless, the Church encourages us to frequently confess even our venial sins in the Sacrament of Reconciliation, since it is of such great benefit to the soul, especially with respect to the grace received.

Sacred Scripture

If we confess our sins, he is faithful and just, and will forgive our sins and cleanse us from all unrighteousness. *1 John 1:9*

Catechism of the Catholic Church

1394 As bodily nourishment restores lost strength, so the Eucharist strengthens our charity, which tends to be weakened in daily life; and this living charity *wipes away venial sins*.[1] By giving himself to us Christ revives our love and enables us to break our disordered attachments to creatures and root ourselves in him.

#C17-18

The Church encourages us to frequently confess even our venial sins in the Sacrament of Reconciliation, since it is of such great benefit to the soul.

Sacred Scripture
Q. 67. Sir 3:30; Jas 5:16.

Catechism of the Catholic Church
Q. 67. Paragraphs **1416**, 1447, **1452**, 1875.

For cross-references with Vatican II, Papal documents & other resources, see Family Wisdom Library on page 196.
For commentaries on each question with Cardinal Arinze, Sr. John Vianney and Fr. Straub (in Spanish), see Appendix C.

#E4-20

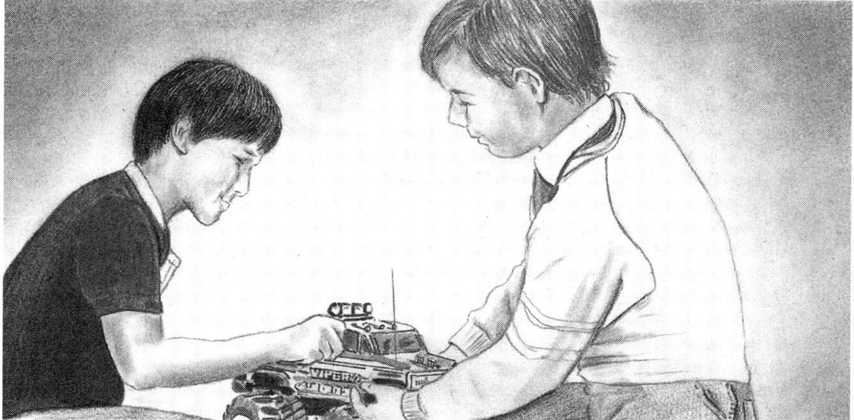

If we confess our sins, he is faithful and just, and will forgive our sins and cleanse us from all unrighteousness. *(1 John 1:9)*

Doctrine • Moral • Worship Exercise

(See Appendix A for answer key, questions 64-67.)

1. Read Luke 15 and 19:1-10 and explain how God's mercy is greater than His justice.
2. God forgives those who are truly sorry for their sins. On our part, what can we do in order to be forgiven?
3. When was the last time you received the Sacrament of Reconciliation? Resolve to go to confession regularly (at least once a month).

Chapter Summary Prayer

Father of our Lord Jesus Christ, in Your unbounded mercy You have revealed the beauty of Your power through Your constant forgiveness of our sins. May the power of this love be in our hearts, so that we may bring Your pardon and Your Kingdom to all we meet.

Your love for us surpasses all our hopes and desires. Forgive our failings, keep us in Your peace and lead us in the way of Salvation. May our obedient service bring us to the fullness of Your redemption.

Father, we see Your infinite power in Your loving plan of Salvation. You came to our rescue by Your power as God, but You wanted us to be saved by one like us. Man refused Your friendship, but it was restored by the sacrificial Death of the God-man, Jesus Christ, Your Son.

Loving Father, our hope and our strength, without You we falter. Help us to follow Christ and to live according to Your will.

Help us remember the sufferings and the Death on the Cross which Your loving Son endured to destroy the effects of sin. Help us also to recall the power of grace which is greater than sin. We hope in the super-abundant love of Your heart which restores the penitent and draws him toward Salvation.

Father, You show Your almighty power in Your mercy and forgiveness. Continue to fill us with Your gifts of love. Help us to hurry toward the eternal life You promise, and to share in the joys of Your Kingdom, where You live forever and ever with Your Divine Son and Holy Spirit. Amen.

Thought Provokers

Please see Appendix B for the answers.

Q. 64: Are our consciences always right?

Q. 65: A. Do we deserve to have our sins forgiven?

B. Why is God willing to forgive our sins?

Q. 66: Think of several ways that God leads people to Salvation through the grace merited for them by the Passion and Death of Jesus.

Q. 67: What advantages are there to confessing venial sins in the Sacrament of Penance?

#S13-25-2

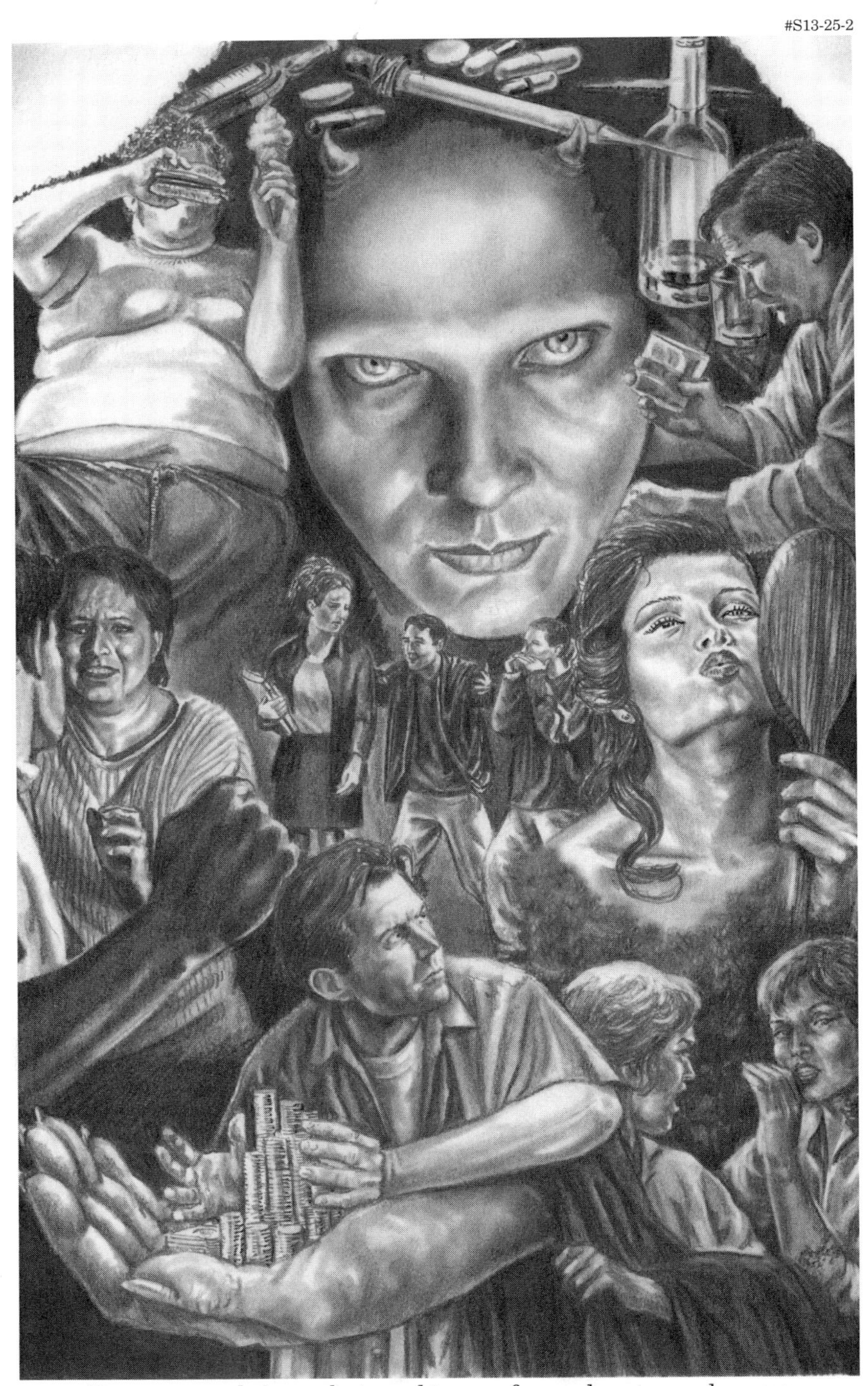

Every personal sin can be traced to one of seven human weaknesses.
These personal sins are called Capital Sins.

CHAPTER SEVENTEEN

Capital Sins

Q. 68. What is a Capital Sin?

Every personal sin can be traced to one of seven human weaknesses. These personal sins are called Capital Sins.

Capital Sins do not necessarily refer to grave sins, but rather to those sins which are the source of all others.

Catechism of the Catholic Church

1866 Vices can be classified according to the virtues they oppose, or also be linked to the *capital sins* which Christian experience has distinguished, following St. John Cassian and St. Gregory the Great. They are called "capital" because they engender other sins, other vices.[1] They are pride, avarice, envy, wrath, lust, gluttony, and sloth or acedia.

Splendor of Truth

Reason and experience not only confirm the weakness of human freedom, they also confirm its tragic aspects. Man comes to realize that his freedom is in some mysterious way inclined to betray this openness to the True and the Good, and that all too often he actually prefers to choose finite, limited and ephemeral goods. *(section 86)*

Q. 69. What are the seven Capital Sins?

The Capital Sins are pride, avarice, envy, anger, lust, gluttony, and sloth.

Pride is seeking after one's own honor. Self-seeking and vanity are examples of pride.

Sacred Scripture

Pride goes before destruction, and a haughty spirit before a fall. *Proverbs 16:18*

Do nothing from selfishness or conceit, but in humility count others better than yourselves. Let each of you look not only to his own interests, but also to the interests of others. *Philippians 2:3-4*

God opposes the proud, but gives grace to the humble. *James 4:6*

Sacred Scripture
Q. 69. Prov 15:27, 23:19-21; Gal 5:19-21; Col 3:8.

Catechism of the Catholic Church
Q. 68. Paragraphs 1876, 2539-2540.
Q. 69. Paragraph 1866, 2094.

For cross-references with Vatican II, Papal documents & other resources, see Family Wisdom Library on page 196.
For commentaries on each question with Cardinal Arinze, Sr. John Vianney and Fr. Straub (in Spanish), see Appendix C.

Avarice is seeking after wealth by stealing, fraud, injustice, and stinginess.

Sacred Scripture

Come now, you rich, weep and howl for the miseries that are coming upon you. Your riches have rotted and your garments are moth-eaten. *James 5:1-2*

Envy is a certain sadness of the mind. It leads to hatred and resentment of others. We are envious when we resent the fact that another is better off than ourselves.

Sacred Scripture

Do not rejoice when your enemy falls, and let not your heart be glad when he stumbles. *Proverbs 24:17*

Catechism of the Catholic Church

2554 The baptized person combats envy through good-will, humility, and abandonment to the providence of God.

Anger, as a Capital Sin, refers to a loss of temper. It is often reflected in fits of rage, quarreling, gossip, profanity, and property damage.

Sacred Scripture

Know this, my beloved brethren. Let every man be quick to hear, slow to speak, slow to anger, for the anger of man does not work the righteousness of God. *James 1:19-20*

#S13-17-2

Gluttony is an excessive consumption of food or drink, which can lead to a lack of self-control.

#S13-28-2

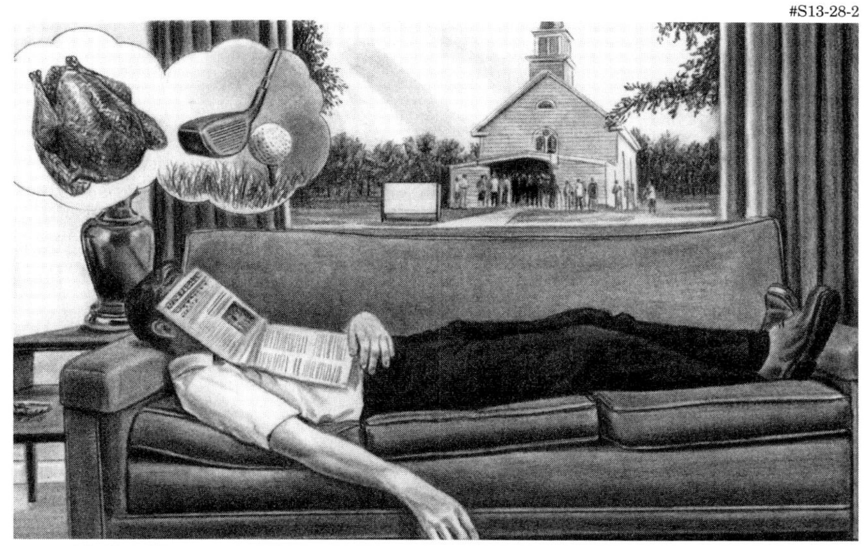

Sloth is laziness in doing one's duty to God and to others because of an unwillingness to sacrifice or exert the effort required to perform the good work.

Lust refers to impurity or sexual sins.

Sacred Scripture

Do not follow your base desires, but restrain your appetites. *Sirach 18:30*

I say to you that every one who looks at a woman lustfully has already committed adultery with her in his heart. *Matthew 5:28*

Gluttony is an excessive consumption of food or drink, which can lead to a lack of self-control.

Sacred Scripture

Wine drunk to excess is bitterness of soul, with provocation and stumbling. Drunkenness increases the anger of a fool to his injury, reducing his strength and adding wounds. *Sirach 31:29-30*

Sloth is laziness in doing one's duty to God and to others because of an unwillingness to sacrifice or exert the effort required to perform the good work. It also refers to the absence of true joy in the face of God's divine goodness and offer of Salvation. Sloth leads to missing Mass and prayer and neglecting work.

Sacred Scripture

The indolent may be compared to a filthy stone, and every one hisses at his disgrace. The indolent may be compared to the filth of dunghills; any one that picks it up will shake it off his hand. *Sirach 22:1-2*

Vatican Council II

The whole of man's history has been the story of dour combat with the powers of evil, stretching, so our Lord tells us, from the very dawn of history until the last day. Finding himself in the midst of the battlefield man has to struggle to do what is right, and it is at great cost to himself, and aided by God's grace, that he succeeds in achieving his own inner integrity. Hence the Church of Christ, trusting in the design of the creator and admitting that progress can contribute to man's true happiness, still feels called upon to echo the words of the apostle: "Do not be conformed to this world" (Rom. 12:2). "World" here means a spirit of vanity and malice whereby human activity from being ordered to the service of God and man is distorted to an instrument of sin.

To the question of how this unhappy situation can be overcome, Christians reply that all these human activities, which are daily endangered by pride and inordinate self-love, must be purified and perfected by the cross and resurrection of Christ. *Gaudium et Spes, 37*

Doctrine • Moral • Worship Exercise

(See Appendix A for answer key, questions 68-69.)

1. What are the seven Capital Sins?
2. Think of the virtue which will best help you to overcome the sin you commit most often.
3. Write a short personal prayer which you can repeat each time you are tempted to commit any of the seven Capital Sins.

Chapter Summary Prayer

Lord, You are the source of unfailing light. Give us true knowledge of Your mercy, that we may renounce our pride, and any of the other Capital Sins of which we are guilty, and that we may be filled with the riches of Your grace. Help us to remember that the Capital Sins are the source of all other sins.

Teach us goodness, discipline, and wisdom. These gifts will keep us from becoming hardened by evil, weakened by laziness, or ignorant because of our foolishness.

God, our Creator, how wonderfully You made man. You transformed dust into Your own image, and gave it a share in Your own nature. Yet You are more wonderful in pardoning the man who has rebelled against You. Grant that where sin abounds, grace may abound even more, so that we can become holier through Your merciful forgiveness, and be more grateful to You, through Jesus Christ our Lord. Amen.

Thought Provokers

Please see Appendix B for the answers.

Q. 68: Is every Capital Sin necessarily a mortal sin?

Q. 69: Why do you think pride, or the unreasonable love of self, is a Capital Sin?

#S13-26-2

God is faithful, and he will not let you be tempted beyond your strength, but with the temptation will also provide the way of escape, that you may be able to endure it.
(1 Corinthians 10:13)

CHAPTER EIGHTEEN

Temptation

Q. 70. What is temptation?

Temptation is an invitation to sin that comes from either within us or from outside us.

Temptations are not sins. Sin occurs only when we consent to a temptation. With God's help we can resist them.

#S13-39-2

Temptations are not sins. With God's help we can resist them.

Sacred Scripture

No temptation has overtaken you that is not common to man. God is faithful, and he will not let you be tempted beyond your strength, but with the temptation will also provide the way of escape, that you may be able to endure it. *1 Corinthians 10:13*

Catechism of the Catholic Church

2847 The Holy Spirit makes us *discern* between trials, which are necessary for the growth of the inner man,[1] and temptation, which leads to sin and death.[2] We must also discern between being tempted and consenting to temptation. Finally, discernment unmasks the lie of temptation, whose object appears to be good, a "delight to the eyes" and desirable,[3] when in reality its fruit is death.

Sacred Scripture
Q. 70. Mk 14:38; 1 Tim 6:9-10; Heb 2:18, 4:14-16.

Catechism of the Catholic Church
Q. 70. Paragraphs **2846-2849**.

For cross-references with Vatican II, Papal documents & other resources, see Family Wisdom Library on page 196.
For commentaries on each question with Cardinal Arinze, Sr. John Vianney and Fr. Straub (in Spanish), see Appendix C.

Splendor of Truth

As universal and daily experience demonstrates, man is tempted to break that harmony: "I do not do what I want, but I do the very thing I hate… I do not do the good I want, but the evil I do not want" (Rom 7:15, 19).

What is the ultimate source of this inner division of man? His history of sin begins when he no longer acknowledges the Lord as his Creator and himself wishes to be the one who determines, with complete independence, what is good and what is evil. "You will be like God, knowing good and evil" (Gen 3:5): this was the first temptation, and it is echoed in all the other temptations to which man is more easily inclined to yield as a result of the original Fall. *(section 102)*

Summary Prayer

God, our help and deliverer, do not abandon us in the many temptations of life, but deliver us from evil and turn our tears and struggles into joy. We ask this through Jesus Christ our Lord and Savior. Amen.

Q. 71. Where do temptations come from?

Not all temptations come from the devil. Many temptations come from the world around us and from the forces within us called passions. Passions are inclinations towards rebelling against God's will.

#H5.1.4-3

We must avoid unnecessary danger—people, places, and things that might lead us to sin.

Sacred Scripture
Q. 71. Lk 4:1-13; Jas 1:12-15.

Catechism of the Catholic Church
Q. 71. Paragraphs **409**, 1520, **1707**, **2514-2516**, 2846-2849.

For cross-references with Vatican II, Papal documents & other resources, see Family Wisdom Library on page 196.
For commentaries on each question with Cardinal Arinze, Sr. John Vianney and Fr. Straub (in Spanish), see Appendix C.

We can conquer temptation, if we want to do so. We gain merit in God's eyes by conquering temptation, and we grow in holiness. We must, however, have God's help to make our weak wills strong. His grace, that is, His help, will be given to us if we ask for it, if we receive Holy Communion often, and if we go to confession regularly. Furthermore, we must avoid unnecessary danger—people, places, and things that might lead us to sin. We should also remember the indwelling Holy Spirit who will give us the grace we need to overcome evil. With His help we can remain true to God and refuse the invitation to commit sin.

Sacred Scripture

Be not envious of evil men, nor desire to be with them. *Proverbs 24:1*

Simon, Simon, behold, Satan demanded to have you, that he might sift you like wheat, but I have prayed for you that your faith may not fail; and when you have turned again, strengthen your brethren. *Luke 22:31, 32*

For the desires of the flesh are against the Spirit, and the desires of the Spirit are against the flesh; for these are opposed to each other, to prevent you from doing what you would. *Galatians 5:17*

Catechism of the Catholic Church

2516 Because man is a *composite being, spirit and body*, there already exists a certain tension in him; a certain struggle of tendencies between "spirit" and "flesh" develops. But in fact this struggle belongs to the heritage of sin. It is a consequence of sin and at the same time a confirmation of it. It is part of the daily experience of the spiritual battle.

Splendor of Truth

But temptations can be overcome, sins can be avoided, because together with the commandments the Lord gives us the possibility of keeping them: "His eyes are on those who fear him, and he knows every deed of man. He has not commanded any one to be ungodly, and he has not given anyone permission to sin" (Sir 15:19-20). Keeping God's law in particular situations can be difficult, extremely difficult, but it is never impossible... For God does not command the impossible, but in commanding he admonishes you to do what you can and to pray for what you cannot, and he gives his aid to enable you. *(section 102)*

Vatican Council II

For when man looks into his own heart he finds that he is drawn towards what is wrong and sunk in many evils which cannot come from his good creator. *Gaudium et Spes, 13*

Man therefore is divided in himself. As a result, the whole life of men, both individual and social, shows itself to be a struggle, and a dramatic one, between good and evil, between light and darkness. Man finds that he is unable of himself to overcome the assaults of evil successfully, so that everyone feels as though bound by chains. But the Lord himself came to free and strengthen man, renewing him inwardly and casting out the "prince of this world" (Jn. 12:13), who held him in the bondage of sin. *Gaudium et Spes, 13*

Catechism by Diagram

#S13-10

Helps to Overcome Temptation. In order to overcome temptation, we should often receive the Sacraments of Holy Communion and Reconciliation, pray daily, especially the Rosary, and think often about the "four last things": death, judgement, Heaven, and Hell. We should pray to the Holy Spirit who dwells in us and will give us the grace (arrows) we need to overcome evil. With God's help we can refuse the invitation to commit sin and can remain true to God and His will.

Summary Prayer

Lord Jesus Christ, remember Your pilgrim Church. Do not let us be drawn into the current of the passing world, but free us from every evil and raise our thoughts to the heavenly Jerusalem. We ask this in Your most holy Name. Amen.

Doctrine • Moral • Worship Exercise

(See Appendix A for answer key, questions 70-71.)

1. God has given us the strength to conquer temptation. How should we cooperate with God so that we can overcome temptations in our daily life?
2. Identify the temptations that you encounter often and think of specific ways to triumph over these temptations.
3. Try to participate in the Holy Mass and receive Holy Communion as often as possible and to go to confession regularly (at least once a month) to obtain God's graces to strengthen your will.

Chapter Summary Prayer

Lord God, the Creation of man was a wonderful work, but his redemption was still more wonderful. May we persevere in right reason against all that entices us to sin, and so attain everlasting joy.

God our Father, by the waters of Baptism You give new life to the faithful. May we not succumb to the influence of evil but remain true to Your gift of life. May we who are redeemed by the suffering and Death of Jesus, Your Son, always rejoice in His Resurrection, for He is Lord forever.

Lord, send Your mercy and Your truth to rescue us from the snares of the devil, and to make us happy to be known as companions of Your Son.

God of strength, You gave Your Son victory over death. Direct Your Church's fight against evil in the world. Clothe us with the weapons of light and unite us under the one banner of love, that we may receive our eternal reward after the battle of earthly life.

Heavenly Father, Who by the Death of Your Son and His glorious rising again, have redeemed us, grant us to die daily to sin that we may live forever in the joy of His Resurrection.

Lord Jesus Christ, in Your suffering You cried out to Your Father and He delivered You out of death. By the power of Your holy Cross, rescue us from the abyss of sin, renew this world of Yours, and flood our minds with the light of Your Resurrection. Amen.

#S13-41-2

Many temptations come from the world around us and from the forces within us called passions.

Thought Provokers

Please see Appendix B for the answers.

Q. 70: Jesus was tempted to sin by the devil, yet He did not yield to the temptations, so He did not sin. Temptation, therefore, is not sin with respect to the person being tempted. What is the difference between temptation and sin?

Q. 71: Name some means of avoiding and overcoming temptations.

By Heart Catechism and Scripture Review™

The "By Heart Catechism and Scripture Review" lists a selected number of questions and Scripture references from "The Apostolate's Family Catechism" to make memorization easier. Q = Question, SR = Scripture Reference

Q. 53. What was the Original Sin? The Original Sin was committed by Adam and Eve when they disobeyed God by eating from the Tree of the Knowledge of Good and Evil.

Q. 54. Why are all men born with Original Sin? All men are born with Original Sin because human nature was affected by the sin of Adam and Eve, in that they lost original holiness and justice. As a result, they passed on this fallen state to their descendants.

Q. 55. What happens in Baptism? In Baptism, God takes away Original Sin and unites the soul to Himself. God's life is poured into the soul.

Q. 56. Was any human being free from Original Sin? Yes, the Blessed Virgin Mary was free from Original Sin from the very moment of her conception.

Q. 57. What is actual or personal sin? Actual or personal sin is the willful disobedience to God's will.

SR 58 Pope Paul VI, *Revision of Indulgences, 4*

By the hidden and kindly mystery of God's Will a supernatural solidarity reigns among men. A consequence of this is that the sin of one person harms other people just as one person's holiness helps others.

Q. 59. What is mortal sin? Mortal sin is choosing to disobey God in a serious matter. Mortal sin destroys God's life in our soul.

SR 59 Romans 6:23

For the wages of sin is death, but the free gift of God is eternal life in Christ Jesus our Lord.

Q. 61. What is venial sin? Venial sin is choosing to disobey God in a small matter. It does not drive God's life out of the soul, but it weakens a person's love for God.

By Heart Catechism and Scripture Review™

The "By Heart Catechism and Scripture Review" lists a selected number of questions and Scripture references from "The Apostolate's Family Catechism" to make memorization easier. Q = Question, SR = Scripture Reference

Q. 62. When does a Christian commit a mortal sin? A Christian commits a mortal sin when he (1) does something seriously wrong, (2) knows that it is seriously wrong, and (3) freely chooses to do it.

SR 62 1 John 5:16-17

If anyone sees his brother committing what is not a mortal sin, he will ask, and God will give him life for those whose sin is not mortal. There is sin which is mortal; I do not say that one is to pray for that. All wrongdoing is sin, but there is sin which is not mortal.

Q. 63. When is an act right or wrong? An act is right when it agrees with God's laws. An act is wrong if it goes against God's laws.

Q. 64. How do we know God's Will? We know God's Will through: (1) our reason, (2) the Bible, (3) Sacred Tradition, and (4) the Magisterium of the Church.

SR 66 John 20:22-23

Receive the Holy Spirit. If you forgive the sins of any, they are forgiven; if you retain the sins of any, they are retained.

Q. 67. How are venial sins forgiven? Venial sins are forgiven by God when we make a sincere act of contrition and will to amend our lives.

Q. 68. What is a Capital Sin? Capital Sins are personal sins that are the source of all other sins.

Q. 69. What are the seven Capital Sins? The Capital Sins are pride, avarice, envy, anger, lust, gluttony and sloth.

SR 69 Proverbs 16:18

Pride goes before destruction, and a haughty spirit before a fall.

Q. 70. What is temptation? Temptation is an invitation to sin.

By Heart Catechism and Scripture Review™

The "By Heart Catechism and Scripture Review" lists a selected number of questions and Scripture references from "The Apostolate's Family Catechism" to make memorization easier. Q = Question, SR = Scripture Reference

SR 70 1 Corinthians 10:13

God is faithful, and he will not let you be tempted beyond your strength, but with the temptation will also provide the way of escape, that you may be able to endure it.

Q. 71. Where do temptations come from? Temptations can come from within us or from outside of us.

Family Wisdom Library™

Papal documents listed below can be viewed at www.vatican.va.
For new cross-references, visit www.familyland.org.

Q. 1. Who is God?

Church Documents

Compendium of the Catechism of the Catholic Church, sect. 39-40, 44-49
Dei Verbum (Dogmatic Constitution on Divine Revelation), Vatican II, sect. 3
Gaudium et Spes (Pastoral Constitution on the Church in the Modern World), Vatican II, sect. 19, 36
God is Love, Benedict XVI, sect. 1
Gospel of Life, John Paul II, sect. 9, 37, 83
Lumen Gentium (Dogmatic Constitution on the Church), Vatican II, sect. 2
On the Dignity and Vocation of Women, John Paul II, sect. 7
On Evangelization in the Modern World, Paul VI, sect. 26
On the Holy Spirit in the Life of the Church and the World, John Paul II, sect. 8-12
On Reconciliation and Penance, John Paul II, sect. 10
Redeemer of Man, John Paul II, sect. 9
The Relationship Between Faith and Reason, John Paul II, sect. 34, 36, 80
Rich in Mercy, John Paul II, sect. 1-2
The Role of the Christian Family in the Modern World, John Paul II, sect. 11
Sacrament of Charity, Benedict XVI, sect. 8
Splendor of Truth, John Paul II, sect. 99
U. S. Catholic Catechism for Adults, [2006] pp. 51-53

Other Resources

Basics of the Faith: A Catholic Catechism, Schreck, pp. 3-14
The Catholic Catechism, Hardon, pp. 68-69
The Church's Confession of Faith, Ignatius Press, pp. 52-54, 63-66
Faith for Today, Hogan and LeVoir, [First Edition] pp. 4-10; [Second Edition] pp. 24-31
Fundamentals of Catholic Dogma, Ott, p. 24
Fundamentals of Catholicism, Baker, Vol. 1, pp. 27-34, Vol. 2, pp. 41-59
Modern Catholic Dictionary, Hardon, see "God"
The Teaching of Christ, Lawler, Wuerl, and Lawler, [First Edition] pp. 48-54; [Second Edition] pp. 36-42; [Third Edition] pp. 31-36

Q. 2. Who made God?

Church Documents

Compendium of the Catechism of the Catholic Church, sect. 39
God is Love, Benedict XVI, sect. 9
U.S. Catholic Catechism for Adults, [2006] p. 4

Other Resources

The Catholic Catechism, Hardon, p. 56
The Church's Confession of Faith, Ignatius Press, pp. 36f, 62, 79
Faith for Today, Hogan and LeVoir, [First Edition] pp. 4-10; [Second Edition] pp. 24-31
Fundamentals of Catholic Dogma, Ott, pp. 36f
Fundamentals of Catholicism, Baker, Vol. 1, p. 35
Modern Catholic Dictionary, Hardon, see "God"
The Teaching of Christ, Lawler, Wuerl, and Lawler, [First Edition] pp. 44-45, 48-49; [Second Edition] pp. 32-33, 36-37; [Third Edition] pp. 28-29, 31-32

Q. 3. Can there be more than one God?

Church Documents

Compendium of the Catechism of the Catholic Church, sect. 37-39
Dei Verbum (Dogmatic Constitution on Divine Revelation), Vatican II, sect. 3, 14
Gaudium et Spes (Pastoral Constitution on the Church in the Modern World), Vatican II, sect. 24
God is Love, Benedict XVI, sect. 9
Gospel of Life, John Paul II, sect. 37
On the Dignity and Vocation of Women, John Paul II, sect. 7
The Relationship Between Faith and Reason, John Paul II, sect. 19
U. S. Catholic Catechism for Adults, [2006] pp. 51-53

Other Resources

Basics of the Faith: A Catholic Catechism, Schreck, pp. 11-13
The Catholic Catechism, Hardon, p. 55
The Church's Confession of Faith, Ignatius Press, pp. 59-61
Faith for Today, Hogan and LeVoir, [First Edition] pp. 4-6; [Second Edition] pp. 24-26
Fundamentals of Catholic Dogma, Ott, p. 32f
Fundamentals of Catholicism, Baker, Vol. 1, pp. 27-29
Modern Catholic Dictionary, Hardon, see "God"
The Teaching of Christ, Lawler, Wuerl, and Lawler, [First Edition] p. 54; [Second Edition] p. 42; [Third Edition] p. 36

Family Wisdom Library™

Papal documents listed below can be viewed at www.vatican.va.
For new cross-references, visit www.familyland.org.

Q. 4. Why must there be a God?

Church Documents

Compendium of the Catechism of the Catholic Church, sect. 3, 4, 39
Gaudium et Spes (Pastoral Constitution on the Church in the Modern World), Vatican II, sect. 19, 36
On the Hundredth Anniversary of Rerum Novarum, John Paul II, sect. 13, 24
The Relationship Between Faith and Reason, John Paul II, sect. 19
U. S. Catholic Catechism for Adults, [2006] pp. 2-5

Other Resources

Basics of the Faith: A Catholic Catechism, Schreck, pp. 3-4
The Catholic Catechism, Hardon, pp. 232-233
The Church's Confession of Faith, Ignatius Press, pp. 28-31
Faith for Today, Hogan and LeVoir, [First Edition] pp. 2-4; [Second Edition] pp. 22-24
Fundamentals of Catholic Dogma, Ott, pp. 14f
Fundamentals of Catholicism, Baker, Vol. 1, pp. 34-36
Modern Catholic Dictionary, Hardon, see "God"
The Teaching of Christ, Lawler, Wuerl, and Lawler, [First Edition] pp. 44-45; [Second Edition] pp. 32-33; [Third Edition] pp. 28-29

Q. 5. Why is God an infinitely perfect Being?

Church Documents

Compendium of the Catechism of the Catholic Church, sect. 39-40
Lumen Gentium (Dogmatic Constitution on the Church), Vatican II, sect. 40
On the Holy Spirit in the Life of the Church and the World, John Paul II, sect. 34
The Relationship Between Faith and Reason, John Paul II, sect. 80
U. S. Catholic Catechism for Adults, [2006] p. 13

Other Resources

The Catholic Catechism, Hardon, pp. 56-57
The Church's Confession of Faith, Ignatius Press, p. 33
Faith for Today, Hogan and LeVoir, [First Edition] pp. 4-10; [Second Edition] pp. 24-31
Fundamentals of Catholic Dogma, Ott, pp. 30-31
Fundamentals of Catholicism, Baker, Vol. 2, pp. 38-41
Modern Catholic Dictionary, Hardon, see "God"
The Teaching of Christ, Lawler, Wuerl, and Lawler, [First Edition] p. 49; [Second Edition] p. 37; [Third Edition] p. 32

Q. 6. What are God's perfections?

Church Documents

Compendium of the Catechism of the Catholic Church, sect. 38-50
Lumen Gentium (Dogmatic Constitution on the Church), Vatican II, sect. 11
On the Holy Spirit in the Life of the Church and the World, John Paul II, sect. 34, 37
The Relationship Between Faith and Reason, John Paul II, sect. 80, 83
Rich in Mercy, John Paul II, sect. 4
U.S. Catholic Catechism for Adults, [2006] pp. 3-4

Other Resources

Basics of the Faith: A Catholic Catechism, Schreck, pp. 9-10
The Catholic Catechism, Hardon, pp. 55-58
The Church's Confession of Faith, Ignatius Press, pp.61-63
Faith for Today, Hogan and LeVoir, [First Edition] pp. 6-10; [Second Edition] pp. 26-31
Fundamentals of Catholic Dogma, Ott, pp. 30-38
Fundamentals of Catholicism, Baker, Vol. 2, pp. 38-41
Modern Catholic Dictionary, Hardon, see "God"
The Teaching of Christ , Lawler, Wuerl, and Lawler, [First Edition] pp. 48-54; [Second Edition] pp. 36-42 [Third Edition] pp. 31-36

Q. 7. Is God infinitely good?

Church Documents

Compendium of the Catechism of the Catholic Church, sect. 40, 58
Dei Verbum (Dogmatic Constitution on Divine Revelation), Vatican II, sect. 2
Gaudium et Spes (Pastoral Constitution on the Church in the Modern World), Vatican II, sect. 13, 16, 38
Lumen Gentium (Dogmatic Constitution on the Church), Vatican II, sect. 2, 46, 52, 62
On the Holy Spirit in the Life of the Church and the World, John Paul II, sect. 34, 37
The Relationship Between Faith and Reason, John Paul II, sect. 83
Sacrament of Charity, Benedict XVI, sect. 8
U.S. Catholic Catechism for Adults, [2006] pp. 327, 495

Other Resources

Basics of the Faith: A Catholic Catechism, Schreck, pp. 13-16;
The Catholic Catechism, Hardon, pp. 81-82

Family Wisdom Library™

Papal documents listed below can be viewed at www.vatican.va.
For new cross-references, visit www.familyland.org.

The Church's Confession of Faith, Ignatius Press, pp. 61-63
Faith for Today, Hogan and LeVoir, [First Edition] pp. 6-8; [Second Edition] pp. 26-29
Fundamentals of Catholic Dogma, Ott, p. 35
Fundamentals of Catholicism, Baker, Vol. 2, pp. 39-40
Modern Catholic Dictionary, Hardon, see "Goodness of God"
The Teaching of Christ, Lawler, Wuerl, and Lawler, [First Edition] pp. 53; [Second Edition] p.42; [Third Edition] p. 36

Q. 8. Is God eternal?

Church Documents

Compendium of the Catechism of the Catholic Church, sect. 39, 41
Gaudium et Spes (Pastoral Constitution on the Church in the Modern World), Vatican II, sect. 45
Gospel of Life, John Paul II, sect. 37, 84
The Relationship Between Faith and Reason, John Paul II, sect. 80
U.S. Catholic Catechism for Adults, [2006] p. 13

Other Resources

Basics of the Faith: A Catholic Catechism, Schreck, p. 10
The Catholic Catechism, Hardon, p. 56
The Church's Confession of Faith, Ignatius Press, p. 82
Faith for Today, Hogan and LeVoir, [First Edition] p. 8; [Second Edition] p. 29
Fundamentals of Catholic Dogma, Ott, pp. 36f
Fundamentals of Catholicism, Baker, Vol. 2, pp. 40, 42, 54
Modern Catholic Dictionary, Hardon, see "Eternity"
The Teaching of Christ, Lawler, Wuerl, and Lawler, [First Edition] p. 51; [Second Edition] pp. 39-40; [Third Edition] p. 34

Q. 9. Why is God all-knowing?

Church Documents

Compendium of the Catechism of the Catholic Church, sect. 41
The Relationship Between Faith and Reason, John Paul II, sect. 80
U.S. Catholic Catechism for Adults, [2006] pp. 61-63

Other Resources

Basics of the Faith: A Catholic Catechism, Schreck, p. 10
The Catholic Catechism, Hardon, pp. 56f, 79
The Church's Confession of Faith, Ignatius Press, pp. 62f
Faith for Today, Hogan and LeVoir, [First Edition] pp.6-7; [Second Edition] pp. 27-28
Fundamentals of Catholic Dogma, Ott, pp. 41-43
Fundamentals of Catholicism, Baker, Vol. 2, p. 40
Modern Catholic Dictionary, Hardon, see "Omniscience"
The Teaching of Christ, Lawler, Wuerl, and Lawler, [First Edition] pp. 49-50; [Second Edition] p. 38; [Third Edition] pp. 32-33
Transformation in Christ, von Hildebrand, p. 191

Q. 10. Is God present everywhere?

Church Documents

Compendium of the Catechism of the Catholic Church, sect. 50
On the Holy Spirit in the Life of the Church and the World, John Paul II, sect. 54
The Relationship Between Faith and Reason, John Paul II, sect. 80
U.S. Catholic Catechism for Adults, [2006] pp. 51-53

Other Resources

Basics of the Faith: A Catholic Catechism, Schreck, p. 10
The Catholic Catechism, Hardon, pp. 56, 185
The Church's Confession of Faith, Ignatius Press, pp. 62-63
Fundamentals of Catholic Dogma, Ott, pp. 37f
Modern Catholic Dictionary, Hardon, see "Omniscience"
The Teaching of Christ, Lawler, Wuerl, and Lawler, [First Edition] p. 52; [Second Edition] p. 40; [Third Edition] pp. 34-35

Q. 11. Is God almighty?

Church Documents

Compendium of the Catechism of the Catholic Church, sect. 50-51
God is Love, Benedict XVI, sect. 1-9
On the Holy Spirit in the Life of the Church and the World, John Paul II, sect. 37
The Relationship Between Faith and Reason, John Paul II, sect. 80
U.S. Catholic Catechism for Adults, [2006] pp. 51-52, 56

Other Resources

Basics of the Faith: A Catholic Catechism, Schreck, p. 10
The Catholic Catechism, Hardon, p. 56

Family Wisdom Library™

Papal documents listed below can be viewed at www.vatican.va.
For new cross-references, visit www.familyland.org.

The Church's Confession of Faith, Ignatius Press, p. 63
Faith for Today, Hogan and LeVoir, [First Edition] p. 6; [Second Edition] p. 27
Fundamentals of Catholic Dogma, Ott, p. 47
Fundamentals of Catholicism, Baker, Vol. 2, pp. 32-34
Modern Catholic Dictionary, Hardon, see "Omnipotence"
The Teaching of Christ, Lawler, Wuerl, and Lawler, [First Edition] pp. 50-51; [Second Edition] p. 39; [Third Edition] pp. 33-34
Transformation in Christ, von Hildebrand, p. 190

Q. 12. Is God all-wise?

Church Documents

Compendium of the Catechism of the Catholic Church, sect. 41, 51, 54
Dei Verbum (Dogmatic Constitution on Divine Revelation), Vatican II, sect. 2
Gospel of Life, John Paul II, sect. 52
Lumen Gentium (Dogmatic Constitution on the Church), Vatican II, sect. 2, 52
The Relationship Between Faith and Reason, John Paul II, sect. 23
U. S. Catholic Catechism for Adults, [2006] p. 53

Other Resources

Basics of the Faith: A Catholic Catechism, Schreck, p. 10
The Catholic Catechism, Hardon, pp. 78, 204
Faith for Today, Hogan and LeVoir, [First Edition] pp. 6-7, 24; [Second Edition] pp. 27-28, 47-48
Fundamentals of Catholic Dogma, Ott, p. 33
Fundamentals of Catholicism, Baker, Vol. 2, p. 39

Q. 13. Why is God all-holy?

Church Documents

Compendium of the Catechism of the Catholic Church, sect. 588
Gaudium et Spes (Pastoral Constitution on the Church in the Modern World), Vatican II, sect. 32
Lumen Gentium (Dogmatic Constitution on the Church), Vatican II, sect. 9
U. S. Catholic Catechism for Adults, [2006] pp. 50-51

Other Resources

The Catholic Catechism, Hardon, p. 66, 214
The Church's Confession of Faith, Ignatius Press, pp. 61, 233
Faith for Today, Hogan and LeVoir, [First Edition] pp. 6, 7, 10, 37; [Second Edition] pp. 26, 27, 31, 62
Fundamentals of Catholic Dogma, Ott, p. 35
Fundamentals of Catholicism, Baker, Vol. 2, pp. 48-50
Modern Catholic Dictionary, Hardon, see "God," "Goodness of God," "Holiness," and "Holiness, Essential"
The Teaching of Christ, Lawler, Wuerl, and Lawler, [First Edition] pp. 52-54; [Second Edition] pp. 41-42; [Third Edition] pp. 35-36

Q. 14. Why is God all-merciful?

Church Documents

Acts and Decrees of the Second Plenary Council of the Philippines, paragraph 54
Compendium of the Catechism of the Catholic Church, sect. 594-595
Dei Verbum (Dogmatic Constitution on Divine Revelation), Vatican II, sect. 15
On the Holy Spirit in the Life of the Church and the World, John Paul II, sect. 38
On Reconciliation and Penance, John Paul II, sect. 7, 10
Rich in Mercy, John Paul II, sect. 8, 10
Splendor of Truth, John Paul II, sect. 104, 118
U. S. Catholic Catechism for Adults, [2006] pp. 51, 92, 312-313

Other Resources

The Catholic Catechism, Hardon, pp. 272, 433, 481
The Church's Confession of Faith, Ignatius Press, p. 63;
Faith for Today, Hogan and LeVoir, [First Edition] pp. 66, 74-75, 194-195; [Second Edition] pp. 94, 104, 105, 236, 237
Fundamentals of Catholic Dogma, Ott, p. 49
Modern Catholic Dictionary, Hardon, see "Divine Mercy" and "Mercy"
The Teaching of Christ, Lawler,Wuerl, and Lawler, [First Edition] pp. 50, 88, 480, 483-484; [Second Edition] pp. 38, 76,470, 473-474; [Third Edition] pp. 66-67, 415, 417-418

Q. 15. Why is God all-just?

Church Documents

Compendium of the Catechism of the Catholic Church, sect. 135, 208
Dei Verbum (Dogmatic Constitution on Divine Revelation), Vatican II, sect. 15
Splendor of Truth, John Paul II, sect. 104
U. S. Catholic Catechism for Adults, [2006] pp. 157, 161, 313

Family Wisdom Library™

Papal documents listed below can be viewed at www.vatican.va.
For new cross-references, visit www.familyland.org.

Other Resources

The Catholic Catechism, Hardon, pp. 256, 268
The Church's Confession of Faith, Ignatius Press, pp. 63, 193
Fundamentals of Catholic Dogma, Ott, p. 48
Fundamentals of Catholicism, Vol. 2, pp. 68-71
Modern Catholic Dictionary, Hardon, see "Divine Justice"
The Teaching of Christ, Lawler, Wuerl, and Lawler, [First Edition] pp. 84-85; [Second Edition] pp. 72-73; [Third Edition] pp. 63-64
Transformation in Christ, von Hildebrand, pp. 291, 423-440

Q. 16. In what ways has God shown His love for us?

Church Documents

Acts and Decrees of the Second Plenary Council of the Philippines, paragraph 58
Catechesis in Our Time, John Paul II, sect. 9
Compendium of the Catechism of the Catholic Church, sect. 41-42, 112, 118-119, 122
Dei Verbum (Dogmatic Constitution on Divine Revelation), Vatican II, sect. 2, 21
Gaudium et Spes (Pastoral Constitution on the Church in the Modern World), Vatican II, sect. 38
God is Love, Benedict XVI, sect. 10, 12
Lumen Gentium (Dogmatic Constitution on the Church), Vatican II, sect. 2
Gospel of Life, John Paul II, sect. 2, 8, 9
Lay Members of Christ's Faithful People, John Paul II, sect. 10-14
On the Christian Meaning of Human Suffering, John Paul II, sect. 3, 19-20
On the Dignity and Vocation of Women, John Paul II, sect. 3
On Evangelization in the Modern World, Paul VI, sect. 6-7, 9
On the Holy Spirit in the Life of the Church and the World, John Paul II, sect. 11-14, 31, 39
On Reconciliation and Penance, John Paul II, sect. 7, 22
Redeemer of Man, John Paul II, sect. 7-10, 18
The Relationship Between Faith and Reason, John Paul II, sect. 7, 10, 12, 13, 60, 93, 107
Rich in Mercy, John Paul II, sect. 7-8, 10
Sacrament of Charity, Benedict XVI, sect. 8
Splendor of Truth, John Paul II, sect. 97
U.S. Catholic Catechism for Adults, [2006] pp. 13-15

Other Resources

Basics of the Faith: A Catholic Catechism, Schreck, pp. 15-16
The Catholic Catechism, Hardon, pp. 168-170, 176-177, 207-208
The Church's Confession of Faith, Ignatius Press, pp. 156-159
Faith for Today, Hogan and LeVoir, [First Edition] pp. 81-85; [Second Edition] pp. 111-115
Fundamentals of Catholic Dogma, Ott, pp. 185-195
Fundamentals of Catholicism, Baker, Vol. 2, pp. 273-276
Modern Catholic Dictionary, Hardon, see "Atonement," "Redemption," and "Sacrament of Salvation"
The Teaching of Christ, Lawler, Wuerl, and Lawler, [First Edition] pp. 50,93-95, 102-103, 107-108; [Second Edition] pp. 38,81-83, 90-91, 95-96; [Third Edition] pp. 33, 71-73, 78-79

Q. 17. How should we respond to God's goodness?

Church Documents

Acts and Decrees of the Second Plenary Council of the Philippines, paragraphs 74, 167, 170, 171, 178, 533
Compendium of the Catechism of the Catholic Church, sect. 112, 123, 165, 300, 427
Gaudium et Spes (Pastoral Constitution on the Church in the Modern World), Vatican II, sect. 45, 57
Gospel of Life, John Paul II, sect. 43, 50, 84
On Reconciliation and Penance, John Paul II, sect. 22
Sacrament of Charity, Benedict XVI, sect. 2
Splendor of Truth, John Paul II, sect. 103
U.S. Catholic Catechism for Adults, [2006] pp. 4-8

Other Resources

Basics of the Faith: A Catholic Catechism, Schreck, pp. 15-16, 19;
The Catholic Catechism, Hardon, pp. 77-78, 442
The Church's Confession of Faith, Ignatius Press, pp. 76, 99, 284
Faith for Today, Hogan and LeVoir, [First Edition] pp. 180, 185; [Second Edition] pp. 220-221, 226
Fundamentals of Catholic Dogma, Ott, p. 412
Fundamentals of Catholicism, Baker, Vol. 2, pp. 234-240

Family Wisdom Library™

Papal documents listed below can be viewed at www.vatican.va.
For new cross-references, visit www.familyland.org.

Modern Catholic Dictionary, Hardon, see "Prayer"
The Teaching of Christ, Lawler, Wuerl, and Lawler, [First Edition] pp. 385, 394;[Second Edition] pp. 375, 384; [Third Edition] pp. 83-84, 341, 375

Q. 18. In what ways do we worship God?

Church Documents

Acts and Decrees of the Second Plenary Council of the Philippines, paragraphs 74, 167, 510, 552
Compendium of the Catechism of the Catholic Church, sect. 221-223, 443-444, 558
Dei Verbum (Dogmatic Constitution on Divine Revelation), Vatican II, sect. 8
Gaudium et Spes (Pastoral Constitution on the Church in the Modern World), Vatican II, sect. 57
God is Love, Benedict XVI, sect. 14
Gospel of Life, John Paul II, sect. 86, 93
Lumen Gentium (Dogmatic Constitution on the Church), Vatican II, sect. 11, 12
On Evangelization in the Modern World, Paul VI, sect. 3
On Human Work, John Paul II, sect. 25
On the Mystery and Worship of the Eucharist, John Paul II, sect. 3
On Social Concern, John Paul II, sect. 30
Redeemer of Man, John Paul II, sect. 21
Sacrament of Charity, Benedict XVI, sect. 70-71
Sacrosanctum Concilium (The Constitution on the Sacred Liturgy), Vatican II, sect. 6, 7
To the Youth of the World, John Paul II, sect. 12
U.S. Catholic Catechism for Adults, [2006] p. 221

Other Resources

The Catholic Catechism, Hardon, pp. 441-449
The Church's Confession of Faith, Ignatius Press, pp. 282-297
Faith for Today, Hogan and LeVoir, [First Edition] pp. 256-257; [Second Edition] pp. 304-306
Fundamentals of Catholic Dogma, Ott, p. 387
Fundamentals of Catholicism, Baker, Vol. 2, pp. 235-237
Modern Catholic Dictionary, Hardon, see "Liturgy""
The Teaching of Christ, Lawler, Wuerl, and Lawler, [First Edition] pp. 402-408; [Second Edition] pp. 392-398; [Third Edition] pp. 347-353

Q. 19. What should we hope to receive from the goodness of God?

Church Documents

Acts and Decrees of the Second Plenary Council of the Philippines, paragraphs 28, 98
Compendium of the Catechism of the Catholic Church, sect. 132, 387, 422-428
Gaudium et Spes (Pastoral Constitution on the Church in the Modern World), Vatican II, sect. 17, 22, 30, 32, 37
Gospel of Life, John Paul II, sect. 25, 32, 44
Lumen Gentium (Dogmatic Constitution on the Church), Vatican II, sect. 8
On the Holy Spirit in the Life of the Church and the World, John Paul II, sect. 31, 37
On Human Work, John Paul II, sect. 25
On the Hundredth Anniversary of Rerum Novarum, John Paul II, sect. 59
On Reconciliation and Penance, John Paul II, sect. 22
On Social Concern, John Paul II, sect. 40
Sacrament of Charity, Benedict XVI, sect. 2, 7-8
Splendor of Truth, John Paul II, sect. 103
U.S. Catholic Catechism for Adults, [2006] p. 333

Other Resources

Basics of the Faith: A Catholic Catechism, Schreck, p. 8
The Catholic Catechism, Hardon, pp. 188-189
The Church's Confession of Faith, Ignatius Press, pp. 114-117,171-172, 327-329, 348-352
Faith for Today, Hogan and LeVoir, [First Edition] p. 219; [Second Edition] pp. 263-364
Fundamentals of Catholic Dogma, Ott, pp. 354-355
Fundamentals of Catholicism, Baker, Vol. 3, pp. 83-86
Modern Catholic Dictionary, Hardon, see "Hope, Act of" and "Hope, Virtue of"
The Teaching of Christ, Lawler, Wuerl, and Lawler, [First Edition] pp. 297-301; [Second Edition] pp. 285-289; [Third Edition] pp. 252-255

Q. 20. Why is it that so few people pay attention to God?

Church Documents

Gaudium et Spes (Pastoral Constitution on the Church in the Modern World), Vatican II, sect. 7, 10, 19, 20, 21, 57
God is Love, Benedict XVI, sect. 5

Family Wisdom Library™

Papal documents listed below can be viewed at www.vatican.va.
For new cross-references, visit www.familyland.org.

Gospel of Life, John Paul II, sect. 21
On the Holy Spirit in the Life of the Church and the World, John Paul II, sect. 36-38, 44, 47, 55-56
The Lay Members of Christ's Faithful People, John Paul II, sect. 4
The Relationship Between Faith and Reason, John Paul II, sect. 5, 46-47, 81, 91
Sacrament of Charity, Benedict XVI, sect. 77
Splendor of Truth, John Paul II, sect. 36
U.S. Catholic Catechism for Adults, [2006] pp. 6-7

Other Resources

Basics of the Faith: A Catholic Catechism, Schreck, pp. 8-9
The Catholic Catechism, Hardon, pp. 426-427
The Church's Confession of Faith, Ignatius Press, pp. 109-114
Faith for Today, Hogan and LeVoir, [First Edition] pp. 69-70; [Second Edition] pp. 98-100
Fundamentals of Catholic Dogma, Ott, pp. 112-113
Fundamentals of Catholicism, Baker, Vol. 2, pp. 159-168
Modern Catholic Dictionary, Hardon, see "Anthropocentrism"
The Teaching of Christ, Lawler, Wuerl, and Lawler, [First Edition] pp. 83-84; [Second Edition] pp. 71-72; [Third Edition] pp. 62-63

Q. 21. Does every man have some desire for God?

Church Documents

Compendium of the Catechism of the Catholic Church, sect. 1-2, 358
Gaudium et Spes (Pastoral Constitution on the Church in the Modern World), Vatican II, sect. 14, 16, 18, 19, 21
God is Love, Benedict XVI, sect. 11
Lumen Gentium (Dogmatic Constitution on the Church), Vatican II, sect. 48
On the Holy Spirit in the Life of the Church and the World, John Paul II, sect. 54
On the Hundredth Anniversary of Rerum Novarum, John Paul II, sect. 13, 24
On Social Concern, John Paul II, sect. 28
The Relationship Between Faith and Reason, John Paul II, opening before introduction, sect. 24, 33
Sacrament of Charity, Benedict XVI, sect. 2
Splendor of Truth, John Paul II, sect. 1
U.S. Catholic Catechism for Adults, [2006] pp. 3-7

Other Resources

Basics of the Faith: A Catholic Catechism, Schreck, pp. 8-9
The Catholic Catechism, Hardon, pp. 448-449
The Church's Confession of Faith, Ignatius Press, pp. 114-117
Fundamentals of Catholic Dogma, Ott, p. 102
Fundamentals of Catholicism, Baker, Vol. 1, pp. 138-141
Modern Catholic Dictionary, Hardon, see "Worship"
The Teaching of Christ, Lawler, Wuerl, and Lawler, [First Edition] pp. 75-76; [Second Edition] pp. 63-64; [Third Edition] pp. 55-56

Q. 22. What is the History of Salvation?

Church Documents

Compendium of the Catechism of the Catholic Church, sect. 1, 67, 72, 75-79, 85, 102-104, 119-120, 131
Dei Verbum (Dogmatic Constitution on Divine Revelation), Vatican II, sect. 1-4, 6
Gaudium et Spes (Pastoral Constitution on the Church in the Modern World), Vatican II, sect. 10, 18, 22, 45, 58, 82
Lumen Gentium (Dogmatic Constitution on the Church), Vatican II, sect. 2, 3, 4
Mother of the Redeemer, John Paul II, sect. 8, 28
On the Dignity and Vocation of Women, John Paul II, sect. 3, 9
On the Hundredth Anniversary of Rerum Novarum, John Paul II, sect. 53
On Reconciliation and Penance, John Paul II, sect. 20
On Social Concern, John Paul II, sect. 30-31
Redeemer of Man, John Paul II, sect. 7-10, 14
The Relationship Between Faith and Reason, John Paul II, sect. 7, 10, 34, 66, 94
Sacrament of Charity, Benedict XVI, sect. 8
Splendor of Truth, John Paul II, sect. 21
U. S. Catholic Catechism for Adults, [2006] pp. 12-15

Other Resources

The Church's Confession of Faith, Ignatius Press, pp. 171, 208

Family Wisdom Library™

Papal documents listed below can be viewed at www.vatican.va.
For new cross-references, visit www.familyland.org.

The Teaching of Christ, Lawler, Wuerl, and Lawler, [First Edition] pp. 48-49, 88, 112, 150-151, 176-177, 421, 538; [Second Edition] pp. 139-140, 164-165; [Third Edition] pp. 31-32, 66-67, 87-88, 121-122, 144-145, 364, 466-467

Q. 23. How did God deal with mankind?

Church Documents

Catechesis in Our Time, John Paul II, sect. 7-8
Compendium of the Catechism of the Catholic Church, sect. 78-79
Dei Verbum (Dogmatic Constitution on Divine Revelation), Vatican II, sect. 7
Gaudium et Spes (Pastoral Constitution on the Church in the Modern World), Vatican II, sect. 22, 32, 38, 41, 58
God is Love, Benedict XVI, sect. 9-11
Gospel of Life, John Paul II, sect. 1, 2, 25, 31, 36, 41, 48, 50, 79, 84, 103
Guardian of the Redeemer, John Paul II, sect. 13
Lumen Gentium (Dogmatic Constitution on the Church), Vatican II, sect. 2
On Reconciliation and Penance, John Paul II, sect. 13
On the Holy Spirit in the Life of the Church and the World, John Paul II, sect. 34
Redeemer of Man, John Paul II, sect. 13-14;
The Relationship Between Faith and Reason, John Paul II, sect. 7, 9, 34, 38, 80
Sacrament of Charity, Benedict XVI, sect. 8-10
U. S. Catholic Catechism for Adults, [2006] pp. 12-15

Other Resources

Basics of the Faith: A Catholic Catechism, Schreck, pp. 19-20
The Catholic Catechism, Hardon, pp. 30-31
The Church's Confession of Faith, Ignatius Press, pp. 34-36,114-117
Fundamentals of Catholic Dogma, Ott, pp. 175-179
Fundamentals of Catholicism, Baker, Vol. 3, pp. 93-98
Modern Catholic Dictionary, Hardon, see "Revelation" and "Soteriology"
The Teaching of Christ, Lawler, Wuerl, and Lawler, [First Edition] pp. 177-179; [Second Edition] pp. 165-167; [Third Edition] pp. 144-146

Q. 24. How did God choose to show Himself to the people of the Old Testament?

Church Documents

Acts and Decrees of the Second Plenary Council of the Philippines, paragraph 54
Compendium of the Catechism of the Catholic Church, sect. 21, 23, 118, 140-142
Dei Verbum (Dogmatic Constitution on Divine Revelation), Vatican II, sect. 2-6, 11-13
Gaudium et Spes (Pastoral Constitution on the Church in the Modern World), Vatican II, sect. 32
God is Love, Benedict XVI, sect. 9
Lumen Gentium (Dogmatic Constitution on the Church), Vatican II, sect. 6
On the Dignity and Vocation of Women, John Paul II, sect. 7
On the Holy Spirit in the Life of the Church and the World, John Paul II, sect. 15-17
The Relationship Between Faith and Reason, John Paul II, sect. 11, 12, 17-20
Sacrament of Charity, Benedict XVI, sect. 10-11
U. S. Catholic Catechism for Adults, [2006] pp. 12-15

Other Resources

Basics of the Faith: A Catholic Catechism, Schreck, pp. 30-47
The Catholic Catechism, Hardon, pp. 41, 44-45
The Church's Confession of Faith, Ignatius Press, pp. 25, 34-35
Faith for Today, Hogan and LeVoir, [First Edition] pp. 63-75; [Second Edition] pp. 92-105
Fundamentals of Catholic Dogma, Ott, pp. 30-49, 53-54
Fundamentals of Catholicism, Baker, Vol. 2, pp. 36-39, 43, 45-46, 48-55
Modern Catholic Dictionary, Hardon, see "Revelation"
The Teaching of Christ, Lawler, Wuerl, and Lawler, [First Edition] pp. 46-54, 248; [Second Edition] pp. 36-46, 236; [Third Edition] pp. 30-36, 206-207

Family Wisdom Library™

Papal documents listed below can be viewed at www.vatican.va.
For new cross-references, visit www.familyland.org.

Q. 25. What is the mystery of the Holy Trinity?

Church Documents

Compendium of the Catechism of the Catholic Church, sect. 44-49
Dei Verbum (Dogmatic Constitution on Divine Revelation), Vatican II, sect. 2
Gaudium et Spes (Pastoral Constitution on the Church in the Modern World), Vatican II, sect. 24
God is Love, Benedict XVI, sect. 19
On the Dignity and Vocation of Women, John Paul II, sect. 7
On the Holy Spirit in the Life of the Church and the World, John Paul II, sect. 8-10
On Social Concern, John Paul II, sect. 40
The Relationship Between Faith and Reason, John Paul II, sect. 13, 66
Sacrament of Charity, Benedict XVI, sect. 8
U. S. Catholic Catechism for Adults, [2006] pp. 51-53

Other Resources

Basics of the Faith: A Catholic Catechism, Schreck, pp. 11-13
The Catholic Catechism, Hardon, pp. 63-67
The Church's Confession of Faith, Ignatius Press, pp. 72-74
Faith for Today, Hogan and LeVoir, [First Edition] pp. 10-20; [Second Edition] pp. 32-43
Fundamentals of Catholic Dogma, Ott, pp. 50-75
Fundamentals of Catholicism, Baker, Vol. 2, pp. 77-118
Modern Catholic Dictionary, Hardon, see "Trinity, The Holy"
The Teaching of Christ, Lawler, Wuerl, and Lawler, [First Edition] pp. 174-175; [Second Edition] pp. 162-163; [Third Edition] pp. 142-143

Q. 26. Why do we believe in the mystery of the Holy Trinity?

Church Documents

Acts and Decrees of the Second Plenary Council of the Philippines, paragraphs 78, 194
Compendium of the Catechism of the Catholic Church, sect. 45;
On the Dignity and Vocation of Women, John Paul II, sect. 7
On the Holy Spirit in the Life of the Church and the World, John Paul II, sect. 8-9
The Relationship Between Faith and Reason, John Paul II, sect. 13, 66
Sacrament of Charity, Benedict XVI, sect. 7-8
U. S. Catholic Catechism for Adults, [2006] pp. 51-53, 62

Other Resources

Basics of the Faith: A Catholic Catechism, Schreck, p. 11
The Catholic Catechism, Hardon, pp. 31, 63-67
The Church's Confession of Faith, Ignatius Press, pp. 72-74
Faith for Today, Hogan and LeVoir, [First Edition] p. 150; [Second Edition] p. 187
Fundamentals of Catholic Dogma, Ott, pp. 59-60, 63-64
Fundamentals of Catholicism, Baker, Vol. 2, pp. 80-82
The Teaching of Christ, Lawler, Wuerl, and Lawler, [First Edition] pp. 177-185; [Second Edition] pp. 165-173; [Third Edition] pp. 144-151

Q. 27. How is the mystery of the Trinity revealed in the New Testament?

Church Documents

Compendium of the Catechism of the Catholic Church, sect. 82-83, 130
Dei Verbum (Dogmatic Constitution on Divine Revelation), Vatican II, sect. 4, 17
God is Love, Benedict XVI, sect. 19
On the Dignity and Vocation of Women, John Paul II, sect. 7
On the Holy Spirit in the Life of the Church and the World, John Paul II, sect. 8-9, 11, 14, 19-24
The Relationship Between Faith and Reason, John Paul II, sect. 7, 13, 66
Sacrament of Charity, Benedict XVI, sect. 8
U. S. Catholic Catechism for Adults, [2006] pp. 104-105

Other Resources

Basics of the Faith: A Catholic Catechism, Schreck, p. 12
The Catholic Catechism, Hardon, pp. 64, 188-189
The Church's Confession of Faith, Ignatius Press, pp. 66-72
Fundamentals of Catholic Dogma, Ott, pp. 55-56
Fundamentals of Catholicism, Baker, Vol. 2, pp. 101, 107, 109-110, 112-118
The Teaching of Christ, Lawler, Wuerl, and Lawler, [First Edition] pp. 178-179; [Second Edition] pp. 166-167; [Third Edition] pp. 145-146

Family Wisdom Library™

Papal documents listed below can be viewed at www.vatican.va.
For new cross-references, visit www.familyland.org.

Q. 28. What did Jesus reveal about Himself?

Church Documents

Compendium of the Catechism of the Catholic Church, sect. 82-84;
Dei Verbum (Dogmatic Constitution on Divine Revelation), Vatican II, sect. 2, 4, 17
Gaudium et Spes (Pastoral Constitution on the Church in the Modern World), Vatican II, sect. 22
Gospel of Life, John Paul II, sect. 50
Lay Members of Christ's Faithful People, John Paul II, sect. 8, 14
Lumen Gentium (Dogmatic Constitution on the Church), Vatican II, sect. 1-4
On the Dignity and Vocation of Women, John Paul II, sect. 7-8
On the Holy Spirit in the Life of the Church and the World, John Paul II, sect. 18-21, 24
The Relationship Between Faith and Reason, John Paul II, sect. 7, 9-13, 33-34, 66
Sacrament of Charity, Benedict XVI, sect. 8-12
U. S. Catholic Catechism for Adults, [2006] pp. 81-83

Other Resources

Basics of the Faith: A Catholic Catechism, Schreck, pp. 56-60
The Catholic Catechism, Hardon, pp. 108-149
The Church's Confession of Faith, Ignatius Press, pp. 123-129, 153-163, 165-180
Faith for Today, Hogan and LeVoir, [First Edition] pp. 85-104; [Second Edition] pp. 115-137
Fundamentals of Catholic Dogma, Ott, pp. 127-150
Fundamentals of Catholicism, Baker, Vol. 2, pp. 197-311
Modern Catholic Dictionary, Hardon, see "Christ, New Testament Names and Titles"
The Teaching of Christ, Lawler, Wuerl, and Lawler, [First Edition] pp. 95-98; [Second Edition] pp. 82-86; [Third Edition] pp. 72-75

Q. 29. How was God the Father revealed by Jesus?

Church Documents

Compendium of the Catechism of the Catholic Church, sect. 46;
Dei Verbum (Dogmatic Constitution on Divine Revelation), Vatican II, sect. 2-4
Gaudium et Spes (Pastoral Constitution on the Church in the Modern World), Vatican II, sect. 22-24, 32
God is Love, Benedict XVI, sect. 12
Gospel of Life, John Paul II, sect. 33, 37, 41
Lumen Gentium (Dogmatic Constitution on the Church), Vatican II, sect. 2-4
On the Eucharist in Its Relationship to the Church, John Paul II, sect. 34-35
On the Holy Spirit in the Life of the Church and the World, John Paul II, sect. 20-21
The Relationship Between Faith and Reason, John Paul II, sect. 7, 11-13, 34, 60
Sacrament of Charity, Benedict XVI, sect. 7-8
U. S. Catholic Catechism for Adults, [2006] pp. 52-53, 62

Other Resources

Basics of the Faith: A Catholic Catechism, Schreck, p. 60
The Catholic Catechism, Hardon, p. 114
The Church's Confession of Faith, Ignatius Press, p. 58
Faith for Today, Hogan and LeVoir, [First Edition] p. 19; [Second Edition] pp. 41-42
Fundamentals of Catholicism, Baker, Vol. 2, p. 85
Fundamentals of Catholic Dogma, Ott, p. 57
The Teaching of Christ, Lawler, Wuerl, and Lawler, [First Edition] p. 98; [Second Edition] p. 86; [Third Edition] p. 75

Q. 30. How did Jesus reveal the Holy Spirit?

Church Documents

Compendium of the Catechism of the Catholic Church, sect. 47
Dei Verbum (Dogmatic Constitution on Divine Revelation), Vatican II, sect. 2-4, 17
Lumen Gentium (Dogmatic Constitution on the Church), Vatican II, sect. 4
On the Eucharist in Its Relationship to the Church, John Paul II, sect. 17
On the Holy Spirit in the Life of the Church and the World, John Paul II, sect. 2-9, 18-24
The Relationship Between Faith and Reason, John Paul II, sect. 7
Sacrament of Charity, Benedict XVI, sect. 12
U. S. Catholic Catechism for Adults, [2006] pp. 102-105, 263

Other Resources

Basics of the Faith: A Catholic Catechism, Schreck, pp. 60-61
The Catholic Catechism, Hardon, pp. 63-67

Family Wisdom Library™

Papal documents listed below can be viewed at www.vatican.va.
For new cross-references, visit www.familyland.org.

The Church's Confession of Faith, Ignatius Press, pp. 70, 72
Fundamentals of Catholic Dogma, Ott, pp. 58-59
Fundamentals of Catholicism, Baker, Vol. 2, pp. 88-89, 91
God is Love, Benedict XVI, sect. 19
Modern Catholic Dictionary, Hardon, see "Holy Spirit" and "Indwelling"
The Teaching of Christ, Lawler, Wuerl, and Lawler, [First Edition] pp. 163-173; [Second Edition] pp. 150-161; [Third Edition] pp. 131-141

Q. 31. What did Jesus teach His disciples about God the Father, God the Son, and God the Holy Spirit?

Church Documents

Acts and Decrees of the Second Plenary Council of the Philippines, paragraphs 64, 556
Catechesis in Our Time, John Paul II, sect. 7-9
Compendium of the Catechism of the Catholic Church, sect. 46-47;
Dei Verbum (Dogmatic Constitution on Divine Revelation), Vatican II, sect. 2-4, 17
God is Love, Benedict XVI, sect. 19
On the Holy Spirit in the Life of the Church and the World, John Paul II, sect. 2-9, 18-24
On Social Concern, John Paul II, sect. 40
The Relationship Between Faith and Reason, John Paul II, sect. 7, 9, 10-13, 34, 60, 80
The Role of the Christian Family in the Modern World, John Paul II, sect. 41
Sacrament of Charity, Benedict XVI, sect. 7-8
Splendor of Truth, John Paul II, sect. 118
U. S. Catholic Catechism for Adults, [2006] pp. 52-53, 62, 81

Other Resources

Basics of the Faith: A Catholic Catechism, Schreck, pp. 60-61
The Catholic Catechism, Hardon, p. 64
The Church's Confession of Faith, Ignatius Press, p. 72
Fundamentals of Catholic Dogma, Ott, pp. 57-59
Fundamentals of Catholicism, Baker, Vol. 2, pp. 85-86, 88-89, 91, 112
The Teaching of Christ, Lawler, Wuerl, and Lawler, [First Edition] pp. 81, 175,178-180; [Second Edition] pp. 163,166-169; [Third Edition] pp. 145-148

Q. 32. Who is God the Father?

Church Documents

Acts and Decrees of the Second Plenary Council of the Philippines, paragraph 39
Compendium of the Catechism of the Catholic Church, sect. 46, 583-585
Dei Verbum (Dogmatic Constitution on Divine Revelation), Vatican II, sect. 3
Gospel of Life, John Paul II, sect. 40, 83, 99
Lumen Gentium (Dogmatic Constitution on the Church), Vatican II, sect. 2
On the Holy Spirit in the Life of the Church and the World, John Paul II, sect. 8, 20-21
The Relationship Between Faith and Reason, John Paul II, sect. 7, 11-13, 34, 60
Sacrament of Charity, Benedict XVI, sect. 7-8
U. S. Catholic Catechism for Adults, [2006] pp. 46, 51-52, 62, 484-485

Other Resources

Basics of the Faith: A Catholic Catechism, Schreck, pp. 60-61
The Catholic Catechism, Hardon, pp. 65-66
The Church's Confession of Faith, Ignatius Press, pp.57-60, 63, 66-69, 77
Faith for Today, Hogan and LeVoir, [First Edition] pp. 16, 18; [Second Edition] pp. 38, 40
Fundamentals of Catholic Dogma, Ott, pp. 56-57
Fundamentals of Catholicism, Baker, Vol. 2, pp. 83-86
Modern Catholic Dictionary, Hardon, see "God the Father" and "Trinity, The Holy"
The Teaching of Christ, Lawler, Wuerl, and Lawler, [First Edition] pp. 179-181 [Second Edition] pp. 167-169; [Third Edition] pp. 146-148

Q. 33. Who is God the Son?

Church Documents

Compendium of the Catechism of the Catholic Church, sect. 81-93
Dei Verbum (Dogmatic Constitution on Divine Revelation), Vatican II, sect. 1, 2, 4
Gaudium et Spes (Pastoral Constitution on the Church in the Modern World), Vatican II, sect. 22
God is Love, Benedict XVI, sect. 12
Gospel of Life, John Paul II, sect. 36

Family Wisdom Library™

Papal documents listed below can be viewed at www.vatican.va.
For new cross-references, visit www.familyland.org.

Lumen Gentium (Dogmatic Constitution on the Church), Vatican II, sect. 2, 3
On the Dignity and Vocation of Women, John Paul II, sect. 25
On the Eucharist in Its Relationship to the Church, John Paul II, sect. 8, 55
On the Holy Spirit in the Life of the Church and the World, John Paul II, sect. 8
The Relationship Between Faith and Reason, John Paul II, sect. 9, 11, 23, 38, 93
Sacrament of Charity, Benedict XVI, sect. 7-12
U. S. Catholic Catechism for Adults, [2006] pp. 79-87

Other Resources

Basics of the Faith: A Catholic Catechism, Schreck, pp. 53-56
The Catholic Catechism, Hardon, pp. 65-67
The Church's Confession of Faith, Ignatius Press, pp. 66-69
Faith for Today, Hogan and LeVoir, [First Edition] pp. 13, 16, 18; [Second Edition] pp. 34, 38, 40
Fundamentals of Catholic Dogma, Ott, pp. 57-58
Fundamentals of Catholicism, Baker, Vol. 2, pp. 86-92
Modern Catholic Dictionary, Hardon, see "God the Son"
The Teaching of Christ, Lawler, Wuerl, and Lawler, [First Edition] pp. 179-181; [Second Edition] pp. 167-169; [Third Edition] pp. 146-148

Q. 34. Who is God the Holy Spirit?

Church Documents

Compendium of the Catechism of the Catholic Church, sect. 47, 136-138, 145-146;
Dei Verbum (Dogmatic Constitution on Divine Revelation), Vatican II, sect. 5
God is Love, Benedict XVI, sect. 19
Gospel of Life, John Paul II, sect. 29, 76, 77
Lumen Gentium (Dogmatic Constitution on the Church), Vatican II, sect. 4, 12
On the Dignity and Vocation of Women, John Paul II, sect. 29
The Relationship Between Faith and Reason, John Paul II, sect. 7, 44
Sacrament of Charity, Benedict XVI, sect. 8, 12-13
U. S. Catholic Catechism for Adults, [2006] pp. 51-53, 104-106

Other Resources

Basics of the Faith: A Catholic Catechism, Schreck, p. 61
The Catholic Catechism, Hardon, pp. 64-65, 188-189
The Church's Confession of Faith, Ignatius Press, pp. 69-72, 184-187
Faith for Today, Hogan and LeVoir, [First Edition] pp. 14, 16, 18; [Second Edition] pp. 35, 38, 40
Fundamentals of Catholic Dogma, Ott, pp. 58-59, 294-296
Fundamentals of Catholicism, Baker, Vol. 2, pp. 86-92
Modern Catholic Dictionary, Hardon, see "God the Holy Spirit"
The Teaching of Christ, Lawler, Wuerl, and Lawler, [First Edition] pp. 161-173; [Second Edition] pp. 150-161; [Third Edition] pp. 131-141

Q. 35. How do we honor the Holy Trinity?

Church Documents

Compendium of the Catechism of the Catholic Church, sect. 48, 221-223, 428
God is Love, Benedict XVI, sect. 19
Lumen Gentium (Dogmatic Constitution on the Church), Vatican II, sect. 4
The Relationship Between Faith and Reason, John Paul II, sect. 13
Sacrament of Charity, Benedict XVI, sect. 70-71, 77
U. S. Catholic Catechism for Adults, [2006] pp. 129, 138-139

Other Resources

The Catholic Catechism, Hardon, pp. 455-456
The Church's Confession of Faith, Ignatius Press, pp. 77-78
Faith for Today, Hogan and LeVoir, [First Edition] pp. 256-257; [Second Edition] pp. 304-306
Fundamentals of Catholicism, Baker, Vol. 1, pp. 95-97, 139-140
Modern Catholic Dictionary, Hardon, see "Adoration" and "Worship"
The Teaching of Christ, Lawler, Wuerl, and Lawler, [First Edition] pp. 184-185; [Second Edition] pp. 172-173; [Third Edition] pp. 150-151

Family Wisdom Library™

Papal documents listed below can be viewed at www.vatican.va.
For new cross-references, visit www.familyland.org.

Q. 36. What is Creation?

Church Documents

Compendium of the Catechism of the Catholic Church, sect. 51-54, 59
Dei Verbum (Dogmatic Constitution on Divine Revelation), Vatican II, sect. 3
Gaudium et Spes (Pastoral Constitution on the Church in the Modern World), Vatican II, sect. 19, 36
God is Love, Benedict XVI, sect. 9
Gospel of Life, John Paul II, sect. 34, 35
Lumen Gentium (Dogmatic Constitution on the Church), Vatican II, sect. 2
On the Dignity and Vocation of Women, John Paul II, sect. 6
On the Holy Spirit in the Life of the Church and the World, John Paul II, sect. 12, 34
On Human Work, John Paul II, sect. 12
The Relationship Between Faith and Reason, John Paul II, sect. 1, 11, 25, 34, 60, 71
Sacrament of Charity, Benedict XVI, sect. 92
U. S. Catholic Catechism for Adults, [2006] pp. 53-57

Other Resources

Basics of the Faith: A Catholic Catechism, Schreck, pp. 16-18
The Catholic Catechism, Hardon, pp. 69-83
The Church's Confession of Faith, Ignatius Press, pp. 80-87
Faith for Today, Hogan and LeVoir, [First Edition] pp. 5-6, 18, 24-47; [Second Edition] pp. 26-27, 40, 47-74
Fundamentals of Catholic Dogma, Ott, pp. 79-86
Fundamentals of Catholicism, Baker, Vol. 2, pp. 121-123
Modern Catholic Dictionary, Hardon, see "Creation"
The Teaching of Christ, Lawler, Wuerl, and Lawler, [First Edition] pp. 56-59; [Second Edition] pp. 44-47; [Third Edition] pp. 38-41

Q. 37. Can we know God through created things?

Church Documents:

Compendium of the Catechism of the Catholic Church, sect. 2, 3, 29, 45
Dei Verbum (Dogmatic Constitution on Divine Revelation), Vatican II, sect. 3, 6
Gaudium et Spes (Pastoral Constitution on the Church in the Modern World), Vatican II, sect. 36
God is Love, Benedict XVI, sect. 17, 18
On the Dignity and Vocation of Women, John Paul II, sect. 7-8
The Relationship Between Faith and Reason, John Paul II, sect. 4, 8-9, 14, 19, 22, 34
Sacrament of Charity, Benedict XVI, sect. 47
U. S. Catholic Catechism for Adults, [2006] p. 4

Other Resources

Basics of the Faith: A Catholic Catechism, Schreck, pp. 3-4
The Catholic Catechism, Hardon, p. 68
The Church's Confession of Faith, Ignatius Press, pp. 24-28
Faith for Today, Hogan and LeVoir, [First Edition] pp. 2-4; [Second Edition] pp. 22-24
Fundamentals of Catholic Dogma, Ott, pp. 18-19
Fundamentals of Catholicism, Baker, Vol. 2, pp. 25-28
Modern Catholic Dictionary, Hardon, see "Revelation"
The Teaching of Christ, Lawler, Wuerl, and Lawler, [First Edition] pp. 45-46; [Second Edition] pp. 33-34; [Third Edition] p. 29

Q. 38. When did the mystery of Salvation begin?

Church Documents

Compendium of the Catechism of the Catholic Church, sect. 51, 53, 65
Dei Verbum (Dogmatic Constitution on Divine Revelation), Vatican II, sect. 3, 6
Lumen Gentium (Dogmatic Constitution on the Church), Vatican II, sect. 2
The Relationship Between Faith and Reason, John Paul II, sect. 7, 10-11, 66
Sacrament of Charity, Benedict XVI, sect. 35
U. S. Catholic Catechism for Adults, [2006] pp. 12-13

Other Resources

Basics of the Faith: A Catholic Catechism, Schreck, pp. 31-33
The Catholic Catechism, Hardon, p. 84
The Church's Confession of Faith, Ignatius Press, pp. 114-117
Faith for Today, Hogan and LeVoir, [First Edition] pp. 63-64; [Second Edition] pp. 92-93
Fundamentals of Catholic Dogma, Ott, pp. 81-82

Family Wisdom Library™

Papal documents listed below can be viewed at www.vatican.va.
For new cross-references, visit www.familyland.org.

Fundamentals of Catholicism, Baker, Vol. 2, pp. 124-127
The Teaching of Christ, Lawler, Wuerl, and Lawler, [First Edition] pp. 66-67, 86-89; [Second Edition] pp. 54-55, 74-77; [Third Edition] pp. 47-48, 65-68

Q. 39. Who are the angels?

Church Documents

Compendium of the Catechism of the Catholic Church, sect. 60-61
U. S. Catholic Catechism for Adults, [2006] pp. 54-55, 62, 153, 157, 219, 468

Other Resources

Basics of the Faith: A Catholic Catechism, Schreck, pp. 16-18, 40
The Catholic Catechism, Hardon, pp. 83-87
The Church's Confession of Faith, Ignatius Press, pp. 92-94
Faith for Today, Hogan and LeVoir, [First Edition] pp. 24-31; [Second Edition] pp. 47-55
Fundamentals of Catholic Dogma, Ott, pp. 114-121
Fundamentals of Catholicism, Baker, Vol. 2, pp. 174-180
Modern Catholic Dictionary, Hardon, see "Angel"
The Teaching of Christ, Lawler, Wuerl, and Lawler, [First Edition] pp. 66-67; [Second Edition] pp. 54-55; [Third Edition] pp. 47-48

Q. 40. Who are the devils?

Church Documents

Compendium of the Catechism of the Catholic Church, sect. 74-75
Gaudium et Spes (Pastoral Constitution on the Church in the Modern World), Vatican II, sect. 13, 22
Gospel of Life, John Paul II, sect. 104
Splendor of Truth, John Paul II, sect. 1
U. S. Catholic Catechism for Adults, [2006] pp. 55, 62, 157, 296, 489

Other Resources

Basics of the Faith: A Catholic Catechism, Schreck, pp. 17-19
The Catholic Catechism, Hardon, pp. 287-290
The Church's Confession of Faith, Ignatius Press, pp. 94-95
Faith for Today, Hogan and LeVoir, [First Edition] pp. 29-30; [Second Edition] pp. 52-54
Fundamentals of Catholic Dogma, Ott, pp. 118-122
Fundamentals of Catholicism, Baker, Vol. 2, pp. 181-187, 190-193
Modern Catholic Dictionary, Hardon, see "Devil"
The Teaching of Christ, Lawler, Wuerl, and Lawler, [First Edition] pp. 86-88; [Second Edition] pp. 74-76; [Third Edition] pp. 65-66

Q. 41. Where are the angels who remained faithful to God?

Church Documents

Compendium of the Catechism of the Catholic Church, sect. 60
U. S. Catholic Catechism for Adults, [2006] pp. 153, 219, 468

Other Resources

The Catholic Catechism, Hardon, pp. 83-90
The Church's Confession of Faith, Ignatius Press, pp. 93-94
Faith for Today, Hogan and LeVoir, [First Edition] pp. 30-31; [Second Edition] pp. 54-55
Fundamentals of Catholic Dogma, Ott, pp. 117-118
Fundamentals of Catholicism, Baker, Vol. 2, p. 182
Modern Catholic Dictionary, Hardon, see "Heaven"
The Teaching of Christ, Lawler, Wuerl, and Lawler, [First Edition] pp. 66-67; [Second Edition] pp. 54-55; [Third Edition] pp. 47-48

Q. 42. How was man created?

Church Documents

Compendium of the Catechism of the Catholic Church, sect. 66-70
Dei Verbum (Dogmatic Constitution on Divine Revelation), Vatican II, sect. 3
Gaudium et Spes (Pastoral Constitution on the Church in the Modern World), Vatican II, sect. 12, 14
God is Love, Benedict XVI, sect. 9-11
Gospel of Life, John Paul II, sect. 35
Lumen Gentium (Dogmatic Constitution on the Church), Vatican II, sect. 2
On the Dignity and Vocation of Women, John Paul II, sect. 6-7
On the Holy Spirit in the Life of the Church and the World, John Paul II, sect. 12, 34
Sacrament of Charity, Benedict XVI, sect. 2, 8
U. S. Catholic Catechism for Adults, [2006] pp. 67-68

Family Wisdom Library™

Papal documents listed below can be viewed at www.vatican.va.
For new cross-references, visit www.familyland.org.

Other Resources

Basics of the Faith: A Catholic Catechism, Schreck, pp. 19-20
The Catholic Catechism, Hardon, pp. 91-103
The Church's Confession of Faith, Ignatius Press, pp. 97-99
Faith for Today, Hogan and LeVoir, [First Edition] pp. 25-41; [Second Edition] pp. 47-66
Fundamentals of Catholic Dogma, Ott, pp. 94-95
Fundamentals of Catholicism, Baker, Vol. 2, pp. 139-142
The Teaching of Christ, Lawler, Wuerl, and Lawler, [First Edition] pp. 68-71; [Second Edition] pp. 56-59; [Third Edition] pp. 49-51

Q. 43. In what way was man created in the image and likeness of God?

Church Documents

Compendium of the Catechism of the Catholic Church, sect. 66
Dei Verbum (Dogmatic Constitution on Divine Revelation), Vatican II, sect. 3
Gaudium et Spes (Pastoral Constitution on the Church in the Modern World), Vatican II, sect. 12, 17, 22, 24, 34, 41
God is Love, Benedict XVI, sect. 5, 9-11
Gospel of Life, John Paul II, sect. 43
Lumen Gentium (Dogmatic Constitution on the Church), Vatican II, sect. 2
The Lay Members of Christ's Faithful People, John Paul II, sect. 37
On the Dignity and Vocation of Women, John Paul II, sect. 6-7
On the Holy Spirit in the Life of the Church and the World, John Paul II, sect. 34
On the Hundredth Anniversary of Rerum Novarum, John Paul II, sect. 24, 53
On Social Concern, John Paul II, sect. 29-30, 47
The Relationship Between Faith and Reason, John Paul II, sect. 80
Sacrament of Charity, Benedict XVI, sect. 2, 8
Splendor of Truth, John Paul II, sect. 41, 49, 50, 86, 90
To the Youth of the World, John Paul II, sect. 4
U. S. Catholic Catechism for Adults, [2006] pp. 67-68

Other Resources

Basics of the Faith: A Catholic Catechism, Schreck, pp. 19-20
The Catholic Catechism, Hardon, pp. 66-67
The Church's Confession of Faith, Ignatius Press, pp. 98-101
Faith for Today, Hogan and LeVoir, [First Edition] pp. 1-4; [Second Edition] pp. 21-24
Fundamentals of Catholic Dogma, Ott, pp. 94-95, 103
Fundamentals of Catholicism, Baker, Vol. 2, pp. 140-143
The Teaching of Christ, Lawler, Wuerl, and Lawler, [First Edition] pp. 68-71; [Second Edition] pp. 56-59; [Third Edition] pp. 49-51

Q. 44. Is the soul directly created by God?

Church Documents

Compendium of the Catechism of the Catholic Church, sect. 70
God is Love, Benedict XVI, sect. 5, 9-11
Gospel of Life, John Paul II, sect. 35
On the Hundredth Anniversary of Rerum Novarum, John Paul II, sect. 39
U. S. Catholic Catechism for Adults, [2006] p. 68

Other Resources

Basics of the Faith: A Catholic Catechism, Schreck, pp. 25-26
The Catholic Catechism, Hardon, pp. 91-99
The Church's Confession of Faith, Ignatius Press, p. 97
Faith for Today, Hogan and LeVoir, [First Edition] pp. 33-34; [Second Edition] pp. 57-59
Fundamentals of Catholic Dogma, Ott, p. 100
Fundamentals of Catholicism, Baker, Vol. 2, pp. 150-151
Modern Catholic Dictionary, Hardon, see "Evolution" and "Soul"
The Teaching of Christ, Lawler, Wuerl, and Lawler, [First Edition] pp. 69-70; [Second Edition] pp. 57-58; [Third Edition] p. 50

Q. 45. What special gifts did Adam and Eve receive?

Church Documents

Compendium of the Catechism of the Catholic Church, sect. 72
Gospel of Life, John Paul II, sect. 35
On the Christian Meaning of Human Suffering, John Paul II, sect. 15
On the Dignity and Vocation of Women, John Paul II, sect. 9
On Human Work, John Paul II, sect. 1
The Relationship Between Faith and Reason, John Paul II, sect. 12, 22

Family Wisdom Library™

Papal documents listed below can be viewed at www.vatican.va.
For new cross-references, visit www.familyland.org.

Splendor of Truth, John Paul II, sect. 10
U. S. Catholic Catechism for Adults, [2006] pp. 69-71, 74

Other Resources

Basics of the Faith: A Catholic Catechism, Schreck, p. 20
The Catholic Catechism, Hardon, p. 101
The Church's Confession of Faith, Ignatius Press, p. 108
Faith for Today, Hogan and LeVoir, [First Edition] pp. 55-56, 219-223; [Second Edition] pp. 82-83, 264-268
Fundamentals of Catholic Dogma, Ott, pp. 103-105
Fundamentals of Catholicism, Baker, Vol. 2, pp. 154-158
Modern Catholic Dictionary, Hardon, see "Fall of Adam"
The Teaching of Christ, Lawler, Wuerl, and Lawler, [First Edition] pp. 74-75; [Second Edition] pp. 62-63; [Third Edition] pp. 54-55
Transformation in Christ, von Hildebrand, pp. 441-450

Q. 46. What commandment did Adam and Eve receive?

Church Documents

Compendium of the Catechism of the Catholic Church, sect. 75
On the Holy Spirit in the Life of the Church and the World, John Paul II, sect. 36
The Relationship Between Faith and Reason, John Paul II, sect. 22
U. S. Catholic Catechism for Adults, [2006] pp. 68-69

Other Resources

Basics of the Faith: A Catholic Catechism, Schreck, p. 20
The Catholic Catechism, Hardon, pp. 99-102
The Church's Confession of Faith, Ignatius Press, p.107
Faith for Today, Hogan and LeVoir, [First Edition] p. 55; [Second Edition] pp. 82-83
Fundamentals of Catholic Dogma, Ott, p. 104
Fundamentals of Catholicism, Baker, Vol. 2, p. 160
Modern Catholic Dictionary, Hardon, see "Adam"
The Teaching of Christ, Lawler, Wuerl, and Lawler, [First Edition] pp. 83-84; [Second Edition] pp. 71-72; [Third Edition] pp. 62-63

Q. 47. What was God's first gift leading to Christ?

Church Documents

Acts and Decrees of the Second Plenary Council of the Philippines, paragraph 13
Compendium of the Catechism of the Catholic Church, sect. 66-72
Dei Verbum (Dogmatic Constitution on Divine Revelation), Vatican II, sect. 3
God is Love, Benedict XVI, sect. 11
Gospel of Life, John Paul II, sect. 34-36
Lumen Gentium (Dogmatic Constitution on the Church), Vatican II, sect. 2
On the Holy Spirit in the Life of the Church and the World, John Paul II, sect. 12, 34
On the Hundredth Anniversary of Rerum Novarum, John Paul II, sect. 24
On Social Concern, John Paul II, sect. 28
Redeemer of Man, John Paul II, sect. 20
The Relationship Between Faith and Reason, John Paul II, sect. 80
Sacrament of Charity, Benedict XVI, sect. 92
To the Youth of the World, John Paul II, sect. 7-8
U. S. Catholic Catechism for Adults, [2006] pp. 67-70

Other Resources

Basics of the Faith: A Catholic Catechism, Schreck, pp. 29-33
The Catholic Catechism, Hardon, pp. 106-107, 179
The Church's Confession of Faith, Ignatius Press, pp. 107-110
Faith for Today, Hogan and LeVoir, [First Edition] pp. 1-4, 63-64; [Second Edition] pp. 21-24, 92-93
Fundamentals of Catholic Dogma, Ott, pp. 94-108
Fundamentals of Catholicism, Baker, Vol. 2, pp. 124-145
Modern Catholic Dictionary, Hardon, see "Adam"
The Teaching of Christ, Lawler, Wuerl, and Lawler, [First Edition] pp. 36-37; [Second Edition] pp. 24-26; [Third Edition] pp. 21-22
Transformation in Christ, von Hildebrand, pp. 441-450

Family Wisdom Library™

Papal documents listed below can be viewed at www.vatican.va.
For new cross-references, visit www.familyland.org.

Q. 48.What did the action of God in the Old Testament show and prove?

Church Documents

Acts and Decrees of the Second Plenary Council of the Philippines, paragraph 422
Compendium of the Catechism of the Catholic Church, sect. 7-8, 21
Dei Verbum (Dogmatic Constitution on Divine Revelation), Vatican II, sect. 3, 4, 14, 15, 16
Gaudium et Spes (Pastoral Constitution on the Church in the Modern World), Vatican II, sect. 32
God is Love, Benedict XVI, sect. 11
The Relationship Between Faith and Reason, John Paul II, sect. 22
Sacrament of Charity, Benedict XVI, sect. 10.
U. S. Catholic Catechism for Adults, [2006] pp. 12-15

Other Resources

Basics of the Faith: A Catholic Catechism, Schreck, p. 29
The Catholic Catechism, Hardon, pp. 72-73, 78-79
The Church's Confession of Faith, Ignatius Press, pp. 86-87
Faith for Today, Hogan and LeVoir, [First Edition] pp. 63-75; [Second Edition] pp. 92-105
Fundamentals of Catholic Dogma, Ott, pp. 88-90
Fundamentals of Catholicism, Baker, Vol. 2, pp. 136-139
The Teaching of Christ, Lawler, Wuerl, and Lawler, [First Edition] pp. 48-54; [Second Edition] pp. 36-42; [Third Edition] pp. 31-36

Q. 49. In what event is God's all-powerful action for our Salvation especially seen?

Church Documents

Compendium of the Catechism of the Catholic Church, sect. 131
Dei Verbum (Dogmatic Constitution on Divine Revelation), Vatican II, sect. 4
Gaudium et Spes (Pastoral Constitution on the Church in the Modern World), Vatican II, sect. 22, 32
God is Love, Benedict XVI, sect. 9-11
Gospel of Life, John Paul II, sect. 29, 82
Lumen Gentium (Dogmatic Constitution on the Church), Vatican II, sect. 5, 7, 8
On the Christian Meaning of Human Suffering, John Paul II, sect. 14-18
On Evangelization in the Modern World, Paul VI, sect. 9, 34
On the Holy Spirit in the Life of the Church and the World, John Paul II, sect. 24
The Relationship Between Faith and Reason, John Paul II, sect. 66, 80
Sacrament of Charity, Benedict XVI, sect. 7-9
Splendor of Truth, John Paul II, sect. 10, 86
U. S. Catholic Catechism for Adults, [2006] pp. 93-95

Other Resources

Basics of the Faith: A Catholic Catechism, Schreck, pp. 53-54
The Catholic Catechism, Hardon, pp. 38, 145-146
The Church's Confession of Faith, Ignatius Press, pp. 165-174
Fundamentals of Catholic Dogma, Ott, pp. 192-193
Fundamentals of Catholicism, Baker, Vol. 2, pp. 304-307
Modern Catholic Dictionary, Hardon, see "Resurrection of Christ"
The Teaching of Christ, Lawler, Wuerl, and Lawler, [First Edition] pp. 148-158; [Second Edition] pp. 137-147; [Third Edition] pp. 120-129

Q. 50. How should we regard Creation?

Church Documents

Compendium of the Catechism of the Catholic Church, sect. 62, 64
Dei Verbum (Dogmatic Constitution on Divine Revelation), Vatican II, sect. 3
Gaudium et Spes (Pastoral Constitution on the Church in the Modern World), Vatican II, sect. 45
God is Love, Benedict XVI, sect. 11
On the Dignity and Vocation of Women, John Paul II, sect. 6-7
On the Holy Spirit in the Life of the Church and the World, John Paul II, sect. 12, 34
On Human Work, John Paul II, sect. 12, 25
Sacrament of Charity, Benedict XVI, sect. 92
U. S. Catholic Catechism for Adults, [2006] pp. 4, 424, 452

Other Resources

Basics of the Faith: A Catholic Catechism, Schreck, pp. 14-16
The Catholic Catechism, Hardon, pp. 78-81
The Church's Confession of Faith, Ignatius Press, pp. 81-90
Faith for Today, Hogan and LeVoir, [First Edition] pp. 24-47; [Second Edition] pp. 47-74
Fundamentals of Catholic Dogma, Ott, p. 87

Family Wisdom Library™

Papal documents listed below can be viewed at www.vatican.va.
For new cross-references, visit www.familyland.org.

Fundamentals of Catholicism, Baker, Vol. 2, pp. 130-139
Modern Catholic Dictionary, Hardon, see "Providence"
The Teaching of Christ, Lawler, Wuerl, and Lawler, [First Edition] pp. 64-67; [Second Edition] pp. 52-55; [Third Edition] pp. 44-47

Q. 51. How was God especially present in the history of man?

Church Documents

Acts and Decrees of the Second Plenary Council of the Philippines, paragraphs 59, 85
Compendium of the Catechism of the Catholic Church, sect. 78-79
Dei Verbum (Dogmatic Constitution on Divine Revelation), Vatican II, sect. 2-4
Gaudium et Spes (Pastoral Constitution on the Church in the Modern World), Vatican II, sect. 18, 22, 32, 38, 41, 78
God is Love, Benedict XVI, sect. 12
Gospel of Life, John Paul II, sect. 31, 39
Lumen Gentium (Dogmatic Constitution on the Church), Vatican II, sect. 3, 5, 7
On the Dignity and Vocation of Women, John Paul II, sect. 6-7
On the Holy Spirit in the Life of the Church and the World, John Paul II, sect. 12, 34
On the Hundredth Anniversary of Rerum Novarum, John Paul II, sect. 5
Sacrament of Charity, Benedict XVI, sect. 7-9
U. S. Catholic Catechism for Adults, [2006] pp. 12-15

Other Resources

Basics of the Faith: A Catholic Catechism, Schreck, pp. 53-54
The Catholic Catechism, Hardon, p. 120
The Church's Confession of Faith, Ignatius Press, pp. 171-172a, 208, 212-218
Faith for Today, Hogan and LeVoir, [First Edition] pp. 63-75; [Second Edition] pp. 92-105
The Teaching of Christ, Lawler, Wuerl, and Lawler, [First Edition] pp. 48, 49, 50, 88, 538-539; [Second Edition] pp. 37, 38, 76, 528-529; [Third Edition] pp. 32, 33, 466-467

Q. 52. How is God present to us in our own day?

Church Documents

Acts and Decrees of the Second Plenary Council of the Philippines, paragraph 62
Compendium of the Catechism of the Catholic Church, sect. 55, 128, 222, 280-282
Dei Verbum (Dogmatic Constitution on Divine Revelation), Vatican II, sect. 4-6
Gaudium et Spes (Pastoral Constitution on the Church in the Modern World), Vatican II, sect. 18, 22, 32, 38, 41, 78
God is Love, Benedict XVI, sect. 11
Gospel of Life, John Paul II, sect. 51, 66
Lumen Gentium (Dogmatic Constitution on the Church), *Vatican II,* sect. 48
On the Holy Spirit in the Life of the Church and the World, John Paul II, sect. 14, 65, 67
On the Hundredth Anniversary of Rerum Novarum, John Paul II, sect. 26
Redeemer of Man, John Paul II, sect. 8-10, 14
The Relationship Between Faith and Reason, John Paul II, sect. 13
U. S. Catholic Catechism for Adults, [2006] pp. 112, 116, 122

Other Resources

Basics of the Faith: A Catholic Catechism, Schreck, pp. 77-78
The Church's Confession of Faith, Ignatius Press, pp. 218-221
Faith for Today, Hogan and LeVoir, [First Edition] pp. 117-144; [Second Edition] pp. 151-181
Fundamentals of Catholic Dogma, Ott, pp. 274-276
Fundamentals of Catholicism, Baker, Vol. 3, pp. 95-98
Modern Catholic Dictionary, Hardon, see "Sacrament of Salvation"
The Teaching of Christ, Lawler, Wuerl, and Lawler, [First Edition] pp. 186-187, 199-200; [Second Edition] pp. 174-175, 187-188; [Third Edition] pp. 152-153, 163-164

Q. 53. What was the Original Sin?

Church Documents

Acts and Decrees of the Second Plenary Council of the Philippines, paragraph 422
Compendium of the Catechism of the Catholic Church, sect. 75-76
Dei Verbum (Dogmatic Constitution on Divine Revelation), Vatican II, sect. 3
Gospel of Life, John Paul II, sect. 7, 36
Lumen Gentium (Dogmatic Constitution on the Church), Vatican II, sect. 2, 56
On the Dignity and Vocation of Women, John Paul II, sect. 9
On the Holy Spirit in the Life of the Church and the World, John Paul II, sect. 33-38

Family Wisdom Library™

Papal documents listed below can be viewed at www.vatican.va.
For new cross-references, visit www.familyland.org.

On the Hundredth Anniversary of Rerum Novarum, John Paul II, sect. 4, 17
Splendor of Truth, John Paul II, sect. 1
The Relationship Between Faith and Reason, John Paul II, sect. 22
U. S. Catholic Catechism for Adults, [2006] pp. 68-69

Other Resources

Basics of the Faith: A Catholic Catechism, Schreck, pp. 20-22
The Catholic Catechism, Hardon, pp. 100-101
The Church's Confession of Faith, Ignatius Press, pp. 109-114
Fundamentals of Catholic Dogma, Ott, pp. 106-107
Fundamentals of Catholicism, Baker, Vol. 2, pp. 159-160
Faith for Today, Hogan and LeVoir, [First Edition] pp. 53-63; [Second Edition] pp. 80-92
Modern Catholic Dictionary, Hardon, see "Adam"
The Teaching of Christ, Lawler, Wuerl, and Lawler, [First Edition] pp. 83-84; [Second Edition] pp. 71-72; [Third Edition] pp. 62-63
Transformation in Christ, von Hildebrand, pp. 441-450

Q. 54. Why are all men conceived and born in Original Sin?

Church Documents

Acts and Decrees of the Second Plenary Council of the Philippines, paragraphs 23, 24, 122, 310
Compendium of the Catechism of the Catholic Church, sect. 76-77
Dei Verbum (Dogmatic Constitution on Divine Revelation), Vatican II, sect. 3
Gaudium et Spes (Pastoral Constitution on the Church in the Modern World), Vatican II, sect. 22
Lumen Gentium (Dogmatic Constitution on the Church), Vatican II, sect. 2
On the Christian Meaning of Human Suffering, John Paul II, sect. 15
On the Holy Spirit in the Life of the Church and the World, John Paul II, sect. 38, 43, 44
On the Hundredth Anniversary of Rerum Novarum, John Paul II, sect. 25
On Reconciliation and Penance, John Paul II, sect. 13
Splendor of Truth, John Paul II, sect. 86
The Relationship Between Faith and Reason, John Paul II, sect. 22
U. S. Catholic Catechism for Adults, [2006] pp. 68-73

Other Resources

Basics of the Faith: A Catholic Catechism, Schreck, pp. 21-23
The Catholic Catechism, Hardon, pp. 100-101
The Church's Confession of Faith, Ignatius Press, pp. 109-114
Faith for Today, Hogan and LeVoir, [First Edition] pp. 56-57, 205-206; [Second Edition] pp. 83-85
Fundamentals of Catholic Dogma, Ott, pp. 111-112
Fundamentals of Catholicism, Baker, Vol. 2, pp. 162-165
Modern Catholic Dictionary, Hardon, see "Sin"
The Teaching of Christ, Lawler, Wuerl, and Lawler, [First Edition] pp. 83-84; [Second Edition] pp. 71-72; [Third Edition] pp. 62-63
Transformation in Christ, von Hildebrand, pp. 441-450

Q. 55. What happens in Baptism?

Church Documents

Compendium of the Catechism of the Catholic Church, sect. 263
Gospel of Life, John Paul II, sect. 79
Lumen Gentium (Dogmatic Constitution on the Church), Vatican II, sect. 7, 11, 14
The Lay Members of Christ's Faithful People, John Paul II, sect. 10-14
On the Holy Spirit in the Life of the Church and the World, John Paul II, sect. 31
On Reconciliation and Penance, John Paul II, sect. 27
U. S. Catholic Catechism for Adults, [2006] pp. 192-195

Other Resources

Basics of the Faith: A Catholic Catechism, Schreck, pp. 155-158
The Catholic Catechism, Hardon, pp. 506-511
The Church's Confession of Faith, Ignatius Press, pp. 272-278
Faith for Today, Hogan and LeVoir, [First Edition] pp. 181-182; [Second Edition] pp. 221-222
Fundamentals of Catholic Dogma, Ott, pp. 354-356
Modern Catholic Dictionary, Hardon, see "Baptism" and "Baptismal Graces"
The Teaching of Christ, Lawler, Wuerl and Lawler, [First Edition] pp. 464-468 [Second Edition] pp. 454-458; [Third Edition] pp. 401-404

Family Wisdom Library™

Papal documents listed below can be viewed at www.vatican.va.
For new cross-references, visit www.familyland.org.

Q. 56. Was anyone exempt from Original Sin?

Church Documents

Compendium of the Catechism of the Catholic Church, sect. 96-97
God is Love, Benedict XVI, sect. 41, 42
Lumen Gentium (Dogmatic Constitution on the Church), Vatican II, sect. 56, 59, 65
Mother of the Redeemer, John Paul II, sect. 10
The Relationship Between Faith and Reason, John Paul II, sect. 108
U. S. Catholic Catechism for Adults, [2006] pp. 143-144, 147

Other Resources

Basics of the Faith: A Catholic Catechism, Schreck, pp. 282-283
The Catholic Catechism, Hardon, pp. 151-152
The Church's Confession of Faith, Ignatius Press, p. 150
Faith for Today, Hogan and LeVoir, [First Edition] pp. 104-106; [Second Edition] pp. 137-139
Fundamentals of Catholic Dogma, Ott, pp. 199-202
Fundamentals of Catholicism, Baker, Vol. 2, pp. 330-333
Modern Catholic Dictionary, Hardon, see "Immaculate Conception"
The Teaching of Christ, Lawler, Wuerl, and Lawler, [First Edition] p. 122; [Second Edition] p. 110; [Third Edition] p. 96

Q. 57. What is actual or personal sin?

Church Documents

Acts and Decrees of the Second Plenary Council of the Philippines, paragraph 81
Compendium of the Catechism of the Catholic Church, sect. 392
Gaudium et Spes (Pastoral Constitution on the Church in the Modern World), Vatican II, sect. 16
On the Holy Spirit in the Life of the Church and the World, John Paul II, sect. 13, 27, 29-30, 32-33, 36, 39, 55
On Reconciliation and Penance, John Paul II, sect.16
The Relationship Between Faith and Reason, John Paul II, sect. 25
Sacrament of Charity, Benedict XVI, sect. 20-21
Splendor of Truth, John Paul II, sect. 72, 73, 84
To the Youth of the World, John Paul II, sect. 6
U. S. Catholic Catechism for Adults, [2006] pp. 69, 71-74, 312-313

Other Resources

Basics of the Faith: A Catholic Catechism, Schreck, p. 217
The Catholic Catechism, Hardon, pp. 283-284, 293-295
The Church's Confession of Faith, Ignatius Press, pp. 116, 298-305
Faith for Today, Hogan and LeVoir, [First Edition] pp. 29, 243-255; [Second Edition] pp. 52-53, 290-304
Fundamentals of Catholicism, Baker, Vol. 3, pp. 283-285
Modern Catholic Dictionary, Hardon, see "Actual Sin"
The Teaching of Christ, Lawler, Wuerl, and Lawler, [First Edition] p. 303; [Second Edition] p. 291; [Third Edition] p. 257

Q. 58. When someone commits a personal sin, what happens?

Church Documents

Acts and Decrees of the Second Plenary Council of the Philippines, paragraph 81
Compendium of the Catechism of the Catholic Church, sect. 392
On the Holy Spirit in the Life of the Church and the World, John Paul II, sect. 32, 41, 43
On Reconciliation and Penance, John Paul II, sect. 5, 14-17
The Relationship Between Faith and Reason, John Paul II, sect. 25
Sacrament of Charity, Benedict XVI, sect. 20-21
Splendor of Truth, John Paul II, sect. 68
U. S. Catholic Catechism for Adults, [2006] pp. 237, 245

Other Resources

Basics of the Faith: A Catholic Catechism, Schreck, p. 217
The Catholic Catechism, Hardon, pp. 293-294
The Church's Confession of Faith, Ignatius Press, p. 303
Faith for Today, Hogan and LeVoir, [First Edition] pp. 251-252; [Second Edition] pp. 299-300
Fundamentals of Catholicism, Baker, Vol. 3, pp. 34-37
Modern Catholic Dictionary, Hardon, see "Sin" and "Venial Sin"
The Teaching of Christ, Lawler, Wuerl, and Lawler, [First Edition] pp. 304-307; [Second Edition] pp. 292-296; [Third Edition] pp. 258-261

Family Wisdom Library™

Papal documents listed below can be viewed at www.vatican.va.
For new cross-references, visit www.familyland.org.

Q. 59. What is mortal sin?

Church Documents

Compendium of the Catechism of the Catholic Church, sect. 393-395
Gospel of Life, John Paul II, sect. 57, 62, 65
On the Holy Spirit in the Life of the Church and the World, John Paul II, sect. 46
On Reconciliation and Penance, John Paul II, sect. 17
The Relationship Between Faith and Reason, John Paul II, sect. 25
Sacrament of Charity, Benedict XVI, sect. 20-21
Splendor of Truth, John Paul II, sect. 65, 67-68, 70, 77-78
U. S. Catholic Catechism for Adults, [2006] pp. 237-238, 313

Other Resources

Basics of the Faith: A Catholic Catechism, Schreck, p. 217
The Church's Confession of Faith, Ignatius Press, p. 303
The Catholic Catechism, Hardon, pp. 293-295
Faith for Today, Hogan and LeVoir, [First Edition] p. 254; [Second Edition] p. 303
Fundamentals of Catholicism, Baker, Vol. 3, p. 32
Modern Catholic Dictionary, Hardon, see "Mortal Sin"
The Teaching of Christ, Lawler, Wuerl, and Lawler, [First Edition] pp. 304-306; [Second Edition] pp. 295-296; [Third Edition] p. 258-260

Q. 60. What are the effects of mortal sin?

Church Documents

Compendium of the Catechism of the Catholic Church, sect. 395
On the Holy Spirit in the Life of the Church and the World, John Paul II, sect. 46
On Reconciliation and Penance, John Paul II, sect. 14
On Social Concern, John Paul II, sect. 36, 46
The Relationship Between Faith and Reason, John Paul II, sect. 25
Sacrament of Charity, Benedict XVI, sect. 20-21
Splendor of Truth, John Paul II, sect. 68
U. S. Catholic Catechism for Adults, [2006] p. 313

Other Resources

Basics of the Faith: A Catholic Catechism, Schreck, p. 217
The Catholic Catechism, Hardon, pp. 183-185
Faith for Today, Hogan and LeVoir, [First Edition] p. 254; [Second Edition] p. 303
Fundamentals of Catholicism, Baker, Vol. 3, p. 32
Modern Catholic Dictionary, Hardon, see "Mortal Sin"
The Teaching of Christ, Lawler, Wuerl, and Lawler, [First Edition] pp. 304-306; [Second Edition] pp. 292-295; [Third Edition] pp. 258-261

Q. 61. What is a venial sin?

Church Documents

Compendium of the Catechism of the Catholic Church, sect. 393, 396
The Relationship Between Faith and Reason, John Paul II, sect. 25
U. S. Catholic Catechism for Adults, [2006] pp. 237-238

Other Resources

Basics of the Faith: A Catholic Catechism, Schreck, pp. 217-218
The Catholic Catechism, Hardon, pp. 183-185
The Church's Confession of Faith, Ignatius Press, p. 303
Faith for Today, Hogan and LeVoir, [First Edition] p. 254; [Second Edition] p. 303
Fundamentals of Catholicism, Baker, Vol. 3, pp. 32, 33, 296
Modern Catholic Dictionary, Hardon, see "Venial Sin"
The Teaching of Christ, Lawler, Wuerl, and Lawler, [First Edition] pp. 306-307; [Second Edition] pp. 295-296; [Third Edition] p. 261

Q. 62. Under what conditions does a Christian commit a mortal sin?

Church Documents

Acts and Decrees of the Second Plenary Council of the Philippines, paragraph 81
Compendium of the Catechism of the Catholic Church, sect. 395;
On the Holy Spirit in the Life of the Church and the World, John Paul II, sect. 46
On Reconciliation and Penance, John Paul II, sect. 6, 17
Splendor of Truth, John Paul II, sect. 62, 67, 68, 70, 73, 77
U. S. Catholic Catechism for Adults, [2006] p. 313

Family Wisdom Library™

Papal documents listed below can be viewed at www.vatican.va.
For new cross-references, visit www.familyland.org.

Other Resources

The Catholic Catechism, Hardon, pp. 293-295
Faith for Today, Hogan and LeVoir, [First Edition] pp. 254-255; [Second Edition] pp. 303-304
Fundamentals of Catholicism, Baker, Vol. 1, pp. 123-129; Vol. 3, pp. 295-297
The Teaching of Christ, Lawler, Wuerl, and Lawler, [First Edition] pp. 304-305; [Second Edition] pp. 292-294; [Third Edition] pp. 258-260

Q. 63. When is an act right or wrong?

Church Documents

Compendium of the Catechism of the Catholic Church, sect. 367-369
Gospel of Life, John Paul II, sect. 28, 62, 65, 70
On the Dignity and Vocation of Women, John Paul II, sect. 9
On the Holy Spirit in the Life of the Church and the World, John Paul II, sect. 36
On Social Concern, John Paul II, sect. 38
The Relationship Between Faith and Reason, John Paul II, sect. 25
U. S. Catholic Catechism for Adults, [2006] pp. 311-312

Other Resources

The Catholic Catechism, Hardon, pp. 293-297
Faith for Today, Hogan and LeVoir, [First Edition] pp. 243-255; [Second Edition] pp. 290-304
Fundamentals of Catholicism, Baker, Vol. 1, pp. 123-126
Modern Catholic Dictionary, Hardon, see "Morality"
The Teaching of Christ, Lawler, Wuerl, and Lawler, [First Edition] pp. 280-292; [Second Edition] pp. 268-280; [Third Edition] 236-247

Q. 64. How do we know God's will?

Church Documents

Compendium of the Catechism of the Catholic Church, sect. 372-375
Gaudium et Spes (Pastoral Constitution on the Church in the Modern World*)*, Vatican II, sect. 34
Gospel of Life, John Paul II, sect. 2, 54, 57, 61, 62, 66
On Human Life (Humanae Vitae), Paul VI, sect. 4
On the Hundredth Anniversary of Rerum Novarum, John Paul II, sect. 5, 51
The Lay Members of Christ's Faithful People, John Paul II, sect. 58
Splendor of Truth, John Paul II, sect. 8-11
U. S. Catholic Catechism for Adults, [2006] pp. 314-315, 318

Other Resources

Basics of the Faith: A Catholic Catechism, Schreck, pp. 235-242
The Catholic Catechism, Hardon, pp. 288-295
The Church's Confession of Faith, Ignatius Press, pp. 258-261
Faith for Today, Hogan and LeVoir, [First Edition] pp. 243-271; [Second Edition] pp. 290-321
Fundamentals of Catholicism, Baker, Vol. 1, pp. 121-138
Modern Catholic Dictionary, Hardon, see "Will of God"
The Teaching of Christ, Lawler, Wuerl, and Lawler, [First Edition] pp. 279-298; [Second Edition] pp. 267-286; [Third Edition] pp. 235-252

Q. 65. Does God forgive our sins?

Church Documents

Compendium of the Catechism of the Catholic Church, sect. 50, 201, 310, 594-595
Gospel of Life, John Paul II, sect. 50
On the Holy Spirit in the Life of the Church and the World, John Paul II, sect. 28-31, 39-42, 45
On the Hundredth Anniversary of Rerum Novarum, John Paul II, sect. 53
On Reconciliation and Penance, John Paul II, sect. 5, 7
Sacrament of Charity, Benedict XVI, sect. 21
U. S. Catholic Catechism for Adults, [2006] pp. 192, 196-197

Other Resources

Basics of the Faith: A Catholic Catechism, Schreck, p. 217
The Catholic Catechism, Hardon, p. 481
Faith for Today, Hogan and LeVoir, [First Edition] pp. 188-190; [Second Edition] pp. 229-232
Fundamentals of Catholic Dogma, Ott, pp. 250f
Fundamentals of Catholicism, Baker, Vol. 3, pp. 280-283
Modern Catholic Dictionary, Hardon, see "Forgiveness"
The Teaching of Christ, Lawler, Wuerl, and Lawler, [First Edition] pp. 480-488; [Second Edition] pp. 470-478; [Third Edition] pp. 415-422

Family Wisdom Library™

Papal documents listed below can be viewed at www.vatican.va.
For new cross-references, visit www.familyland.org.

Q. 66. How does God draw the sinner to Salvation?

Church Documents

Acts and Decrees of the Second Plenary Council of the Philippines, paragraphs 272, 275, 422
Compendium of the Catechism of the Catholic Church, sect. 422-425
Gaudium et Spes (Pastoral Constitution on the Church in the Modern World), Vatican II, sect. 17, 25, 30, 32, 34, 37, 57
Lumen Gentium (Dogmatic Constitution on the Church), Vatican II, sect. 9
On the Holy Spirit in the Life of the Church and the World, John Paul II, sect. 27-45, 48
On the Hundredth Anniversary of Rerum Novarum, John Paul II, sect. 51
On Reconciliation and Penance, John Paul II, sect. 27-34
Redeemer of Man, John Paul II, sect. 20
The Relationship Between Faith and Reason, John Paul II, sect. 26
The Role of the Christian Family in the Modern World, John Paul II, sect. 41
Sacrament of Charity, Benedict XVI, sect. 7-9
Sacrosanctum Concilium (Constitution on the Sacred Liturgy), Vatican II, sect. 8, 9
Splendor of Truth, John Paul II, sect. 8, 73, 103, 107
U. S. Catholic Catechism for Adults, [2006] pp. 37-38, 44-45, 328-330

Other Resources

Basics of the Faith: A Catholic Catechism, Schreck, pp. 222-224
The Catholic Catechism, Hardon, pp. 487-488
The Church's Confession of Faith, Ignatius Press, pp. 196-203
Faith for Today, Hogan and LeVoir, [First Edition] pp. 224-226; [Second Edition] pp. 269-272
Fundamentals of Catholic Dogma, Ott, pp. 252ff
Fundamentals of Catholicism, Baker, Vol. 3, pp. 22-25
Modern Catholic Dictionary, Hardon, see "Justifying Grace"
The Teaching of Christ, Lawler, Wuerl, and Lawler, [First Edition] p. 482; [Second Edition] pp. 472; [Third Edition] pp. 416

Q. 67. How are venial sins forgiven?

Church Documents

Compendium of the Catechism of the Catholic Church, sect. 292, 304, 306
On the Holy Spirit in the Life of the Church and the World, John Paul II, sect. 45-48
On Reconciliation and Penance, John Paul II, sect. 27-30
Redeemer of Man, John Paul II, sect. 20
Splendor of Truth, John Paul II, sect. 86
U. S. Catholic Catechism for Adults, [2006] pp. 237-238

Other Resources

The Catholic Catechism, Hardon, pp. 478-479, 495
The Church's Confession of Faith, Ignatius Press, pp. 303-305
Fundamentals of Catholic Dogma, Ott, p. 433
Fundamentals of Catholicism, Baker, Vol. 3, pp. 296-297
Modern Catholic Dictionary, Hardon, see "Repentance"
The Teaching of Christ, Lawler, Wuerl, and Lawler, [First Edition] pp. 484-488; [Second Edition] pp. 474-478; [Third Edition] pp. 418-422

Q. 68. What is a Capital Sin?

Church Documents

Acts and Decrees of the Second Plenary Council of the Philippines, paragraph 81
Compendium of the Catechism of the Catholic Church, sect. 398
Splendor of Truth, John Paul II, sect. 86
U. S. Catholic Catechism for Adults, [2006] p. 317

Other Resources

Basics of the Faith: A Catholic Catechism, Schreck, p. 217
Modern Catholic Dictionary, Hardon, see "Capital Sins"
The Teaching of Christ, Lawler, Wuerl, and Lawler, [First Edition] p. 378; [Second Edition] p. 368; [Third Edition]; p. 327

Q. 69. What are the seven Capital Sins?

Church Documents

Compendium of the Catechism of the Catholic Church, sect. 398
On the Hundredth Anniversary of Rerum Novarum, John Paul II, sect. 42
On Social Concern, John Paul II, sect. 37
U. S. Catholic Catechism for Adults, [2006] p. 317

Other Resources

Basics of the Faith: A Catholic Catechism, Schreck, p. 217
Faith for Today, Hogan and LeVoir, [First Edition] p. 270; [Second Edition] p. 321

Family Wisdom Library™

Papal documents listed below can be viewed at www.vatican.va.
For new cross-references, visit www.familyland.org.

Modern Catholic Dictionary, Hardon, see "Capital Sins"
The Teaching of Christ, Lawler, Wuerl, and Lawler, [First Edition] p. 378; [Second Edition] p. 368; [Third Edition] p. 327
Transformation in Christ, von Hildebrand, pp. 149-157, 170-175, 281-282

Q. 70. What is temptation?

Church Documents

Compendium of the Catechism of the Catholic Church, sect. 75, 596
On the Holy Spirit in the Life of the Church and the World, John Paul II, sect. 36
U. S. Catholic Catechism for Adults, [2006] pp. 55, 62

Other Resources

Basics of the Faith: A Catholic Catechism, Schreck, pp. 220-222
Modern Catholic Dictionary, Hardon, see "Temptation"

Q. 71. Where do temptations come from?

Church Documents

Acts and Decrees of the Second Plenary Council of the Philippines, paragraphs 83, 532
Compendium of the Catechism of the Catholic Church, sect. 75, 596
On the Holy Spirit in the Life of the Church and the World, John Paul II, sect. 38
Splendor of Truth, John Paul II, sect. 86, 103, 105
U. S. Catholic Catechism for Adults, [2006] pp. 488-489

Other Resources

Basics of the Faith: A Catholic Catechism, Schreck, pp. 220-221
The Catholic Catechism, Hardon, pp. 87-90, pp. 220-221
The Church's Confession of Faith, Ignatius Press, p. 94
Faith for Today, Hogan and LeVoir, [First Edition] pp. 29-30; [Second Edition] pp. 53-54
Fundamentals of Catholic Dogma, Ott, pp. 106f, 121f
Fundamentals of Catholicism, Baker, Vol. 2, pp. 190-193
Modern Catholic Dictionary, Hardon, see "Temptation"
The Teaching of Christ, Lawler, Wuerl, and Lawler, [First Edition] p. 87; [Second Edition] p. 75; [Third Edition] p. 65

Jesus Christ, Son of God, Savior

"...We believe in one Lord, Jesus Christ, the only Son of God eternally begotten of the Father, God from God, Light from Light, true God from true God, begotten, not made, one in Being with the Father. Through Him all things were made. For us men and for our Salvation He came down from Heaven: by the power of the Holy Spirit He was born of the Virgin Mary, and became man.

"For our sake He was crucified under Pontius Pilate; He suffered, died, and was buried. On the third day He rose again in fulfillment of the Scriptures; He ascended into Heaven and is seated at the right hand of the Father. He will come again in glory to judge the living and the dead, and His Kingdom will have no end."

#R2.1-13

The angel of the Lord declared unto Mary.

#M3-248-2

And she conceived by the Holy Spirit.

The Angelus

V. The angel of the Lord declared unto Mary;
R. And she conceived by the Holy Spirit. *Hail Mary…*
V. Behold the handmaid of the Lord;
R. Be it done unto me according to your word. *Hail Mary…*
V. And the Word was made flesh;
R. And dwelt among us. *Hail Mary…*
V. Pray for us, O holy Mother of God;
R. That we may be made worthy of the promises of Christ.

Let us pray:

Pour forth, we beseech Thee, O Lord, Thy grace into Thy hearts, that we to whom the Incarnation of Christ Thy Son, was made known by the message of an angel, may by His Passion and Cross, be brought to the glory of His Resurrection, through the same Christ Our Lord. Amen.

The Incarnation

#R2.1-7

The Incarnation means that the Second Person of the Blessed Trinity, the Son of God, became man and came to live among us.

CHAPTER NINETEEN

The Incarnation

Q. 72. Of all of God's works, which is the greatest?

The Incarnation is the greatest of God's works. The Incarnation refers to the mystery of Jesus Christ, the eternal Son of God the Father, uniting His divine nature with a complete human nature.

Sacred Scripture

But when the time had fully come, God sent forth his Son, born of woman, born under the law, to redeem those who were under the law, so that we might receive adoption as sons. *Galatians 4:4-5*

And the Word became flesh and dwelt among us, full of grace and truth; we have beheld his glory, glory as of the only Son from the Father. *John 1:14*

Catechism of the Catholic Church

461 Taking up St. John's expression, "The Word became flesh,"[1] the Church calls "Incarnation" the fact that the Son of God assumed a human nature in order to accomplish our salvation in it. In a hymn cited by St. Paul, the Church sings the mystery of the Incarnation: "Have this mind among yourselves, which is yours in Christ Jesus, who, though he was in the form of God, did not count equality with God a thing to be grasped, but emptied himself, taking the form of a servant, being born in the likeness of men. And being found in human form he humbled himself and became obedient unto death, even death on a cross."[2]

Splendor of Truth

Christ came not to condemn but to forgive, to show mercy (cf. Mt. 9:13). And the greatest mercy of all is found in his being in our midst and calling us to meet him and to confess with Peter, that he is "the Son of the living God" (Mt 16:16). *(section 118)*

Vatican Council II

In order to establish a relationship of peace and communion with himself, and in order to bring about brotherly union among men, and they sinners, God decided to enter into the history of mankind in a new and definitive manner, by sending his own Son in human flesh, so that through him he might snatch men from the power of darkness and of Satan (cf. Col. 1:13; Acts 10:38) and in him reconcile the world to himself. *Missionary Activity, 3*

For when the time had fully come (cf. Gal. 4:4), the Word became flesh and dwelt among us full of grace and truth (cf. Jn. 1:14). *Dei Verbum, 17*

Sacred Scripture
Q. 72. Phil 2:5-8.

Catechism of the Catholic Church
Q. 72. Paragraphs **456-483**.

For cross-references with Vatican II, Papal documents & other resources, see Family Wisdom Library on page 370.
For commentaries on each question with Cardinal Arinze, Sr. John Vianney and Fr. Straub (in Spanish), see Appendix C.

Summary Prayer

Jesus, the Divine Word of God, we believe that God's greatest work was Your taking on our human nature when You became man and came to live among us. At Mary's consent to Your Father's request, You became man in her immaculate womb by means of the Holy Spirit. To You be all honor and glory, now and forever. Amen.

Q. 73. What does the Incarnation mean?

The Incarnation means that the Second Person of the Blessed Trinity, the Son of God (the Divine Word), became man and came to live among us.

#R2.1-18

The Angel said, "You will conceive in your womb and bear a son, and you shall call his name Jesus" *(Luke 1:31).*

"And Mary said, 'Behold, I am the handmaid of the Lord; let it be to me according to your word'" (Luke 1:38). At that very moment Jesus Christ, God's own Son, became man in the Blessed Virgin Mary.

The Son is begotten from the Father, and the Holy Spirit proceeds from the Father and the Son. By an act of His almighty power, God the Son united His own divine nature to a true human nature,

Sacred Scripture
Q. 73. Mt 1:18-23; Lk 2:8-12.

Catechism of the Catholic Church
Q. 73. Paragraphs **461-464**.

For cross-references with Vatican II, Papal documents & other resources, see Family Wisdom Library on page 370.
For commentaries on each question with Cardinal Arinze, Sr. John Vianney and Fr. Straub (in Spanish), see Appendix C.

to a body and soul like ours. The two natures were united in one divine Person. Mary is the Mother of God because she is the Mother of God the Son, Who became man in her womb.

Mary gave her free consent to become the Mother of Jesus. At that moment, by the operation of the Holy Spirit, she conceived Jesus within her womb. The result was one divine Person with one divine and one human nature.

#R2.1-16

Mary gave her free consent to become the Mother of Jesus and at that moment "the Word became flesh" *(John 1:14).*

Sacred Scripture

And he [the angel Gabriel] came to her and said, "Hail, full of grace, the Lord is with you!"..."And behold, you will conceive in your womb and bear a son, and you shall call his name Jesus."...And Mary said to the angel, "How can this be, since I have no husband?" And the angel said to her, "The Holy Spirit will come upon you, and the power of the Most High will overshadow you; therefore the child to be born will be called holy, the Son of God." *Luke 1:28, 31, 34-35*

Catechism of the Catholic Church

463 Belief in the true Incarnation of the Son of God is the distinctive sign of Christian faith: "By this you know the Spirit of God: every spirit which confesses that Jesus Christ has come in the flesh is of God."[1] Such is the joyous conviction of the Church from her beginning whenever she sings "the mystery of our religion": "He was manifested in the flesh."[2]

744 In the fullness of time the Holy Spirit completes in Mary all the preparations for Christ's coming among the People of God. By the action of the Holy Spirit in her, the Father gives the world Emmanuel, "God- with-us"[1].

Catechism by Diagram

#J2-273

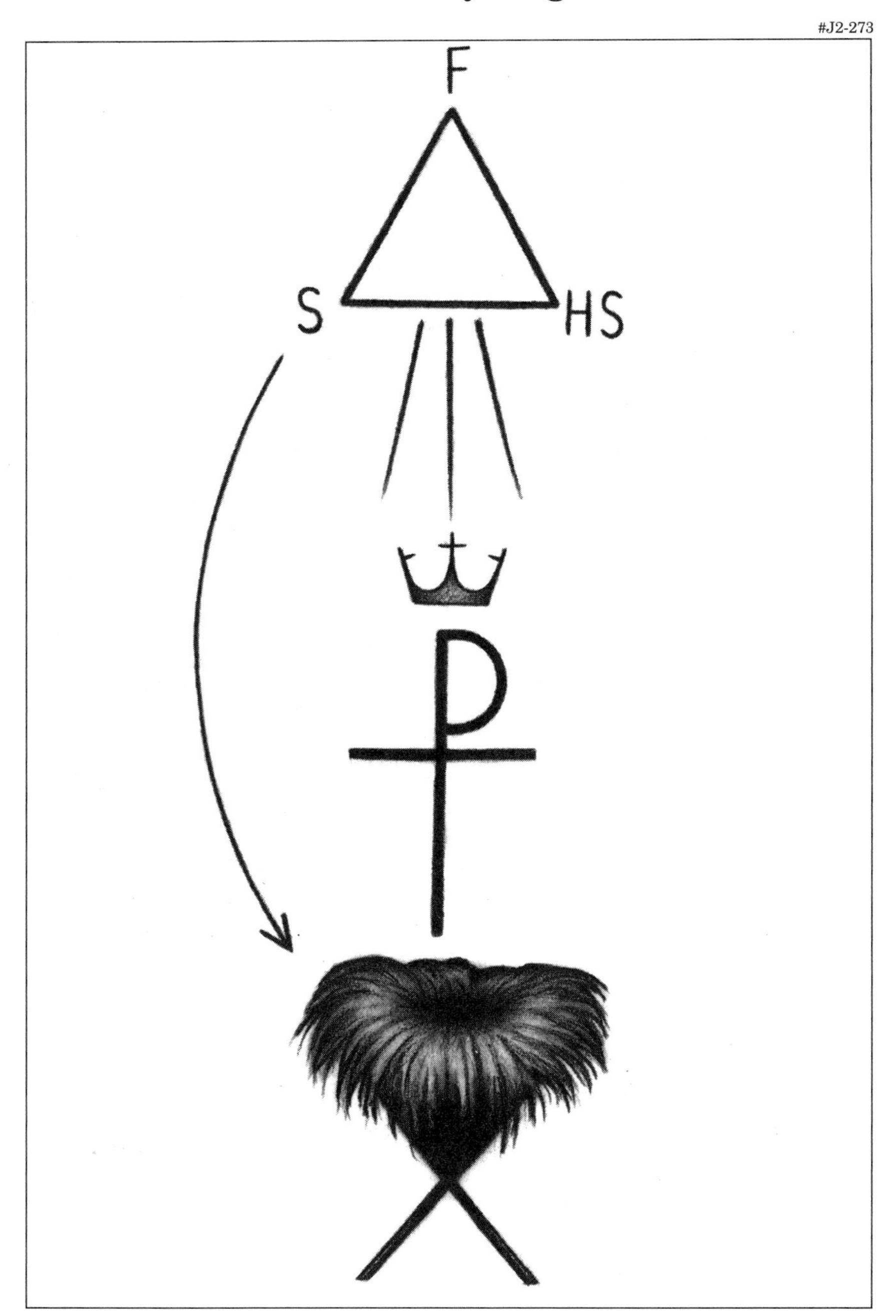

The Birth of Jesus. Jesus Christ is true God (triangle, S), Who became man and dwelt among us. Nine months after the message of the angel, Mary gave birth to her first-born Son in Bethlehem and laid Him in a manger. Christ (monogram) is the First-born of all Creation, exalted as Lord of all (crown).

Vatican Council II

In reality it is only in the mystery of the Word made flesh that the mystery of man truly becomes clear. For Adam, the first man, was a type of him who was to come, Christ the Lord, Christ the new Adam, in the very revelation of the mystery of the Father and of his love, fully reveals man to himself and brings to light his most high calling. *Gaudium et Spes, 22*

The sacred writings of the Old and New Testaments, as well as venerable tradition, show the role of the Mother of the Saviour in the plan of salvation in an ever clearer light and call our attention to it. *Lumen Gentium, 55*

The Father of mercies willed that the Incarnation should be preceded by assent on the part of the predestined mother, so that just as a woman had a share in bringing about death, so also a woman should contribute to life. *Lumen Gentium, 56*

#R2.3-12-2

But when the time had fully come, God sent forth his Son, born of woman. *(Galatians 4:4)*

Summary Prayer

Eternal Word of God, in the Incarnation You have brought to our eyes of faith a new and radiant vision of Your glory. In You we see God made visible. We recognize in You the revelation of God's love. Before all ages, You were predestined to be born in time. You have come to lift up all things to Yourself, restore unity to Creation, and lead mankind from exile into Your heavenly Kingdom.

We welcome You as Lord, the true light of the world. Bring us to eternal joy in the Kingdom of Heaven where You live and reign forever and ever. Amen.

Doctrine • Moral • Worship Exercise

(See Appendix A for answer key, questions 72-73.)

1. What does "Incarnation" mean?
2. Jesus lived among us to reveal to us what it means to be man. What transformation in your life do you think you have to make to pattern your life after Jesus' life as a human being?
3. The Angelus reminds us of the Incarnation, the greatest of God's works. Take a moment now to pray the Angelus with gratitude and reverence. Try to pray it three times daily.

Q. 74. Why did God the Son come into the world?

God the Son became incarnate and came into the world: (1) to bring us His own divine life; (2) to save us from sin; and (3) to renew the world.

1. God the Son came into the world to bring us His own divine life.

Born of the Virgin Mary, the Son of God truly became one of us. He was like us in all things except sin. Through the sin of our first parents, the human race lost God's life of grace. Because of His love for mankind, Jesus brought grace back to us by His life, Passion, Death, and Resurrection.

Sacred Scripture	**Catechism of the Catholic Church**
Q. 74. Mt 9:10-13; Rom 5:10-11; 1 Tim 1:12-17.	Q. 74. Paragraphs **456-460**.

For cross-references with Vatican II, Papal documents & other resources, see Family Wisdom Library on page 370.
For commentaries on each question with Cardinal Arinze, Sr. John Vianney and Fr. Straub (in Spanish), see Appendix C.

#S13-21-2

Through the sin of our first parents, the human race lost God's life of grace. Because of His love for mankind, Jesus brought grace back to us by His life, Passion, Death, and Resurrection.

2. God the Son came into the world to save us from sin.

By offering His life on the Cross for us, Jesus gave the highest of gifts to His Father. Thus, He redeemed the entire world. Our Lord's Passion and Death reveals to us the great evil of sin. It was sin that caused His great suffering and agonizing Death. But He took away our sins and made us free to serve God and to reach Heaven with the help of divine grace.

3. God the Son came into the world to renew the world.

Through the Catholic Church, with its truths and sacraments, we are able to keep a life of grace in our souls. With sanctifying grace we are united with God in this world and in Heaven. Through this grace, Jesus is for us the source of eternal life and Salvation; in this way He renews the world.

Sacred Scripture

For God so loved the world that he gave his only Son, that whoever believes in him should not perish but have eternal life. For God sent the Son into the world, not to condemn the world, but that the world might be saved through him. *John 3:16-17*

His divine power has granted to us all things that pertain to life and godliness, through the knowledge of him who called us to his own glory and excellence, by which he has granted to us his precious and very great promises, that through these you may escape from the corruption that is in the world because of passion, and become partakers of the divine nature. *2 Peter 1:3-4*

Catechism by Diagram

#C41-1

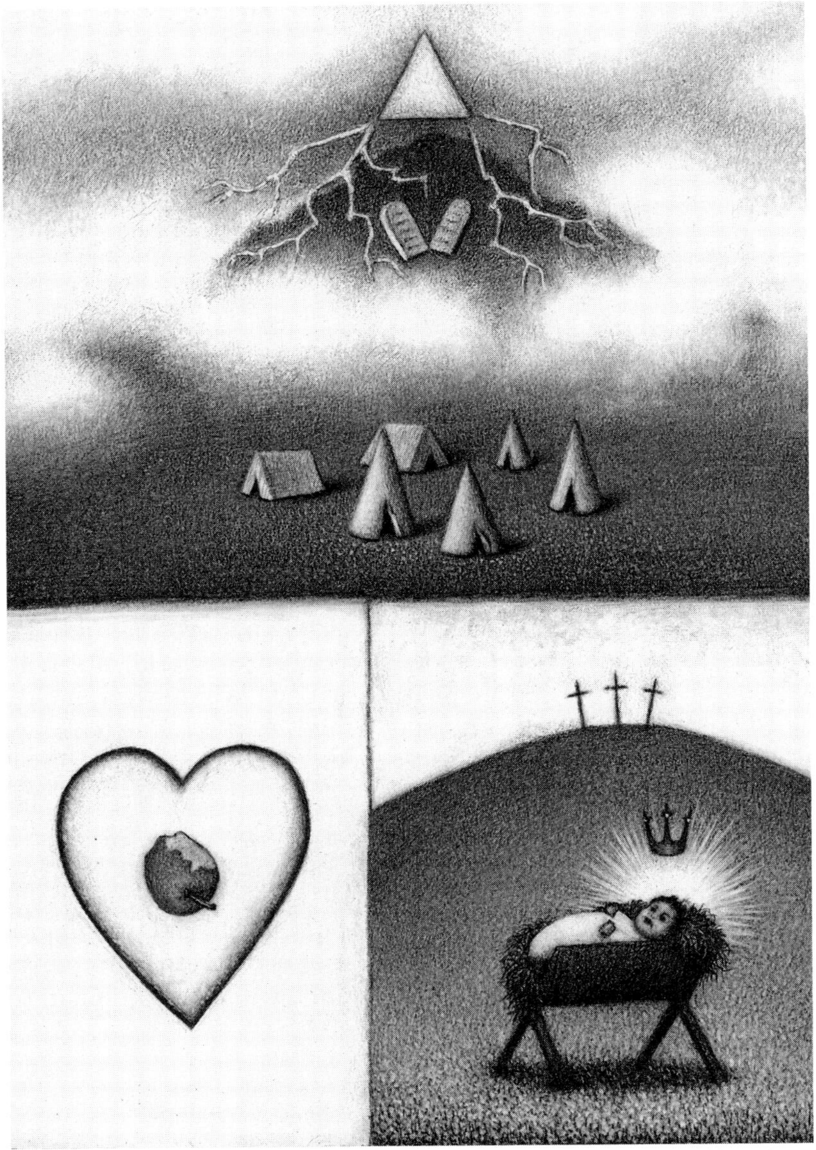

The Two Covenants. In the Old Testament, God revealed Himself as the one true God, making a covenant of commandments (tablets) with the Hebrew people (tents). Being subject to the effects of Original Sin (apple inside the heart), they were now given special assistance. Centuries later, the Son of God was made flesh, that He might make all men sharers in the divine nature and give His life as a ransom for all (Calvary). In this way, He established a new, universal and everlasting covenant, renewing the world.

Catechism of the Catholic Church

458 The Word became flesh *so that thus we might know God's love*: "In this the love of God was made manifest among us, that God sent his only Son into the world, so that we might live through him."[1] "For God so loved the world that he gave his only Son, that whoever believes in him should not perish but have eternal life."[2]

Vatican Council II

So the Son of God entered the world by means of a true incarnation that he might make men sharers in the divine nature; though rich, he was made poor for our sake, that by his poverty we might become rich (2 Cor. 8:9). The Son of man did not come to be served, but to serve and to give his life as a ransom for many, that is for all (cf. Mk. 10:45). *Missionary Activity, 3*

Through the Catholic Church, with its truths and sacraments, we are able to keep a life of grace in our souls. Through this grace, Jesus is for us the source of eternal life and Salvation.

Doctrine • Moral • Worship Exercise

(See Appendix A for answer key, question 74.)

1. In what way does Jesus renew the world?
2. One of the fruits of the coming of Jesus to the earth is the life of grace in our souls. On your part, how can you keep the life of grace in your soul?
3. Read and memorize John 3:16. What does this verse inspire you to do?

Chapter Summary Prayer

Jesus, divine Savior, we believe that You came to earth to bring to the world Your divine life, to save us from sin, and to make the world new again. We thank You for Your mercy and generosity.

When You came to us as man, You, the Son of God, scattered the darkness of this world, and filled it with Your glorious light. God of infinite goodness, scatter the darkness of sin and brighten our hearts with holiness. When You, the Divine Word, became man, earth was joined to Heaven. Give us Your peace and good will. Give us a foretaste of the joy that You will grant us when the fullness of Your glory has filled the earth.

Jesus, born of a virgin, in coming to us, You show the world the splendor of Your glory. Give us true faith and love to celebrate You properly Who are God made man. All glory be to You, to the Father, and to the Holy Spirit. Amen.

Thought Provokers

Please see Appendix B for the answers.

Q. 72: Why is the Incarnation regarded as the greatest of God's works?

Q. 73: As God made man, Jesus had a beginning and was given the name of Jesus. As God, He always was and is. Jesus is known by many titles. What are some of these titles?.

Q. 74: What do we mean when we say Jesus is the New Adam?

CHAPTER TWENTY

Jesus Is God

Q. 75. Is Jesus Christ true God?

Yes, Jesus Christ is true God because He is a divine Person having a divine nature.

Jesus Christ is the Divine Word of God made man. But He is only one Person, and that Person is the Second Person of the Holy Trinity.

#T3-25-2

Jesus Christ is true God because He is a divine Person having a divine nature.

Sacred Scripture

Behold, a virgin shall conceive and bear a son, and his name shall be called Emmanuel (which means, God with us). *Matthew 1:23*

Therefore the Lord himself will give you a sign. Behold, a young woman shall conceive and bear a son, and shall call his name Immanuel. *Isaiah 7:14*

Behold, your God will come with vengeance, with the recompense of God. He will come and save you. *Isaiah 35:4*

And we know that the Son of God has come and has given us understanding, to know him who is true; and we are in him who is true, in his Son Jesus Christ. This is the true God and eternal life. *1 John 5:20*

Sacred Scripture
Q. 75. Is 9:6; Mt 17:1-5; Mk 1:9-11; 2 Pet 1:16-18.

Catechism of the Catholic Church
Q. 75. Paragraphs **461-469**.

For cross-references with Vatican II, Papal documents & other resources, see Family Wisdom Library on page 370.
For commentaries on each question with Cardinal Arinze, Sr. John Vianney and Fr. Straub (in Spanish), see Appendix C.

#H1-230-2

God with us. *(Matthew 1:23)*

Catechism of the Catholic Church

468 After the Council of Chalcedon, some made of Christ's human nature a kind of personal subject. Against them, the fifth ecumenical council at Constantinople in 553 confessed that "there is but one *hypostasis* [or person], which is our Lord Jesus Christ, one of the Trinity."[1] Thus everything in Christ's human nature is to be attributed to his divine person as its proper subject, not only his miracles but also his sufferings and even his death: "He who was crucified in the flesh, our Lord Jesus Christ, is true God, Lord of glory, and *one of the Holy Trinity*."[2]

Vatican Council II

Jesus Christ was sent into the world as the true Mediator between God and men. Since he is God, all the fullness of the divine nature dwells in him bodily (Col. 2:9). *Missionary Activity, 3*

Summary Prayer

Lord Jesus Christ, we believe that You are the true God because You are God's only begotten Son. In You there is the fullness of divinity. You are the Divine Word of God made man. In You there is only one Person, the Second Person of the Blessed Trinity. May we give You glory now and forever. Amen.

Q. 76. How does the Nicene Creed express our faith in Christ's divinity?

Speaking of Christ's divinity, the Nicene Creed states that He is: "God from God, Light from Light, true God from true God, begotten not made, one in Being with the Father."

Catechism by Diagram

#J2-391

Declaration of Christ's Divinity. Left side: In God's only-begotten Son (monogram) is the fullness of divinity. At Jesus' baptism (water, shell), the Father spoke, "This is my beloved Son, with whom I am well pleased" (Mt 3:17). The Spirit of God descended like a dove and hovered over Him. Right side: When Jesus was transfigured on the mountain, the Father's voice was heard, "This is my beloved Son, with whom I am well pleased; listen to him" (Mt 17:5). Moses (tablets of the Law) and Elijah (scroll of the prophets) talked with Jesus. Middle: To Caiaphas, (C) Jesus (monogram) said, "You will see the Son of man seated at the right hand of Power, and coming on the clouds of heaven" (Mt 26:64). To Pilate (seat of judgement, symbol of law), Jesus said, "My kingship is not of this world" (Jn 18:36).

The principal teaching of the Catholic Church about Jesus Christ is that He is God made man. He is the God-man Whom we hear speaking to us in the Gospels and Whom we receive in the Holy Eucharist.

Catechism of the Catholic Church
Q. 76. Paragraphs 184-185, **465**.

For cross-references with Vatican II, Papal documents & other resources, see Family Wisdom Library on page 370.
For commentaries on each question with Cardinal Arinze, Sr. John Vianney and Fr. Straub (in Spanish), see Appendix C.

It is to Jesus with the Father and the Holy Spirit that we pray: "Glory be to the Father, and to the Son, and to the Holy Spirit."

Sacred Scripture

In the beginning was the Word, and the Word was with God, and the Word was God. He was in the beginning with God; all things were made through him, and without him was not anything made that was made. In him was life, and the life was the light of men. *John 1:1-4*

Catechism of the Catholic Church

242 Following this apostolic tradition, the Church confessed at the first ecumenical council at Nicaea (325) that the Son is "consubstantial" with the Father, that is, one only God with him.[1] The second ecumenical council, held at Constantinople in 381, kept this expression in its formulation of the Nicene Creed and confessed "the only-begotten Son of God, eternally begotten of the Father, light from light, true God from true God, begotten not made, consubstantial with the Father."[2]

Vatican Council II

This plan flows from "fountain-like love," the love of God the Father. As the principle without principle from whom the Son is generated and from whom the Holy Spirit proceeds through the Son. *Missionary Activity, 2*

Summary Prayer

Jesus, You are the way to God. By getting to know You, we meet God in human form and really see His love for us in action. Finding You, we reach the very presence of our Heavenly Father.

You brought to us a whole new life. This new life, which is sanctifying grace, is a participation in God's own life and is communicated to us by the Holy Spirit. Because You are the Son of God, You are able to give us a share in divine life and make us adopted children of God through the gift of the Holy Spirit Whom You give us.

To enlighten the world, You, the Divine Word, came to us as the Sun of Truth and Justice shining upon mankind. Illumine our eyes that we may discern Your glory in the many works of Your hand. May Your presence bring lasting light to the People of God that we may pray to You with deep faith.

"God from God, Light from Light, true God from true God, begotten not made, one in Being with the Father," may we love You forever. Amen.

Q. 77. Did Jesus say He was God?

Yes, Jesus said He was God. For instance, He said to the Jews: "I and the Father are one" (John 10:30), and "If God were your Father, you would love me, for I proceeded and came forth from God; I came not of my own accord, but he sent me... But you have not known him; I know him. If I said, I do not know him, I should be a liar like you; but I do know him and I keep his word... Truly, truly, I say to you, before Abraham was, I am" [i.e. Pure Existence having neither beginning nor ending, existing only in the eternal present] (John 8:42, 55, 58).

#R19.3-8

Jesus said He was God. For instance, He said to the Jews: "I and the Father are one" *(John 10:30).*

Men come to believe in God because He shows something of Himself to them. Catholics believe in what the Catholic Church teaches about Christ because they have the supernatural gift of faith. Thus, God the Son revealed Himself in what He said and did, how He lived with others, and by what He revealed of His thoughts and feelings. He revealed more of Himself than we can fully understand. Nevertheless, through faith and the virtue of love, we can understand a great deal about Him.

Sacred Scripture
Q. 77. Jn 14:1-11, 20:24-30.

Catechism of the Catholic Church
Q. 77. Paragraph 590.

For cross-references with Vatican II, Papal documents & other resources, see Family Wisdom Library on page 370.
For commentaries on each question with Cardinal Arinze, Sr. John Vianney and Fr. Straub (in Spanish), see Appendix C.

Jesus is the center of our Catholic faith. Everything that He said and did is important, because in Him we find God our Father and come to believe in Him. Jesus is our Way, our Truth, and our Life (cf. John 14:6).

When men had fallen in Adam, the eternal Father did not abandon them, but held out to them the means of salvation. *(Lumen Gentium, 2)*

Sacred Scripture

And this is eternal life, that they know thee the only true God, and Jesus Christ whom thou hast sent. *John 17:3*

Catechism of the Catholic Church

589 Jesus gave scandal above all when he identified his merciful conduct toward sinners with God's own attitude toward them.[1] He went so far as to hint that by sharing the table of sinners he was admitting them to the messianic banquet.[2] But it was most especially by forgiving sins that Jesus placed the religious authorities of Israel on the horns of a dilemma. Were they not entitled to demand in consternation, "Who can forgive sins but God alone?"[3] By forgiving sins Jesus either is blaspheming as a man who made himself God's equal or is speaking the truth, and his person really does make present and reveal God's name.[4]

Splendor of Truth

The light of God's face shines in all its beauty on the countenance of Jesus Christ, "the image of the invisible God" (Col 1:15), the "reflection of God's glory" (Heb 1:3), "full of grace and truth" (Jn 1:14). Christ is "the way, and the truth, and the life" (Jn 14:6). Consequently the decisive answer to every one of man's questions, his religious and moral questions in particular, is given by Jesus Christ, or rather is Jesus Christ himself. *(section 2)*

Vatican Council II

The eternal Father, in accordance with the utterly gratuitous and mysterious design of his wisdom and goodness, created the whole universe, and chose to raise up men to share in his own divine life; and when they had fallen in Adam, he did not abandon them, but at all times held out to them the means of salvation, bestowed in consideration of Christ, the Redeemer, "who is the image of the invisible God, the firstborn of every creature" (Col. 1:15). All the elect, before time began, the Father foreknew and also predestined to become conformed to the image of his Son, that he should be the firstborn among many brethren" (Rom. 8:29). *Lumen Gentium, 2*

Summary Prayer

Jesus, we firmly believe, by the gift of faith, that You are the Son of God. Your words and Your deeds also attest to Your divine nature. On the holy mountain of Tabor, You revealed Your glorified body in Your wondrous Transfiguration in the presence of Your disciples. You revealed Your glory to the disciples to strengthen them for the scandal of the Cross. You wanted to teach them, through the Law and the Prophets, that the long-awaited Christ had first to suffer before coming to the glory of the Resurrection.

Jesus, in You, the Father has renewed all things and has given us all a share in Your riches. Though Your nature was divine, You stripped Yourself of all glory, and by shedding Your Blood on the Cross, You brought Your peace to the world. Therefore, You are exalted above all Creation and have become the source of eternal life to all who serve You. With all the choirs of angels in Heaven, we proclaim Your glory and profess our faith in You as Peter did when he said: "You are the Christ, the Son of the living God!" (Matthew 16:16). All glory and honor be to You, to the Father, and to the Holy Spirit. Amen.

Doctrine • Moral • Worship Exercise

(See Appendix A for answer key, questions 75-77.)

1. Read John 1:1-4. What significant truth about Jesus is revealed through these verses?
2. Cite an instance in your life in which you manifested your faith in Jesus as Lord and God.
3. In silence, express your trust in Jesus' word that He is God.

Q. 78. During His Passion, did Jesus say He was God?

Yes, the night before He died, at the Last Supper, Jesus spoke as being equal to His Father when He said He had power to give eternal life.

#R19.4-9

At the Last Supper Jesus prayed, "Father, the hour has come; glorify thy Son that the Son may glorify thee, since thou hast given him power over all flesh, to give eternal life to all whom thou hast given him" *(John 17:1).*

Sacred Scripture

When Jesus had spoken these words, he lifted up his eyes to heaven and said, "Father, the hour has come; glorify thy Son that the Son may glorify thee, since thou hast given him power over all flesh, to give eternal life to all whom thou hast given him." *John 17:1-2*

Father, I desire that they also, whom thou hast given me, may be with me where I am, to behold my glory which thou hast given me in thy love for me before the foundation of the world. *John 17:24*

Catechism of the Catholic Church

591 Jesus asked the religious authorities of Jerusalem to believe in him because of the Father's works which he accomplished.[1] But such an act of faith must go through a mysterious death to self, for a new "birth from above" under the influence of divine grace.[2] Such a demand for conversion in the face of so surprising a fulfillment of the promises[3] allows one to understand the Sanhedrin's tragic misunderstanding of Jesus: they judged that he deserved

Catechism of the Catholic Church
Q. 78. Paragraph 610.

For cross-references with Vatican II, Papal documents & other resources, see Family Wisdom Library on page 370.
For commentaries on each question with Cardinal Arinze, Sr. John Vianney and Fr. Straub (in Spanish), see Appendix C.

the death sentence as a blasphemer.[4] The members of the Sanhedrin were thus acting at the same time out of "ignorance" and the "hardness" of their "unbelief."[5]

Vatican Council II

What has revealed the love of God among us is that the only-begotten Son of God has been sent by the Father into the world, so that, being made man, he might by his redemption of the entire human race give new life to it and unify it. Before offering himself up as a spotless victim upon the altar of the cross, he prayed to his Father for those who believe: "that all may be one, as you, Father, are in me, and I in you; I pray that they may be one in us, that the world may believe that you sent me" (Jn. 17:21). In his Church he instituted the wonderful sacrament of the Eucharist by which the unity of the Church is both signified and brought about. He gave his followers a new commandment to love one another, and promised the Spirit, their Advocate, who, as Lord and life-giver, should remain with them forever." *Ecumenism, 2*

Summary Prayer

Jesus, in the high-priestly prayer which You uttered at the Last Supper, You spoke to Your Father as Your equal. You prayed that He might glorify You. You prayed for Your disciples and for those who, through the teachings of these disciples, would believe in You, that they all might be one even as You and the Father are one.

Jesus, we believe that You are the Word through Whom God the Father made the universe. You are also the Savior He sent to redeem us. By the power of the Holy Spirit, You took on flesh and were born of the Virgin Mary. For our sake You opened Your arms on the Cross; You put an end to death and revealed the Resurrection. In this way, You fulfilled Your Father's will and won for Him a holy people.

Divine Redeemer, we believe that You are the Son of God and that we will see You "seated at the right hand of Power, and coming on the clouds of heaven" (Matthew 26:64). You have ascended into Heaven and have taken Your seat in majesty at the right hand of the Father. When You appear as Judge, may we be pleasing forever in Your sight. Amen.

Doctrine • Moral • Worship Exercise

(See Appendix A for answer key, question 78.)

1. The prayer of Jesus before His Passion shows that He is truly God. Write two verses from John 17 which help us to know that Jesus is God.
2. How can you show by your example that the Death of Jesus on the Cross has borne redemptive fruit in your life?
3. Meditate on this faith affirmation: Lord, by Your Cross and Resurrection, You have set us free, You are the Savior of the world.

Q. 79. Does the Catholic Church teach that Jesus is truly God?

Yes, the Catholic Church has always taught, and will always teach, that Jesus is truly God, existing from all eternity together with the Father and the Holy Spirit. It is He who, upholding the universe with His almighty power, came and "dwelt among us" (John 1:14), as the Word made flesh.

St. John said, "The life was made manifest, and we saw it, and testify to it, and proclaim to you the eternal life which was with the Father and was made manifest to us." (1 John 1:2), and "But these are written that you may believe that Jesus is the Christ, the Son of God, and that believing you may have life in his name" (John 20:31).

In the Prologue to St. John's Gospel, Jesus, the Word of God, is referred to as a divine Person, existing in the beginning with God the Father. St. John said: "In the beginning was the Word, and the Word was with God, and the Word was God...all things were made through him, and without him was not anything made that was made… And the Word became flesh and dwelt among us, full of grace and truth; we have beheld his glory, glory as of the only Son from the Father" (John 1:1, 3, 14).

Jesus the man, then, is also the eternal Word of God.

Catechism of the Catholic Church
Q. 79. Paragraph 464-469.

#T3-33-2

The Catholic Church has always taught, and will always teach, that Jesus is truly God, existing from all eternity together with the Father and the Holy Spirit.

Catechism of the Catholic Church

464 The unique and altogether singular event of the Incarnation of the Son of God does not mean that Jesus Christ is part God and part man, nor does it imply that he is the result of a confused mixture of the divine and the human. He became truly man while remaining truly God. Jesus Christ is true God and true man. During the first centuries, the Church had to defend and clarify this truth of faith against the heresies that falsified it.

Vatican Council II

Jesus Christ was sent into the world as the true Mediator between God and men. Since he is God, all the fullness of the divine nature dwells in him bodily (Col. 2:9). *Missionary Activity, 3*

Summary Prayer

Our Father in Heaven, You sent us Your only begotten Son, Your Word, when He took flesh from the Virgin Mary and became man. Give us the light of faith that we may always acknowledge Jesus as our God and our Redeemer. Open our hearts to receive His life, and increase our faith in Him. May we become more like Him and share in His life completely by living as He taught.

With gratitude, we adore His humanity, containing the human life He shared with us. May the power of His divinity help us answer His call to receive forgiveness and life. May we welcome Christ as our Redeemer, and meet Him with confidence when He comes to be our Judge.

May we share in the glory of His Incarnation, see Him in His heavenly Kingdom, and enjoy His presence forever.

You have shown men the splendor of Jesus Christ, our Light. We love Him as Lord, the true Light of the world.

May we come to live more fully the life we profess, and come to the glory of His Kingdom where He lives and reigns forever and ever. Amen.

Q. 80. Is there any further evidence in the New Testament pointing to Jesus as God?

There are several passages, apart from those already cited, in which Jesus' divinity is taught:

1. Expressing his faith in the Resurrection, St. Thomas cried out: "My Lord and my God!" (John 20:28).

#R4.1-11

Jesus' divinity is taught in the New Testament when St. Thomas, expressing his faith in the Resurrection, cried out: "My Lord and my God!" *(John 20:28).*

Catechism of the Catholic Church
Q. 80. Paragraphs 461, **590**, 635, 1130.

For cross-references with Vatican II, Papal documents & other resources, see Family Wisdom Library on page 370.
For commentaries on each question with Cardinal Arinze, Sr. John Vianney and Fr. Straub (in Spanish), see Appendix C.

2. God the Father, speaking to Christ, addresses Him as God in the following words: "Of the Son he says, 'Thy throne, O God, is for ever and ever!'" (Hebrews 1:8).

3. "To them [i.e., belonging to the Israelites] belong the patriarchs, and of their race, according to the flesh, is the Christ, who is God over all, blessed for ever. Amen" (Romans 9:5).

#J2-537

Very often in the Gospels people address Jesus as "Lord." This title testifies to the respect and trust of those who approach him for help and healing.
(Catechism of the Catholic Church, 448)

4. "Have this mind among yourselves, which was in Christ Jesus, who, though he was in the form of God, did not count equality with God a thing to be grasped" (Philippians 2:5-6).

5. Christian life is lived in eager anticipation, "awaiting our blessed hope, the appearing of the glory of our great God and Savior Jesus Christ" (Titus 2:13; see also 2 Peter 1:1).

6. Most frequently the title "Lord" is given to Jesus. He is called this because His divinity is acknowledged. "That at the name of Jesus every knee should bow, in heaven and on earth and under the earth, and every tongue confess that Jesus Christ is Lord, to the glory of God the Father" (Philippians 2:10-11).

7. Jesus also applies terms to Himself which are proper to God, such as "I am," already noted in question 77. This refers to God's eternal existence and being. "Before Abraham was, I am" (John 8:58; cf. Exodus 3:14).

Catechism of the Catholic Church

448 Very often in the Gospels people address Jesus as "Lord." This title testifies to the respect and trust of those who approach him for help and healing.[1] At the prompting of the Holy Spirit, "Lord" expresses the recognition of the divine mystery of Jesus.[2] In the encounter with the risen Jesus, this title becomes adoration: "My Lord and my God!" It thus takes on a connotation of love and affection that remains proper to the Christian tradition: "It is the Lord!"[3]

449 By attributing to Jesus the divine title "Lord," the first confessions of the Church's faith affirm from the beginning that the power, honor, and glory due to God the Father are due also to Jesus, because "he was in the form of God,"[1] and the Father manifested the sovereignty of Jesus by raising him from the dead and exalting him into his glory.[2]

Summary Prayer

Father, flood our hearts with the Gospel of Christ, Your matchless image, and transform us more and more into His very likeness, that like Jesus and through Jesus we may always give You glory. Amen.

Q. 81. How does the New Testament portray Jesus?

Throughout the New Testament, Jesus is portrayed as divine. For instance, He is described as the "Word made flesh" that is, God Who assumed human nature. He is also spoken of as Creator. St. John said: "All things were made through him" (John 1:3).

St. Paul wrote, "For in him all things were created, in heaven and on earth, visible and invisible... all things were created through him and for him. He is before all things, and in him all things hold together" (Colossians 1:16-17).

Salvation and forgiveness are found only in God. Thus Jesus is called the Savior of all, Who personally forgives sins by His own authority (cf. Luke 5:10-25).

Catechism of the Catholic Church

151 For a Christian, believing in God cannot be separated from believing in the One he sent, his "beloved Son," in whom the Father is "well pleased"; God tells us to listen to him.[1] The Lord himself said to his disciples: "Believe in God, believe also in me."[2] We can believe in Jesus Christ because he is himself God, the Word made flesh: "No one has ever seen God; the only Son, who is in the bosom of the Father, he has made him known."[3] Because he "has seen the Father," Jesus Christ is the only one who knows him and can reveal him.[4]

Catechism of the Catholic Church
Q. 81. Paragraphs 291.

For cross-references with Vatican II, Papal documents & other resources, see Family Wisdom Library on page 370.
For commentaries on each question with Cardinal Arinze, Sr. John Vianney and Fr. Straub (in Spanish), see Appendix C.

#J2-372

Jesus is called the Savior of all, Who personally forgives sins by His own authority *(cf. Luke 5:17-25)*.

#R2.4-5

Jesus is described as the "Word made flesh" that is, God Who assumed human nature.

Vatican Council II

It pleased God, in his goodness and wisdom, to reveal himself and to make known the mystery of his will (cf. Eph. 1:9). His will was that men should have access to the Father, through Christ, the Word made flesh, in the Holy Spirit, and thus become sharers in the divine nature (cf. Eph. 2:18; 2 Pet. 1:4). By this revelation, then, the invisible God (cf. Col. 1:15; 1 Tim. 1:17), from the fullness of his love, addresses men as his friends (cf. Ex. 33:11; Jn. 15:14-15), and moves among them (cf. Bar. 3:38), in order to invite and receive them into his own company. *Dei Verbum, 2*

Summary Prayer

God of love, Father of all, the darkness that covered the earth has given way to the bright dawn of Your Word made flesh. Make us followers of this Light. Make us faithful to Your Word. We ask this in His most powerful and holy Name. Amen.

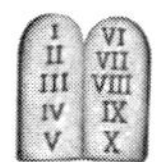

Doctrine • Moral • Worship Exercise

(See Appendix A for answer key, questions 79-81.)

1. Cite two passages from the New Testament which show that Jesus is God.
2. In the Angelus we pray, "The Word was made flesh and dwelt among us." What has our Faith taught us about

the meaning of these words, and what do they mean for you personally?

3. If you have a friend who does not believe that Jesus is God, which of your actions in your daily life help him to know that you are a Christian?

#N1.1-18-2

"For in him all things were created, in heaven and on earth, visible and invisible... all things were created through him and for him. He is before all things, and in him all things hold together" *(Colossians 1:16-17).*

Chapter Summary Prayer

Heavenly Father, keep before us the wisdom and love You have revealed in Your Son. Help us to be like Him in our thoughts, words, and deeds. Open our eyes to His deeds, and our ears to the sound of His words in the Gospel, so that all the acts of our lives may increase our sharing in the life He has offered us.

Form us in the likeness of Your Son and deepen His life within us. Help us to live His example of love.

Help us to be like Christ, Your Son, Who loved the world and died for our Salvation. Inspire us by His love, and guide us by His example. Change our selfishness into self-giving, that we may imitate His sacrifice of love.

May we always remain one with Jesus. Give us the grace to follow Him more faithfully so that we may come to the joy of His Kingdom forever and ever. Amen.

Thought Provokers

Please see Appendix B for the answers.

Q. 75: Was there ever a time that Jesus was not fully divine? Explain your answer.

Q. 76: "God from God, Light from Light, true God from true God, begotten not made, of one substance with the Father." What basic truth is the Nicene Creed conveying by these words?

Q. 77: What evidence is there that Jesus is God?

Q. 78: If, contrary to fact, Jesus were only a man, what effect would His Passion have on mankind?

Q. 79: In the New Testament, Jesus is referred to as "Our Lord Jesus Christ" (cf. Galatians 6:18), and we also find the expression, "Jesus Christ is Lord" (Philippians 2:11). What precisely does the title "Lord" mean in these passages?

Q. 80: One of the clearest passages in the Bible indicating Jesus the man is also God is found in John 20:28. In this passage, St. Thomas the Apostle exclaims to the Risen Jesus, "My Lord and my God." But, in fact, Thomas, having just been invited by Our Lord to probe His Wounds, became convinced only of the fact that Jesus was no phantom. How did this incident lead him to further believe in Jesus' divinity?

Q. 81: Some claim Jesus was only a moral teacher, that is, a teacher much like Confucius or the Buddha who taught their followers how to lead good lives. But what, in fact, does the New Testament teach us about Jesus to indicate that He was much more than a moral teacher?

By Heart Catechism and Scripture Review™

The "By Heart Catechism and Scripture Review" lists a selected number of questions and Scripture references from "The Apostolate's Family Catechism" to make memorization easier. Q = Question, SR = Scripture Reference

Q. 73. What does the Incarnation mean? The Incarnation means that the Second Person of the Holy Trinity became a man.

Q. 74. Why did God the Son come into the world? God the Son came into the world (1) to give us a share in His own life, (2) to save us from sin, and (3) to renew the world.

Q. 75. Is Jesus Christ true God? Yes, Jesus is true God because He is the Second Person of the Holy Trinity and so possesses a divine nature.

SR 76 John 1:1–4

In the beginning was the Word, and the Word was with God, and the Word was God. He was in the beginning with God; all things were made through him, and without him was not anything made that was made. In him was life, and the life was the light of men.

Q. 77. Did Jesus say that He was God? Yes, Jesus said that He was God, for example, He said, "I and the Father are one" (John 10:30).

SR 81 Colossians 1:16-17

For in him all things were created, in heaven and on earth, visible and invisible...all things were created through him and for him. He is before all things, and in him all things hold together.

#J2-351-2

Jesus said, “I am the good shepherd... My sheep...follow me, and I give them eternal life... and no one shall snatch them out of my hand” *(John 10:11, 27-28).*

Jesus Is True Man and Our Redeemer

#J2-310-2

He worked with human hands, he thought with a human mind. He acted with a human will, and with a human heart he loved. *(Gaudium et Spes, 22)*

CHAPTER TWENTY-ONE

Jesus Is True Man

Q. 82. Is Jesus Christ true man?

Jesus, the Son of God, became a real man, having real flesh, a human body and soul.

Jesus is a man just as we are, with the exception of sin. Jesus felt the joys and sorrows and the pleasures and pains that we feel as human beings. As a man, Jesus had a human mind, a human will, and a physical, mortal body.

#H1-232-2

Christ possesses two wills and two natural operations, divine and human. *(Catechism of the Catholic Church, 475)*

Jesus Christ is also true God, Who became man and dwelt among us. St. John says, "And the Word became flesh [i.e., the Incarnation] and dwelt among us" (John 1:14).

The ancient Fathers of the Church proclaimed that what Christ took up was our entire human nature, though without our sin. He was directly conceived by the Holy Spirit in the womb of Mary and was born in the normal course of events. Because of this extraordinary

Catechism of the Catholic Church
Q. 82. Paragraphs **464-470, 476, 478.**

For cross-references with Vatican II, Papal documents & other resources, see Family Wisdom Library on page 370.
For commentaries on each question with Cardinal Arinze, Sr. John Vianney and Fr. Straub (in Spanish), see Appendix C.

action of God, Mary is called the Blessed Virgin. Christ had no human father. Joseph was Mary's husband, and acted as virgin father to Jesus during His childhood.

#J2-553

Jesus is a man just as we are, with the exception of sin. Jesus felt the joys and sorrows and the pleasures and pains that we feel as human beings.

The greatest proof of God's goodness and love toward us is His gift of His only beloved Son. All love tends toward that which it loves. Jesus, the Son of God, loved man, therefore, He became man. Infinite love and mercy caused Him to leave the Kingdom of eternal bliss; to descend from the throne of His majesty, power and glory; to become a helpless child; to suffer and to die for us, that we might live forever in Heaven. In the crib we see the love of God, as He humbles Himself, so low as to beg the love of our hearts. When He was only forty days old, Mary brought Him to the Temple to offer Him to God as the Victim for our Redemption.

Sacred Scripture

The child to be born will be called holy, the Son of God. *Luke 1:35*

But the free gift is not like the trespass. For if many died through one man's trespass, much more have the grace of God and the free gift in the grace of that one man Jesus Christ abounded for many. *Romans 5:15*

The light shines in darkness, and the darkness has not overcome it. There was a man sent from God, whose name was John. He came for testimony, to bear witness to the light, that all might believe through him. He was not the light, but came to bear witness to the light. The true light that enlightens every man was coming into the world. He was in the world, and the world was made through him, yet the world knew him not. He came to his own home, and his own people received him not. But to all who received him, who believed in his name, he gave power to become children of God; who were born, not of blood nor of the will of the flesh nor of the will of man, but of God.

And the Word became flesh and dwelt among us, full of grace and truth; we have beheld his glory, glory as of the only Son from the Father. (John bore witness to him, and cried, "This was he of whom I said, 'He who comes after me ranks before me, for he was before me.'") And from his fullness have we all received, grace upon grace. For the law was given through Moses; grace and truth came through Jesus Christ. No one has ever seen God; the only Son, who is in the bosom of the Father, he has made him known. *John 1:5-18*

Catechism of the Catholic Church

475 Similarly, at the sixth ecumenical council, Constantinople III in 681, the Church confessed that Christ possesses two wills and two natural operations, divine and human. They are not opposed to each other, but cooperate in such a way that the Word made flesh willed humanly in obedience to his Father all that he had decided divinely with the Father and the Holy Spirit for our salvation.[1] Christ's human will "does not resist or oppose but rather submits to his divine and almighty will."[2]

#H1-231-2

Joseph was Mary's husband, and acted as virgin father to Jesus during His childhood.

Vatican Council II

For, by his incarnation, he, the son of God, has in a certain way united himself with each man. He worked with human hands, he thought with a human mind. He acted with a human will, and with a human heart he loved. Born of the Virgin Mary, he has truly been made one of us, like to us in all things except sin. *Gaudium et Spes, 22*

Summary Prayer

Jesus, we believe that You are true man. You, the Son of God, became a real man, having real flesh, a human body and soul. With gratitude we recall Your humanity, the life You share with the sons of men. You felt the joys and sorrows that we feel as human beings. You took our entire human nature, though without sin, and lived among us. Infinite love and mercy caused You to come to us as a helpless child, and to suffer and die for us, that we might have eternal life.

Jesus, may we, who celebrate Your coming as man, share more fully in Your divine life. May the power of Your divinity help us answer Your call to receive forgiveness and life.

Divine Word become man, born of the Virgin Mary, Who humbled Yourself to share our human nature, may we come to share increasingly Your divinity.

Fill our hearts with Your love. Lead us through Your suffering and Death to the glory of Your Resurrection. When You come again in glory, reward us with eternal life. May we meet You with confidence when You come to be our Judge. In Your coming, You gave us a new vision of Your glory. You were born of the Virgin Mary and came to share our life. May we come to share Your eternal life in the glory of Your Kingdom. Amen.

Doctrine • Moral • Worship Exercise

(See Appendix A for answer key, question 82.)

1. How is Jesus a true man?
2. By becoming man, Jesus proved His love for us. Think of situations in your life in which you can love Jesus in return.
3. Express in prayer your faith that Jesus enlightens and strengthens us so that we may resist every temptation that comes our way.

Q. 83. In what ways did Jesus show His concern for us?

Jesus showed His divine concern for us by means of His human nature. In His humanity we see God's love for man. We cannot see God, but since God sent His divine Son to live among us and to save us by His Death on the Cross, we can see how much God really loves us. During Jesus' public ministry, He worked many miracles to help people.

#R19.3-2

Jesus loved everyone and spent His life trying to help them. He traveled all over Israel, teaching the people about His Father, His heavenly Kingdom, and the need for repentance.

Jesus loved everyone and spent His life trying to help them in their need, even those who opposed Him. He traveled all over Israel, teaching the people about His Father, His heavenly Kingdom, and the need for repentance. He also taught about the necessity of loving God with one's whole heart, soul, and mind, and of loving one's neighbor as one's self. He loved especially the poor, the sick, and the troubled. Jesus loved sinners and forgave their sins. He offered His life to save all mankind.

Sacred Scripture

For in him all the fullness of God was pleased to dwell, and through him to reconcile to himself all things, whether on earth or in heaven, making peace by the blood of his cross. And you, who once were estranged and hostile in

Sacred Scripture
Q. 83. Jn 3:16-17; Rom 5:6-8.

Catechism of the Catholic Church
Q. 83. Paragraphs **478, 595-617**.

For cross-references with Vatican II, Papal documents & other resources, see Family Wisdom Library on page 370.
For commentaries on each question with Cardinal Arinze, Sr. John Vianney and Fr. Straub (in Spanish), see Appendix C.

mind, doing evil deeds, he has now reconciled in his body of flesh by his death, in order to present you holy and blameless and irreproachable before him. *Colossians 1:19-22*

And Jesus went about all the cities and villages, teaching in their synagogues and preaching the gospel of the kingdom, and healing every disease and every infirmity. When he saw the crowds, he had compassion for them, because they were harassed and helpless, like sheep without a shepherd. *Matthew 9:35-36*

Catechism of the Catholic Church

607 The desire to embrace his Father's plan of redeeming love inspired Jesus' whole life,[1] for his redemptive passion was the very reason for his Incarnation. And so he asked, "And what shall I say? 'Father, save me from this hour'? No, for this purpose I have come to this hour."[2] And again, "Shall I not drink the cup which the Father has given me?"[3] From the cross, just before "It is finished," he said, "I thirst."[4]

#R19.3-4

During Jesus' public ministry, He worked many miracles to help people, such as raising Lazurus from the dead.

Vatican Council II

God sent his Son, whom he appointed heir of all things (cf. Heb. 1:2), that he might be teacher, king and priest of all, the head of the new and universal People of God's sons. *Lumen Gentium, 13*

In assuming human nature he [Christ] has united to himself all humanity in a supernatural solidarity which makes of it one single family. He has made charity the distinguishing mark of his disciples, in the words: "By this will all men know you are my disciples, by the love you bear one another" (Jn. 13:35). *Lay People, 8*

Catechism by Diagram

#M8-7

"He is risen."
"Receive sight."
"Be open!"
"He spoke."
"Walk!"
"Rise!"
"Depart!"
"Be still!"
A Ω

The Miracles of Jesus. By becoming man, Jesus reached out to all. For our benefit He worked many miracles. He gave sight to the blind, hearing to the deaf, speech to the dumb, health to the sick, life to the dead, freedom to those possessed of the devil, calmness to the sea. His greatest miracle was His own Resurrection from the dead.

Summary Prayer

Lord Jesus, in Your concern for people during Your public life on earth, we see both the divine and human love for man. We see this love especially in Your Passion and Death. In the Gospels we read of Your tender acts of compassion for people. You loved the poor, the sick, the sinners, and children. That is why You could say "Come to me, all who labor and are heavy laden, and I will give you rest. Take my yoke upon you, and learn from me; for I am gentle and lowly in heart, and you will find rest for your souls" (Matthew 11:28-29). Please, Jesus, help us in our needs. Amen.

#J2-315-2

Jesus loved especially the poor, the sick, and the troubled. He offered His life to save all mankind.

Doctrine • Moral • Worship Exercise

(See Appendix A for answer key, question 83.)

1. As a true human being, Jesus has shown His concern for us in many ways. What are some of the ways?
2. Have you experienced Jesus' concern in your life? List the things that He has done for you.
3. Through your actions, how can you thank Jesus for His concern for you?

Chapter Summary Prayer

Savior of mankind, You loved the children of the lands You walked, and You enriched them with the witness of justice and truth. You lived and died that we might be reborn in the Spirit and be filled with love of all men. You came to earth to relieve the pain of our exile; You took our natural limitations as Your own. Uphold us when our hearts grow faint. May we receive forgiveness and mercy through Your coming.

Lord Jesus, our Savior and our God, give us always the water of life to drink, the free gift of the Spirit flowing from Your Sacred Heart, for You are all good and You love mankind. We glorify You, and Your eternal Father, and Your life-giving Spirit.

Lord Jesus Christ, in virtue of Your saving passover from death to life, pour Your Holy Spirit into our hearts and fill us with awe and reverence for You, and love and compassion for our neighbor, for Yours is the power and the glory forever and ever. Amen.

Thought Provokers

Please see Appendix B for the answers.

Q. 82: Today many people have difficulty believing Jesus is divine. On the other hand, during the first centuries of the Church's existence, there were many who had difficulty believing Jesus was a true man. Why, during this period, was His humanity questioned and denied?

Q. 83: Our deliberate sins, especially our mortal sins, indicate our rejection of God's will. Yet, in spite of Jesus' full knowledge of this rejection, He assumed human nature so that we could enjoy true happiness both in this life and in the next. Why, in spite of our repeated rejections of His will, do you think He voluntarily suffered for us by accepting cruel scourging and an agonizing Crucifixion?

#J2-359

The Son of God became man in order to be our Savior and Redeemer.
God the Father sent His Son to free man from the power of Satan
and to make peace between God and man.

CHAPTER TWENTY-TWO

Jesus Our Savior and Redeemer

Q. 84. Why did the Son of God become man?

The Son of God became man in order to be our Savior and Redeemer. God the Father sent His Son to free man from the power of Satan and to make peace between God and man. To do this Jesus became man, to preach His truth about the Kingdom of His Father.

#R3.4-5

By His freely offered sacrificial Death on the Cross, Jesus became our Savior.

Jesus continued preaching even though the religious leaders of the Jewish people were trying to harm Him. They finally arranged to have Him put to death by the Romans because He claimed to be God. By His freely offered sacrificial Death on the Cross, Jesus became our Savior.

Sacred Scripture

"The Spirit of the Lord is upon me, because he has anointed me to preach good news to the poor. He has sent me to proclaim release to the captives and recovering of sight to the blind, to set at liberty those who are oppressed, to proclaim the acceptable year of the Lord." And he closed the book, and gave

Catechism of the Catholic Church
Q. 84. Paragraphs **456-460**.

For cross-references with Vatican II, Papal documents & other resources, see Family Wisdom Library on page 370.
For commentaries on each question with Cardinal Arinze, Sr. John Vianney and Fr. Straub (in Spanish), see Appendix C.

it back to the attendant, and sat down; and the eyes of all in the synagogue were fixed on him. And he began to say to them, "Today this scripture has been fulfilled in your hearing." *Luke 4:18-21*

He was in the world, and the world was made through him, yet the world knew him not. He came to his own home, and his own people received him not. But to all who received him, who believed in his name, he gave power to become children of God; who were born, not of blood nor of the will of the flesh nor of the will of man, but of God. *John 1:10-13*

For I through the law died to the law, that I might live to God. I have been crucified with Christ; it is no longer I who live, but Christ who lives in me; and the life I now live in the flesh I live by faith in the Son of God, who loved me and gave himself for me. *Galatians 2:19-20*

For to this you have been called, because Christ also suffered for you, leaving you an example, that you should follow in his steps. *1 Peter 2:21*

#J2-368

For to this you have been called, because Christ also suffered for you, leaving you an example, that you should follow in his steps. *(1 Peter 2:21)*

Catechism of the Catholic Church

608 After agreeing to baptize him along with the sinners, John the Baptist looked at Jesus and pointed him out as the "Lamb of God, who takes away the sin of the world."[1] By doing so, he reveals that Jesus is at the same time the suffering Servant who silently allows himself to be led to the slaughter and who bears the sin of the multitudes, and also the Paschal Lamb, the symbol of Israel's redemption at the first Passover.[2] Christ's whole life expresses his mission: "to serve and to give his life as a ransom for many."[3]

Splendor of Truth

Called to salvation through faith in Jesus Christ, "the true light that enlightens everyone" (Jn 1:9), people become "light in the Lord" and "children of light" (Eph 5:8), and are made holy by "obedience to the truth" (1 Pet 1:22). *(section 1)*

#R19.5-8

Christ's whole life expresses his mission: "to serve and to give his life as a ransom for many." *(Catechism of the Catholic Church, 608)*

Vatican Council II

After God had spoken many times and in various ways through the prophets, "in these last days he has spoken to us by a Son" (Hebrews 1:1-2). For he sent his Son, the eternal Word who enlightens all men, to dwell among men and to tell them about the inner life of God. *Dei Verbum, 4*

Summary Prayer

Jesus, we acknowledge You as our Savior and Redeemer because, as God made man, You preached the Gospel of the Kingdom of God and gave Yourself up to death out of love for Your Father and for us. You freed all creatures from the slavery of sin, and You made peace between God and man. We thank You for Your love for all mankind, and for each and every one of us in particular. We, too, wish to give our lives to You in faithful service. All glory and honor be to the Father, to the Son, and to the Holy Spirit forever and ever. Amen.

Q. 85. What do we mean when we say that Jesus is our Savior?

Jesus is our Savior because through Him all mankind can be saved from the slavery of sin and be saved for everlasting life with God.

St. Paul refers to sin as a slavery. Jesus Christ is our Savior because He saved us from sin. St. Paul said, "For you did not receive the spirit of slavery to fall back into fear, but you have received the spirit of sonship. When we cry, 'Abba! Father!' it is the Spirit himself bearing witness with our spirit that we are children of God" (Romans 8:15-16), and "Stand fast therefore, and do not submit again to a yoke of slavery" (Galatians 5:1).

#L3-17-2

Jesus is our Savior because through Him all mankind can be saved from the slavery of sin and be saved for everlasting life with God.

Sacred Scripture

For the creation waits with eager longing for the revealing of the sons of God; for the creation was subjected to futility, not of its own will but by the will of him who subjected it in hope; because the creation itself will be set free from its bondage to decay and obtain the glorious liberty of the children of God. *Romans 8:19-21*

So Jesus again said to them, "...I am the door; if any one enters by me, he will be saved, and will go in and out and find pasture... I came that they may have life, and have it abundantly. I am the good shepherd. The good shepherd lays down his life for the sheep." *John 10:7-11*

Catechism of the Catholic Church
Q. 85. Paragraphs 421, 601, 605-617, 714.

For cross-references with Vatican II, Papal documents & other resources, see Family Wisdom Library on page 370.
For commentaries on each question with Cardinal Arinze, Sr. John Vianney and Fr. Straub (in Spanish), see Appendix C.

#R3.4-10

Jesus said, "I am the good shepherd. The good shepherd lays down his life for the sheep" *(John 10:11).*

Catechism of the Catholic Church

549 By freeing some individuals from the earthly evils of hunger, injustice, illness, and death,[1] Jesus performed messianic signs. Nevertheless he did not come to abolish all evils here below,[2] but to free men from the gravest slavery, sin, which thwarts them in their vocation as God's sons and causes all forms of human bondage.[3]

Vatican Council II

However, in order to establish a relationship of peace and communion with himself, and in order to bring about brotherly union among men, and they [sic] sinners, God decided to enter into the history of mankind in a new and definitive manner, by sending his own Son in human flesh, so that through him he might snatch men from the power of darkness and of Satan (cf. Col. 1:13; Acts 10:38). *Missionary Activity, 3*

Through preaching and the celebration of the sacraments, of which the holy Eucharist is the center and summit, missionary activity makes Christ present, he who is the author of salvation. *Missionary Activity, 9*

Summary Prayer

Praise to You, our Savior. By Your Death You have opened for us the way of Salvation. Guide Your people to walk in Your ways. Teach them to see Your Passion in their sufferings, and to show to others Your power to save. To You be all honor and glory now and forever. Amen.

Q. 86. Is there any other Savior besides Jesus?

There is no Salvation in anyone but Jesus Christ, nor has there ever been, nor will there ever be.

By his own power no one is freed from the slavery of sin. Scripture says that there is no Salvation in anyone else but Christ Jesus (cf. Acts 4:12). Until Jesus died upon the Cross and paid the price for man's sin, no human soul could enter Heaven.

#J2-311-2

Until Jesus died upon the Cross and paid the price for man's sin, no human soul could enter Heaven.

St. Paul says, "God was in Christ reconciling the world to himself, not counting their trespasses against them, and entrusting to us the message of reconciliation" (2 Corinthians 5:19).

The mystery of Christ appears in the history of men and of the world—a history subject to sin—not only as the mystery of the Incarnation, but also as the mystery of Salvation and redemption. God the Father so loved sinners that He gave His Son, reconciling the world to Himself. Christ, in His boundless love, freely underwent His Passion and Death because of the sins of all men, so that all might attain Salvation.

Our Lord's life shows God's own love for us because all that He said and did, His whole life and Death, was for the sake of others. He spent His life teaching men the truth about His Father and about

Sacred Scripture
Q. 86. Jn 1:29; Rom 5:19.

Catechism of the Catholic Church
Q. 86. Paragraph 452.

For cross-references with Vatican II, Papal documents & other resources, see Family Wisdom Library on page 370.
For commentaries on each question with Cardinal Arinze, Sr. John Vianney and Fr. Straub (in Spanish), see Appendix C.

themselves; He shared their lives and suffering, and He healed their illnesses. He did all this out of love for them and for His Father, Who called Him to this service. The life of Jesus shows us in a human way that God's life is a life of love. Father, Son, and Holy Spirit are forever giving Themselves to each other. Having received from Jesus a perfect human life of love, the Father now gives His own life to people who turn to Him in faith.

Sacred Scripture

I am the way, and the truth, and the life; no one comes to the Father, but by me. If you had known me, you would have known my Father also, henceforth you know him and have seen him. *John 14:6-7*

We have an advocate with the Father, Jesus Christ the righteous; and he is the expiation for our sins, and not for ours only but also for the sins of the whole world. *1 John 2:1-2*

Catechism of the Catholic Church

430 Jesus means in Hebrew: "God saves." At the annunciation, the angel Gabriel gave him the name Jesus as his proper name, which expresses both his identity and his mission.[1] Since God alone can forgive sins, it is God who, in Jesus his eternal Son made man, "will save his people from their sins."[2] In Jesus, God recapitulates all of his history of salvation on behalf of men.

Vatican Council II

Christ, whom the Father sanctified or consecrated and sent into the world, "gave himself for us to redeem us from all iniquity and to purify for himself a people of his own who are zealous for good deeds" (Tit. 2:14), and in this way through his passion entered into his glory. *Priests, 12*

#E4.4-11

Having received from Jesus a perfect human life of love, the Father now gives His own life to people who turn to Him in faith.

Catechism by Diagram

#J2-436

Salvation through Christ. God (triangle) saved all men (man drowning) through His Son (monogram), Who came to earth to suffer and die for our sins. He brings us Salvation through His Church (boat), especially through the sacraments (lifesaver), to save us from eternal death. In the Church, Christ is the source of grace and eternal life.

Summary Prayer

Jesus, we believe that there is no Salvation in anyone but You. You are the Word through Whom God made the universe; You are the Savior He sent to redeem us. By the power of the Holy Spirit, You took flesh and were born of the Virgin Mary. For our sake You opened Your arms on the Cross; You put an end to death and revealed the Resurrection. In this You fulfilled Your Father's will and won for Him a holy people.

Savior of mankind, You destroyed death, and by rising again, restored life. Sanctify Your people, redeemed by Your blood. Give us a greater share in Your Passion through a deeper spirit of repentance, so that we may share the glory of Your Resurrection.

As You offered Your body on the Cross, Your perfect sacrifice fulfilled all others. As You gave Yourself into the hands of Your heavenly Father for our Salvation, You showed Yourself to be the Priest and the Lamb of Sacrifice. Sustain us by Your love, for You offered Yourself as a perfect sacrifice on the Cross, and You are Lord forever.

By Your blood, You have set all men free and saved us from death. Continue Your work of love within us. By constantly celebrating the mystery of our Salvation, which is re-enacted in the Holy Sacrifice of the Mass, may we reach the eternal life it promises. All glory and honor be unto You now and forever. Amen.

Q. 87. How did Jesus Christ redeem us?

Jesus Christ redeemed us by His Passion, Death, Resurrection, and Ascension. To "redeem" means to buy back something that has been lost, sold or given away. Because of Original Sin and our personal sins, we were slaves of the devil. But Jesus freed us, giving us the freedom of the children of God, for, by His Resurrection, He destroyed death and gave us the life of grace.

#J2-321-2

By His Death and Resurrection, Jesus Christ redeemed us from slavery to sin and Satan.

Jesus obeyed the will of His Father by delivering Himself up for us by means of His Passion and Death. Afterwards He raised Himself up from the dead, in order to redeem us and make us acceptable to the Father. He is the Messiah, God's own Son. He said that He did these things so that the Scriptures might be fulfilled and that His Father's will would be accomplished.

Through sin, man had lost his birthright of eternal union with God—eternal happiness in Heaven. The Son of God made man gave that birthright back to us, by offering Himself to His heavenly Father as a victim for our redemption. The Old Testament sacrifices were only symbols of the new sacrifice of the Lamb—the Lamb of God—Who was sacrificed to give worthy honor and reparation to

Sacred Scripture
Q. 87. Col 1:13-20.

Catechism of the Catholic Church
Q. 87. Paragraphs **517**, **613**, **616**-617.

For cross-references with Vatican II, Papal documents & other resources, see Family Wisdom Library on page 370.
For commentaries on each question with Cardinal Arinze, Sr. John Vianney and Fr. Straub (in Spanish), see Appendix C.

His Father. That is why He is called the Redeemer and why His work is called the work of redemption.

He offered His life for love of us and for the glory of His Father. He did His Father's will to honor Him and to make people happy forever in God's Kingdom. The Father now gives His own divine life of grace to people who turn to Him in faith.

By sinning, man failed to love God, but Christ's work of redemption was an act of infinitely perfect love and obedience, which made up His whole life on earth. His infancy spent in Egypt and His thirty years at home in Nazareth were as much a part of our redemption as were the three years of His active life and His Death. His Death on the Cross was the climax of His earthly lifetime of obedience to the will of the Father.

Whatever God does is of infinite value. Because Christ is God, the very least of His works or sufferings is enough to make up for man's sins. But in the plan of the Father, His Son would carry His act of perfect obedience to the point of giving Himself up to death on Calvary.

#J2-550

You were ransomed from the futile ways inherited from your fathers, not with perishable things such as silver or gold, but with the precious blood of Christ. *(1 Peter 1:18-19)*

Catechism by Diagram

#J2-394

Jesus, The Redeemer. Out of love for His Father and for us, Jesus gave Himself up to suffering (pillar of scourging) and death (Calvary), having been crucified by the Romans (Roman banner). The sun was darkened and there was an earthquake (break in line of Mt. Calvary). Christ rose from the dead (tomb), destroying death by His Death and Resurrection, and gave us life so as to become children of God. He created in Himself a new humanity.

Sacred Scripture

For there is one God, and there is one mediator between God and men, the man Christ Jesus, who gave himself as a ransom for all, the testimony to which was borne at the proper time. *1 Timothy 2:5-6*

You know that you were ransomed from the futile ways inherited from your fathers, not with perishable things such as silver or gold, but with the precious blood of Christ, like that of a lamb without blemish or spot. *1 Peter 1:18-19*

Catechism of the Catholic Church

561 "The whole of Christ's life was a continual teaching: his silences, his miracles, his gestures, his prayer, his love for people, his special affection for the little and the poor, his acceptance of the total sacrifice on the Cross for the redemption of the world, and his Resurrection are the actualization of his word and the fulfillment of Revelation."[1]

Splendor of Truth

Furthermore, Jesus reveals by his whole life, and not only by his words, that freedom is acquired in love, that is, in the gift of self. The one who says: "Greater love has no man than this, that a man lay down his life for his friends" (Jn 15:13), freely goes out to meet his Passion (cf. Mt 26:46), and in obedience to the Father gives his life on the Cross for all men (cf. Phil 2:6-11).

Contemplation of Jesus Crucified is thus the highroad which the Church must tread every day if she wishes to understand the full meaning of freedom: the gift of self in service to God and one's brethren. *(section 87)*

Vatican Council II

The Lord himself came to free and strengthen man, renewing him inwardly and casting out the "prince of this world" (Jn. 12:31), who held bondage of sin. For sin brought man to a lower state, forcing him away from the completeness that is his to attain. *Gaudium et Spes, 13*

Summary Prayer

Jesus, we believe that by Your Death and Resurrection You redeemed mankind from slavery to sin and the devil. There is no Salvation in anyone but You.

Your Father loved the world so much that He gave You, His only Son, to free us from the ancient power of sin and from death. Help us who wait for Your coming, and lead us to true liberty. In Your Father's plan of Salvation, You accepted the Cross and freed us from the power of the enemy. Your Father decreed that man should be saved through the wood of the Cross. The tree of man's defeat was replaced by the wood of the Cross, a tree of victory; where life was lost, there life has been restored through You. May we come to share in the glory of Your Resurrection. We ask this in Your most powerful and holy Name. Amen.

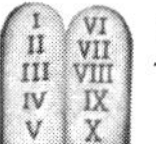

Doctrine • Moral • Worship Exercise

(See Appendix A for answer key, questions 84-87.)

1. By becoming man and offering His sacrificial Death on the Cross, Jesus became our Savior. From what did Jesus save us? For what did He save us?
2. How can you cooperate with the saving act of Jesus' Death and Resurrection? Write out two specific things that you will do to cooperate with Him in your daily life.
3. Thank Jesus for freeing you from the slavery of sin. Express your gratitude by continually cooperating with His saving act.

Catechism by Diagram

#J2-395

Reconciliation between God and Man. God (triangle) so loved mankind that He gave His Son. Jesus came into the world as God made man, to be its Savior and Redeemer. He came as our Brother to teach us and to show us what it means to love God and to belong to Him (handshake). This was done through His life on earth and His Death on Calvary (cross) and through His glorious Resurrection. Christ fulfilled Old Testament prophecy and history, fulfilling the covenant (tablets of commandments) of God with His people through the Incarnation (Gospel verse translated from Latin: "In the beginning was the Word...the Word was made flesh."). In this way, God reconciled the world to Himself.

Chapter Summary Prayer

Jesus, Mediator of the New Covenant, in the Sacrifice of the Mass may we come to You, find Salvation in the sprinkling of Your Blood, and draw closer to the Kingdom where You are Lord forever.

You renew us with the food and drink of Salvation in Holy Communion. May Your Blood be for us a fountain of water springing up to eternal life. Through this sacrament defend us from those who threaten us with evil, for You have set us free and saved us from death by Your Precious Blood. Hear us during times of trouble and protect us by the power of Your Name, that we who share Your struggle on earth, may merit a share in Your victory.

Lord Jesus, Redeemer of all and Author of our Salvation, by Your sacrificial Death, You conquered death. Hear the prayers of Your family and lift us from our slavery to evil, that we may be redeemed by You and see Your Father's glory. Teach us to seek for imperishable goods and to have confidence in Your Blood, poured out as the price of our redemption.

Lord Jesus, You have revealed Your justice to all nations. We stood condemned, but You came to be judged in our place. Send Your saving power to us, and, when You come in glory, bring Your mercy to those for whom You were condemned. To You be all power, honor and glory. Amen.

Thought Provokers

Please see Appendix B for the answers.

Q. 84: What does Jesus' obedience to his earthly parents teach us?

Q. 85: Reflect on the following words of St. Paul: "Why, one will hardly die for a righteous man—though perhaps for a good man one will dare even to die. But God shows his love for us in that while we were yet sinners Christ died for us" (Romans 5:7–8).

Q. 86: A. Is there any other Savior than Jesus Christ?

B. What does the Catholic Church mean when it refers to being saved?

Q. 87: What is meant when it is said that Jesus redeemed us?

#R4.1-15

We like sheep have gone astray; we have turned every one to his own way; and the Lord has laid on him the iniquity of us all. *(Isaiah 53:4-6)*

CHAPTER TWENTY-THREE

The Passion of Our Lord: The Agony on Mount Olivet

"Then Jesus went with them to a place called Gethsemane, and he said to his disciples, 'Sit here, while I go yonder and pray.' And taking with him Peter and the two sons of Zebedee, he began to be sorrowful and troubled. Then he said to them, 'My soul is very sorrowful, even to death; remain here, and watch with me.'

"And going a little farther, he fell on his face and prayed, 'My Father, if it be possible, let this cup pass from me; nevertheless, not as I will, but as thou wilt.'

#R3.1-12

In the Garden of Gethsemane, Jesus told his Apostles, "My soul is very sorrowful, even to death; remain here, and watch with me" *(Matthew 26:38).*

"And he came to the disciples and found them sleeping; and he said to Peter, 'So, could you not watch with me one hour? Watch and pray that you may not enter into temptation; the spirit indeed is willing, but the flesh is weak.'

"Again, for the second time, he went away and prayed, 'My Father, if this cannot pass unless I drink it, thy will be done.' And again he came and found them sleeping, for their eyes were heavy. So, leaving them again, he went away and prayed for the third time, saying the same words.

"Then he came to the disciples and said to them, 'Are you still sleeping and taking your rest? Behold, the hour is at hand, and the Son of man is betrayed into the hands of sinners. Rise, let us be going; see, my betrayer is at hand'" (Matthew 26:36-46).

Q. 88. What did the agony and prayer in the garden express?

The agony and prayer of Jesus in the Garden of the Mount of Olives expressed His desire to do His Father's will at all costs. "Yet not what I will, but what thou wilt" (Mark 14:36).

It also expressed all the spiritual torment Jesus experienced for our sake, as He placed Himself fully in the Father's hands. The torment He experienced due to mankind's rejection of Him caused Him unimaginable pain.

#J2-322-2

The agony and prayer of Jesus in the Garden of the Mount of Olives expressed His desire to do His Father's will at all costs.

Sacred Scripture

He was in the world, and the world was made through him, yet the world knew him not. He came to his own home, and his own people received him not. *John 1:10-11*

Catechism of the Catholic Church

612 The cup of the New Covenant, which Jesus anticipated when he offered himself at the Last Supper, is afterwards accepted by him from his Father's hands in his agony in the garden at Gethsemani,[1] making himself "obedient

Sacred Scripture
Q. 88. Paragraphs 539, 555, 607.

For cross-references with Vatican II, Papal documents & other resources, see Family Wisdom Library on page 370.
For commentaries on each question with Cardinal Arinze, Sr. John Vianney and Fr. Straub (in Spanish), see Appendix C.

unto death."[1] Jesus prays: "My Father, if it be possible, let this cup pass from me...."[2] Thus he expresses the horror that death represented for his human nature. Like ours, his human nature is destined for eternal life; but unlike ours, it is perfectly exempt from sin, the cause of death.[3] Above all, his human nature has been assumed by the divine person of the "Author of life," the "Living One."[4] By accepting in his human will that the Father's will be done, he accepts his death as redemptive, for "he himself bore our sins in his body on the tree."[5]

#R3.1-7

Jesus fell on his face and prayed, "My Father, if it be possible, let this cup pass from me, nevertheless, not as I will but as thou wilt." *(Matthew 26:39)*

Q. 89. Why were the sufferings Christ bore for us so severe?

The sufferings Christ bore for us were extremely severe, in large measure, because of our rejection of His infinite love for us.

Sacred Scripture

In this is love, not that we loved God but that he loved us and sent his Son to be the expiation for our sins. *1 John 4:10*

Surely he has borne our griefs and carried our sorrows; yet we esteemed him stricken, smitten by God, and afflicted. But he was wounded for our transgressions, he was bruised for our iniquities; upon him was the chastisement that made us whole, and with his stripes we are healed. All we like sheep have gone astray; we have turned every one to his own way; and the Lord has laid on him the iniquity of us all. *Isaiah 53:4-6*

Catechism of the Catholic Church

1851 It is precisely in the Passion, when the mercy of Christ is about to vanquish it, that sin most clearly manifests its violence and its many forms: unbelief, murderous hatred, shunning and mockery by the leaders and the

Sacred Scripture
Q. 89. Is 53:7-12; Heb 12:3.

Catechism of the Catholic Church
Q. 89. Paragraphs 312, 572, 766.

For cross-references with Vatican II, Papal documents & other resources, see Family Wisdom Library on page 370.
For commentaries on each question with Cardinal Arinze, Sr. John Vianney and Fr. Straub (in Spanish), see Appendix C.

people, Pilate's cowardice and the cruelty of the soldiers, Judas' betrayal—so bitter to Jesus, Peter's denial and the disciples' flight. However, at the very hour of darkness, the hour of the prince of this world,[1] the sacrifice of Christ secretly becomes the source from which the forgiveness of our sins will pour forth inexhaustibly.

#R3.1-5

The sufferings Christ bore for us were extremely severe, in large measure, because of our rejection of His infinite love for us.

Vatican Council II

The Church always held and continues to hold that Christ out of infinite love freely underwent suffering and death because of the sins of all men, so that all might attain salvation. It is the duty of the Church, therefore, in her preaching to proclaim the cross of Christ as the sign of God's universal love and the source of all grace. *Non-Christian Religions, 4*

Doctrine • Moral • Worship Exercise

(See Appendix A for answer key, questions 88-89.)

1. Jesus prayed in the Garden at the beginning of His Passion. What did He pray for?
2. Recall the last time that you risked hardship or persecution to do God's will.
3. Think of situations in your role as a daughter, son, parent, friend, worker, or citizen in which you encounter challenges in fulfilling God's will. List the things that you can do as a Christian to meet these challenges.

Chapter Summary Prayer

Jesus, Your Passion begins. Yours is the suffering of the soul. Fear takes hold of You; fear caused by the certainty and nearness of Your Death and by the sufferings which will bring it about. You experience disgust at the thought of the sins for which You are to suffer so much. How terrible are the sins of all men and nations and ages, in all their vileness and malice, as compared with God's supreme authority, infinite goodness, justice, and beauty!

Sadness fills the very depths of Your soul—sadness caused by Your knowledge of those who will ultimately reject what You will gain by all Your sacrifices. You foresee that men will neglect Your Church, or misuse it, to their own ruin. All these dreadful pictures rise before You and cut You to Your very heart. You are sorrowful unto death. We humbly beg You to forgive us for our part in this agony of Your soul by committing our many sins.

Humble obedience to Your Father and tender love for us made You willing to suffer even the greatest torments. Help us to show that we are grateful for Your generosity by granting us true contrition for our sins and a burning love for You, our best Friend and our God, now and forever. Amen.

#R3.1-3

Christ out of infinite love freely underwent suffering and death because of the sins of all men. *(Non-Christian Religions, 4)*

Thought Provokers

Please see Appendix B for the answers.

Q. 88: In the Garden of Gethsemane, Jesus expressed His natural fear of the tremendous physical and emotional suffering he was about to undergo (cf. Matthew 26:36–46). God the Father willed that Jesus' suffering be so intense in order to make clear how evil sin really is. But the Father also wanted to redeem suffering and turned Jesus' intense torment into a supreme good, for it became, together with His Death, the means of our Redemption. But what about our suffering? Does it have any positive value, morally speaking?

Q. 89: Who among the Christians have demonstrated the greatest love for God and for mankind?

CHAPTER TWENTY-FOUR

The Passion of Our Lord: Jesus before Pilate

"Then he released for them Barabbas, and having scourged Jesus, delivered him to be crucified. Then the soldiers of the governor took Jesus into the praetorium, and they gathered the whole battalion before him. And they stripped him and put a scarlet robe upon him, and plaiting a crown of thorns they put it on his head, and put a reed in his right hand. And kneeling before him they mocked him, saying, 'Hail, King of the Jews!' And they spat upon him, and took the reed and struck him on the head" (Matthew 27:26-30).

#J2-334-2

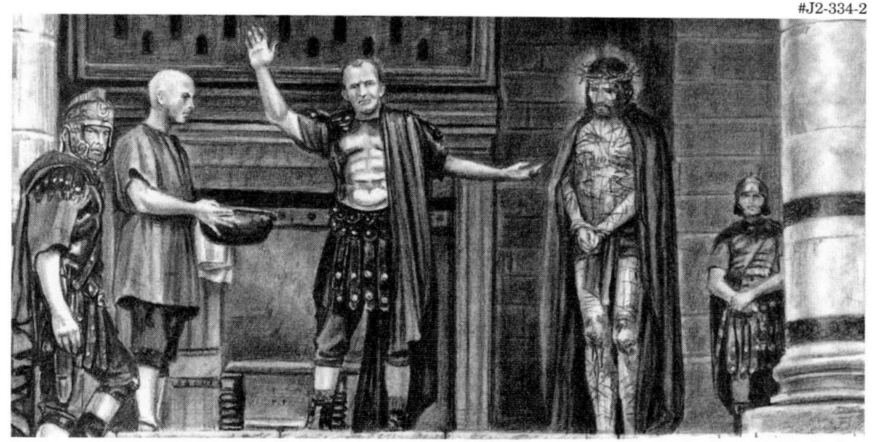

Pilate said to the Jews, "Here is your King!" They cried out, "Away with him, away with him, crucify him!"... Then he handed him over to them to be crucified. *(John 19:14-16)*

"Pilate went out again, and said to them, 'Behold, I am bringing him out to you, that you may know that I find no crime in him.' So Jesus came out, wearing the crown of thorns and the purple robe. Pilate said to them, 'Here is the man!'

"When the chief priests and the officers saw him, they cried out, 'Crucify him, crucify him!' Pilate said to them, 'Take him yourselves and crucify him, for I find no crime in him.' The Jews answered him, 'We have a law, and by that law he ought to die, because he has made himself the Son of God.' When Pilate heard these words, he was the more afraid; he entered the praetorium again and said to Jesus, 'Where are you from?' But Jesus gave no answer. Pilate therefore said to him, 'You will not speak to me? Do you not know that I have power to release you, and power to crucify you?' Jesus answered him, 'You would have no power over me unless it had been given you from above; therefore he who delivered me to you has the greater sin.'

#R3.3-9

He was in the world, and the world was made through him, yet the world knew him not. He came to his own home, and his own people received him not. *(John 1:10-11)*

"Upon this Pilate sought to release him, but the Jews cried out, 'If you release this man, you are not Caesar's friend; every one who makes himself a king sets himself against Caesar.' When Pilate heard these words, he brought Jesus out and sat down on the judgment seat at a place called The Pavement, and in Hebrew, Gabbatha. Now it was the day of Preparation of the Passover; it was about the sixth hour. He said to the Jews, 'Here is your King!' They cried out, 'Away with him, away with him, crucify him!' Pilate said to them, 'Shall I crucify your King?' The chief priests answered, 'We have no king but Caesar.' Then he handed him over to them to be crucified" (John 19:4-16).

Q. 90. Before His Death what trials did Jesus undergo?

Before He was crucified, Jesus was falsely accused and mocked by the soldiers. He was also tried and cruelly treated by (1) the chief priests and elders; (2) the Tetrarch Herod; and (3) Pontius Pilate, the Roman governor. It was Pontius Pilate who condemned Him to die on the Cross as a common criminal.

"And taking the twelve, he said to them, 'Behold, we are going up to Jerusalem, and everything that is written of the Son of man by the prophets will be accomplished. For he will be delivered to the Gentiles, and will be mocked and shamefully treated and spit upon, they will scourge him and kill him, and on the third day he will rise'" (Luke 18:31-33). But His disciples could not begin to understand this mystery of redemption (cf. Luke 18:34) until it had been accomplished (cf. Luke 24:25).

Jesus, whose very name means "Savior," had the Cross always "before his eyes." Jesus longed for the Cross, for by it, only, would the fire of His love be enkindled on earth (cf. Luke 12:49); by it He would "gather into one the children of God who are scattered abroad" (John 11:52).

#R3-96

Before He was crucified, Jesus was falsely accused and mocked by the soldiers. He was also tried and cruelly treated by the chief priests and elders.

Catechism of the Catholic Church
Q. 90. Paragraphs **571-597.**

For cross-references with Vatican II, Papal documents & other resources, see Family Wisdom Library on page 370.
For commentaries on each question with Cardinal Arinze, Sr. John Vianney and Fr. Straub (in Spanish), see Appendix C.

#R3.2-3

He will be delivered to the Gentiles, and will be mocked and shamefully treated and spit upon, they will scourge him and kill him, and on the third day he will rise. *(Luke 18:31-33)*

Sacred Scripture

When the days drew near for him to be received up, he set his face to go to Jerusalem. And he sent messengers ahead of him.... [There He was to undergo the bitter and saving baptism of the Cross:] "I came to cast fire upon the earth; and would that it were already kindled! I have a baptism to be baptized with; and how I am constrained until it is accomplished!" *Luke 9:51-52, 12:49-50*

Catechism of the Catholic Church

574 From the beginning of Jesus' public ministry, certain Pharisees and partisans of Herod together with priests and scribes agreed together to destroy him.[1] Because of certain of his acts — expelling demons, forgiving sins, healing on the sabbath day, his novel interpretation of the precepts of the Law regarding purity, and his familiarity with tax collectors and public sinners[2] — some ill-intentioned persons suspected Jesus of demonic possession.[3] He is accused of blasphemy and false prophecy, religious crimes which the Law punished with death by stoning.[4]

Summary Prayer

Jesus, the soldiers lashed Your body with scourges, Jews lashed Your soul with their tongues, and we lash You with our sins. Each repeated stroke of our sins shocks Your whole nervous system, resounds in Your Father's heavenly court, and pleads for our pardon. Each drop of Your precious

Blood that painfully forces its way from Your bruised skin and flesh is offered up for us. You answer these bloody scourges with love for us who dealt them to You. To You be eternal praise and thanksgiving. Amen.

Q. 91. What was Christ's mission on earth?

Christ's mission on earth, given to Him by His Father, was to save us from the horrors of Hell, and to bring us to the joys of eternal life in the Kingdom of Heaven. He did this through His suffering and dying on the Cross.

#J2-316-2

The Word became flesh for us in order to save us by reconciling us with God, who "loved us and sent his Son to be the expiation for our sins."
(Catechism of the Catholic Church, 457)

We can also say that the Son of God became man to save us from Satan, sin, and death. In the Nicene Creed we say: "For us men and for our Salvation He came down from Heaven... For our sake He was crucified under Pontius Pilate; He suffered, died, and was buried."

Sacred Scripture

Christ Jesus, Who, though he was in the form of God, did not count equality with God a thing to be grasped, but emptied himself, taking the form of a servant, being born in the likeness of men. And being found in human form

Catechism of the Catholic Church
Q. 91. Paragraphs **456-460**.

For cross-references with Vatican II, Papal documents & other resources, see Family Wisdom Library on page 370.
For commentaries on each question with Cardinal Arinze, Sr. John Vianney and Fr. Straub (in Spanish), see Appendix C.

he humbled himself and became obedient unto death, even death on a cross. Therefore God has highly exalted him and bestowed on him the name which is above every name, that at the name of Jesus every knee should bow, in heaven and on earth, and under the earth, and every tongue confess that Jesus Christ is Lord, to the glory of God the Father. *Philippians 2:5-11*

Christ's mission on earth, given to Him by His Father, was to save us from the horrors of Hell, and to bring us to the joys of eternal life in the Kingdom of Heaven. He did this through His suffering and dying on the Cross.

Catechism of the Catholic Church

457 The Word became flesh for us *in order to save us by reconciling us with God*, who "loved us and sent his Son to be the expiation for our sins": "the Father has sent his Son as the Savior of the world," and "he was revealed to take away sins":[1] "Sick, our nature demanded to be healed; fallen, to be raised up; dead, to rise again. We had lost the possession of the good; it was necessary for it to be given back to us. Closed in the darkness, it was necessary to bring us the light; captives, we awaited a Savior; prisoners, help; slaves, a liberator. Are these things minor or insignificant? Did they not move God to descend to human nature and visit it since humanity was in so miserable and unhappy a state?"[2]

Q. 92. In what sense do we speak of the necessity of the Passion and Death of Jesus?

We speak of the necessity of the Passion and Death of Jesus in the sense that it was God's will that man's redemption be achieved in this particular manner. The Passion of our Lord was not something which absolutely had to be. Our redemption could have been obtained in a variety of other ways had God so desired it.

#J2-347-2

We speak of the necessity of the Passion and Death of Jesus in the sense that it was God's will that man's redemption be achieved in this particular manner.

Sacred Scripture

"Do you think that I cannot appeal to my Father, and he will at once send me more than twelve legions of angels? But how then should the scriptures be fulfilled, that it must be so?" At that hour Jesus said to the crowds, "Have you come out as against a robber, with swords and clubs to capture me? Day after day I sat in the temple teaching, and you did not seize me. But all this has taken place, that the scriptures of the prophets might be fulfilled. *Matthew 26:53-56*

Yet it was the will of the Lord to bruise him; he has put him to grief; when he makes himself an offering for sin, he shall see his offspring, he shall prolong his days. *Isaiah 53:10*

Catechism of the Catholic Church

599 Jesus' violent death was not the result of chance in an unfortunate coincidence of circumstances, but is part of the mystery of God's plan, as St. Peter explains to the Jews of Jerusalem in his first sermon on Pentecost: "This

Sacred Scripture
Q. 92. Rom 3:23-26.

Catechism of the Catholic Church
Q. 92. Paragraph 572.

For cross-references with Vatican II, Papal documents & other resources, see Family Wisdom Library on page 370.
For commentaries on each question with Cardinal Arinze, Sr. John Vianney and Fr. Straub (in Spanish), see Appendix C.

Jesus [was] delivered up according to the definite plan and foreknowledge of God.'[1] This Biblical language does not mean that those who handed him over were merely passive players in a scenario written in advance by God."[2]

Q. 93. Did Jesus Himself declare that He had to suffer?

Yes, Jesus stated that it was necessary for Him to suffer in order to bring us eternal life. Thus, He said, "And as Moses lifted up the serpent in the wilderness, so must the Son of man be lifted up, that whoever believes in him may have eternal life" (John 3:14-15).

#R3.4-4

Speaking of His heavenly Father's will for Him, Jesus exclaimed, "For this reason the Father loves me, because I lay down my life, that I may take it again" *(John 10:17)*.

After His Resurrection, Jesus said, "Was it not necessary that the Christ should suffer these things and enter into his glory?" (Luke 24:26).

Centuries before Christ's Passion and Death, the Old Testament prophets prophesied them. The Suffering Servant passages of Isaiah are particularly noteworthy (cf. Isaiah 53). Speaking of the fulfillment of these ancient prophecies, Jesus said, "Everything written about me in the law of Moses and the prophets and the psalms must be fulfilled" (Luke 24:44).

Catechism of the Catholic Church
Q. 93. Paragraph 572.

For cross-references with Vatican II, Papal documents & other resources, see Family Wisdom Library on page 370.
For commentaries on each question with Cardinal Arinze, Sr. John Vianney and Fr. Straub (in Spanish), see Appendix C.

#R3.4-6

From the first moment of his Incarnation the Son embraces the Father's plan of divine salvation in his redemptive mission: "My food is to do the will of him who sent me, and to accomplish his work." *(Catechism of the Catholic Church, 606)*

Speaking of His heavenly Father's will for Him, Jesus exclaimed, "For this reason the Father loves me, because I lay down my life, that I may take it again" (John 10:17). Jesus, with perfect freedom, lovingly accepted this heavy burden placed upon Him so that we might be saved. "No one takes it from me, but I lay it down of my own accord. I have power to lay it down, and I have power to take it again; this charge I have received from my Father" (John 10:18).

Sacred Scripture

But I do as the Father has commanded me, so that the world may know that I love the Father. *John 14:31*

By this we know love, that he laid down his life for us; and we ought to lay down our lives for the brethren. *1 John 3:16*

Catechism of the Catholic Church

606 The Son of God, who came down "from heaven, not to do [his] own will, but the will of him who sent [him],"[1] said on coming into the world, "Lo, I have come to do your will, O God." "And by that will we have been sanctified through the offering of the body of Jesus Christ once for all."[2] From the first moment of his Incarnation the Son embraces the Father's plan of divine salvation in his redemptive mission: "My food is to do the will of him who sent me, and to accomplish his work."[3] The sacrifice of Jesus "for the sins of the whole world"[4] expresses his loving communion with the Father. "The Father loves me, because I lay down my life," said the Lord, "[for] I do as the Father has commanded me, so that the world may know that I love the Father."[5]

Splendor of Truth

Jesus, then, is the living, personal summation of perfect freedom in total obedience to the will of God. His crucified flesh fully reveals the unbreakable bond between freedom and truth. *(section 87)*

Vatican Council II

No one is freed from sin by himself or by his own efforts, no one is raised above himself or completely delivered from his own weakness, solitude or slavery; all have need of Christ who is the model, master, liberator, saviour, and giver of life. *Missionary Activity, 8*

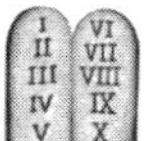

Doctrine • Moral • Worship Exercise

(See Appendix A for answer key, questions 90-93.)

1. Jesus had to suffer to bring us eternal life. What did Jesus prove by doing this?
2. Meditate on the Scripture verse, "By this we know love, that he laid down his life for us; and we ought to lay down our lives for the brethren" (1 John 3:16). Write down your reflections.
3. What actions will you take to be able to lay down your life for Jesus and for your brothers and sisters?

Chapter Summary Prayer

Jesus, You reject the crown of gold and kingly robes to accept instead a crown of thorns and the purple rags of mockery and scorn. You consent to be a mock king, when, in fact, You are the true King of our souls.

We subject ourselves entirely to Your divine kingship of love. We would rather be fools in the eyes of men for Your sake and have You reign over us than be rulers of the world and slaves of the prince of darkness. We pledge unending loyalty to You, our King, and we beg You to reign supremely in our hearts, in our lives, and in the hearts of all men.

Jesus, help us to be devoted subjects of Your kingship, ennobled by the divine powers of Your grace to do good and avoid evil; to love God with our whole heart, our whole soul, all our strength, and to love our neighbor as ourselves; to wield mastery over the evil promptings of the world, the flesh, and the devil. As children of the royal family of God through grace, we claim a loving right to be admitted to Your intimate friendship, with the privilege of feeling the sacred

influence of Your holy love which has transformed us into God-like beings, making our innermost thoughts and affections like Your own. To You be all glory and praise forever and ever. Amen.

Thought Provokers

Please see Appendix B for the answers.

Q. 90: What sort of sufferings can we offer to the Father in union with Jesus' self-sacrifice in order to help repair for the sins of the world?

Q. 91: We have learned that Christ's mission to earth was to save us from sin, death and Hell, and also to save us for eternal life with God and with the angels and saints. Why couldn't God have appointed someone like Moses to accomplish this for us instead of sending His own divine Son?

Q. 92: Although Jesus could have redeemed and saved us in a manner other than undergoing His Passion and Death, why do you think this way was taken?

Q. 93: Jesus told all who would be His followers that they must deny themselves, take up their crosses and follow Him. (cf. Matthew 16:24). In other words, Jesus said that His true followers would suffer simply by leading a Christian life. Why?

#J2-331-2

In him we have redemption through his blood, the forgiveness of our trespasses, according to the riches of his grace which he lavished upon us. *(Ephesians 1:7-8)*

CHAPTER TWENTY-FIVE

The Passion of Our Lord: The Crucifixion of Jesus

#J2-549

When Jesus saw his mother, and the disciple whom he loved standing near, he said to his mother, "Woman, behold your son!" Then he said to the disciple, "Behold, your mother!" *(John 19:26-27)*

"So they took Jesus, and he went out, bearing his own cross, to the place called the place of a skull, which is called in Hebrew Golgotha. There they crucified him, and with him two others, one on either side, and Jesus between them. Pilate also wrote a title and put it on the cross; it read, 'Jesus of Nazareth, the King of the Jews.'

"Many of the Jews read this title, for the place where Jesus was crucified was near the city; and it was written in Hebrew, in Latin, and in Greek. The chief priests of the Jews then said to Pilate, 'Do not write "The King of the Jews," but, "This man said, 'I am King of the Jews.'" Pilate answered, 'What I have written I have written.'

"When the soldiers had crucified Jesus they took his garments and made four parts, one for each soldier; also his tunic. But the tunic was without seam, woven from top to bottom; so they said to one another, 'Let us not tear it, but cast lots for it to see whose it shall be.' This was to fulfill the scripture, 'They parted my garments among them, and for my clothing they cast lots.' So the soldiers did this.

"But standing by the cross of Jesus were his mother, and his mother's sister, Mary the wife of Clopas, and Mary Magdalene. When Jesus saw his mother, and the disciple whom he loved standing near, he said to his mother, 'Woman, behold your son!' Then he said to the disciple, 'Behold, your mother!' And from that hour the disciple took her to his own home.

"After this Jesus, knowing that all was now finished, said (to fulfill the scripture), 'I thirst.' A bowl full of vinegar stood there; so they put a sponge full of the vinegar on hyssop and held it to his mouth. When Jesus had received the vinegar, he said, 'It is finished'; and he bowed his head and gave up his spirit" (John 19:17-30).

Q. 94. What did Jesus suffer upon the Cross?

Jesus suffered inexpressible physical and spiritual agony upon the Cross.

#J2-338-2

Jesus suffered inexpressible physical and spiritual agony upon the Cross.

Crucifixion was such a horrible instrument of death that the Roman authorities would not use it on their own citizens. Added to this torment was that indescribable pain of rejected love. He was rejected not only by those in Palestine, but also by all those who prefer sinful life-styles to the will of God.

Catechism of the Catholic Church
Q. 94. Paragraphs 478, 599, 766.

For cross-references with Vatican II, Papal documents & other resources, see Family Wisdom Library on page 370.
For commentaries on each question with Cardinal Arinze, Sr. John Vianney and Fr. Straub (in Spanish), see Appendix C.

Upon the Cross, Jesus suffered not only extreme physical pain, but also loneliness and desolation, and the anguish of seeing inexpressible sorrow in the one He loved most deeply, His Mother Mary.

Even in the terrible torment of those hours, Jesus, the Son of God and High Priest of our Salvation, retained patience and greatness of soul.

#J2-554

Added to the torment of the Crucifixion was that indescribable pain of rejected love. Jesus was rejected not only by those in Palestine, but also by all those who prefer sinful life-styles to the will of God.

Sacred Scripture

Let us run with perseverance the race that is set before us, looking to Jesus the pioneer and perfecter of our faith, who for the joy that was set before him endured the cross, despising the shame, and is seated at the right hand of the throne of God. Consider him who endured from sinners such hostility against himself, so that you may not grow weary or fainthearted. In your struggle against sin you have not yet resisted to the point of shedding your blood. *Hebrews 12:1-4*

Catechism of the Catholic Church

603 Jesus did not experience reprobation as if he himself had sinned.[1] But in the redeeming love that always united him to the Father, he assumed us in the state of our waywardness of sin, to the point that he could say in our name from the cross: "My God, my God, why have you forsaken me?"[2] Having thus established him in solidarity with us sinners, God "did not spare his own Son but gave him up for us all," so that we might be "reconciled to God by the death of his Son."[3]

Summary Prayer

Jesus, You were not alone in offering Your sacrifice. To have followed You to Calvary was the most certain proof of love. That is the reason why Mary, Your loving Mother, stood beneath Your Cross, nailed to it in spirit, as a co-victim with You. No one ever loved You as Your Blessed Mother did; therefore, no one ever suffered for You as she did. May we always enjoy her maternal love and protection. Amen.

Q. 95. What are the "seven last words" of Jesus as recorded in the Gospels?

The "seven last words" of Jesus as recorded in the Gospels are:

1. "Father, forgive them; for they know not what they do" (Luke 23:34).
2. To a thief who had been crucified with him and who asked for mercy, He said, "Truly, I say to you, today you will be with me in Paradise" (Luke 23:43).

#R3.5-21

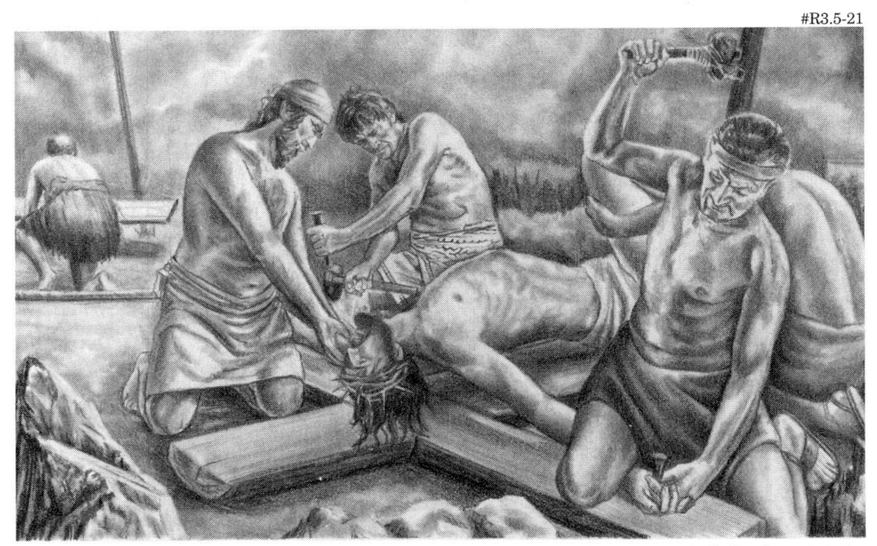

Jesus said, "Father, forgive them; for they know not what they do" *(Luke 23:34).*

Catechism of the Catholic Church
Q. 95. Paragraphs 2605.

For cross-references with Vatican II, Papal documents & other resources, see Family Wisdom Library on page 370.
For commentaries on each question with Cardinal Arinze, Sr. John Vianney and Fr. Straub (in Spanish), see Appendix C.

#J2-343-2

Jesus said, "I thirst" *(John 19:28)*.

3. To His Mother He said, "Woman, behold, your son!" And to St. John, Jesus exclaimed, "Behold, your mother!" (John 19:26, 27).
4. To His Father, in the prayerful words drawn from a prophetic Psalm, He said, "My God, my God, why hast thou forsaken me?" (Matthew 27:46; Psalm 22:1).
5. "I thirst" (John 19:28).
6. "It is finished" (John 19:30).
7. "Father, into thy hands I commit my spirit!" (Luke 23:46; cf. Psalm 31:5).

Summary Prayer

Jesus, You are our Redeemer, Advocate, and Victim for sinners. You begin Your last words amid the deafening yell of triumphant hate, amidst the hissing curses and grim delight of Your enemies. You asked not for justice for them, but for mercy when You pleaded as a Son with Your Father, "Father, forgive them; for they know not what they do" (Luke 23:34). Lord, we sinners also plead for Your mercy and the grace to live lives worthy of Your heavenly Kingdom now and forever. Amen.

Q. 96. How did Jesus die?

Jesus died by crucifixion. Having been nailed to the Cross for about three hours, He bowed His head and gave up His spirit (cf. John 19:30). Thus, the Son of God died for us sinners.

#J2-336-2

God shows his love for us in that while we were yet sinners Christ died for us. *(Romans 5:8)*

St. Paul wrote, "Why, one will hardly die for a righteous man—though perhaps for a good man one will dare even to die. But God shows his love for us in that while we were yet sinners Christ died for us" (Romans 5:7-8).

Catechism of the Catholic Church

618 The cross is the unique sacrifice of Christ, the "one mediator between God and men."[1] But because in his incarnate divine person he has in some way united himself to every man, "the possibility of being made partners in a way known to God, in the paschal mystery" is offered to all men.[2] He calls his disciples to "take up [their] cross and follow [him],"[3] for "Christ also suffered for [us], leaving [us] an example so that [we] should follow in his steps."[4] In fact Jesus desires to associate with his redeeming sacrifice those who were to be its first beneficiaries.[5] This is achieved supremely in the case of his mother, who was associated more intimately than any other person in the mystery of his redemptive suffering.[6]

"Apart from the cross there is no other ladder by which we may get to heaven."[7]

Catechism of the Catholic Church
Q. 96. Paragraphs 607, 609-610, **616-618**, **623**, 2605.

For cross-references with Vatican II, Papal documents & other resources, see Family Wisdom Library on page 370.
For commentaries on each question with Cardinal Arinze, Sr. John Vianney and Fr. Straub (in Spanish), see Appendix C.

Summary Prayer

Jesus, have pity on our souls, for which You bore all this pain, and for which You died in bloody agony. Forgive us, for we did not know what we were doing. Amen.

Q. 97. What effects did the Passion of Jesus have?

The Passion of Jesus has eternal effects. His suffering saved us from sin and all its consequences, and we have received every grace and gift leading to eternal life.

This liberation won for us by Jesus in His Passion has effects even in this world. Redemption is not only in the soul's inner life of love and grace. Men freed from sin can, with God's grace, transform this world also into a kingdom of greater freedom, justice, and peace—into God's Kingdom.

#J2-324-2

Jesus' suffering saved us from sin and all its consequences, and we have received every grace and gift leading to eternal life.

Sacred Scripture

In him we have redemption through his blood, the forgiveness of our trespasses, according to the riches of his grace which he lavished upon us. *Ephesians 1:7-8*

Since all have sinned and fall short of the glory of God, they are justified by his grace as a gift, through the redemption which is in Christ Jesus, whom God put forward as an expiation by his blood, to be received by faith. *Romans 3:23-25*

Catechism of the Catholic Church
Q. 97. Paragraphs 601, **613-615**, 1020-1029, 1987-1996.

For cross-references with Vatican II, Papal documents & other resources, see Family Wisdom Library on page 370.
For commentaries on each question with Cardinal Arinze, Sr. John Vianney and Fr. Straub (in Spanish), see Appendix C.

Catechism of the Catholic Church

1026 By his death and Resurrection, Jesus Christ has "opened" heaven to us. The life of the blessed consists in the full and perfect possession of the fruits of the redemption accomplished by Christ. He makes partners in his heavenly glorification those who have believed in him and remained faithful to his will. Heaven is the blessed community of all who are perfectly incorporated into Christ.

#J2-318-2

Christ makes partners in his heavenly glorification those who have believed in him and remained faithful to his will. *(Catechism of the Catholic Church, 1026)*

Splendor of Truth

Christian morality consists...in following Jesus Christ, in abandoning oneself to him, in letting oneself be transformed by his grace and renewed by his mercy, gifts which come to us in the living communion of his Church. *(section 119)*

Vatican Council II

Since Jesus, the Son of God, showed his love by laying down his life for us, no one has greater love than he who lays down his life for him and for his brothers (cf. 1 Jn. 3:16; Jn. 15:13). *Lumen Gentium, 42*

Doctrine • Moral • Worship Exercise

(See Appendix A for answer key, questions 94-97.)

1. Upon the Cross, Jesus suffered not only extreme physical pain but also the indescribable pain of rejected love. Who rejected the love of Jesus?
2. In what ways have you rejected Jesus' love?
3. How can you respond more generously to the love of Jesus?

Chapter Summary Prayer

Jesus, You offered Yourself to God as a Victim for the sins of the world, and for our sins. Your bleeding wounds are proof of a love unto death. We see Your head bent down to reach us in our sinfulness; Your arms extended to embrace us, though it was we who nailed them there; Your body hanging to redeem us, though we sometimes hardly seem to care. We do not belong to ourselves, but to You, Who have purchased us at such a price.

We are Your parting gift of love to Your Mother. Your Mother is Your parting gift of love to us. She is the dearest and loveliest of mothers, who You have created for Yourself according to Your own divine desires. She has been created in every way immensely superior to all other mothers, the outstanding blessed one among women.

We thank You for giving us so good and amiable a Mother. May we love her as much as she deserves to be loved, according to the way You love her. May we, like John, take her to be our very own, that in life she may make us Your very own, and in Heaven, God's very own for all eternity.

Into Your hands we commend unreservedly and forever our spirits, our souls with all their powers, our bodies with all their senses, our whole beings, to be owned and ruled by Your Holy Spirit in all things during life. Teach us to do Your will in all things and to recognize Your divine providence in all that may befall us. May we be ever united with You in love and confidence till our last breath, so that, mindful of Your own Death for us upon the Cross, we may bow our heads in humble submission to God's will, and reverently commend our souls into Your Father's hands forever and ever. Amen.

Thought Provokers

Please see Appendix B for the answers.

Q. 94: Jesus suffered with extreme intensity on the Cross, but did He experience it in His divine nature?

Q. 95: Quoting Psalm 22, Jesus cried out from the Cross, "My God, my God, why hast thou forsaken me?" Doesn't this suggest that Jesus believed He has been abandoned by His Father?

Q. 96: Why did Jesus die on a cross?

Q. 97: Is Jesus' Redemption available for everyone?

By Heart Catechism and Scripture Review™

The "By Heart Catechism and Scripture Review" lists a selected number of questions and Scripture references from "The Apostolate's Family Catechism" to make memorization easier. Q = Question, SR = Scripture Reference

Q. 82. Is Jesus Christ true man? Yes, Jesus Christ, the Son of God, became a real man, with a human body and soul.

Q. 85. What do we mean when we say that Jesus is our Savior? Jesus is our Savior means that through Jesus all mankind can be saved from the slavery of sin and saved for everlasting life with God.

Q. 86. Is there any other Savior besides Jesus? There is no Savior but Jesus.

SR 86 Acts 4:12

And there is salvation in no one else, for there is no other name under heaven given among men by which we must be saved.

Q. 87. How did Jesus Christ redeem mankind? Jesus Christ redeemed mankind from slavery to sin and Satan by His Passion, Death, Resurrection, and Ascension.

SR 87 1 Timothy 2:5-6

For there is one God, and there is one mediator between God and men, the man Christ Jesus, who gave himself as a ransom for all, the testimony to which was born at the proper time.

Q. 89. Why were the sufferings of Jesus so great? The sufferings of Jesus were so great because of our rejection of His infinite love for us.

Q. 90. Before His Death, what trials did Jesus undergo? Before His Death, Jesus suffered the agony in the garden and was falsely accused, mocked by the soldiers, and mistreated by the chief priests, elders, Herod, and Pontius Pilate.

Q. 94. What did Jesus suffer on the Cross? On the Cross, Jesus suffered great pains in His body and soul, including the pains of rejection, loneliness and sorrow.

By Heart Catechism and Scripture Review™

The "By Heart Catechism and Scripture Review" lists a selected number of questions and Scripture references from "The Apostolate's Family Catechism" to make memorization easier. Q = Question, SR = Scripture Reference

Q. 96. How did Jesus die? Jesus died by painful crucifixion.

SR 96 Romans 5:7-8

Why, one will hardly die for a righteous man — though perhaps for a good man one will dare even to die. But God shows his love for us in that while we were yet sinners Christ died for us.

#J2-309-2

Jesus Christ, sent as "a man among men", "speaks the words of God" and accomplishes the saving work which the Father gave him to do. *(Dei Verbum, 4)*

The Resurrection and the Ascension

#J2-329-2

Jesus' power as the Son of God was revealed to us through His Resurrection.

CHAPTER TWENTY-SIX

The Resurrection

"Now after the sabbath, toward the dawn of the first day of the week, Mary Magdalene and the other Mary went to see the sepulcher.

"And behold, there was a great earthquake; for an angel of the Lord descended from heaven and came and rolled back the stone, and sat upon it. His appearance was like lightning, and his raiment white as snow. And for fear of him the guards trembled and became like dead men.

And behold, there was a great earthquake; for an angel of the Lord descended from heaven and came and rolled back the stone, and sat upon it. *(Matthew 28:2)*

"But the angel said to the women, 'Do not be afraid; for I know that you seek Jesus who was crucified. He is not here; for he has risen, as he said. Come, see the place where he lay. Then go quickly and tell his disciples that he has risen from the dead, and behold, he is going before you to Galilee; there you will see him. Lo, I have told you.'

"So they departed quickly from the tomb with fear and great joy, and ran to tell his disciples.

"And behold, Jesus met them and said, 'Hail!' And they came up and took hold of his feet and worshiped him. Then Jesus said to them, 'Do not be afraid; go and tell my brethren to go to Galilee, and there they will see me'" (Matthew 28:1-10).

Q. 98. How did Jesus Christ show the power He has as the Son of God?

Jesus' power as the Son of God was revealed to us through His Resurrection.

#J2-355-2

Jesus raised Himself from the dead on the third day as He had promised He would. His Resurrection gave the final proof that He was God's Son.

Until the Resurrection, He remained humbly obedient even unto death, and by gloriously raising Himself from the dead, He was exalted as Lord of all. Jesus raised Himself from the dead on the third day as He had promised He would. His Resurrection gave the final proof that He was God's Son, as He had claimed to be. By conquering bodily death through His own power, Jesus showed Himself to be master of life and death. He is truly our God and Savior.

In the many centuries from Adam until Jesus, there were great numbers of men and women throughout the world who believed in God and obeyed His laws. Since such souls were not deserving of eternal punishment, they lived after death in a state of happiness but without any vision of God.

Jesus appeared with His human soul to these souls while His body lay in the tomb, to announce to them the glad tidings of the redemption, and to bring them to God the Father (cf. *Catechism of the Catholic Church*, 631-637). During this time, His divine Person remained united both to His body and to His soul. In the Apostles' Creed we say: "He descended into Hell."

Sacred Scripture
Q. 98. Acts 2:23-24; 13:34-35.

Catechism of the Catholic Church
Q. 98. Paragraphs 428, 444, 631-637, **648-649**, **651**.

For cross-references with Vatican II, Papal documents & other resources, see Family Wisdom Library on page 370.
For commentaries on each question with Cardinal Arinze, Sr. John Vianney and Fr. Straub (in Spanish), see Appendix C.

Jesus rose from the dead in a glorified body, a body glorified even as the bodies of the just will be after their resurrection at the end of the world. It was a body that could no longer suffer or die; a body that showed forth the brightness and beauty of a soul united with God; a body that could pass from place to place with the speed of thought; a body that could pass through a solid wall; a body that needed neither food, nor drink, nor sleep. It is in and through His risen and glorified body that Jesus makes Himself available to mankind through His Church. His divine power is at work especially in the sacraments, providing the grace we need for Salvation and sanctification.

#J2-366-2

Before His Ressurection, Jesus appeared with His human soul to those who, from the time of Adam, had died believing in God and obeying his laws.

Sacred Scripture

This Jesus God raised up, and of that we all are witnesses. *Acts: 2:32*

And what is the immeasurable greatness of his power in us who believe, according to the working of his great might which he accomplished in Christ when he raised him from the dead and made him sit at his right hand in the heavenly places. *Ephesians 1:19-20*

Catechism of the Catholic Church

445 After his Resurrection, Jesus' divine sonship becomes manifest in the power of his glorified humanity. He was "designated Son of God in power according to the Spirit of holiness by his Resurrection from the dead."[1] The apostles can confess: "We have beheld his glory, glory as of the only Son from the Father, full of grace and truth."[2]

Vatican Council II

The wonderful works of God among the people of the Old Testament were but a prelude to the work of Christ Our Lord in redeeming mankind and giving perfect glory to God. He achieved his task principally by the paschal mystery of his blessed passion, resurrection from the dead, and glorious ascension, whereby "dying, he destroyed our death, and rising, restored our life." *Sacrosanctum Concilium, 5*

Summary Prayer

Jesus, we believe that in Your Resurrection Your body was glorified by being united again to Your glorified soul. You rose triumphantly by Your own power. Your body took on spiritual qualities: immortality, beauty, glory, freedom and the power to move about with speed and without hindrance. Divinity shines forth from Your glorified body, and floods of joy pour into Your soul and Your Sacred Heart. At Your Second Coming, grant that we also, through Your great mercy, may have glorified bodies, which, with our souls, will share forever in Your love, joy and peace. Amen.

Q. 99. Why is the Resurrection of our Lord so important?

The Resurrection of our Lord is very important because it not only confirms the Church's faith, but is the central mystery through which God calls us to life everlasting.

The Church celebrates the Resurrection of Jesus with great joy. Not only on Easter, but every Sunday of the year is a celebration of our Lord's Resurrection.

This is the day when Jesus Christ broke the chains of death and rose triumphant from the grave. Faith in the Resurrection is the basis for hope in "an inheritance which is imperishable, undefiled, and unfading, kept in heaven for you" (1 Peter 1:4).

Sacred Scripture

I am the resurrection and the life; he who believes in me, though he die, yet shall he live, and whoever lives and believes in me shall never die. *John 11:25 26*

If for this life only we have hoped in Christ, we are of all men most to be pitied. But in fact Christ has been raised from the dead, the first fruits of those who have fallen asleep. For as by a man came death, by a man has come also the

Catechism of the Catholic Church
Q. 99. Paragraphs **638, 651-658**.

For cross-references with Vatican II, Papal documents & other resources, see Family Wisdom Library on page 370.
For commentaries on each question with Cardinal Arinze, Sr. John Vianney and Fr. Straub (in Spanish), see Appendix C.

resurrection of the dead. For as in Adam all die, so also in Christ shall all be made alive. *1 Corinthians 15:19-22*

Now faith is the assurance of things hoped for, the conviction of things not seen. *Hebrews 11:1*

#J3-26

Faith in the Resurrection is the basis for hope in "an inheritance which is imperishable, undefiled, and unfading, kept in heaven for you" *(1 Peter 1:4)*.

Catechism of the Catholic Church

653 The truth of Jesus' divinity is confirmed by his Resurrection. He had said: "When you have lifted up the Son of man, then you will know that I am he."[1] The Resurrection of the crucified one shows that he was truly "I Am," the Son of God and God himself. So St. Paul could declare to the Jews: "What God promised to the fathers, this he has fulfilled to us their children by raising Jesus; as also it is written in the second psalm, 'You are my Son, today I have begotten you.'"[2] Christ's Resurrection is closely linked to the Incarnation of God's Son and is its fulfillment in accordance with God's eternal plan.

#E4-72

Not only on Easter, but every Sunday of the year is a celebration of our Lord's Resurrection.

Summary Prayer

Jesus, what great love You showed to the pious women! They followed You to Calvary, and wished to be with You even when they believed You were in the grave. In reward for this love and fidelity, You appeared to them soon after Your Resurrection. Through Your graces, may we share in their love and fidelity, and be with You forever in Heaven. Amen.

Q. 100. Why does the Resurrection of Jesus play a central part in the life of faith?

The Resurrection plays a central part in the life of faith because it is the key event underlying the Church's faith in Jesus as Savior and Redeemer.

The historical, bodily, and perpetual resurrection of Jesus from the dead is evidence that Jesus has conquered mankind's enemies of sin and death. The Resurrection also confirms that all Jesus taught about His divinity and messianic mission is true. Moreover, the Resurrection points to the triumph over sin and death which belongs to those who fully accept Jesus as their Savior.

The Apostles and disciples considered the Resurrection so important that they risked imprisonment, torture, and death in proclaiming the historical reality of the Resurrection.

#A18-19-2

The Apostles and disciples considered the Resurrection so important that they risked imprisonment, torture, and death in proclaiming the historical reality of the Resurrection.

Sacred Scripture

If Christ has not been raised, then our preaching is in vain and your faith is in vain...If Christ has not been raised, your faith is fútile and you are still in your sins. *1 Corinthians 15:14, 17*

Sacred Scripture
Q. 100. 1 Cor 15:20-28.

Catechism of the Catholic Church
Q. 100. Paragraphs 651-655.

For cross-references with Vatican II, Papal documents & other resources, see Family Wisdom Library on page 370.
For commentaries on each question with Cardinal Arinze, Sr. John Vianney and Fr. Straub (in Spanish), see Appendix C.

If then you have been raised with Christ, seek the things that are above, where Christ is, seated at the right hand of God. Set your minds on things that are above, not on things that are on earth. *Colossians 3:1-2*

Catechism of the Catholic Church

638 "We bring you the good news that what God promised to the fathers, this day he has fulfilled to us their children by raising Jesus."[1] The Resurrection of Jesus is the crowning truth of our faith in Christ, a faith believed and lived as the central truth by the first Christian community; handed on as fundamental by Tradition; established by the documents of the New Testament; and preached as an essential part of the Paschal mystery along with the cross:

> Christ is risen from the dead!
> Dying, he conquered death;
> To the dead, he has given life.[2]

Summary Prayer

Jesus, we believe that by Your divine power You rose, as You had promised, as a glorious Victor. The earth quaked as You came forth from the tomb, and the guards trembled with fear. Your body now shines like the sun. The wounds of Your hands and feet sparkle like precious jewels. Death is conquered, its victory broken, its sting destroyed. You triumph not for Yourself alone, but that we too may triumph over the grave.

This mystery strengthens our hope in another and better life after death, in the resurrection of our bodies on the last day, and in an eternity of happiness. We firmly hope that we may die in the state of grace so that You can raise us up glorified. Through Your glorious Resurrection, we hope that You will make our bodies like Your own in glory, and permit us to dwell with You in Heaven for all eternity.

We adore Your sacred humanity which receives this eternal kingdom of honor, power, joy, and glory. We rejoice with You, our Master; immortal, all-glorious, and all-powerful. Amen.

The Resurrection plays a central part in the life of faith because it is the key event underlying the Church's faith in Jesus as Savior and Redeemer.

Q. 101. What was the Easter proclamation?

The Easter proclamation was the words of the angel to the holy women, "He is not here, but has risen" (Luke 24:5).

#R4.1-18

The angel said to the women, "He is not here, but has risen" *(Luke 24:5).*

Sacred Scripture

Now I would remind you, brethren, in what terms I preached to you the gospel, which you received, in which you stand, by which you are saved, if you hold it fast—unless you believed in vain. For I delivered to you as of first importance what I also received, that Christ died for our sins in accordance with the scriptures, that he was buried, that he was raised on the third day in accordance with the scriptures, and that he appeared to Cephas, then to the twelve. *1 Corinthians 15:1-5*

Catechism of the Catholic Church

640 "Why do you seek the living among the dead? He is not here, but has risen."[1] The first element we encounter in the framework of the Easter events is the empty tomb. In itself it is not a direct proof of Resurrection; the absence of Christ's body from the tomb could be explained otherwise.[2] Nonetheless the empty tomb was still an essential sign for all. Its discovery by the disciples was the first step toward recognizing the very fact of the Resurrection. This was the case, first with the holy women, and then with Peter.[3] The disciple "whom Jesus loved" affirmed that when he entered the empty tomb and discovered "the linen cloths lying there," "he saw and believed."[4] This suggests that he

Catechism of the Catholic Church
Q. 101. Paragraph 640.

For cross-references with Vatican II, Papal documents & other resources, see Family Wisdom Library on page 370.
For commentaries on each question with Cardinal Arinze, Sr. John Vianney and Fr. Straub (in Spanish), see Appendix C.

realized from the empty tomb's condition that the absence of Jesus' body could not have been of human doing and that Jesus had not simply returned to earthly life as had been the case with Lazarus.[5]

Vatican Council II

After God had spoken many times and in various ways through the prophets, "in these last days he has spoken to us by a Son" (Heb. 1:1-2). For he sent his Son, the eternal Word who enlightens all men, to dwell among men and to tell them about the inner life of God. Hence, Jesus Christ, sent as "a man among men," "speaks the words of God" (Jn. 3:34), and accomplishes the saving work which the Father gave him to do (cf. Jn. 5:36; 17:4). As a result, he himself—to see whom is to see the Father (cf. Jn. 14:9)—completed and perfected Revelation and confirmed it with divine guarantees. He did this by the total fact of his presence and self-manifestation—by words and works, signs and miracles, but above all by his death and glorious resurrection from the dead, and finally by sending the Spirit of truth. He revealed that God was with us, to deliver us from the darkness of sin and death, and to raise us up to eternal life. *Dei Verbum, 4*

#R4.1-20

Jesus, it was but a matter of course, after Your Resurrection, that You would appear to Your holy Mother, for she is Your nearest and dearest in the order of nature and of grace.

Doctrine • Moral • Worship Exercise

(See Appendix A for answer key, questions 98-101.)

1. What truths did Jesus reveal through His Resurrection?
2. What should we hope for from the Resurrection of Jesus? How do you manifest this hope in your everyday actions?
3. How does the Resurrection of Jesus influence your daily decisions?

Chapter Summary Prayer

Jesus, You are infinitely good to all, and never fail to reward those who wish to please You. Your goodness will be made manifest also in us, if we remain faithful in all sufferings and temptations. How often have we been unfaithful to You; how often, in times of sorrow and trial, have we forsaken You. We promise to be more faithful to You in the future. Give us a true love for You; an ardent, self-sacrificing love, that seeks to please You perfectly and to become like You in suffering.

Jesus, it was but a matter of course that You would appear to Your holy Mother, for she is Your nearest and dearest in the order of nature and of grace. You received from her the life that is now so glorious.

She has the most intimate share in Your mysteries, of which this glory of Your Resurrection is the exceedingly great reward. She shared more than anyone else in the sorrow and bitterness of Your Passion, and so she shares more than all others in the glory of Your triumph. It is, therefore, fitting that she should now have a special share in Your glory.

Lord Jesus, early in the morning of Your Resurrection, You made Your love known and brought the first light of dawn to those who dwelt in darkness. Your Death has opened a path for us. Do not enter into judgment with Your servants; let Your Holy Spirit guide us into the land of justice and heavenly bliss. This we ask in Your most holy and powerful Name. Amen.

Thought Provokers

Please see Appendix B for the answers.

Q. 98: A. What historical evidence is there for Jesus' bodily Resurrection from the dead?

B. What was their earthly reward for insisting on the truth of the Resurrection?

Q. 99: The bodily resurrection of Jesus from the dead is a central dogma of the Catholic Faith, attested to, as we noted above, by the heroic witness of the Apostles. If, contrary to fact, the Resurrection proclaimed by the Catholic Church were not true, what would be some of the consequences?

Q. 100: Think for a few moments of some of the implications for you and your family, if Jesus had not been raised from the dead and ascended bodily into Heaven.

Q. 101: Why is Easter the most important feast in the Church's calendar?

CHAPTER TWENTY-SEVEN

Jesus Appears to the Apostles

"On the evening of that day, the first day of the week, the doors being shut where the disciples were, for fear of the Jews, Jesus came and stood among them and said to them, 'Peace be with you.' When he had said this, he showed them his hands and his side. Then the disciples were glad when they saw the Lord.

"Jesus said to them again, 'Peace be with you. As the Father has sent me, even so I send you.' And when he had said this, he breathed on them, and said to them, 'Receive the Holy Spirit. If you forgive the sins of any, they are forgiven; if you retain the sins of any, they are retained.'

#R4.1-13

Jesus came and stood among them and said to them, 'Peace be with you' *(John 20:19).*

"Now Thomas, one of the twelve, called the Twin, was not with them when Jesus came. So the other disciples told him, 'We have seen the Lord.' But he said to them, 'Unless I see in his hands the print of the nails, and place my finger in the mark of the nails, and place my hand in his side, I will not believe.'

"Eight days later, his disciples were again in the house, and Thomas was with them. The doors were shut, but Jesus came and stood among them, and said, 'Peace be with you.' Then he said to Thomas,

'Put your finger here, and see my hands; and put out your hand, and place it in my side; do not be faithless, but believing.' Thomas answered him, 'My Lord and my God!' Jesus said to him, 'Have you believed because you have seen me? Blessed are those who have not seen and yet believe'" (John 20:19-29).

Q. 102. How did Jesus lead His Apostles to faith in His Resurrection?

Jesus led His Apostles to believe in His Resurrection by His being present among His followers for forty days in His resurrected and glorified body, by eating with them, by speaking to them, and by allowing Himself to be touched and felt. Clearly He, Whom they saw, touched, and heard, was neither a disembodied spirit nor an illusion.

#R4.1-5-2

Jesus said to his Apostles, "See my hands and my feet, that it is I myself; handle me, and see; for a spirit has not flesh and bones as you see that I have" *(Luke 24:39).*

Sacred Scripture

To them he presented himself alive after his Passion by many proofs, appearing to them during forty days, and speaking of the kingdom of God. *Acts 1:3*

Jesus himself stood among them, and said to them, "Peace to you." But they were startled and frightened, and supposed that they saw a spirit. And he said to them, "Why are you troubled, and why do questionings rise in your hearts? See my hands and my feet, that it is I myself; handle me, and see; for a spirit has not flesh and bones as you see that I have." And when he had said this he

Catechism of the Catholic Church
Q. 102. Paragraph 641-645.

For cross-references with Vatican II, Papal documents & other resources, see Family Wisdom Library on page 370.
For commentaries on each question with Cardinal Arinze, Sr. John Vianney and Fr. Straub (in Spanish), see Appendix C.

showed them his hands and his feet. And while they still disbelieved for joy, and wondered, he said to them, "Have you anything here to eat?" They gave him a piece of broiled fish, and he took it and ate before them. *Luke 24:36-43*

#R4.1-10

As witnesses of the Risen One, they remain the foundation stones of his Church. *(Catechism of the Catholic Church, 642)*

Catechism of the Catholic Church

642 Everything that happened during those Paschal days involves each of the apostles—and Peter in particular—in the building of the new era begun on Easter morning. As witnesses of the Risen One, they remain the foundation stones of his Church. The faith of the first community of believers is based on the witness of concrete men known to the Christians and for the most part still living among them. Peter and the Twelve are the primary "witnesses to his Resurrection," but they are not the only ones—Paul speaks clearly of more than five hundred persons to whom Jesus appeared on a single occasion and also of James and of all the apostles.[1]

Summary Prayer

Most gentle Prince of Peace, Who gave peace to Your Apostles, we beg You, from the fullness of Your Sacred Heart, give us that peace which the world cannot give, that we may faithfully keep Your commandments and serve You without fear of our enemies.

Jesus, before Your Death, You informed Peter and the other Apostles that in Your Church they would be given power to bind and loose with respect to sins. When appearing to Your Apostles after Your Resurrection, You actually gave them the power to forgive sins and the authority to judge. This power was given not only to them, but also to their lawful successors.

Jesus, may the loving way in which You brought Thomas to believe, strengthen in us the spirit of love, confidence, and faith in Your Real Presence in the Blessed Sacrament, where we cannot see You. May that faith be proven by our fervent devotion at Mass and Holy Communion and by our visits to the tabernacle. We ask this in Your most powerful and holy Name. Amen.

Q. 103. How did the Holy Spirit lead the Apostles towards faith in the Resurrection of Jesus?

The Holy Spirit, by the means of the inner gift of faith, confirmed the Apostles in their outward acceptance of Jesus' Resurrection, as evidenced by St. Thomas and all the Apostles during the early days and years of the Church.

#R4.1-7-2

The Apostles' faith in the Resurrection was born, under the action of divine grace, from their direct experience of the reality of the risen Jesus.
(Catechism of the Catholic Church, 644)

Sacred Scripture
Q. 103. Lk 24:36-49.

Catechism of the Catholic Church
Q. 103. Paragraph 640-645.

For cross-references with Vatican II, Papal documents & other resources, see Family Wisdom Library on page 370.
For commentaries on each question with Cardinal Arinze, Sr. John Vianney and Fr. Straub (in Spanish), see Appendix C.

#A18-17-2

With great power the apostles gave their testimony to the resurrection of the Lord Jesus, and great grace was upon them all. *(Acts 4:33)*

Sacred Scripture

And with great power the apostles gave their testimony to the resurrection of the Lord Jesus, and great grace was upon them all. *Acts 4:33*

And we are witnesses to these things, and so is the Holy Spirit whom God has given to those who obey him. *Acts 5:32*

Catechism of the Catholic Church

644 Even when faced with the reality of the risen Jesus the disciples are still doubtful, so impossible did the thing seem: they thought they were seeing a ghost. "In their joy they were still disbelieving and still wondering."[1] Thomas will also experience the test of doubt and St. Matthew relates that during the risen Lord's last appearance in Galilee "some doubted."[2] Therefore the hypothesis that the Resurrection was produced by the Apostles' faith (or credulity) will not hold up. On the contrary their faith in the Resurrection was born, under the action of divine grace, from their direct experience of the reality of the risen Jesus.

Vatican Council II

Holy Mother Church believes that it is for her to celebrate the saving work of her divine Spouse in a sacred commemoration on certain days throughout the course of the year. Once each week, on the day which she has called the Lord's Day, she keeps the memory of the Lord's resurrection. She also celebrates it once every year, together with his blessed passion, at Easter, that most solemn of all feasts.

In the course of the year, moreover, she unfolds the whole mystery of Christ from the incarnation and nativity to the ascension, to pentecost and the expectation of the blessed hope of the coming of the Lord.

Thus recalling the mysteries of the redemption, she opens up to the faithful the riches of her Lord's powers and merits, so that these are in some way made present for all time; the faithful lay hold of them and are filled with saving grace." *Sacrosanctum Concilium, 102*

Doctrine • Moral • Worship Exercise

(See Appendix A for answer key, questions 102-103.)

1. What did Jesus do after His Resurrection to strengthen His disciples' faith?
2. Meditate on the Scripture verse, "Blessed are those who have not seen and yet believe" (John 20:29).
3. What specific steps can you take to strengthen your faith in the Resurrection?

Chapter Summary Prayer

Jesus, You instructed the Apostles that it was necessary that You should suffer, and, on the third day, rise from the dead. If it was necessary that You should suffer in order to enter into the glory of Heaven, there certainly is no other way for us. We have been redeemed by the Cross, and by this sign we must work out our own Salvation and the Salvation of others. Without the Cross there is no Salvation.

Strengthen us with Your grace that, after following Your example and that of Your words in Scripture, and for the love of You, we may patiently bear the trials and sufferings that our work may bring us. In the same measure in which we share Your suffering, shall we share in Your glory in the life after death. Grant us the grace of sharing Your glory in the everlasting bliss of Heaven.

We thank You for the inestimable benefit of the institution of the Sacrament of Penance. Through frequent confession, You give us an increase of sanctifying grace, a firm confidence in God, peace of conscience, the strength to resist temptation, ease to perform good works, and a lasting joy.

In this sacrament we receive the price of Your Precious Blood and Your five sacred wounds. We thank You for all the graces we have ever received in this sacrament, by which You have rendered spiritual resurrection possible for us. Help us to make use of this great means of grace with confidence, joy, and zeal.

How kind and patient You are in bearing with our faults and in bringing good out of them. When we reflect upon how You have sought us, wandering faithless disciples, and upon how You have visited us with Your grace, we, in admiration of Your loving kindness, exclaim, "My Lord and my God!" Amen.

Thought Provokers

Please see Appendix B for the answers.

Q. 102: Why do you suppose that the Apostles at first doubted Jesus' bodily Resurrection from the dead, even though He had foretold it?

Q. 103: The Holy Spirit, through the gift of faith, enabled the Apostles to believe that the resurrected Jesus was the Messiah Who had conquered sin and death. But couldn't their senses and unaided reason alone also have led them to the same firm and certain conviction?

#R4.1-28

The Paschal mystery has two aspects: by his death, Christ liberates us from sin; by his Resurrection, he opens for us the way to a new life.
(*Catechism of the Catholic Church, 654*)

CHAPTER TWENTY-EIGHT

Belief in the Resurrection

Q. 104. What does the Church teach about the Resurrection?

The Catholic Church teaches that Jesus was raised bodily from the dead by the power of the Father and by His own power.

#T3-39-2

Jesus is conclusively revealed as "Son of God in power according to the Spirit of holiness by his Resurrection from the dead." *(Catechism of the Catholic Church, 648)*

Sacred Scripture

For this reason the Father loves me, because I lay down my life, that I may take it again. No one takes it from me, but I lay it down of my own accord. I have power to lay it down, and I have power to take it again; this charge I have received from my Father. *John 10:17-18*

Sacred Scripture
Q. 104. Acts 2:22-36.

Catechism of the Catholic Church
Q. 104. Paragraph 649.

For cross-references with Vatican II, Papal documents & other resources, see Family Wisdom Library on page 370.
For commentaries on each question with Cardinal Arinze, Sr. John Vianney and Fr. Straub (in Spanish), see Appendix C.

Catechism of the Catholic Church

648 Christ's Resurrection is an object of faith in that it is a transcendent intervention of God himself in creation and history. In it the three divine persons act together as one, and manifest their own proper characteristics. The Father's power "raised up" Christ his Son and by doing so perfectly introduced his Son's humanity, including his body, into the Trinity. Jesus is conclusively revealed as "Son of God in power according to the Spirit of holiness by his Resurrection from the dead."[1] St. Paul insists on the manifestation of God's power[2] through the working of the Spirit who gave life to Jesus' dead humanity and called it to the glorious state of Lordship.

Q. 105. What does it mean to believe in the bodily Resurrection of Jesus from the dead?

To believe in the bodily Resurrection of Jesus from the dead is to believe that God, Who became man, has conquered sin and death. We must also believe that this victory is made available to us through His Church.

#T3-34-2

Jesus has conquered sin and death and this victory is made available to us through His Church.

Sacred Scripture

"Death is swallowed up in victory. O death, where is thy victory? O death, where is thy sting?" The sting of death is sin, and the power of sin is the law. But thanks be to God, who gives us the victory through our Lord Jesus Christ. *1 Corinthians 15:54-57*

Sacred Scripture
Q. 105. Eph 2:4-7; Rom 6:3-11.

Catechism of the Catholic Church
Q. 105. Paragraphs 651-655.

For cross-references with Vatican II, Papal documents & other resources, see Family Wisdom Library on page 370.
For commentaries on each question with Cardinal Arinze, Sr. John Vianney and Fr. Straub (in Spanish), see Appendix C.

Catechism of the Catholic Church

654 The Paschal mystery has two aspects: by his death, Christ liberates us from sin; by his Resurrection, he opens for us the way to a new life. This new life is above all justification that reinstates us in God's grace, "so that as Christ was raised from the dead by the glory of the Father, we too might walk in newness of life."[1] Justification consists in both victory over the death caused by sin and a new participation in grace.[2] It brings about filial adoption so that men become Christ's brethren, as Jesus himself called his disciples after his Resurrection: "Go and tell my brethren."[3] We are brethren not by nature, but by the gift of grace, because that adoptive filiation gains us a real share in the life of the only Son, which was fully revealed in his Resurrection.

Vatican Council II

When Jesus, having died on the cross for men, rose again from the dead, he was seen to be constituted as Lord, the Christ, and as Priest for ever (cf. Acts 2:36; Heb. 5:6; 7:17-21), and he poured out on his disciples the Spirit promised by the Father (cf. Acts 2:23). Henceforward the Church, endowed with the gifts of her founder and faithfully observing his precepts of charity, humility and self-denial, receives the mission of proclaiming and establishing among all peoples the kingdom of Christ and of God, and she is, on earth, the seed and the beginning of that kingdom. *Lumen Gentium, 5*

Doctrine • Moral • Worship Exercise

(See Appendix A for answer key, questions 104-105.)

1. What did Jesus conquer by His Resurrection?
2. How can this triumph of Jesus at His Resurrection help you in facing life's trials and struggles?
3. Ask Jesus to give you the strength to conquer sin and death through His Resurrection.

Chapter Summary Prayer

Jesus, hitherto Peter had only received the promise of the primacy (cf. Matthew 16:15-19), but after that morning meal, You finally conferred it upon him in all its fullness and majesty, in the presence of the other Apostles. We firmly believe that this primacy is a divinely bestowed office, divine in its origin and nature, for it represents You; divine in its extent, for it embraces the whole Church, the learning body (lay faithful) as well as the teaching body (hierarchical). It also includes the entire and supreme power, divine in its operation and significance, since the whole Church—its being, attributes, stability, life, growth, and work—stands or falls with the primacy.

Jesus, after having conferred upon Peter the highest dignity in Your Church, You predicted to him that he would be taken prisoner in his old age, bound, and led to the martyrdom of the cross. All this is a proof of his love for You and for his flock, as the good shepherd he was.

We thank You for the graces and privileges You have bestowed upon us as Catholics. Help us to use these graces well and to be grateful for each token of Your tender love. Give us a generous love like Peter's for You. Help us to love You when we have to suffer, as well as when we are able to rejoice. We ask this in Your most holy and powerful Name. Amen.

Thought Provokers

Please see Appendix B for the answers.

Q. 104: The Second Ecumenical Council of Lyons in 1274, for instance, definitively taught: "The third day He rose from the dead by a true resurrection of the body. With the body of His resurrection and with His soul, He ascended into Heaven on the fortieth day after the Resurrection."

Q. 105: What connection is there between Jesus' Resurrection and our resurrection which will take place at the time of the Final Judgment?

CHAPTER TWENTY-NINE

The Benefits of the Resurrection

Q. 106. What has Jesus Christ done for us through His Resurrection?

When Christ passed from death to life, He made possible our passing from the death of sin to life in Him. Being the firstborn of the dead, Jesus Christ offers eternal life to all. In Him we are made spiritually renewed persons.

#J3-10-2

When Christ passed from death to life, He made possible our passing from the death of sin to life in Him.

We receive the new life of grace in Baptism, where we become God's children. St. Peter says, "Blessed be the God and Father of our Lord Jesus Christ! By his great mercy we have been born anew to a living hope through the resurrection of Jesus Christ from the dead, and to an inheritance which is imperishable, undefiled, and unfading, kept in heaven for you" (1 Peter 1:3-4).

Sacred Scripture
Q. 106. 1 Cor 15:35-53; 2 Cor 5:14-17.

Catechism of the Catholic Church
Q. 106. Paragraphs 638, 651, 653-655, **989**, 994, **1003**-1004.

For cross-references with Vatican II, Papal documents & other resources, see Family Wisdom Library on page 370.
For commentaries on each question with Cardinal Arinze, Sr. John Vianney and Fr. Straub (in Spanish), see Appendix C.

Sacred Scripture

Although he was a Son, he learned obedience through what he suffered; and being made perfect he became the source of eternal salvation to all who obey him. *Hebrews 5:8-9*

For those whom he foreknew he also predestined to be conformed to the image of his Son, in order that he might be the first-born among many brethren. *Romans 8:29*

Baptism, which corresponds to this, now saves you, not as a removal of dirt from the body but as an appeal to God for a clear conscience, through the resurrection of Jesus Christ. *1 Peter 3:21*

Catechism of the Catholic Church

995 To be a witness to Christ is to be a "witness to his Resurrection," to "[have eaten and drunk] with him after he rose from the dead."[1] Encounters with the risen Christ characterize the Christian hope of resurrection. We shall rise like Christ, with him, and through him.

Splendor of Truth

The Christian, thanks to God's Revelation and to faith, is aware of the "newness" which characterizes the morality of his actions: these actions are called to show either consistency or inconsistency with that dignity and vocation which have been bestowed on him by grace. *(section 73)*

Vatican Council II

In the human nature united to himself, the son of God, by overcoming death through his own death and resurrection, redeemed man and changed him into a new creation (cf. Gal. 6:15; 2 Cor. 5:17). *Lumen Gentium, 7*

Summary Prayer

Jesus, we believe that through Your Resurrection You are the firstborn of the dead and give eternal life to all. In You we are made spiritually renewed persons. You give us the divine life of grace and pour out Your Holy Spirit upon us.

We praise You, Lord, with greater joy than ever for Your Resurrection when You became our paschal sacrifice. You are the true Lamb Who takes away the sins of the world. By dying You destroyed our death; by rising You restored our life. You have opened the gates of Heaven to receive Your faithful people. Your Death is our ransom from death; Your Resurrection is our rising to life. May we, Your unworthy servants, remain in this life, now and forever. Amen.

Q. 107. How does the risen Jesus help us now?

The risen Jesus helps us by: (1) giving us the supernatural life of grace and (2) pouring out His Holy Spirit upon us.

1. The risen Jesus helps us by giving us the supernatural life of grace.

By dying and rising, our Lord Jesus saved us from death and restored us to life. He continues to give us the supernatural life of grace through the sacraments, beginning with Baptism.

#B6-5b

Jesus continues to give us the supernatural life of grace through the sacraments, beginning with Baptism.

2. The risen Jesus helps us by pouring out His Holy Spirit upon us to make us holy and pleasing to God.

We should model our lives after Jesus. The Father gives His own life to all who turn to Him in faith and love. The Father, Son, and Holy Spirit come and share Their love with those who give themselves to Jesus. Jesus sends us the Holy Spirit to guide and strengthen us, to make us holy. "And I will pray the Father, and He will give you another Counselor, to be with you forever" (John 14:16).

Sacred Scripture
Q. 107. Jn 4:7-14.

Catechism of the Catholic Church
Q. 107. Paragraphs 989, 1262-1270, 1988-2005.

For cross-references with Vatican II, Papal documents & other resources, see Family Wisdom Library on page 370.
For commentaries on each question with Cardinal Arinze, Sr. John Vianney and Fr. Straub (in Spanish), see Appendix C.

Sacred Scripture

Now this he said about the Spirit, which those who believed in him were to receive; for as yet the Spirit had not been given, because Jesus was not yet glorified. *John 7:39*

Being therefore exalted at the right hand of God, and having received from the Father the promise of the Holy Spirit, he has poured out this which you see and hear. *Acts 2:33*

If the Spirit of him who raised Jesus from the dead dwells in you, he who raised Christ Jesus from the dead will give life to your mortal bodies also through his Spirit who dwells in you. *Romans 8:11*

#F1-53-2

Jesus sends us the Holy Spirit to guide and strengthen us, to make us holy.

Catechism of the Catholic Church

1997 Grace is a *participation in the life of God*. It introduces us into the intimacy of Trinitarian life: by Baptism the Christian participates in the grace of Christ, the Head of his Body. As an "adopted son" he can henceforth call God "Father," in union with the only Son. He receives the life of the Spirit who breathes charity into him and who forms the Church.

Vatican Council II

And this is in order that non-Christians, whose heart is being opened by the Holy Spirit (cf. Acts 16:4), might, while believing, freely turn to the Lord who, since he is the "way, the truth and the life" (John 14:6), will satisfy all their inner hopes, or rather infinitely surpass them.

This conversion is, indeed, only initial; sufficient however to make a man realize that he has been snatched from sin, and is being led into the mystery of God's love, who invites him to establish a personal relationship with him in Christ. Under the movement of divine grace the new convert sets out on a spiritual journey by means of which, while already sharing through faith in the mystery of the death and resurrection, he passes from the old man to the new man who has been made perfect in Christ (cf. Col. 3:5-10; Eph. 4:20-24). *Missionary Activity, 13*

Catechism by Diagram

#J2-396

God's Justice Satisfied. Jesus Christ is the firstborn among the many brethren, because by dying, He destroyed our death, and by rising, He restored our life. As the Risen Lord, He now shares with us His divine life of grace, especially through the sacraments, and gives us His Holy Spirit to make us holy and pleasing to God. All this is possible because Jesus has paid the debt of our sinfulness by His suffering and Death (Calvary). Through Him, all creatures can be saved from the slavery of corruption and sin (apple). As our Redeemer, He paid our debt (cross on scale) for sin and bought Heaven back for us, and in this way He fulfilled our obligation to the justice of God (scale). In Him comes perfect satisfaction for us, that we might be reconciled with God.

Summary Prayer

Lord Jesus, by Your victory You broke the power of evil and destroyed sin and death. Make us victorious over sin all the days of our lives. You laid death low and bought us new life. To You be all honor and glory, now and forever. Amen.

#J2-341-2

Christ our Savior, send down Your abundant blessings upon Your people who devoutly recall Your Death and Resurrection at Holy Mass in the sure hope of the resurrection in the world to come.

Doctrine • Moral • Worship Exercise

(See Appendix A for answer key, questions 106-107.)

1. After His Resurrection, Jesus continues to help us. In what ways?
2. How can you cooperate with the grace of the Resurrection?
3. How can you show your gratitude to Jesus by word and action for His victorious and continuous presence in us today?

Chapter Summary Prayer

Christ our Savior, in conquering death You brought us joy, in rising again You raised us up and filled us with the abundance of Your gifts. Stir up our hearts and sanctify us through the gifts of Your Holy Spirit.

You have restored us to life by Your triumphant Death and Resurrection. Continue this healing work within us. May we who participate in the mystery of the Eucharistic Sacrifice never cease to serve You. Send down Your abundant blessings upon Your people who devoutly recall Your Death and Resurrection at Holy Mass in the sure hope of the resurrection in the world to come.

Lord Jesus Christ, risen Savior, You chose to suffer and be overwhelmed by death in order to open the gates of eternal life in triumph. Stay with us to help us on our pilgrimage. Free us from all evil by the power of Your Resurrection. In the company of Your saints, and constantly remembering Your love for us, may we be worthy to praise You forever in Your Father's house. May our mortal life be crowned by the ultimate joy of rising with You. Amen.

Thought Provokers

Please see Appendix B for the answers.

Q. 106: Through Jesus' Resurrection, what is made available to us?

Q. 107: What does the risen Lord help us become?

#R4.2-1-2

While he blessed them, he parted from them and was carried up into heaven.
(Luke 24:51)

CHAPTER THIRTY

The Ascension: Jesus Returns to the Father

"Then he opened their minds to understand the scriptures, and said to them, 'Thus it is written, that the Christ should suffer and on the third day rise from the dead, and that repentance and forgiveness of sins should be preached in his name to all nations, beginning from Jerusalem. You are witnesses of these things. And behold, I send the promise of my Father upon you; but stay in the city, until you are clothed with power from on high.'

#R4.2-4

Before He ascended into Heaven Jesus said, "Repentance and forgiveness of sins should be preached in his name to all nations" *(Luke 24:47).*

"Then he led them out as far as Bethany, and lifting up his hands he blessed them. While he blessed them, he parted from them and was carried up into heaven. And they worshiped him, and returned to Jerusalem with great joy, and were continually in the temple blessing God" (Luke 24:45-53).

Q. 108. What is the meaning of the Ascension of Christ?

The Ascension of Christ means that Jesus "was lifted up, and a cloud took him out of their [the disciples'] sight" (Acts 1:9). His glorified body and soul, which had risen from the dead, now ascended into Heaven.

#R4.3-8

In Heaven, Jesus Christ "intercedes constantly for us as the mediator who assures us of the permanent outpouring of the Holy Spirit" *(Catechism of the Catholic Church, 667).*

Sacred Scripture

So then the Lord Jesus, after he had spoken to them, was taken up into heaven, and sat down at the right hand of God. *Mark 16:19*

Catechism of the Catholic Church

667 Jesus Christ, having entered the sanctuary of heaven once and for all, intercedes constantly for us as the mediator who assures us of the permanent outpouring of the Holy Spirit.

Summary Prayer

Jesus, in Your risen Body You plainly showed Yourself to Your disciples, and then You were taken up to Heaven in their sight to claim for us a share in Your divine life. May we follow You into the new creation, for Your Ascension is our glory and our hope. All praise, glory, and honor be to You now and forever. Amen.

Sacred Scripture
Q. 108. Acts 1:9-11

Catechism of the Catholic Church
Q. 108. Paragraphs **659-667**.

For cross-references with Vatican II, Papal documents & other resources, see Family Wisdom Library on page 370.
For commentaries on each question with Cardinal Arinze, Sr. John Vianney and Fr. Straub (in Spanish), see Appendix C.

Catechism by Diagram

#J2-437

The Way to Glory. Jesus is the Messiah, God's own Son, Who fulfilled Old Testament prophecy, as He carried out His mission on earth. This was the will of His Father (Triangle, rays). God's way of life has begun among men, and they are called to enter it (road to Heaven). Original Sin broke all contact with God (dotted line). Jesus is the Way. He became man and was born on this earth (manger). He spent thirty years in a hidden life of prayer and work (hatchet, saw). After three years of preaching God's Kingdom, He offered His life on the Cross (Calvary) for our Salvation to deliver us from sin and death (serpent, tree). He rose from the dead and, after forty days, ascended into Heaven (monogram).

Q. 109. What are the two distinctive aspects of the mystery of the Ascension?

The two distinctive aspects of the mystery of the Ascension are: (1) the fullness of the glorification of Jesus' victorious humanity in Heaven and (2) the completion of His visible ministry on earth.

#J2-386-2

Therefore God has highly exalted him and bestowed on him the name which is above every name, that at the name of Jesus every knee should bow.
(Philippians 2:9-11)

Sacred Scripture

And what is the immeasurable greatness of his power in us who believe, according to the working of his great might which he accomplished in Christ when he raised him from the dead and made him sit at his right hand in the heavenly places. *Ephesians 1:19-20*

In saying, "He ascended," what does it mean but that he had also descended into the lower parts of the earth? He who descended is he who also ascended far above all the heavens, that he might fill all things. *Ephesians 4:9-10*

He was manifested in the flesh, vindicated in the Spirit, seen by angels, preached among the nations, believed on in the world, taken up in glory. *1 Timothy 3:16*

Therefore God has highly exalted him and bestowed on him the name which is above every name, that at the name of Jesus every knee should bow, in heaven and on earth and under the earth, and every tongue confess that Jesus Christ is Lord, to the glory of God the Father. *Philippians 2:9-11*

Catechism of the Catholic Church
Q. 109. Paragraphs 660, **2749**.

For cross-references with Vatican II, Papal documents & other resources, see Family Wisdom Library on page 370.
For commentaries on each question with Cardinal Arinze, Sr. John Vianney and Fr. Straub (in Spanish), see Appendix C.

Catechism of the Catholic Church

659 "So then the Lord Jesus, after he had spoken to them, was taken up into heaven, and sat down at the right hand of God."[1] Christ's body was glorified at the moment of his Resurrection, as proved by the new and supernatural properties it subsequently and permanently enjoys.[2] But during the forty days when he eats and drinks familiarly with his disciples and teaches them about the kingdom, his glory remains veiled under the appearance of ordinary humanity.[3] Jesus' final apparition ends with the irreversible entry of his humanity into divine glory, symbolized by the cloud and by heaven, where he is seated from that time forward at God's right hand.[4] Only in a wholly exceptional and unique way would Jesus show himself to Paul "as to one untimely born," in a last apparition that established him as an apostle.[5]

Summary Prayer

Jesus, You ascended into Heaven to enter into Your glory. While on earth You always enjoyed the vision of God, but the glory of Your sacred humanity showed forth only at Your Transfiguration and in the Resurrection. When You ascended into Heaven, You took Your place as triumphant beside Your heavenly Father and are exalted above all other creatures. We rejoice at the glory into which You entered to reign as King of Heaven and earth. When the struggle of our lives is over, give us the grace to share Your joy forever in Heaven. Amen.

Q. 110. What has Christ done for us through His Ascension?

Through His Ascension, Christ has claimed for us a participation in His divine life. He has ascended into Heaven to prepare a place for us. However, He has not abandoned us here on earth.

Sacred Scripture

Let not your hearts be troubled; believe in God, believe also in me. In my Father's house are many rooms; if it were not so, would I have told you that I go to prepare a place for you? *John 14:1-2*

And lo, I am with you always, to the close of the age. *Matthew 28:20*

Catechism of the Catholic Church

788 When his visible presence was taken from them, Jesus did not leave his disciples orphans. He promised to remain with them until the end of time; he sent them his Spirit.[1] As a result communion with Jesus has become, in a way, more intense: "By communicating his Spirit, Christ mystically constitutes as his body those brothers of his who are called together from every nation."[2]

Sacred Scripture
Q. 110. Jn 14:16-18; Heb 9:24; 1 Jn 2:1-2.

Catechism of the Catholic Church
Q. 110. Paragraphs 662, **668**-670, 2743.

For cross-references with Vatican II, Papal documents & other resources, see Family Wisdom Library on page 370.
For commentaries on each question with Cardinal Arinze, Sr. John Vianney and Fr. Straub (in Spanish), see Appendix C.

Splendor of Truth

We must first of all show the inviting splendor of that truth which is Jesus Christ himself. In him, who is the Truth (cf. Jn 14:6), man can understand fully and live perfectly, through his good actions, his vocation to freedom in obedience to the divine law summarized in the commandment of love of God and neighbor. *(section 83)*

#R4.2-13

Jesus has ascended into Heaven to prepare a place for us.

Q. 111. How is Christ present with the Church?

Christ is present with the Church through God the Holy Spirit. It is through the Holy Spirit that Christ is present to us in the sacraments, especially in the Holy Eucharist. He is also present in the souls of all who love Him and who are striving to do His will.

Sacred Scripture

And I will pray the Father, and he will give you another Counselor, to be with you for ever, even the Spirit of truth, whom the world cannot receive, because it neither sees him nor knows him; you know him, for he dwells with you, and will be in you. I will not leave you desolate; I will come to you. *John 14:16-18*

Catechism of the Catholic Church

737 The mission of Christ and the Holy Spirit is brought to completion in the Church, which is the Body of Christ and the Temple of the Holy Spirit. This joint mission henceforth brings Christ's faithful to share in his communion with the Father in the Holy Spirit. The Spirit *prepares* men and goes out to them with his grace, in order to draw them to Christ. The Spirit *manifests* the risen Lord to them, recalls his word to them and opens their minds to the understanding of his Death and Resurrection. He *makes present* the mystery of Christ, supremely in the Eucharist, in order to reconcile them, to *bring them into communion* with God, that they may "bear much fruit."[1]

#S13-38-2

Christ is present in the souls of all who love Him and who are striving to do His will.

Catechism of the Catholic Church
Q. 111. Paragraphs **737-741**.

For cross-references with Vatican II, Papal documents & other resources, see Family Wisdom Library on page 370.
For commentaries on each question with Cardinal Arinze, Sr. John Vianney and Fr. Straub (in Spanish), see Appendix C.

Vatican Council II

From the fact of their union with Christ the head flows the laymen's right and duty to be apostles. Inserted as they are in the Mystical Body of Christ by baptism and strengthened by the power of the Holy Spirit in confirmation, it is by the Lord himself that they are assigned to the apostolate. If they are consecrated a kingly priesthood and a holy nation (cf. 1 Pet. 2:4-10), it is in order that they may in all their actions offer spiritual sacrifices and bear witness to Christ all the world over. Charity, which is, as it were, the soul of the whole apostolate, is given to them and nourished in them by the sacraments, the Eucharist above all.

The apostolate is lived in faith, hope and charity poured out by the Holy Spirit into the hearts of all the members of the Church. And the precept of charity, which is the Lord's greatest commandment, urges all Christians to work for the glory of God through the coming of his kingdom and for the communication of eternal life to all men, that they may know the only true God and Jesus Christ whom he has sent (cf. Jn. 17:3). *Lay People, 3*

Summary Prayer

Jesus, complete the work of Your grace and raise up in our days many apostolic men and women who, imbued with a burning zeal for souls and with true wisdom, will go forth to preach the Gospel to nominal Christians, the unchurched, and the lapsed. Increase the number of devoted missionaries and give to them Your Holy Spirit to guide and direct them. We ask this in Your most powerful and holy Name. Amen.

Doctrine • Moral • Worship Exercise

(See Appendix A for answer key, questions 108-111.)

1. Although Jesus ascended into Heaven, He has not abandoned us. Where on earth is He especially present now?
2. Jesus is also present in the souls of those who love Him. How can you make Him more present in your life? Think of specific things that you can do.
3. Through His Ascension, Jesus has prepared a place for us in Heaven. Let the thought of this inspire you to carry out faithfully the things that you listed in your previous answer.

Chapter Summary Prayer

Jesus, we believe in the mystery of the most Holy Trinity, that there is one God in three Persons: the Father, the Son, and the Holy Spirit, each existing separately and distinctly in the one divine nature.

We believe that because of Your redemption we share, through grace, in the divine nature and have become sons of God by adoption. We are Your younger brothers and sisters, so we belong to Your family and have God as our Father.

Since You have promised to be with Your Church until the end of the world, the Church is infallible in doctrinal and moral matters. Because You are with her and support her, she cannot err in her office as teacher and interpreter of Your revelation. We thank You for the glorious blessings and privileges which You have conferred upon Your Church to assure our Salvation. Fill our hearts with gratitude for the benefits of our Catholic faith. Give us respect for, and submission to the ecclesiastical hierarchy, which is invested with such glorious and truly divine power. We ask this in Your all-glorious and all-holy Name. Amen.

Thought Provokers

Please see Appendix B for the answers.

Q. 108: What relationship does the Ascension have with the Resurrection?

Q. 109: What does Jesus' Ascension (body and soul) into Heaven tell us about human destiny?

Q. 110: Weren't the Apostles and other disciples of Jesus privileged since they knew Him while he was on earth?

Q. 111: In addition to the Holy Eucharist, what are some other ways in which Christ is present in His Church?

#F3-55

Since Christ is the center of all of God's works of Salvation, through Him all Creation can give glory to God.

CHAPTER THIRTY-ONE

Christ the King: Center of Our Life

"Then they led Jesus from the house of Caiaphas to the praetorium. It was early. They themselves did not enter the praetorium, so that they might not be defiled, but might eat the passover. So Pilate went out to them and said, 'What accusation do you bring against this man?' They answered him, 'If this were not an evildoer, we would not have handed him over.' Pilate said to them, 'Take him yourselves and judge him by your own law.' The Jews said to him, 'It is not lawful for us to put any man to death.' This was to fulfill the word which Jesus had spoken to show by what death he was to die.

#R19.3-9

The Father loves the Son, and has given all things into his hand. He who believes in the Son has eternal life. *(John 3:35-36)*

Pilate entered the praetorium again and called Jesus, and said to him, 'Are you the King of the Jews?' Jesus answered, 'Do you say this of your own accord, or did others say it to you about me?' Pilate answered, 'Am I a Jew? Your own nation and the chief priests have handed you over to me; what have you done?' Jesus answered, 'My kingship is not of this world; if my kingship were of this world, my servants would fight, that I might not be handed over to the Jews; but my kingship is not from the world.' Pilate said to him, 'So you are a king?' Jesus answered, 'You say that I am a king. For this I was born, and for this I have come into the world, to bear witness to the truth. Every one who is of the truth hears my voice.' Pilate said to him, 'What is truth?' After he had said this, he went out to the Jews again, and told them, 'I find no crime in him'" (John 18:28-38).

Q. 112. What plan does God have for mankind?

In general, God's plan for us is the carrying out of our Salvation, which is to culminate in forming His faithful followers to become one in mind and will with Him for all eternity. Thus, we become permanent members of the new People of God, with Jesus as our Head—we become the "Whole Christ."

#J2-365

Jesus asks us to believe in Him, to put our hope in Him for the future, and to love Him with all our hearts.

In the Creed we say, "He sits at the right hand of God, the Father Almighty." Being God, Jesus is in all things the Father's equal; as man, He is above all the saints in the closeness of His union with God the Father.

Since Christ is the center of all of God's works of Salvation, through Him all Creation can give glory to God. Jesus asks us to believe in

Sacred Scripture
Q. 112. Mt 25:31-46; Eph 4:4-8; 1 Pet 2:9-10.

Catechism of the Catholic Church
Q. 112. Paragraphs **1067**, 1372, 1442.

For cross-references with Vatican II, Papal documents & other resources, see Family Wisdom Library on page 370.
For commentaries on each question with Cardinal Arinze, Sr. John Vianney and Fr. Straub (in Spanish), see Appendix C.

Him, to put our hope in Him for the future, and to love Him with all our hearts. In this, we humans glorify God and obtain our Salvation. He said, "The Father loves the Son, and has given all things into his hand. He who believes in the Son has eternal life" (John 3:35-36).

During His Passion, Jesus Christ gave Himself for us in order to redeem us from sin and make us pleasing to God. Then He sent us His Spirit, the Spirit of adoption, making us children of God. Thus, He made in Himself a new people, a people filled with the grace of God. The new People of God, united to Jesus, their Head, make up "the whole Christ." He offers them to His Father and gives Him glory. This is God the Father's plan for the Salvation of all men.

#W2-18

The state of this people is that of the dignity and freedom of the sons of God, in whose hearts the Holy Spirit dwells as in a temple. Its law is the new commandment to love as Christ loved us. *(Lumen Gentium, 9)*

Sacred Scripture

And his gifts were that some should be apostles, some prophets, some evangelists, some pastors and teachers, for the equipment of the saints, for the work of ministry, for building up the body of Christ, until we all attain to the unity of the faith and of the knowledge of the Son of God, to mature manhood, to the measure of the stature of the fullness of Christ. *Ephesians 4:11-13*

So if there is any encouragement in Christ, any incentive of love, any participation in the Spirit, any affection and sympathy, complete my joy by being of the same mind, having the same love, being in full accord and of one mind. *Philippians 2:1-2*

Now to him who by the power at work within us is able to do far more abundantly than all that we ask or think, to him be glory in the church and in Christ Jesus to all generations, for ever and ever. Amen. *Ephesians 3:20*

Catechism of the Catholic Church

436 The word "Christ" comes from the Greek translation of the Hebrew *Messiah*, which means "anointed." It became the name proper to Jesus only because he accomplished perfectly the divine mission that "Christ" signifies. In effect, in Israel those consecrated to God for a mission that he gave were anointed in his name. This was the case for kings, for priests and, in rare instances, for prophets.[1] This had to be the case all the more so for the Messiah whom God would send to inaugurate his kingdom definitively.[2] It was necessary that the Messiah be anointed by the Spirit of the Lord at once as king and priest, and also as prophet.[3] Jesus fulfilled the messianic hope of Israel in his threefold office of priest, prophet, and king.

1066 In the Symbol of the faith the Church confesses the mystery of the Holy Trinity and of the plan of God's "good pleasure" for all creation: the Father accomplishes the "mystery of his will" by giving his beloved Son and his Holy Spirit for the salvation of the world and for the glory of his name.[1] Such is the mystery of Christ, revealed and fulfilled in history according to the wisely ordered plan that St. Paul calls the "plan of the mystery"[2] and the patristic tradition will call the "economy of the Word incarnate" or the "economy of salvation."

Splendor of Truth

The Church, and each of her members, is thus called to share in the *munus regale* of Crucified Christ (cf. Jn 12:32), to share in the grace and in the responsibility of the Son of man who came "not to be served but to serve, and to give his life as a ransom for many" (Mt.20:28). *(section 87)*

Vatican Council II

That messianic people has as its head Christ, "who was delivered up for our sins and rose again for our justification" (Rom. 4:25), and now, having acquired the name which is above all names, reigns gloriously in heaven. The state of this people is that of the dignity and freedom of the sons of God, in whose hearts the Holy Spirit dwells as in a temple. Its law is the new commandment to love as Christ loved us (cf. Jn. 13:34). Its destiny is the kingdom of God which has been begun by God himself on earth and which must be further extended until it is brought to perfection by him at the end of time when Christ our life (cf. Col. 3:4) will appear and "creation itself also will be delivered from its slavery to corruption into the freedom of the glory of the sons of God" (Rom. 8:21). Hence that messianic people, although it does not actually include all men, and at times may appear as a small flock, is however, a most sure seed of unity, hope and salvation for the whole human race. Established by Christ as a communion of life, love and truth, it is taken up by him also as the instrument for the salvation of all; as the light of the world and the salt of the earth (cf. Mt. 5:13-16) it is sent forth into the whole world. *Lumen Gentium, 9*

God's plan for us is to culminate in forming His faithful followers to become one in mind and will with Him for all eternity. With Jesus as our Head—we become the "Whole Christ."

Summary Prayer

Jesus, as God You stand before Your creatures. You are humble and submissive as You speak of Your Kingdom. You declare that Your Kingdom is upon the earth, but not of the earth; it is a spiritual, supernatural kingdom, the Kingdom of Truth. It fights with spiritual weapons and conquers by this means the hearts that by all rights belong to it. You are witness to this truth, and You Yourself are the Truth. May we always be subjects of Your Kingdom. Amen.

Q. 113. Is Jesus Christ the center of all of God's saving work?

Yes, Jesus Christ is the center of all of God's saving work, because the Father chose Him to be so in view of His Incarnation, birth, Death, and Resurrection.

Jesus Christ became man so that He might save all men and re-establish in Himself all things which were hurt by the fall of man. Thus, by His Death and Resurrection, He was given by His Father all power in Heaven and on earth, and He founded the Catholic Church as the means of our Salvation. In Christ, our Savior and Redeemer, we are united to all men. Jesus said, "The Father loves the Son, and has given all things into his hand. He who believes in the Son has eternal life" (John 3:35-36).

The whole work of Salvation receives its meaning from Jesus Christ, the Incarnate Word. That work, beginning with the Creation, showed itself in Christ's coming, in His life on earth, and in His Death and Resurrection, and it will be completed in His glorious Second Coming. Thus, God was powerfully at work in the history of Israel, and in the life, Death and Resurrection of His Incarnate Son.

Sacred Scripture

Blessed be the God and Father of our Lord Jesus Christ, who has blessed us in Christ with every spiritual blessing in the heavenly places, even as he chose us in him before the foundation of the world, that we should be holy and blameless before him.

He destined us in love to be his sons through Jesus Christ, according to the purpose of his will, to the praise of his glorious grace which he freely bestowed on us in the Beloved.

In him we have redemption through his blood, the forgiveness of our trespasses, according to the riches of his grace which he lavished upon us. For

Sacred Scripture
Q. 113. Jn 15:5; Eph 2:4-10; Heb 7:25; Rev 22:13-16.

Catechism of the Catholic Church
Q. 113. Paragraphs 457, 461, **571**.

For cross-references with Vatican II, Papal documents & other resources, see Family Wisdom Library on page 370.
For commentaries on each question with Cardinal Arinze, Sr. John Vianney and Fr. Straub (in Spanish), see Appendix C.

he has made known to us in all wisdom and insight the mystery of his will, according to his purpose which he set forth in Christ as a plan for the fullness of time, to unite all things in him, things in heaven and things on earth. *Ephesians 1:3-1*

When all things are subjected to him, then the Son himself will also be subjected to him who put all things under him, that God may be everything to every one. *1 Corinthians 15:28*

#J2-370-2

Jesus Christ is the center of all of God's saving work.

Catechism of the Catholic Church

2074 Jesus says: "I am the vine, you are the branches. He who abides in me, and I in him, he it is that bears much fruit, for apart from me you can do nothing."[1] The fruit referred to in this saying is the holiness of a life made fruitful by union with Christ. When we believe in Jesus Christ, partake of his mysteries, and keep his commandments, the Savior himself comes to love, in us, his Father and his brethren, our Father and our brethren. His person becomes, through the Spirit, the living and interior rule of our activity. "This is my commandment, that you love one another as I have loved you."[2]

Catechism by Diagram

#J2-398

Christ the King. By conquering death through His own power in His Resurrection (empty tomb), Jesus has shown Himself master of life and death; therefore, Jesus Christ, the Son of God, the Second Person of the Trinity, is true God and true man. For forty days (dotted line), He appeared to His disciples to complete their training. On Mt. Olivet, He gave His Apostles the final command to preach the Gospel to the whole world. He ascended into Heaven (monogram, arrow) and sits at the right hand (throne) of His Father (triangle), where He reigns with Him and the Holy Spirit (dove) in eternal glory. He is King of Kings (crown) and Lord of Lords, our own Savior. Christ's passage from death to life brought about our passage from death in sin to life in Christ. God has restored all things in Christ.

Vatican Council II

The Word of God, through whom all things were made, was made flesh, so that as a perfect man he could save all men and sum up all things in himself. The Lord is the goal of human history, the focal point of the desires of history and civilization, the center of mankind, the joy of all hearts, and the fulfillment of all aspirations. *Gaudium et Spes, 45*

When Jesus, having died on the cross for men, rose again from the dead, he was seen to be constituted as Lord, the Christ, and as Priest for ever (cf. Acts 2:36; Heb. 5:6; 7:17-21), and he poured out on his disciples the Spirit promised by the Father (cf. Acts 2:23). Henceforward the Church, endowed with the gifts of her founder and faithfully observing his precepts of charity, humility and self-denial, receives the mission of proclaiming and establishing among all peoples the kingdom of Christ and of God, and she is, on earth, the seed and the beginning of that kingdom. *Lumen Gentium, 5*

Summary Prayer

Jesus, Your Ascension is the assurance of our own bodily ascension into Heaven after the Last Judgment, if we remain faithful to You, dying in the state of grace. You entered into Your glorious Kingdom to prepare a place for us, for You promised to come again to take us to Yourself. Let us ascend into the heavens with You. Grant that we may detach ourselves from all the passing things on earth, so that we may seek only the joys that are true and lasting. To You be all honor and glory, now and forever. Amen.

Doctrine • Moral • Worship Exercise

(See Appendix A for answer key, questions 112-113.)

1. Think about times you have allowed Jesus to be King of your life.
2. In what ways can you cooperate with God in carrying out His plan for us so that Jesus will truly become the King and center of your Christian life?
3. Pray to Jesus that mankind will cooperate fully with God in the accomplishment of His plan.

Chapter Summary Prayer

Jesus, You are truly a king because You have come into the world to institute among men the rule of God; every man owes You a loyal and undivided allegiance.

Jesus, as Catholics, we are members of Your Kingdom, and You are our King. To You we owe loyalty, obedience, and love. Help us to carry out these most sacred duties toward You. We wish to listen to Your voice and gladly follow You in all things. We accept You as our King and submit to Your authority.

Reign supremely in our hearts and in our lives. Your reign is heavenly peace; Your law is love. Help us to pray and work that Your Kingdom may come into every soul, every family, and every nation.

Jesus, You ascended into Heaven to be our Mediator with Your Father. There, pointing to the wounds which You received for the glory of God and for the Salvation of souls, You are ever pleading for us.

Jesus, King of all Creation, Your Father anointed You with the oil of gladness as the Eternal Priest and Universal King. As Priest, You offered Your life on the altar of the Cross and redeemed the human race by this one perfect sacrifice of peace. As King, You claim dominion over all Creation, that You may present to Your Father an eternal and universal Kingdom: a Kingdom of truth and life, a Kingdom of holiness and grace, and a Kingdom of justice, love and peace.

Jesus, in the hour of our own homecoming, when we appear before Your Father to give account of our lives on earth, have mercy on us. May we be able to say, as You did: "I glorified thee on earth, having accomplished the work which thou gavest me to do" (John 17:4). Amen.

Thought Provokers

Please see Appendix B for the answers.

Q. 112: How can we discover God's particular plan for us as individuals?

Q. 113: How should we regard Jesus?

Jesus, You are our King. To You we owe loyalty, obedience, and love.
We wish to listen to Your voice and gladly follow You in all things.

By Heart Catechism and Scripture Review™

The "By Heart Catechism and Scripture Review" lists a selected number of questions and Scripture references from "The Apostolate's Family Catechism" to make memorization easier. Q = Question, SR = Scripture Reference

Q. 98. How did Jesus Christ show His power as the Son of God? Jesus showed His power as the Son of God by His Resurrection.

Q. 99. Why is the Resurrection of Jesus so important? The Resurrection of Jesus is important because it proves that Jesus is God and that He has the power to give us eternal life.

Q. 101. What was the Easter proclamation? The Easter proclamation was the words of the angel to the holy women, "He is not here, but has risen." (Lk 24:5)

Q. 102. How did Jesus lead His Apostles to faith in the Resurrection? After His Resurrection, Jesus ate with the Apostles, spoke with them, and allowed them to touch His body.

SR 102 John 20:29

Jesus said to him, "Have you believed because you have seen me? Blessed are those who have not seen and yet believe."

Q. 103. How did the Holy Spirit lead the Apostles to believe in the Resurrection of Jesus? The Holy Spirit led the Apostles to believe in the Resurrection of Jesus by giving them the gift of faith.

SR 103 Acts 5:32

And we are witnesses to these things, and so is the Holy Spirit, whom God has given to those who obey him.

Q. 106. What has Jesus Christ done for us through His Resurrection? Through His Resurrection, Jesus opened the way for us to become children of God and to have eternal life.

Q. 107. How does the Risen Jesus help us now? The Risen Jesus helps us now by: (1) giving us the supernatural life of grace through the sacraments, and (2) pouring out His Holy Spirit upon us.

By Heart Catechism and Scripture Review™

The "By Heart Catechism and Scripture Review" lists a selected number of questions and Scripture references from "The Apostolate's Family Catechism" to make memorization easier. Q = Question, SR = Scripture Reference

SR 107 Romans 8:11

If the Spirit of him who raised Jesus from the dead dwells in you, he who raised Christ Jesus from the dead will give life to your mortal bodies also through his Spirit who dwells in you.

Q. 108. What is the meaning of the Ascension of Christ? The Ascension of Christ means that Jesus went up to Heaven in His Risen Body.

Q. 109. What are the two distinctive aspects of the mystery of the Ascension? The two distinctive aspects of the mystery of the Ascension are: (1) that the human nature of Jesus was perfectly glorified, and (2) that Jesus had finished His work on earth.

Q. 110. What has Jesus done for us through the Ascension? Through the Ascension, Jesus in Heaven is preparing a place for each of us.

Family Wisdom Library™

Papal documents listed below can be viewed at www.vatican.va. For new cross-references, visit www.familyland.org

Q. 72. Of all of God's works, which is the greatest?

Church Documents

Compendium of the Catechism of the Catholic Church, sect. 85-86, 89
Dei Verbum (Dogmatic Constitution on Divine Revelation), Vatican II, sect. 2, 4, 17-18
Gaudium et Spes (Pastoral Constitution on the Church in the Modern World), Vatican II, sect. 22, 58, 78
God is Love, Benedict XVI, sect. 12
Gospel of Life, John Paul II, sect. 2
Lumen Gentium (Dogmatic Constitution on the Church), Vatican II, sect. 65
Mother of the Redeemer, John Paul II, sect. 1, 9-11
On the Dignity and Vocation of Women, John Paul II, sect. 3-4
On the Holy Spirit in the Life of the Church and the World, John Paul II, sect. 50
The Relationship Between Faith and Reason, John Paul II, sect. 80
Sacrament of Charity, Benedict XVI, sect. 7-8
U. S. Catholic Catechism for Adults, [2006] pp. 81-83, 85-86

Other Resources

Basics of the Faith: A Catholic Catechism, Schreck, pp. 53-56
The Catholic Catechism, Hardon, pp. 38, 145-146
The Church's Confession of Faith, Ignatius Press, pp. 134-138
Faith for Today, Hogan and LeVoir, [First Edition] pp. 81-85; [Second Edition] pp. 111-115
Modern Catholic Dictionary, Hardon, see "Incarnation"
The Teaching of Christ, Lawler, Wuerl, and Lawler, [First Edition] pp. 93-94; [Second Edition] pp. 81-82 [Third Edition] pp. 71-72

Q. 73. What does the Incarnation mean?

Church Documents

Compendium of the Catechism of the Catholic Church, sect. 86
Gaudium et Spes (Pastoral Constitution on the Church in the Modern World), Vatican II, sect. 22, 58, 78
God is Love, Benedict XVI, sect. 41-42
Mother of the Redeemer, John Paul II, sect. 1, 9
On the Dignity and Vocation of Women, John Paul II, sect. 3-4
On the Holy Spirit in the Life of the Church and the World, John Paul II, sect. 49-50
The Relationship Between Faith and Reason, John Paul II, sect. 80, 93
Sacrament of Charity, Benedict XVI, sect. 7-8
U. S. Catholic Catechism for Adults, [2006] pp. 83, 86-87

Other Resources

Basics of the Faith: A Catholic Catechism, Schreck, pp. 53-54
The Catholic Catechism, Hardon, pp. 108-149
The Church's Confession of Faith, Ignatius Press, pp. 135-137
Faith for Today, Hogan and LeVoir, [First Edition] pp. 83-85; [Second Edition] pp. 113-115
Fundamentals of Catholicism, Baker, Vol. 2, pp. 219-246
Fundamentals of Catholic Dogma, Ott, pp. 143-146
Modern Catholic Dictionary, Hardon, see "Incarnation"
The Teaching of Christ, Lawler, Wuerl, and Lawler, [First Edition] pp. 93-108; [Second Edition] pp. 81-96; [Third Edition] pp. 71-84

Q. 74. Why did God the Son come into the world?

Church Documents

Acts and Decrees of the Second Plenary Council of the Philippines, paragraphs 37, 61, 135
Compendium of the Catechism of the Catholic Church, sect. 85
Dei Verbum (Dogmatic Constitution on Divine Revelation), Vatican II, sect. 2-3, 4, 17
Gaudium et Spes (Pastoral Constitution on the Church in the Modern World), Vatican II, sect. 21- 22, 32, 37, 45, 78
God is Love, Benedict XVI, sect. 19
Gospel of Life, John Paul II, sect. 3, 28
Lumen Gentium (Dogmatic Constitution on the Church), Vatican II, sect. 48
Mother of the Redeemer, John Paul II, sect. 1
On the Dignity and Vocation of Women, John Paul II, sect. 3
On the Holy Spirit in the Life of the Church and the World, John Paul II, sect. 24, 31
On Human Work, John Paul II, sect. 27
The Relationship Between Faith and Reason, John Paul II, sect. 2, 10-12, 80
Sacrament of Charity, Benedict XVI, sect. 7-8

Family Wisdom Library™

Papal documents listed below can be viewed at www.vatican.va.
For new cross-references, visit www.familyland.org

Sacrosanctum Concilium (Constitution on the Sacred Liturgy), Vatican II, sect. 5
Splendor of Truth, John Paul II, sect. 103, 118
U. S. Catholic Catechism for Adults, [2006] pp. 86-87, 427

Other Resources

Basics of the Faith: A Catholic Catechism, Schreck, pp. 53-54
The Catholic Catechism, Hardon, pp.108-110
The Church's Confession of Faith, Ignatius Press, p. 136
Faith for Today, Hogan and LeVoir, [First Edition] pp. 81-85; [Second Edition] pp. 111-115
Fundamentals of Catholic Dogma, Ott, pp. 186-189
Fundamentals of Catholicism, Baker, Vol. 2, pp. 269-272
Modern Catholic Dictionary, Hardon, see "Atonement", "Incarnation", "Sacrament of God"
The Teaching of Christ, Lawler, Wuerl, and Lawler, [First Edition] pp. 136-147; [Second Edition] pp.125-136; [Third Edition] pp. 109-119

Q. 75. Is Jesus Christ true God?

Church Documents

Compendium of the Catechism of the Catholic Church, sect. 87
Gaudium et Spes (Pastoral Constitution on the Church in the Modern World), Vatican II, sect. 22
Gospel of Life, John Paul II, sect 36
Lumen Gentium (Dogmatic Constitution on the Church), Vatican II, sect. 5
On the Dignity and Vocation of Women, John Paul II, sect. 3-4
On the Holy Spirit in the Life of the Church and the World, John Paul II, sect. 33
The Relationship Between Faith and Reason, John Paul II, sect. 80
Sacrament of Charity, Benedict XVI, sect. 7-8
U. S. Catholic Catechism for Adults, [2006] p. 81

Other Resources

Basics of the Faith: A Catholic Catechism, Schreck, pp. 54-56
The Catholic Catechism, Hardon, pp. 132-138
The Church's Confession of Faith, Ignatius Press, pp.133-138
Faith for Today, Hogan and LeVoir, [First Edition] pp. 88-89; [Second Edition] pp. 119-120
Fundamentals of Catholic Dogma, Ott, pp. 132-161
Fundamentals of Catholicism, Baker, Vol. 2, pp. 197-199
Modern Catholic Dictionary, Hardon, see "Hypostatic Union"
The Teaching of Christ, Lawler, Wuerl, and Lawler, [First Edition] pp. 95-98, 115-117; [Second Edition] pp. 83-86, 103-105; [Third Edition] 73-75, 90-92

Q. 76. How does the Nicene Creed express our faith in Christ's divinity?

Church Documents

Catechesis in Our Time, John Paul II, sect. 28
Compendium of the Catechism of the Catholic Church, sect. 81-84
Gospel of Life, John Paul II, sect 103
On the Holy Spirit in the Life of the Church and the World, John Paul II, sect. 49
On the Mystery and Worship of the Eucharist, John Paul II, sect. 9, 11
U. S. Catholic Catechism for Adults, [2006] p. 82

Other Resources

Basics of the Faith: A Catholic Catechism, Schreck, p. 52
The Catholic Catechism, Hardon, pp. 128-130
The Church's Confession of Faith, Ignatius Press, p. 69
Fundamentals of Catholic Dogma, Ott, p. 51
Fundamentals of Catholicism, Baker, Vol. 2, pp.197-198
Modern Catholic Dictionary, Hardon, see "Nicene Creed"
The Teaching of Christ, Lawler, Wuerl, and Lawler, [First Edition] p. 95; [Second Edition] p. 83; [Third Edition] p. 73

Q. 77. Did Jesus say He was God?

Church Documents

Compendium of the Catechism of the Catholic Church, sect. 82-84, 113, 116
U. S. Catholic Catechism for Adults, [2006] pp. 79-80

Other Resources

The Catholic Catechism, Hardon, p. 124
The Church's Confession of Faith, Ignatius Press, p. 68

Family Wisdom Library™

Papal documents listed below can be viewed at www.vatican.va.
For new cross-references, visit www.familyland.org

Faith for Today, Hogan and LeVoir, [First Edition] p. 19; [Second Edition] p. 41
Fundamentals of Catholic Dogma, Ott, pp. 133-134
Fundamentals of Catholicism, Baker, Vol. 2, pp. 205-206
The Teaching of Christ, Lawler, Wuerl, and Lawler, [First Edition] p. 97; [Second Edition] p. 85; [Third Edition] p. 74

Q. 78. During His Passion, did Jesus say He was God ?

Church Documents

Compendium of the Catechism of the Catholic Church, sect. 113, 116

Other Resources

The Church's Confession of Faith, Ignatius Press, pp. 230-231
Fundamentals of Catholic Dogma, Ott, p. 133
The Teaching of Christ, Lawler, Wuerl, and Lawler, [First Edition] p. 302; [Second Edition] p. 290; [Third Edition] pp. 255-257

Q. 79. Does the Catholic Church teach that Jesus is truly God?

Church Documents

Compendium of the Catechism of the Catholic Church, sect. 88-89
God is Love, Benedict XVI, sect. 12
Gospel of Life, John Paul II, sect. 3, 36, 76
On the Dignity and Vocation of Women, John Paul II, sect 3-4
On the Mercy of God, John Paul II, sect. 2
Sacrament of Charity, Benedict XVI, sect. 7-8
U. S. Catholic Catechism for Adults, [2006] pp. 81-83

Other Resources

Basics of the Faith: A Catholic Catechism, Schreck, pp. 52, 54-59
The Catholic Catechism, Hardon, pp. 138-141
The Church's Confession of Faith, Ignatius Press, pp. 133-137
Faith for Today, Hogan and LeVoir, [First Edition] pp. 19-20, 81-94; [Second Edition] pp. 41-42, 111-126
Fundamentals of Catholic Dogma, Ott, p. 127
Fundamentals of Catholicism, Baker, Vol. 2, pp. 197-200
Modern Catholic Dictionary, Hardon, see pp. 579-580
The Teaching of Christ, Lawler, Wuerl, and Lawler, [First Edition] pp. 101-103; [Second Edition] pp. 89-91; [Third Edition] pp. 77-79

Q. 80. Is there any further evidence in the New Testament pointing to Jesus as God?

Church Documents

Compendium of the Catechism of the Catholic Church, sect. 108, 127
Dei Verbum (Dogmatic Constitution on Divine Revelation), Vatican II, sect. 17-20
On the Dignity and Vocation of Women, John Paul II, sect. 12-13
On the Holy Spirit in the Life of the Church and the World, John Paul II, sect. 24
U. S. Catholic Catechism for Adults, [2006] pp. 79-80, 94-99

Other Resources

The Catholic Catechism, Hardon, pp. 124-125
The Church's Confession of Faith, Ignatius Press, pp. 134-137
Fundamentals of Catholic Dogma, Ott, pp. 57-58;
Fundamentals of Catholicism, Baker, Vol. 2, pp. 203-209
Modern Catholic Dictionary, Hardon, see "Logos"
The Teaching of Christ, Lawler, Wuerl, and Lawler, [First Edition] pp. 98-102; [Second Edition] pp. 86-90; [Third Edition] pp. 75-78

Q. 81. How does the New Testament portray Jesus?

Church Documents

Catechesis in Our Time, John Paul II, sect. 7-8
Compendium of the Catechism of the Catholic Church, sect. 103, 105-132
Dei Verbum (Dogmatic Constitution on Divine Revelation), Vatican II, sect. 17-20
God is Love, Benedict XVI, sect. 12
Gospel of Life, John Paul II, sect. 3
The Lay Members of Christ's Faithful People, John Paul II, sect. 7
On the Dignity and Vocation of Women, John Paul II, sect. 12
On the Holy Spirit in the Life of the Church and the World, John Paul II, sect. 24-25, 27-30
The Relationship Between Faith and Reason, John Paul II, sect. 23
U. S. Catholic Catechism for Adults, [2006] pp. 79-80

Other Resources

The Catholic Catechism, Hardon, pp. 108-125;
The Church's Confession of Faith, Ignatius Press, pp. 121-152

Family Wisdom Library™

Papal documents listed below can be viewed at www.vatican.va.
For new cross-references, visit www.familyland.org

Faith for Today, Hogan and LeVoir, [First Edition] pp. 81-104; [Second Edition] pp. 111-137
Fundamentals of Catholic Dogma, Ott, pp.57-58
Fundamentals of Catholicism, Baker, Vol. 2, pp. 203-209
Modern Catholic Dictionary, Hardon, see "Son of God" and "Son of Man"
The Teaching of Christ, Lawler, Wuerl, and Lawler, [First Edition] pp. 98-102; [Second Edition] pp. 86-90; [Third Edition] pp. 75-78

Q. 82. Is Jesus Christ true man?

Church Documents

Compendium of the Catechism of the Catholic Church, sect. 87-88, 92
Dei Verbum (Dogmatic Constitution on Divine Revelation), Vatican II, sect. 2, 4, 13, 17
Gaudium et Spes (Pastoral Constitution on the Church in the Modern World), Vatican II, sect. 22
God is Love, Benedict XVI, sect. 12, 14, 17
Gospel of Life, John Paul II, sect. 3
Lumen Gentium (Dogmatic Constitution on the Church), Vatican II, sect. 5
On the Dignity and Vocation of Women, John Paul II, sect. 3, 11, 25
On the Holy Spirit in the Life of the Church and the World, John Paul II, sect. 49-50
The Relationship Between Faith and Reason, John Paul II, sect. 11-12, 60, 66, 80, 93
U. S. Catholic Catechism for Adults, [2006] p. 81

Other Resources

Basics of the Faith: A Catholic Catechism, Schreck, pp. 54-56
The Church's Confession of Faith, Ignatius Press, pp. 131-133
Faith for Today, Hogan and LeVoir, [First Edition] pp. 85-94; [Second Edition] pp. 115-126
Fundamentals of Catholic Dogma, Ott, pp.144-152
Fundamentals of Catholicism, Baker, Vol. 2, pp. 48-50
Modern Catholic Dictionary, Hardon, see "Hypo-static Union"
The Teaching of Christ, Lawler, Wuerl, and Lawler, [First Edition] pp. 94-95; [Second Edition] pp. 82-83; [Third Edition] pp. 72-73

Q. 83. In what ways did Jesus show His concern for us?

Church Documents

Catechesis in Our Time, John Paul II, sect. 9
Compendium of the Catechism of the Catholic Church, sect. 79, 85
Dei Verbum (Dogmatic Constitution on Divine Revelation), Vatican II, sect. 2, 4, 13, 17
Gaudium et Spes (Pastoral Constitution on the Church in the Modern World), Vatican II, sect. 22
God is Love, Benedict XVI, sect. 12, 14, 17
Gospel of Life, John Paul II, sect. 2
The Lay Members of Christ's Faithful People, John Paul II, sect. 53
Lumen Gentium (Dogmatic Constitution on the Church), Vatican II, sect. 7
On the Dignity and Vocation of Women, John Paul II, sect. 12-13
On Evangelization in the Modern World, Paul VI, sect. 6-9, 12
On the Holy Spirit in the Life of the Church and the World, John Paul II, sect. 39
Redeemer of Man, John Paul II, sect. 8
The Relationship Between Faith and Reason, John Paul II, sect. 11-12, 23, 60, 66, 80, 93
Sacrament of Charity, Benedict XVI, sect. 7-11
Splendor of Truth, John Paul II, sect. 8
To the Youth of the World, John Paul II, sect. 7-8
U. S. Catholic Catechism for Adults, [2006] pp. 91-93

Other Resources

Basics of the Faith: A Catholic Catechism, Schreck, pp. 58-61
The Catholic Catechism, Hardon, pp. 108-125
The Church's Confession of Faith, Ignatius Press, pp. 129-130, 153-163
Faith for Today, Hogan and LeVoir, [First Edition] pp. 81-85, 94-104; [Second Edition] 111-115, 126-137
Fundamentals of Catholic Dogma, Ott, p. 49
Fundamentals of Catholicism, Baker, Vol. 2, pp. 269-301
Modern Catholic Dictionary, Hardon, see "Redemption"
The Teaching of Christ, Lawler, Wuerl, and Lawler, [First Edition] pp. 124-150; [Second Edition] pp. 112-140; [Third Edition] pp. 98-122

Family Wisdom Library™

Papal documents listed below can be viewed at www.vatican.va.
For new cross-references, visit www.familyland.org

Q. 84. Why did the Son of God become man?

Church Documents

Compendium of the Catechism of the Catholic Church, sect. 78-79, 81, 85
Dei Verbum (Dogmatic Constitution on Divine Revelation), Vatican II, sect. 2-4
Gaudium et Spes (Pastoral Constitution on the Church in the Modern World), Vatican II, sect. 22
God is Love, Benedict XVI, sect. 12
Gospel of Life, John Paul II, sect. 2, 28
Lumen Gentium (Dogmatic Constitution on the Church), Vatican II, sect. 3, 5, 48
Mother of the Redeemer, John Paul II, sect. 1
On the Dignity and Vocation of Women, John Paul II, sect. 3-4
On Evangelization in the Modern World, Paul VI, sect. 8
On the Holy Spirit in the Life of the Church and the World, John Paul II, sect. 50
On Human Work, John Paul II, sect. 26
On the Hundredth Anniversary of Rerum Novarum, John Paul II, sect. 25
On Reconciliation and Penance, John Paul II, sect. 7
Redeemer of Man, John Paul II, sect. 9
The Relationship Between Faith and Reason, John Paul II, sect. 7, 11-12, 23, 60, 66, 80, 93
Sacrament of Charity, Benedict XVI, sect. 7-9
Sacrosanctum Concilium (Constitution on the Sacred Liturgy), Vatican II, sect. 5
Splendor of Truth, John Paul II, sect. 1
U. S. Catholic Catechism for Adults, [2006] pp. 86-87

Other Resources

Basics of the Faith: A Catholic Catechism, Schreck, p.53
The Catholic Catechism, Hardon, pp. 256, 268
The Church's Confession of Faith, Ignatius Press, pp. 131-133
Faith for Today, Hogan and LeVoir, [First Edition] pp. 81-85; [Second Edition] pp. 111-115
Fundamentals of Catholic Dogma, Ott, p. 175
Fundamentals of Catholicism, Baker, Vol. 2, pp. 269-272
Modern Catholic Dictionary, Hardon, see "Incarnation"
The Teaching of Christ, Lawler, Wuerl, and Lawler, [First Edition] pp. 265-274; [Second Edition] pp. 253-262; [Third Edition] pp. 223-231

Q. 85. What do we mean when we say that Jesus is our Savior?

Church Documents

Compendium of the Catechism of the Catholic Church, sect. 81-82, 422-423
Dei Verbum (Dogmatic Constitution on Divine Revelation), Vatican II, sect. 2-4
Gaudium et Spes (Pastoral Constitution on the Church in the Modern World), Vatican II, sect. 22
God is Love, Benedict XVI, sect. 12
Lumen Gentium (Dogmatic Constitution on the Church), Vatican II, sect. 3, 5, 48
On the Dignity and Vocation of Women, John Paul II, sect. 4
On Evangelization in the Modern World, Paul VI, sect. 33-34
On the Holy Spirit in the Life of the Church and the World, John Paul II, sect. 24
On the Hundredth Anniversary of Rerum Novarum, John Paul II, sect. 55
On Reconciliation and Penance, John Paul II, sect. 7
Redeemer of Man, John Paul II, sect. 9
The Relationship Between Faith and Reason, John Paul II, sect. 7, 9, 11, 70, 80
Rich in Mercy, John Paul II, sect. 7-8
Sacrament of Charity, Benedict XVI, sect. 86
Sacrosanctum Concilium (Constitution on the Sacred Liturgy), Vatican II, sect. 5
U. S. Catholic Catechism for Adults, [2006] pp. 91-92

Other Resources

The Catholic Catechism, Hardon, pp. 115-122
The Church's Confession of Faith, Ignatius Press, pp. 153-161
Faith for Today, Hogan and LeVoir, [First Edition] pp. 81-82; [Second Edition] pp. 111-112
Fundamentals of Catholic Dogma, Ott, pp. 185-186
Fundamentals of Catholicism, Baker, Vol. 2, pp. 273-276
Modern Catholic Dictionary, Hardon, see "Redemption" and "Sacrament of God"
The Teaching of Christ, Lawler, Wuerl, and Lawler, [First Edition] pp. 136-147; [Second Edition] pp. 125-136; [Third Edition] pp. 109-119

Family Wisdom Library™

Papal documents listed below can be viewed at www.vatican.va.
For new cross-references, visit www.familyland.org

Q. 86. Is there any other Savior besides Jesus?

Church Documents

Compendium of the Catechism of the Catholic Church, sect. 81
Dei Verbum (Dogmatic Constitution on Divine Revelation), Vatican II, sect. 2-4
Lumen Gentium (Dogmatic Constitution on the Church), Vatican II, sect. 3, 5
Redeemer of Man, John Paul II, sect. 7-8
Sacrament of Charity, Benedict XVI, sect. 86
Sacrosanctum Concilium (Constitution on the Sacred Liturgy), Vatican II, sect. 5
Splendor of Truth, John Paul II, sect. 1
U. S. Catholic Catechism for Adults, [2006] pp. 38, 68

Other Resources

Basics of the Faith: A Catholic Catechism, Schreck, p. 53
The Catholic Catechism, Hardon, pp. 256, 268
The Church's Confession of Faith, Ignatius Press, pp. 131-133
Faith for Today, Hogan and LeVoir, [First Edition] pp. 81-85 [Second Edition] pp. 111-115
Fundamentals of Catholic Dogma, Ott, p. 175
Fundamentals of Catholicism, Baker, Vol. 2, pp. 269-272
Modern Catholic Dictionary, Hardon, see "Incarnation"
The Teaching of Christ, Lawler, Wuerl, and Lawler, [First Edition] pp. 265-274; [Second Edition] pp. 253-262; [Third Edition] pp. 223-231

Q. 87. How did Jesus Christ redeem us?

Church Documents

Compendium of the Catechism of the Catholic Church, sect. 118-122
Dei Verbum (Dogmatic Constitution on Divine Revelation), Vatican II, sect. 2-4, 17, 19
Gaudium et Spes (Pastoral Constitution on the Church in the Modern World), Vatican II, sect. 2, 13, 22, 32, 37, 78
God is Love, Benedict XVI, sect. 12
Gospel of Life, John Paul II, sect. 82
Guardian of the Redeemer, John Paul II, sect. 7-9
Lumen Gentium (Dogmatic Constitution on the Church), Vatican II, sect. 2, 3, 5, 48
On the Dignity and Vocation of Women, John Paul II, sect. 3-4, 11-12
On Evangelization in the Modern World, Paul VI, sect. 33-34
On the Holy Spirit in the Life of the Church and the World, John Paul II, sect. 24, 40
Redeemer of Man, John Paul II, sect. 8
The Relationship Between Faith and Reason, John Paul II, sect. 11-12, 23, 93
Sacrament of Charity, Benedict XVI, sect. 86
Sacrosanctum Concilium (Constitution on the Sacred Liturgy), Vatican II, sect. 5
Splendor of Truth, John Paul II, sect. 18, 85
U. S. Catholic Catechism for Adults, [2006] pp. 91-92

Other Resources

Basics of the Faith: A Catholic Catechism, Schreck, pp. 67-69
The Catholic Catechism, Hardon, pp. 431-432
The Church's Confession of Faith, Ignatius Press, pp. 153-161
Faith for Today, Hogan and LeVoir, [First Edition] pp. 81-82 99-100; [Second Edition] pp. 111-112, 131-133
Fundamentals of Catholic Dogma, Ott, p. 148
Fundamentals of Catholicism, Baker, Vol. 2, pp. 273-276
Modern Catholic Dictionary, Hardon, see "Passion" and "Redemption"
The Teaching of Christ, Lawler, Wuerl, and Lawler, [First Edition] pp. 136-160; [Second Edition] p. 125-139; [Third Edition] pp. 109-130

Q. 88. What did the agony and prayer in the garden express?

Church Documents

Compendium of the Catechism of the Catholic Church, sect. 121
On the Christian Meaning of Human Suffering, John Paul II, sect. 18

Other Resources

The Church's Confession of Faith, Ignatius Press, pp. 154-155
Faith for Today, Hogan and LeVoir, [First Edition] p. 100; [Second Edition] pp. 132-133
Fundamentals of Catholic Dogma, Ott, p. 148
Fundamentals of Catholicism, Baker, Vol. 2, p. 248
The Teaching of Christ, Lawler, Wuerl, and Lawler, [First Edition] p. 141; [Second Edition] p. 130 [Third Edition] p. 113

Family Wisdom Library™

Papal documents listed below can be viewed at www.vatican.va.
For new cross-references, visit www.familyland.org

Q. 89. Why were the sufferings Christ bore for us so severe?

Church Documents

Compendium of the Catechism of the Catholic Church, sect. 122
God is Love, Benedict XVI, sect. 9-12, 17
On the Christian Meaning of Human Suffering, John Paul II, sect. 14-19
On the Holy Spirit in the Life of the Church and the World, John Paul II, sect. 31-32, 39
U. S. Catholic Catechism for Adults, [2006] pp. 91-93

Other Resources

Basics of the Faith: A Catholic Catechism, Schreck, pp. 66-67
The Catholic Catechism, Hardon, p. 110
The Church's Confession of Faith, Ignatius Press pp. 156-157
Faith for Today, Hogan and LeVoir, [First Edition] pp. 99-100; [Second Edition] pp. 131-133
Fundamentals of Catholic Dogma, Ott, pp. 173-174
Fundamentals of Catholicism, Baker, Vol. 2, pp. 266-267, 292
The Teaching of Christ, Lawler, Wuerl, and Lawler, [First Edition] pp. 137-140; [Second Edition] pp. 126-129; [Third Edition] pp. 110-112

Q. 90. Before His Death what trials did Jesus undergo?

Church Documents

Compendium of the Catechism of the Catholic Church, sect. 106, 113, 115, 117, 121, 122
On the Christian Meaning of Human Suffering, John Paul II, sect. 15-18
Redeemer of Man, John Paul II, sect. 12
U. S. Catholic Catechism for Adults, [2006] pp. 91-92

Other Resources

The Church's Confession of Faith, Ignatius Press, pp. 154-155
The Teaching of Christ, Lawler, Wuerl, and Lawler, [First Edition] pp. 141-142; [Second Edition] pp. 130-131; [Third Edition] pp. 113-114

Q. 91. What was Christ's mission on earth?

Church Documents

Compendium of the Catechism of the Catholic Church, sect. 85-86
Dei Verbum (Dogmatic Constitution on Divine Revelation), Vatican II, sect. 2-4, 17, 19
Gaudium et Spes (Pastoral Constitution on the Church in the Modern World), Vatican II, sect. 22
God is Love, Benedict XVI, sect. 12
Gospel of Life, John Paul II, sect. 47
Lumen Gentium (Dogmatic Constitution on the Church), Vatican II, sect. 2, 3, 5, 48
On the Christian Meaning of Human Suffering, John Paul II, sect. 14-18
On Evangelization in the Modern World, Paul VI, sect. 8
On Human Work, John Paul II, sect. 27
On the Hundredth Anniversary of Rerum Novarum, John Paul II, sect. 25
The Relationship Between Faith and Reason, John Paul II, sect. 11-12, 23, 60, 66, 93
Sacrament of Charity, Benedict XVI, sect. 7-12
Sacrosanctum Concilium (Constitution on the Sacred Liturgy), Vatican II, sect. 5
U. S. Catholic Catechism for Adults, [2006] pp. 79-80

Other Resources

Basics of the Faith: A Catholic Catechism, Schreck, pp. 53-54
The Catholic Catechism, Hardon, pp. 108-110
The Church's Confession of Faith, Ignatius Press, pp. 124-138
Faith for Today, Hogan and LeVoir, [First Edition] pp. 81-85; [Second Edition] pp. 111-115
Fundamentals of Catholic Dogma, Ott, pp. 175-195
Fundamentals of Catholicism, Baker, Vol. 2, pp. 269-272
The Teaching of Christ, Lawler, Wuerl, and Lawler, [First Edition] pp. 136-137, 265-266; [Second Edition] pp. 125-126, 253-254; [Third Edition] pp. 109-110, 223-224

Q. 92. In what sense do we speak of the necessity of the Passion and Death of Jesus?

Church Documents

Compendium of the Catechism of the Catholic Church, sect. 118-120
Lumen Gentium (Dogmatic Constitution on the Church), Vatican II, sect. 3
On the Holy Spirit in the Life of the Church and the World, John Paul II, sect. 27-32

Family Wisdom Library™

Papal documents listed below can be viewed at www.vatican.va.
For new cross-references, visit www.familyland.org

On Reconciliation and Penance, John Paul II, sect. 7
Redeemer of Man, John Paul II, sect. 8-9
U. S. Catholic Catechism for Adults, [2006] pp. 72-75

Other Resources

The Catholic Catechism, Hardon, pp. 108-109
Fundamentals of Catholic Dogma, Ott, pp. 178-179
Fundamentals of Catholicism, Baker, Vol. 2, pp. 276-279
The Teaching of Christ, Lawler, Wuerl, and Lawler, [First Edition] p.137-138; [Second Edition] pp. 126-127; [Third Edition] p. 110

Q. 93. Did Jesus Himself declare that He had to suffer?

Church Documents

Catechesis in Our Time, John Paul II, sect. 9
Compendium of the Catechism of the Catholic Church, sect. 120-121
Redeemer of Man, John Paul II, sect. 8-9
To the Youth of the World, John Paul II, sect. 5
U. S. Catholic Catechism for Adults, [2006] p. 91

Other Resources

Basics of the Faith: A Catholic Catechism, Schreck, p. 67
The Catholic Catechism, Hardon, p. 124
The Church's Confession of Faith, Ignatius Press, p. 158
Fundamentals of Catholic Dogma, Ott, pp. 184-185
The Teaching of Christ, Lawler, Wuerl, and Lawler, [First Edition] pp. 137-138; [Second Edition] pp. 126-127; [Third Edition] p. 110

Q. 94. What did Jesus suffer upon the Cross?

Church Documents

Compendium of the Catechism of the Catholic Church, sect. 121-122
Gospel of Life, John Paul II, sect. 25, 49, 50, 51
U. S. Catholic Catechism for Adults, [2006] pp. 91-92

Other Resources

The Catholic Catechism, Hardon, p. 123
The Church's Confession of Faith, Ignatius Press, p.155
Fundamentals of Catholicism, Baker, Vol. 2, pp. 248-249
The Teaching of Christ, Lawler, Wuerl, and Lawler, [First Edition] p. 142; [Second Edition p. 131; [Third Edition] p. 114

Q. 95. What are the "seven last words" of Jesus as recorded in the Gospels?

Church Documents

On the Christian Meaning of Human Suffering, John Paul II, sect. 18

Other Resources

The Church's Confession of Faith, Ignatius Press, p. 159
Fundamentals of Catholicism, Baker, Vol. 2, p. 357
The Teaching of Christ, Lawler, Wuerl, and Lawler, [First Edition] p. 142; [Second Edition] p. 131; [Third Edition] p. 114

Q. 96. How did Jesus die?

Church Documents

Compendium of the Catechism of the Catholic Church, sect. 119, 122, 124
God is Love, Benedict XVI, sect. 12, 17
Gospel of Life, John Paul II, sect. 33
Lumen Gentium (Dogmatic Constitution on the Church), Vatican II, sect. 3, 5, 58, 61
Sacrosanctum Concilium (Constitution on the Sacred Liturgy), Vatican II, sect. 5
U. S. Catholic Catechism for Adults, [2006] pp. 91-92

Other Resources

The Catholic Catechism, Hardon, pp. 465-466
The Church's Confession of Faith, Ignatius Press, pp. 153-156
Faith for Today, Hogan and LeVoir, [First Edition] pp. 98-100 pp. 130-133
Fundamentals of Catholicism, Baker, Vol. 2, pp. 289-292
Modern Catholic Dictionary, Hardon, see "Crucifixion"
The Teaching of Christ, Lawler, Wuerl, and Lawler, [First Edition] p. 142; [Second Edition] pp. 131-132; [Third Edition] p. 114

Q. 97. What effects did the Passion of Jesus have?

Church Documents

Compendium of the Catechism of the Catholic Church, sect. 118, 131
Gaudium et Spes (Pastoral Constitution on the Church in the Modern World), Vatican II, sect. 22

Family Wisdom Library™

Papal documents listed below can be viewed at www.vatican.va.
For new cross-references, visit www.familyland.org

Guardian of the Redeemer, John Paul II, sect. 8
Lumen Gentium (Dogmatic Constitution on the Church), Vatican II, sect. 3, 5, 48
The Relationship Between Faith and Reason, John Paul II, sect. 12, 93
Sacrament of Charity, Benedict XVI, sect. 9
Sacrosanctum Concilium (Constitution on the Sacred Liturgy), Vatican II, sect. 5-6
Splendor of Truth, John Paul II, sect. 87, 103
U. S. Catholic Catechism for Adults, [2006] pp. 93-96

Other Resources

The Catholic Catechism, Hardon, pp. 431-432
The Church's Confession of Faith, Ignatius Press, pp. 156-161
Faith for Today, Hogan and LeVoir, [First Edition] pp. 82-100, 228-229; [Second Edition] pp. 112-113, 132-133, 273-275
Fundamentals of Catholic Dogma, Ott, pp. 184-189
Fundamentals of Catholicism, Baker, Vol. 2, pp. 292-295, 298-301
Modern Catholic Dictionary, Hardon, see "Redemption"
The Teaching of Christ, Lawler, Wuerl, and Lawler, [First Edition] pp. 142-143; [Second Edition] p. 132; [Third Edition] p. 115

Q. 98. How did Jesus Christ show the power He has as the Son of God?

Church Documents

Compendium of the Catechism of the Catholic Church, sect. 108, 128-131
Gaudium et Spes (Pastoral Constitution on the Church in the Modern World), Vatican II, sect. 22, 32, 37-38
Lumen Gentium (Dogmatic Constitution on the Church), Vatican II, sect. 7, 48
On the Holy Spirit in the Life of the Church and the World, John Paul II, sect. 24
The Relationship Between Faith and Reason, John Paul II, sect. 11-12
Sacrament of Charity, Benedict XVI, sect. 72
Sacrosanctum Concilium (Constitution on the Sacred Liturgy), Vatican II, sect. 5, 6
U. S. Catholic Catechism for Adults, [2006] pp. 79-80

Other Resources

The Catholic Catechism, Hardon, p. 38
The Church's Confession of Faith, Ignatius Press, pp. 165-174
Faith for Today, Hogan and LeVoir, [First Edition] p. 85; [Second Edition] p. 115
Fundamentals of Catholic Dogma, Ott, pp. 192-193
Fundamentals of Catholicism, Baker, Vol. 2, pp. 304-307
Modern Catholic Dictionary, Hardon, see "Resurrection of Christ"
The Teaching of Christ, Lawler, Wuerl, and Lawler, [First Edition] pp. 148-158; [Second Edition] pp. 137-147; [Third Edition] pp. 120-129

Q. 99. Why is the Resurrection of our Lord so important?

Church Documents

Compendium of the Catechism of the Catholic Church, sect. 126, 128, 131
Dei Verbum (Dogmatic Constitution on Divine Revelation), Vatican II, sect. 4, 17
Gaudium et Spes (Pastoral Constitution on the Church in the Modern World), Vatican II, sect. 22, 38
Gospel of Life, John Paul II, sect. 82, 97, 104
Lumen Gentium (Dogmatic Constitution on the Church), Vatican II, sect. 7, 48
On the Holy Spirit in the Life of the Church and the World, John Paul II, sect. 24-25
The Relationship Between Faith and Reason, John Paul II, sect. 11-12, 26
Sacrament of Charity, Benedict XVI, sect. 72
Sacrosanctum Concilium (Constitution on the Sacred Liturgy), Vatican II, sect. 5-6
U. S. Catholic Catechism for Adults, [2006] pp. 93-97

Other Resources

Basics of the Faith: A Catholic Catechism, Schreck, pp. 69-70
The Catholic Catechism, Hardon, p. 38
The Church's Confession of Faith, Ignatius Press, pp.172-174
Fundamentals of Catholic Dogma, Ott, p.193
Fundamentals of Catholicism, Baker, Vol. 2, p. 307
Modern Catholic Dictionary, Hardon, see "Resurrection of Christ"
The Teaching of Christ, Lawler, Wuerl, and Lawler, [First Edition] pp. 148-158; [Second Edition] pp. 137-147; [Third Edition] pp. 120-128

Family Wisdom Library™

Papal documents listed below can be viewed at www.vatican.va.
For new cross-references, visit www.familyland.org

Q. 100. Why does the Resurrection of Jesus play a central part in the life of faith?

Church Documents

Acts and Decrees of the Second Plenary Council of the Philippines, paragraph 234;
Catechesis in Our Time, John Paul II, sect. 10
Compendium of the Catechism of the Catholic Church, sect. 131
Dei Verbum (Dogmatic Constitution on Divine Revelation), Vatican II, sect. 4, 17
Gaudium et Spes (Pastoral Constitution on the Church in the Modern World), Vatican II, sect. 22, 37
God is Love, Benedict XVI, sect. 6
Lumen Gentium (Dogmatic Constitution on the Church), Vatican II, sect. 7, 48
On the Holy Spirit in the Life of the Church and the World, John Paul II, sect. 24, 58
On Human Work, John Paul II, sect. 27
The Relationship Between Faith and Reason, John Paul II, sect. 11-12, 26
Sacrament of Charity, Benedict XVI, sect. 72-73
Sacrosanctum Concilium (Constitution on the Sacred Liturgy), Vatican II, sect. 5
U. S. Catholic Catechism for Adults, [2006] pp. 95-96

Other Resources

Basics of the Faith: A Catholic Catechism, Schreck, pp. 69-70
The Catholic Catechism, Hardon, p. 38
Fundamentals of Catholic Dogma, Ott, p.193
Fundamentals of Catholicism, Baker, Vol. 2, p. 307
The Church's Confession of Faith, Ignatius Press, pp. 172-174
The Teaching of Christ, Lawler, Wuerl, and Lawler, [First Edition] p. 149; [Second Edition] p. 138; [Third Edition] p. 121

Q. 101. What was the Easter proclamation?

Church Documents

Acts and Decrees of the Second Plenary Council of the Philippines, paragraph 51
On the Dignity and Vocation of Women, John Paul II, sect. 16
Sacrosanctum Concilium (Constitution on the Sacred Liturgy), Vatican II, sect. 5
U. S. Catholic Catechism for Adults, [2006] pp. 93-94

Other Resources

The Church's Confession of Faith, Ignatius Press, pp. 166-169
The Teaching of Christ, Lawler, Wuerl, and Lawler, [First Edition] pp. 148-149; [Second Edition] pp. 137-138; [Third Edition] pp. 120-121

Q. 102. How did Jesus lead His Apostles to faith in His Resurrection?

Church Documents

Compendium of the Catechism of the Catholic Church, sect. 127
Sacrament of Charity, Benedict XVI, sect. 72
Sacrosanctum Concilium (Constitution on the Sacred Liturgy), Vatican II, sect. 5
U. S. Catholic Catechism for Adults, [2006] pp. 95-97

Other Resources

Basics of the Faith: A Catholic Catechism, Schreck, pp. 70-71
The Church's Confession of Faith, Ignatius Press, pp. 168-170
Fundamentals of Catholic Dogma, Ott, p. 193
Fundamentals of Catholicism, Baker, Vol. 2, pp. 306-307
The Teaching of Christ, Lawler, Wuerl, and Lawler, [First Edition] pp.151-152; [Second Edition] pp. 140-141; [Third Edition] pp. 122-124

Q. 103. How did the Holy Spirit lead the Apostles towards faith in the Resurrection of Jesus?

Church Documents

Compendium of the Catechism of the Catholic Church, sect. 137
Dei Verbum (Dogmatic Constitution on Divine Revelation), Vatican II, sect. 5, 17-20
Gaudium et Spes (Pastoral Constitution on the Church in the Modern World), Vatican II, sect. 22, 37
God is Love, Benedict XVI, sect. 19
Lumen Gentium (Dogmatic Constitution on the Church), Vatican II, sect. 48
On the Holy Spirit in the Life of the Church and the World, John Paul II, sect. 24
Sacrament of Charity, Benedict XVI, sect. 12
Sacrosanctum Concilium (Constitution on the Sacred Liturgy), Vatican II, sect. 5
U. S. Catholic Catechism for Adults, [2006] pp. 102-104

Family Wisdom Library™

Papal documents listed below can be viewed at www.vatican.va.
For new cross-references, visit www.familyland.org

Other Resources

Basics of the Faith: A Catholic Catechism, Schreck, pp. 71-74
The Catholic Catechism, Hardon, p. 208
The Teaching of Christ, Lawler, Wuerl, and Lawler, [First Edition] p. 151; [Second Edition] p. 140; [Third Edition] p. 122

Q. 104. What does the Church teach about the Resurrection?

Church Documents

Compendium of the Catechism of the Catholic Church, sect. 126-131
Gaudium et Spes (Pastoral Constitution on the Church in the Modern World), Vatican II, sect. 38
Lumen Gentium (Dogmatic Constitution on the Church), Vatican II, sect. 7, 48
On the Holy Spirit in the Life of the Church and the World, John Paul II, sect. 24
Sacrament of Charity, Benedict XVI, sect. 72
Sacrosanctum Concilium (Constitution on the Sacred Liturgy), Vatican II, sect. 5
U. S. Catholic Catechism for Adults, [2006] pp. 96-98

Other Resources

The Church's Confession of Faith, Ignatius Press, pp. 168, 171-172
Fundamentals of Catholic Dogma, Ott, pp. 192-193
Fundamentals of Catholicism, Baker, Vol. 2, pp. 304-307
The Teaching of Christ, Lawler, Wuerl, and Lawler, [First Edition] pp. 149-150; [Second Edition] pp. 138-139; [Third Edition] p. 122

Q. 105. What does it mean to believe in the bodily Resurrection of Jesus from the dead?

Church Documents

Compendium of the Catechism of the Catholic Church, sect. 131
Gaudium et Spes (Pastoral Constitution on the Church in the Modern World), Vatican II, sect. 32, 37
Gospel of Life, John Paul II, sect. 28
Lumen Gentium (Dogmatic Constitution on the Church), Vatican II, sect. 48
Sacrosanctum Concilium (Constitution on the Sacred Liturgy), Vatican II, sect. 5
U. S. Catholic Catechism for Adults, [2006] pp. 96-97, 183-184

Other Resources

Basics of the Faith: A Catholic Catechism, Schreck, pp. 70-71
The Catholic Catechism, Hardon, pp. 207-208
The Church's Confession of Faith, Ignatius Press, pp. 171-174
Fundamentals of Catholic Dogma, Ott, p.193
Fundamentals of Catholicism, Baker, Vol. 2, p. 307
Modern Catholic Dictionary, Hardon, see "Resurrection"
The Teaching of Christ, Lawler, Wuerl, and Lawler, [First Edition] pp. 153-155; [Second Edition] pp. 142-144; [Third Edition] pp. 124-125

Q. 106. What has Jesus Christ done for us through His Resurrection?

Church Documents

Compendium of the Catechism of the Catholic Church, sect. 131, 202-204
Gaudium et Spes (Pastoral Constitution on the Church in the Modern World), Vatican II, sect. 32, 37-38, 41, 78
Gospel of Life, John Paul II, sect. 38, 67
The Lay Members of Christ's Faithful People, John Paul II, sect. 37
Lumen Gentium (Dogmatic Constitution on the Church), Vatican II, sect. 7, 48
Sacrament of Charity, Benedict XVI, sect. 72-73
Sacrosanctum Concilium (Constitution on the Sacred Liturgy), Vatican II, sect. 5
U. S. Catholic Catechism for Adults, [2006] pp. 95-96, 183-184, 221

Other Resources

Basics of the Faith: A Catholic Catechism, Schreck, p. 70
The Catholic Catechism, Hardon, p. 208
The Teaching of Christ, Lawler, Wuerl, and Lawler, [First Edition] pp. 157-158; [Second Edition] pp. 146-147; [Third Edition] pp. 128-129

Q. 107. How does the risen Jesus help us now?

Church Documents

Compendium of the Catechism of the Catholic Church, sect. 131, 146, 156-158
Gaudium et Spes (Pastoral Constitution on the Church in the Modern World), Vatican II, sect. 32, 37-38, 78
God is Love, Benedict XVI, sect. 19
Gospel of Life, John Paul II, sect. 84

Family Wisdom Library™

Papal documents listed below can be viewed at www.vatican.va.
For new cross-references, visit www.familyland.org

Guardian of the Redeemer, John Paul II, sect. 7
Lumen Gentium (Dogmatic Constitution on the Church), Vatican II, sect. 5, 7, 48
On Reconciliation and Penance, John Paul II, sect. 20
Sacrament of Charity, Benedict XVI, sect. 12, 37
Sacrosanctum Concilium (Constitution on the Sacred Liturgy), Vatican II, sect. 5-6
Splendor of Truth, John Paul II, sect. 118
U. S. Catholic Catechism for Adults, [2006] pp. 102-106, 167, 264

Other Resources

Basics of the Faith: A Catholic Catechism, Schreck, p. 72
The Catholic Catechism, Hardon, pp. 207-208
The Church's Confession of Faith, Ignatius Press, pp. 262-266
Faith for Today, Hogan and LeVoir, [First Edition] pp. 177-178; [Second Edition] pp. 217-218
Fundamentals of Catholic Dogma, Ott, pp. 274-275
Fundamentals of Catholicism, Baker, Vol. 3, p. 95
The Teaching of Christ, Lawler, Wuerl, and Lawler, [First Edition] p. 414; [Second Edition] p. 404; [Third Edition] p. 358

Q. 108. What is the meaning of the Ascension of Christ?

Church Documents

Compendium of the Catechism of the Catholic Church, sect. 132
Dei Verbum (Dogmatic Constitution on Divine Revelation), Vatican II, sect. 17
Sacrosanctum Concilium (Constitution on the Sacred Liturgy), Vatican II, sect. 5
U. S. Catholic Catechism for Adults, [2006] pp. 96-97

Other Resources

Basics of the Faith: A Catholic Catechism, Schreck, p. 72
The Church's Confession of Faith, Ignatius Press, pp. 174-176
Fundamentals of Catholicism, Baker, Vol. 2, pp. 308-311
Fundamentals of Catholic Dogma, Ott, pp.194-195
Modern Catholic Dictionary, Hardon, see "Ascension"
The Teaching of Christ, Lawler, Wuerl, and Lawler, [First Edition] pp. 158-160; [Second Edition] pp. 148-149; [Third Edition] pp. 129-130

Q. 109. What are the two distinctive aspects of the mystery of the Ascension?

Church Documents

Compendium of the Catechism of the Catholic Church, sect. 132
U. S. Catholic Catechism for Adults, [2006] pp. 96-97

Other Resources

Basics of the Faith: A Catholic Catechism, Schreck, p. 71
The Church's Confession of Faith, Ignatius Press, pp. 174-175
Fundamentals of Catholic Dogma, Ott, pp. 194-195
Fundamentals of Catholicism, Baker, Vol. 2, pp. 308-309
Modern Catholic Dictionary, Hardon, see "Ascension"
The Teaching of Christ, Lawler, Wuerl, and Lawler, [First Edition] p. 159; [Second Edition] p. 148; [Third Edition] p. 129

Q. 110. What has Christ done for us through His Ascension?

Church Documents

Compendium of the Catechism of the Catholic Church, sect. 132
Dei Verbum (Dogmatic Constitution on Divine Revelation), Vatican II, sect. 17
The Relationship Between Faith and Reason, John Paul II, sect. 93
Sacrosanctum Concilium (Constitution on the Sacred Liturgy), Vatican II, sect. 5
U. S. Catholic Catechism for Adults, [2006] pp. 96-97

Other Resources

The Church's Confession of Faith, Ignatius Press, pp. 174-178
Fundamentals of Catholic Dogma, Ott, pp. 194-195
Fundamentals of Catholicism, Baker, Vol. 2, p. 310
The Teaching of Christ, Lawler, Wuerl, and Lawler, [First Edition] pp. 158-160; [Second Edition] pp. 148-149; [Third Edition] pp. 129-130

Q. 111. How is Christ present with the Church?

Church Documents

Compendium of the Catechism of the Catholic Church, sect. 146, 156-158

Family Wisdom Library™

Papal documents listed below can be viewed at www.vatican.va.
For new cross-references, visit www.familyland.org

Gaudium et Spes (Pastoral Constitution on the Church in the Modern World), Vatican II, sect. 1, 3, 15, 21-22, 37-38, 43, 92, 93
God is Love, Benedict XVI, sect. 13-14, 17, 19
Gospel of Life, John Paul II, sect. 84
Lumen Gentium (Dogmatic Constitution on the Church), Vatican II, sect. 3, 7
On the Holy Spirit in the Life of the Church and the World, John Paul II, sect. 61-64
On the Mystery and Worship of the Eucharist, John Paul II, sect. 3
On Reconciliation and Penance, John Paul II, sect. 24
The Relationship Between Faith and Reason, John Paul II, sect. 7
Sacrament of Charity, Benedict XVI, sect. 14-16
U. S. Catholic Catechism for Adults, [2006] pp. 102-109, 114-115

Other Resources

Basics of the Faith: A Catholic Catechism, Schreck, p. 72
The Catholic Catechism, Hardon, pp. 446-447
The Church's Confession of Faith, Ignatius Press, pp. 176-178
Faith for Today, Hogan and LeVoir, [First Edition] pp. 177-236; [Second Edition] pp. 217-283
Fundamentals of Catholic Dogma, Ott, pp. 194-195
Fundamentals of Catholicism, Baker, Vol. 3, pp. 95-100
The Teaching of Christ, Lawler, Wuerl, and Lawler, [First Edition] pp. 159-160; [Second Edition] p. 149; [Third Edition] p. 130

Q. 112. What plan does God have for mankind?

Church Documents

Compendium of the Catechism of the Catholic Church, sect. 1
Gaudium et Spes (Pastoral Constitution on the Church in the Modern World), Vatican II, sect. 22, 24, 37, 43, 45, 92
Gospel of Life, John Paul II, sect. 6, 36, 44, 66
Lumen Gentium (Dogmatic Constitution on the Church), Vatican II, sect. 1- 2, 5, 7-9, 48
On Human Work, John Paul II, sect. 24
The Relationship Between Faith and Reason, John Paul II, sect. 13, 81
Sacrament of Charity, Benedict XVI, sect. 70-72, 77
Sacrosanctum Concilium (Constitution on the Sacred Liturgy), Vatican II, sect. 5
Splendor of Truth, John Paul II, sect. 2
U. S. Catholic Catechism for Adults, [2006] pp. 116-119

Other Resources

Basics of the Faith: A Catholic Catechism, Schreck, pp. 30-31
The Catholic Catechism, Hardon, pp. 78-81, 425-428
The Church's Confession of Faith, Ignatius Press, pp. 88-90
Faith for Today, Hogan and LeVoir, [First Edition] pp. 63-75, 102, 109, 142, 233; [Second Edition] pp. 92-105, 135, 142-143, 279
Fundamentals of Catholic Dogma, Ott, pp. 89-91
Fundamentals of Catholicism, Baker, Vol. 2, pp. 136-139
Modern Catholic Dictionary, Hardon, see "Providence"
The Teaching of Christ, Lawler, Wuerl, and Lawler, [First Edition] pp. 275-293; [Second Edition] pp. 263-281; [Third Edition] pp. 232-238

Q. 113. Is Jesus Christ the center of all of God's saving work?

Church Documents

Compendium of the Catechism of the Catholic Church, sect. 6, 78-86
Dei Verbum (Dogmatic Constitution on Divine Revelation), Vatican II, sect. 2, 4
Gaudium et Spes (Pastoral Constitution on the Church in the Modern World), Vatican II, sect. 22, 41, 58, 78
Lumen Gentium (Dogmatic Constitution on the Church), Vatican II, sect. 1-2, 5, 7-9, 48
On the Dignity and Vocation of Women, John Paul II, sect. 3
Redeemer of Man, John Paul II, sect. 12
Sacrament of Charity, Benedict XVI, sect. 7-8
Sacrosanctum Concilium (Constitution on the Sacred Liturgy), *Vatican II,* sect. 5
U. S. Catholic Catechism for Adults, [2006] pp. 38, 68, 91-92

Other Resources

Basics of the Faith: A Catholic Catechism, Schreck, pp. 52-54
The Church's Confession of Faith, Ignatius Press, pp. 57-59, 104-106

Family Wisdom Library™

Papal documents listed below can be viewed at www.vatican.va.
For new cross-references, visit www.familyland.org

Faith for Today, Hogan and LeVoir, [First Edition] pp. 81-85; [Second Edition] pp. 111-115

Fundamentals of Catholic Dogma, Ott, pp. 292-293

Fundamentals of Catholicism, Baker, Vol. 2, pp. 310-311

The Teaching of Christ, Lawler, Wuerl, and Lawler, [First Edition] pp. 265-293; [Second Edition] pp. 253-281; [Third Edition] pp. 223-248

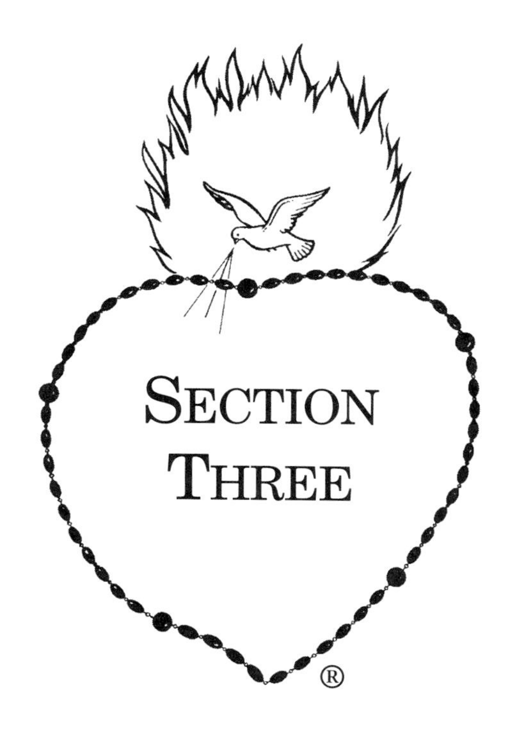

The Holy Spirit

"...We believe in the Holy Spirit, the Lord, the giver of life, Who proceeds from the Father and the Son. With the Father and the Son, He is worshiped and glorified. He has spoken through the Prophets."

#R19.1-4

No one comprehends the thoughts of God except the Spirit of God. Now we have received not the spirit of the world, but the Spirit which is from God, that we might understand the gifts bestowed on us by God. *(1 Corinthians 2:10-12)*

SECTION THREE
Part One

The Person of the Holy Spirit

#M3-354

God, the Holy Spirit, divine Spirit of love and light proceeding from the Father and the Son, we adore You as the Third Person of the adorable Trinity.

CHAPTER THIRTY-TWO

The Holy Spirit

Q. 114. Who is God the Holy Spirit?

God the Holy Spirit, the Third Person of the Blessed Trinity, is God just as the Father and the Son are God.

He is called the Paraclete (or Comforter) and the Advocate, because He pleads mankind's cause with God. He is also called the Spirit of Truth, the Spirit of God, and the Spirit of Love. The Holy Spirit comes to us when we are baptized, and He continues to dwell within us and sanctify us as long as we do not shut Him out by mortal sin.

#H5-29

The Holy Spirit is called the Paraclete and the Advocate, because He pleads mankind's cause with God.

Sacred Scripture

God has revealed to us through the Spirit. For the Spirit searches everything, even the depths of God. For what person knows a man's thoughts except the spirit of the man which is in him? So also no one comprehends the thoughts of God except the Spirit of God. Now we have received not the spirit of the world, but the Spirit which is from God, that we might understand the gifts bestowed on us by God. *1 Corinthians 2:10-12*

Do you not know that your body is a temple of the Holy Spirit within you, which you have from God? You are not your own; you were bought with a price. So glorify God in your body. *1 Corinthians 6:19-20*

Sacred Scripture
Q. 114. Jn 14:16-17; Gal 4:6.

For cross-references with Vatican II, Papal documents & other resources, see Family Wisdom Library on page 513.
For commentaries on each question with Cardinal Arinze, Sr. John Vianney and Fr. Straub (in Spanish), see Appendix C.

Catechism of the Catholic Church

684 Through his grace, the Holy Spirit is the first to awaken faith in us and to communicate to us the new life, which is to "know the Father and the one whom he has sent, Jesus Christ."[1] But the Spirit is the last of the persons of the Holy Trinity to be revealed. St. Gregory of Nazianzus, the Theologian, explains this progression in terms of the pedagogy of divine "condescension": "The Old Testament proclaimed the Father clearly, but the Son more obscurely. The New Testament revealed the Son and gave us a glimpse of the divinity of the Spirit. Now the Spirit dwells among us and grants us a clearer vision of himself. It was not prudent, when the divinity of the Father had not yet been confessed, to proclaim the Son openly and, when the divinity of the Son was not yet admitted, to add the Holy Spirit as an extra burden, to speak somewhat daringly.... By advancing and progressing 'from glory to glory,' the light of the Trinity will shine in ever more brilliant rays."[2]

743 From the beginning to the end of time, whenever God sends his Son, he always sends his Spirit: their mission is conjoined and inseparable.

#H5-22-2

The Holy Spirit comes to us when we are baptized, and He continues to dwell within us and sanctify us as long as we do not shut Him out by mortal sin.

Summary Prayer

God, the Holy Spirit, divine Spirit of love and light proceeding from the Father and the Son, we adore You as the Third Person of the adorable Trinity, our very God. In the same way as we adore God the Father and God the Son, we adore You in union with the angels and saints who surround Your throne on high. May You be praised and glorified now and forever. Amen.

Q. 115. The Holy Spirit proceeds from the Father and the Son. What is meant by this?

God the Father and God the Son behold the infinite lovableness of each other. There flows between these two divine Persons a Love which is divine and personal. It is a Love so perfect that it is a living Love. This Love is God, the Holy Spirit, the Third Person of the Blessed Trinity.

#T3-35-2

There flows between God the Father and God the Son a Love which is divine and personal. This Love is God, the Holy Spirit, the Third Person of the Blessed Trinity.

The Father and the Son eternally give this personal Love (God the Holy Spirit) to one another. God's love for us has led Him to make us sharers in His own divine life. We can say that the Spirit of Love, God the Holy Spirit, is the One Who makes this possible. Since the work of making souls holy is especially a work of divine Love, we say that the Holy Spirit is the Sanctifier, the One Who makes us holy; yet what one Person in the Trinity does, all three do.

Sacred Scripture

Nevertheless I tell you the truth: it is to your advantage that I go away, for if I do not go away, the Counselor will not come to you; but if I go, I will send him to you. *John 16:7*

When the Spirit of truth comes, he will guide you into all the truth; for he will not speak on his own authority, but whatever he hears he will speak, and he will declare to you the things that are to come. He will glorify me, for he will

Sacred Scripture
Q. 115. Rom 8:9; Eph1:13-14.

For cross-references with Vatican II, Papal documents & other resources, see Family Wisdom Library on page 513.
For commentaries on each question with Cardinal Arinze, Sr. John Vianney and Fr. Straub (in Spanish), see Appendix C.

take what is mine and declare it to you. All that the Father has is mine; therefore I said that he will take what is mine and declare it to you. *John 16:13-15*

Catechism of the Catholic Church

248 At the outset the Eastern tradition expresses the Father's character as first origin of the Spirit. By confessing the Spirit as he "who proceeds from the Father," it affirms that he *comes from* the Father *through* the Son.[1] The Western tradition expresses first the consubstantial communion between Father and Son, by saying that the Spirit proceeds from the Father and the Son *(filioque)*. It says this, "legitimately and with good reason,"[2] for the eternal order of the divine persons in their consubstantial communion implies that the Father, as "the principle without principle,"[3] is the first origin of the Spirit, but also that as Father of the only Son, he is, with the Son, the single principle from which the Holy Spirit proceeds.[4] This legitimate complementarity, provided it does not become rigid, does not affect the identity of faith in the reality of the same mystery confessed.

#C11-108

Since the work of making souls holy is especially a work of divine Love, we say that the Holy Spirit is the Sanctifier, the One Who makes us holy; yet what one Person in the Trinity does, all three do.

Splendor of Truth

This is what takes place through the gift of the Holy Spirit, the Spirit of truth, of freedom and of love: in him we are enabled to interiorize the law, to receive it and to live it as the motivating force of true personal freedom: "the perfect law, the law of liberty." *(section 83)*

Vatican Council II

Now, what was once preached by the Lord, or fulfilled in him for the salvation of mankind, must be proclaimed and spread to the ends of the earth (Acts 1:8), starting from Jerusalem (cf. Luke 24:27), so that what was accomplished for the salvation of all men may, in the course of time, achieve its universal effect.

To do this, Christ sent the Holy Spirit from the Father to exercise inwardly his saving influence, and to promote the spread of the Church. Without doubt, the Holy Spirit was at work in the world before Christ was glorified. On the day of Pentecost, however, he came down on the disciples that he might remain with them forever (cf. Jn. 14:16); on that day the Church was openly displayed to the crowds and the spread of the Gospel among the nations, through preaching, was begun. *Missionary Activity, 3, 4*

#Y1-10

Jesus said, "When the Spirit of truth comes, he will guide you into all the truth." *(John 16:13)*

Summary Prayer

God the Holy Spirit, we believe that in the divinity itself, You are the completion of the inner life of God. By contemplating Himself, the Father begets the idea of the living, perfect and perpetual "mirror image" of Himself. This is God the Son, Who is the expression of the Father's infinite self-knowledge. The Father and the Son see each other in their divine beauty and embrace each other in infinite love. You are this Love Who proceeds from the Father and the Son. You are Their blissful surrender to one another, and Their reposing in one another. You are the bond and unity, the embrace and kiss, the streaming joy, the jubilant happiness, and the silent blessed repose of the Trinity.

Your very name, "Spirit," signifies that You are the "Breathing Forth" of God the Father and God the Son. You are the "Holy" Spirit, because by virtue of Your origin You are the holiness of God, and God's holiness is one with His infinite love of Himself. Though You are the mutual love of the Father and the Son, still, like Them, You are God, equal to Them in all things. As God, You never had a beginning; You always were. As God, You are worthy of adoration, love, and devotion.

Divine Love, the One Who unites the Father and the Son, Spirit of power, faithful Consoler of the afflicted, let the splendor of Your light penetrate our hearts to their very depths. Send the heavenly rays of Your love into the sanctuary of our souls that, penetrating them, they may enkindle divine love and there consume all our weaknesses and our negligences.

Holy Spirit, have mercy on us. Make our souls docile and upright. Show pity toward our weaknesses with such clemency that our nothingness may find grace before Your infinite greatness, that our helplessness may find mercy before Your almighty power, and that our offenses may find forgiveness before the multitude of Your mercies, through our Lord and Savior, Jesus Christ. Amen.

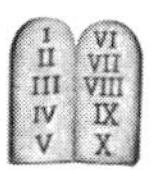

Doctrine • Moral • Worship Exercise

(See Appendix A for answer key, questions 114-115.)

1. Who is the Holy Spirit?
2. In what way can you worship and glorify the Father, Son and Holy Spirit in your daily life?
3. Name a prayer that mentions the Father, Son and Holy Spirit. Slowly read the Summary Prayer after question 115, and make it your own prayer.

Q. 116. What did Jesus Christ say about the Holy Spirit?

Jesus promised that He would send the Holy Spirit and that this Spirit would remain with us.

Jesus said to the Apostles the night of the Last Supper, "And I will pray the Father, and he will give you another Counselor, to be with you for ever, even the Spirit of truth, whom the world cannot receive, because it neither sees him nor knows him; you know him, for he dwells with you, and will be in you" (John 14:16-17).

#J2-357-2

The Lord promised his disciples the Holy Spirit, who would "bring to their remembrance" and teach them to understand his commandments, and who would be the principle and constant source of a new life in the world.
(Splendor of Truth, 25)

Sacred Scripture

These things I have spoken to you, while I am still with you. But the Counselor, the Holy Spirit, whom the Father will send in my name, he will teach you all things, and bring to your remembrance all that I have said to you.
John 14:25-26

But when the Counselor comes, whom I shall send to you from the Father, even the Spirit of truth, who proceeds from the Father, he will bear witness to me.
John 15:26

Jesus stood up and proclaimed, "If any one thirst, let him come to me and drink. He who believes in me, as the scripture has said, 'Out of his heart shall flow rivers of living water.'" Now this he said about the Spirit, which those who

Sacred Scripture
Q. 116. Acts 1:1-8.

Catechism of the Catholic Church
Q. 116. Paragraphs 692, 728, 2615.

For cross-references with Vatican II, Papal documents & other resources, see Family Wisdom Library on page 513.
For commentaries on each question with Cardinal Arinze, Sr. John Vianney and Fr. Straub (in Spanish), see Appendix C.

believed in him were to receive; for as yet the Spirit had not been given, because Jesus was not yet glorified. *John 7:37-39*

Catechism of the Catholic Church

729 Only when the hour has arrived for his glorification does Jesus *promise* the coming of the Holy Spirit, since his Death and Resurrection will fulfill the promise made to the fathers.[1] The Spirit of truth, the other Paraclete, will be given by the Father in answer to Jesus' prayer; he will be sent by the Father in Jesus' name; and Jesus will send him from the Father's side, since he comes from the Father. The Holy Spirit will come and we shall know him; he will be with us for ever; he will remain with us. The Spirit will teach us everything, remind us of all that Christ said to us and bear witness to him. The Holy Spirit will lead us into all truth and will glorify Christ. He will prove the world wrong about sin, righteousness, and judgment.

Most Holy Spirit, we entrust our minds to Your guidance and our hearts to Your inspirations. Let us be witnesses to Jesus Christ in the world, especially by our good example.

Splendor of Truth

The Lord promised his disciples the Holy Spirit, who would "bring to their remembrance" and teach them to understand his commandments (cf. Jn 14:26), and who would be the principle and constant source of a new life in the world (cf. Jn 3:5-8; Rom 8:1-13). *(section 25)*

Vatican Council II

Before freely laying down his life for the world, the Lord Jesus organized the apostolic ministry and promised to send the Holy Spirit, in such a way that both would be always and everywhere associated in the fulfillment of the work of salvation. *Missionary Activity, 4*

Summary Prayer

Most Holy Spirit of God, Jesus spoke of You as the "Paraclete" or "Advocate" as He prepared to call You from Heaven. Your mission was to act as Christ's Witness before the world, by defending His character, authority, and doctrine. To assure our eternal Salvation, we entrust our minds to Your guidance and our hearts to Your inspirations. Let us be witnesses to Jesus Christ in the world, especially by our good example. We ask this through the same Christ our Lord. Amen.

Doctrine • Moral • Worship Exercise

(See Appendix A for answer key, question 116.)

1. In the Scripture verses John 14:16-17 and 25-26, what does our Lord Jesus say about the Holy Spirit?
2. "Paraclete" means "He who is called to help." Recall occasions when you experienced the help of the Holy Spirit. Describe one of your experiences in writing.
3. Read John 14:16-17 again. Thank the Father and Jesus for the gift of the Holy Spirit. Ask the Holy Spirit to remain with you always and to inspire, strengthen, and guide you to greater intimacy with Jesus.

Chapter Summary Prayer

Holy Spirit of God, the Incarnation of Jesus, which is the most important of the whole work of Salvation, and the deepest proof of God's love for us, was wrought by Your divine power. The Incarnation was the highest union of a human nature with God and is the source of all holiness.

Spirit of Life, Your divine breath filled the sanctuary of Mary's womb and brought into existence the union of the eternal Word of God with His human nature. You were the mysterious heartbeat of His inner life, moving it in its wonderful depths of devotion.

We believe that Jesus Christ's divine and human natures are united in one divine Person, the eternal Word of God, the Second Person of the adorable Trinity. Creator Spirit, You effected this wonderful union. Your infinite power created the human soul of the Savior and conceived His sacred Body in the womb of His Most Holy Mother. The angel spoke to Mary, "The Holy Spirit will come upon you, and the power of the Most High will overshadow you; therefore the child to be born will be called holy, the Son of God" (Luke 1:35).

Most infinite Spirit of love and life, we praise and thank You also for Your constant work within Jesus' soul, which, with His cooperation, brought forth marvelous increases of grace, wisdom, holiness and glory. May we, as sharers in Your divine life by virtue of Baptism, also be always open to Your will and to Your grace. We ask this through Jesus Christ our Lord and Savior. Amen.

Thought Provokers

Please see Appendix B for the answers.

Q. 114: Where in the Bible is the divinity of God the Holy Spirit clearly taught?

Q. 115: What are the basic similarities and differences between the love exchanged between a Christian husband and wife in the state of grace and that exchanged between God the Father and God the Son?

Q. 116: How do we know when God the Holy Spirit is dwelling in us helping us to become holy?

By Heart Catechism and Scripture Review™

The "By Heart Catechism and Scripture Review" lists a selected number of questions and Scripture references from "The Apostolate's Family Catechism" to make memorization easier. Q = Question, SR = Scripture Reference

SR 114 1 Corinthians 6:19-20

Do you not know that your body is a temple of the Holy Spirit within you, which you have from God? You are not your own; you were bought with a price. So glorify God in your body.

Q. 115. What do we mean when we say, "The Holy Spirit proceeds from the Father and the Son"? We mean that the Holy Spirit is the endless, living love that flows between God the Father and God the Son.

#C15-24

For theirs is a community composed of men, who, united in Christ and guided by the Holy Spirit, press onward towards the kingdom of the Father and are bearers of a message of salvation intended for all men. *(Gaudium et Spes, 1)*

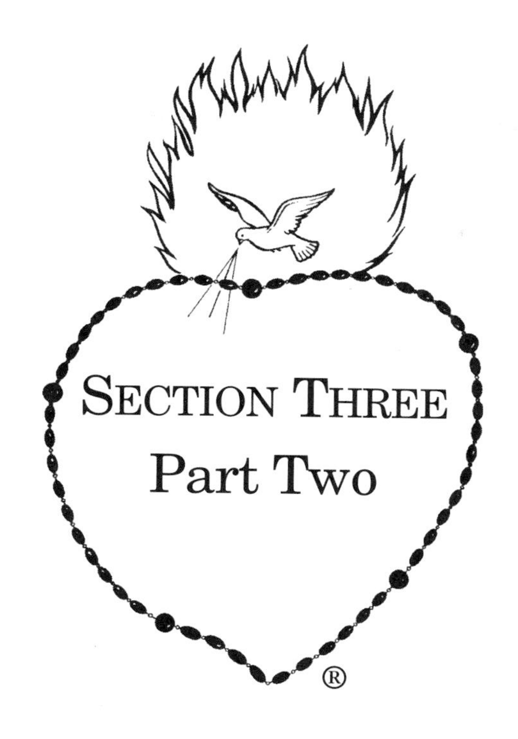

The Holy Spirit in the Life of the Church

#H5-35

To finish the work of the Salvation of all men, Jesus sends the Holy Spirit from the Father. The Spirit now carries out His work of Salvation in the souls of men and spreads the Church throughout the world.

CHAPTER THIRTY-THREE

The Work of the Holy Spirit in the Church

Q. 117. When did the Holy Spirit descend upon the Church?

In a mighty wind and tongues of fire, God the Holy Spirit descended upon the early Church on Pentecost, fifty days after Easter and ten days after Jesus ascended into Heaven. The Holy Spirit transformed the Apostles from timid, fearful men to the courageous men of faith through whom Christ wanted to evangelize the world.

#R4.3-18

In a mighty wind and tongues of fire, God the Holy Spirit descended upon the early Church on Pentecost, fifty days after Easter.

Sacred Scripture

When the day of Pentecost had come, they were all together in one place. And suddenly a sound came from heaven like the rush of a mighty wind, and it filled all the house where they were sitting. And there appeared to them tongues as of fire, distributed and resting on each one of them. And they were all filled with the Holy Spirit and began to speak in other tongues, as the Spirit gave them utterance. *Acts 2:1-4*

Catechism of the Catholic Church
Q. 117. Paragraph 732.

For cross-references with Vatican II, Papal documents & other resources, see Family Wisdom Library on page 513.
For commentaries on each question with Cardinal Arinze, Sr. John Vianney and Fr. Straub (in Spanish), see Appendix C.

#A18-21-2

The Holy Spirit transformed the Apostles from timid, fearful men to the courageous men of faith through whom Christ wanted to evangelize the world.

Catechism of the Catholic Church

731 On the day of Pentecost when the seven weeks of Easter had come to an end, Christ's Passover is fulfilled in the outpouring of the Holy Spirit, manifested, given, and communicated as a divine person: of his fullness, Christ, the Lord, pours out the Spirit in abundance.[1]

Vatican Council II

When the work which the Father gave the Son to do on earth (cf. Jn. 17:4) was accomplished, the Holy Spirit was sent on the day of Pentecost in order that he might continually sanctify the Church, and that, consequently, those who believe might have access through Christ in one Spirit to the Father (cf. Eph. 2:18). He is the Spirit of life, the fountain of water springing up to eternal life (cf. Jn. 4:47; 7:38-39). To men, dead in sin, the Father gives life through him, until the day when, in Christ, he raises to life their mortal bodies (cf. Rom. 8:10-11). *Lumen Gentium, 4*

Summary Prayer

Most Holy Spirit, on the Feast of Pentecost, You laid the foundation of the Church of Christ by coming down upon the Apostles. You confirmed them in faith and charity so that, without fear, they could preach the name of Jesus to both Jews and Gentiles.

Spirit of Truth, You preserve the Church from error by investing its visible head, the Pope, with the gift of infallibility in matters of faith and morals. You are truly the Soul of the Catholic Church. May You always be the life of our souls. Amen.

Catechism by Diagram

#H5-43

The Spirit is Present in the Church. The Spirit (dove) is present in a special way in the Church (boat). He was sent to give life to the Church. The Holy Spirit guides the Pope (tiara), the bishops, and the priests in their work for Christ—teaching His doctrines, guiding souls, and bringing grace to the people through the sacraments. He directs all the work of Christ in the Church. He is the very Soul of the Catholic Church.

Q. 118. How does the Holy Spirit carry out Christ's work in the Church?

The Holy Spirit carries out Christ's work in the Church when persons are willing to answer God's invitation to love Him and one another.

#B7-6

The Holy Spirit carries out Christ's work in the Church when persons are willing to answer God's invitation to love Him and one another.

As Jesus Christ is the center of the History of Salvation, so the mystery of God is the center from which this history takes its origin and to which it is ordered to its last end. Our crucified and risen Lord draws men to the Father by sending His Spirit upon the Church.

The Holy Spirit was already at work in the world before Jesus rose from the dead and ascended into Heaven. But to finish the work of the Salvation of all men, Jesus sent the Holy Spirit from the Father. The Spirit now carries out His work of Salvation in the souls of men and spreads the Church throughout the world.

Sacred Scripture

By this we know that we abide in him and he in us, because he has given us of his own Spirit. And we have seen and testify that the Father has sent his Son as the Savior of the world. *1 John 4:13-14*

Sacred Scripture
Q. 118. John 16:13-15; Rom 15:15-19.

Catechism of the Catholic Church
Q. 118. Paragraphs **257**, **259**, 485, 494, 1824, 2055.

For cross-references with Vatican II, Papal documents & other resources, see Family Wisdom Library on page 513.
For commentaries on each question with Cardinal Arinze, Sr. John Vianney and Fr. Straub (in Spanish), see Appendix C.

Catechism of the Catholic Church

243 Before his Passover, Jesus announced the sending of "another Paraclete" (Advocate), the Holy Spirit. At work since creation, having previously "spoken through the prophets," the Spirit will now be with and in the disciples, to teach them and guide them "into all the truth."[1] The Holy Spirit is thus revealed as another divine person with Jesus and the Father.

1110 In the liturgy of the Church, God the Father is blessed and adored as the source of all the blessings of creation and salvation with which he has blessed us in his Son, in order to give us the Spirit of filial adoption.

Vatican Council II

The joy and hope, the grief and anguish of the men of our time, especially of those who are poor or afflicted in any way, are the joy and hope, the grief and anguish of the followers of Christ as well. Nothing that is genuinely human fails to find an echo in their hearts. For theirs is a community composed of men, who, united in Christ and guided by the Holy Spirit, press onward towards the kingdom of the Father and are bearers of a message of salvation intended for all men. *Gaudium et Spes, 1*

#W2-4

The joy and hope, the grief and anguish of the men of our time, especially of those who are poor or afflicted in any way, are the joy and hope, the grief and anguish of the followers of Christ as well. *(Gaudium et Spes, 1)*

Summary Prayer

Father, Your Son ascended above all the heavens, and from His throne at Your right hand, He poured into the hearts of Your adopted children the Holy Spirit of Your promise. You give Your gifts of grace for every time and season, as You guide the Church in the marvelous ways of Your providence. Give us Your Holy Spirit to help us always by His power, so that with loving trust we may turn to You in all our troubles, and give You thanks in all our joys.

Holy Spirit, You are one God with the Father and the Son. You are the mutual Love between Them both. You formed the sacred humanity of our Lord Jesus Christ and enriched it with the fullness of Your gifts and graces. Under Your guidance, He, an innocent Victim for the sins of the world, ascended the altar of the Cross.

God our Father, by raising Christ Your Son, You conquered the power of death and opened for us the way to eternal life. Raise us up and renew our lives by the Spirit that is within us, especially through the sacrifice of the Mass.

Your Spirit made us Your children, confident to call You Father. Increase Your Spirit of love within us and bring us to our promised inheritance.

Through the power of the Spirit, purify our hearts and strengthen us in Your love. Send Your Spirit to live in our hearts and make us temples of His glory. May we, by Your help, never lose the gifts and graces You have given us through Him. We ask this through Jesus Christ our Lord. Amen.

Doctrine • Moral • Worship Exercise

(See Appendix A for answer key, questions 117-118.)

1. What does our Catholic faith tell us about Pentecost? Why is the feast of Pentecost very significant for us as Christians?
2. How can you and your family answer God's invitation to love Him and one another? Be specific.
3. Slowly read the Summary Prayer after question 117. Then close your eyes and pray to the Holy Spirit in your own words.

Q. 119. Where is God the Holy Spirit especially present?

God the Holy Spirit is especially present in the Catholic Church.

The Holy Spirit gives His divine life of grace to the Catholic Church, making it pleasing to God. He is present to help the Church to carry on the work of Christ in the world. He moves people by His grace to unite themselves in sincere love with God and their fellow men, and to serve Him and one another. By the power of the Gospel message, He makes the Church grow. With His gifts, He renews it and leads it to a perfect union with Christ.

#C15-16-2

God the Holy Spirit is especially present in the Catholic Church. The Holy Spirit gives His divine life of grace to the Catholic Church, making it pleasing to God.

The Holy Spirit is also present outside the Catholic Church in other Christian churches and ecclesial communities. Moreover, He is active in what is known as the Ecumenical Movement, which promotes the union of all Christians in the fullness of truth, as revealed by Christ and His Apostles.

God the Holy Spirit is active as well among other believers. He helps them to seek and find truth and goodness. Moreover, He guides the efforts of the Catholic Church in her relationship with other believers.

Sacred Scripture
Q. 119. Mt 28:19; Jn 17:20-23.

Catechism of the Catholic Church
Q. 119. Paragraphs 748, 750, **767-768**, **813**, 819, 822, **845**.

For cross-references with Vatican II, Papal documents & other resources, see Family Wisdom Library on page 513.
For commentaries on each question with Cardinal Arinze, Sr. John Vianney and Fr. Straub (in Spanish), see Appendix C.

Sacred Scripture

Nevertheless I tell you the truth; it is to your advantage that I go away, for if I do not go away, the Counselor will not come to you; but if I go, I will send him to you. *John 16:7*

Catechism of the Catholic Church

749 The article concerning the Church also depends entirely on the article about the Holy Spirit, which immediately precedes it. "Indeed, having shown that the Spirit is the source and giver of all holiness, we now confess that it is he who has endowed the Church with holiness."[1] The Church is, in a phrase used by the Fathers, the place "where the Spirit flourishes."[2]

Splendor of Truth

The Church, as the People of God among the nations, while attentive to the new challenges of history and to mankind's efforts to discover the meaning of life, offers to everyone the answer which comes from the truth about Jesus Christ and his Gospel. *(section 2)*

#E5-33

The Holy Spirit is present to help the Church to carry on the work of Christ in the world.

Vatican Council II

On the day of Pentecost, however, he came down on the disciples that he might remain with them forever (cf. Jn. 14:16); on that day the Church was openly displayed to the crowds and the spread of the Gospel among the nations, through preaching, was begun. Finally, on that day was foreshadowed the union of all peoples in the catholicity of the faith by means of the Church of the New Alliance, a Church which speaks every language, understands and embraces all tongues in charity, and thus overcomes the dispersion of Babel. The "acts of the apostles" began with Pentecost, just as Christ was conceived in the Virgin Mary with the coming of the Holy Spirit and was moved to begin his ministry by the descent of the same Holy Spirit, who

came down upon him while he was praying. Before freely laying down his life for the world, the Lord Jesus organized the apostolic ministry and promised to send the Holy Spirit, in such a way that both would be always and everywhere associated in the fulfillment of the work of salvation. *Missionary Activity, 4*

#C36-1-2

The Holy Spirit moves people by His grace to unite themselves in sincere love with God and their fellow men, and to serve Him and one another.

Summary Prayer

Holy Spirit, Finger of God's right hand, in thousands of ways in the early days of Christianity, You showed Yourself to be the Soul and Heart of the Church. You gave it supernatural strength and beauty. Your divine influence explains its irresistible attraction, that is, its power to draw souls. You worked in the early Church, bringing forth signs of new life in strength, beauty, and fruitfulness. Praise and thanks be to You, life-giving Spirit, for the wonderful power of Your grace.

Divine Fire, enkindle in all those who share Your apostolate the flames which transformed the disciples in the Upper Room. They will then no longer be ordinary men, but men living to transfuse Your divine life to the souls of their fellow men. Enkindle in their wills an ardent desire for the inner life, since their apostolate will be successful only in the measure that they themselves live that supernatural life of which You are the sovereign principle and Jesus Christ the source.

Be merciful to all the children of the Holy Catholic Church, that they may be faithful to its teaching and thereby save their souls.

Look graciously upon the Holy Souls in Purgatory. Comfort and refresh them with the graces which flow from Your merciful love.

Be merciful to other Christians, to those belonging to non-Christian religions, and to agnostics, atheists, and sinners. Grant them grace to recognize You, with the Father and the Son, as the only source of true happiness, and to love You with their whole hearts. All this we ask through Christ our Lord. Amen.

Doctrine • Moral • Worship Exercise

(See Appendix A for answer key, question 119.)

1. The Holy Spirit is present in the Catholic Church through His divine life of grace. What does this grace enable us to do?
2. The Holy Spirit is also present outside the Catholic Church. What can you do to promote the unity of all Christians?
3. Read John 17:11-12. Pray for the unity of all Christians. If possible, invite your family to join you.

#C15-43

The Holy Spirit guides the efforts of the Catholic Church in her relationship with other believers.

Q. 120. What does God the Holy Spirit accomplish for the Church?

Through God the Holy Spirit, the Church is able to accomplish the work of Salvation which Christ gave her at her birth.

#M1-8

The Holy Spirit guides the Pope, bishops and priests in their work and enables the People of God to know the truth.

The Holy Spirit came in order to remain with the Church forever. At Pentecost, the Church was publicly made known to those gathered in Jerusalem. From there, the Gospel began to spread throughout the nations. Today, the Holy Spirit is still the Soul of the Church's apostolate. He gives His divine life of grace to the Church.

The Holy Spirit guides the Pope, the bishops, and the priests of the Church in their work of teaching the Faith, guiding souls, dispensing God's grace, caring for the sick, teaching children, guiding the youth, comforting the sorrowful, and supporting the needy.

The Holy Spirit enables the People of God to know the truth. He prays in them and helps them to remember that they are adopted children of God. He unites the Church in love and worship.

Catechism of the Catholic Church
Q. 120. Paragraphs 686, 688, 692, 1996-**1997**, **1999**.

For cross-references with Vatican II, Papal documents & other resources, see Family Wisdom Library on page 513.
For commentaries on each question with Cardinal Arinze, Sr. John Vianney and Fr. Straub (in Spanish), see Appendix C.

Sacred Scripture

The Counselor, the Holy Spirit, whom the Father will send in my name, he will teach you all things, and bring to your remembrance all that I have said to you. *John 14:26*

He [Jesus] breathed on them, and said to them, "Receive the Holy Spirit. If you forgive the sins of any, they are forgiven; if you retain the sins of any, they are retained." *John 20:22-23*

For by one Spirit we were all baptized into one body...and all were made to drink of one Spirit. *1 Corinthians 12:13*

Catechism of the Catholic Church

976 The Apostle's Creed associates faith in the forgiveness of sins not only with faith in the Holy Spirit, but also with faith in the Church and in the communion of saints. It was when he gave the Holy Spirit to his apostles that the risen Christ conferred on them his own divine power to forgive sins: "Receive the Holy Spirit. If you forgive the sins of any, they are forgiven; if you retain the sins of any, they are retained."[1]

Vatican Council II

The Spirit dwells in the Church and in the hearts of the faithful, as in a temple (cf. 1 Cor. 3:16; 6:19). In them he prays and bears witness to their adoptive sonship (cf. Gal. 4:6; Rom. 8:15-16 and 26). *Lumen Gentium, 4*

Before freely laying down his life for the world, the Lord Jesus organized the apostolic ministry and promised to send the Holy Spirit, in such a way that both would be always and everywhere associated in the fulfillment of the work of salvation. *Missionary Activity, 4*

Summary Prayer

God our Father, how wonderful are the works of the Holy Spirit which are revealed in so many gifts!

How marvelous is the unity the Spirit creates from Your children's diversity as He dwells in their hearts, thus filling the whole Church with His presence and guiding it with His wisdom. May we always be attentive to His inspirations and trust in His never-failing strength.

Life-giving Spirit, our Creator and Sanctifier, You have given us life and being, and have led us into the fullness of Christ's revelation, which He gave to His Catholic Church. You have adorned our souls with sanctifying grace, made them Your temples, enriched them with heavenly virtues, and sanctified them through the holy sacraments. All these benefits have come to us through the Holy Catholic Church. We thank You for having made us children of this Church which is animated and directed by You in union with the Father and the Son, now and forever. Amen.

Q. 121. Why is the Holy Spirit called the Soul of the Church?

The Holy Spirit is called the Soul of the Church because He animates it with His divine presence, giving supernatural life to all its parts.

#C15-35

The Holy Spirit is called the Soul of the Church because He animates it with His divine presence, giving supernatural life to all its parts.

Sacred Scripture

And I will pray the Father, and he will give you another Counselor, to be with you for ever, even the Spirit of truth, whom the world cannot receive, because it neither sees him nor knows him; you know him, for he dwells with you, and will be in you. *John 14:16-17*

Do you not know that you are God's temple and that God's Spirit dwells in you? *1 Corinthians 3:16*

Catechism of the Catholic Church

797 "What the soul is to the human body, the Holy Spirit is to the Body of Christ, which is the Church."[1] "To this Spirit of Christ, as an invisible principle, is to be ascribed the fact that all the parts of the body are joined one with the other and with their exalted head; for the whole Spirit of Christ is in the head, the whole Spirit is in the body, and the whole Spirit is in each of the members."[2] The Holy Spirit makes the Church "the temple of the living God":[3]

Sacred Scripture
Q. 121. Rom 8:9-17.

Catechism of the Catholic Church
Q. 121. Paragraphs 692, **809**, 813.

For cross-references with Vatican II, Papal documents & other resources, see Family Wisdom Library on page 513.
For commentaries on each question with Cardinal Arinze, Sr. John Vianney and Fr. Straub (in Spanish), see Appendix C.

"Indeed, it is to the Church herself that the 'Gift of God' has been entrusted.... In it is in her that communion with Christ has been deposited, that is to say: the Holy Spirit, the pledge of incorruptibility, the strengthening of our faith and the ladder of our ascent to God.... For where the Church is, there also is God's Spirit; where God's Spirit is, there is the Church and every grace."[4]

Splendor of Truth

No matter how many and great the obstacles put in his way by human frailty and sin, the Spirit, who renews the face of the earth (cf. Ps 104:30), makes possible the miracle of the perfect accomplishment of the good. This renewal, which gives the ability to do what is good, noble, beautiful, pleasing to God and in conformity with his will, is in some way the flowering of the gift of mercy, which offers liberation from the slavery of evil and gives the strength to sin no more." *(section 118)*

Vatican Council II

In order that we might be unceasingly renewed in him [i.e. Jesus] (cf. Eph.4:23), he has shared with us his Spirit who, being one and the same in head and members, gives life to, unifies and moves the whole body. Consequently, his work could be compared by the Fathers to the function that the principle of life, the soul, fulfills in the human body. *Lumen Gentium, 7*

Summary Prayer

Heavenly Father, through Christ, You have given the Holy Spirit to all peoples. Fill our hearts with His love. May the fire of Your Spirit, which filled the hearts of the disciples of Jesus with courage and love, make our thoughts, words and deeds holy so that our whole life may be pleasing to You.

Send the Holy Spirit of Pentecost into our hearts to keep us always in Your love, that we may perfectly love You and fittingly praise You. May we live in holiness and be Your witnesses to the world.

Fill with the Spirit of Christ those whom You call to live in the midst of the world and its concerns. Help them by their work on earth to build up Your eternal Kingdom. May they be effective witnesses to the truth of the Gospel and make Your Church a living and vibrant presence in the midst of the world.

Through Your Holy Spirit, the Soul of the Church, increase Your spiritual gifts to the Church so that Your faithful people may continue to grow in holiness in imitation of Your beloved Son.

Holy Spirit, Creator, mercifully assist Your Catholic Church, and by Your heavenly power, strengthen and establish her against the assaults of her enemies. By Your love and grace,

renew the spirit of Your servants whom You have anointed, that in You they may glorify the Father and His only-begotten Son, Jesus Christ our Lord.

Help us to be ever obedient to the Holy Father, the Pope, who teaches infallibly in matters of faith and morals. Make us faithful children of the Catholic Church, which is the pillar and ground of truth. Help us to always uphold her doctrines, seek her interests, and defend her rights. We ask this in Jesus' name. Amen.

#H5-26

Heavenly Father, send the Holy Spirit of Pentecost into our hearts to keep us always in Your love, that we may perfectly love You and fittingly praise You.

Doctrine • Moral • Worship Exercise

(See Appendix A for answer key, questions 120-121.)

1. How does the Holy Spirit animate and nourish the Church in her life of grace so that she can continue the work of Salvation begun by Christ?
2. In what concrete ways can you and your family take part in the work of the Church to bring the good news of God's love to others?
3. Pray the Summary Prayer after question 121. Thank the Holy Spirit for His work in the Church.

Q. 122. What is the task of the Holy Spirit in the Church?

The Holy Spirit (1) preserves the Church as the Body of Christ and as the Bride of Christ so that she can remain faithful to Him in holiness until the end of time; and (2) assists the Church in purifying and renewing herself and her members.

#R4.3-11

The Holy Spirit preserves the Church as the Body of Christ. He brings about a union between Christ and His members

1. The Holy Spirit preserves the Church as the Body of Christ.

The Holy Spirit, Whom Jesus sent from the Father to His Church at Pentecost, continues His work in the Church, and will do so until the end of time. He brings about a union between Christ and His members, which St. Paul describes as "the Body of Christ." Each member of the Body is united to each other, with Christ as the Head, by a strong interior bond, which is the Holy Spirit.

2. The Holy Spirit assists the Church in purifying and renewing herself and her members.

Every Christian receives the Holy Spirit in the Sacrament of Baptism and in the Sacrament of Confirmation. The Holy Spirit, with the Father and the Son, actually lives in the Christian. Jesus

Sacred Scripture
Q. 122. Rom 12:3-8.

Catechism of the Catholic Church
Q. 122. Paragraphs 687, 696, **733-741**, 797-801.

For cross-references with Vatican II, Papal documents & other resources, see Family Wisdom Library on page 513.
For commentaries on each question with Cardinal Arinze, Sr. John Vianney and Fr. Straub (in Spanish), see Appendix C.

said, "If a man loves me, he will keep my word, and my Father will love him, and we will come to him and make our home with him" (John 14:23).

Through the Holy Spirit, a Christian shares in the life of grace, which is God's life in his soul. St. Paul reminds the Christian that he is holy because the Holy Spirit dwells in him. "Do you not know that you are God's temple and that God's Spirit dwells in you? If any one destroys God's temple, God will destroy him. For God's temple is holy, and that temple you are" (1 Corinthians 3:16-17).

The Holy Spirit enlightens our minds to accept and believe the teaching of Jesus and gives us the strength to live according to it. An openness to God and a willingness to respond to the guidance of His Holy Spirit is necessary for holiness. St. Paul says, "Do not quench the Spirit" (1 Thessalonians 5:19).

Holiness is expected from the whole Church. Giving Himself to all, God makes it possible for everyone to give himself completely to Him and to his fellow man. All are called to holiness, according to the gifts and talents each possesses.

St. Paul also speaks of charisms, that is, "gifts of grace," which are blessings, freely given, of an extraordinary and transitory nature that the Holy Spirit confers directly on certain individuals for the good of others (cf. 1 Corinthians 12:4-11). These blessings may also benefit indirectly the one who possesses them, but their immediate purpose is the spiritual welfare of the Christian community.

So that we may live well as God's children, the Holy Spirit helps us in many ways. He gives us "actual graces" to help us to think, desire and do things pleasing to God. Without His grace it is impossible to do anything to achieve our Salvation or the Salvation of others. With the help of the grace of the Holy Spirit, the Church is constantly purified and renewed spiritually.

Sacred Scripture

Now there are varieties of gifts, but the same Spirit; and there are varieties of service, but the same Lord; and there are varieties of working, but it is the same God who inspires them all in every one. To each is given the manifestation of the Spirit for the common good. To one is given through the Spirit the utterance of wisdom, and to another the utterance of knowledge according to the same Spirit, to another faith by the same Spirit, to another gifts of healing by the one Spirit, to another the working of miracles, to another prophecy, to another the ability to distinguish between spirits, to another various kinds of tongues, to another the interpretation of tongues. All these are inspired by one and the same Spirit, who apportions to each one individually as he wills. *1 Corinthians 12:4-11*

#H5-28-2

So that we may live well as God's children, the Holy Spirit helps us in many ways. The Holy Spirit gives us "actual graces" to help us to think, desire and do things pleasing to God.

Holiness is expected from the whole Church. Giving Himself to all, God makes it possible for everyone to give himself completely to Him and to his fellow man.

Catechism of the Catholic Church

737 The mission of Christ and the Holy Spirit is brought to completion in the Church, which is the Body of Christ and the Temple of the Holy Spirit. This joint mission henceforth brings Christ's faithful to share in his communion with the Father in the Holy Spirit. The Spirit *prepares* men and goes out to them with his grace, in order to draw them to Christ. The Spirit *manifests* the risen Lord to them, recalls his word to them and opens their minds to the understanding of his Death and Resurrection. He *makes present* the mystery of Christ, supremely in the Eucharist, in order to reconcile them, to *bring them into communion* with God, that they may "bear much fruit."[1]

1989 The first work of the grace of the Holy Spirit is *conversion*, effecting justification in accordance with Jesus' proclamation at the beginning of the Gospel: "Repent, for the kingdom of heaven is at hand."[1] Moved by grace, man turns toward God and away from sin, thus accepting forgiveness and righteousness from on high. "Justification is not only the remission of sins, but also the sanctification and renewal of the interior man."[2]

Splendor of Truth

In the Holy Spirit, the Church receives and hands down the Scripture as the witness to the "great things" which God has done in history (cf. Lk 1:49); she professes by the lips of her Fathers and Doctors the truth of the Word made flesh, puts his precepts and love into practice in the lives of her Saints and in the sacrifice of her Martyrs, and celebrates her hope in him in the Liturgy. *(section 27)*

At the heart of the new evangelization and of the new moral life which it proposes and awakens by its fruits of holiness and missionary zeal, there is the Spirit of Christ, the principle and strength of the fruitfulness of Holy Mother Church. As Pope Paul VI reminded us: "Evangelization will never be possible without the action of the Holy Spirit." *(section 108)*

Vatican Council II

Guiding the Church in the way of all truth (cf. Jn. 16:13) and unifying her in communion and in the works of ministry, he [the Holy Spirit] bestows upon her varied hierarchic and charismatic gifts, and in this way directs her; and he adorns her with his fruits (cf. Eph. 4:11-12; 1 Cor. 12:4; Gal. 5:22). By the power of the Gospel he permits the Church to keep the freshness of youth. Constantly he renews her and leads her to perfect union with her Spouse. For the Spirit and the Bride both say to Jesus, the Lord: "Come!" (cf. Apoc. 22:17). Hence the universal Church is seen to be "a people brought into unity from the unity of the Father, the Son and the Holy Spirit." *Lumen Gentium, 4*

Doctrine • Moral • Worship Exercise

(See Appendix A for answer key, question 122.)

1. Why is the Catholic Church called the Body of Christ? What is the role of the Holy Spirit in the Body of Christ?
2. As a member of the Body of Christ, in what specific ways do you strive to become a worthy member of the Body of Christ?
3. Each day, ask the Holy Spirit to help you and your family in your efforts to become holy, worthy members of the Body of Christ.

Chapter Summary Prayer

Come, O Creator Spirit blest, And in our souls take up Thy rest; Come with Thy grace and heavenly aid To fill the hearts which Thou hast made.

Great Paraclete, to Thee we cry, O highest gift of God most high! O font of life! O fire of love! And sweet anointing from above.

Thou in Thy sevenfold gifts art known, The finger of God's hand we own; The promise of the Father, Thou! Who dost the tongue with power endow.

Kindle our senses from above, And make our hearts o'erflow with love; With patience firm and virtue high The weakness of our flesh supply.

Far from us drive the foe we dread, And grant us Thy true peace instead; So shall we not, with Thee for guide, Turn from the path of life aside.

O may Thy grace on us bestow The Father and the Son to know, And Thee through endless times confessed Of both the eternal Spirit blest.

All glory while the ages run Be to the Father and the Son, Who rose from death; the same to Thee, O Holy Ghost, eternally. Amen.

Catechism by Diagram

#H5-39

Justified or Unjustified. Left diagram: God's indwelling in the soul (triangle in heart) is a great grace. A sinner is justified by God, given new life by the Holy Spirit (dove), and given a share in Christ's life. He enters into close communion with the Holy Trinity. Thus, a soul in the state of grace (rays) is made holy and justified by the Holy Spirit; he becomes a child of God the Father, a brother of Jesus Christ, a friend of the Holy Spirit, and an heir in Heaven. Right Diagram: A soul in the state of mortal sin is deprived of grace because of sin (black heart). He is an unjustified sinner, an enemy of God, separated from Jesus Christ, spiritually dead, and excluded from Heaven unless he repents.

Thought Provokers

Please see Appendix B for the answers.

Q. 117: When does God the Holy Spirit first dwell intimately in the lives of most Christians?

Q. 118: On the level of everyday living, how does God the Holy Spirit help us?

Q. 119: In a general sense, where can the Holy Spirit be found?

Q. 120: What is sanctifying grace?

Q. 121: As the "Soul of the Church," God the Holy Spirit gives it life. What does this mean?

Q. 122: How can individual Christians help the Holy Spirit in His work of purifying and renewing the Church?

#T3-28

The Holy Spirit should be loved and honored as our God, just as the Father and the Son are honored.

CHAPTER THIRTY-FOUR

Devotion to the Holy Spirit

Q. 123. How should the Holy Spirit be honored?

The Holy Spirit should be loved and honored as our God, just as the Father and the Son are honored.

We should also allow the Holy Spirit to guide our lives. By prayer, we learn to discern His inspirations in our souls. His inspirations bring peace.

We should recognize the importance of the Holy Spirit and His work in the Church and in our lives. Every Christian receives the Holy Spirit in the Sacrament of Baptism and in the Sacrament of Confirmation. By His presence men are continually moved to have communion with God and one another and to fulfill their duties.

United in Christ, the followers of Jesus are led by the Holy Spirit on their journey to the Kingdom of their Father and the Son. We should often ask him for the light and strength we need to live a holy life and to save our souls.

#H5-34-2

By the presence of the Holy Spirit, men are continually moved to have communion with God and one another and to fulfill their duties.

Catechism of the Catholic Church
Q. 123. Paragraphs 684, 739.

For cross-references with Vatican II, Papal documents & other resources, see Family Wisdom Library on page 513.
For commentaries on each question with Cardinal Arinze, Sr. John Vianney and Fr. Straub (in Spanish), see Appendix C.

Sacred Scripture

But Peter said, "Ananias, why has Satan filled your heart to lie to the Holy Spirit...You have not lied to men but to God." *Acts 5:3-4*

I therefore, a prisoner for the Lord, beg you to lead a life worthy of the calling to which you have been called, with all lowliness and meekness, with patience, forbearing one another in love, eager to maintain the unity of the Spirit in the bond of peace. There is one body and one Spirit, just as you were called to the one hope that belongs to your call. *Ephesians 4:1-4*

And do not grieve the Holy Spirit of God, in whom you were sealed for the day of redemption. Let all bitterness and wrath and anger and clamor and slander be put away from you, with all malice, and be kind to one another, tenderhearted, forgiving one another, as God in Christ forgave you. *Ephesians 4:30-32*

#Y1-1-2

We should also allow the Holy Spirit to guide our lives. By prayer, we learn to discern His inspirations in our souls. His inspirations bring peace.

Catechism of the Catholic Church

685 To believe in the Holy Spirit is to profess that the Holy Spirit is one of the persons of the Holy Trinity, consubstantial with the Father and the Son: "with the Father and the Son he is worshiped and glorified."1 For this reason, the divine mystery of Holy Spirit was already treated in the context of Trinitarian "theology." Here, however, we have to do with the Holy Spirit only in the divine "economy."

Splendor of Truth

It is the Holy Spirit "who confirmed the hearts and minds of the disciples, who revealed the mysteries of the Gospel, who shed upon them the light of things divine." *(section 108)*

Vatican Council II

When the work which the Father gave the Son to do on earth (cf. Jn. 17:4) was accomplished, the Holy Spirit was sent on the day of Pentecost in order that he might continually sanctify the Church, and that, consequently, those who believe might have access through Christ in one Spirit to the Father (cf. Eph. 2:18). He is the Spirit of life, the fountain of water springing up to eternal life (cf. Jn. 4:47; 7:38-39). To men, dead in sin, the Father gives life through him, until the day when, in Christ, he raises to life their mortal bodies (cf. Rom. 8:10-11). The Spirit dwells in the Church and in the hearts of the faithful, as in a temple (cf. 1 Cor. 3:16; 6:19). In them he prays and bears witness to their adoptive sonship (cf. Gal. 4:6; Rom. 8:15-16 and 26). *Lumen Gentium, 4*

Summary Prayer

Holy Spirit, our God and Sanctifier, O that we would not always move on the surface of our souls, but would delve into the depths where You dwell! Our dearest Guest, You have allowed us to look into this sacred sanctuary where You hide Yourself. Help us to try to be aware of Your presence in our souls and of the working of Your grace within us, that we may receive strength and consolation: strength to do good and overcome evil; and consolation to enable us to accept the crosses and sorrows of life patiently and cheerfully.

Free our souls from attachment to earthly things which so often hamper us from doing Your will. Let us think of You within our souls when we are dealing with others who work and live with us, so that the thought of You may help to increase and preserve the peace of our souls. Make us triumph over difficulties, confirm our confidence in You, and bless all our sacrifices and labors. We ask this through Jesus Christ our Lord. Amen.

#B7-5a

We should recognize the importance of the Holy Spirit and His work in the Church and in our lives.

Doctrine • Moral • Worship Exercise

(See Appendix A for answer key, question 123.)

1. Describe some of the ways in which you can honor the Holy Spirit.
2. When making decisions, how do you discern what will be most pleasing to God?
3. Be aware of God's presence in your heart right now. Thank Him for the many times when you have experienced His protection, guidance, and strength. If you know the following song, "Come Holy Spirit, I Need You," sing it softly. If not, read it slowly and say the words from your heart. You may add additional verses.

Come, Holy Spirit, I need You
Come, Holy Spirit, I pray.
Come with Your strength and Your power
Come in Your own special way.

Come, Holy Spirit, I need You
Come, Holy Spirit, I pray.
Come with Your light and Your guidance
Come in Your own special way.

Holy Spirit of God, help us to appreciate the great and inestimable happiness of being children of Holy Mother Church. Give us the courage and zeal to fulfill our vocation as messengers of Christ to the world.

Chapter Summary Prayer

O Holy Spirit, You are the living Soul of God's holy Church. In You alone, dwelling in the Church as in a living tabernacle, the great mystery of the Church of Christ is made possible.

Holy Spirit of God, help us to appreciate the great and inestimable happiness of being children of Holy Mother Church. Through Confirmation, in which You give us the fullness of Yourself, give us the courage and zeal to fulfill our vocation as messengers of Christ to the world. Make us sincere apostles by helping us to be faithful to our duty of proclaiming the Gospel and making its influence felt in the lives of others.

Spirit of Truth, keep us always in a spirit of devoted love and submission to Holy Mother Church. Help us to do our part in bringing about the unity of all men under God. We ask this in the most powerful and holy name of Jesus. Amen.

Thought Provokers

Please see Appendix B for the answers.

Q. 123: Why should we honor the Holy Spirit?

By Heart Catechism and Scripture Review™

The "By Heart Catechism and Scripture Review" lists a selected number of questions and Scripture references from "The Apostolate's Family Catechism" to make memorization easier. Q = Question, SR = Scripture Reference

Q. 117. When did the Holy Spirit descend upon the Church? The Holy Spirit descended upon the Church in a mighty wind and in tongues of fire on Pentecost, fifty days after Easter.

Q. 119. Where is God the Holy Spirit especially present? God the Holy Spirit is especially present in the Catholic Church.

SR 120 John 14:26

But the Counselor, the Holy Spirit, whom the Father will send in my name, he will teach you all things, and bring to your remembrance all that I have said to you.

#L3-44

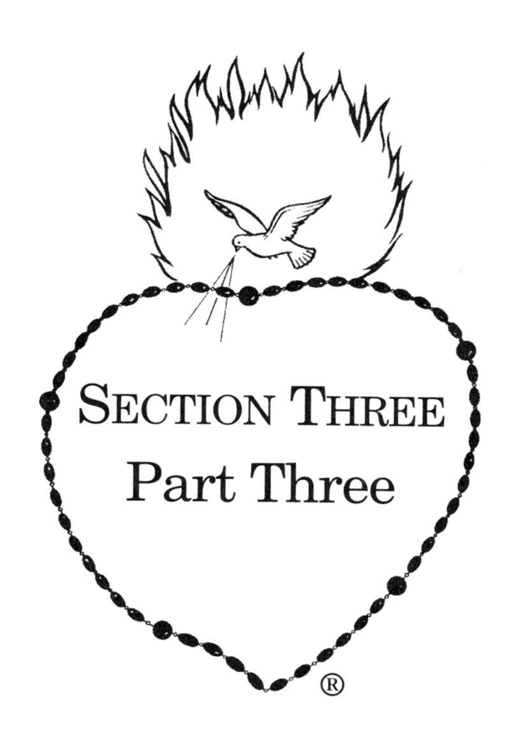

SECTION THREE
Part Three

The Holy Spirit in the Life of the Christian

#T3-30-2

When a person accepts the Spirit of Christ, he receives the power to become an adopted child of God. He truly shares in God's own divine nature and in the fellowship of the divine Persons.

CHAPTER THIRTY-FIVE

Sanctifying Grace

Q. 124. What takes place when a person accepts the Spirit of Christ?

When a person accepts the Spirit of Christ, he receives the power to become an adopted child of God. He truly shares in God's own divine nature and in the fellowship of the divine Persons. He is then led by God to a new way of life. The power to become God's child is called sanctifying grace.

All three Persons of the Holy Trinity have a part in the work of distributing grace to man. This, however, is particularly the task of God the Holy Spirit since it is a work of love, and the Holy Spirit is the personal Love of the Father and the Son. It is the Holy Spirit, the Spirit of Love, Who makes our souls holy through the gift of grace.

Sacred Scripture

For the wages of sin is death, but the free gift of God is eternal life in Christ Jesus our Lord. *Romans 6:23*

If a man loves me, he will keep my word, and my Father will love him, and we will come to him and will make our home with him. *John 14:23*

Catechism of the Catholic Church

1966 The New Law is the grace of the Holy Spirit given to the faithful through faith in Christ. It works through charity; it uses the Sermon on the Mount to teach us what must be done and makes use of the sacraments to give us the grace to do it: "If anyone should meditate with devotion and perspicacity on the sermon our Lord gave on the mount, as we read in the Gospel of Saint Matthew, he will doubtless find there...the perfect way of the Christian life.... This sermon contains...all the precepts needed to shape one's life."[1]

Splendor of Truth

The more one obeys the new law of the Holy Spirit, the more one grows in the freedom to which he or she is called by the service of truth, charity and justice. *(section 107)*

The Spirit of Jesus, received by the humble and docile heart of the believer, brings about the flourishing of Christian moral life and the witness of holiness amid the great variety of vocations, gifts, responsibilities, conditions and life situations. *(section 108)*

Sacred Scripture
Q. 124. Jn 1:12; Rom 8:14-17; Gal 4:5; Tit 3:4-7; 2 Pet 1:4; 1 Jn 1:3.

Catechism of the Catholic Church
Q. 124. Paragraphs **1265-1266**, 1997-1999, 2002-**2003**.

For cross-references with Vatican II, Papal documents & other resources, see Family Wisdom Library on page 513.
For commentaries on each question with Cardinal Arinze, Sr. John Vianney and Fr. Straub (in Spanish), see Appendix C.

Vatican Council II

All Christians by the example of their lives and the witness of the word, wherever they live, have an obligation to manifest the new man which they put on in baptism, and to reveal the power of the Holy Spirit by whom they were strengthened at confirmation, so that others, seeing their good works, might glorify the Father (cf. Matt. 5:16) and more perfectly perceive the true meaning of human life and the universal solidarity of mankind. *Missionary Activity, 11*

#B7-5b

The more one obeys the new law of the Holy Spirit, the more one grows in the freedom to which he or she is called by the service of truth, charity and justice. *(Splendor of Truth, 107)*

Summary Prayer

Divine Spirit, You are our Sanctifier. By Your holy grace, You wish to make us more like Jesus, our Savior. We can be holy only in so far as we become similar to Him Who is "the Way, the Truth, and the Life." God has laid no other foundation for our Salvation, perfection and glory. You alone can bring us to Christ and effect the union of our souls with the Son of God. Infuse Your grace into our minds and hearts.

O Holy Spirit, Living Fire, we desire to offer ourselves to You with the same love with which Jesus offers Himself in all the Holy Masses that are celebrated throughout the world. We beg You, through the merits of this Holy Sacrifice, have mercy on us and make us a living, pleasing sacrifice to You. Transform our souls into the image and likeness of Jesus, and grant that we may have a share in the abundance of graces hidden in His Sacred Heart. Come and live in our hearts as You live in the Sacred Heart of Jesus, that the fullness of Your light and the power of Your grace may reign in us.

Spirit of the Father and of the Son, let the might of Your love be felt forevermore in the hearts of men. Let Your light shine upon the souls of those who are wandering in darkness. Turn them to the life-giving Heart of Jesus and to the healing streams of His Most Precious Blood. Strengthen souls that love You. Perfect in them Your seven gifts and Your twelve fruits. Make them Your temples here, that You may be adored by them forever in Heaven. Amen.

Doctrine • Moral • Worship Exercise

(See Appendix A for answer key, question 124.)

1. Which sacrament gives us the Spirit of Christ?
2. How can you show the people in your family, school, workplace, or community that you live "according to the Spirit of Christ"?
3. Light a candle; then renew your Baptismal vows and ask the Holy Spirit to guide and strengthen you to live a truly Christian life.

   Baptismal vows:

   Do you reject Satan and all his works and all his empty promises?

   Do you believe in God, the Father Almighty, Creator of Heaven and earth?

   Do you believe in Jesus Christ, his only Son, our Lord, who was born of the Virgin Mary, was crucified, died, and was buried, rose from the dead, and is now seated at the right hand of the Father?

   Do you believe in the Holy Spirit, the holy catholic Church, the Communion of Saints, the forgiveness of sins, the resurrection of the body, and life everlasting?

   (Taken from "The Rites of the Catholic Church," Pueblo Publishing Company, New York, 1976)

Q. 125. What is sanctifying grace?

Sanctifying or habitual grace is a gift of God enabling us to be holy and pleasing to God. It confers on us a true share in God's own divine nature and the fellowship of the divine Persons.

By sanctifying grace, our souls participate and share in God's very own life even while we live on earth. This grace helps us to live as God's obedient children.

#W2-13

Sanctifying grace is a gift of God enabling us to be holy and pleasing to God. By sanctifying grace, our souls participate and share in God's very own life even while we live on earth.

Sacred Scripture

But we believe that we shall be saved through the grace of the Lord Jesus. *Acts 15:11*

And from his fullness have we all received, grace upon grace. For the law was given through Moses; grace and truth came through Jesus Christ. *John 1:16-17*

Catechism of the Catholic Church

1266 The Most Holy Trinity gives the baptized sanctifying grace, the grace of justification:

– enabling them to believe in God, to hope in him, and to love him through the theological virtues;

– giving them the power to live and act under the prompting of the Holy Spirit through the gifts of the Holy Spirit;

– allowing them to grow in goodness through the moral virtues.

Thus the whole organism of the Christian's supernatural life has its roots in Baptism.

Sacred Scripture
Q. 125. Jn 4:14; 2 Pet 1:3-4; 1 Jn 1:3.

Catechism of the Catholic Church
Q. 125. Paragraphs **1996-2000, 2023**.

For cross-references with Vatican II, Papal documents & other resources, see Family Wisdom Library on page 513.
For commentaries on each question with Cardinal Arinze, Sr. John Vianney and Fr. Straub (in Spanish), see Appendix C.

Vatican Council II

It pleased God, in his goodness and wisdom, to reveal himself and to make known the mystery of his will (cf. Eph. 1:9). His will was that men should have access to the Father, through Christ, the Word made flesh, in the Holy Spirit, and thus become sharers in the divine nature (cf. Eph. 2:18; 2 Pet. 1:4). *Dei Verbum, 2*

Summary Prayer

Creator Spirit, in nature You changed disorder into order and beauty. You formed and fashioned the universe. You called the seas, the skies, and the earth into existence by a mere act of Your will. All created things are the work of Your creative hand. We adore and praise You!

Living Spirit of God, in the order of grace You have performed wonderful deeds. By Your divine power, You perform the work of Salvation by uniting us to God in love and holiness even as You unite the Father and the Son within the Trinity. Teach us to realize that the loving union of our souls with God through sanctifying grace is the work of Your mercy. We receive grace "because God's love has been poured into our hearts through the Holy Spirit who has been given to us" (Romans 5:5).

Dearest Holy Spirit, help us to hold in highest esteem this priceless gift of sanctifying grace which was infused into our souls when we were baptized. Give us Your grace, that we may never offend or lose You through sin but may keep the promises which were made then on our behalf. May our souls walk in You and live through You and be led by You, even as the Savior Himself was led, so that we may always live in a manner befitting a child of God and a member of His Catholic Church and thus obtain hereafter the inheritance of Heaven. All glory and praise be to You, to the Father and to the Son, One God, world without end. Amen.

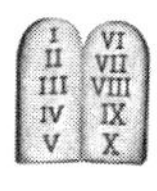

Doctrine • Moral • Worship Exercise

(See Appendix A for answer key, question 125.)

1. How can you explain sanctifying grace to a friend?
2. In what ways can you grow in holiness so that you can better live as God's child?
3. Read Ephesians 1:7 and 2:7. Thank God for sharing His divine life with you and with all people.

Q. 126. What does this new life of sanctifying grace do for man?

This new life of sanctifying grace gives man the ability to participate and share in God's own life, uniting him to the Father and to Christ in a union of love that not even death can separate.

#F1-70-2

The Spirit brings God's own life to man and to everything that He does so that he is said to live in the "state of grace".

Jesus said, "If a man loves me, he will keep my word, and my Father will love him, and we will come to him and make our home with him" (John 14:23).

The Spirit brings God's own life to man and to everything that He does so that he is said to live in the "state of grace," or the "state of sanctifying grace." Sanctifying grace is a gift of God that allows us to live in Him. This life, the life of grace, is a sharing in God's very own life.

Faith is a gift of the Holy Spirit which enables us to accept God's Word and to realize that God loves us and that we can completely trust in Him.

We can hope because God has promised us His love and care forever, through His Son, Jesus Christ. He will never leave us as long as we remain united with Him.

Catechism of the Catholic Church
Q. 126. Paragraphs 1997, **1999-2000**, 2020.

For cross-references with Vatican II, Papal documents & other resources, see Family Wisdom Library on page 513.
For commentaries on each question with Cardinal Arinze, Sr. John Vianney and Fr. Straub (in Spanish), see Appendix C.

Charity is the ability to love both God and man, because all men belong to God. The Holy Spirit's presence in us means we are able to love with a love similar to God's. We can even love our enemies.

Sacred Scripture

I am the vine, you are the branches. He who abides in me, and I in him, he it is that bears much fruit, for apart from me you can do nothing. *John 15:5*

So we know and believe the love God has for us. God is love, and he who abides in love abides in God, and God abides in him. *1 John 4:16*

Catechism of the Catholic Church

2021 Grace is the help that God gives us to respond to our vocation of becoming his adopted sons. It introduces us into the intimacy of the Trinitarian life.

Splendor of Truth

Faith is a decision involving one's whole existence. It is an encounter, a dialogue, a communion of love and of life between the believer and Jesus Christ, the Way, and the Truth, and the Life (cf. Jn. 14:6). It entails an act of trusting abandonment to Christ, which enables us to live as he lived (cf. Gal 2:20), in profound love of God and of our brothers and sisters. *(section 88)*

#C37-7

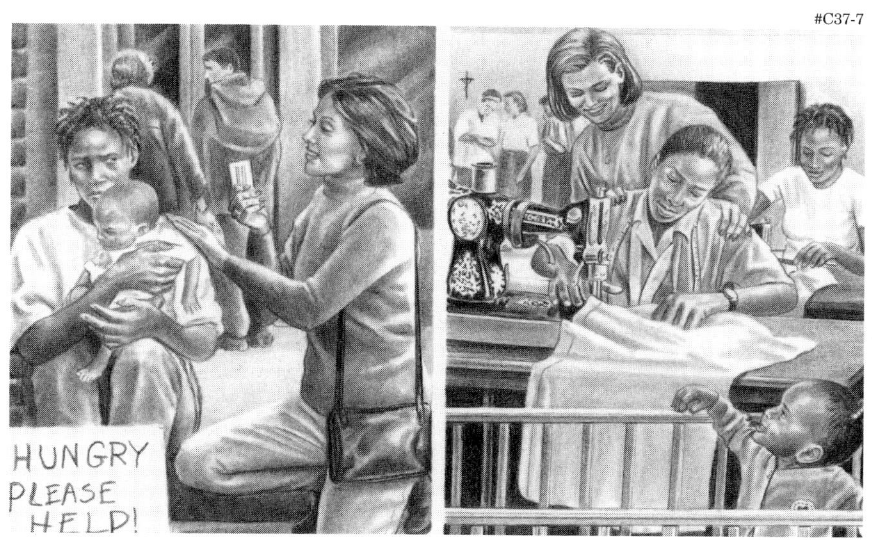

Charity is the ability to love both God and man, because all men belong to God. The Holy Spirit's presence in us means we are able to love with a love similar to God's.

Vatican Council II

All children of the Church should...remember that their exalted condition results, not from their own merits, but from the grace of Christ. If they fail to respond in thought, word and deed to that grace, not only shall they not be saved, but they shall be the more severely judged. *Lumen Gentium, 14*

#C11-103-2

We can hope because God has promised us His love and care forever, through His Son, Jesus Christ. He will never leave us as long as we remain united with Him.

Summary Prayer

Jesus, we believe that through Your Holy Spirit You have given us sanctifying grace. We believe that this new way of life gives us the power to share in God's own life and to be joined to the Father and to You in a union of love which not even death can break. Jesus, we thank You for having made us ready for Your gift of grace. By it we share with You in the divine nature, in the life of God Himself. Help us to appreciate the dignity that is ours.

We trust in the power of Your grace and in the power of Your infinite mercy to preserve us from the misfortune of offending You and of losing Your divine life by mortal sin. May we always thank You for Your infinite love for us, and daily grow in grace.

Jesus, You are the vine, and we are the branches. The vine and the branches have one and the same life. They are nourished by the same sap, that is, the sap of Your grace, which the vine transmits to the branches and which makes them bear fruit.

Sin has made us like wild growth. But You have grafted us onto Yourself, the Divine Vine, and now we have become one with You, sharing in Your divine life. You are the Head, and we are the members of Your Mystical Body. As the same blood gives life to the head and to the members of a human body, the same sanctifying grace flows from You into all those who are united to You by love.

You want us to abide in You. This is also our most earnest wish. You are the Way, the Truth and the Life. Without You we can do nothing; we are like dead branches which should be cast into the fire. Help us ever to abide in You through sanctifying grace. Increase in our souls the virtues of faith, hope and charity. We ask this in Your most holy Name. Amen.

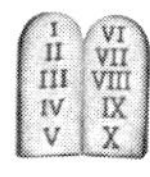

Doctrine • Moral • Worship Exercise

(See Appendix A for answer key, question 126.)

1. What does it mean to say that a person is in the “state of sanctifying grace” or in the “state of grace”? When can one say that he or she is not in the state of grace?
2. How do you strive to remain in the state of grace?
3. Pray the Summary Prayer after question 126.

#H5-24-2

I am the vine, you are the branches. He who abides in me, and I in him, he it is that bears much fruit, for apart from me you can do nothing. *(John 15:5)*

Q. 127. What does God's gift of grace do for us?

God's gift of grace: (1) helps us to overcome sin and live with God, (2) enables us to be closely united to the Blessed Trinity through the Theological Virtues, and (3) helps us to live as adopted children of God.

1. God's gift of grace (especially actual grace) helps us to overcome sin and live with God.

The grace we receive through the Holy Spirit gives us the strength to make the sacrifices necessary to avoid everything that would lead us to sin. With God's help we can conquer our desire to do what is against God's commandments.

#H5-32-2

The Holy Spirit gives us the strength to make the sacrifices necessary to avoid everything that would lead us to sin.

2. God's gift of grace (especially sanctifying grace) enables us to be closely united to the Blessed Trinity through the Theological Virtues.

St. Paul reminds us that we are the temple of God: "Do you not know that you are God's temple and that God's Spirit dwells in you?" (1 Corinthians 3:16).

The Holy Spirit was sent in order that He might make the Church holy. Through Him the Father gives supernatural life to men who are willing to give up sin, because He is the Spirit of life. United in Jesus as His followers, we are led by the Holy Spirit in our journey to the Kingdom of our heavenly Father. He helps us to fulfill our

Sacred Scripture
Q. 127. Eph 1:3-10; Tit 2:11-14.

Catechism of the Catholic Church
Q. 127. Paragraphs **1996-2005**.

For cross-references with Vatican II, Papal documents & other resources, see Family Wisdom Library on page 513.
For commentaries on each question with Cardinal Arinze, Sr. John Vianney and Fr. Straub (in Spanish), see Appendix C.

duties. He prompts us to strive for what is good. He encourages us to pray. His grace unites us to the Most Holy Trinity by the virtues of faith, hope, and charity, especially charity.

#F1-61-2

The Holy Spirit helps us to fulfill our duties.

3. God's gift of grace helps us to live as adopted children of God.

In Baptism, we became the children of God. At that time, we received the new life of grace. As St. Paul says, "For all who are led by the Spirit of God are sons of God" (Romans 8:14).

Sacred Scripture

Truly, truly, I say to you, unless one is born of water and the Spirit, he cannot enter the Kingdom of God. *John 3:5*

Working together with him, then, we entreat you not to accept the grace of God in vain. *2 Corinthians 6:1*

Catechism of the Catholic Church

2003 Grace is first and foremost the gift of the Spirit who justifies and sanctifies us. But grace also includes the gifts that the Spirit grants us to associate us with his work, to enable us to collaborate in the salvation of others and in the growth of the Body of Christ, the Church. There are *sacramental* graces, gifts proper to the different sacraments. There are furthermore *special graces*, also called *charisms*...meaning "favor," "gratuitous gift," "benefit."1 Whatever their character — sometimes it is extraordinary, such as the gift of miracles or of tongues — charisms are oriented toward sanctifying grace and are intended for the common good of the Church. They are at the service of charity which builds up the Church.[2]

2022 The divine initiative in the work of grace precedes, prepares, and elicits the free response of man. Grace responds to the deepest yearnings of human freedom, calls freedom to cooperate with it, and perfects freedom.

Splendor of Truth

This mercy reaches its fullness in the gift of the Spirit who bestows new life and demands that it be lived... Through the gift of new life, Jesus makes us sharers in his love and leads us to the Father in the Spirit. *(section 118)*

Summary Prayer

Holy Spirit, we thank You for the gift of sanctifying grace, which enables us to die to sin, to share in the divine life of God as His children, and to be closely united with the Most Holy Trinity by love.

Divine Healer, beautify our souls by casting out sin. From the fullness of Your gifts and graces, pour upon us the heavenly remedy against sin.

No one needs Your divine remedy more than we. We are often blinded by our passions, chilled by obstinate lukewarmness, and defiled by many imperfections. Come and enlighten us; kindle our fervor and destroy in us all that is displeasing to You. The greater our miseries, the more glorious will be Your triumph over our wickedness. How marvelous and glorious You are. May You be forever praised. Amen.

Doctrine • Moral • Worship Exercise

(See Appendix A for answer key, question 127.)

1. What does Holy Mother Church teach us about sin? How does the Holy Spirit help us to die to sin and to live with God?
2. Recall the occasions in the past month (or since your last confession) when you sinned against God by doing something that displeased Him or by failing to do something that He wanted you to do.
3. Ask God's forgiveness for the times when you did not cooperate with His grace. Promise God that you will go to confession as soon as you can. Ask the Holy Spirit to give you the strength to overcome temptation and to practice the virtue that will overcome your primary fault.

Chapter Summary Prayer

O Holy Spirit, come and create in us new hearts that will give themselves to God and not to the world. We offer You anew the chalice of our souls in love and reverence, in order that You may fill them with Your divine life.

Delightful Guest of our soul, throughout our life, as members of the Church, You are ever present within us, inspiring and leading us on to that goal for which we were created: union with God. Whenever we pass from sin to grace, whenever we resist temptation, whenever we perform a good act which leads to Salvation, You are at work. You are the Creator of this world of wonders and glories, as St. Paul reminds us: "All these are inspired by one and the same Spirit, who apportions to each one individually as he wills" (1 Corinthians 12:11). May You, the Divine Fire which filled the hearts of Jesus' disciples with courage and love, make us holy. Plant Your grace deep within us, so that we can serve You with chaste bodies and please You with pure minds forever and ever. Amen.

Thought Provokers

Please see Appendix B for the answers.

Q. 124: St. Paul says that Christians are "temples of God the Holy Spirit" (cf. 1 Corinthians 6:19). What does this mean?

Q. 125: A. After we are baptized, is it possible to receive more sanctifying grace?
B. What are the benefits of receiving additional sanctifying grace?

Q. 126: Once lost through mortal sin, can sanctifying grace be recovered?

Q. 127: How does being in the state of grace, or sanctifying grace, affect our view of reality?

#P26-17-2

Man always has before him the spiritual horizon of hope, thanks to the help of divine grace and with the cooperation of human freedom.
(Splendor of Truth, 103)

CHAPTER THIRTY-SIX

Actual Grace

Q. 128. What is actual grace?

Actual grace is that special help which the Holy Spirit gives us to enlighten our minds and to inspire and guide our wills to do good and to avoid evil in particular situations. It consists in temporary gifts of divine light for our minds and divine powers for our hearts.

#H5-37-2

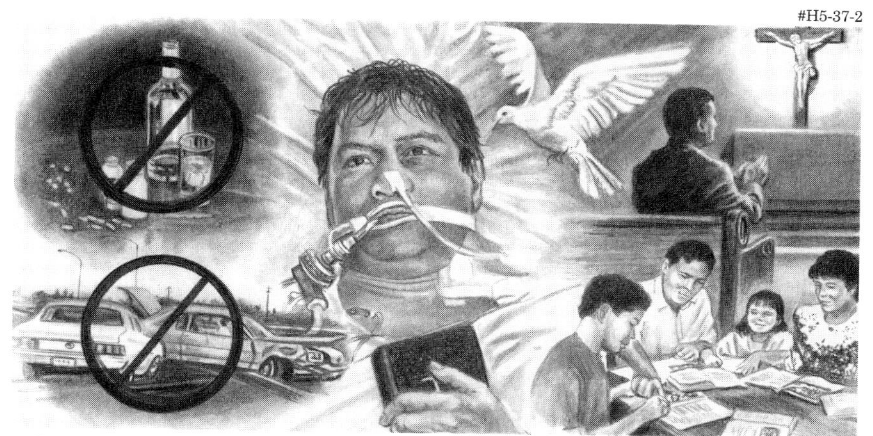

It is the actual grace of Jesus that gives us the light to see what we must do, and the strength of will to do it.

St. John tells us that God comes to illumine every man born into this world, and he quotes the words of Christ about the divine call to the mind that must precede any following of the Master. “No one can come to me unless the Father who sent me draws him; and I will raise him up at the last day” (John 6:44).

In the Book of Revelation, St. John speaks of actual grace operating on the will: “Behold, I stand at the door and knock; if any one hears my voice and opens the door, I will come in to him and eat with him, and he with me” (Revelation 3:20).

The Corinthians are reminded of the same effect when St. Paul says, “I planted, Apollos watered, but God gave the growth” (1 Corinthians 3:6). Paul and Apollos were only the instruments of

Catechism of the Catholic Church
Q. 128. Paragraph 2024.

For cross-references with Vatican II, Papal documents & other resources, see Family Wisdom Library on page 513.
For commentaries on each question with Cardinal Arinze, Sr. John Vianney and Fr. Straub (in Spanish), see Appendix C.

Jesus. But because they cooperated with His actual graces, the Church in Corinth continued to grow in sanctity.

"But by the grace of God I am what I am, and his grace toward me was not in vain. On the contrary, I worked harder than any of them, though it was not I, but the grace of God which is with me. Whether then it was I or they, so we preach and so you believed" (1 Corinthians 15:10-11).

Jesus told His disciples: "Abide in me, and I in you. As the branch cannot bear fruit by itself, unless it abides in the vine, neither can you, unless you abide in me. I am the vine, you are the branches. He who abides in me, and I in him, he it is that bears much fruit, for apart from me you can do nothing" (John 15:4-5).

It is the actual grace of Jesus that gives us the light to see what we must do, and the strength of will to do it. Without this help we cannot live a holy life. Therefore, actual grace is a divine help enabling us to obtain, retain, or grow in sanctifying grace and in the life of God.

#H9-6

Actual grace is that special help which the Holy Spirit gives us to enlighten our minds and to inspire and guide our wills to do good and to avoid evil in particular situations.

Catechism by Diagram

#G6.2-1

Actual Grace. The indwelling Holy Spirit (dove) gives a man guidance and courage on his way to Heaven and shows him the road that is right or wrong, good or bad. The Holy Spirit, through actual grace, helps man to do good, to avoid evil, to walk in the way of virtue. The Holy Spirit helps man to live according to the spirit of Jesus (monogram), to love God and his neighbor (heart), to pray (book), and to be ready for any temptation (umbrella—ready for rain).

Catechism of the Catholic Church

2000 Sanctifying grace is an habitual gift, a stable and supernatural disposition that perfects the soul itself to enable it to live with God, to act by his love. *Habitual grace*, the permanent disposition to live and act in keeping with God's call, is distinguished from *actual graces* which refer to God's interventions, whether at the beginning of conversion or in the course of the work of sanctification.

2010 Since the initiative belongs to God in the order of grace, no one can merit the initial grace of forgiveness and justification, at the beginning of conversion. Moved by the Holy Spirit and by charity, we can then merit for ourselves and for others the graces needed for our sanctification, for the increase of grace and charity, and for the attainment of eternal life. Even temporal goods like health and friendship can be merited in accordance with God's wisdom. These graces and goods are the object of Christian prayer. Prayer attends to the grace we need for meritorious actions.

Splendor of Truth

Man always has before him the spiritual horizon of hope, thanks to the help of divine grace and with the cooperation of human freedom. *(section 103)*

Summary Prayer

Spirit of Jesus, You are our heart and soul, our innermost life and deepest strength. You unite us to the Son of God. We realize now that we cannot come to a special union with Jesus and be His own without also possessing You. St. Paul reminds us that, "if the Spirit of him who raised Jesus from the dead dwells in you, he who raised Christ Jesus from the dead will give life to your mortal bodies also through his Spirit who dwells in you" (Romans 8:11).

We cannot be transformed into the image of the Savior except by Your grace. Especially through frequent Holy Communion, help us to think, desire, speak, and act like Christ. In this sacred union, may His love and ours become one, for the glory of God and for the Salvation of our souls. We need the help that the actual graces You send can give us. Support us by Your power. May everything that we do begin with Your Inspiration, continue with Your help, and reach perfection under Your guidance. With Your loving care, give us the graces that we need to persevere with love and sincerity. May we grow in Your love and service and become more pleasing to God. We ask this through Jesus Christ our Lord. Amen.

Doctrine • Moral • Worship Exercise

(See Appendix A for answer key, question 128.)

1. Picture this situation in your mind. You are inside a locked room. Jesus is outside and wishes to enter. Only you can open the door because it has no knob on the outside. How does this situation relate to actual grace?
2. What are some signs that you have let Jesus into your life?
3. If you know the following song, sing it softly. If not, read it slowly and say the words from your heart.

    Day by day, Day by day,
    Oh, dear Lord, three things I pray:
    To see You more clearly,
    Love You more dearly,
    Follow You more nearly,
    Day by day.

Thought Provokers

Please see Appendix B for the answers.

Q. 128: Is actual grace necessary for every good act we perform?

#L3-44

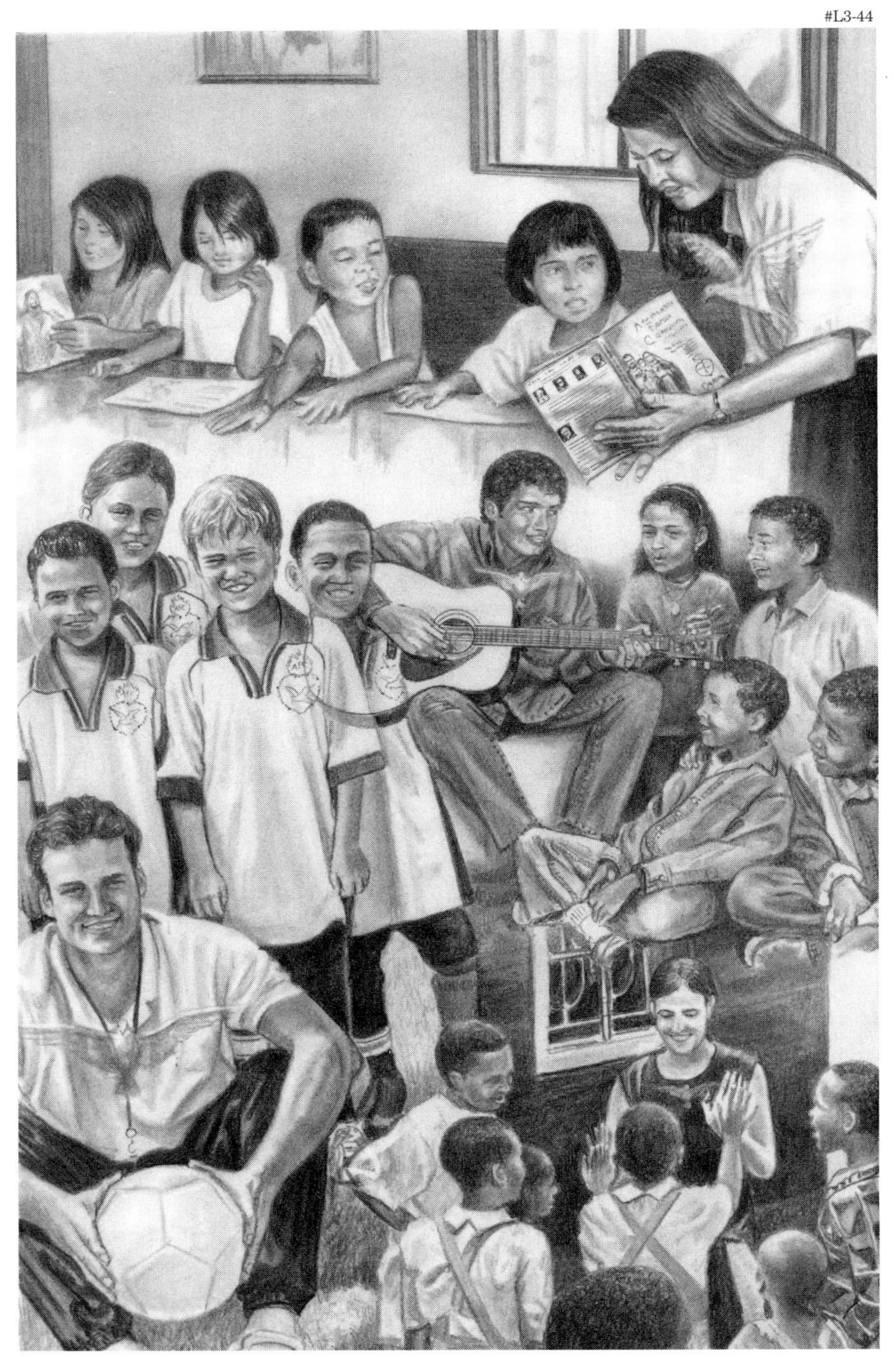

By the indwelling of the Holy Spirit, we are given sanctifying grace, the seven Gifts of the Holy Spirit, and the Theological and Cardinal Virtues.

CHAPTER THIRTY-SEVEN

The Indwelling of the Holy Spirit in Man

Q. 129. What does the indwelling of the Holy Spirit do for man?

By the indwelling of the Holy Spirit: (1) we are given sanctifying grace, the seven Gifts of the Holy Spirit, and the Theological and Cardinal Virtues; (2) our weakness of soul is healed; (3) we are helped to overcome our evil desires and selfishness and to practice virtues such as charity and patience; and (4) our prayers and lives are made pleasing to God.

1. By the indwelling of the Holy Spirit, we are given sanctifying grace, the seven Gifts of the Holy Spirit, and the Theological and Cardinal Virtues.

Sanctifying grace is a sharing in God's own divine nature and life. The seven Gifts of the Holy Spirit are capacities to receive and use seven kinds of divine light from Christ's fullness of truth. The Theological and Cardinal Virtues are capacities to receive and use seven kinds of divine power from Christ's fullness of grace (cf. Jn 1:14, 16). In order to live in us, the Holy Spirit gives us these supernatural gifts.

2. By the indwelling of the Holy Spirit, our weakness of soul is healed.

The Holy Spirit gives us actual graces, those special divine lights, powers, and helps that enlighten our minds and strengthen our wills so that we can do good and avoid evil. The seven Gifts of the Holy Spirit and the Theological and Cardinal Virtues give us the capacity to receive and use these graces in order to make acts and develop habits of the gifts and virtues.

3. By the indwelling of the Holy Spirit we are helped to overcome our evil desires and selfishness and to practice virtues such as charity and patience.

As a result of Original Sin, the desires and tendencies of our bodies tempt us to do things unworthy of a Christian. These tendencies are

Sacred Scripture
Q. 129. Rom 5:1-6; 8:26.

Catechism of the Catholic Church
Q. 129. Paragraphs 683-685, **733-736, 797-801**, 1266.

For cross-references with Vatican II, Papal documents & other resources, see Family Wisdom Library on page 513.
For commentaries on each question with Cardinal Arinze, Sr. John Vianney and Fr. Straub (in Spanish), see Appendix C.

called Capital Sins—sins of impurity, sloth, gluttony, anger, envy, pride, and avarice. Evil persons, places, and things can also lead us into sin. We need the help of the Holy Spirit to lead good Christian lives. If we allow the Holy Spirit to guide us, and if we use the help of His actual graces, we will overcome these Capital Sins, preserve God's divine life of sanctifying grace in our souls, live as His children, and grow in the habits of the Gifts of the Holy Spirit and of the Theological and Cardinal Virtues.

#L3-26-2

By the indwelling of the Holy Spirit, we are helped to overcome our evil desires and selfishness and to practice virtues such as charity and patience.

4. By the indwelling of the Holy Spirit, our prayers and lives are made pleasing to God.

The Holy Spirit helps us to develop our love of God and to keep and deepen our friendship with Him by prayer. Because it is the Holy Spirit Himself who inspires and guides our prayers, they are pleasing to God. The graces we receive in prayer help us to grow in our imitation of Jesus and our resemblance to Him, making our lives pleasing to God.

Sacred Scripture

But the fruit of the Spirit is love, joy, peace, patience, kindness, goodness, faithfulness, gentleness, self-control; against such there is no law. *Galatians 5:22-23*

For he who sows to his own flesh will from the flesh reap corruption; but he who sows to the Spirit will from the Spirit reap eternal life. *Galatians 6:8*

#H5-20-2

But the fruit of the Spirit is love, joy, peace, patience, kindness, goodness, faithfulness, gentleness, self-control; against such there is no law.
(Galatians 5:22-23)

Catechism of the Catholic Church

736 By this power of the Spirit, God's children can bear much fruit. He who has grafted us onto the true vine will make us bear "the fruit of the Spirit: ...love, joy, peace, patience, kindness, goodness, faithfulness, gentleness, self-control."[1] "We live by the Spirit"; the more we renounce ourselves, the more we "walk by the Spirit."[2]

Through the Holy Spirit we are restored to paradise, led back to the Kingdom of heaven, and adopted as children, given confidence to call God "Father" and to share in Christ's grace, called children of light and given a share in eternal glory.[3]

1803 "Whatever is true, whatever is honorable, whatever is just, whatever is pure, whatever is lovely, whatever is gracious, if there is any excellence, if there is anything worthy of praise, think about these things."[1]

A virtue is an habitual and firm disposition to do the good. It allows the person not only to perform good acts, but to give the best of himself. The virtuous person tends toward the good with all his sensory and spiritual powers; he pursues the good and chooses it in concrete actions.

The goal of a virtuous life is to become like God.[3]

Splendor of Truth

All people must take great care not to allow themselves to be tainted by the attitude of the Pharisee, which would seek to eliminate awareness of one's own limits and of one's own sin. In our own day this attitude is expressed particularly in the attempt to adapt the moral norm to one's own capacities and personal interests, and even in the rejection of the very idea of a norm. Accepting, on the other hand, the "disproportion" between the law and human ability (that is, the capacity of the moral forces of man left to himself) kindles the desire for grace and prepares one to receive it. *(section 105)*

Vatican Council II

Before this faith can be exercised, man must have the grace of God to move and assist him; he must have the interior helps of the Holy Spirit, who moves the heart and converts it to God, who opens the eyes of the mind and "makes it easy for all to accept and believe the truth." The same Holy Spirit constantly perfects faith by his gifts. *Dei Verbum, 5*

Summary Prayer

Indwelling Holy Spirit, give us hope and courage. Heal the weaknesses of our souls. Help us to overcome our evil desires and selfishness. Through Your grace, aid us in the practice of virtue and make our prayers more pleasing to God.

Fill our souls with the wisdom and knowledge of Christ's teachings; sanctify us in Your grace as You sanctified the saints. Pour into our hearts a love for those virtues which You especially require of us. Imbue us, above all, with the spirit of self-sacrifice, that we may make any sacrifice to which Your grace invites us, for Your own glorification, for the honor of the Father and the Son, and for the Salvation of immortal souls.

Loving Comforter, we beg You for the grace of a personal, constant, and daily devotion to You. We were entrusted to Your care in Baptism, and we received You in a special manner at Confirmation. Be then our Guide, our Friend, our Counselor, and our Guardian. Keep us far from sin and all its occasions.

Holy Spirit, bestow upon us a love of chastity, that with tender care we may watch over the purity of our bodies and souls. As You dispense Your graces through prayer and the sacraments, grant that we may rightly love and esteem these precious means of grace and zealously make use of them.

Glory be to the Father, our Creator; glory be to the Son, our Redeemer; glory be to You, Holy Spirit, our Sanctifier, now and forever. Amen.

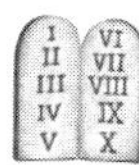

Doctrine • Moral • Worship Exercise

(See Appendix A for answer key, question 129.)

1. How does the Holy Spirit help us to lead good Christian lives?
2. Do you allow the Holy Spirit to guide you in your daily life? List the things that you will do to become more receptive to the grace of the Holy Spirit.
3. Compose a personal prayer to the Holy Spirit. Make at least two copies. Keep one in your room so that you can use it, especially when you are feeling spiritually weak or discouraged. Insert one in your calendar, planner/organizer, or schedule/school notebook so that you can pray it whenever you make your plans.

Q. 130. What is our greatest dignity?

Our greatest dignity as Christians consists in the fact that we are children of God and have God's life in our souls through the grace of our Lord Jesus Christ.

#F1-123

Our greatest dignity as Christians consists in the fact that we are children of God and have God's life in our souls through the grace of our Lord Jesus Christ.

Sacred Scripture
Q. 130. Gen 1:26-27; Gal 4:6-7; 1 Jn 3:1-3.

Catechism of the Catholic Church
Q. 130. Paragraphs **1996-1999**.

For cross-references with Vatican II, Papal documents & other resources, see Family Wisdom Library on page 513.
For commentaries on each question with Cardinal Arinze, Sr. John Vianney and Fr. Straub (in Spanish), see Appendix C.

#B6-2-2

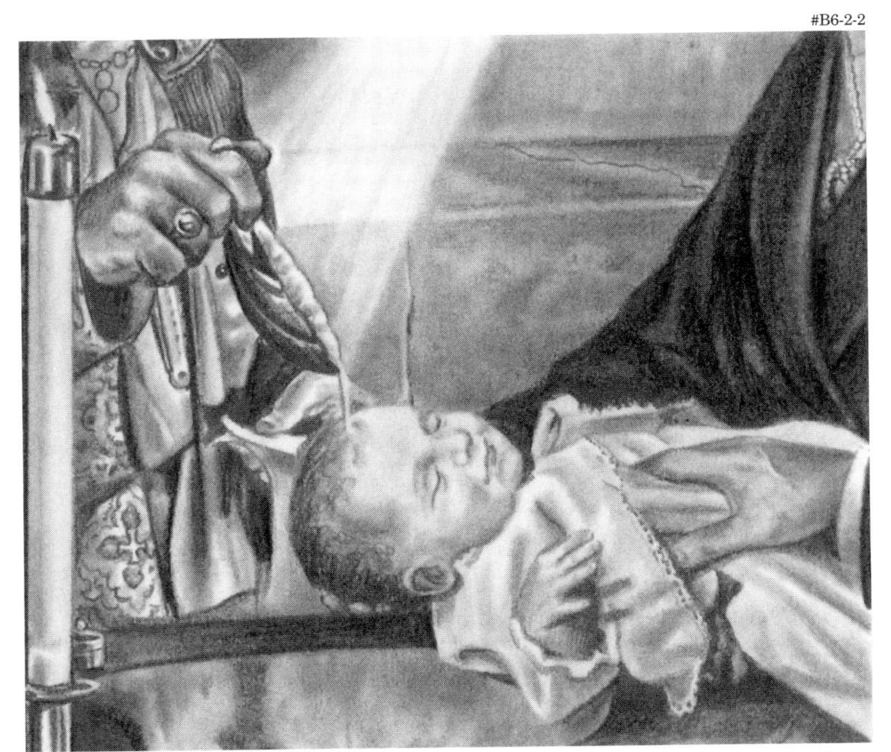

We receive two lives from God. One is the natural life we receive at conception. The other is the supernatural life we receive when we are baptized as Christians.

We must try to live holy lives and strive always to keep God's grace as our most precious treasure. We need to ask the Holy Spirit to help us live according to our great dignity as children of God and as true Christians.

We receive two lives from God. One is the natural life we receive at conception. The other is the supernatural life we receive when we are baptized as Christians. Jesus said to Nicodemus, "Truly, truly, I say to you, unless one is born anew, he cannot see the kingdom of God" (John 3:3).

We believe in things unseen and hope for the reward promised to those who love God. As a result, we witness the action of a superhuman power, which is divine grace operating on our minds and wills, that enables us to see and want what the purely natural man cannot understand or desire. The gifts of nature are common to the good and bad, but supernatural grace is the proper gift of the elect. They who are adorned with it are esteemed worthy of eternal life.

The Trinitarian God is the source of supernatural grace. Indeed man's greatest dignity is that he is meant to possess supernatural life from the Father, through the Son, and in union with the Holy Spirit.

We could never earn this grace. Jesus bought supernatural grace for all men by His suffering, Death, and Resurrection. Through supernatural grace we can gain eternal life.

Sacred Scripture

By which he [Jesus] has granted to us his precious and very great promises, that through these you may escape from the corruption that is in the world because of passion, and become partakers of the divine nature. *2 Peter 1:4*

It is the Spirit himself bearing witness with our spirit that we are children of God, and if children, then heirs, heirs of God and fellow heirs with Christ, provided we suffer with him in order that we may also be glorified with him. *Romans 8:16-17*

#L3-20

All children of the Church should nevertheless remember that their exalted condition results, not from their own merits, but from the grace of Christ. *(Lumen Gentium, 14)*

Catechism of the Catholic Church

1700 The dignity of the human person is rooted in his creation in the image and likeness of God *(article 1)*; it is fulfilled in his vocation to divine beatitude *(article 2)*. It is essential to a human being freely to direct himself to this fulfillment *(article 3)*. By his deliberate actions *(article 4)*, the human person does, or does not, conform to the good promised by God and attested by moral conscience *(article 5)*. Human beings make their own contribution to their interior growth; they make their whole sentient and spiritual lives into means of this growth *(article 6)*. With the help of grace they grow in virtue *(article 7)*, avoid sin, and if they sin they entrust themselves as did the prodigal son[1] to the mercy of our Father in heaven *(article 8)*. In this way they attain to the perfection of charity.

1711 Endowed with a spiritual soul, with intellect and with free will, the human person is from his very conception ordered to God and destined for eternal beatitude. He pursues his perfection in "seeking and loving what is true and good."[1]

Splendor of Truth

The relationship between faith and morality shines forth with all its brilliance in the unconditional respect due to the insistent demands of the personal dignity of every man. *(section 90)*

#R1-6

The dignity of man rests above all on the fact that he is called to communion with God... For if man exists it is because God has created him through love, and through love continues to hold him in existence. *(Gaudium et Spes, 19)*

Vatican Council II

The dignity of man rests above all on the fact that he is called to communion with God. The invitation to converse with God is addressed to man as soon as he comes into being. For if man exists it is because God has created him through love, and through love continues to hold him in existence. He cannot live fully according to truth unless he freely acknowledges that love and entrusts himself to his creator. *Gaudium et Spes, 19*

All men are endowed with a rational soul and are created in God's image; they have the same nature and origin and, being redeemed by Christ, they enjoy the same divine calling and destiny; there is here a basic equality between all men and it must be given ever greater recognition.

...Furthermore, while there are rightful differences between people, their equal dignity as persons demands that we strive for fairer and more humane conditions. Excessive economic and social disparity between individuals and peoples of the one human race is a source of scandal and militates against social justice, equity, human dignity, as well as social and international peace. *Gaudium et Spes, 29*

All children of the Church should nevertheless remember that their exalted condition results, not from their own merits, but from the grace of Christ. If they fail to respond in thought, word and deed to that grace, not only shall they not be saved, but they shall be the more severely judged. *Lumen Gentium, 14*

Summary Prayer

Holy Spirit, with all the humility and love of which we are capable, we invite You to come into our hearts. We are overwhelmed by Your divine goodness and condescension in wishing to leave the splendors of Your throne of supreme majesty and glory, in order to stoop to such miserable beings as ourselves. Our greatest dignity is that You dwell in our souls through grace.

As we cast ourselves down in humble adoration before You, we most earnestly beg You to take complete possession of our souls and make them Your own. We are Yours because You created us. All that we have are Your free gifts to us. Our wondrous bodies, with all their senses, are so very marvelous and perfect in their operations. Still more wondrous are our souls, spiritual and immortal, and their sublime faculties of understanding, memory, and will. All these You have given us. Our one desire is to return them entirely to You, that You may make them Your own and take forevermore complete and unreserved possession of our entire being. Amen.

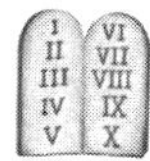

Doctrine • Moral • Worship Exercise

(See Appendix A for answer key, question 130.)

1. When did we become children of God? What are the implications of our being children of God—for our relationship to Him, to others, and to the earth on which we live?
2. List some specific things that you will do in order to live according to your great dignity as a child of God.
3. Be aware of God's presence and thank God the Father for the great dignity of being His child. Ask the Holy Spirit for the grace to think, feel, and act according to the values and teachings of Christ, your Brother, as set forth in Sacred Scripture and the "Catechism of the Catholic Church."

Chapter Summary Prayer

We wish to be Yours, Divine Spirit, by the gift of sanctifying grace. You have made us Your temple and have illumined and warmed us by Your most enlivening presence. We wish to be Yours by experiencing the infusion of Your divine grace in our souls and by living the three Theological virtues of faith, hope, and charity. We wish to be Yours by sharing in Your seven gifts and twelve fruits, and by receiving the grace You give us to practice the acquired virtues.

Our indwelling God, stay with us forever. Strengthen us by Your all-powerful grace against the awful possibility, which we tremble even to think about, of ever driving You out of our souls by mortal sin. Help us to keep the temples of our souls pure and, as far as poor human frailty will permit, sinless in Your sight. Thus, may You be pleased to dwell there forever with blessed delight until we see You face to face in Your heavenly Kingdom. Amen.

Thought Provokers

Please see Appendix B for the answers.

Q. 129: A. What does "indwelling of the Holy Spirit" mean?

B. Is God the Holy Spirit present even in great sinners?

Q. 130: In addition to the existence of the state of Original Sin and the existence of actual sins, what other condition makes men unworthy of sharing in God's own life?

By Heart Catechism and Scripture Review™

The "By Heart Catechism and Scripture Review" lists a selected number of questions and Scripture references from "The Apostolate's Family Catechism" to make memorization easier. Q = Question, SR = Scripture Reference

SR 124 John 14:23

If a man loves me, he will keep my word, and my Father will love him, and we will come to him and make our home with him.

Q. 125. What is sanctifying grace? Sanctifying grace is the gift of God's own life which enables us to be holy and pleasing to God.

SR 127 John 3:5

Truly, truly, I say to you, unless one is born of water and the Spirit, he cannot enter the kingdom of God.

Q. 128. What is actual grace? Actual grace is a special help which the Holy Spirit gives us so that we can know and do God's Will.

SR 129 Galatians 5:22-23

But the fruit of the Spirit is love, joy, peace, patience, kindness, goodness, faithfulness, gentleness, self-control; against such there is no law.

Q. 130. What is our greatest dignity? Our greatest dignity is that we are children of God with God's own life, His grace, in our souls.

#J2-371

He looked up and saw the rich putting their gifts into the treasury; and he saw a poor widow put in two copper coins. And he said, "Truly I tell you, this poor widow has put in more than all of them; for they all contributed out of their abundance, but she out of her poverty put in all the living that she had."
(Luke 21:1-4)

The Theological and Cardinal Virtues and the Seven Gifts of the Holy Spirit

---

#L3-4-2

The Theological virtues unite us directly to God. God infuses them into our souls, along with sanctifying grace, in the Sacrament of Baptism.

CHAPTER THIRTY-EIGHT

The Theological Virtues

Q. 131. What are the Theological Virtues?

The Theological Virtues are faith, hope, and charity. These virtues are supernatural capacities to receive three divine powers from Jesus' fullness of grace.

These virtues are called theological, or divine, because they unite us directly to God. God infuses them into our souls, along with sanctifying grace, in the Sacrament of Baptism.

The Theological Virtues, along with the Gifts of the Holy Spirit and the Cardinal Virtues, are the means God gives us in Baptism for activating and developing the share in His divine nature and life that sanctifying grace confers. These virtues and gifts enable us to function and live in the dimension of God's own life, of God's own acts of consciousness, intellect and will.

By making repeated acts of these virtues, we develop strong habits of them. These habits enable us to grow constantly in our union with Christ in the Holy Spirit, and with the Father through Christ. The Theological Virtues give us the power to share Jesus' own possession of and obedience to the truth, His commitment to His Father's will and plan, and His habit of saying "yes" to all God gives Him and asks of Him. They are also our most fundamental weapons in the battle against evil and our strongest protection against the wiles of the devil.

Sacred Scripture

So faith, hope, love abide, these three; but the greatest of these is love. *1 Corinthians 13:13*

We give thanks to God always for you all, constantly mentioning you in our prayers, remembering before our God and Father your work of faith and labor of love and steadfastness of hope in our Lord Jesus Christ. *1 Thessalonians 1:2-3*

But, since we belong to the day, let us be sober, and put on the breastplate of faith and love, and for a helmet the hope of salvation. *1 Thessalonians 5:8*

Catechism of the Catholic Church
Q. 131. Paragraphs **1812-1829**.

For cross-references with Vatican II, Papal documents & other resources, see Family Wisdom Library on page 513.
For commentaries on each question with Cardinal Arinze, Sr. John Vianney and Fr. Straub (in Spanish), see Appendix C.

Catechism by Diagram

#V4-1

Theological Virtues. The Theological Virtues are faith (F), which guides (arrow) us to God, hope (H), and love (L). They raise us to God. We believe in God, we hope in Him, and we love Him. These three virtues are infused into our souls (heart) in the Sacrament of Baptism. Through these virtues, the grace of God comes into our soul and is increased there (long rays).

Catechism of the Catholic Church

1813 The theological virtues are the foundation of Christian moral activity; they animate it and give it its special character. They inform and give life to all the moral virtues. They are infused by God into the souls of the faithful to make them capable of acting as his children and of meriting eternal life. They are the pledge of the presence and action of the Holy Spirit in the faculties of the human being. There are three theological virtues: faith, hope, and charity.[1]

Vatican Council II

The forms and tasks of life are many but holiness is one—that sanctity which is cultivated by all who act under God's Spirit and, obeying the Father's voice and adoring God the Father in spirit and in truth, follow Christ, poor, humble and cross-bearing, that they may deserve to be partakers of his glory. Each one, however, according to his own gifts and duties must steadfastly advance along the way of a living faith, which arouses hope and works through love. *Lumen Gentium, 41*

#L3-22

The Theological Virtues enable us to grow constantly in our union with Christ in the Holy Spirit, and with the Father through Christ.

Summary Prayer

Most Holy Spirit, we firmly believe that You are really a Person and that You abide in our souls through sanctifying grace. You are co-equal and co-eternal with the Father and the Son. Never let us forget that You are always living and working in our souls to make us holy by increasing in us the virtues of faith, hope, and charity. What You desire most of all is our sanctification. May Your desire evoke the same desire in our souls.

Most Loving Friend, by Your indwelling in our souls, You make an abode with us as the Protector and Giver of all spiritual gifts and virtues. As the Spirit of adoption in a child of God, You are the cause and fountain of supernatural life and the seal of the promised full and beatific possession of God in Heaven. Your indwelling in us differs only in degree from that by which You beatify the saints in Heaven.

Divine Author and Giver of all grace, although Your divine working in our souls is secret, hidden, and unseen, and although we do not feel Your presence there, let us never become indifferent to You. Rather, let us adore You as the dearest Guest of our souls, give You thanks for Your blessings, and listen to Your inspirations. Fill our souls with the fullness of Your gifts and virtues, especially the virtues of faith, hope, and charity. Give us peace and consolation. Direct us with Your inspirations; govern our conduct; raise us above the restlessness of this world; help us to overcome our temptations; heal our souls and inflame them with the fire of Your love; and guide us to a home of everlasting beauty in the Kingdom of God. Amen.

Doctrine • Moral • Worship Exercise

(See Appendix A for answer key, question 131.)

1. Name the three Theological Virtues. Why are they called Theological Virtues? How do they help us in our daily lives?
2. Recall occasions in your life when you acted as a person who believes in God, who hopes in God, and who loves God and other people for His sake.
3. Pray the Apostles' Creed, one Our Father, and three Hail Marys for an increase of faith, hope and charity, and pray one Glory Be in honor of the Most Holy Trinity.

Q. 132. What is the Theological Virtue of faith?

The Theological Virtue of faith is the supernatural virtue by which we firmly believe in our hearts all the truths God has revealed.

The virtue of faith enables us to accept as true and choose to live by the body of truths that are found in the Creeds and in the teachings of the Church, for these are based upon divine Revelation, which includes both Sacred Scripture and Sacred Tradition. The power of faith is essentially the power to believe in God's revelation of Himself and His will for us and to obey that revelation and will.

#A2.3-2

The Theological Virtue of faith is the supernatural virtue by which we firmly believe in our hearts all the truths God has revealed.

An act of supernatural faith is thus the assent of the mind to what God has revealed. Such an act requires divine grace, either actual or sanctifying or both. The mind needs the light of Christ's knowledge before it can give this assent. This is made available to it by the Holy Spirit's gift of knowledge.

When made in the state of grace, an act of faith is meritorious before God. A simple act of faith is, "My God, I believe in You and all that Your Church teaches, because You have said it, and Your word is true."

Catechism of the Catholic Church
Q. 132. Paragraphs **1814-1815**.

For cross-references with Vatican II, Papal documents & other resources, see Family Wisdom Library on page 513.
For commentaries on each question with Cardinal Arinze, Sr. John Vianney and Fr. Straub (in Spanish), see Appendix C.

The virtue or capacity of faith is infused into our souls, along with sanctifying grace, when the Sacrament of Baptism is received. Even the baptized infant possesses this virtue, although he will not be able to exercise it fully until he reaches the age of reason.

The effect of faith is something called justification. This means that faith perfected by the Theological Virtue of charity brings man from a stage of separation from God into communion with Him and with his fellow men in God.

Faith is the permanent capacity to share in the power of Jesus' obedience to the Truth revealed by God, and to use this power to develop habits of supernatural faith. These habits enable us to live our lives in God's Truth and to adhere to His plan and New Covenant for our Salvation.

Catechism by Diagram

#T9.2.1-1

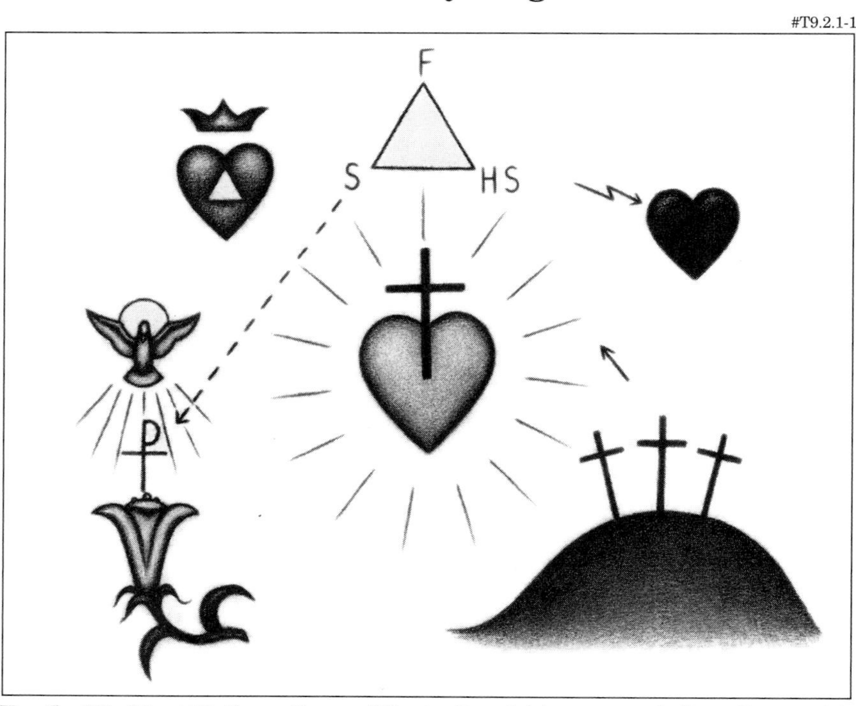

Truths We Must Believe. Some of the truths which we must believe (heart with cross) with an act of faith are: (1) the existence of God, Who will reward good deeds (crown, heart with triangle—grace) and punish evil (black heart—grace driven out of the heart of sinners); (2) the principal mysteries of our Faith: the Holy Trinity—three Persons in one God (triangle, F, S, HS); the Incarnation—the Son of God (S) becomes man (dotted line from S to monogram) in the womb of the Blessed Virgin Mary (lily), through the overshadowing of the Holy Spirit (dove); the Redemption—the Son of God dies to redeem the world (cross of Calvary).

#P26-14-2

A simple act of faith is, "My God, I believe in You and all that Your Church teaches, because You have said it, and Your word is true."

Sacred Scripture

Because, if you confess with your lips that Jesus is Lord and believe in your heart that God raised him from the dead, you will be saved. For man believes with his heart and so is justified, and he confesses with his lips and so is saved. *Romans 10:9-10*

No one can come to me unless the Father who sent me draws him; and I will raise him up at the last day. *John 6:44*

Since all have sinned and fall short of the glory of God, they are justified by his grace as a gift, through the redemption which is in Christ Jesus, whom God put forward as an expiation by his blood, to be received by faith. This was to show God's righteousness, because in his divine forbearance he had passed over former sins. *Romans 3:23-25*

For through the Spirit, by faith, we wait for the hope of righteousness. For in Christ Jesus neither circumcision nor uncircumcision is of any avail, but faith working through love. *Galatians 5:5-6*

Catechism of the Catholic Church

1816 The disciple of Christ must not only keep the faith and live on it, but also profess it, confidently bear witness to it, and spread it: "All however must be prepared to confess Christ before men and to follow him along the way of the Cross, amidst the persecutions which the Church never lacks."[1] Service of and witness to the faith are necessary for salvation: "So every one who acknowledges me before men, I also will acknowledge before my Father who is in heaven; but whoever denies me before men, I also will deny before my Father who is in heaven."[2]

181 "Believing" is an ecclesial act. The Church's faith precedes, engenders, supports, and nourishes our faith. The Church is the mother of all believers. "No one can have God as Father who does not have the Church as Mother."[1]

Splendor of Truth

It is a question of the decision of faith, of the obedience of faith (cf. Rom 16:26) "by which man makes a total and free self-commitment to God offering 'the full submission of intellect and will to God as he reveals.'" This faith, which works through love (cf. Gal 5:6), comes from the core of man, from his "heart" (cf. Rom 10:10), whence it is called to bear fruit in works (cf. Mt 12:33-35; Lk 6:43-45; Rom 8:5-10; Gal 5:22). *(section 66)*

Faith is a lived knowledge of Christ, a living remembrance of his commandments, and a truth to be lived out. A word, in any event, is not truly received until it passes into action, until it is put into practice. *(section 88)*

Faith...gives rise to and calls for a consistent life commitment; it entails and brings to perfection the acceptance and observance of God's commandments...Through the moral life, faith becomes "confession," not only before God but also before men: it becomes witness. *(section 89)*

Vatican Council II

The act of faith is of its very nature a free act. Man, redeemed by Christ the Saviour and called through Jesus Christ to be an adopted son of God, cannot give his adherence to God when he reveals himself unless, drawn by the Father, he submits to God with a faith that is reasonable and free. *Liberty, 10*

Only the light of faith and meditation on the Word of God can enable us to find everywhere and always the God "in whom we live and exist" (Acts 17:28); only thus can we seek his will in everything, see Christ in all men, acquaintance or stranger, make sound judgments on the true meaning and value of temporal realities both in themselves and in relation to man's end. *Lay People, 4*

Catechism by Diagram

#T9.2.1-2

An Act of Faith. Christ gave His Church the power to teach, to sanctify, and to govern spiritually in His name when He sent His Holy Spirit (dove) upon it. The instructed Catholic can make an act of supernatural faith by believing firmly and completely all the truths which God has revealed through His Son (I=intellect; W=will). The Holy Spirit gives light to his understanding and strength to his will to accept (credo) God's truth (heart).

Summary Prayer

Our God, we firmly believe that You are one God in three divine Persons: Father, Son, and Holy Spirit. We believe that God the Son became man and died for our sins, and that He will come to judge the living and the dead. We believe these and all the truths which the Holy Catholic Church teaches, because You have revealed them, and You can neither deceive nor be deceived.

Divine Spirit, pour Your heavenly light into our souls that we may, to some degree, understand these truths and the end and object of our being in this world. Enlighten our minds by the light of the Church's teaching, for You keep intact the Deposit of Faith and guard the teaching Church from the possibility of error.

Guide our minds also by the interior light of Your divine inspirations, by the virtue of faith, by the infusion of Your gifts, and by the actual graces You impart to us.

May we, who have received Your gift of faith, share forever in the new life of Christ. Restore us by Your sacraments. May Your grace bring us eternal joy. In loving us, You have brought us from evil to good and from misery to happiness. Through Your blessings of grace, give the courage of perseverance to the ones You have called and justified by faith.

Holy Spirit, our God, by the coming of the Divine Word, Jesus, among us, may the light of faith shine in our words and actions. Open our hearts to receive Jesus' life and increase our vision of faith, that our life may be filled forever with Your glory and Your peace. Amen.

Doctrine • Moral • Worship Exercise

(See Appendix A for answer key, question 132.)

1. When did you receive the virtue of faith for the first time? What is the meaning of faith?
2. List specific steps that you can take to deepen your knowledge of the truths of our Catholic faith.
3. Read and meditate on a Scripture passage for ten minutes. For another ten minutes, read a sound Catholic formation book such as the "Catechism of the Catholic Church," "The Apostolate's Family Catechism" or Church documents and writings. Try to set aside time each day for this type of spiritual reading.

Q. 133. What is the Theological Virtue of hope?

Hope is the supernatural virtue by which we firmly commit ourselves in our hearts to fulfill God's covenant and plan for our lives while firmly trusting that He, Who is all-powerful and faithful to His promises, will, in His mercy, give us eternal happiness and the means to obtain it, if we keep this commitment. These promises are given to us through the merits of the sufferings and works of Jesus Christ.

#F1-66-2

Hope gives one the confidence that he will receive the graces necessary to reach Heaven, and the will to do whatever it takes to achieve it.

Hope belongs to the will and makes a person desire and commit oneself to obtaining eternal life, which is the heavenly vision of God. Hope gives one the confidence that he will receive the graces necessary to reach Heaven, and the will to do whatever it takes to achieve it.

"For in this hope we were saved. Now hope that is seen is not hope. For who hopes for what he sees? But if we hope for what we do not see, we wait for it with patience" (Romans 8:24-25).

The grounds of hope are the omnipotence of God, the goodness of God, and the fidelity of God to what He has promised. "But they who wait for the Lord shall renew their strength, they shall mount up with wings like eagles, they shall run and not be weary, they shall walk and not faint" (Isaiah 40:31).

Catechism of the Catholic Church
Q. 133. Paragraphs **1817-1821**.

For cross-references with Vatican II, Papal documents & other resources, see Family Wisdom Library on page 513.
For commentaries on each question with Cardinal Arinze, Sr. John Vianney and Fr. Straub (in Spanish), see Appendix C.

#P26-25-2

Acts of hope are required in times of temptation to discouragement or despair, and are implicit in every supernaturally good work.

The virtue of hope is infused at Baptism, together with sanctifying grace, and is necessary for Salvation. Individual acts of hope are also necessary for Salvation and are commanded by God for all who have come to the age of reason. "But, since we belong to the day, let us be sober, and put on the breastplate of faith and love, and for a helmet the hope of salvation" (1 Thessalonians 5:8).

Acts of hope are required in times of temptation to discouragement or despair, and are implicit in every supernaturally good work. "My steadfast love shall not depart from you, and my covenant of peace shall not be removed, says the Lord, who has compassion on you" (Isaiah 54:10).

The virtue of hope is the permanent capacity to receive the power of Jesus' trusting commitment to His Father's plan and New Covenant. It is the capacity to use this power to develop habits of supernatural hope. These habits cause our hearts to perseveringly and trustingly commit ourselves to God and His Kingdom of Love—a commitment that, with Baptism, incorporates us into Christ's Mystical Body and God's Kingdom.

We can make an act of hope by saying, "My God I hope in You. I desire and firmly commit myself to obtain and achieve all you are promising me and inviting me to achieve. With trust in your promises, your mercy and your power, I ask for all that you want to give me for carrying out your plan and your New Covenant with me."

Catechism of the Catholic Church

1817 Hope is the theological virtue by which we desire the kingdom of heaven and eternal life as our happiness, placing our trust in Christ's promises and relying not on our own strength, but on the help of the grace of the Holy Spirit. "Let us hold fast the confession of our hope without wavering, for he who promised is faithful."[1] "The Holy Spirit... he poured out upon us richly through Jesus Christ our Savior, so that we might be justified by his grace and become heirs in hope of eternal life."[2]

Splendor of Truth

Man always has before him the spiritual horizon of hope, thanks to the help of divine grace and with the cooperation of human freedom. It is in the saving Cross of Jesus, in the gift of the Holy Spirit, in the sacraments which flow forth from the pierced side of the Redeemer (cf. Jn 19:34), that believers find the grace and the strength always to keep God's holy law, even amid the gravest of hardships. *(section 103)*

Vatican Council II

Those with such a faith live in the hope of the revelation of the sons of God, keeping in mind the cross and resurrection of the Lord. On life's pilgrimage they are hidden with Christ in God, are free from the slavery of riches, are in search of the goods that last for ever. Generously they exert all their energies in extending God's kingdom, in making the Christian spirit a vital energizing force in the temporal sphere. In life's trials they draw courage from hope, "convinced that present sufferings are no measure of the future glory to be revealed in us" (Rom. 8:18). *Lay People, 4*

Hope in a life to come does not take away from the importance of the duties of this life on earth but rather adds to it by giving new motives for fulfilling those duties. When, on the other hand, man is left without this divine support and without hope of eternal life his dignity is deeply wounded, as may so often be seen today. The problems of life and death, of guilt and of suffering, remain unsolved, so that men are not rarely cast into despair. *Gaudium et Spes, 21*

In life's trials they draw courage from hope, "convinced that present sufferings are no measure of the future glory to be revealed in us" (Rom. 8:18). *(Lay People, 4)*

Catechism by Diagram

#T9.2.2-1

An Act of Hope. Divine hope is the virtue by which we firmly trust that God (triangle), who is all-powerful and faithful to His promises, will in His mercy, through the merits of the sufferings and works of Jesus Christ (monogram), give us eternal life (anchor—sign of Salvation, joined to God) when we cooperate with His grace by performing good works (glass of water, poor box).

Summary Prayer

Holy Spirit, You are the Paraclete, the mighty Comforter, the One Whom Jesus Christ, while still on earth, promised to send to His Apostles, and through them, to us. We put our hope in You. You have come to us as You came to them.

You are the Living Spring in Whose purifying and refreshing waters our souls are cleansed, sanctified, and quickened. You are the Sweet Unction that fills all the powers of our souls and bodies with the oil of gladness, and gives to them spiritual strength and energy.

Holy Spirit, You know our weaknesses and how insistently the enemy of our Salvation strives to bring about our destruction. Without Your all-powerful aid, we are unable to defend ourselves against the malice, treachery, and power of such a terrible foe. With Your help, we can do all things and have nothing to fear.

Divine Spirit, with hope we turn to You, not only for protection from our spiritual enemies, but also for that true interior peace of which You are the source. Our life on earth must necessarily be a warfare; foes within and foes without are ever seeking to destroy our peace. Yet down in the depths of our souls we shall have peace, for You make Your dwelling there by giving us sanctifying grace. Our indwelling God, fill our inmost souls with peace, hope, and joy, so that nothing can disturb us. Like the little child who holds his father's hand and never thinks of fear so long as he is thus protected, help us to walk confidently upon the way to Heaven.

Holy Spirit, amidst the sorrows, trials, temptations, disappointments, and mental and physical sufferings of life, we ask for Your comfort and consolation. Console us by the sacraments, especially by the Eucharist and the Sacrament of Penance. Console us by Your actual graces. Sweeten the toils and sorrows of our lives, enlighten our understanding to know the value of suffering, and strengthen our wills to embrace that suffering with courage and joy. Console us by the thought of Heaven and of the blissful reward that awaits us. Thank you, Spirit of peace and joy, for Your indwelling in our souls. Knowing that You are with us is the source of our hope. Amen.

Doctrine • Moral • Worship Exercise

(See Appendix A for answer key, question 133.)

1. If we have the virtue of hope, what do we desire, and what do we receive through this desire? What is the basis of our hope?
2. What are some signs that one is indeed a person full of hope?
3. Copy the following prayer and try to memorize it so you can pray it often, especially in times of suffering or discouragement:

My God, I hope in You, for grace and for glory, because of Your promises, Your mercy and Your power. Amen.

Q. 134. What is the Theological Virtue of charity?

Charity is the supernatural virtue by which we love God above all things for His own sake, and our neighbor as ourselves as part of our love of God.

"You shall love the Lord your God with all your heart, and with all your soul, and with all your mind. This is the great and first commandment. And a second is like it, You shall love your neighbor as yourself" (Matthew 22:37-39).

Because charity is infused into the soul at Baptism, along with sanctifying grace, it is often identified with the state of grace. A person who has lost the supernatural virtue of charity has lost the state of grace, although he may still possess the virtues of hope and faith.

An act of charity is a supernatural act, based on faith, in which God is loved for Himself and not for any hope of reward. This act requires divine grace, either sanctifying or actual, or both. It is also the normal way of growing in the virtue or habit of charity.

A simple act of charity can be made in these words, "My God, because You are so good, I love You with all my heart. As part of my love for You, I love my neighbor as myself, since You have so loved us as to create us, redeem us, reconcile us to Yourself, and adopt us as your own children destined for your heavenly Kingdom."

Sacred Scripture
Q. 134. Mt 5:43-47; 1 Jn 3:23.

Catechism of the Catholic Church
Q. 134. Paragraphs **1822-1829**.

For cross-references with Vatican II, Papal documents & other resources, see Family Wisdom Library on page 513.
For commentaries on each question with Cardinal Arinze, Sr. John Vianney and Fr. Straub (in Spanish), see Appendix C.

#E4.4-7

Charity is the supernatural virtue by which we love God above all things for His own sake, and our neighbor as ourselves as part of our love of God.

Supernatural love resides primarily in the will, not in the emotions. To love God means that we are willing to give up anything rather than offend God by mortal sin.

We may have a genuine, supernatural love for our neighbor even though on the natural level we feel a strong distaste for him. Thus, we forgive for God's sake the wrong he has done. We pray for him and stand ready to help him if he should be in need. We then have a supernatural love for our neighbor.

The virtue of charity is the permanent capacity to receive the power of Jesus' love and self-giving. It is the capacity to use this power to develop habits of supernatural charity based on the reality of our identity with and in Christ, the Father and the Holy Spirit, and with Mary, St. Joseph, the angels, the saints, and each other in Jesus. These habits of charity cause our hearts to say "yes" to Jesus and to all He wants to give us and ask of us. This "yes" allows Jesus to begin living and growing in us individually and collectively, and us to live and grow in Him.

Sacred Scripture

Love one another with brotherly affection; outdo one another in showing honor. Never flag in zeal, be aglow with the Spirit, serve the Lord. Rejoice in your hope, be patient in tribulation, be constant in prayer. Contribute to the needs of the saints, practice hospitality. Bless those who persecute you; bless and do not curse them. Rejoice with those who rejoice, weep with those who weep. *Romans 12:10-15*

So then, as we have opportunity, let us do good to all men, and especially to those who are of the household of faith. *Galatians 6:10*

Love is patient and kind; love is not jealous or boastful; it is not arrogant or rude. Love does not insist on its own way; it is not irritable or resentful; it does not rejoice at wrong, but rejoices in the right. Love bears all things, believes all things, hopes all things, endures all things. *1 Corinthians 13:4-7*

Catechism of the Catholic Church

1823 Jesus makes charity the *new commandment*.[1] By loving his own "to the end,"[2] he makes manifest the Father's love which he receives. By loving one another, the disciples imitate the love of Jesus which they themselves receive. Whence Jesus says: "As the Father has loved me, so have I loved you; abide in my love." And again: "This is my commandment, that you love one another as I have loved you."[3]

1827 The practice of all the virtues is animated and inspired by charity, which "binds everything together in perfect harmony"[1]; it is the *form of the virtues*; it articulates and orders them among themselves; it is the source and the goal of their Christian practice. Charity upholds and purifies our human ability to love, and raises it to the supernatural perfection of divine love.

#Y1-2

Supernatural love resides primarily in the will, not in the emotions. Thus, we forgive for God's sake the wrong our neighbor has done. We pray for him and stand ready to help him if he should be in need.

Splendor of Truth

Both the Old and the New Testaments explicitly affirm that without love of neighbor, made concrete in keeping the commandments, genuine love for God is not possible. *(section 14)*

Charity, in conformity with the radical demands of the Gospel, can lead the believer to the supreme witness of martyrdom. Once again this means imitating Jesus who died on the Cross: "Be imitators of God, as beloved children," Paul writes to the Christians of Ephesus, "and walk in love, as Christ loved us and gave himself up for us, a fragrant offering and sacrifice to God" (Eph 5:1-2). *(section 89)*

Jesus asks us to follow him and to imitate him along the path of love, a love which gives itself completely to the brethren out of love for God: "This is my commandment, that you love one another as I have loved you" (Jn 15:12). *(section 20)*

Catechism by Diagram

#H9-5

An Act of Charity. Charity is the virtue by which we love God (triangle) above all things for His own sake and our neighbor as ourselves for the love of God. God gives us the privilege of sharing His divine life by giving us grace (white heart); He dwells in our souls (triangle in heart). God's grace is given us by the Holy Spirit (dove), and thus we are able to deserve a reward in Heaven (coins of merit placed into bank, arrow to Heaven).

Vatican Council II

"God is love, and he who abides in love abides in God, and God abides in him" (1 Jn. 4:16). God has poured out his love into our hearts through the Holy Spirit who has been given to us (cf. Rom. 5:5); therefore the first and most necessary gift is charity, by which we love God above all things and our neighbor because of him. But if charity is to grow and fructify in the soul like a good seed, each of the faithful must willingly hear the word of God and carry out his will with deeds, with the help of his grace; he must frequently partake of the sacraments, chiefly the Eucharist, and take part in the liturgy; he must constantly apply himself to prayer, self-denial, active brotherly service and the practice of all virtues. This is because love, as the bond of perfection and fullness of the law (cf. Col. 3:14; Rom. 13:10), governs, gives meaning to, and perfects all the means of sanctification. Hence the true disciple of Christ is marked by love both of God and of his neighbor. *Lumen Gentium, 42*

#M5-1-2

To love God means that we are willing to give up anything rather than offend God by mortal sin.

Summary Prayer

Holy Spirit, inflame our hearts with charity so that we may love You, our God, above and before all things and love our neighbor as ourselves. You are the Spirit of Love. Kindle in our hearts Your ardent flame of love.

Holy Spirit, help us to love the heavenly Father with a strong and sincere love, whereby we may realize that He is not only our Creator but also our Father. His paternal love for us is infinite, and therefore, we should love and reverence it with all the tender, filial confidence and trust He deserves. All this we ask through our Lord and Savior Jesus Christ. Amen.

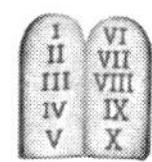

Doctrine • Moral • Worship Exercise

(See Appendix A for answer key, question 134.)

1. What is the greatest commandment and what does it mean? What does it mean to love your neighbor as yourself or to love your neighbor as God has loved you?
2. Read 1 John 4:20-21. Spend five minutes or more in silence reflecting on the times in your life when you experienced God's love and the love of the people around you. Thank God for those experiences. Ask the Holy Spirit to inspire you to think of concrete ways by which you can show your love for others—especially for those who are difficult to love. Write down your inspirations.
3. Next time that you go to Mass, be aware of the special moments in the liturgy that show and celebrate God's love for you.

Chapter Summary Prayer

Our God, we love You above all things with our whole heart and soul, because You are all-good and worthy of all love. We love our neighbor as ourselves for the love of You. We forgive all who have injured us and ask pardon of all whom we have injured.

Enable us, Holy Spirit, to know and love Jesus Christ, the eternal Son of God, the Second Person of the ever blessed Trinity, with all the fervor and energy of our souls. He is our Savior and our Redeemer. To know Him is eternal life, for within His Sacred Heart are all the graces of Redemption that we need to save and sanctify our souls.

Grant us, Holy Spirit, a more intimate knowledge and more fervent love for You by showing us Your infinite perfections, Your wondrous attributes, and Your marvelous gifts. Grant us the grace to know You and love You daily more and more. Throughout life, give us the grace to more ardently cultivate devotion to You. Thus, through You, may we come to know and love the Father and the Son, to Whom, with You, all praise, honor, and glory belongs. Amen.

Thought Provokers

Please see Appendix B for the answers.

Q. 131: A person in the state of mortal sin is deprived of the Theological Virtue of charity. Is this also true of faith and hope?

Q. 132: What can lead people to lose their gift of faith?

Q. 133: How can a person lose the Theological Virtue of hope?

Q. 134: How does a person lose the Theological Virtue of charity?

CHAPTER THIRTY-NINE

The Cardinal Virtues

Q. 135. What are the Cardinal Virtues?

The Cardinal Virtues are prudence, justice, temperance, and fortitude of heart. Along with the Gifts of the Holy Spirit, these Cardinal Virtues enable us to express, prove, and grow in our love of God by implementing His plan and covenant in a practical way.

#F1-62-2

The Cardinal Virtues are prudence, justice, temperance, and fortitude of heart. The virtue of prudence is the power to make right judgments.

"And if anyone loves righteousness, her [Wisdom's] labors are virtues; for she teaches self-control and prudence, justice and courage; nothing in life is more profitable for men than these" (Wisdom 8:7).

The virtue of prudence is the power to make right judgments. It is the permanent capacity to receive Jesus' power of prudence and to use this power to develop habits of supernatural prudence. These habits lead our hearts to set goals, make plans, and choose projects for implementing God's plan for us.

Catechism of the Catholic Church
Q. 135. Paragraphs 1805-1809.

For cross-references with Vatican II, Papal documents & other resources, see Family Wisdom Library on page 513.
For commentaries on each question with Cardinal Arinze, Sr. John Vianney and Fr. Straub (in Spanish), see Appendix C.

#C37-5

The virtue of justice helps us to see the need to protect the rights of our fellow man.

The virtue of justice helps us to see the need to protect the rights of our fellow man. It is the permanent capacity to receive Jesus' power of justice and to use this power to develop habits of supernatural justice. These habits lead our hearts to always choose to do the right thing, consistently giving ourselves firm commands to do God's will and to keep our New Covenant with Him.

The virtue of temperance helps us to control our desires, especially the desires that might keep us from using correctly the things which appeal to our senses. It is the permanent capacity to receive Jesus' power of temperance and to use this power to develop habits of supernatural temperance. These habits lead us to toughen our wills and commitments by focusing Jesus' or Mary's own delight, desire, and joy on them; and their dismay, aversion, and sorrow on any temptation to neglect or abandon these commitments.

"My son, test your soul while you live; see what is bad for it and do not give it that" (Sirach 37:27). "But take heed to yourselves lest your hearts be weighed down with dissipation and drunkenness and cares of this life, and that day come upon you suddenly like a snare" (Luke 21:34).

Fortitude gives us the strength to do what is good in spite of every difficulty. It is the permanent capacity to receive Jesus' power of fortitude of heart and to use this power to develop habits of supernatural fortitude. By these habits, we imitate Jesus and Mary

in focusing the emotions of courage, trusting commitment, and enthusiasm on doing God's will and the emotions of fear, despair, and anger on sin, false hopes, and Satan.

Sanctifying grace gives us a certain readiness for the practice of all of the virtues, together with a supernatural merit each time we practice them.

Catechism of the Catholic Church

1804 *Human virtues* are firm attitudes, stable dispositions, habitual perfections of intellect and will that govern our actions, order our passions, and guide our conduct according to reason and faith. They make possible ease, self-mastery, and joy in leading a morally good life. The virtuous man is he who freely practices the good.

The moral virtues are acquired by human effort. They are the fruit and seed of morally good acts; they dispose all the powers of the human being for communion with divine love.

Splendor of Truth

Respect for human dignity requires the practice of the virtue of temperance, to moderate our attachment to the goods of this world; of the virtue of justice, to preserve our neighbor's rights and to render what is his or her due. *(section 100)*

Vatican Council II

Justice and equity also demand that the livelihood of individuals and their families should not become insecure and precarious through a kind of mobility which is a necessary feature of developing economies. All kinds of discrimination in wages and working conditions should be avoided in regard to workers who come from other countries or areas and contribute their work to the economic development of a people or a region. *Gaudium et Spes, 66*

The virtue of temperance helps us to control our desires, especially the desires that might keep us from using correctly the things which appeal to our senses.

Catechism by Diagram

#V5-1

The Cardinal Moral Virtues. The virtue of religion is like the framework of a doorway threshold. The four hinges of the door are prudence, justice, fortitude, and temperance. They are called Cardinal Virtues (Latin: "cardo" means hinge). The Cardinal Virtues support the other virtues. They contain within themselves the seeds of all the other virtues. Through this doorway, evil (serpent) must not enter our souls (heart).

Summary Prayer

Holy Spirit, help us to practice the Cardinal Virtues, which will enable us to lead a good life, by helping us to treat persons and things in the right way, according to God's will. Give us the virtue of prudence, that we may be able to make right judgments; the virtue of justice, that we may be able to protect the rights of our fellow men; the virtue of fortitude, that we may have the strength to do what is good and the willingness to make any sacrifice You require; the virtue of temperance, that we may be able to control our desires and use correctly the things which appeal to our senses.

We believe that when we are in the state of sanctifying grace, we bear Your image within our inmost being. By granting us sanctifying grace, pierce the center of our hearts and render our thoughts and actions both spiritual and supernatural. By the divine infused virtues of faith, hope, and charity, and the acquired virtues, which include humility and obedience, control our understanding and our will, and enable them to elicit supernatural acts. By bestowing Your gifts on us, set these supernatural acts in motion, guide us in them, and by Your actual graces render our performance of them easier.

Truly, You are the very source and center of our spiritual life. For this we give You our humble thanks, through Christ Our Lord. Amen.

Fortitude gives us the strength to do what is good in spite of every difficulty.

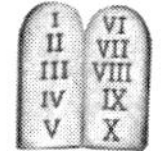

Doctrine • Moral • Worship Exercise

(See Appendix A for answer key, question 135.)

1. Name the four Cardinal Virtues. How do each of these virtues help us in our lives?
2. Think of specific times in your daily life when you will need to practice the Cardinal Virtues.
3. Pray the Summary Prayer after question 135, with a deep desire that you and your family practice the Cardinal Virtues.

Q. 136. Why are prudence, justice, temperance, and fortitude called Cardinal Virtues?

Prudence, justice, temperance, and fortitude are called Cardinal Virtues because they are the key virtues upon which all the other virtues hinge or depend. In Latin, "cardo" means "hinge." The other virtues of human morality, such as obedience, patience, humility, truthfulness, and patriotism, are related to the Cardinal Virtues.

#L3-28

A virtue acquired by our own efforts — that is, through our conscious development of a particular good habit — is called a natural virtue.

A virtue begins as the *capacity* to make particular virtuous acts. Repeated acts become *habits* or permanent dispositions inclining us to do a particular good and to avoid a particular evil.

A virtue acquired by our own efforts—that is, through our conscious development of a particular good habit—is called a natural virtue. Supernatural virtues, on the other hand, are capacities or habits which God directly infuses into our souls, with no effort on our part. We need to ask Jesus for the fullness of grace of these virtues. Even when God gives us the grace of supernatural virtues, we must work to strengthen our virtues, bringing them to maturity and perfection.

Sacred Scripture

A fool despises his father's instruction, but he who heeds admonition is prudent. *Proverbs 15:5*

Bid the older men be temperate, serious, sensible, sound in faith, in love, and in steadfastness. *Titus 2:2*

Sacred Scripture
Q. 136. Ps 89:14; Wis 8:7.

Catechism of the Catholic Church
Q. 136. Paragraph 1805.

For cross-references with Vatican II, Papal documents & other resources, see Family Wisdom Library on page 513.
For commentaries on each question with Cardinal Arinze, Sr. John Vianney and Fr. Straub (in Spanish), see Appendix C.

#B7-1-2

Prudence, justice, temperance, and fortitude are called Cardinal Virtues because they are the key virtues upon which all the other virtues hinge or depend.

Catechism of the Catholic Church

1810 Human virtues acquired by education, by deliberate acts and by a perseverance ever-renewed in repeated efforts are purified and elevated by divine grace. With God's help, they forge character and give facility in the practice of the good. The virtuous man is happy to practice them.

Vatican Council II

Anyone who in obedience to Christ seeks first the kingdom of God will derive from it a stronger and purer love for helping all his brethren and for accomplishing the task of justice under the inspiration of charity. *Gaudium et Spes, 72*

#C11-109

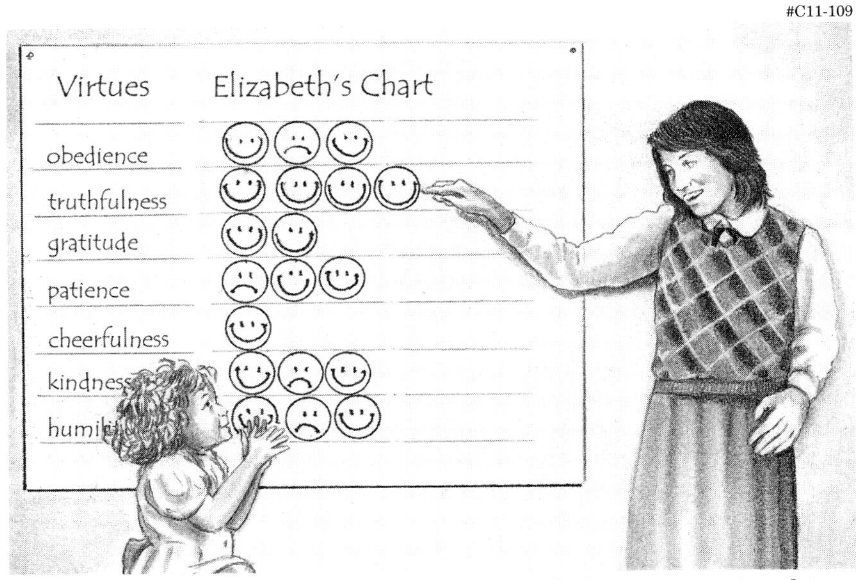

Even when God gives us the grace of supernatural virtues, we must work to strengthen our virtues, bringing them to maturity and perfection.

Summary Prayer

Holy Spirit, Divine Spirit of light and love, we consecrate to You our understanding, our hearts, our wills, and our whole beings for time and for eternity. May our understanding always be submissive to Your heavenly inspirations and to the teachings of the Catholic Church, of which You are the infallible Guide. May our hearts ever be inflamed with love for God and for our neighbors; may our wills ever be conformed to the divine will; may our lives be faithful to the imitation of the life and virtues of our Lord and Savior Jesus Christ, to Whom, with the Father and Yourself, we give honor and glory forever. Amen.

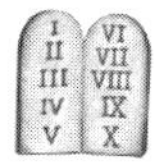

Doctrine • Moral • Worship Exercise

(See Appendix A for answer key, question 136.)

1. What is a virtue? How might you explain in simple terms the meaning of the theological and Cardinal Virtues? What are some other moral virtues?
2. Which virtue is the most difficult for you to practice? Think of concrete steps by which you can develop this virtue.
3. Write down on a piece of paper the virtue you wish to focus on for a month. Include a Scripture passage that will help you practice that virtue. Post it in your room and pray to the Holy Spirit to inspire and strengthen you in developing that virtue. Try to make it a habit to write a different virtue and Scripture passage each month on which to focus.

Chapter Summary Prayer

O Holy Spirit, Infinite Love of the Father and the Son, through the pure hands of Mary, Your Immaculate Spouse, we place ourselves this day and all the days of our life upon Your chosen altar, the divine Heart of Jesus. May we be a pleasing sacrifice to You, O Consuming Fire, as we are firmly resolved, now more than ever, to hear Your voice and to do in all things Your most holy and adorable will.

Holy Spirit, Divine Light, illumine our souls with Your brightness; fill them with love, gladness, and life; warm them and quicken them into vigorous action in God's service.

Holy Spirit, Spirit of Truth, come into our hearts. Abide in us and grant that we may ever abide in You forever, through Jesus Christ, our only Lord and Savior. Amen.

Thought Provokers

Please see Appendix B for the answers.

Q. 135: How are moral virtues received?

Q. 136: What does each of the four Cardinal Virtues mean?

#P26-15-2

The Gifts of the Holy Spirit are the qualities God gives our souls to make them responsive to the grace of God. They help us practice virtue.

CHAPTER FORTY

The Seven Gifts of the Holy Spirit

Q. 137. What are the seven Gifts of the Holy Spirit?

The seven Gifts of the Holy Spirit are wisdom, understanding, counsel, fortitude, knowledge, piety, and fear of the Lord. They are the gifts listed in Isaiah 11 which were to characterize the Just Man—the Messiah.

The Gifts of the Holy Spirit are the qualities God gives our souls to make them responsive to the grace of God. They help us practice virtue. These gifts were imparted to us in Baptism as permanent capacities for receiving seven different kinds of supernatural light from the fullness of truth in Jesus Christ (cf. John 1:14, 16). They are also capacities for using these lights as the necessary foundation for developing habits of the infused virtues.

The Gifts of the Holy Spirit implant in us the forms and paths which our spiritual development and our service of God will take, while the infused virtues drive and bring about in us that development and service. Developing the habits of the gifts and virtues will put to death in us the seven Capital Sins, or tendencies to sin. If we give in to the seven Capital Sins, they will block or kill in us the life of the gifts and virtues.

1. The gift of *wisdom* strengthens our faith, fortifies our hope, perfects our charity, and promotes our practice of virtue to the highest degree. Just as charity (the most perfect of virtues) embraces all the other virtues, wisdom is the most perfect of gifts, since it embodies all the other gifts. Wisdom enlightens our minds to discern and relish things divine, so that the appreciation of earthly joys loses its savor, while the Cross of Christ yields a divine sweetness.

This gift is the permanent capacity to receive the light of Jesus' wisdom and to use it to develop supernatural wisdom—enabling our minds to see, in God's plan, where we have come from, where we are going, and how to get there.

Sacred Scripture
Q. 137. Prov 2:1-11; Sir 1:14-20.

Catechism of the Catholic Church
Q. 137. Paragraphs **1831**-1832.

For cross-references with Vatican II, Papal documents & other resources, see Family Wisdom Library on page 513.
For commentaries on each question with Cardinal Arinze, Sr. John Vianney and Fr. Straub (in Spanish), see Appendix C.

The gift of wisdom is especially necessary for developing the virtue of prudence, by which we set goals and priorities, plan projects and programs, etc.

2. The gift of *understanding* helps us to grasp the meaning of the truths of our holy religion. By faith we know these truths, but by understanding we learn to appreciate and relish them. Understanding enables us to penetrate the inner meaning of revealed truths, thus quickening us to the newness of life.

#Y1-3-2

The gift of understanding helps us to grasp the meaning of the truths of our holy religion.

This gift is the permanent capacity to receive the light of Jesus' understanding and to use it to develop supernatural understanding—enabling our minds to grasp that which God wants us to understand, especially the meaning for each of us personally and of our relationships with the divine Trinity, Mary, St. Joseph, the angels, the saints, and each other.

The gift of understanding is especially necessary for developing habits of the virtue of hope, by which we commit ourselves firmly to God's will and plan.

3. The gift of *counsel* endows our souls with the supernatural light we need to judge promptly and rightly what must be done, especially in difficult circumstances. Counsel applies the principles furnished by wisdom, prudence, knowledge, and understanding, to the innumerable concrete cases which confront us in the course of our daily duty. Counsel is supernatural common sense.

This gift is the permanent capacity to receive the light of Jesus' counsel and to use it to develop supernatural counsel—enabling our minds to discern what God wants us to think, say or do at each moment, and to plan and carry out a daily agenda.

The gift of counsel is particularly necessary for developing habits of the virtue of justice, by which we always do the right thing.

4. The gift of *fortitude* strengthens our souls against natural fear, allowing us to undertake the most arduous tasks, to face dangers, to trample underfoot worldly considerations, and to endure without complaint the crosses of daily life.

#M10-4-2

The gift of fortitude strengthens our souls against natural fear, allowing us to undertake the most arduous tasks, to face dangers, to trample underfoot worldly considerations, and to endure without complaint the crosses of daily life.

This gift is the permanent capacity to receive the light of Jesus' mental fortitude (fortitude of mind) and to use it to develop supernatural fortitude—enabling us to control our imaginations and memories and fill them with images of Jesus, Mary, the angels and the saints. These images help us develop and focus our emotions of courage, trusting commitment, and enthusiasm on doing God's will and carrying out His plan, and our emotions of fear, despair and anger on whatever would prevent or divert us from doing these things.

The gift of fortitude is especially necessary for developing habits of the virtue of fortitude.

5. The gift of *knowledge* enables us to learn the truths which God has revealed, so that we may believe them and live by them. Knowledge enables our souls to evaluate created things for their true worth, that is, in their relationship to God. This gift unmasks the pretense of creatures, reveals their shallowness, and points out their only true purpose as instruments in the service of God. It shows us the loving care God has for us, even in times of adversity. Knowledge directs us to glorify God in every circumstance of life. Guided by the light of knowledge, we put God first and prize our friendship with Him above all else.

#F1.9-3

The gift of knowledge enables us to learn the truths which God has revealed, so that we may believe them and live by them.

This gift is the permanent capacity to receive the light of Jesus' knowledge and to use it to develop supernatural knowledge—enabling our minds to grasp that which God wants us to know, especially the realities of who God is and who we are in relationship to Him, of God's call and plan for our Salvation, of our renewed divine adoption, and of God's New Covenant with us that activates that plan.

The gift of knowledge is essential for developing habits of the virtue of faith.

6. The gift of *piety* begets in our hearts a childlike affection for God as our most loving Father. Piety inspires us to love and respect, for God's sake, persons and things consecrated to Him, as well as those who are vested with His authority, i.e., the Blessed Virgin and the saints; the Church and its visible head, the Pope; our parents and superiors; and our country with its rulers. He who is filled with the gift of piety finds the practice of his religion, not a burdensome duty, but a delightful service.

#C11-110

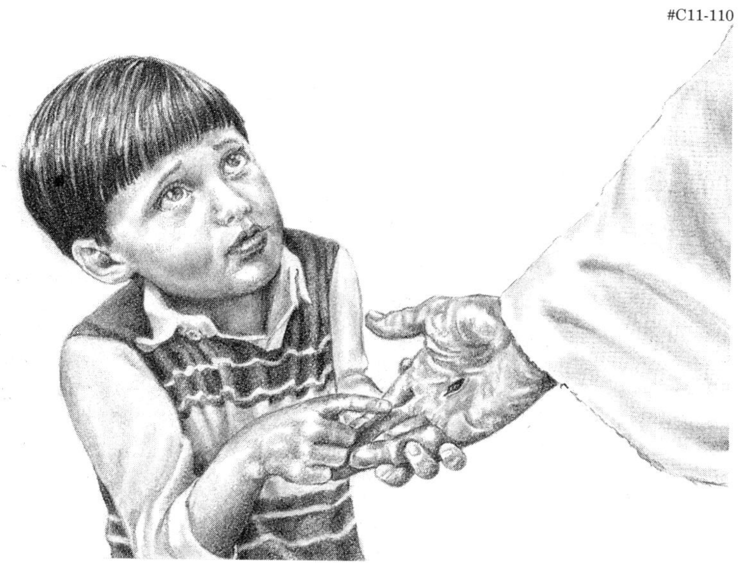

The gift of piety begets in our hearts a childlike affection for God as our most loving Father. He who is filled with the gift of piety finds the practice of his religion, not a burdensome duty, but a delightful service.

This gift is the permanent capacity to receive the light of Jesus' piety and to use it to develop supernatural piety—enabling our minds to share Jesus' own vision of our identity with and in the divine Persons and with Mary, St. Joseph, the angels, the saints, and each other.

The gift of piety is necessary for developing strong habits of the virtue of charity.

#D1-12-2

The gift of fear of the Lord fills us with a sovereign respect for God and makes us dread, above all, offending God by sin. Fear of the Lord is the beginning of wisdom, because it detaches us from worldly pleasures that can separate us from God.

7. The gift of *fear of the Lord* fills us with a sovereign respect for God and makes us dread, above all, offending God by sin. Fear of the Lord rises, not from the thought of Hell, but from reverence and childlike submission to our heavenly Father. Fear of the Lord is the beginning of wisdom, because it detaches us from worldly pleasures that can separate us from God.

This gift is the permanent capacity to receive the light of Jesus' reverence for God and of Jesus' compassion for others and to use this light to develop supernatural fear of the Lord—enabling us to fill our minds with images from the lives of Jesus, Mary, the angels and the saints. These images help us develop and focus our emotions of delight, desire, and joy on God's goodness, will and plan for our Salvation, and our emotions of dismay, aversion and sorrow on sin and whatever would turn us away from God.

The gift of fear of the Lord is necessary for developing strong habits of the virtue of temperance.

Sacred Scripture

And the spirit of the Lord shall rest upon him, the spirit of wisdom and understanding, the spirit of counsel and might, the spirit of knowledge and the fear of the Lord. And his delight shall be in the fear of the Lord. *Isaiah 11:2-3*

The unspiritual man does not receive the gifts of the Spirit of God, for they are folly to him, and he is not able to understand them because they are spiritually discerned. *1 Corinthians 2:14*

Catechism of the Catholic Church

1709 He who believes in Christ become a son of God. This filial adoption transforms him by giving him the ability to follow the example of Christ. It makes him capable of acting rightly and doing good. In union with his Savior, the disciple attains the perfection of charity which is holiness. Having matured in grace, the moral life blossoms into eternal life in the glory of heaven.

1830 The moral life of Christians is sustained by the gifts of the Holy Spirit. These are permanent dispositions which make man docile in following the promptings of the Holy Spirit.

Splendor of Truth

Strengthened by his (Holy Spirit's) gift, they (disciples) did not fear either prisons or chains for the name of the Lord; indeed they even trampled upon the powers and torments of the world, armed and strengthened by him, having in themselves the gifts which this same Spirit bestows and directs like jewels to the Church, the Bride of Christ. *(section 108)*

Although martyrdom represents the high point of the witness to moral truth, and one to which relatively few people are called, there is nonetheless a consistent witness which all Christians must daily be ready to make, even at the cost of suffering and grave sacrifice. Indeed, faced with the many difficulties which fidelity to the moral order can demand, even in the most ordinary circumstances, the Christian is called, with the grace of God invoked in prayer, to a sometimes heroic commitment. In this he or she is sustained by the virtue of fortitude, whereby...one can actually "love the difficulties of this world for the sake of eternal rewards." *(section 93)*

#Y1-1

The moral life of Christians is sustained by the gifts of the Holy Spirit. These are permanent dispositions which make man docile in following the promptings of the Holy Spirit. *(Catechism of the Catholic Church, 1830)*

Vatican Council II

It is not only through the sacraments and the ministrations of the Church that the Holy Spirit makes holy the People, leads them and enriches them with his virtues. Allotting his gifts according as he wills (cf. Cor. 12:11), he also distributes special graces among the faithful of every rank. By these gifts he makes them fit and ready to undertake various tasks and offices for the renewal and building up of the Church, as it is written, "the manifestation of the Spirit is given to everyone for profit" (1 Corinthians 12:7). Whether these charisms be very remarkable or more simple and widely diffused, they are to be received with thanksgiving and consolation since they are fitting and useful for the needs of the Church. Extraordinary gifts are not to be rashly desired, nor is it from them that the fruits of apostolic labors are to be presumptuously expected. Those who have charge over the Church should judge the genuineness and proper use of these gifts, through their office not indeed to extinguish the Spirit, but to test all things and hold fast to what is good (cf. 1 Thes. 5:12 and 19-21). *Lumen Gentium, 12*

Summary Prayer

O God, grant us Your Spirit of Wisdom, that He may reveal to us the enemies we ought to fear and the dangers we ought to avoid amidst the deceptive appearances of this world. May He help us to choose, in every circumstance, what is most useful for the preservation and increase of divine life in us and for the Salvation of our souls.

O God, send us Your Spirit of Understanding, that He may help us to understand the beauty, the sweetness, and the fruitfulness of the holy truths that light our paths in this world. You, Heavenly Father, reveal these truths with much love to the humble, while You hide them from the proud.

O God, send us Your Spirit of Counsel, that in moments of action He may always incline us to the most opportune and prudent reflections, that He may make us perfectly docile to Your secret inspirations, and that He may also make us, in time of need, courageous and self-denying counselors for our neighbors.

O God, send us Your Spirit of Fortitude, that He may change our weaknesses into strengths and make us apostles full of burning zeal.

O God, send us Your Spirit of Knowledge, that He may inspire us with a horror of lying and of error. May He inflame us with a noble and holy love of all the truths that You have taught us. May He guard these truths by placing in our hearts a constant memory of them, just as the most holy Virgin, our beloved Mother, held all Your truths in her heart.

O God, give us Your Spirit of Piety, that He may enkindle in us the fire of Your love, which makes us love Your divine will ardently, even in the smallest of our duties. That love will lead us even to heroism and will secure for us strength, perseverance, and victory in all things by means of prayer.

O God, fill us with Your Spirit of Fear, that He may never allow us to forget the reverence which is due Your infinite majesty, Your boundless power, and Your dread judgment. Send us the Spirit of Fear, that He may keep us ever under Your gaze, Your direction, and Your sovereign dominion. Above all, form in our hearts a sublime and heavenly union of respect and love with You. May the Holy Spirit help us to see that the only real misfortune for the creature is the ingratitude which is contracted through sin. All this we ask through Christ our Lord. Amen.

Doctrine • Moral • Worship Exercise

(See Appendix A for answer key, question 137.)

1. Name the seven Gifts of the Holy Spirit. What does each gift do for us?
2. Recall some occasions in your life when you concretely experienced the Gifts of the Holy Spirit. Write these down in a reflection notebook or spiritual journal.
3. Slowly pray the Summary Prayer after question 137. Invite your family to pray it with you. Pray also for your religious and civil leaders, that they may receive the seven Gifts of the Holy Spirit.

Chapter Summary Prayer

Come, Spirit of Wisdom, reveal to our souls the mysteries of heavenly things and their exceeding greatness, power, and beauty. Teach us to love heavenly things above and beyond all the passing joys of earth. Help us to attain them and possess them forever.

Come, Spirit of Understanding, enlighten our minds, that we may know and believe all the mysteries of Salvation. May we merit at last to see the eternal light in Your light; and in the light of glory, may we have a clear vision of You, the Father, and the Son.

Come, Spirit of Counsel, help and guide us in all our ways, that we may always do Your holy will. Incline our hearts to that which is good and turn them away from what is evil. Direct us by the straight path of Your commandments to that goal of eternal life for which we long.

Come, Blessed Spirit of Fortitude, uphold our souls in time of trouble and adversity, sustain our efforts toward holiness, and strengthen our weaknesses. Give us courage against all the assaults of our enemies, that we may never be overcome and separated from You, our God and greatest Good.

Come, Blessed Spirit of Knowledge, grant that we may perceive the will of the Father. Show us the nothingness of earthly things, that we may realize their vanity and use them only for Your glory and our own Salvation. May we always look beyond them to You and Your eternal rewards.

Come, Blessed Spirit of Piety, possess our hearts. Enkindle in them such a love for God that we may find satisfaction only in His service, and that, for His sake, we may lovingly submit to all legitimate authority.

Come, Blessed Spirit of holy Fear, penetrate our inmost hearts, that we may set You, our Lord and God, before our face forever. Help us to shun all things which can offend You, and make us worthy to appear before the pure majesty of God. All this we ask through Jesus Christ our Lord and Savior. Amen.

Thought Provokers

Please see Appendix B for the answers.

Q. 137: The consistent use of the Gifts of the Holy Spirit is said to produce in the soul the desirable trait of docility. Precisely what is docility?

By Heart Catechism and Scripture Review™

The "By Heart Catechism and Scripture Review" lists a selected number of questions and Scripture references from "The Apostolate's Family Catechism" to make memorization easier. Q = Question, SR = Scripture Reference

Q. 131. What are the Theological Virtues? The Theological Virtues of faith, hope, and charity are good habits that are placed in the soul by God, along with sanctifying grace.

Q. 132. What is the Theological Virtue of faith? Faith is the supernatural virtue that gives us the power to firmly believe all the truths God has revealed.

Q. 133. What is hope? Hope is the supernatural virtue that gives us the power to firmly commit ourselves to God's plan for our lives and to trust in Him.

Q. 134. What is charity? Charity is the supernatural virtue that gives us the power to love God above all things for His own sake and our neighbor as ourselves out of love for God.

Q. 135. What are the Cardinal Virtues? The Cardinal Virtues are prudence, justice, temperance and fortitude.

Q. 136. Why are prudence, justice, fortitude, and temperance called the Cardinal Virtues? They are called Cardinal Virtues because all other virtues hinge, or depend, upon them.

Q. 137. What are the seven Gifts of the Holy Spirit? The seven Gifts of the Holy Spirit are wisdom, understanding, counsel, fortitude, knowledge, piety, and fear of the Lord.

Family Wisdom Library™

Papal documents listed below can be viewed at www.vatican.va.
For new cross-references, visit www.familyland.org

Q. 114. Who is God the Holy Spirit?

Church Documents

Compendium of the Catechism of the Catholic Church, sect. 47, 136-137
Dei Verbum (Dogmatic Constitution on Divine Revelation), Vatican II, sect. 2, 4-5, 17, 20
Gaudium et Spes (Pastoral Constitution on the Church in the Modern World), Vatican II, sect. 1, 3, 10-11, 21-22, 32, 37-38, 42-43, 92-93
God is Love, Benedict XVI, sect. 19
Lumen Gentium (Dogmatic Constitution on the Church), Vatican II, sect. 4, 12, 24, 40, 42, 48
On the Dignity and Vocation of Women, John Paul II, sect. 29
On the Holy Spirit in the Life of the Church and the World, John Paul II, see entire document
The Relationship Between Faith and Reason, John Paul II, sect. 44
Sacrament of Charity, Benedict XVI, sect. 7-8, 12-13
U. S. Catholic Catechism for Adults, [2006] pp. 104-105

Other Resources

Basics of the Faith: A Catholic Catechism, Schreck, pp. 11-13
The Catholic Catechism, Hardon, pp. 64-66, 136
The Church's Confession of Faith, Ignatius Press, pp. 69-72, 184-187
Faith for Today, Hogan and LeVoir, [First Edition] p. 16; [Second Edition] p. 38
Fundamentals of Catholic Dogma, Ott, pp. 54, 58, 69
Fundamentals of Catholicism, Baker, Vol.1, pp. 90-92; Vol. 2. pp. 86-89
Modern Catholic Dictionary, Hardon, see "Holy Spirit"
The Teaching of Christ, Lawler, Wuerl, and Lawler, [First Edition] pp.161-173; [Second Edition] pp. 150-161; [Third Edition] pp. 131-141

Q. 115. The Holy Spirit proceeds from the Father and the Son. What is meant by this?

Church Documents

Compendium of the Catechism of the Catholic Church, sect. 47
God is Love, Benedict XVI, sect. 1, 6-11, 19
On the Holy Spirit in the Life of the Church and the World, John Paul II, sect. 8
The Relationship Between Faith and Reason, John Paul II, sect. 7, 44
Sacrament of Charity, Benedict XVI, sect. 7-8
U. S. Catholic Catechism for Adults, [2006] p. 53

Other Resources

The Catholic Catechism, Hardon, pp. 64-65
The Church's Confession of Faith, Ignatius Press, pp. 70-71
Faith for Today, Hogan and LeVoir, [First Edition] pp. 13-14; [Second Edition] pp. 34-35
Fundamentals of Catholic Dogma, Ott, pp. 61-64, 66-67
Fundamentals of Catholicism, Baker, Vol. 1, pp. 92-94; Vol. 2 pp. 89-92
Modern Catholic Dictionary, Hardon, see "Holy Spirit" and "Divine Procession"
The Teaching of Christ, Lawler, Wuerl, and Lawler, [First Edition] pp. 164-166; [Second Edition] pp. 153-155; [Third Edition] pp. 134-135

Q. 116. What did Jesus Christ say about the Holy Spirit?

Church Documents

Compendium of the Catechism of the Catholic Church, sect. 47, 138, 144
Dei Verbum (Dogmatic Constitution on Divine Revelation), Vatican II, sect. 2, 5, 8, 17
Lumen Gentium (Dogmatic Constitution on the Church), Vatican II, sect. 4
On the Dignity and Vocation of Women, John Paul II, sect. 15
On the Holy Spirit in the Life of the Church and the World, John Paul II, sect. 30
Sacrament of Charity, Benedict XVI, sect. 12
Splendor of Truth, John Paul II, sect. 83
U. S. Catholic Catechism for Adults, [2006] pp. 102-105

Other Resources

Basics of the Faith: A Catholic Catechism, Schreck, p. 61
The Catholic Catechism, Hardon, p. 185
Fundamentals of Catholic Dogma, Ott, p. 58
Fundamentals of Catholicism, Baker, Vol. 2, p. 113; Vol. 3, p. 135
The Teaching of Christ, Lawler, Wuerl, and Lawler, [First Edition] p. 164; [Second Edition] p. 153

Family Wisdom Library™

Papal documents listed below can be viewed at www.vatican.va.
For new cross-references, visit www.familyland.org

Q. 117. When did the Holy Spirit descend upon the Church?

Church Documents

Compendium of the Catechism of the Catholic Church, sect. 144
Dei Verbum (Dogmatic Constitution on Divine Revelation), Vatican II, sect. 17
God is Love, Benedict XVI, sect. 19
Lumen Gentium (Dogmatic Constitution on the Church), Vatican II, sect. 4, 12, 19, 24, 59
On the Holy Spirit in the Life of the Church and the World, John Paul II, sect. 25
The Relationship Between Faith and Reason, John Paul II, sect. 44
Sacrament of Charity, Benedict XVI, sect. 12
Sacrosanctum Concilium (Constitution on the Sacred Liturgy), Vatican II, sect. 6
U. S. Catholic Catechism for Adults, [2006] pp. 102-103

Other Resources

Basics of the Faith: A Catholic Catechism, Schreck, pp. 72, 79
The Catholic Catechism, Hardon, p. 208
The Church's Confession of Faith, Ignatius Press, pp. 184-185, 214
Fundamentals of Catholic Dogma, Ott, pp. 294-295
Fundamentals of Catholicism, Baker, Vol. 3, p. 141
Modern Catholic Dictionary, Hardon, see "Pentecost"
The Teaching of Christ, Lawler, Wuerl, and Lawler, [First Edition] pp. 166-167; [Second Edition] pp. 155-156; [Third Edition] pp. 132, 135-136

Q. 118. How does the Holy Spirit carry out Christ's work in the Church?

Church Documents

Compendium of the Catechism of the Catholic Church, sect. 145-146
Dei Verbum (Dogmatic Constitution on Divine Revelation), Vatican II, sect. 2, 5, 8, 17
Gaudium et Spes (Pastoral Constitution on the Church in the Modern World), Vatican II, sect. 3, 15, 21, 37-38, 43, 92-93
God is Love, Benedict XVI, sect. 19
Lumen Gentium (Dogmatic Constitution on the Church), Vatican II, sect. 4, 5, 7, 9, 12, 48
On Evangelization in the Modern World, Paul VI, sect. 75
On the Holy Spirit in the Life of the Church and the World, John Paul II, sect. 67
The Relationship Between Faith and Reason, John Paul II, sect. 44
Sacrament of Charity, Benedict XVI, sect. 16
U. S. Catholic Catechism for Adults, [2006] pp. 114-116

Other Resources

Basics of the Faith: A Catholic Catechism, Schreck, pp. 79, 103
The Catholic Catechism, Hardon, p. 188
The Church's Confession of Faith, Ignatius Press, pp. 69-71, 183-187
Faith for Today, Hogan and LeVoir, [First Edition] pp. 20, 204; [Second Edition] pp. 42, 247
Fundamentals of Catholic Dogma, Ott, p. 254
Fundamentals of Catholicism, Baker, Vol. 2, pp. 109-111
Modern Catholic Dictionary, Hardon, see "Holy Spirit"
The Teaching of Christ, Lawler, Wuerl, and Lawler, [First Edition] pp. 162,167-168; [Second Edition] pp. 151,156-157; [Third Edition] pp 136-137

Q. 119. Where is God the Holy Spirit most present?

Church Documents

Catechesis in Our Time, John Paul II, sect. 24
Compendium of the Catechism of the Catholic Church, sect. 145-146
Dei Verbum (Dogmatic Constitution on Divine Revelation), Vatican II, sect. 2, 5, 8, 17
Gaudium et Spes (Pastoral Constitution on the Church in the Modern World), Vatican II, sect. 3, 15, 21, 37-38, 40, 42-44, 92-93
Lumen Gentium (Dogmatic Constitution on the Church), Vatican II, sect. 4, 9
On Evangelization in the Modern World, Paul VI, sect. 75
On the Holy Spirit in the Life of the Church and the World, John Paul II, sect. 25
The Lay Members of Christ's Faithful People, John Paul II, sect. 18-20
The Relationship Between Faith and Reason, John Paul II, sect. 44
Sacrament of Charity, Benedict XVI, sect. 16
Splendor of Truth, John Paul II, sect. 103
U. S. Catholic Catechism for Adults, [2006] pp. 114-116, 119

Family Wisdom Library™

Papal documents listed below can be viewed at www.vatican.va.
For new cross-references, visit www.familyland.org

Other Resources

Basics of the Faith: A Catholic Catechism, Schreck, p. 74
The Catholic Catechism, Hardon, p. 234
The Church's Confession of Faith, Ignatius Press, pp. 211, 223, 228
Faith for Today, Hogan and LeVoir, [First Edition] p.121; [Second Edition] pp. 155-156
Fundamentals of Catholic Dogma, Ott, pp. 294-296
Fundamentals of Catholicism, Baker, Vol. 3, pp. 128-131
The Teaching of Christ, Lawler, Wuerl, and Lawler, [First Edition] pp.167-168; [Second Edition] pp. 156-157; [Third Edition] pp. 136-137

Q. 120. What does God the Holy Spirit accomplish for the Church?

Church Documents

Compendium of the Catechism of the Catholic Church, sect. 145
Dei Verbum (Dogmatic Constitution on Divine Revelation), Vatican II, sect. 2, 5, 7-8, 10, 17
Gaudium et Spes (Pastoral Constitution on the Church in the Modern World), Vatican II, sect. 3, 15, 21, 37-38, 43, 92-93
Lumen Gentium (Dogmatic Constitution on the Church), Vatican II, sect. 4, 5, 7, 9, 12, 48
On the Dignity and Vocation of Women, John Paul II, sect. 29
On the Holy Spirit in the Life of the Church and the World, John Paul II, sect. 7, 25
The Relationship Between Faith and Reason, John Paul II, sect. 44
Sacrament of Charity, Benedict XVI, sect. 16
U. S. Catholic Catechism for Adults, [2006] pp. 114-116, 119

Other Resources

Basics of the Faith: A Catholic Catechism, Schreck, pp. 79, 103, 119-129
The Catholic Catechism, Hardon, p. 238
The Church's Confession of Faith, Ignatius Press, pp. 49, 70, 184, 214, 228-231, 234, 236-238, 259-260, 312
Faith for Today, Hogan and LeVoir, [First Edition] pp. 121, 130; [Second Edition] pp. 155-156, 165-166
Fundamentals of Catholic Dogma, Ott, pp. 294-295
Fundamentals of Catholicism, Baker, Vol. 3, pp. 100, 129-137, 140-142
The Teaching of Christ, Lawler, Wuerl, and Lawler, [First Edition] pp. 167-168; [Second Edition] pp. 156-157; [Third Edition] pp. 136-137
Transformation in Christ, von Hildebrand, pp. 232-233

Q. 121. Why is the Holy Spirit called the Soul of the Church?

Church Documents

Compendium of the Catechism of the Catholic Church, sect. 145
Dei Verbum (Dogmatic Constitution on Divine Revelation), Vatican II, sect. 2, 5, 8, 17
Gaudium et Spes (Pastoral Constitution on the Church in the Modern World), Vatican II, sect. 3, 15, 21, 37-38, 43, 92-93
Lumen Gentium (Dogmatic Constitution on the Church), Vatican II, sect. 4-5, 7, 9, 12, 48
On Evangelization in the Modern World, Paul VI, sect. 75
On the Holy Spirit in the Life of the Church and the World, John Paul II, sect. 25-26
The Relationship Between Faith and Reason, John Paul II, sect. 44
Sacrament of Charity, Benedict XVI, sect. 16
U. S. Catholic Catechism for Adults, [2006] p. 120

Other Resources

The Church's Confession of Faith, Ignatius Press, pp. 214, 228
Fundamentals of Catholic Dogma, Ott, pp. 294-295
Fundamentals of Catholicism, Baker, Vol. 3, pp. 100, 128-131
Modern Catholic Dictionary, Hardon, see "Soul of the Church"
The Teaching of Christ, Lawler, Wuerl, and Lawler, [First Edition] p. 168; [Second Edition] p. 157; [Third Edition] p. 137

Q. 122. What is the task of the Holy Spirit in the Church?

Church Documents

Compendium of the Catechism of the Catholic Church, sect. 145
Dei Verbum (Dogmatic Constitution on Divine Revelation), Vatican II, sect. 2, 5, 8, 17
Gaudium et Spes (Pastoral Constitution on the Church in the Modern World), Vatican II, sect. 3, 15, 21, 37-38, 43, 92-93

Family Wisdom Library™

Papal documents listed below can be viewed at www.vatican.va.
For new cross-references, visit www.familyland.org

Lumen Gentium (Dogmatic Constitution on the Church), Vatican II, sect. 4, 5, 7, 9, 12, 48
On Evangelization in the Modern World, Paul VI, sect. 75
On the Holy Spirit in the Life of the Church and the World, John Paul II, sect. 7, 25, 27
The Lay Members of Christ's Faithful People, John Paul II, sect. 16-17
The Relationship Between Faith and Reason, John Paul II, sect. 44
Sacrament of Charity, Benedict XVI, sect. 12-16
Splendor of Truth, John Paul II, sect. 103, 118
U. S. Catholic Catechism for Adults, [2006] pp. 115-116, 129

Other Resources

The Catholic Catechism, Hardon, pp. 210-211, 214-215, 225
The Church's Confession of Faith, Ignatius Press, pp. 184-187, 228-230
Faith for Today, Hogan and LeVoir, [First Edition] pp.121, 204, 208; [Second Edition] pp. 155-156, 247, 251
Fundamentals of Catholic Dogma, Ott, pp. 294-295
Fundamentals of Catholicism, Baker, Vol. 3, pp. 100, 128-131
The Teaching of Christ, Lawler, Wuerl, and Lawler, [First Edition] pp. 167-172; [Second Edition] pp. 156-161; [Third Edition] pp. 136-140

Q. 123. How should the Holy Spirit be honored?

Church Documents

Compendium of the Catechism of the Catholic Church, sect. 136
Lumen Gentium (Dogmatic Constitution on the Church), Vatican II, sect. 12
The Relationship Between Faith and Reason, John Paul II, sect. 44
Sacrament of Charity, Benedict XVI, sect. 70-72, 77
U. S. Catholic Catechism for Adults, [2006] pp. 129, 328-330

Other Resources

The Church's Confession of Faith, Ignatius Press, p. 78
Fundamentals of Catholicism, Baker, Vol. 1, pp. 95-97
The Teaching of Christ, Lawler, Wuerl, and Lawler, [First Edition] p. 166; [Second Edition] p. 155; [Third Edition] p. 135

Q. 124. What takes place when a person accepts the Spirit of Christ?

Church Documents

Compendium of the Catechism of the Catholic Church, sect. 145, 420
Dei Verbum (Dogmatic Constitution on Divine Revelation), Vatican II, sect. 5
Gaudium et Spes (Pastoral Constitution on the Church in the Modern World), Vatican II, sect. 22
The Lay Members of Christ's Faithful People, John Paul II, sect. 13
Lumen Gentium (Dogmatic Constitution on the Church), Vatican II, sect. 4-5, 7, 9, 12, 14, 48
On the Holy Spirit in the Life of the Church and the World, John Paul II, sect. 48
On Social Concern, John Paul II, sect. 40
The Relationship Between Faith and Reason, John Paul II, sect. 44
Sacrament of Charity, Benedict XVI, sect. 70-72, 77
U. S. Catholic Catechism for Adults, [2006] pp. 328-331

Other Resources

The Catholic Catechism, Hardon, p. 183
The Church's Confession of Faith, Ignatius Press, pp. 205-210
Faith for Today, Hogan and LeVoir, [First Edition] pp. 20, 121-122, 208-209; [Second Edition] pp. 42, 155-156, 251-252
Fundamentals of Catholic Dogma, Ott, pp. 219, 254, 259, 295-296
Fundamentals of Catholicism, Baker, Vol. 2, pp. 113-114; Vol. 3, pp. 56-59
Modern Catholic Dictionary, Hardon, see "Justification" and "Sanctification"
The Teaching of Christ, Lawler, Wuerl, and Lawler, [First Edition] pp. 169, 269, 371-373; [Second Edition] pp. 158, 257, 361-363; [Third Edition] pp. 138, 226, 321-322

Q. 125. What is sanctifying grace?

Church Documents

Compendium of the Catechism of the Catholic Church, sect. 422-423
Dei Verbum (Dogmatic Constitution on Divine Revelation), Vatican II, sect. 5

Family Wisdom Library™

Papal documents listed below can be viewed at www.vatican.va.
For new cross-references, visit www.familyland.org

Gaudium et Spes (Pastoral Constitution on the Church in the Modern World), Vatican II, sect. 22, 25, 32, 37, 49, 57, 89
Lumen Gentium (Dogmatic Constitution on the Church), Vatican II, sect. 11-14
On the Holy Spirit in the Life of the Church and the World, John Paul II, sect. 9
The Relationship Between Faith and Reason, John Paul II, sect. 9
Sacrosanctum Concilium (Constitution on the Sacred Liturgy), Vatican II, sect. 10
U. S. Catholic Catechism for Adults, [2006] pp. 193, 329

Other Resources

The Catholic Catechism, Hardon, pp. 176, 178, 193, 200
The Church's Confession of Faith, Ignatius Press, p. 206
Faith for Today, Hogan and LeVoir, [First Edition] pp. 204-237; [Second Edition] pp. 247-283
Fundamentals of Catholic Dogma, Ott, pp. 254-257;
Fundamentals of Catholicism, Baker, Vol. 3, pp. 16, 18, 20, 22, 56-59
Modern Catholic Dictionary, Hardon, see "Sanctifying Grace", "Habitual Grace" and "Justifying Grace"
The Teaching of Christ, Lawler, Wuerl, and Lawler, [First Edition] pp. 268, 373; [Second Edition] pp. 256, 363; [Third Edition] pp. 226, 323-325

Q. 126. What does this new life of sanctifying grace do for man?

Church Documents

Compendium of the Catechism of the Catholic Church, sect. 425, 427-428
Dei Verbum (Dogmatic Constitution on Divine Revelation), Vatican II, sect. 5
Gaudium et Spes (Pastoral Constitution on the Church in the Modern World), Vatican II, sect. 22, 25, 32, 37, 49, 57, 89
Gospel of Life, John Paul II, sect. 29, 37, 51
Lumen Gentium (Dogmatic Constitution on the Church), Vatican II, sect. 9, 11-12, 14
On the Holy Spirit in the Life of the Church and the World, John Paul II, sect. 9, 58
Sacrosanctum Concilium (Constitution on the Sacred Liturgy), Vatican II, sect. 10
U. S. Catholic Catechism for Adults, [2006] pp. 328-330

Other Resources

The Catholic Catechism, Hardon, pp. 175-177, 187, 189, 193
The Church's Confession of Faith, Ignatius Press, pp. 205-210
Faith for Today, Hogan and LeVoir, [First Edition] pp. 204-237; [Second Edition] pp. 247-283
Fundamentals of Catholic Dogma, Ott, pp. 257-261
Fundamentals of Catholicism, Baker, Vol. 3, pp. 65-68
Modern Catholic Dictionary, Hardon, see "Sanctifying Grace", "Habitual Grace" and "Justifying Grace"
The Teaching of Christ, Lawler, Wuerl, and Lawler, [First Edition] pp. 268-269, 374-376; [Second Edition] pp. 256-257, 364-366; [Third Edition] pp. 226, 323-325
Transformation in Christ, von Hildebrand, pp. 232-233

Q. 127. What does God's gift of grace do for us?

Church Documents

Compendium of the Catechism of the Catholic Church, sect. 423, 425
Gaudium et Spes (Pastoral Constitution on the Church in the Modern World), Vatican II, sect. 22, 25, 32, 37, 49, 57, 89
Gospel of Life, John Paul II, sect. 2, 78, 80
Lumen Gentium (Dogmatic Constitution on the Church), Vatican II, sect. 9
On the Holy Spirit in the Life of the Church and the World, John Paul II, sect. 58;
On the Hundredth Anniversary of Rerum Novarum, John Paul II, sect. 50
The Role of the Christian Family in the Modern World, John Paul II, sect. 41
Sacrament of Charity, Benedict XVI, sect. 16, 71
Splendor of Truth, John Paul II, sect. 25, 103
U. S. Catholic Catechism for Adults, [2006] pp. 328-330

Other Resources

The Church's Confession of Faith, Ignatius Press, pp. 206, 209-210
Faith for Today, Hogan and LeVoir, [First Edition] pp. 204-236; [Second Edition] pp.247-283
Fundamentals of Catholic Dogma, Ott, pp. 257-261
Fundamentals of Catholicism, Baker, Vol. 3, pp. 68-74
Modern Catholic Dictionary, Hardon, see "Grace"

Family Wisdom Library™

Papal documents listed below can be viewed at www.vatican.va.
For new cross-references, visit www.familyland.org

The Teaching of Christ, Lawler, Wuerl and Lawler, [First Edition] pp. 269-271, 373-374; [Second Edition] pp. 257-259, 363-364; [Third Edition] pp. 227-228, 322-323

Transformation in Christ, von Hildebrand, pp. 232-233

Q. 128. What is actual grace?

Church Documents

Compendium of the Catechism of the Catholic Church, sect. 424

Gaudium et Spes (Pastoral Constitution on the Church in the Modern World), Vatican II, sect. 17, 22, 25, 32, 37, 49, 57, 89

On Evangelization in the Modern World, Paul VI, sect. 75

Sacrament of Charity, Benedict XVI, sect. 12,77

U. S. Catholic Catechism for Adults, [2006] p. 329

Other Resources

The Catholic Catechism, Hardon, pp. 178, 189-193

The Church's Confession of Faith, Ignatius Press, p. 206

Faith for Today, Hogan and LeVoir, [First Edition] p. 226; [Second Edition] p. 271

Fundamentals of Catholic Dogma, Ott, pp. 222, 225-233

Fundamentals of Catholicism, Baker, Vol. 3, pp. 16-25

Modern Catholic Dictionary, Hardon, see "Actual Grace"

The Teaching of Christ, Lawler, Wuerl, and Lawler, [First Edition] p. 377; [Second Edition] p. 367; [Third Edition] p. 326

Q. 129. What do we receive from the indwelling of the Holy Spirit?

Church Documents

Compendium of the Catechism of the Catholic Church, sect. 145-146, 378, 422

Dei Verbum (Dogmatic Constitution on Divine Revelation), Vatican II, sect. 5

Gaudium et Spes (Pastoral Constitution on the Church in the Modern World), Vatican II, sect. 22, 25, 32, 37, 49, 57, 89

Lumen Gentium (Dogmatic Constitution on the Church), Vatican II, sect. 4-5, 7, 9, 11, 12, 14

On the Christian Meaning of Human Suffering, John Paul II, sect. 22

On the Dignity and Vocation of Women, John Paul II, sect. 27-28

On Evangelization in the Modern World, Paul VI, sect. 75

On the Holy Spirit in the Life of the Church and the World, John Paul II, sect. 48, 58-60

On Reconciliation and Penance, John Paul II, sect. 6, 22

Sacrament of Charity, Benedict XVI, sect. 12, 77

U. S. Catholic Catechism for Adults, [2006] pp. 193, 195-197, 328-330

Other Resources

The Catholic Catechism, Hardon, pp. 172, 187-189

The Church's Confession of Faith, Ignatius Press, pp. 186-187, 205-206

Faith for Today, Hogan and LeVoir, [First Edition] pp. 204-237; [Second Edition] pp. 247-283

Fundamentals of Catholic Dogma, Ott, pp. 254-261

Fundamentals of Catholicism, Baker, Vol. 2, pp. 112-115

Modern Catholic Dictionary, Hardon, see "Indwelling"

The Teaching of Christ, Lawler, Wuerl, and Lawler, [First Edition] pp. 169, 269, 372-373; [Second Edition] pp. 158, 257, 362-363; [Third Edition] pp. 138, 321-322

Transformation in Christ, von Hildebrand, pp. 315-335

Q. 130. What is our greatest dignity?

Church Documents

Compendium of the Catechism of the Catholic Church, sect. 66, 358

Dei Verbum (Dogmatic Constitution on Divine Revelation), Vatican II, sect. 5, 8

Gaudium et Spes (Pastoral Constitution on the Church in the Modern World), Vatican II, sect. 22, 25, 32, 37, 49, 57, 89

Gospel of Life, John Paul II, sect. 37, 38

The Lay Members of Christ's Faithful People, John Paul II, sect. 5, 37, 39

Lumen Gentium (Dogmatic Constitution on the Church), Vatican II, sect. 9, 11

On the Dignity and Vocation of Women, John Paul II, sect. 3, 13, 25, 29

On the Holy Spirit in the Life of the Church and the World, John Paul II, sect. 34, 60

On the Mercy of God, John Paul II, sect. 6-8

Sacrament of Charity, Benedict XVI, sect. 7-8

U. S. Catholic Catechism for Adults, [2006] pp. 67-68

Family Wisdom Library™

Papal documents listed below can be viewed at www.vatican.va.
For new cross-references, visit www.familyland.org

Other Resources

The Church's Confession of Faith, Ignatius Press, pp. 97-106, 206
Faith for Today, Hogan and LeVoir, [First Edition] pp. 204-205, 216, 223, 228-229; [Second Edition] pp. 247-248, 261, 268-269, 273-274
The Teaching of Christ, Lawler, Wuerl and Lawler, [First Edition] pp. 68-77, 370; [Second Edition] pp. 56-65, 360; [Third Edition] pp. 49-57, 320
Transformation in Christ, von Hildebrand, pp. 163-164

Q. 131. What are the Theological Virtues?

Church Documents

Compendium of the Catechism of the Catholic Church, sect. 384-385
Dei Verbum (Dogmatic Constitution on Divine Revelation), Vatican II, sect. 1
Gaudium et Spes (Pastoral Constitution on the Church in the Modern World), Vatican II, sect. 48
God is Love, Benedict XVI, sect. 39
The Lay Members of Christ's Faithful People, John Paul II, sect. 41
Lumen Gentium (Dogmatic Constitution on the Church), Vatican II, sect. 8, 31, 41, 61, 63-65
Splendor of Truth, John Paul II, sect. 64
U. S. Catholic Catechism for Adults, [2006] pp. 315-317

Other Resources

The Catholic Catechism, Hardon, pp. 33, 193-197;
The Church's Confession of Faith, Ignatius Press, p. 206
Faith for Today, Hogan and LeVoir, [First Edition] pp. 218-220; [Second Edition] pp. 263-265
Fundamentals of Catholic Dogma, Ott, p. 260
Fundamentals of Catholicism, Baker, Vol. 3, pp. 71-72
Modern Catholic Dictionary, Hardon, see "Theological Virtue"
The Teaching of Christ, Lawler, Wuerl, and Lawler, [First Edition] pp. 294, 375; [Second Edition] pp. 282, 365; [Third Edition] pp. 249, 324
Transformation in Christ, von Hildebrand, pp. 333, 400, 461-462, 478-479

Q. 132. What is the Theological Virtue of faith?

Church Documents

Compendium of the Catechism of the Catholic Church, sect. 386
Dei Verbum (Dogmatic Constitution on Divine Revelation), Vatican II, sect. 5
Gaudium et Spes (Pastoral Constitution on the Church in the Modern World), Vatican II, sect. 7, 11, 15, 18-19, 21, 32, 36, 38, 40, 42, 48, 59
God is Love, Benedict XVI, sect. 39
Lumen Gentium (Dogmatic Constitution on the Church), Vatican II, sect. 5, 9, 12, 24, 31-32, 35, 40-41, 56, 61, 63-64
On the Holy Spirit in the Life of the Church and the World, John Paul II, sect. 6, 51
On Social Concern, John Paul II, sect. 31, 35
The Relationship Between Faith and Reason, John Paul II, sect. 9, 12, 32, 42-43, 98
Splendor of Truth, John Paul II, sect. 27, 109
U. S. Catholic Catechism for Adults, [2006] pp. 315-317, 342

Other Resources

The Catholic Catechism, Hardon, pp. 32-37
The Church's Confession of Faith, Ignatius Press, p. 207
Faith for Today, Hogan and LeVoir, [First Edition] pp. 218-219; [Second Edition] pp. 263-264
Fundamentals of Catholic Dogma, Ott, pp. 229-230, 260, 263
Fundamentals of Catholicism, Baker, Vol. 3, p. 72
Modern Catholic Dictionary, Hardon, see "Faith, Virtue of"
The Teaching of Christ, Lawler, Wuerl, and Lawler, [First Edition] pp. 294-297, 375; [Second Edition] pp. 282-285, 365; [Third Edition] pp. 249-252, 324

Q. 133. What is the Theological Virtue of hope?

Church Documents

Compendium of the Catechism of the Catholic Church, sect. 387
Dei Verbum (Dogmatic Constitution on Divine Revelation), Vatican II, sect. 3, 14, 26
Gaudium et Spes (Pastoral Constitution on the Church in the Modern World), Vatican II, sect. 18, 21-22, 39, 48, 82, 93

Family Wisdom Library™

Papal documents listed below can be viewed at www.vatican.va.
For new cross-references, visit www.familyland.org

God is Love, Benedict XVI, sect. 39
The Lay Members of Christ's Faithful People, John Paul II, sect. 7
Lumen Gentium (Dogmatic Constitution on the Church), Vatican II, sect. 32, 35, 41, 48, 55, 61, 64-65, 68
On Human Work, John Paul II, sect. 27
On the Mercy of God, John Paul II, sect. 7-8
On Reconciliation and Penance, John Paul II, sect. 22
Splendor of Truth, John Paul II, sect. 102, 118
U. S. Catholic Catechism for Adults, [2006] pp. 315-317, 343

Other Resources

The Catholic Catechism, Hardon, p. 197
The Church's Confession of Faith, Ignatius Press, p. 207
Faith for Today, Hogan and LeVoir, [First Edition] p. 219; [Second Edition] pp. 263-264
Fundamentals of Catholic Dogma, Ott, pp. 260. 263
Fundamentals of Catholicism, Baker, Vol. 3, p. 72
Modern Catholic Dictionary, Hardon, see "Hope, Virtue of"
The Teaching of Christ, Lawler, Wuerl, and Lawler, [First Edition] pp. 297-301, 375; [Second Edition] pp. 285-289, 365; [Third Edition] pp. 252-255, 324
Transformation in Christ, von Hildebrand, pp. 333, 451-462, 478-479

Q. 134. What is the Theological Virtue of charity?

Church Documents

Compendium of the Catechism of the Catholic Church, sect. 388
Dei Verbum (Dogmatic Constitution on Divine Revelation), Vatican II, sect. 23
Gaudium et Spes (Pastoral Constitution on the Church in the Modern World), Vatican II, sect. 16, 21-22, 24, 28, 32, 38-39, 42-43, 48-49, 57, 67, 69, 72, 75-76, 88, 90, 92
God is Love, Benedict XVI, sect. 19-22
The Lay Members of Christ's Faithful People, John Paul II, sect. 41
Lumen Gentium (Dogmatic Constitution on the Church), Vatican II, sect. 14, 31-32, 41-42, 44, 48, 51, 64-65
On the Hundredth Anniversary of Rerum Novarum, John Paul II, sect. 57
On Social Concern, John Paul II, sect. 42
Splendor of Truth, John Paul II, sect. 10
U. S. Catholic Catechism for Adults, [2006] pp. 315-317, 343

Other Resources

The Church's Confession of Faith, Ignatius Press, pp. 207-208
Faith for Today, Hogan and LeVoir, [First Edition] p. 219; [Second Edition] p. 264
Fundamentals of Catholic Dogma, Ott, pp. 256, 258, 260, 263
Fundamentals of Catholicism, Baker, Vol. 3, p. 72
Modern Catholic Dictionary, Hardon, see "Charity"
The Teaching of Christ, Lawler, Wuerl, and Lawler, [First Edition] pp. 301-303, 375; [Second Edition], pp. 289-291,365; [Third Edition] pp. 255-257, 324
Transformation in Christ, von Hildebrand, pp. 333-334, 400

Q. 135. What are the Cardinal Virtues?

Church Documents

Compendium of the Catechism of the Catholic Church, sect. 379
Lumen Gentium (Dogmatic Constitution on the Church), Vatican II, sect. 11, 42
On the Hundredth Anniversary of Rerum Novarum, John Paul II, sect. 32
On Social Concern, John Paul II, sect. 38-40
Splendor of Truth, John Paul II, sect. 64, 67
U. S. Catholic Catechism for Adults, [2006] pp. 193, 316-317

Other Resources

The Catholic Catechism, Hardon, pp. 193-194, 197-200
Faith for Today, Hogan and LeVoir, [First Edition] pp. 218-223, 226-227; [Second Edition] pp. 263-268, 272-273
Fundamentals of Catholic Dogma, Ott, pp. 260-261
Fundamentals of Catholicism, Baker, Vol. 3, pp. 72-73
The Teaching of Christ, Lawler, Wuerl, and Lawler, [First Edition] p. 375; [Second Edition] p. 365; [Third Edition] p. 324

Q. 136. Why are prudence, justice, fortitude and temperance called Cardinal Virtues?

Church Documents

Compendium of the Catechism of the Catholic Church, sect. 379-383

Family Wisdom Library™

Papal documents listed below can be viewed at www.vatican.va.
For new cross-references, visit www.familyland.org

U. S. Catholic Catechism for Adults, [2006] p. 317

Other Resources

The Catholic Catechism, Hardon, p. 194

Q. 137. What are the seven Gifts of the Holy Spirit?

Church Documents

Compendium of the Catechism of the Catholic Church, sect. 389

Gaudium et Spes (Pastoral Constitution on the Church in the Modern World), Vatican II, sect. 38

Lumen Gentium (Dogmatic Constitution on the Church), Vatican II, sect. 11-12, 42

On Reconciliation and Penance, John Paul II, sect. 21

Splendor of Truth, John Paul II, sect. 88;

U. S. Catholic Catechism for Adults, [2006] pp. 108, 205, 207-209

Other Resources

The Catholic Catechism, Hardon, pp. 200-205

Faith for Today, Hogan and LeVoir, [First Edition] pp. 222-223; [Second Edition] p. 268

Fundamentals of Catholic Dogma, Ott, p. 261

Fundamentals of Catholicism, Baker, Vol. 3, p. 73

Modern Catholic Dictionary, Hardon, see "Gifts of the Holy Spirit"

The Teaching of Christ, Lawler, Wuerl, and Lawler, [First Edition] pp. 169-170, 375; [Second Edition] pp. 158-159, 365; [Third Edition] pp. 138, 324

The Church, the Communion of Saints, and the Forgiveness of Sins

---

"...We believe in one, holy, catholic, and apostolic Church. We acknowledge one Baptism for the forgiveness of sins."

#E4-86-2

The Church

#C15-36

The Catholic Church is the community of all baptized persons united in the same true faith, the same sacrifice, the same sacraments, under the authority of the Sovereign Pontiff, the Bishop of Rome, and the bishops in communion with him.

CHAPTER FORTY-ONE

What Is the Catholic Church?

Q. 138. What is the Catholic Church?

The Catholic Church is the community of all baptized persons united in the same true faith, the same sacrifice, the same sacraments, under the authority of the Sovereign Pontiff, the Bishop of Rome, and the bishops in communion with him.

In the Old Testament, God made Israel the first People of God. He made Israel a sacred community, dearer to Him than all other nations. They were to be the bearers of God's blessings to the world and His instruments to reunite a torn and divided mankind. To help them faithfully endure their trials, He reminded them that He was caring for them as a loving Father.

God remained faithful to them even when they sinned. He brought them out of Egypt and fed them in the desert. He said that He would always care for them as His special possession, and He asked them to accept His love and be His adopted children. After the Children of Israel had wandered in the desert for forty years, God led them into the land originally promised to Abraham.

Although Israel as a whole failed in its devotion to God, a few people remained faithful. They were the remnant of the once great Israel, and they depended on God alone. Through them, He would keep His promise to send the world a Savior Who would draw all men into the family of God.

Jesus Christ, the Son of God born of Mary, was a descendant of the great Israelite king, David. With the scattered fragments of Israel, Jesus established a new kingdom, the Church, intended for all peoples. He brought peace to His people and freed them from the bondage of sin and the sadness due to sin. He is our Savior.

Our Lord Jesus formed His followers, the community of believers, into one body to proclaim the Gospel to all men. He called this body the Church, which is the Catholic Church. This was to be the new People of God.

Sacred Scripture
Q. 138. Gen 12:1-3, 15:5-6; Acts 10:34-43.

Catechism of the Catholic Church
Q. 138. Paragraphs **758-786**.

For cross-references with Vatican II, Papal documents & other resources, see Family Wisdom Library on page 734.
For commentaries on each question with Cardinal Arinze, Sr. John Vianney and Fr. Straub (in Spanish), see Appendix C.

#A18-20-2

Jesus Christ, the Son of God born of Mary, was a descendant of the great Israelite king, David. With the scattered fragments of Israel, Jesus established a new kingdom, the Church, intended for all peoples.

At the Second Vatican Council (1962-1965), this concept of the Catholic Church was qualified to include, but not fully, all who are baptized and profess their faith in Jesus Christ. Their possession of truth and holiness, elements belonging by right to the Catholic Church, is the principle which propels them to unite ever more fully with that Church founded by Christ Himself.

God has chosen the new People of God to be His own and has bestowed the special graces of His providence on them.

Sacred Scripture

And he has put all things under his feet and has made him the head over all things for the church. *Ephesians 1:22*

Now you are the body of Christ and individually members of it. *1 Corinthians 12:27*

But you are a chosen race, a royal priesthood, a holy nation, God's own people, that you may declare the wonderful deeds of him who called you out of darkness into his marvelous light. Once you were no people but now you are God's people; once you had not received mercy but now you have received mercy. *1 Peter 2:9-10*

Catechism of the Catholic Church

751 The word "Church" (Latin *ecclesia*, from the Greek *ek-ka-lein*, to "call out of") means a convocation or an assembly. It designates the assemblies of the people, usually for a religious purpose.[1] *Ekklesia* is used frequently in the Greek Old Testament for the assembly of the Chosen People before God, above all for their assembly on Mount Sinai where Israel received the Law and was established by God as his holy people.[2] By calling itself "Church," the first community of Christian believers recognized itself as heir to that assembly. In the Church, God is "calling together" his people from all the ends of the earth. The equivalent Greek term *Kyriake*, from which the English word *Church* and the German *Kirche* are derived, means "what belongs to the Lord."

839 "Those who have not yet received the Gospel are related to the People of God in various ways."[1] *"The relationship of the Church with the Jewish People.* When she delves into her own mystery, the Church, the People of God in the New Covenant, discovers her link with the Jewish People,[2] 'the first to hear the Word of God.'[3] The Jewish faith, unlike other non-Christian religions, is already a response to God's revelation in the Old Covenant. To the Jews 'belong the sonship, the glory, the covenants, the giving of the law, the worship, and the promises; to them belong the patriarchs, and of their race, according to the flesh, is the Christ';[4] 'for the gifts and the call of God are irrevocable.'"[5]

#C15-22-2

God has chosen the new People of God to be His own and has bestowed the special graces of His providence on them.

Vatican Council II

Hence the universal Church is seen to be "a people brought into unity from the unity of the Father, the Son and the Holy Spirit." *Lumen Gentium, 4*

In the Old Testament the revelation of the kingdom is often made under the forms of symbols. In similar fashion the inner nature of the Church is now made known to us in various images. Taken either from the life of the shepherd or from cultivation of the land, from the art of building or from family life and marriage, these images have their preparation in the books of the prophets. *Lumen Gentium, 6*

#E4-29

But you are a chosen race, a royal priesthood, a holy nation, God's own people, that you may declare the wonderful deeds of him who called you out of darkness into his marvelous light. *(1 Peter 2:9)*

But, the society structured with hierarchical organs and the mystical body of Christ, the visible society and the spiritual community, the earthly Church and the Church endowed with heavenly riches, are not to be thought of as two realities. On the contrary, they form one complex reality which comes together from a human and a divine element. *Lumen Gentium, 8*

The Church is compared, in a powerful analogy, to the mystery of the incarnate Word. As the assumed nature, inseparably united to him, serves the divine Word as a living organ of salvation, so, in a somewhat similar way, does the social structure of the Church serve the Spirit of Christ who vivifies it, in the building up of the body (cf. Eph. 4:15). *Lumen Gentium, 8*

As Israel according to the flesh which wandered in the desert was already called the Church of God (2 Esd.; 13:1 cf. Num. 20:4; Deut. 23:1 ff.), so too, the new Israel, which advances in this present era in search of a future and permanent city (cf. Heb. 13:14), is called also the Church of Christ (cf. Mt. 16:18). It is Christ indeed who had purchased it with his own blood (cf. Acts 20:28); he has filled it with his Spirit; he has provided means adapted to its visible and social union. *Lumen Gentium, 9*

Catechism by Diagram

#C15-57

The Church, Founded by Jesus Christ. The Church is the new People of God, prepared for in the Old Testament and given life, growth, and direction by Christ (monogram) in the Holy Spirit (dove). Founded by Christ upon the Apostles, it had its origin in Jesus' death and Resurrection (cross). In order to proclaim the message of Salvation, to extend His kingdom (arrows pointing to all directions), to be present in the world (earth) for all people, to teach us, to shepherd us, and to pour His grace upon us, Jesus entrusted to His twelve Apostles (twelve circles) the power, right, and duty in His Church (St. Peter's Basilica) to teach, guide, and sanctify (rays from triangle) all men. God speaks to us (horn) through Jesus Christ, the Apostles, and His Church, guided by the Holy Spirit. The Church preaches the faith (I believe) in every part of the world.

Summary Prayer

Heavenly Father, even today we see the wonders of the miracles You worked long ago. Once You saved a single nation from their slavery in Egypt. Now through Baptism, You offer everyone eternal Salvation from the slavery of sin. May the peoples of the world become true sons of Abraham and prove worthy of the heritage of Israel.

Father in Heaven, from the days of Abraham and Moses until this gathering of Your Church in prayer, You have formed a people in the image of Your Son. Bless this people with the gift of Your Kingdom. May we serve You with our every desire and show love for one another even as You have loved us.

Almighty God, ever-living mystery of unity and Trinity, You gave life to the new Israel by birth from water and the Spirit, and made it a chosen race, a royal priesthood, a people set apart as Your eternal possession. May all those whom You have called to walk in the splendor of the new light render You fitting service and adoration.

Enable us to live honorably and unselfishly in this world, and so arrive at the glories of the heavenly city where, in union with all the blessed company of Heaven, we shall sing of Your majestic deeds forever and ever. Amen.

Doctrine • Moral • Worship Exercise

(See Appendix A for answer key, question 138.)

1. Why is the Catholic Church called the "new People of God"? What sets the Catholic Church apart from other religious bodies?
2. How can you concretely show your gratitude to God for having made you a member of the Catholic Church?
3. Thank Jesus from the depths of your heart for His gift of the Catholic Church.

Q. 139. When did Jesus start the Catholic Church?

Jesus started the Catholic Church at the time of His Death and Resurrection, more than two thousand years ago.

Jesus earned for us the privilege of belonging to God's holy family, the Church, by His death and Resurrection. In order to enter that family, we must have sanctifying grace, which we first receive at Baptism and which cleanses our soul from sin and restores our friendship with God.

By the power of Baptism, we become members of the Church, the Mystical Body of Christ. Thus we become united to one another through our union with Christ, Who is the Head of the Body. Incorporated into Christ, we are freed from sin's dominion.

#J2-332-2

Jesus started the Catholic Church at the time of His Death and Resurrection, more than two thousand years ago.

Sacred Scripture

And Jesus came and said to them [Apostles], "All authority in heaven and on earth has been given to me. Go therefore and make disciples of all nations, baptizing them in the name of the Father and of the Son and of the Holy Spirit, teaching them to observe all that I have commanded you; and lo, I am with you always, to the close of the age." *Matthew 28:18-20*

Sacred Scripture
Q. 139. Mt 16:18; 1 Pet 3:18-22.

Catechism of the Catholic Church
Q. 139. Paragraphs **763-768**, 787-791.

For cross-references with Vatican II, Papal documents & other resources, see Family Wisdom Library on page 734.
For commentaries on each question with Cardinal Arinze, Sr. John Vianney and Fr. Straub (in Spanish), see Appendix C.

#J2-356-2

The Church has been manifested as the mystery of salvation by the outpouring of the Holy Spirit. (*Catechism of the Catholic Church, 778)*

Catechism of the Catholic Church

778 The Church is both the means and the goal of God's plan: prefigured in creation, prepared for in the Old Covenant, founded by the words and actions of Jesus Christ, fulfilled by his redeeming cross and his Resurrection, the Church has been manifested as the mystery of salvation by the outpouring of the Holy Spirit. She will be perfected in the glory of heaven as the assembly of all the redeemed of the earth.[1]

Vatican Council II

The mystery of the holy Church is already brought to light in the way it was founded. For the Lord Jesus inaugurated his Church by preaching the Good News, that is, the coming of the kingdom of God, promised over the ages in the scriptures: "The time is fulfilled and the kingdom of God is at hand" (Mk. 1:15; Mt. 4:17). This kingdom shone out before men in the word, in the works and in the presence of Christ. *Lumen Gentium, 5*

For it was from the side of Christ as he slept the sleep of death upon the cross that there came forth "the wondrous sacrament of the whole Church." *Sacrosanctum Concilium, 5*

Often, too, the Church is called the building of God (1 Cor. 3:9). The Lord compared himself to the stone which the builders rejected, but which was made into the cornerstone (Mt. 21:42; cf. Acts 4:11; 1 Pet. 2:7; Ps. 117:22). On this foundation the Church is built by the apostles (cf. 1 Cor. 3:11) and from it the Church receives solidity and unity. This edifice has many names to describe it: the house of God in which his family dwells; the household of God in the Spirit (Eph. 2:19, 22); the dwelling-place of God among men (Apoc. 21:3); and, especially, the holy temple. This temple, symbolized in places of worship built out of stone, is praised by the Fathers and, not without reason, is compared in the liturgy to the Holy City, the New Jerusalem. As

living stones we here on earth are built into it (1 Pet. 2:5). It is this holy city that is seen by John as it comes down out of heaven from God when the world is made anew, prepared like a bride adorned for her husband (Apoc. 21:1 f.).
Lumen Gentium, 6

Summary Prayer

Lord Jesus Christ, faithful witness and first-born from the dead, be our Life and our Resurrection. High Priest of the new and eternal covenant, intercede for Your holy Church. You Who loved us and washed away our sins in Your blood, make us holy so that we may serve our God worthily.

When You rose from the dead, Lord Jesus, You formed the Church into Your Mystical Body and made of it the new Jerusalem, united in Your Spirit. Give us peace in our day. Guide all nations into Your Church so that they may share Your gifts in fellowship, render You thanks without end, and come to Your eternal city. We ask this in Your most powerful and holy Name. Amen.

#R4.3-4

The Lord compared himself to the stone which the builders rejected, but which was made into the cornerstone (Mt. 21:42; cf. Acts 4:11; 1 Pet. 2:7; Ps. 117:22). On this foundation the Church is built by the apostles (cf. 1 Cor. 3:11) and from it the Church receives solidity and unity. *(Lumen Gentium, 6)*

The Lord Jesus inaugurated his Church by preaching the Good News, that is, the coming of the kingdom of God, promised over the ages in the scriptures. *(Lumen Gentium, 5)*

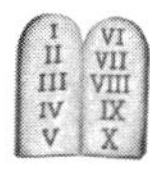

Doctrine • Moral • Worship Exercise

(See Appendix A for answer key, question 139.)

1. When and how did Christ lay the foundations of the Catholic Church? How does one become a member of the Catholic Church, the Mystical Body of Christ?
2. What should our attitude be towards all members of the Church? How can we remain united with Christ and with one another?
3. Renew the promises which were made at your Baptism. Thank the Lord for making you part of His family and ask Him for the grace to remain faithful to your baptismal promises.

Chapter Summary Prayer

Lord Jesus our Savior, build up the faith of Your pilgrim Church on earth, that it may bear witness to Your Resurrection before the whole world. Fill our minds with the light of faith. Through Your Resurrection, You opened for us the way to eternal life; sustain us with the hope of glory. You sent the Holy Spirit into the world; set our hearts on fire with spiritual love.

Lord Jesus, in You, Who has risen from the dead, God has opened for us the way to everlasting life. Through Your victory, save the people You have redeemed.

The Father has established in You the foundation of all our hope and the principle of our resurrection. We rejoice with You, King of Glory, and we thank You for the privilege of belonging to the Church which You have founded and which began at the time of Your death and Resurrection. You were crucified to set us free; be our Salvation and redemption.

Be with Your Church on its pilgrimage through life. Do not let us be slow to believe, but help us, as members of Your Church, to be ready to proclaim You as Victor over sin and death forever and ever. Amen.

Thought Provokers

Please see Appendix B for the answers.

Q. 138: Is the Church, the new People of God, a continuation of the old People of God, that is, the Jews of the Old Testament period?

Q. 139: Sometimes the Church is said to have begun at Pentecost; and sometimes, with Jesus' death upon the Cross. Why is this?

#E4-23

The Catholic Church is nourished by God's saving truth, the sacraments, and the apostolic ministry.

CHAPTER FORTY-TWO

Gifts of God to the Catholic Church

Q. 140. What are some of the basic gifts given by God to the Catholic Church?

Some of the basic gifts given by God to the Catholic Church are: (1) the apostolic ministries of bishops, priests, and deacons, (2) the truths of the Faith, and (3) the Seven Sacraments.

1. Among the basic gifts given by God to the Catholic Church are the apostolic ministries of bishops, priests, and deacons.

Christ gave the Apostles and their successors, the bishops, assisted by priests and deacons, the power to be His witnesses in the world. Jesus said to His Apostles before ascending into Heaven, "You shall receive power when the Holy Spirit has come upon you; and you shall be my witnesses in Jerusalem and in all Judea and Samaria and to the end of the earth" (Acts 1:8).

#R6-10

Among the basic gifts given by God to the Catholic Church are the apostolic ministries of bishops, priests, and deacons.

Sacred Scripture
Q. 140. Jn 20:21; Rom 10:14-18.

Catechism of the Catholic Church
Q. 140. Paragraphs 14, 185-186, **861-862**, **873-896**, 949-951, **1210-1211**.

For cross-references with Vatican II, Papal documents & other resources, see Family Wisdom Library on page 734.
For commentaries on each question with Cardinal Arinze, Sr. John Vianney and Fr. Straub (in Spanish), see Appendix C.

Catechism by Diagram

#C15-58

The Church, the Deposit of Faith. In the Catholic Church is found the Deposit of Faith (St. Peter's Basilica). The deposit contains the truths which God has revealed. The Holy Spirit preserves the Church as the Body of Christ, His bride, and the protector of revealed truths, so that despite the sins of its members or the persecution of its enemies, the devil will never destroy it (broken arrows). Jesus said to Peter, "And I tell you, you are Peter, and on this rock I will build my church and the powers of death shall not prevail against it" (Matthew 16:18). The kingdom of darkness and sin (spotted sphere) is constantly opposed to the kingdom of light (white sphere) and grace. The Church is like the sun giving the truth (rays) and the warmth of God's grace to the world.

2. Among the basic gifts given by God to the Catholic Church are the truths of the faith.

In order that His teaching might be carried on, Jesus gave the Apostles the authority and responsibility to teach the truths of the faith to the whole world. They were appointed as the chief teachers of the Church, as shepherds, so that through them and their successors, Christ could guide the peoples of the world to the Kingdom of Heaven with the manna of His heavenly doctrine.

Our Lord Jesus said, "He who hears you hears me, and he who rejects you rejects me, and he who rejects me rejects him who sent me" (Luke 10:16). "Truly, I say to you, whatever you bind on earth shall be bound in heaven, and whatever you loose on earth shall be loosed in heaven" (Matthew 18:18).

3. Among the basic gifts given by God to the Catholic Church are the Seven Sacraments.

Christ taught the Apostles that through them His grace was to be given to men, especially by means of the Seven Sacraments. For example, through the Apostles, He would forgive sins through the Sacrament of Penance: "If you forgive the sins of any, they are forgiven; if you retain the sins of any, they are retained" (John 20:23).

Through the Apostles, Christ would also give the world the precious gift of His Body and Blood. "And he took bread, and when he had given thanks he broke it and gave it to them, saying, 'This is my body which is given for you. Do this in remembrance of me.' And likewise the cup after supper, saying, 'This cup which is poured out for you is the new covenant in my blood'" (Luke 22:19-20).

Through the authority and power to dispense grace that Christ gave to the Apostles and their successors, together with the priests and deacons, the Catholic Church administers the Seven Sacraments for the Salvation of the People of God.

Jesus continues, through the gifts of His Apostles and their successors, to be King, Priest, and Teacher to His people. Through the Apostles and their successors, believers are gathered into the Catholic Church and are united to Christ and to each other.

#C12-154-2

It is through Christ's Catholic Church alone, which is the universal help towards salvation, that the fullness of the means of salvation can be obtained.
(Ecumenism, 3)

Splendor of Truth

People today need to turn to Christ once again in order to receive from him the answer to their questions about what is good and what is evil. Christ is the Teacher, the Risen One who has life in himself and who is always present in his Church and in the world. It is he who opens up to the faithful the book of the Scriptures and, by fully revealing the Father's will, teaches the truth about moral action. *(section 8)*

Vatican Council II

All men are called to belong to the new People of God. This People therefore, whilst remaining one and only one, is to be spread throughout the whole world and to all ages in order that the design of God's will may be fulfilled. *Lumen Gentium, 13*

It is through the faithful preaching of the Gospel by the Apostles and their successors–the bishops with Peter's successor at their head– through their administering the sacraments, and through their governing in love, that Jesus Christ wishes his people to increase, under the action of the Holy Spirit; and he perfects its fellowship in unity: in the confession of one faith, in the common celebration of divine worship, and in the fraternal harmony of the family of God. *Ecumenism, 2*

It is through Christ's Catholic Church alone, which is the universal help towards salvation, that the fullness of the means of salvation can be obtained. It was to the apostolic college alone, of which Peter is the head, that we believe that our Lord entrusted all the blessings of the New Covenant, in order to establish on earth the one Body of Christ into which all those should be fully incorporated who belong in any way to the People of God. *Ecumenism, 3*

The Catholic Church is by the will of Christ the teacher of truth. It is her duty to proclaim and teach with authority the truth which is Christ and, at the same time, to declare and confirm by her authority the principles of the moral order which spring from human nature itself. *Liberty, 14*

Summary Prayer

God of might and majesty, the strength of those who hope in You, rescue the troubled and afflicted, set us free from our sins, and preserve us in Your truth which is given to us in Your Church. Your light of truth guides us on the way to Christ. May all who follow Him reject what is contrary to the Gospel. We ask this through Jesus Christ our only Lord and Savior, to Whom with You and the Holy Spirit be all honor and glory. Amen.

Doctrine • Moral • Worship Exercise

(See Appendix A for answer key, question 140.)

1. God has given us gifts in the Catholic Church. What are these gifts? How does each of these gifts help us in our daily life?
2. Resolve to receive the sacraments more frequently and with greater devotion. Think of ways to help your family members do the same.
3. Pray that more families will receive the sacraments with fervor and devotion. Reflect on the goodness of God in giving us His gifts in the Catholic Church.

Q. 141. What are the two sources of Divine Truth which constitute the truths of the faith?

The two sources of Divine Truth are: (1) Holy Scripture and (2) Sacred Tradition (also known as Apostolic Tradition or simply Tradition).

#C15-1-2

Both Scripture and Tradition must be accepted and honored with equal feelings of devotion and reverence. *(Dei Verbum, 9)*

Catechism of the Catholic Church
Q. 141. Paragraphs **74-82**, 101-105.

For cross-references with Vatican II, Papal documents & other resources, see Family Wisdom Library on page 734.
For commentaries on each question with Cardinal Arinze, Sr. John Vianney and Fr. Straub (in Spanish), see Appendix C.

1. One source of Divine Truth is Holy Scripture.

Holy Scripture (or the Bible) is the collection of books accepted as definitive by the Catholic Church. Sacred Scripture is the authentic, inspired record of the revelations made to mankind by God about Himself and about His Will for men. It is divided into the Old and New Testaments in order to distinguish between the earlier Covenant between God and the Jewish nation, given to Moses on Mount Sinai, and the later definitive Covenant between God and the followers of Jesus Christ throughout the world.

#P26-6-2

The four Gospels in the New Testament (Matthew, Mark, Luke, and John) are the heart of all the Scriptures because they encompass the life and teachings of our Savior, Jesus Christ.

In the New Testament, the Old Testament is generally spoken of as "the Scriptures" or the "sacred writings" (cf. Matthew 21:42). Gradually the word "Scripture" has become a synonym for the Bible as a whole. "Testament" has the meaning of "covenant," with reference to the two covenants which God established with His People in human history.

The Catholic Church has, more than once, taught which books are to be regarded as inspired, and which, therefore, belong to the Bible. The complete list of sacred books in the Bible is called the canon of Scripture. It is made up of forty-six books for the Old Testament and twenty-seven books for the New Testament. The four Gospels in the New Testament (Matthew, Mark, Luke, and John) are the heart of all the Scriptures because they encompass the life and teachings of our Savior, Jesus Christ.

At the Ecumenical Council of Trent, in 1546, the biblical canon was solemnly defined, and the Latin Vulgate version of the Bible, written by St. Jerome, was declared to be authentic. In 1943, Pope Pius XII reconfirmed the biblical canon and the authenticity of the Vulgate. But he made some important declarations which encouraged other translations of the Bible based on the Hebrew and Greek manuscripts.

2. The second source of Divine Truth is Sacred Tradition (also known as Apostolic Tradition or simply Tradition).

The term "tradition" literally means, a "handing on," referring to the passing down of God's revealed word. It has two distinct meanings.

#A18-16-2

Tradition means all of divine revelation, as it has been passed on from one generation of believers to the next, and as it is preserved under divine guidance by the Church established by Christ.

First, Tradition means all of divine revelation, from the dawn of human history to the end of the apostolic age, as it has been passed on from one generation of believers to the next, and as it is preserved under divine guidance by the Church established by Christ.

Tradition also means, within all transmitted revelation, that part of God's revealed word which is not contained in Sacred Scripture. The Second Vatican Council tells us how Sacred Tradition was handed on: "It was done by the apostles who handed on, by the spoken word of their preaching, by the example they gave, by the institutions they established, what they themselves had received–whether from the lips of Christ, from his way of life and his works, or whether they had learned it at the prompting of the Holy Spirit" (*Dei Verbum, 7).*

#E5-1

Tradition also means, within all transmitted revelation, that part of God's revealed word which is not contained in Sacred Scripture and was handed on by the Apostles.

Sacred Scripture

"I commend you because you remember me in everything and maintain the traditions even as I have delivered them to you." *1 Corinthians 11:2*

So then, brethren, stand firm and hold to the traditions which you were taught by us, either by word of mouth or by letter. *2 Thessalonians 2:15*

All scripture is inspired by God and profitable for teaching, for reproof, for correction, and for training in righteousness. *2 Timothy 3:16*

For the word of God is living and active, sharper than any two-edged sword, piercing to the division of soul and spirit, of joints and marrow, and discerning the thoughts and intentions of the heart. *Hebrews 4:12*

#S2-261

So then, brethren, stand firm and hold to the traditions which you were taught by us, either by word of mouth or by letter. *(2 Thessalonians 2:15)*

Catechism of the Catholic Church

81 "*Sacred Scripture* is the speech of God as it is put down in writing under the breath of the Holy Spirit."[1]

"And [Holy] *Tradition* transmits in its entirety the Word of God which has been entrusted to the apostles by Christ the Lord and the Holy Spirit. It transmits it to the successors of the apostles so that, enlightened by the Spirit of truth, they may faithfully preserve, expound, and spread it abroad by their preaching."[2]

Splendor of Truth

"This Tradition which comes from the Apostles, progresses in the Church under the assistance of the Holy Spirit." In the Holy Spirit, the Church receives and hands down the Scripture as the witness to the "great things" which God has done in history (cf. Lk 1:49).

...Within Tradition, the authentic interpretation of the Lord's law develops, with the help of the Holy Spirit. The same Spirit who is at the origin of the Revelation of Jesus' commandments and teachings, guarantees that they will be reverently preserved, faithfully expounded and correctly applied in different times and places. *(section 27)*

Christians have a great help for the formation of conscience in the Church and her Magisterium. As the Council affirms: "In forming their consciences the Christian faithful must give careful attention to the sacred and certain teaching of the Church. For the Catholic Church is by the will of Christ the teacher of truth. Her charge is to announce and teach authentically that truth which is Christ, and at the same time with her authority to declare and confirm the principles of the moral order which derive from human nature itself." *(section 64)*

Catechism by Diagram

#C15-59

The Church and the Bible. It is necessary that the living voice of Christ in His Church (St. Peter's Basilica), to which He sent His Holy Spirit (dove), interprets Sacred Scripture for us (Old and New Testament books). Sacred Scripture and Tradition, dating from Christ or His Apostles, are equally important as sources of Divine Truth. They are not two separate sources of Christian truth. Tradition is a complement to the Bible. We nourish our souls not only on Christ present in the Eucharist, but also on the Word of God as it is presented to us in the Bible and in Sacred Tradition. God inspired the writers of the biblical books to write what He wanted written and preserved them from error. Through the infallible authority of His Church, God showed which books, of all the books that had been written, were the ones inspired by Him and, therefore, were a part of Sacred Scripture.

#F1-68-2

Christians have a great help for the formation of conscience in the Church and her Magisterium. *(Splendor of Truth, 64)*

Vatican Council II

The Christian economy, therefore, since it is the new and definitive covenant, will never pass away; and no new public revelation is to be expected before the glorious manifestation of our Lord, Jesus Christ (cf. 1 Tim. 6:14 and Tit. 2:13). *Dei Verbum, 4*

Sacred Tradition and sacred Scripture, then, are bound closely together, and communicate one with the other. For both of them, flowing out from the same divine well-spring, come together in some fashion to form one thing, and move towards the same goal. Sacred Scripture is the speech of God as it is put down in writing under the breath of the Holy Spirit. And Tradition transmits in its entirety the Word of God which has been entrusted to the apostles by Christ the Lord and the Holy Spirit. It transmits it to the successors of the apostles so that, enlightened by the Spirit of truth, they may faithfully preserve, expound and spread it abroad by their preaching. Thus it comes about that the Church does not draw her certainty about all revealed truths from the holy Scriptures alone. Hence, both Scripture and Tradition must be accepted and honored with equal feelings of devotion and reverence. *Dei Verbum, 9*

The task of giving an authentic interpretation of the Word of God, whether in its written form or in the form of Tradition, has been entrusted to the living teaching office of the Church alone. Its authority in this matter is exercised in the name of Jesus Christ. Yet this Magisterium [teaching authority] is not superior to the Word of God, but is its servant. It teaches only what has been handed on to it. At the divine command and with the help of the Holy Spirit, it listens to this devotedly, guards it with dedication and expounds it faithfully. All that it proposes for belief as being divinely revealed is drawn from this single deposit of faith. *Dei Verbum, 10*

Catechism by Diagram

#T8-1

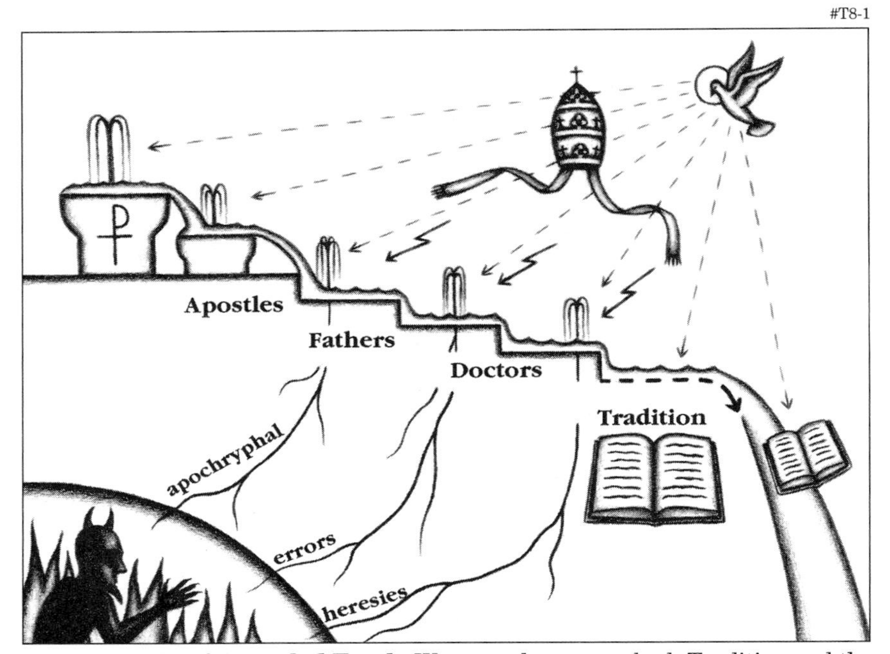

The Fountain of Revealed Truth. We must draw upon both Tradition and the Bible for a full knowledge of Christ and His teachings. The oral teachings of the Apostles have been handed on, from generation to generation, through the popes and bishops of the Catholic Church (tiara of the Pope). These teachings were put into writing by the early Christian writers, whom we call the Fathers of the Church. Christian writers and theologians called Doctors further explained these truths. Much of the Tradition of the Church has been given to us in the decrees of the Church councils and pronouncements of the popes (Holy Spirit guiding the Pope and the Church). Only the Church can say which truths are a part of Tradition. The devil and enemies of the Church have always tried to poison the water of truth (errors, heresies). The revealed truths are like pure waters coming from the fountain of Christ Who said, "I am the Truth" (fountain with monogram, water flowing down).

> Holy Mother Church, relying on the faith of the apostolic age, accepts as sacred and canonical the books of the Old and the New Testaments, whole and entire, with all their parts, on the grounds that, written under the inspiration of the Holy Spirit (cf. Jn. 20:31; 2 Tim. 3:16; 2 Pet. 1:19-21; 3:15-16), they have God as their author, and have been handed on as such to the Church herself. To compose the sacred books, God chose certain men who, all the while he employed them in this task, made full use of their powers and faculties so that, though he acted in them and by them, it was as true authors that they consigned to writing whatever he wanted written, and no more.
>
> Since, therefore, all that the inspired authors, or sacred writers, affirm should be regarded as affirmed by the Holy Spirit, we must acknowledge that the books of Scripture, firmly, faithfully and without error, teach that truth which

God, for the sake of our salvation, wished to see confided to the sacred Scriptures. *Dei Verbum, 11*

It is common knowledge that among all the inspired writings, even among those of the New Testament, the Gospels have a special place, and rightly so, because they are our principal source for the life and teaching of the Incarnate Word, our Saviour. *Dei Verbum, 18*

The Church has always venerated the divine Scriptures as she venerated the Body of the Lord, in so far as she never ceases, particularly in the sacred liturgy, to partake of the bread of life and to offer it to the faithful from the one table of the Word of God and the Body of Christ. *Dei Verbum, 21*

So may it come that, by the reading and study of the sacred books "the Word of God may speed on and triumph" (2 Th. 3:1) and the treasure of Revelation entrusted to the Church may more and more fill the hearts of men. Just as from constant attendance at the eucharistic mystery the life of the Church draws increase, so a new impulse of spiritual life may be expected from increased veneration of the Word of God, which "stands forever" (Is. 40:8; cf. 1 Pet. 1:23-25). *Dei Verbum, 26*

Sacred scripture is of the greatest importance in the celebration of the liturgy. For it is from it that lessons are read and explained in the homily, and psalms are sung. It is from the scriptures that the prayers, collects, and hymns draw their inspiration and their force, and that actions and signs derive their meaning. *Sacrosanctum Concilium, 24*

#B3-1-2

Holy Mother Church, relying on the faith of the apostolic age, accepts as sacred and canonical the books of the Old and the New Testaments, whole and entire, written under the inspiration of the Holy Spirit, they have God as their author, and have been handed on as such to the Church herself. *(Dei Verbum, 11)*

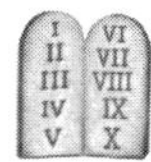

Doctrine • Moral • Worship Exercise

(See Appendix A for answer key, question 141.)

1. Why must Sacred Scripture and Sacred Tradition be accepted and honored with equal devotion and reverence?
2. Make a concrete action plan which will enable you and your family to meditate on the Bible frequently and deepen your understanding of Sacred Tradition by reading books endorsed by the Magisterium, the teaching office of the Church. Write down your action plan for your family and put it in a place where you will see it every day. Ask God for the grace to faithfully carry out your action plan.
3. Read 2 Timothy 3:16, 2 Thess. 2:15, and Divine Revelation, section 26 (see the references after question 141). Thank God for revealing Himself and His plan for our Salvation through Sacred Scripture and Sacred Tradition.

Summary Prayer

Heavenly Father, You inspired the writers of the biblical books to write what You wanted written, and You preserved them from error. You nourish our souls through Christ present in the Eucharist and through Your Word as it is presented to us in the Bible. But You have also given us Tradition as a complement to the Bible and as an equally important source of Your truth. Give us Your Holy Spirit that He may help us to draw from the Bible and Tradition a better knowledge of Christ and His teachings.

Almighty God, You Who first ordered light to shine in darkness, flood our hearts with the glorious Gospel of Christ, Your matchless image, and transform us more and more into His very likeness. Only Your Son, our Savior, is the true Teacher of Righteousness; help us to grasp the inner meaning of His Gospel and the happiness that it promises. May we hunger for Your Word more than for bodily food. Fill our hearts with His light. May we always acknowledge Christ as our Savior and be more faithful to His Gospel. We ask this in His most holy Name. Amen.

Q. 142. What are some other gifts of the Catholic Church besides the truths of the faith?

Other gifts of the Catholic Church besides the truths of the faith are the sacraments (cf. Q. 140).

Jesus taught the Apostles that His grace was to be given to men through them. It would be through the Apostles and their successors, for example, that He would forgive sin and give the world His Precious Body and Blood in the Holy Eucharist.

#S11-27

Jesus taught the Apostles that His grace was to be given to men through them.

In the Person of Jesus Christ, God first laid the foundation of His Church. This was a task spread over three years, from Jesus' first public miracle at Cana until His ascent into Heaven. During this time Jesus chose His twelve Apostles, whom He had destined to be the first bishops of His Church. He instructed and trained them for their duties and prepared them for the task of establishing the Kingdom of God. During that time, Jesus gave His Church the Seven Sacraments—the seven channels through which the graces He would gain for mankind upon the Cross would flow into men's souls.

Catechism of the Catholic Church
Q. 142. Paragraphs 1278, 1284, 1316-1320, 1407-1412, 1446, 1480, 1531-1532.

For cross-references with Vatican II, Papal documents & other resources, see Family Wisdom Library on page 734.
For commentaries on each question with Cardinal Arinze, Sr. John Vianney and Fr. Straub (in Spanish), see Appendix C.

Q. 143. Are there other gifts of the Church besides the truths of the faith and the sacraments?

Yes, the other gifts of the Church besides the truths of the faith and the sacraments are the ministries inherited from the Apostles (cf. Q. 140).

#F1-58-2

Today the Church continues, through the Pope and its bishops and aided by priests and deacons who are in union with the Holy Father in Rome, to be a community in Christ.

St. Peter was Christ's chief ambassador on earth. The whole Church was entrusted to his care. The Apostles shared their responsibility with others, called bishops. Today the Church continues, through the Pope and its bishops and aided by priests and deacons who are in union with the Holy Father in Rome, to be a community in Christ. They serve people by giving Christ's saving truth and His divine life to them through grace and the sacraments. The Catholic Church inherited these ministries from the Apostles.

With the powers given to them by Christ, the Apostles were His witnesses in the world. He said to them before ascending into Heaven, "But you shall receive power when the Holy Spirit has come upon you; and you shall be my witnesses in Jerusalem and in all Judea and Samaria and to the end of the earth" (Acts 1:8).

Splendor of Truth

The Church's Pastors, in communion with the Successor of Peter, are close to the faithful in this effort; they guide and accompany them by their authoritative teaching, finding ever new ways of speaking with love and mercy not only to believers but to all people of good will. *(section 3)*

Catechism of the Catholic Church
Q. 143. Paragraphs **880-896**.

For cross-references with Vatican II, Papal documents & other resources, see Family Wisdom Library on page 734.
For commentaries on each question with Cardinal Arinze, Sr. John Vianney and Fr. Straub (in Spanish), see Appendix C.

Summary Prayer

Lord, You are always present in Your Church. Through Your Holy Spirit, guide it into all truth.

Father, You established Your ancient covenant by signs and wonders, but You confirmed the new one in a more wonderful way through the sacrifice of Your Son. Guide Your Church in the pathways of life, that we may be led to the land of promise and celebrate Your Name with lasting praise.

You sustain us with the Word and the Body of Your Son. Watch over us with loving care; help the Church to grow in faith, holiness, charity, and loving service. You have set us firm within Your Church, which You built upon the rock of Peter's faith. Bless us with a faith that never falters.

We celebrate the memorial of the love of Your Son in the Eucharist. May His saving work bring Salvation to all the world through the ministry of Your Church. We ask this in the name of Jesus Christ our Lord. Amen.

Q. 144. By means of these gifts, what does the Catholic Church do for mankind?

By means of these gifts, the Catholic Church can act and grow as a community in Christ, by serving men and giving them His saving word and activity.

The Catholic Church is nourished by God's saving truth, the sacraments, and the apostolic ministry. Through these gifts, the Church Militant (the Church on earth) is able to grow and to continue Christ's saving work in the world.

Sacred Scripture

I hope to come to you soon, but I am writing these instructions to you so that, if I am delayed, you may know how one ought to behave in the household of God, which is the church of the living God, the pillar and the bulwark of the truth. *1 Timothy 3:14-15*

Vatican Council II

In the human nature united to himself, the son of God, by overcoming death through his own death and resurrection, redeemed man and changed him into a new creation (cf. Gal. 6:15; 2 Cor. 5:17). For by communicating his Spirit,

Sacred Scripture
Q. 144. Jn 6:35-59; Acts 13:26-42.

Catechism of the Catholic Church
Q. 144. Paragraphs 14, 874, 876-878, **1216**, 1226, 1241, **1288**, 1336, **1428**, **1449**, **1458**, 1520-1521, 1576, **1585-1587**, **1641**, 1652, 1664.

For cross-references with Vatican II, Papal documents & other resources, see Family Wisdom Library on page 734.
For commentaries on each question with Cardinal Arinze, Sr. John Vianney and Fr. Straub (in Spanish), see Appendix C.

Christ mystically constitutes as his body those brothers of his who are called together from every nation. In that body the life of Christ is communicated to those who believe and who, through the sacraments, are united in a hidden and real way to Christ in his passion and glorification. *Lumen Gentium, 7*

#B7-2-2

By means of the gifts of the apostolic ministries, the truths of the Faith and the Seven Sacraments, the Catholic Church can act and grow as a community in Christ, by serving men and giving them His saving word and activity.

Doctrine • Moral • Worship Exercise

(See Appendix A for answer key, questions 142-144.)

1. What does the Catholic Church do for mankind through the truths, ministries, and sacraments entrusted to her by God?
2. Do you try to get to know the bishop of your diocese and the priest(s) in your parish? How can you and your family show support for your parish priest in word and deed?
3. Reflect on the important role of the Pope, bishops and priests in our Christian lives. Try to pray for their protection and guidance every day.

Chapter Summary Prayer

Lord, our faithful God, You permitted the great Temple in Jerusalem, the symbol of the Old Covenant, to be destroyed and Your people to be persecuted by unbelievers. Do not forget the New Covenant, sealed with the Blood of Your Son. Make the Church Your spiritual house and make us living stones built upon Christ so that a full and lasting temple may be built at last.

Heavenly Father, You anointed Your servant Jesus with holy oil and raised Him higher than all kings on earth. In this anointing You fulfilled the promise made to David's descendants and established a lasting covenant through Your first-born Son. Remember Your covenant, so that we, who are signed with the Blood of Your Son, may sing Your mercies forever.

Purify and renew Your Church through Your gifts of truth and the sacraments, that she may give an ever greater witness to You. Your word of life gives us a new birth; may we receive it with open hearts, live it with joy, and express it in love. May we grow in the life of Christ through the sacraments of the Church, especially the Holy Eucharist. Keep us faithful to Your Son, Who alone has the words of eternal life and is Himself the Bread of Life, that He may lead us as the loyal sheep of His flock to the eternal joys of Your Kingdom. We ask this through Jesus our Savior. Amen.

Thought Provokers

Please see Appendix B for the answers.

Q. 140: What is the most basic and important gift of God to His Church?

Q. 141: Does the Bible give us any hint of the existence of Holy Tradition?

Q. 142: What constitutes a valid sacrament?

Q. 143: With the exception of the auxiliary bishops of the Diocese of Rome, and those who serve in the Roman Curia, are the Bishops of the Catholic Church representatives of the Bishop of Rome, the Pope?

Q. 144: How should we receive Our Lord's divine gifts to us?

#C15-26

And he has put all things under his feet and has made him the head over all things for the church, which is his body, the fullness of him who fills all in all. *(Ephesians 1:22)*

CHAPTER FORTY-THREE

The Catholic Church Belongs to Christ

Q. 145. Why does the Catholic Church belong entirely to Christ?

The Catholic Church belongs entirely to Christ, because He is the Head of the Church, its Founder, its Spouse, and its Savior. He continues to do His saving work in and through the Church.

In the New Testament we see Christ's preparation for the Church, His promises concerning it, and the beginning of their rich fulfillment.

#C15-40

The Catholic Church belongs entirely to Christ, because He is the Head of the Church, its Founder, its Spouse, and its Savior.

Sacred Scripture
Q. 145. Jn 8:12, 14:5-7.

Catechism of the Catholic Church
Q. 145. Paragraphs 763, 765-**766**, 768, 786, **792**, **795-796**, 926, 973.

For cross-references with Vatican II, Papal documents & other resources, see Family Wisdom Library on page 734.
For commentaries on each question with Cardinal Arinze, Sr. John Vianney and Fr. Straub (in Spanish), see Appendix C.

Christ is the Light of the world. The Church receives its being and mission from Him. The Church is not merely a society of men; it has a certain sacred dimension because of the inseparable union which Christ established between it and Himself.

#R4.1-8-2

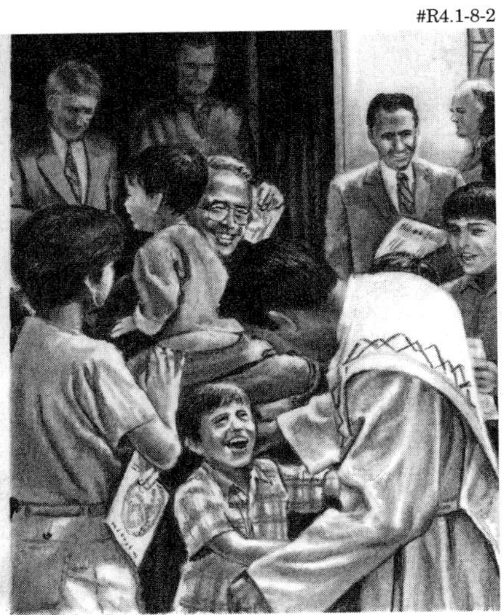

Christ is the Light of the world. The Church receives its being and mission from Him.

Sacred Scripture

"And I tell you, you are Peter, and on this rock I will build my church, and the powers of death shall not prevail against it." *Matthew 16:18*

And he has put all things under his feet and has made him the head over all things for the church, which is his body, the fullness of him who fills all in all. *Ephesians 1:22*

For the husband is the head of the wife as Christ is the head of the church, his body, and is himself its Savior. *Ephesians 5:23*

Catechism of the Catholic Church

789 The comparison of the Church with the body casts light on the intimate bond between Christ and his Church. Not only is she gathered *around him*; she is united *in him*, in his body. Three aspects of the Church as the Body of Christ are to be more specifically noted: the unity of all her members with each other as a result of their union with Christ; Christ as the head of the Body; and the Church as bride of Christ.

Q. 146. How does the Catholic see the Church?

The Catholic always sees the Church in its relationship to Christ. It is not the Church as such that is the primary object of Catholic faith. The Catholic believes in Christ and in His Father and in the Holy Spirit. In the Creed, the Catholic professes his belief in "the holy catholic Church" precisely because he sees the Church as a presence of Christ and of His Spirit.

The Catholic believes what the Church teaches precisely because he recognizes Christ's authority in the Church.

The Catholic recognizes a duty to further the work of the Church precisely because he sees the mission of the Church as a continuation of Christ's work in the world.

#T3-53

The Catholic believes in Christ and in His Father and in the Holy Spirit. He professes his belief in "the holy catholic Church" precisely because he sees the Church as a presence of Christ and of His Spirit.

Sacred Scripture
Q. 146. 1 Cor 1:10; Eph 2:14-22.

Catechism of the Catholic Church
Q. 146. Paragraphs 749, 763-766, **771**.

For cross-references with Vatican II, Papal documents & other resources, see Family Wisdom Library on page 734.
For commentaries on each question with Cardinal Arinze, Sr. John Vianney and Fr. Straub (in Spanish), see Appendix C.

Sacred Scripture

For just as the body is one and has many members, and all the members of the body, though many, are one body, so it is with Christ. For by one Spirit we were all baptized into one body...and all were made to drink of one Spirit.
1 Corinthians 12:12-13

Q. 147. Why is the Catholic Church a living continuation of Christ on earth?

The Church is a living continuation of Christ on earth because Christ spiritually and mystically lives and acts through the Church. It is a living organism, not just an organization.

#S11-8-2

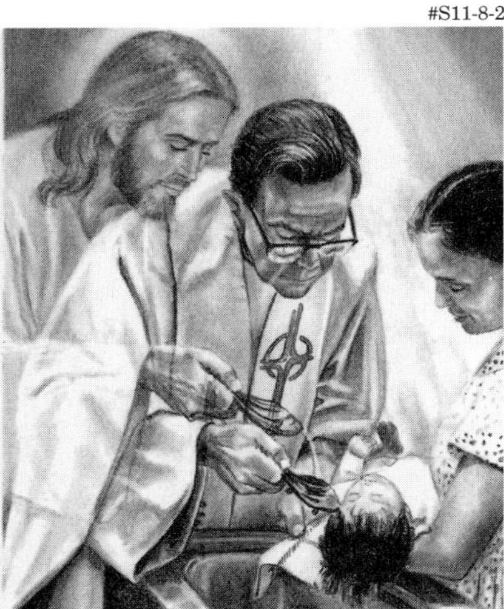

Christ organized the Church to carry on His work in the world and to bring His ministry and truth to all men and all ages.

Christ organized the Church to carry on His work in the world and to bring His ministry and truth to all men and all ages.

It is Christ Who accomplishes all that is done in the Church for man's Salvation. The institution which is the Church survives because it comes from Christ, and because He promises to be with it to the end of time (cf. Matthew 18:20).

The Church is a living continuation on earth of its divine Founder. Jesus is indeed the Son of God, but He is truly a man too, the Son of Mary. Similarly, in the Church, the Mystical Body of Christ, is found the presence of Christ, its Head, and His Holy Spirit, the

Sacred Scripture
Q. 147. Jn 15:1-11.

Catechism of the Catholic Church
Q. 147. Paragraphs 785, 789, **792**, **795**, 809, 863, 865.

For cross-references with Vatican II, Papal documents & other resources, see Family Wisdom Library on page 734.
For commentaries on each question with Cardinal Arinze, Sr. John Vianney and Fr. Straub (in Spanish), see Appendix C.

bearer of heavenly gifts. Yet, the Church is also very human. Its sublime mission is carried out by its baptized members. Among them are the ordained priests, who perform sacred ceremonies, called the sacraments, with ordinary realities of human life such as bread, water, wine, and oil. These ceremonies have been entrusted to the priests by Christ.

The Church acts for Christ. When a priest gives us a sacrament, it is Christ Who gives us the sacrament through the priest. When the Church speaks His word to us, it is Christ Who speaks to us and calls us to faith. The teaching and ruling authority of the Church is the shepherding of Christ.

He is the image of the invisible God and in him all things came into being. He is the head of the body which is the Church. All the members must be formed in his likeness, until Christ be formed in them (cf. Gal. 4:19). *(Lumen Gentium, 7)*

Catechism of the Catholic Church

864 "Christ, sent by the Father, is the source of the Church's whole apostolate"; thus the fruitfulness of apostolate for ordained ministers as well as for lay people clearly depends on their vital union with Christ.[1] In keeping with their vocations, the demands of the times and the various gifts of the Holy Spirit, the apostolate assumes the most varied forms. But charity, drawn from the Eucharist above all, is always "as it were, the soul of the whole apostolate."[2]

Splendor of Truth

Jesus Christ, the "light of the nations," shines upon the face of his Church, which he sends forth to the whole world to proclaim the Gospel to every creature (cf. Mk 16:15). *(section 2)*

Vatican Council II

The head of this body is Christ. He is the image of the invisible God and in him all things came into being. He is before all creatures and in him all things hold together. He is the head of the body which is the Church. He is the beginning, the firstborn from the dead, that in all things he might hold the primacy (cf. Col. 1:15-18). By the greatness of his power he rules heaven and earth, and with his all-surpassing perfection and activity he fills the whole body with the riches of his glory (cf. Eph. 1:18-23). All the members must be formed in his likeness, until Christ be formed in them (cf. Gal. 4:19). Lumen Gentium, 7

Q. 148. Why is the Catholic Church called the sacrament of Christ?

The Church is called the sacrament of Christ because it is a visible reality which Christ has formed in this world as a sacred sign of His presence. It is the sign and also the means He uses to give us the unity and holiness He actually confers through it. It is a sacrament of His presence because He is really present in it.

As a family called to share in the life of the Trinity, the Church has an eternal destiny. But in its time of pilgrimage on earth, it also has a visible, sacramental dimension: it exists also as a sign. Because the Church is a sign, it leads us to what it signifies, that is, to Christ, our God. When we finally come to God in eternity, the Church, as a material and time bound instrument of God's will and grace, will have no further reason to exist. It will have accomplished what God put it on earth to do.

The sacrament, which is the visible Church, is now, in time, a precious indispensable gift of Christ. It is the work of Christ. It will last, as He promises, until the end of the world, when it will reach its fulfillment in glorious union in Christ. Its task on earth will not be finished until Christ brings His redemptive work to completion and God has become, as St. Paul put it, "all, and in all" (Colossians 3:11).

Sacred Scripture

For we are God's fellow workers; you are God's field, God's building... For no other foundation can any one lay than that which is laid, which is Jesus Christ. *1 Corinthians 3:9, 11*

Catechism of the Catholic Church

775 "The Church, in Christ, is like a sacrament—a sign and instrument, that is, of communion with God and of unity among all men."[1] The Church's first purpose is to be the sacrament of the *inner union of men with God.* Because men's communion with one another is rooted in that union with God, the Church is also the sacrament of the *unity of the human race.* In her, this unity is already begun, since she gathers men "from every nation, from all tribes and peoples and tongues";[2] at the same time, the Church is the "sign and instrument" of the full realization of the unity yet to come.

Sacred Scripture
Q. 148. Eph 1:20-23, 2:19-22; Col 1:18-19.

Catechism of the Catholic Church
Q. 148. Paragraphs 766, **774**, 776.

For cross-references with Vatican II, Papal documents & other resources, see Family Wisdom Library on page 734.
For commentaries on each question with Cardinal Arinze, Sr. John Vianney and Fr. Straub (in Spanish), see Appendix C.

The Church is called the sacrament of Christ because it is a visible reality which Christ has formed in this world as a sacred sign of His presence.

Summary Prayer

Jesus, in Your questions to Peter before bestowing on him the primacy of authority over Your Church, we sense three great yearnings of Your Sacred Heart: the yearning to prove to us Your love, the yearning for our love in return, and the yearning for us to be able to find You and love You in souls.

Christian love is self-giving, Christian love is sacrificial, and Christian love is expressed in deeds rather than in words. Your Heart loves souls with an everlasting love, a love greater than that of any human being, a love that is both divine and human, a love that is symbolized by Your Sacred Heart. May Your great love flood our souls and bring us to the rewards of eternal life. Amen.

Q. 149. What do we mean when we speak of the Church in Heaven?

When we speak of the Church in Heaven, we do not mean the Church in the condition in which it is a sign, with ministers and sacraments; these will cease. As signs and instruments, they will be absorbed into the heavenly realities which they now serve. When we speak of the Church in Heaven, we mean the union of the saints with Christ and the life they have in Him, with the Father and the Holy Spirit.

#E4.4-10

When we speak of the Church in Heaven, we do not mean the Church in the condition in which it is a sign, with ministers and sacraments; these will cease. We mean the union of the saints with Christ and the life they have in Him, with the Father and the Holy Spirit.

Sacred Scripture

For he will render to every man according to his works: to those who by patience in well-doing seek for glory and honor and immortality, he will give eternal life. *Romans 2:6-7*

For now we see in a mirror dimly, but then face to face. Now I know in part; then I shall understand fully, even as I have been fully understood. *1 Corinthians 13:12*

We shall be like him, for we shall see him as he is. *1 John 3:2*

Sacred Scripture
Q. 149. Jn 14:1-3; 1 Thess 4:16-17; Rev 7:13-17.

Catechism of the Catholic Church
Q. 149. Paragraphs **1023-1029**.

For cross-references with Vatican II, Papal documents & other resources, see Family Wisdom Library on page 734.
For commentaries on each question with Cardinal Arinze, Sr. John Vianney and Fr. Straub (in Spanish), see Appendix C.

Catechism of the Catholic Church

1026 By his death and Resurrection, Jesus Christ has "opened" heaven to us. The life of the blessed consists in the full and perfect possession of the fruits of the redemption accomplished by Christ. He makes partners in his heavenly glorification those who have believed in him and remained faithful to his will. Heaven is the blessed community of all who are perfectly incorporated into Christ.

Vatican Council II

Already the final age of the world is with us (cf. 1 Cor. 10:11) and the renewal of the world is irrevocably under way; it is even now anticipated in a certain real way, for the Church on earth is endowed already with a sanctity that is real though imperfect. However, until there be realized new heavens and a new earth in which justice dwells (cf. 2 Pet. 3:13) the pilgrim Church, in its sacraments and institutions, which belong to this present age, carries the mark of this world which will pass, and she herself takes her place among the creatures which groan and travail yet and await the revelation of the sons of God (cf. Rom. 8:19-22). *Lumen Gentium, 48*

We must all appear "before the judgment seat of Christ, so that each one may receive good or evil, according to what he has done in the body" (2 Cor. 5:10). *Lumen Gentium, 48*

#M3-254

For now we see in a mirror dimly, but then face to face. Now I know in part; then I shall understand fully, even as I have been fully understood.
(1 Corinthians 13:12)

Summary Prayer

Surround Your people, Lord Jesus, within the safety of Your Church, which You preserve on its rock foundation. Let us neither reach out our hands to evil deeds, nor be destroyed by the insidious snares of the enemy; instead, bring us to share the love of the saints in light. We ask this in Your most holy Name. Amen.

Doctrine • Moral • Worship Exercise

(See Appendix A for answer key, questions 145–149.)

1. How does the Catholic Church finish the work begun by Christ?
2. How can you be a sacrament of Christ's presence in your family, school, and workplace?
3. Using the Chapter Summary Prayer, praise Jesus for His sacred presence in the Church.

Chapter Summary Prayer

Lord God, Your only Son wept over ancient Jerusalem, which was soon to be destroyed for its lack of faith. He established the new Jerusalem firmly upon the rock and made it the Mother of the faithful. Make us rejoice in Your Church and grant that all people may be reborn in the freedom of Your Spirit. Grant us always to seek the wisdom of the Cross and the blessing of those who suffer for the sake of justice. May we always be filled with Your happiness and remain safe under the guidance and care of the shepherds to whom You have entrusted Your flock.

May the faithful respect and love the Pope and the bishops in union with him and the priests and deacons who assist them in the care of Your Church. Help all pastors to edify, both by word and example, those over whom they have charge, that they may reach everlasting life together with the flocks entrusted to them. Be their light, their strength, and their consolation.

Lord our God, King of the universe, Creator of light and darkness, origin and preserver of all that exists, remember Your Church, protect it from all evil, perfect it in Your love, gather it from the four winds, and bring it into Your Kingdom, for Yours is the power and the glory forever and ever. Amen.

Thought Provokers

Please see Appendix B for the answers.

Q. 145: If the Catholic Church belongs entirely to Christ, what about her members?

Q. 146: How should Catholics respect the Church?

Q. 147: A. The Catholic Church is a living continuation of Christ in space and time. What does this truth imply for us her living members?

B. Can you think of several things that Jesus expects of us to reach out to others?

Q. 148: Can we Catholics be regarded as sacraments of Christ?

Q. 149: In what does the happiness of Heaven chiefly consist?

#P2-1

The Catholic Church is a hierarchical society. It is a people guided by its bishops, who are in union with the Pope, the Bishop of Rome.

CHAPTER FORTY-FOUR

Leaders of the Catholic Church

Q. 150. Does the Catholic Church have leaders?

Yes, in God's plan, the Catholic Church is a hierarchical society. It is a people guided by its bishops, who are in union with the Pope, the Bishop of Rome.

By means of the Sacrament of Holy Orders, bishops (the successors of the Apostles) and priests have received the powers of Jesus Christ. Bishops and priests, together with deacons, are those in the Church who have been given the authority to teach for Christ, to distribute His sacramental graces to mankind, and to watch over His flock. Christ continues His work in the Church, in a special way, through the ministry of His bishops, priests, and deacons.

#R6-9-2

Bishops and priests, together with deacons, are those in the Church who have been given the authority to teach for Christ, to distribute His sacramental graces to mankind, and to watch over His flock.

Sacred Scripture

If he refuses to listen to them, tell it to the church; and if he refuses to listen even to the church, let him be to you as a Gentile and a tax collector. *Matthew 18:17*

Sacred Scripture
Q. 150. Mt 28:18-20; Lk 10:16; Acts 1:8, 14:21-23.

Catechism of the Catholic Church
Q. 150. Paragraphs **877-887**.

For cross-references with Vatican II, Papal documents & other resources, see Family Wisdom Library on page 734.
For commentaries on each question with Cardinal Arinze, Sr. John Vianney and Fr. Straub (in Spanish), see Appendix C.

Catechism by Diagram

#C15-79

The Catholic Church, a Society with Leaders. By God's design, the Catholic Church is a society with leaders—with a hierarchy. The Church is a people guided by the bishops who are in union with the Pope. Christ (large cross) conferred on the Apostles and their successors the duty of teaching, sanctifying, and ruling in His name and power. The Pope is the Bishop of Rome (St. Peter's Basilica), the Vicar of Christ. He is the successor to the office of Peter. The whole flock of Christ is in his care and under his guidance, and he is the head (tiara) of the College of the Bishops (miters). The Pope is the highest Christian teaching authority in the world; he is the supreme ruler or shepherd of the Catholic Church.

Remember your leaders, those who spoke to you the word of God; consider the outcome of their life, and imitate their faith. Jesus Christ is the same yesterday and today and for ever. *Hebrews 13:7-8*

Catechism of the Catholic Church

876 Intrinsically linked to the sacramental nature of ecclesial ministry is *its character as service*. Entirely dependent on Christ who gives mission and authority, ministers are truly "slaves of Christ,"[1] in the image of him who freely took "the form of a slave" for us.[2] Because the word and grace of which they are ministers are not their own, but are given to them by Christ for the sake of others, they must freely become the slaves of all.[3]

#C15-13-2

In order that the episcopate itself, however, might be one and undivided he put Peter at the head of the other apostles, and in him he set up a lasting and visible source and foundation of the unity both of faith and of communion.
(Lumen Gentium, 18)

Vatican Council II

"This Church, constituted and organized as a society in the present world, subsists in the Catholic Church, which is governed by the successor of Peter and by the bishops in communion with him. Nevertheless, many elements of sanctification and of truth are found outside its visible confines. Since these are gifts belonging to the Church of Christ, they are forces impelling towards Catholic unity. *Lumen Gentium, 8*

"This sacred synod, following in the steps of the First Vatican Council, teaches and declares with it that Jesus Christ, the eternal pastor, set up the holy Church by entrusting the apostles with their mission as he himself had been sent by the Father (cf. Jn. 20:21). He willed that their successors, the bishops namely, should be the shepherds in his Church until the end of the world. In order that the episcopate itself, however, might be one and undivided he put Peter at the head of the other apostles, and in him he set up a lasting and visible source and foundation of the unity both of faith and of communion." *Lumen Gentium, 18*

Summary Prayer

Jesus our High Priest, on Holy Thursday we celebrate the memory of the first Eucharist, at which time You shared with Your Apostles, and now share with Your bishops and priests, Your offices of priestly service in Your Church. Help bishops and priests to renew their dedication to You as priests of Your New Covenant.

May their word and example inspire and guide the Church, may they and all those entrusted to their care come to the joy of everlasting life. Enrich them with the gifts and virtues of true apostles for the good of Your people. You have chosen them to be shepherds of Your flock in the tradition of the Apostles. By governing with fidelity those entrusted to their care, may they guide Your Church as a sign of Salvation for the world.

Give the fullness of Your blessing to the College of Bishops and keep all those entrusted to their care faithful to the teachings of the Apostles. We ask this though the power of Your most Precious Blood. Amen.

Q. 151. Who is the Holy Father, the Pope?

Our Holy Father, the Pope, the Bishop of Rome, is the Vicar of Christ. He is the successor of Peter and holds the office of supreme authority over all the Church, appointed by Christ for the guidance and care of His flock.

The Pope is the head of the College of Bishops. Our Lord solemnly told Peter he was to be supreme shepherd, the head of the Church. "And I tell you, you are Peter, and on this rock I will build my church, and the powers of death shall not prevail against it" (Matthew 16:18).

Christ gave Peter the holy task of giving the entire People of God His teaching and His grace. After His Resurrection Jesus said to Simon Peter, "'Simon, son of John, do you love me more than these?' He said to him, 'Yes, Lord; you know that I love you.' He said to him, 'Feed my lambs.' A second time he said to him, 'Simon, son of John, do you love me?' He said to him, 'Yes, Lord; You know that I love you.' He said to him, 'Tend my sheep'" (John 21:15-16).

Catechism of the Catholic Church
Q. 151. Paragraphs **880-883**.

For cross-references with Vatican II, Papal documents & other resources, see Family Wisdom Library on page 734.
For commentaries on each question with Cardinal Arinze, Sr. John Vianney and Fr. Straub (in Spanish), see Appendix C.

The Pope, as the successor of St. Peter, holds the highest Christian teaching authority in the world; he is the supreme shepherd of the Catholic Church.

#C15-33

Our Holy Father, the Pope, the Bishop of Rome, is the Vicar of Christ. He is the successor of Peter and holds the office of supreme authority over all the Church, appointed by Christ for the guidance and care of His flock.

Catechism of the Catholic Church

881 The Lord made Simon alone, whom he named Peter, the "rock" of his Church. He gave him the keys of his Church and instituted him shepherd of the whole flock.[1] "The office of binding and loosing which was given to Peter was also assigned to the college of apostles united to its head."[2] This pastoral office of Peter and the other apostles belongs to the Church's very foundation and is continued by the bishops under the primacy of the Pope.

Splendor of Truth

At all times, but particularly in the last two centuries, the Popes, whether individually or together with the College of Bishops, have developed and proposed a moral teaching regarding the many different spheres of human life. In Christ's name and with his authority they have exhorted, passed judgment and explained. In their efforts on behalf of humanity, in fidelity to their mission, they have confirmed, supported and consoled. With the guarantee of assistance from the Spirit of truth they have contributed to a better understanding of moral demands in the areas of human sexuality, the family, and social, economic and political life. In the tradition of the Church and in the history of humanity, their teaching represents a constant deepening of knowledge with regard to morality. *(section 4)*

Catechism by Diagram

#C15-80

The Church Gives Christian Witness. Jesus told Peter that he was to be the supreme shepherd, the head of His Church: "You are Peter, and on this rock I will build my church" (rock, St. Peter's Basilica), "and the powers of death (jagged arrows) shall not prevail against it" (Matthew 16:18). The Catholic Church has the Deposit of Faith, the sacraments, and the ministries which it inherited from the Apostles (tiara). Through these gifts of God, the Church is able to act and grow as a community in Christ, by serving mankind and giving men His saving word and activity. The Church witnesses to Christ in every part of the world (boat of the missionary).

#C15-51-2

Christ gave Peter the holy task of giving the entire People of God His teaching and His grace. The Pope, as the successor of St. Peter, holds the highest Christian teaching authority in the world; he is the supreme shepherd of the Catholic Church.

Vatican Council II

In this Church of Christ the Roman Pontiff, as the successor of Peter, to whom Christ entrusted the care of his sheep and his lambs, has been granted by God supreme, full, immediate and universal power in the care of souls. As pastor of all the faithful his mission is to promote the common good of the universal Church and the particular good of all the churches. He is therefore endowed with the primacy of ordinary power over all the churches. *Bishops, 2*

In exercising his supreme, full and immediate authority over the universal Church the Roman Pontiff employs the various departments of the Roman Curia, which act in his name and by his authority for the good of the churches and in the service of the sacred pastors. *Bishops, 9*

Summary Prayer

Heavenly Father, look with love on our Pope, Your appointed successor to St. Peter, on whom You built Your Church. Assist him in his position as the visible center and foundation of our unity in faith and love. May his word and example inspire and guide the Church, and may he and all those who are entrusted to his care come to the joy of everlasting life. We ask this in the name of Jesus, the Lord. Amen.

Q. 152. Who are the bishops of the Church?

The Pope is the successor of St. Peter; the Catholic bishops are the successors of the Apostles. Collectively, the bishops constitute what is known as the Episcopal College, with the Pope as its head.

#C15-38

The Pope is the successor of St. Peter; the Catholic bishops are the successors of the Apostles.

Christ made the Apostles as a stable group, or college. They were jointly responsible for spreading the Gospel of Christ in the whole world. To the whole college, Christ addressed His great missionary command, "Go therefore and make disciples of all nations, baptizing them in the name of the Father and of the Son and of the Holy Spirit, teaching them to observe all that I have commanded you; and lo, I am with you always, to the close of the age" (Matthew 28:19-20).

Jesus said to Peter, "But I have prayed for you that your faith may not fail; and when you have turned again, strengthen your brethren" (Luke 22:32).

When the first council of the Church was held in Jerusalem in the first century, the Apostles, as a college, decided the question

Sacred Scripture
Q. 152. Mt 10:1; Jn 20:19-23; Acts 20:17, 28.

Catechism of the Catholic Church
Q. 152. Paragraphs 880-**893**, 896, 1576.

For cross-references with Vatican II, Papal documents & other resources, see Family Wisdom Library on page 734.
For commentaries on each question with Cardinal Arinze, Sr. John Vianney and Fr. Straub (in Spanish), see Appendix C.

whether Jewish customs should be imposed on non-Jewish converts: "For it has seemed good to the Holy Spirit and to us to lay upon you no greater burden than these necessary things: that you abstain from what has been sacrificed to idols and from blood and from what is strangled and from unchastity. If you keep yourselves from these, you will do well. Farewell" (Acts 15:28-29).

Sacred Scripture

And with great power the apostles gave their testimony to the resurrection of the Lord Jesus, and great grace was upon them all. *Acts 4:33*

For a bishop, as God's steward, must be blameless;... a lover of goodness, master of himself, upright, holy, and self-controlled; he must hold firm to the sure word as taught, so that he may be able to give instruction in sound doctrine and also to confute those who contradict it. *Titus 1:7, 9*

Catechism of the Catholic Church

862 "Just as the office which the Lord confided to Peter alone, as first of the apostles, destined to be transmitted to his successors, is a permanent one, so also endures the office, which the apostles received, of shepherding the Church, a charge destined to be exercised without interruption by the sacred order of bishops."[1] Hence the Church teaches that "the bishops have by divine institution taken the place of the apostles as pastors of the Church, in such wise that whoever listens to them is listening to Christ and whoever despises them despises Christ and him who sent Christ."[2]

#C15-31

Collectively, the bishops constitute what is known as the Episcopal College, with the Pope as its head.

Splendor of Truth

"For the bishops are the heralds of the faith who bring new disciples to Christ. They are authentic teachers, that is, teachers endowed with the authority of Christ, who preach to the people entrusted to them the faith to be believed and put into practice; they illustrate this faith in the light of the Holy Spirit, drawing out of the treasury of Revelation things old and new (cf. Mt 13:52); they make it bear fruit and they vigilantly ward off errors that are threatening their flock (cf. 2 Tim 4:1-4)." *(section 114)*

#C15-50

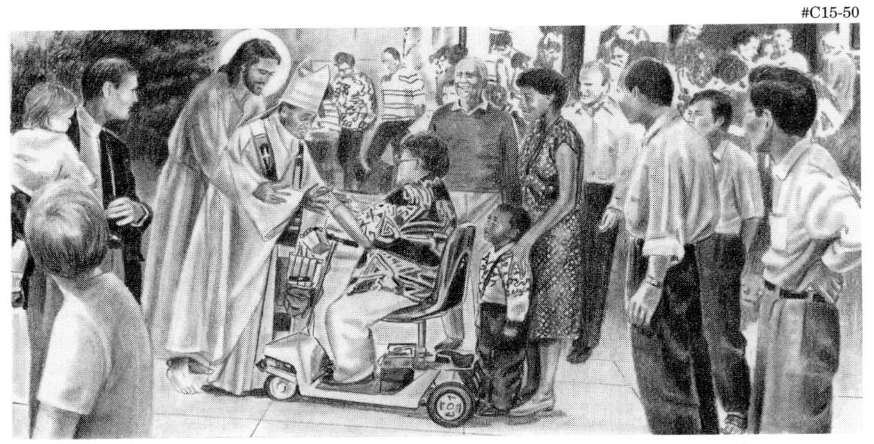

In the person of the bishops, then, to whom the priests render assistance, the Lord Jesus Christ, supreme high priest, is present in the midst of the faithful. *(Lumen Gentium, 21)*

Vatican Council II

By preaching everywhere the Gospel (cf. Mk. 16:20), welcomed and received under the influence of the Holy Spirit by those who hear it, the apostles gather together the universal Church, which the Lord founded upon the apostles and built upon blessed Peter their leader, the chief cornerstone being Christ Jesus himself (cf. Apoc. 21:14; Mt. 16:18; Eph. 2:20). *Lumen Gentium, 19*

Moreover, just as the office which the Lord confided to Peter alone, as first of the apostles, destined to be transmitted to his successors, is a permanent one, so also endures the office, which the apostles received, of shepherding the Church, a charge destined to be exercised without interruption by the sacred order of bishops. The sacred synod consequently teaches that the bishops have by divine institution taken the place of the apostles as pastors of the Church, in such wise that whoever listens to them is listening to Christ and whoever despises them despises Christ and him who sent Christ (cf. Lk. 10:16). *Lumen Gentium, 20*

In the person of the bishops, then, to whom the priests render assistance, the Lord Jesus Christ, supreme high priest, is present in the midst of the faithful. *Lumen Gentium, 21*

The bishop, invested with the fullness of the sacrament of Orders, "is the steward of the grace of the supreme priesthood," above all in the Eucharist, which he himself offers, or ensures that it is offered, from which the Church ever derives its life and on which it thrives. *Lumen Gentium, 26*

Summary Prayer

God, Eternal Shepherd, You tend Your Church in many ways and rule us with love. Help Your chosen servants, the bishops of Your Church as pastors for Christ, to watch over Your flock. Help them to be faithful teachers, wise administrators, and holy priests. We ask this through Jesus Christ, our Lord, to Whom with You and the Holy Spirit be all honor and glory. Amen.

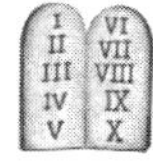

Doctrine • Moral • Worship Exercise

(See Appendix A for answer key, questions 150–152.)

1. What is the role of the Pope in the Church? Who gives him his authority?
2. How can you show your loyalty and obedience to the Pope in your family, school, workplace, and parish community?
3. Thank Jesus for giving us a Pope to lead us to unity with Him and with each other. Pray every day for the intentions of our Holy Father and for his spiritual and physical well being.

#A18-24

By preaching everywhere the Gospel, ...the apostles gather together the universal Church. *(Lumen Gentium, 19)*

Q. 153. What are the chief responsibilities of the Pope and bishops of the Catholic Church?

The chief responsibilities of the Pope and the bishops are to teach, sanctify, and govern the People of God. This authority and power was given to them by Jesus, beginning with that received by St. Peter and the other Apostles.

#C18-3

The chief responsibilities of the Pope and the bishops are to teach, sanctify, and govern the People of God.

After His Resurrection, Jesus demanded of Peter a profession of love. "He said to him the third time, 'Simon, son of John, do you love me?'...And he said to him, 'Lord you know everything; you know that I love you.' Jesus said to him, 'Feed my sheep'" (John 21:17).

Jesus willed that the bishops, the successors of the Apostles, should be shepherds in His Church. He placed Peter over the other Apostles and instituted him as a permanent source and foundation of unity, faith, and fellowship.

Sacred Scripture
Q. 153. 2 Thess 2:15; 1 Tim 1:1-7, 4:6-16.

Catechism of the Catholic Church
Q. 153. Paragraph **888-896**.

For cross-references with Vatican II, Papal documents & other resources, see Family Wisdom Library on page 734.
For commentaries on each question with Cardinal Arinze, Sr. John Vianney and Fr. Straub (in Spanish), see Appendix C.

#C15-49

Infallibility is a gift of the Holy Spirit which protects the Church's faith from error. Jesus said, "And I tell you, you are Peter, and on this rock I will build my church, and the powers of death shall not prevail against it" *(Matthew 16:18)*.

#C15-27

When the Catholic Church teaches solemnly in the name of God in matters of faith and morals, the teaching is infallible; that is, it cannot be mistaken.

"And I tell you, you are Peter, and on this rock I will build my church, and the powers of death shall not prevail against it. I will give you the keys of the kingdom of heaven, and whatever you bind on earth shall be bound in heaven, and whatever you loose on earth shall be loosed in heaven" (Matthew 16:18-19).

The Roman Pontiff, the head of the College of Bishops, is guaranteed doctrinal infallibility in virtue of his office, when, as the supreme shepherd and teacher of all the faithful, he proclaims by a definitive act some doctrine of faith and morals.

Infallibility is a gift of the Holy Spirit which protects the Church's faith from error. The Holy Spirit remains in the Catholic Church to enable it to continue the saving work of Jesus in the world. He guides the bishops, priests, and deacons in their holy work of teaching Christ's doctrine, shepherding souls, and giving grace to the people through the sacraments.

When the Catholic Church teaches solemnly in the name of God in matters of faith and morals, the teaching is infallible; that is, it cannot be mistaken. When the Pope teaches solemnly as head of the Church, or when bishops assembled with the Pope in council solemnly pronounce upon a matter of faith or morals, that doctrine is the infallible teaching of the Church. It must receive the assent of faith.

Moreover, when the Pope and the bishops throughout the world who are in union with him teach that a certain doctrine has been revealed by God, this teaching is infallible, even though it has not been solemnly defined, for it is still Christ teaching through His universal Church. When the Pope speaks to the whole Church on a matter of faith or morals, but not *ex cathedra*, his teaching, nevertheless, demands respect, obedience, and assent.

Sacred Scripture

"Simon, Simon, behold, Satan demanded to have you, that he might sift you like wheat, but I have prayed for you that your faith may not fail; and when you have turned again, strengthen your brethren.'" *Luke 22:31-32*

Follow the pattern of the sound words which you have heard from me, in the faith and love which are in Christ Jesus; guard the truth that has been entrusted to you by the Holy Spirit who dwells within us. *2 Timothy 1:13-14*

Catechism of the Catholic Church

894 "The bishops, as vicars and legates of Christ, govern the particular Churches assigned to them by their counsels, exhortations, and example, but over and above that also by the authority and sacred power" which indeed they ought to exercise so as to edify, in the spirit of service which is that of their Master.[1]

#C15-52

When the Pope and the bishops throughout the world who are in union with him teach that a certain doctrine has been revealed by God, this teaching is infallible, even though it has not been solemnly defined.

Catechism by Diagram

#C15-61

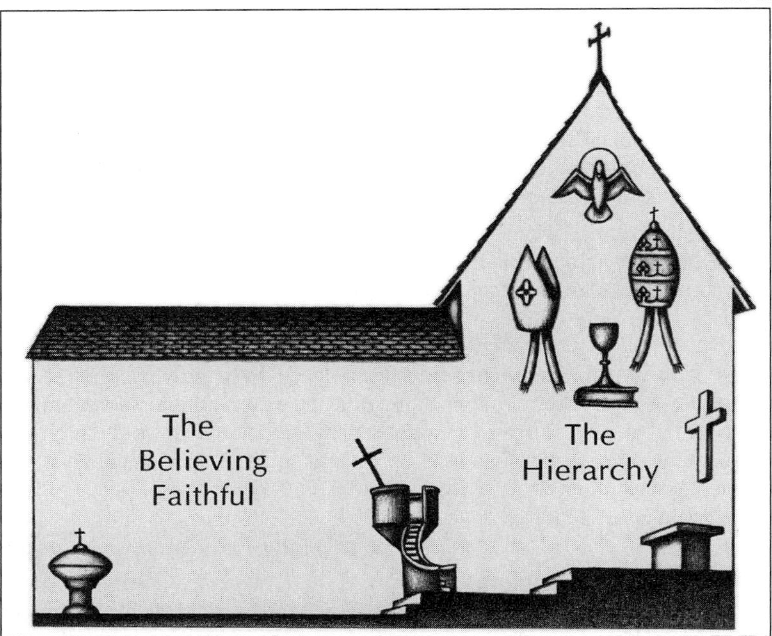

The Catholic Church. The Catholic Church is the community of all baptized persons (baptismal font) who are united in the same true faith (pulpit and cross), the same sacrifice (altar), the same sacraments (altar, baptismal font), and governed by the same authority of the Sovereign Pontiff (tiara) and the bishops who are in communion with him (miter). The Pope and the bishops make up the hierarchy. They are assisted by the priests, who share the powers of the priesthood (chalice, gospel book). All have the same Christ-life of grace (cross) which is given to them by the Holy Spirit (dove), the Sanctifier. The believing laity have a true apostolate in bringing the Gospel and holiness to men. Incorporated into Christ's Mystical Body through Baptism and Confirmation, they are assigned to this apostolate by the Lord Himself.

Splendor of Truth

Responsibility for the faith and the life of faith of the People of God is particularly incumbent upon the Church's Pastors. *(section 114)*

We have the duty, as bishops, to be vigilant that the word of God is faithfully taught. My Brothers in the Episcopate, it is part of our pastoral ministry to see to it that this moral teaching is faithfully handed down and to have recourse to appropriate measures to ensure that the faithful are guarded from every doctrine and theory contrary to it. In carrying out this task we are all assisted by theologians; even so, theological opinions constitute neither the rule nor the norm of our teaching. Its authority is derived, by the assistance of the Holy Spirit and in communion cum Petro et sub Petro, from our fidelity to the Catholic faith which comes from the Apostles. As bishops, we have the "grave obligation" to be personally vigilant that the "sound doctrine" (1 Tim 1:10) of faith and morals is taught in our dioceses. *(section 116)*

Vatican Council II

Although the bishops, taken individually, do not enjoy the privilege of infallibility, they do, however, proclaim infallibly the doctrine of Christ on the following conditions: namely, when, even though dispersed throughout the world but preserving for all that amongst themselves and with Peter's successor the bond of communion, in their authoritative teaching concerning matters of faith and morals, they are in agreement that a particular teaching is to be held definitively and absolutely. This is still more clearly the case when, assembled in an ecumenical council, they are, for the universal Church, teachers of and judges in matters of faith and morals, whose decisions must be adhered to with the loyal and obedient assent of faith. *Lumen Gentium, 25*

Among the more important duties of bishops that of preaching the Gospel has pride of place. For the bishops are heralds of the faith, who draw new disciples to Christ; they are authentic teachers, that is, teachers endowed with the authority of Christ, who preach the faith to the people assigned to them, the faith which is destined to inform their thinking and direct their conduct; and under the light of the Holy Spirit they make that faith shine forth, drawing from the storehouse of revelation new things and old (cf. Mt. 13:52); they make it bear fruit and with watchfulness they ward off whatever errors threaten their flock (cf. 2 Tim. 4:1-4). *Lumen Gentium, 25*

This infallibility, however, with which the divine redeemer wished to endow his Church in defining doctrine pertaining to faith and morals, is co-extensive with the deposit of revelation, which must be religiously guarded and loyally and courageously expounded. The Roman Pontiff, head of the college of bishops, enjoys this infallibility in virtue of his office, when, as supreme pastor and teacher of all the faithful—who confirms his brethren in the faith (cf. Lk. 22:32)—he proclaims in an absolute decision a doctrine pertaining to faith or morals. *Lumen Gentium, 25*

#R4.1-27

Jesus willed that the bishops, the successors of the Apostles, should be shepherds in His Church. He placed Peter over the other Apostles and instituted him as a permanent source and foundation of unity, faith, and fellowship.

Q. 154. Who directs Christ's work in the Catholic Church?

The Pope and the bishops direct Christ's work in the Catholic Church, in every rite and diocese.

#C15-29

The Pope is chief representative of Christ in the Church; he is its principal symbol of unity.

The Pope is chief representative of Christ in the Church; he is its principal symbol of unity. He enjoys the primacy of jurisdiction over the Church and is the head of the College of Bishops. He is the chief teacher and ruler over the Church.

The bishops are visible signs of Christ and the symbols of unity in their respective dioceses. Each diocesan bishop, or ordinary, is the principal teacher, priest, and shepherd of the Church in his diocese. Collectively, all the bishops, with the Pope as their head, are the teachers of the faith for the whole Church. They are responsible for its well-being throughout the world.

Catechism of the Catholic Church
Q. 154. Paragraph 879.

For cross-references with Vatican II, Papal documents & other resources, see Family Wisdom Library on page 734.
For commentaries on each question with Cardinal Arinze, Sr. John Vianney and Fr. Straub (in Spanish), see Appendix C.

Vatican Council II

This sacred synod, following in the steps of the First Vatican Council, teaches and declares with it that Jesus Christ, the eternal pastor, set up the holy Church by entrusting the apostles with their mission as he himself had been sent by the Father (cf. Jn. 20:21). He willed that their successors, the bishops namely, should be the shepherds in his Church until the end of the world. In order that the episcopate itself, however, might be one and undivided he put Peter at the head of the other apostles, and in him he set up a lasting and visible source and foundation of the unity both of faith and of communion. *Lumen Gentium, 18*

Just as, in accordance with the Lord's decree, St. Peter and the rest of the apostles constitute a unique apostolic college, so in like fashion the Roman Pontiff, Peter's successor, and the bishops, the successors of the apostles, are related with and united to one another. *Lumen Gentium, 22*

The order of bishops is the successor to the college of the apostles in their role as teachers and pastors, and in it the apostolic college is perpetuated. Together with their head, the Supreme Pontiff, and never apart from him, they have supreme and full authority over the universal Church; but this power cannot be exercised without the agreement of the Roman Pontiff. *Lumen Gentium, 22*

The supreme authority over the whole Church, which this college possesses, is exercised in a solemn way in an ecumenical council. *Lumen Gentium, 22*

#C15-30-2

The bishops are visible signs of Christ and the symbols of unity in their respective dioceses. Collectively, all the bishops, with the Pope as their head, are the teachers of the faith for the whole Church.

#L10-2

The Pope and the bishops direct Christ's work in the Catholic Church, in every rite and diocese.

Doctrine • Moral • Worship Exercise

(See Appendix A for answer key, questions 153–154.)

1. What does it mean to say that the Church and the Pope are infallible in their teachings? In what instances are the Church and the Pope infallible?
2 Do you strive to know and remain loyal to the teachings of the Church regarding moral issues? How can you keep informed of the Pope's stand on contemporary moral issues?
3. Allot 5-10 minutes a day to reflect on one of the Holy Father's encyclicals or apostolic letters (e.g., "Letter to Children," "Guardian of the Redeemer" or "Lay Members of Christ's Faithful").

Chapter Summary Prayer

Most Holy Trinity, by the power of the Eucharist, make Your Church firm in unity and love and grant strength and Salvation to Your servant, our Holy Father, the Pope and Supreme Shepherd, together with the flock You have entrusted to his care. Give to Your shepherd a spirit of courage, right judgment, knowledge, and love. By governing with fidelity those entrusted to his care, may he, as successor to the Apostle Peter and the Vicar of Christ, guide us in building up Your Church, which is a sacrament of unity, love, and peace for all the world.

God our Father, You guide all things by Your Word; You govern all Christian people. In Your love, protect the Pope You have chosen for us. Under his leadership, may we deepen our faith and become better Christians through Jesus our Lord. Amen.

Thought Provokers

Please see Appendix B for the answers.

Q. 150: Members of the Catholic Church belong also to civil or temporal societies. Doesn't this fact tend to cause divided and conflicting loyalties?

Q. 151: It is sometimes said that the Pope teaches without error in matters pertaining to faith and morals only when he exercises his extraordinary or *ex cathedra* teaching authority or magisterium. Is this correct?

Q. 152: The Church teaches that Catholic bishops enjoy the fullness of the Sacrament of Holy Orders. What does this mean?

Q. 153: The Pope, as the Successor of St. Peter and the Vicar of Christ, enjoys full, supreme, and universal power over the entire Church. Among other things, this means that the Pope may govern the Church without the consent of the other bishops. Do the other bishops, in any sense, as successors of the Apostles, share with the Pope in the government of the whole Church?

Q. 154: Who directs all work in the cause of Christ in the Catholic home?

#E4-21

To be a Catholic means to believe that Jesus Christ, the Son of God, established the Church to continue His work of redemption throughout all ages.

CHAPTER FORTY-FIVE

Members of the Catholic Church

Q. 155. What is owed to the Pope and bishops by the faithful?

The Pope and the bishops are owed honor, respect, obedience and love by the faithful.

We obey the fourth commandment of God, and thus serve Him and His Church, when we honor, love, respect, and obey the Pope and the bishops in union with him.

#C15-44

The Pope and the bishops are owed honor, respect, obedience and love by the faithful.

To be a Catholic means to believe that Jesus Christ, the Son of God, established the Church to continue His work of redemption throughout all ages. Since the average Catholic cannot probe the depths of philosophical and theological arguments, he turns with security and peace to the teaching authority of the Church, to which Our Lord promised immunity from error through the help of the Holy Spirit, to learn with assurance what he must believe and do to attain Salvation.

Catechism of the Catholic Church
Q. 155. Paragraphs **1899-1900.**

For cross-references with Vatican II, Papal documents & other resources, see Family Wisdom Library on page 734.
For commentaries on each question with Cardinal Arinze, Sr. John Vianney and Fr. Straub (in Spanish), see Appendix C.

#P30-1

Bishops who teach in communion with the Roman Pontiff are to be revered by all as witnesses of divine and Catholic truth; the faithful... are obliged to submit to their bishops' decision, made in the name of Christ, in matters of faith and morals. *(Lumen Gentium, 25)*

Catechism of the Catholic Church

1900 The duty of obedience requires all to give due honor to authority and to treat those who are charged to exercise it with respect, and, insofar as it is deserved, with gratitude and good-will: "Pope St. Clement of Rome provides the Church's most ancient prayer for political authorities:[1] 'Grant to them, Lord, health, peace, concord, and stability, so that they may exercise without offense the sovereignty that you have given them. Master, heavenly King of the ages, you give glory, honor, and power over the things of earth to the sons of men. Direct, Lord, their counsel, following what is pleasing and acceptable in your sight, so that by exercising with devotion and in peace and gentleness the power that you have given to them, they may find favor with you.'"[2]

Vatican Council II

Bishops who teach in communion with the Roman Pontiff are to be revered by all as witnesses of divine and Catholic truth; the faithful, for their part, are obliged to submit to their bishops' decision, made in the name of Christ, in matters of faith and morals, and to adhere to it with a ready and respectful allegiance of mind. This loyal submission of the will and intellect must be given, in a special way, to the authentic teaching authority of the Roman Pontiff, even when he does not speak *ex cathedra* in such wise, indeed, that his supreme teaching authority be acknowledged with respect, and that one sincerely adhere to decisions made by him, conformably with his manifest mind and intention. *Lumen Gentium, 25*

Q. 156. Why is respect owed to everyone in the Church?

Everyone in the Church deserves our deepest respect since, through Baptism, we are united to Christ in His Mystical Body and become His brothers and sisters. Every human person is created in the image and likeness of God and is precious in His eyes. Our Lord said, "Truly, I say to you, as you did it to one of the least of these my brethren, you did it to me" (Matthew 25:40). We should love and honor each of our brothers and sisters in Christ.

Consecration to Christ implies obedience to the Commandments, fulfillment of our duties of state, offering up our sufferings in union with Christ, perseverance in doing all for the love of God, and sacrificing our time, talents, and resources to make Christ known in the world. As Christians we are called to love and respect our brothers and sisters, who have been created in the image and likeness of God, and who, through Baptism, have become children of God and members of Christ's Mystical Body.

#L10-5

As Christians we are called to love and respect our brothers and sisters, who have been created in the image and likeness of God.

Sacred Scripture
Q. 156. Eph 4:31-5:2.

Catechism of the Catholic Church
Q. 156. Paragraphs 782-795, **1701-1702.**

For cross-references with Vatican II, Papal documents & other resources, see Family Wisdom Library on page 734.
For commentaries on each question with Cardinal Arinze, Sr. John Vianney and Fr. Straub (in Spanish), see Appendix C.

Sacred Scripture

So God created man in his own image, in the image of God he created him; male and female he created them. *Genesis 1:27*

It is the Spirit himself bearing witness with our spirit that we are children of God, and if children, then heirs, heirs of God and fellow heirs with Christ, provided we suffer with him in order that we may also be glorified with him. *Romans 8:16-17*

Catechism of the Catholic Church

1934 Created in the image of the one God and equally endowed with rational souls, all men have the same nature and the same origin. Redeemed by the sacrifice of Christ, all are called to participate in the same divine beatitude: all therefore enjoy an equal dignity.

Vatican Council II

Mutual esteem for all forms of the Church's apostolate, and good coordination, preserving nevertheless the character special to each, are in fact absolutely necessary for promoting that spirit of unity which will cause fraternal charity to shine out in the Church's whole apostolate, common aims to be reached and ruinous rivalries avoided. *Lay People, 23*

This Church of Christ is really present in all legitimately organized local groups of the faithful, which, in so far as they are united to their pastors, are also quite appropriately called Churches in the New Testament. *Lumen Gentium, 26*

#R19.3-1

Our Lord said, "Truly, I say to you, as you did it to one of the least of these my brethren, you did it to me" *(Matthew 25:40).*

Q. 157. Why is the Catholic Church a community?

The Catholic Church is a community since its members share Christ's life with one another; it is a people brought together by God.

When we describe the Church as the People of God and as the Mystical Body of Christ, it helps each of us to see himself as one with a group to whose destiny we are tied and whose welfare we share.

The Church is a community of those throughout the world whom God has called to give witness to Christ and to the new life He has brought to man. This assembly is called the "People of God" and the "Mystical Body of Christ."

When we describe the Church as the People of God and as the Mystical Body of Christ, it helps each of us to see himself as one with a group to whose destiny we are tied and whose welfare we share. This is the reality of our Baptism: we are joined to the whole Christ, that is, joined to Christ and His people, the Church.

If we are thus joined in Christ, He is truly one with us in a very intimate sense. The Church is seen as the successor to ancient Israel, and Jesus, the Messiah and Head of the new People of God, is seen as rooted in humanity by His physical birth, life, death, and Resurrection. The infant Jesus is the Son of Mary and the Son of God. He is of the people of Israel, of the tribe of Judah, of the house of David.

Sacred Scripture
Q. 157. Eph 4:15-16; 1 Pet 2:9-10.

Catechism of the Catholic Church
Q. 157. Paragraphs 782, 787, 804-805.

For cross-references with Vatican II, Papal documents & other resources, see Family Wisdom Library on page 734.
For commentaries on each question with Cardinal Arinze, Sr. John Vianney and Fr. Straub (in Spanish), see Appendix C.

#P25-9-2

The Church is a community of those throughout the world whom God has called to give witness to Christ and to the new life He has brought to man.

Through His humanity we are each united to Christ as our Savior. The divinity of Christ must not be slighted; still, that does not cancel out His true humanity. When we use the phrase the "People of God," we see Christ, prefigured in Moses. Jesus shares a truly human nature with Moses and, like him, leads the People of God from slavery to freedom, from death to life. Christ is our Passover. When we think about the Blessed Virgin Mary, the daughter of Zion, whose Son is Jesus, we clearly see that Jesus is one of us, truly Emmanuel, our "God with us."

God has called this community to give witness to His Son Jesus and to live the new life He has brought to men. As members of this community, we are joined to Christ through Baptism; we share in His divine life through grace, which reaches us especially in the sacraments.

Sacred Scripture

For the body does not consist of one member but of many... But as it is, God arranged the organs in the body, each one of them, as he chose. If all were a single organ, where would the body be? As it is, there are many parts, yet one body... But God has so adjusted the body, giving the greater honor to the inferior part, that there may be no discord in the body, but that the members may have the same care for one another. If one member suffers, all suffer together; if one member is honored, all rejoice together." *1 Corinthians 12:14, 18-20, 24-26*

Catechism of the Catholic Church

805 The Church is the Body of Christ. Through the Spirit and his action in the sacraments, above all the Eucharist, Christ, who once was dead and is now risen, establishes the community of believers as his own Body.

Splendor of Truth

The first Christians, coming both from the Jewish people and from the Gentiles, differed from the pagans not only in their faith and their liturgy but also in the witness of their moral conduct, which was inspired by the New Law. The Church is in fact a communion both of faith and of life; her rule of life is "faith working through love" (Gal 5:6). *(section 26)*

Vatican Council II

Fully incorporated into the Church are those who, possessing the Spirit of Christ, accept all the means of salvation given to the Church together with her entire organization, and who – by the bonds constituted by the profession of faith, the sacraments, ecclesiastical government, and communion—are joined in the visible structure of the Church of Christ, who rules her through the Supreme Pontiff and the bishops. *Lumen Gentium, 14*

Catechism by Diagram

#C15-62

A Community Sharing the Life of Christ. The Catholic Church is a community (three circles) that shares the life of Christ (monogram, large cross). By Baptism the faithful are made one body with Christ and also members of the People of God. This union with Christ is especially brought about through the Holy Sacrifice of the Mass (altar, host, chalice), in which the faithful join Christ (monogram) in His sacrifice on Calvary (cross). By His grace, they are sanctified (white heart), forgiven of their sins (spotted heart), and aided in avoiding mortal sin (black heart). The Church Militant is aided by the life of Christ's grace. The Church Suffering in Purgatory receives the benefits of the Mass.

The Church knows that she is joined in many ways to the baptized who are honored by the name of Christian, but who do not however profess the Catholic faith in its entirety or have not preserved unity or communion under the successor of Peter. For there are many who hold sacred scripture in honor as a rule of faith and of life, who have a sincere religious zeal, who lovingly believe in God the Father Almighty and in Christ, the Son of God and the Savior, who are sealed by baptism which unites them to Christ, and who indeed recognize and receive other sacraments in their own Churches or ecclesiastical communities. Many of them possess the episcopate, celebrate the holy Eucharist and cultivate devotion of the Virgin Mother of God. There is furthermore a sharing in prayer and spiritual benefits; these Christians are indeed in some real way joined to us in the Holy Spirit. *Lumen Gentium, 15*

Summary Prayer

Lord God, eternal Shepherd, You have so tended the vineyard You planted that it now extends its branches to the farthest lands. Look down on Your Church and come to us. Help us to remain in Your Son like branches that are planted firmly on the vine of Your love, that we may testify before the whole world to Your great power working everywhere. We ask this through and in the Sacred Heart of Jesus. Amen.

Doctrine • Moral • Worship Exercise

(See Appendix A for answer key, questions 155–157.)

1. How is the Church a community?
2. How can you and your family use your time, talents, and possessions to build up your parish community?
3. Pray for all the members of the Catholic Church, that all may contribute to the strengthening of the Christian community.

Q. 158. Is everyone in the Church equal?

All the members of the Church are equal, but they have different duties and roles. They are united to each other as the one People of God whose Head is Christ.

#C15-39

All the members of the Church are equal, but they have different duties and roles. They are united to each other as the one People of God whose Head is Christ.

Describing the Church as the "People of God" emphasizes the fact that the Church is composed of people, including the Pope, bishops, priests, deacons, and the laity. As the Second Vatican Council said, the Church is "a people brought into unity from the unity of the Father, the Son and the Holy Spirit" (cf. St. John Chrysostom, De Oratio Domino, 23). In this assembly of people, there is a basic equality of all persons.

Just as God made Moses the leader of His people in the Old Testament, so Christ gave His Apostles and their successors the right to teach and to command in His Name. This authority is given to them for the service and welfare of the People of God.

Sacred Scripture
Q. 158. Eph 4:4-16.

Catechism of the Catholic Church
Q. 158. Paragraph **1934**.

For cross-references with Vatican II, Papal documents & other resources, see Family Wisdom Library on page 734.
For commentaries on each question with Cardinal Arinze, Sr. John Vianney and Fr. Straub (in Spanish), see Appendix C.

The Church is also a "priestly people," but the ministerial priesthood is essentially different from "the priesthood of the faithful." All, however, are equal and united as the one People of God.

By Baptism, the laity are made one body with Christ and members of the People of God. Sharing, in their own way, in the priestly, prophetic, and kingly functions of Christ, they play a vital role in carrying out the mission of the Church in the world. St. Peter says, "But you are a chosen race, a royal priesthood, a holy nation, God's own people, that you may declare the wonderful deeds of him who called you out of darkness into his marvelous light" (1 Peter 2:9).

The baptized, therefore, by regeneration and the anointing of the Holy Spirit, are consecrated to be a spiritual house and a holy priesthood. Through all the works of Christians, they may offer spiritual sacrifices to and proclaim the perfection of Him Who has called them out of darkness into His marvelous light. Thus all Christians, persevering in prayer and praising God, should offer themselves as sacrifices, holy and pleasing to God. They should bear witness to Christ (cf. Romans 12:1) and always be ready to give an answer to everyone who asks a reason for the hope of an eternal life which is theirs (cf. 1 Peter 3:15).

#L3-9-2

The laity are called by God to work for the sanctification of the world like a leaven, from within, by carrying out their proper tasks according to the spirit of the Gospel.

The laity are distinguished by their "secular character." Although those in Holy Orders can at times be engaged in secular activities and professions, they are, by reason of their vocation, especially ordained to the sacred ministry. The laity are called by God to work for the sanctification of the world like a leaven, from within, by carrying out their proper tasks according to the spirit of the Gospel. They are consecrated into a royal priesthood and a holy people so that they too might offer spiritual sacrifices of everything they do, and in this manner witness to Christ in the world.

Priests should minister to the needs of one another and of the laity. The laity should enthusiastically cooperate with and support their priests. All clergy, religious, and laity are brothers and sisters in the Mystical Body of Christ. Thus, while there is a basic equality among all members of the Church, there is a diversity of functions and responsibilities.

#C11-111-2

The equality of men rests essentially on their dignity as persons and the rights that flow from it. *(Catechism of the Catholic Church, 1935)*

Sacred Scripture

I bid every one among you not to think of himself more highly than he ought to think, but to think with sober judgment, each according to the measure of faith which God has assigned him. For as in one body we have many members, and all the members do not have the same function, so we, though many, are one body in Christ, and individually members one of another. Having gifts that differ according to the grace given to us, let us use them. *Romans 12:3-6*

As each has received a gift, employ it for one another, as good stewards of God's varied grace. *1 Peter 4:10*

To him who loves us and has freed us from our sins by his blood and made us a kingdom, priests to his God and Father, to him be glory and dominion for ever and ever. Amen." *Revelation 1:5-6*

#H5-25

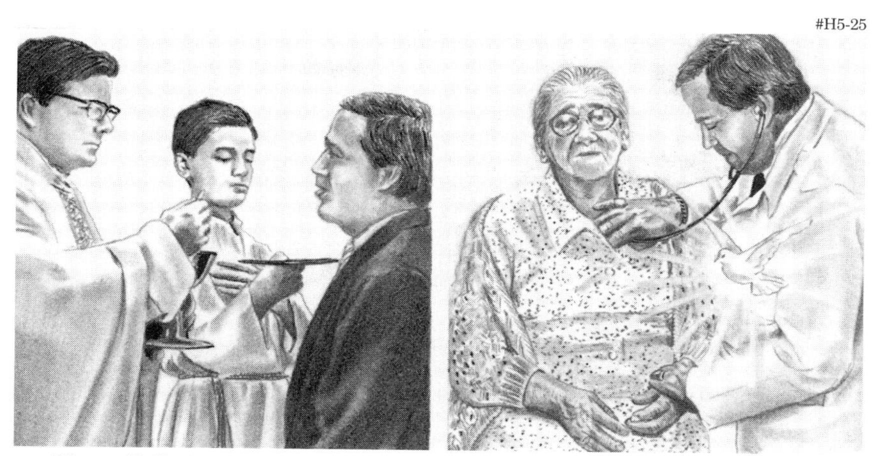

Thus all Christians, persevering in prayer and praising God, should offer themselves as sacrifices, holy and pleasing to God.

Catechism of the Catholic Church

1935 The equality of men rests essentially on their dignity as persons and the rights that flow from it: "Every form of social or cultural discrimination in fundamental personal rights on the grounds of sex, race, color, social conditions, language, or religion must be curbed and eradicated as incompatible with God's design."[1]

Vatican Council II

Though they differ essentially and not only in degree, the common priesthood of the faithful and the ministerial or hierarchical priesthood are nonetheless ordered one to another; each in its own proper way shares in the one priesthood of Christ. *Lumen Gentium, 10*

The social nature of man shows that there is an interdependence between personal betterment and the improvement of society. Insofar as man by his very nature stands completely in need of life in society, he is and he ought to be the beginning, the subject and the object of every social organization. Life in society is not something accessory to man himself: through his dealing with others, through mutual service, and through fraternal dialogue, man develops all his talents and becomes able to rise to his destiny.

Among the social ties necessary for man's development some correspond more immediately to his innermost nature—the family, for instance, and the political community; others flow rather from his free choice. Nowadays for various reasons mutual relationships and interdependence increase from day to day and give rise to a variety of associations and organizations, both public and private. Socialization, as it is called, is not without its dangers, but it brings with it many advantages for the strengthening and betterment of human qualities and for the protection of human rights. *Gaudium et Spes, 25*

Summary Prayer

Heavenly Father, in the New Testament You shed light on the miracles You worked in ancient times: the Red Sea is seen as a symbol of our Baptism, and the nation You freed from slavery is a sign of Your Christian people. May every nation share the faith and privilege of Israel by coming to new birth in the Holy Spirit and becoming one people in Christ. We ask this in His most powerful and holy Name. Amen.

Q. 159. Who in the Church is called to a life of holiness?

In the Church each member has a vocation to lead a life of holiness.

When God created man, He gave him the gifts of supernatural life, of divine sonship. Man was alive with the very life of God, but by sin, he lost this gift of divine life. Left to himself, man was incapable of winning back the divine life. But God, in His infinite mercy, conceived the wonderful plan of the Redemption and sent His only-begotten Son, Jesus, into the world to save mankind.

#C37-9

We open our hearts to Christ so that He may live in us His own life of love and self-surrender to the Father. We strive to imitate His life so that in all things we become like Him.

Sacred Scripture
Q. 159. Heb 12:14.

Catechism of the Catholic Church
Q. 159. Paragraphs **825**, 1713, 1720, 2012, 2014-2016.

For cross-references with Vatican II, Papal documents & other resources, see Family Wisdom Library on page 734.
For commentaries on each question with Cardinal Arinze, Sr. John Vianney and Fr. Straub (in Spanish), see Appendix C.

#L3-31

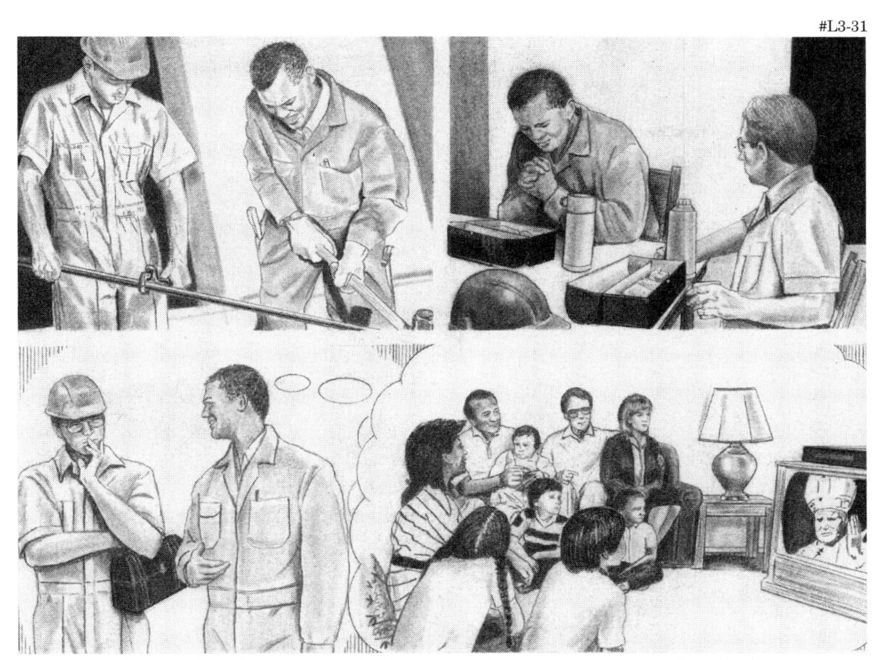

It is therefore quite clear that all Christians in any state or walk of life are called to the fullness of Christian life and to the perfection of love.
(Lumen Gentium, 40)

Christ became man and took man's sinfulness upon Himself. He stood in the place of all men before His Father. By accepting His death on Calvary, He paid the penalty for all men's sins. Since He was God's Son, the bonds of death could not hold Him. He rose to life. With Him all mankind passed from death to life, returned to the Father's sonship, and again enjoyed the intimacy of His love.

In Christ we have already died to sin and risen to new life. He infuses into our souls that very life of divine sonship which filled Him at His own Resurrection. He does this through the sacraments which He instituted for the Church. Christ wills to carry on His life within us for the glory of the Father. This life of Christ within us is that state of holiness to which we are all called by God.

This Christ-life means that we can open our minds to Him by faith so that we may have the same outlook that He had. We open our hearts to Him so that He may live in us His own life of love and self-surrender to the Father. We strive to imitate His life so that in all things we become like Him. St. Paul said, "I have been crucified with Christ; it is no longer I who live, but Christ who lives in me; and the life I now live in the flesh I live by faith in the Son of God, who loved me and gave himself for me" (Galatians 2:20).

#L3-21-2

I...beg you to lead a life worthy of the calling to which you have been called, with all lowliness and meekness, with patience, forbearing one another in love, eager to maintain the unity of the Spirit in the bond of peace. *(Ephesians 4:1-3)*

Sacred Scripture

I...beg you to lead a life worthy of the calling to which you have been called, with all lowliness and meekness, with patience, forbearing one another in love, eager to maintain the unity of the Spirit in the bond of peace...There is one body and one Spirit, just as you were called to the one hope that belongs to your call, one Lord, one faith, one baptism, one God and Father of us all, who is above all and through all and in all. *Ephesians 4:1-6*

As obedient children, do not be conformed to the passions of your former ignorance, but as he who called you is holy, be holy yourselves in all your conduct; since it is written, "You shall be holy, for I am holy." And if you invoke as Father him who judges each one impartially according to his deeds, conduct yourselves with fear throughout the time of your exile. *1 Peter 1:14-17*

Catechism of the Catholic Church

2013 "All Christians in any state or walk of life are called to the fullness of Christian life and to the perfection of charity."[1] All are called to holiness: "Be perfect, as your heavenly Father is perfect."[2] "In order to reach this perfection the faithful should use the strength dealt out to them by Christ's gift, so that... doing the will of the Father in everything, they may wholeheartedly devote themselves to the glory of God and to the service of their neighbor. Thus the holiness of the People of God will grow in fruitful abundance, as is clearly shown in the history of the Church through the lives of so many saints."[3]

Splendor of Truth

His [every Christian's] moral life has the value of a "spiritual worship" (Rom 12:1; cf. Phil 3:3), flowing from and nourished by that inexhaustible source of holiness and glorification of God which is found in the sacraments, especially in the Eucharist: by sharing in the sacrifice of the Cross, the Christian partakes of Christ's self-giving love and is equipped and committed to live this same charity in all his thoughts and deeds. *(section 107)*

Vatican Council II

It is therefore quite clear that all Christians in any state or walk of life are called to the fullness of Christian life and to the perfection of love. *Lumen Gentium, 40*

Summary Prayer

Lord, You are the fullness of life, holiness, and joy. Fill our days and nights with the love of Your wisdom, that we, the People of God, may bear fruit in the beauty of holiness, like a tree that is watered by running streams.

Almighty God, You are our Father and we are Your people. You keep constant guard over us. Protect us from hidden snares and make us holy, that we may praise and thank You, and so live in righteousness before You.

So that Your people might walk in innocence and holiness, You gave us our Lord Jesus Christ. Help Your children to love what is truly perfect, so that we may neither speak what is evil nor do what is wrong. Let us stand in Your sight and always celebrate Your love and justice, through our Lord and Savior Jesus Christ. Amen.

Doctrine • Moral • Worship Exercise

(See Appendix A for answer key, questions 158–159.)

1. In what sense are the members of the Church equal?
2. As a lay person, what is your distinct role and responsibility in the Church? Describe specific ways in which you can fulfill these responsibilities.
3. Foster a fervent and constant desire for holiness in the fulfillment of your daily duties.

Chapter Summary Prayer

Most Holy Trinity, Father, Son, and Holy Spirit, we beg of You, have mercy on Your Holy Catholic Church. Protect and bless the Pope and all bishops, priests, and deacons. Fill them with wisdom, strength, and virtue, that they may live lives worthy of their sublime vocation and guide their flocks to eternal Salvation. Visit all of the faithful with Your sanctifying grace, so that by leading pure and holy lives, they may persevere in Your love.

Stretch forth Your mighty arm and protect Your holy Church against all attacks of the enemy; destroy their power so that, in peace and security, we may work out our Salvation and spread Your holy Faith. Exalt and glorify Your Church with the splendor of holiness so that, as the Bride of Christ, she may give praise to You forever and ever. Amen.

Thought Provokers

Please see Appendix B for the answers.

Q. 155: In addition to respect and obedience, how else should we provide help for the Pope and for our bishops, priests, and deacons?

Q. 156: Every human person deserves our respect. Why?

Q. 157: In what sense is the Christian family a community?

Q. 158: What did St. Paul mean when he wrote: "For in Christ Jesus you are all sons of God, through faith. For as many of you as were baptized into Christ have put on Christ. There is neither Jew nor Greek, there is neither slave nor free, there is neither male nor female; for you are all one in Christ Jesus."? (Galatians 3:26–28)

Q. 159: Why is growth in holiness, or sanctity, so hard to achieve?

CHAPTER FORTY-SIX

The Role of the Catholic Church

Q. 160. Why is the Catholic Church essentially missionary?

The Catholic Church is missionary because every member shares the command from Christ to carry the Good News of His teaching to all mankind by word and example.

#Y1-11

The Church, as a community of believers and brotherly love, bears Christian witness by its preaching of the Gospel and its service to others.

The Church, as a community of believers and brotherly love, bears Christian witness by its preaching of the Gospel and its service to others.

God has called to be witnesses all those who believe He has revealed and given Himself to men in Jesus Christ. The Church gives this witness by proclaiming in the world, by word and deed, what God has done in Jesus Christ. The Church must live the life of Jesus in His Spirit and show His love, by her life of brotherhood and service to others.

Sacred Scripture
Q. 160. Jas 1:22-25; 1 Pet 4:8-11.

Catechism of the Catholic Church
Q. 160. Paragraphs **2044**.

For cross-references with Vatican II, Papal documents & other resources, see Family Wisdom Library on page 734.
For commentaries on each question with Cardinal Arinze, Sr. John Vianney and Fr. Straub (in Spanish), see Appendix C.

#S5-1

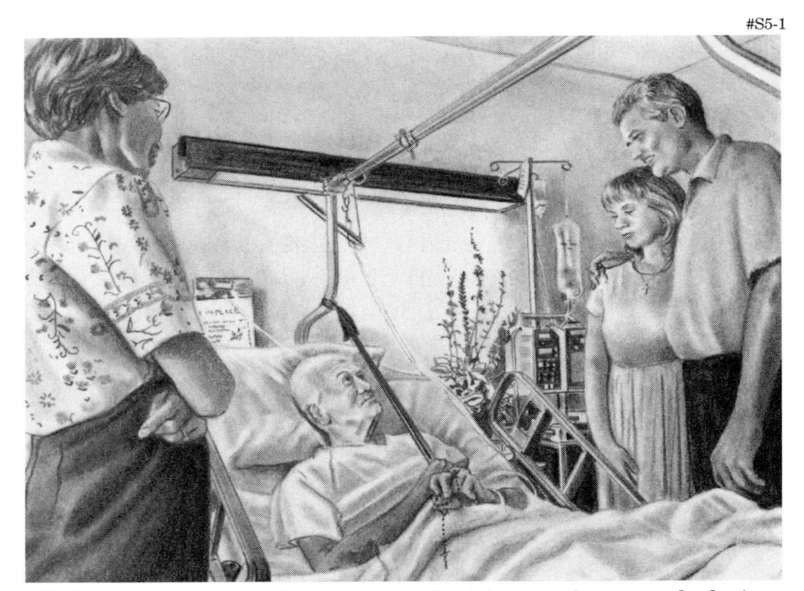

Christian witness, or missionary activity, gives testimony to the loving presence of God in the world.

Jesus said to the Apostles, "All authority in heaven and on earth has been given to me. Go therefore and make disciples of all nations, baptizing them in the name of the Father and of the Son and of the Holy Spirit, teaching them to observe all that I have commanded you; and lo, I am with you always, to the close of the age" (Matthew 28:18-20).

In reality, the Church is its members. The Christian community should follow the example of its founder, Jesus Christ—serving the larger human community by sharing the riches of its faith and reaching out to help all those in need. Christian witness, or missionary activity, gives testimony to the loving presence of God in the world.

St. Luke says of the first Christians, "And they devoted themselves to the apostles' teaching and fellowship, to the breaking of bread and the prayers" (Acts 2:42).

Sacred Scripture

But how are men to call upon him in whom they have not believed? And how are they to believe in him of whom they have never heard? And how are they to hear without a preacher? And how can men preach unless they are sent? As it is written, "How beautiful are the feet of those who preach good news!" But they have not all heeded the gospel; for Isaiah says, "Lord, who has believed what he has heard from us?" So faith comes from what is heard, and what is heard comes by the preaching of Christ. *Romans 10:14-17*

Preach the word, be urgent in season and out of season, convince, rebuke, and exhort, be unfailing in patience and in teaching. *2 Timothy 4:2*

Catechism of the Catholic Church

863 The whole Church is apostolic, in that she remains, through the successors of St. Peter and the other apostles, in communion of faith and life with her origin: and in that she is "sent out" into the whole world. All members of the Church share in this mission, though in various ways. "The Christian vocation is, of its nature, a vocation to the apostolate as well." Indeed, we call an apostolate "every activity of the Mystical Body" that aims "to spread the Kingdom of Christ over all the earth."[1]

905 Lay people also fulfill their prophetic mission by evangelization, "that is, the proclamation of Christ by word and the testimony of life." For lay people, "this evangelization... acquires a specific property and peculiar efficacy because it is accomplished in the ordinary circumstances of the world."[1]

"This witness of life, however, is not the sole element in the apostolate; the true apostle is on the lookout for occasions of announcing Christ by word, either to unbelievers... or to the faithful."[2]

Splendor of Truth

The new evangelization will show its authenticity and unleash all its missionary force when it is carried out through the gift not only of the word proclaimed but also of the word lived. *(section 107)*

#E5-10-2

"The Christian vocation is, of its nature, a vocation to the apostolate as well."
Indeed, we call an apostolate "every activity of the Mystical Body"
that aims "to spread the Kingdom of Christ over all the earth."
(Catechism of the Catholic Church, 863)

#E5-36

Lay people also fulfill their prophetic mission by evangelization, "that is, the proclamation of Christ by word and the testimony of life."
(Catechism of the Catholic Church, 905)

Vatican Council II

Having been divinely sent to the nations that she might be "the universal sacrament of salvation," the Church, in obedience to the command of her founder (Mk. 16:15) and because it is demanded by her own essential universality, strives to preach the Gospel to all men...In the present state of things which gives rise to a new situation for mankind, the Church, the salt of the earth and the light of the world (cf. Mt. 5:13-14), is even more urgently called upon to save and renew every creature, so that all things might be restored in Christ, and so that in him men might form one family and one people of God. *Missionary Activity, 1*

Missionary activity extends the saving faith of the Church, it expands and perfects its catholic unity, it is sustained by its apostolicity, it activates the collegiate sense of its hierarchy, and bears witness to its sanctity which it both extends and promotes. *Missionary Activity, 6*

All Christians, by the example of their lives and the witness of the word, wherever they live, have an obligation to manifest the new man which they put on in baptism, and to reveal the power of the Holy Spirit by whom they were strengthened at confirmation, so that others, seeing their good works, might glorify the Father (cf. Matt. 5:16) and more perfectly perceive the true meaning of human life and the universal solidarity of mankind. *Missionary Activity, 11*

#H5-30

The Christian community should follow the example of its founder, Jesus Christ—serving the larger human community by sharing the riches of its faith and reaching out to help all those in need.

Q. 161. What is the role of the Church in the world?

The role of the Church is to make Christ known and loved, to spread the knowledge of Salvation everywhere, and to pray and suffer for the Salvation of souls.

#E5-34

Much of the effective work of bringing the Gospel of Christ to the world must be done by the laity.

Christ gave His Church the commission to spread the message of Salvation to the ends of the earth. The greatest gift which God has given to man is the gift of the good news of the Gospel. In the Gospel, God brings to fulfillment His hidden plan, prophesied and prefigured in the Old Testament, to save mankind and to give each man a share in His divine life through Jesus Christ His Son. Therefore the Church both speaks and listens to the world, without being conformed to it. It tries to show the world how to be faithful to the Gospel and how to journey toward Heaven.

For these reasons, the Church makes "a judgment about economic and social matters when the fundamental rights of the person or the salvation of souls requires it" (*Catechism of the Catholic Church*, 2458). The Church issues public statements or encyclicals on how these matters impact the common good and are to be ordered to God, man's ultimate end and sovereign Good.

Catechism of the Catholic Church
Q. 161. Paragraphs 756, **771**, 780, **782**, 785, 1886.

For cross-references with Vatican II, Papal documents & other resources, see Family Wisdom Library on page 734.
For commentaries on each question with Cardinal Arinze, Sr. John Vianney and Fr. Straub (in Spanish), see Appendix C.

Much of the effective work of bringing the Gospel of Christ to the world must be done by the laity. The laity are challenged to make holy the actual world in which they live; they discover Christ as the Way, the Truth, and the Life, and then bring Him into the world. As citizens of both the Church and the world, the laity are meant to be the bridge that connects them. The priest stands between God and man; the laity stand between the Church and the world.

Sacred Scripture

I appeal to you therefore, brethren, by the mercies of God, to present your bodies as a living sacrifice, holy and acceptable to God, which is your spiritual worship. Do not be conformed to this world but be transformed by the renewal of your mind, that you may prove what is the will of God, what is good and acceptable and perfect. *Romans 12:1-2*

For if I preach the gospel, that gives me no ground for boasting. For necessity is laid upon me. Woe to me if I do not preach the gospel! *1 Corinthians 9:16*

Catechism of the Catholic Church

2044 The fidelity of the baptized is a primordial condition for the proclamation of the Gospel and for the *Church's mission in the world.* In order that the message of salvation can show the power of its truth and radiance before men, it must be authenticated by the witness of the life of Christians. "The witness of a Christian life and good works done in a supernatural spirit have great power to draw men to the faith and to God."[1]

Splendor of Truth

At times, in the discussions about new and complex moral problems, it can seem that Christian morality is in itself too demanding, difficult to understand and almost impossible to practice. This is untrue, since Christian morality consists, in the simplicity of the Gospel, in following Jesus Christ, in abandoning oneself to him, in letting oneself be transformed by his grace and renewed by his mercy, gifts which come to us in the living communion of his Church. *(section 119)*

#L3-36-2

The laity are challenged to make holy the actual world in which they live.

Vatican Council II

The presence of Christians among these human groups should be one that is animated by that love with which we are loved by God, who desires that we should love each other with that self-same love (cf. 1 Jn 4:11). Christian charity is extended to all without distinction of race, social condition, or religion, and seeks neither gain nor gratitude. Just as God loves us with a gratuitous love, so too the faithful, in their charity, should be concerned for mankind, loving it with that same love with which God sought man. As Christ went about all the towns and villages healing every sickness and infirmity, as a sign that the kingdom of God had come (cf. Mt. 9:35 ff; Acts 10:38), so the Church, through its children, joins itself with men of every condition, but especially with the poor and afflicted, and willingly spends herself for them (cf. 2 Cor. 12:15). It shares their joys and sorrows, it is familiar with the hopes and problems of life, it suffers with them in the anguish of death. It wishes to enter into fraternal dialogue with those who are working for peace, and to bring them the peace and light of the Gospel. *Missionary Activity, 12*

#P26-11-2

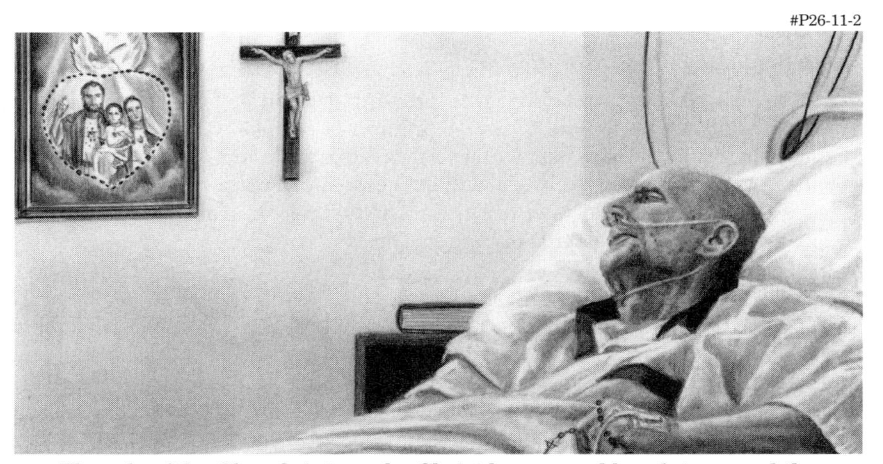

The role of the Church is to make Christ known and loved, to spread the knowledge of Salvation everywhere, and to pray and suffer for the Salvation of souls.

Proceeding from the love of the eternal Father, the Church was founded by Christ in time and gathered into one by the Holy Spirit. It has a saving and eschatological purpose which can be fully attained only in the next life. But it is now present here on earth and is composed of men; they, the members of the earthly city, are called to form the family of the children of God even in this present history of mankind and to increase it continually until the Lord comes. Made one in view of heavenly benefits and enriched by them, this family has been "constituted and organized as a society in the present world" by Christ and "provided with means adapted to its visible and social union." Thus the Church, at once "a visible organization and a spiritual community," travels the same journey as all mankind and shares the same earthly lot with the world: it is to be a leaven and, as it were, the soul of human society in its renewal by Christ and transformation into the family of God. *Gaudium et Spes, 40*

In their pilgrimage to the heavenly city, Christians are to seek and relish the things that are above: this involves not a lesser, but rather a greater commitment to working with all men towards the establishment of a world that is more human. *Gaudium et Spes, 57*

Catechism by Diagram

#C15-64

The Light of Revealed Truth. Jesus said, "I am the light of the world." Jesus (candle) brought the light of His truth to the world at His birth (manger); the Apostles drew from this light and passed it on to their successors—the bishops, priests, and deacons (men with candles)—for Jesus said, "You are the light of the world." This light—the truths of faith—was gathered by the Apostles and evangelists and put into writing (Bible) or orally passed on as Tradition. These truths were explained by the Fathers and Doctors of the Church (ring with rays). All members of the Church should bring this light to the world by their teaching and good example.

Summary Prayer

Heavenly Father, Your Son, Jesus Christ, said that He is the Light of the world. He told us, His followers, to be like lights for the whole world. May our light shine before people, so that they will see the good things we do and praise You. This is the will of Your Son. Send us Your Holy Spirit to make us holy so that the brightness of our good example, even more than our words or learning, may scatter the darkness of the spirit of the world and radiate the ideal of true happiness found in Your divine teaching. We ask this in the name of Jesus our Lord. Amen.

Q. 162. How does the Catholic Church minister to our spiritual needs?

The Catholic Church ministers to our spiritual needs by providing a community of faith, where we can find help and guidance in seeking God.

The Holy Spirit gives and strengthens the life of God in the Church community through its teaching, the sacraments, prayer, and works of service. The sacraments are special actions in the Church through which the life of God is communicated to His people. The Church is Christ still active in the world.

#C17-19

The Catholic Church ministers to our spiritual needs by providing a community of faith, where we can find help and guidance in seeking God.

Catechism of the Catholic Church

798 The Holy Spirit is "the principle of every vital and truly saving action in each part of the Body."[1] He works in many ways to build up the whole Body in charity:[2] by God's Word "which is able to build you up";[3] by Baptism, through which he forms Christ's Body;[4] by the sacraments, which give growth and healing to Christ's members; by "the grace of the apostles, which holds first place among his gifts";[5] by the virtues, which make us act according to what is good; finally, by the many special graces (called "charisms"), by which he makes the faithful "fit and ready to undertake various tasks and offices for the renewal and building up of the Church."[6]

Vatican Council II

Education is, in a very special way, the concern of the Church, not only because the Church must be recognized as a human society capable of imparting education, but especially it has the duty of proclaiming the way of

Catechism of the Catholic Church
Q. 162. Paragraphs 799, **1113-1134**, 1143, 1146, 1198.

For cross-references with Vatican II, Papal documents & other resources, see Family Wisdom Library on page 734.
For commentaries on each question with Cardinal Arinze, Sr. John Vianney and Fr. Straub (in Spanish), see Appendix C.

salvation to all men, of revealing the life of Christ to those who believe, and of assisting them with unremitting care so that they may be able to attain to the fullness of that life.

The Church as a mother is under an obligation, therefore, to provide for its children an education by virtue of which their whole lives may be inspired by the spirit of Christ. At the same time it will offer its assistance to all peoples for the promotion of a well-balanced perfection of the human personality, for the good of society in this world and for the development of a world more worthy of man. *Christian Education, 3*

Q. 163. How does the Catholic Church minister to the bodily needs of people?

The Catholic Church ministers extensively to the bodily needs of people by helping those in need, by seeking to relieve the causes of suffering, and by building up a better life for man. Its vast health care and social welfare systems are found throughout the world.

Although the Church is deeply involved in ministering to the bodily needs of people, it always has Heaven in view and continues to be a light to lead people to eternal life with God.

#W2-10

For I was hungry and you gave me food, I was thirsty and you gave me drink, I was a stranger and you welcomed me. *(Matthew 25:35)*

Sacred Scripture
Q. 163. Mt 20:26-28; Acts 6:1-6.

Catechism of the Catholic Church
Q. 163. Paragraphs **1928-1948**, 2288-2289, 2297-2298, 2300, **2447**, 2449.

For cross-references with Vatican II, Papal documents & other resources, see Family Wisdom Library on page 734.
For commentaries on each question with Cardinal Arinze, Sr. John Vianney and Fr. Straub (in Spanish), see Appendix C.

The Church is the answer to our Lord's appeal, "Come to me, all who labor and are heavy laden, and I will give you rest. Take my yoke upon you, and learn from me; for I am gentle and lowly in heart, and you will find rest for your souls. For my yoke is easy, and my burden is light" (Matthew 11:28-30).

#W2-6

The Catholic Church ministers extensively to the bodily needs of people by helping those in need, by seeking to relieve the causes of suffering, and by building up a better life for man.

Sacred Scripture

For I was hungry and you gave me food, I was thirsty and you gave me drink, I was a stranger and you welcomed me, I was naked and you clothed me, I was sick and you visited me, I was in prison and you came to me. *Matthew 25:35-36*

Catechism of the Catholic Church

786 Finally, the People of God shares in the *royal* office of Christ. He exercises his kingship by drawing all men to himself through his death and Resurrection.[1] Christ, King and Lord of the universe, made himself the servant of all, for he came "not to be served but to serve, and to give his life as a ransom for many."[2] For the Christian, "to reign is to serve him," particularly when serving "the poor and the suffering, in whom the Church recognizes the image of her poor and suffering founder."[3] The People of God fulfills its royal dignity by a life in keeping with its vocation to serve with Christ: "The sign of the cross makes kings of all those reborn in Christ and the anointing of the Holy Spirit consecrates them as priests, so that, apart from the particular service of our ministry, all spiritual and rational Christians are recognized as members of this royal race and sharers in Christ's priestly office. What, indeed, is as royal for a soul as to govern the body in obedience to God? And what is as priestly as to dedicate a pure conscience to the Lord and to offer the spotless offerings of devotion on the altar of the heart?"[4]

Vatican Council II

Charitable action today can and should reach all men and all needs. *Lay People, 8*

Indeed it is a duty for the whole people of God, under the teaching and example of the bishops, to alleviate the hardships of our times within the limits of its means, giving generously, as was the ancient custom of the Church, not merely out of what is superfluous, but also out of what is necessary. *Gaudium et Spes, 88*

The Church ought to be present in the community of peoples, to foster and stimulate cooperation among men; motivated by the sole desire of serving all men, it contributes both by means of its official channels and through the full and sincere collaboration of all Christians. This goal will be more effectively brought about if all the faithful are conscious of their responsibility as men and as Christians and work in their own environments to arouse generous cooperation with the international community. *Gaudium et Spes, 89*

Q. 164. How can we help unbelievers find God?

We can help unbelievers find God by the witness of our lives of firm faith in God and personal love of Christ, and by our goodness and love towards unbelievers.

#C37-3

The very witness of a Christian life, and good works done in a supernatural spirit, are effective in drawing men to the faith and to God. *(Lay People, 6)*

We can help people to turn to God if we give them a good example of our own deep faith in God. If people see our love for Christ in our good deeds, they will be moved to love Him also. God has willed that

Catechism of the Catholic Church
Q. 164. Paragraphs **849-856**, 863-864, **905**, **2105**, 2205, 2225.

For cross-references with Vatican II, Papal documents & other resources, see Family Wisdom Library on page 734.
For commentaries on each question with Cardinal Arinze, Sr. John Vianney and Fr. Straub (in Spanish), see Appendix C.

all men should make up one family and treat one another in a spirit of brotherhood, for all men are called to the same goal—God Himself. By our love for one another for the love of God and by other good works, we can help those who do not believe in God to find Him.

#E5-5

Evangelization is the most powerful and stirring challenge which the Church has been called to face from her very beginning. *(Splendor of Truth, 106)*

Sacred Scripture

"A new commandment I give to you, that you love one another; even as I have loved you, that you also love one another. By this all men will know that you are my disciples, if you have love for one another." *John 13:34-35*

Above all hold unfailing your love for one another, since love covers a multitude of sins. Practice hospitality ungrudgingly to one another. *1 Peter 4:8-9*

Catechism of the Catholic Church

851 *Missionary motivation*. It is from God's love for all men that the Church in every age receives both the obligation and the vigor of her missionary dynamism, "for the love of Christ urges us on."[1] Indeed, God "desires all men to be saved and to come to the knowledge of the truth";[2] that is, God wills the salvation of everyone through the knowledge of the truth. Salvation is found in the truth. Those who obey the prompting of the Spirit of truth are already on the way of salvation. But the Church, to whom this truth has been entrusted, must go out to meet their desire, so as to bring them the truth. Because she believes in God's universal plan of salvation, the Church must be missionary.

Splendor of Truth

Evangelization is the most powerful and stirring challenge which the Church has been called to face from her very beginning. The present time is instead marked by a formidable challenge to undertake a "new evangelization," a proclamation of the Gospel which is always new and always the bearer of new things, an evangelization which must be "new in its ardor, methods, and expression." Dechristianization, which weighs heavily upon entire peoples and communities once rich in faith and Christian life, involves not only the loss of faith or in any event its becoming irrelevant for everyday life, but also, and of necessity, a decline or obscuring of the moral sense. This comes about both as a result of a loss of awareness of the originality of Gospel morality and as a result of an eclipse of fundamental principles and ethical values themselves. *(section 106)*

Vatican Council II

Laymen have countless opportunities for exercising the apostolate of evangelization and sanctification. The very witness of a Christian life, and good works done in a supernatural spirit, are effective in drawing men to the faith and to God; and that is what the Lord has said: "Your light must shine so brightly before men that they can see your good works and glorify your Father who is in heaven" (Mt. 5:16).

This witness of life, however, is not the sole element in the apostolate; the true apostle is on the lookout for occasions of announcing Christ by word, either to unbelievers to draw them towards the faith, or to the faithful to instruct them, strengthen them, [or] incite them to a more fervent life. *Lay People, 6*

#E5-3

The true apostle is on the lookout for occasions of announcing Christ by word, either to unbelievers to draw them towards the faith, or to the faithful to instruct them, strengthen them, [or] incite them to a more fervent life. *(Lay People, 6)*

Q. 165. What is our duty towards the world?

As Christians, we must help men to solve their problems as much as possible. We show our love for God by loving our neighbors—the people around us.

#W2-7

Love for our neighbor makes us do all we can to help those who need our assistance and to make the world better.

Love for our neighbor makes us do all we can to help those who need our assistance and to make the world better. Jesus said, "You are the light of the world. A city set on a hill cannot be hid... Let your light so shine before men, that they may see your good works and give glory to your Father who is in heaven" (Matthew 5:14, 16).

As Christians, we must take an active part in all aspects of temporal life—economic, political, and social, for we and our fellow men are in fact the authors, center, and goal of this life. Concretely, this participation includes working to make sure that the goods God has created for everyone do in fact reach everyone, both now and in the future, as justice and charity require.

Sacred Scripture
Q. 165. Sir 29:1-3, 8-12; Mk 12:28-31.

Catechism of the Catholic Church
Q. 165. Paragraphs **2419-2430**.

For cross-references with Vatican II, Papal documents & other resources, see Family Wisdom Library on page 734.
For commentaries on each question with Cardinal Arinze; Sr. John Vianney and Fr. Straub (in Spanish), see Appendix C.

Closely connected with this obligation is the people's right to information based on truth, freedom, and justice. Without it, citizens cannot rightly fulfill their duties. Christians, therefore, need to be involved in the work of gathering, evaluating, commenting on, and disseminating this information. Similarly they need to be involved in the entertainment industry and in the use of the social communications media.

In all this, justice and charity require us to practice moderation and discipline, so that society is not undermined by false, useless, and evil talk, or the needless publication of scandalous information. Our rule and guide must be the words of Paul to the Ephesians: "Guard against foul talk; let your words be for the improvement of others, as occasion offers, and do good to your listeners, otherwise you will only be grieving the Holy Spirit of God who has marked you with his seal for you to be set free when the day comes. Never have grudges against others, or lose your temper, or raise your voice to anyone, or call each other names, or allow any sort of spitefulness. Be friends with one another, and kind, forgiving each other as readily as God forgave you in Christ" (Eph 4:29–32, The New Jerusalem Bible).

#C37-6

Economic life is not meant solely to multiply goods produced and increase profit or power; it is ordered first of all to the service of persons, of the whole man, and of the entire human community. *(Catechism of the Catholic Church, 2426)*

Sacred Scripture

And the word of the Lord came to Zechariah, saying, "Thus says the Lord of hosts, Render true judgments, show kindness and mercy each to his brother, do not oppress the widow, the fatherless, the sojourner, or the poor; and let none of you devise evil against his brother in your heart." *Zechariah 7:8-10*

In this is love, not that we loved God but that he loved us and sent his Son to be the expiation for our sins. Beloved, if God so loved us, we also ought to love one another. No man has ever seen God; if we love one another, God abides in us and his love is perfected in us. *1 John 4:10-12*

#W2-5

Render true judgments, show kindness and mercy each to his brother, do not oppress the widow, the fatherless, the sojourner, or the poor; and let none of you devise evil against his brother in your heart. *(Zechariah 7:8-10)*

Catechism of the Catholic Church

1928 Society ensures social justice when it provides the conditions that allow associations or individuals to obtain what is their due, according to their nature and their vocation. Social justice is linked to the common good and the exercise of authority.

2426 The development of economic activity and growth in production are meant to provide for the needs of human beings. Economic life is not meant solely to multiply goods produced and increase profit or power; it is ordered first of all to the service of persons, of the whole man, and of the entire human community. Economic activity, conducted according to its own proper methods, is to be exercised within the limits of the moral order, in keeping with social justice so as to correspond to God's plan for man.[1]

2427 Human work proceeds directly from persons created in the image of God and called to prolong the work of creation by subduing the earth, both with and for one another.1 Hence work is a duty: "If any one will not work, let him not eat."2 Work honors the Creator's gifts and the talents received from him. It can also be redemptive. By enduring the hardship of work3 in union with Jesus, the carpenter of Nazareth and the one crucified on Calvary, man collaborates in a certain fashion with the Son of God in his redemptive work.

He shows himself to be a disciple of Christ by carrying the cross, daily, in the work he is called to accomplish.[4] Work can be a means of sanctification and a way of animating earthly realities with the Spirit of Christ.

Vatican Council II

Human work which is exercised in the production and exchange of goods or in the provision of economic services, surpasses all other elements of economic life, for the latter are only means to an end.

Human work, whether exercised independently or in subordination to another, proceeds from the human person, who as it were impresses his seal on the things of nature and reduces them to his will. By his work a man ordinarily provides for himself and his family, associates with others as his brothers, and renders them service; he can exercise genuine charity and be a partner in the work of bringing divine creation to perfection. Moreover, we believe by faith that through the homage of work offered to God man is associated with the redemptive work of Jesus Christ, whose labor with his hands at Nazareth greatly ennobled the dignity of work. This is the source of every man's duty to work loyally as well as his right to work; moreover, it is the duty of society to see to it that, according to the prevailing circumstances, all citizens have the opportunity of finding employment. Finally, remuneration for work should guarantee man the opportunity to provide a dignified livelihood for himself and his family on the material, social, cultural and spiritual level to correspond to the role and the productivity of each, the relevant economic factors in his employment, and the common good. *Gaudium et Spes, 67*

Doctrine • Moral • Worship Exercise

(See Appendix A for answer key, questions 160-165.)

1. What does it mean to be a missionary? How does a Catholic fulfill his or her task of being a missionary?
2. In the ordinary circumstances of your life, how can you be a missionary to the people around you? Write down concrete things that you and your family can do to bring Christ to others (in your neighborhood, parish community, school, or workplace).
3. Frequently pray that all Christians respond generously to the call to make Christ known by spreading the knowledge of Salvation everywhere and by praying and offering our daily trials for the Salvation of souls.

Chapter Summary Prayer

God Our Father, we pray for those who do not believe in Christ, that the light of the Holy Spirit may show them the way to Salvation. Enable those who do not acknowledge Christ to find the truth, as they walk before You in sincerity of heart. Help us to grow in love for one another, to grasp more fully the mystery of Your Godhead, and to become more perfect witnesses of Your love in the sight of men.

Lord God, we pray for those who do not believe in You. May they find You by sincerely following all that is right. You created mankind so that they might long to find You, and then have peace when You are found. Grant that, in spite of the worldly things that stand in their way, they may all recognize in the lives of Christians the tokens of Your love and mercy, and so gladly acknowledge You as the one true God and Father of us all. We ask this through Jesus Christ, our Lord and Savior. Amen.

Thought Provokers

Please see Appendix B for the answers.

Q. 160: How do we receive the Catholic Faith?

Q. 161: Why did Jesus refer to the devil as the prince of this world? (cf. John 12:31)

Q. 162: How can parents minister to the spiritual needs of their children?

Q. 163: In what concrete ways has the Church shown concern for the bodily needs of people?

Q. 164: How can we speak to unbelievers about God?

Q. 165: How can the laity help bring the world back under the loving and merciful dominion of God?

CHAPTER FORTY-SEVEN

Christian Unity

Q. 166. Why is the unity of Christians in faith and love God's will?

Christian unity in faith and love is God's will because Jesus prayed that all who believe in Him should be one, in order that the whole world would know that His Father sent Him.

#C15-34-2

Christian unity in faith and love is God's will because Jesus prayed that all who believe in Him should be one.

The night before He suffered His Passion and death, Jesus prayed for Christian unity. "I do not pray for these only, but also for those who believe in me through their word, that they may all be one; even as thou, Father, art in me, and I in thee, that they also may be in us, so that the world may believe that thou hast sent me" (John 17:20-21).

Seeing how the early Christians loved and honored one another, the pagans came to believe that the Christian God was the true God.

Catechism of the Catholic Church
Q. 166. Paragraphs 1815-1816, 1826-**1827**.

For cross-references with Vatican II, Papal documents & other resources, see Family Wisdom Library on page 734.
For commentaries on each question with Cardinal Arinze, Sr. John Vianney and Fr. Straub (in Spanish), see Appendix C.

Jesus said, “I am the good shepherd; I know my own and my own know me, as the Father knows me and I know the Father; and I lay down my life for the sheep. And I have other sheep, that are not of this fold; I must bring them also, and they will heed my voice. So there shall be one flock, one shepherd” (John 10:14-16).

Jesus founded but one Church, that which is built upon Peter the Rock. Moreover, Jesus brought the same Good News to all men, and called all to the same new life. His Church subsists in the Catholic Church, which is the world-wide community of the followers of Jesus united around the Pope.

#P26-35

Today, in many parts of the world, under the influence of the grace of the Holy Spirit, many efforts are being made in prayer, word and action to attain that fullness of unity which Jesus Christ desires. *(Ecumenism, 4)*

Vatican Council II

The condition of the modern world lends greater urgency to this duty of the Church; for, while men of the present day are drawn ever more closely together by social, technical and cultural bonds, it still remains for them to achieve full unity in Christ. *Lumen Gentium, 1*

Today, in many parts of the world, under the influence of the grace of the Holy Spirit, many efforts are being made in prayer, word and action to attain that fullness of unity which Jesus Christ desires. The sacred Council exhorts, therefore, all the Catholic faithful to recognize the signs of the times and to take an active and intelligent part in the work of ecumenism. *Ecumenism, 4*

Q. 167. How is Christian unity promoted by Catholics?

In order to promote Christian unity, Catholics should take the first steps in seeking to overcome the unfortunate divisions existing between Christians. They should strive to make Christians more faithful to Christ and to be effective witnesses to the truths received from the Apostles.

#M3-253-2

The Church is one because there is only one Jesus. At the same time, the Church is not one, because historical differences and bitterness have driven the followers of Jesus apart.

The Church is one because there is only one Jesus, Who communicates the same life of God through the Holy Spirit to all who believe in Him. At this level, all Christians are truly united, and the Church is one. If our love for Christ is sincere, we shall do all in our power, by prayer and work, so that Christ's will and prayer for unity may be realized: "That they may all be one" (John 17:21).

At the same time, the Church is not one, because historical differences and bitterness have driven the followers of Jesus apart. Consequently, much of their Christian lives is not shared with one another. Besides, men's understanding of Jesus and the meaning of His life and teaching differ, and sometimes these differences prevent Christians from coming together.

As a result, divisions and separate groups have appeared. These groups are principally the Roman Catholic Church, the Eastern Orthodox Church, the Anglican Church, and the various Protestant

Sacred Scripture
Q. 167. 1 Cor 12:12-13; Eph 4:1-3.

Catechism of the Catholic Church
Q. 167. Paragraphs **815**, **821**, 855.

For cross-references with Vatican II, Papal documents & other resources, see Family Wisdom Library on page 734.
For commentaries on each question with Cardinal Arinze, Sr. John Vianney and Fr. Straub (in Spanish), see Appendix C.

communities. As Catholics, we should show our deep concern for this sad condition by praying and working for Christian unity.

Ecumenism is the acceptance of the basic unity of the Church and the effort to make this unity present and visible in the whole life of the Church. We Catholics partake of Christ's unfathomable riches, and we should lovingly share them with others.

#P26-36

In certain circumstances, such as in prayer services "for unity" and during ecumenical gatherings, it is allowable, indeed desirable that Catholics should join in prayer with their separated brethren. *(Ecumenism, 8)*

Sacred Scripture

I appeal to you, brethren, by the name of our Lord Jesus Christ, that all of you agree and that there be no dissensions among you, but that you be united in the same mind and the same judgment." *1 Corinthians 1:10*

Catechism of the Catholic Church

822 Concern for achieving unity "involves the whole Church, faithful and clergy alike."[1] But we must realize "that this holy objective—the reconciliation of all Christians in the unity of the one and only Church of Christ—transcends human powers and gifts." That is why we place all our hope "in the prayer of Christ for the Church, in the love of the Father for us, and in the power of the Holy Spirit."

Vatican Council II

The Church knows that she is joined in many ways to the baptized who are honored by the name of Christian, but who do not however profess the Catholic faith in its entirety or have not preserved unity or communion under the successor of Peter. For there are many who hold sacred scripture in honor as a rule of faith and of life, who have a sincere religious zeal, who lovingly believe in God the Father Almighty and in Christ, the Son of God and the Savior, who are sealed by baptism which unites them to Christ, and who indeed recognize and receive other sacraments in their own Churches or ecclesiastical communities. Many of them possess the episcopate, celebrate the holy Eucharist and cultivate devotion of the Virgin Mother of God. There is furthermore a sharing in prayer and spiritual benefits; these Christians are indeed in some real way joined to us in the Holy Spirit for, by his gifts and graces, his sanctifying power is also active in them and he has strengthened some of them even to the shedding of their blood. *Lumen Gentium, 15*

Certainly, such division openly contradicts the will of Christ, scandalizes the world, and damages that most holy cause, the preaching of the Gospel to every creature. *Ecumenism, 1*

This change of heart and holiness of life, along with public and private prayer for the unity of Christians, should be regarded as the soul of the whole ecumenical movement, and merits the name, "spiritual ecumenism." *Ecumenism, 8*

In certain circumstances, such as in prayer services "for unity" and during ecumenical gatherings, it is allowable, indeed desirable that Catholics should join in prayer with their separated brethren. Such prayers in common are certainly a very effective means of petitioning for the grace of unity, and they are a genuine expression of the ties which still bind Catholics to their separated brethren. "For where two or three are gathered in my name, there am I in the midst of them" (Mt. 18:20). *Ecumenism, 8*

#P26-65

If our love for Christ is sincere, we shall do all in our power, by prayer and work, so that Christ's will and prayer for unity may be realized: "That they may all be one" *(John 17:21).*

Summary Prayer

Heavenly Father, gather all our brothers and sisters who share our faith in Jesus Christ. Gather and keep together in one Church all those who seek the truth with sincerity. Look kindly on all those who follow Jesus Your Son. We are all consecrated to You by our common Baptism. Make us one in the fullness of faith, and keep us one in the fellowship of love, through Jesus Christ our Lord, to Whom with You and the Holy Spirit be all honor and glory. Amen.

Q. 168. Why should we respect all men of good will?

We should respect all men of good will because man was created for God in His image and likeness; as a human being he possesses a special dignity and value. Man, having a spiritual soul and being a more perfect image of God, has dominion over all other earthly creatures. He has a free will and is immortal. For these reasons alone, all men are deserving of our respect. The Catholic Church rejects as un-Christian any unjust discrimination or injustice because of race, national origin, ethnic origin, color, sex, class, condition in life, or religion.

The story of the Good Samaritan teaches us that our neighbor is every man, not only those who belong to our race, our country, or our religion. We should love even those who hate us and injure us. The Divine Master gave us the example when He said, "This is my commandment, that you love one another as I have loved you" (John 15:12).

#W2-3-2

The story of the Good Samaritan teaches us that our neighbor is every man, not only those who belong to our race, our country, or our religion.

Sacred Scripture

If anyone says, "I love God," and hates his brother, he is a liar; for he who does not love his brother whom he has seen, cannot love God whom he has not seen. *1 John 4:20*

Sacred Scripture
Q. 168. Gen 1:27; Lk 10:29-37.

Catechism of the Catholic Church
Q. 168. Paragraphs 842, **1931-1933**.

For cross-references with Vatican II, Papal documents & other resources, see Family Wisdom Library on page 734.
For commentaries on each question with Cardinal Arinze, Sr. John Vianney and Fr. Straub (in Spanish), see Appendix C.

#C37-1

In his fatherly care for all of us, God desired that all men should form one family and deal with each other in a spirit of brotherhood. *(Gaudium et Spes, 24)*

Catechism of the Catholic Church

1930 Respect for the human person entails respect for the rights that flow from his dignity as a creature. These rights are prior to society and must be recognized by it. They are the basis of the moral legitimacy of every authority: by flouting them, or refusing to recognize them in its positive legislation, a society undermines its own moral legitimacy.[1] If it does not respect them, authority can rely only on force or violence to obtain obedience from its subjects. It is the Church's role to remind men of good will of these rights and to distinguish them from unwarranted or false claims.

Splendor of Truth

Jesus' way of acting and his words, his deeds and his precepts constitute the moral rule of Christian life. Indeed, his actions, and in particular his Passion and Death on the Cross, are the living revelation of his love for the Father and for others. *(section 20)*

Vatican Council II

And so the Spirit stirs up desires and actions in all of Christ's disciples in order that all may be peaceably united, as Christ ordained, in one flock under one shepherd. Mother Church never ceases to pray, hope and work that this may be achieved. *Lumen Gentium, 15*

It is through the faithful preaching of the Gospel by the Apostles and their successors—the bishops with Peter's successor at their head—through their administering the sacraments, and through their governing in love, that Jesus Christ wishes his people to increase, under the action of the Holy Spirit; and he perfects its fellowship in unity: in the confession of one faith, in the common celebration of divine worship, and in the fraternal harmony of the family of God. *Ecumenism, 2*

In his fatherly care for all of us, God desired that all men should form one family and deal with each other in a spirit of brotherhood. *Gaudium et Spes, 24*

Therefore, the Church reproves, as foreign to the mind of Christ, any discrimination against people or any harassment of them on the basis of their race, color, condition in life or religion. Accordingly, following the footsteps of the holy apostles Peter and Paul, the sacred Council earnestly begs the Christian faithful to "conduct themselves well among Gentiles" (1 Pet. 2:12) and if possible, as far as depends on them, to be at peace with all men (cf. Rom. 12:18) and in that way to be true sons of the Father who is in heaven (cf. Mt. 5:45). *Non-Christian Religions, 5*

#Y1-4-2

The Catholic Church rejects as un-Christian any unjust discrimination or injustice because of race, national origin, ethnic origin, color, sex, class, condition in life, or religion.

Doctrine • Moral • Worship Exercise

(See Appendix A for answer key, questions 166–168.)

1. Cite two passages in Sacred Scripture which show that Jesus wants all people to be united in faith in the one true Catholic Church which He founded? What does ecumenism mean?
2. One way to promote Christian unity is to lead others to the knowledge of the one true faith. What can you and your family do to teach or lead others to the truths of our Catholic Church?
3. Pray for Christian unity and that all may come to the knowledge of the one true Catholic faith.

Chapter Summary Prayer

Father, You gather the nations to praise Your Name. May all who are reborn in Baptism be one in faith and love. Grant Your continuing protection to all those who have received new life in Baptism. The perfect sacrifice of Jesus Christ made us Your people. In Your love grant peace and unity to Your Church. You are the strength of the people. Unite us as one in Your holy Church, so that we may attain the peace our hearts desire. Jesus, Divine Shepherd, Your life's last concern was that the Apostles, upon whom You would confer the Holy Spirit, would be able, by God's grace and their own word and example, to lead Your scattered sheep into the one true fold. You prayed to Your Father for this unity the night before You died. Help us to maintain this unity by remaining always faithful to the Holy Father, the Pope, and to all the bishops united to him in faith and charity. We ask this in Your most powerful and holy Name. Amen.

Thought Provokers

Please see Appendix B for the answers.

Q. 166: Where should Christian unity in faith and love begin?

Q. 167: In addition to showing a deep love for our Christian, but non-Catholic, family members, friends, and acquaintances, how else can we Catholics promote Christian unity with them, as well as with other non-Catholic Christians?

Q. 168: Why should we show respect to those who profess good will but who, nonetheless, hold views which are contrary to Christianity?

#C15-32

Catholics firmly believe that Jesus Christ made His Catholic Church the ordinary means of Salvation. We should desire to share the Church's fullness with all mankind.

CHAPTER FORTY-EIGHT

The Catholic Church: Means of Salvation

Q. 169. What do we believe about the Catholic Church and Salvation?

We firmly believe that Jesus Christ made His Catholic Church the ordinary means of Salvation. We should desire to share the Church's fullness with all mankind.

#C15-41-2

Catholics believe that Jesus Christ placed the work of Salvation in the care of His Church.

Catholics believe that Jesus Christ placed the work of Salvation in the care of His Church. Speaking to His disciples, Jesus said, "He who hears you hears me, and he who rejects you rejects me, and he who rejects me rejects him who sent me" (Luke 10:16). Not to the individual, but to the Church, was the promise made by Christ:

Catechism of the Catholic Church
Q. 169. Paragraphs **168-169**, **847**, 1257, 1260.

For cross-references with Vatican II, Papal documents & other resources, see Family Wisdom Library on page 734.
For commentaries on each question with Cardinal Arinze, Sr. John Vianney and Fr. Straub (in Spanish), see Appendix C.

"And I will pray the Father, and he will give you another Counselor, to be with you for ever" (John 14:16).

On Pentecost, the Holy Spirit descended upon the Apostles in tongues of fire and transformed those men into the strong foundation upon which Christ's Church was to be built. The once ignorant, weak, and timid Apostles now went bravely forward to confront the world and to save it for their Master.

Catholics believe that only through the Church can we find full security and certainty about the meaning and destiny of human life, and know fully what God wills us to believe and do, thus attaining Salvation. Without the Church, religion becomes merely a matter of opinion and conjecture, and we have no assurance as to what is true or false.

#P26-73

Catholics believe that only through the Church can we find full security and certainty about the meaning and destiny of human life, and know fully what God wills us to believe and do, thus attaining Salvation.

Our lives as Catholic Christians are not meaningless. We are not at the mercy of a blind, unreasonable fate. We know that we are walking in the sunlight of truth, under the loving care of our heavenly Father and with the guidance of the Church, our spiritual mother upon earth. As we recognize the unique fullness of the Catholic Church, we should thank our Lord for this great gift, "the pillar and bulwark of the truth" (1 Timothy 3:15).

#F1-74-2

God our Savior… desires all men to be saved and to come to the knowledge of the truth. *(1 Timothy 2:3, 4)*

Sacred Scripture

So Jesus again said to them, "Truly, truly I say to you…I am the door; if any one enters by me, he will be saved, and will go in and out and find pasture… I am the good shepherd; I know my own and my own know me." *John 10:7, 9, 14*

God our Savior… desires all men to be saved and to come to the knowledge of the truth. *1 Timothy 2:3, 4*

Catechism of the Catholic Church

"Outside the Church there is no salvation"

846 How are we to understand this affirmation, often repeated by the Church Fathers?[1] Re-formulated positively, it means that all salvation comes from Christ the Head through the Church which is his Body: "Basing itself on Scripture and Tradition, the Council teaches that the Church, a pilgrim now on earth, is necessary for salvation: the one Christ is the mediator and the way of salvation; he is present to us in his body which is the Church. He himself explicitly asserted the necessity of faith and Baptism, and thereby affirmed at the same time the necessity of the Church which men enter through Baptism as through a door. Hence they could not be saved who, knowing that the Catholic Church was founded as necessary by God through Christ, would refuse either to enter it or to remain in it."[2]

847 This affirmation is not aimed at those who, through no fault of their own, do not know Christ and his Church: "Those who, through no fault of their own, do not know the Gospel of Christ or his Church, but who nevertheless seek God with a sincere heart, and, moved by grace, try in their actions to do his will as they know it through the dictates of their conscience—those too may achieve eternal salvation."[1]

Splendor of Truth

Precisely on the questions frequently debated in moral theology today and with regard to which new tendencies and theories have developed, the Magisterium, in fidelity to Jesus Christ and in continuity with the Church's tradition, senses more urgently the duty to offer its own discernment and teaching, in order to help man in his journey towards truth and freedom. *(section 27)*

Vatican Council II

The Church is... a sheepfold, the sole and necessary gateway to which is Christ (Jn. 10:1-10). It is also a flock, of which God foretold that he would himself be the shepherd (cf. Is. 40:11; Ex. 34:11 f), and whose sheep, although watched over by human shepherds, are nevertheless at all times led and brought to pasture by Christ himself, the Good Shepherd and prince of shepherds (cf. Jn. 10:11; 1 Pet. 5:4), who gave his life for his sheep (cf. Jn. 10:11-16). *Lumen Gentium, 6*

All those, who in faith look towards Jesus, the author of salvation and the principle of unity and peace, God has gathered together and established as the Church, that it may be for each and everyone the visible sacrament of this saving unity. *Lumen Gentium, 9*

It is through Christ's Catholic Church alone, which is the universal help towards salvation, that the fullness of the means of salvation can be obtained. It was to the apostolic college alone, of which Peter is the head, that we believe that Our Lord entrusted all the blessings of the New Covenant, in order to establish on earth the one Body of Christ into which all those should be fully incorporated who belong in any way to the people of God. *Ecumenism, 3*

Whether it aids the world or whether it benefits from it, the Church has but one sole purpose – that the kingdom of God may come and the salvation of the human race may be accomplished. Every benefit the people of God can confer on mankind during its earthly pilgrimage is rooted in the Church's being "the universal sacrament of salvation," at once manifesting and actualizing the mystery of God's love for men. *Gadium et Spes, 45*

Summary Prayer

Lord God, guide us with Your love through the Church. Keep us faithful, that we may be helped through life and be brought to Salvation through its teaching and sacraments. We ask this in the Name of Jesus Christ our Lord and Savior. Amen.

Q. 170. How do the laity share in Christ's mission?

As Christ sent His Apostles to teach and to be witnesses to Him in the world, so too, He wants the laity to share in this mission.

The duty of proclaiming the Gospel and of making its power felt in the lives of men belongs not only to bishops, priests, deacons, and religious, but also to the laity in the Church.

#L3-34

As Christ sent His Apostles to teach and to be witnesses to Him in the world, so too, He wants the laity to share in this mission.

The laity are called to be Christ's witnesses in the world of social, economic, and political activity. They must contribute to the growth of the Kingdom of God by bringing the love and truth of Christ to the world.

In the small circle of their families and neighborhoods, the Catholic laity are called to help guide the world heavenward. They must work in the making of laws and in the shaping of social doctrines and practice, contribute to their country's development, and minister to the spiritual and material needs of the poor.

The vocation of the laity is to continue Christ's work of transforming the kingdom of the world into the Kingdom of God, consecrating the world for Christ. By living truly Christ-centered lives of generous service to others, they can help bring about the unity of all men under God.

Catechism of the Catholic Church
Q. 170. Paragraphs 863, 905, **2044**, **2472**.

For cross-references with Vatican II, Papal documents & other resources, see Family Wisdom Library on page 734.
For commentaries on each question with Cardinal Arinze, Sr. John Vianney and Fr. Straub (in Spanish), see Appendix C.

#F1-77

The Catholic laity must work in the making of laws and in the shaping of social doctrines and practice, contribute to their country's development, and minister to the spiritual and material needs of the poor.

As our Lord sent His Apostles to teach and be His witnesses in the world, so too He would have the Catholic laity participate in this mission of living and proclaiming the Gospel. This mission can only be accomplished in and through love. As our Lord said, "By this all men will know that you are my disciples, if you have love for one another" (John 13:35).

Sacred Scripture

They are not of the world, even as I am not of the world... As thou didst send me into the world, so I have sent them into the world. *John 17:16, 18*

Whatever your task, work heartily, as serving the Lord and not men, knowing that from the Lord you will receive the inheritance as your reward; you are serving the Lord Christ. *Colossians 3:23-24*

Catechism of the Catholic Church

900 Since, like all the faithful, lay Christians are entrusted by God with the apostolate by virtue of their Baptism and Confirmation, they have the right and duty, individually or grouped in associations, to work so that the divine message of salvation may be known and accepted by all men throughout the earth. This duty is the more pressing when it is only through them that men can hear the Gospel and know Christ. Their activity in ecclesial communities is so necessary that, for the most part, the apostolate of the pastors cannot be fully effective without it.[1]

Splendor of Truth

Evangelization—and therefore the "new evangelization"—also involves the proclamation and presentation of morality. Jesus himself, even as he preached the Kingdom of God and its saving love, called people to faith and conversion (cf. Mk 1:15). And when Peter, with the other Apostles, proclaimed the Resurrection of Jesus of Nazareth from the dead, he held out a new life to be lived, a "way" to be followed, for those who would be disciples of the Risen One (cf. Acts 2:37-41; 3:17-20).

The life of holiness which is resplendent in so many members of the People of God, humble and often unseen, constitutes the simplest and most attractive way to perceive at once the beauty of truth, the liberating force of God's love, and the value of unconditional fidelity to all the demands of the Lord's law, even in the most difficult situations. *(section 107)*

Vatican Council II

The holy People of God shares also in Christ's prophetic office: it spreads abroad a living witness to him, especially by a life of faith and love and by offering to God a sacrifice of praise, the fruit of lips praising his name (cf. Heb. 13:15). *Lumen Gentium, 12*

The term "laity" is here understood to mean all the faithful except those in Holy Orders and those who belong to a religious state approved by the Church. That is, the faithful who by Baptism are incorporated into Christ, are placed in the People of God and, in their own way share the priestly, prophetic and kingly office of Christ, and to the best of their ability carry on the mission of the whole Christian people in the Church and in the world. Their secular character is proper and peculiar to the laity. *Lumen Gentium, 31*

#P26-69

By living truly Christ-centered lives of generous service to others, the laity can help bring about the unity of all men under God.

Although by Christ's will some are established as teachers, dispensers of the mysteries and pastors for the others, there remains, nevertheless, a true equality between all with regard to the dignity and to the activity which is common to all the faithful in the building up of the Body of Christ. The distinction which the Lord has made between the sacred ministers and the rest of the People of God involves union, for the pastors and the other faithful are joined together by a close relationship: the pastors of the Church—following the example of the Lord—should minister to each other and to the rest of the faithful; the latter should eagerly collaborate with the pastors and teachers. And so amid variety all will bear witness to the wonderful unity in the Body of Christ: this very diversity of graces, of ministries and of works gathers the sons of God into one, for "all these things are the work of the one and the same Spirit (1 Cor. 12:11)." *Lumen Gentium, 32*

Gathered together in the People of God and established in the one Body of Christ under one head, the laity—no matter who they are—have, as living members, the vocation of applying to the building up of the Church and to its continual sanctification all the powers which they have received from the goodness of the Creator and from the grace of the Redeemer. *Lumen Gentium, 33*

The apostolate of the laity is a sharing in the salvific mission of the Church. Through Baptism and Confirmation all are appointed to this apostolate by the Lord himself. Moreover, by the sacraments, and especially by the Eucharist, that love of God and man which is the soul of the apostolate is communicated and nourished. The laity, however, are given this special vocation: to make the Church present and fruitful in those places and circumstances where it is only through them that she can become the salt of the earth. *Lumen Gentium, 33*

Each individual layman must be a witness before the world to the resurrection and life of the Lord Jesus, and a sign of the living God. All together, and each one to the best of his ability, must nourish the world with spiritual fruits (cf. Gal. 5:22). They must diffuse in the world the spirit which animates those poor, meek and peace-makers whom the Lord in the Gospel proclaimed blessed (cf. Mt. 5:3-9). In a word: "what the soul is in the body, let Christians be in the world." *Lumen Gentium, 38*

The Church can never be without the lay apostolate; it is something that derives from the layman's very vocation as a Christian. *Lay People, 1*

#E5-15

The laity, however, are given this special vocation: to make the Church present and fruitful in those places and circumstances where it is only through them that she can become the salt of the earth. *(Lumen Gentium, 33)*

#C15-46-2

Bulletin Announcement

Parish Pastoral Council Meeting
Saturday, 1:30-3:30PM

Be Not Afraid Family Hours
and Confessions
Wednesdays, 7-8PM

The pastors of the Church—following the example of the Lord—should minister to each other and to the rest of the faithful; the latter should eagerly collaborate with the pastors and teachers. *(Lumen Gentium, 32)*

In the Church there is diversity of ministry but unity of mission. To the apostles and their successors Christ has entrusted the office of teaching, sanctifying and governing in his name and by his power. But the laity are made to share in the priestly, prophetical and kingly office of Christ; they have therefore, in the Church and in the world, their own assignment in the mission of the whole People of God. *Lay People, 2*

The Church was founded to spread the kingdom of Christ over all the earth for the glory of God the Father, to make all men partakers in redemption and salvation, and through them to establish the right relationship of the entire world to Christ. Every activity of the Mystical Body with this in view goes by the name of "apostolate"; the Church exercises it through all its members, though in various ways. In fact, the Christian vocation is, of its nature, a vocation to the apostolate as well. *Lay People, 2*

The hierarchy entrusts the laity with certain charges more closely connected with the duties of pastors: in the teaching of Christian doctrine, for example, in certain liturgical actions, in the care of souls. In virtue of this mission the laity are fully subject to superior ecclesiastical control in regard to the exercise of these charges. *Lay People, 24*

Summary Prayer

God our Father, inspire the hearts of all Your people to continue the saving work of Christ everywhere until the end of the world. The suffering and death of Christ Your Son won Your Salvation for all the world. May the suffering and death of Your Son sanctify the Church so that it can be an instrument of Salvation for the world. May the prayers and the Eucharistic sacrifice of Your Church come to You and be pleasing in Your sight. Make us holy by the Eucharist we share at Your table. Through the sacraments of Your Church, may all people receive the Salvation Your Son brought us through His suffering and death on the Cross. We ask this through our Lord and Savior Jesus Christ. Amen.

Q. 171. How is the Catholic Church an institution of Salvation?

The Catholic Church is an institution for Salvation since (1) it is a community of the faithful with our Savior Jesus Christ as its Head, and (2) it has been given the mission of communicating the Good News of Salvation to all mankind.

1. The Catholic Church is an institution of Salvation because it is a community of the faithful with our Savior Jesus Christ as its Head.

The Church is a fellowship of life, charity and truth. Through Jesus Christ, we have become members of the family of God, the People of God. We are intimately united to Christ and to one another in a union which our Lord compared to the sublime union of the Blessed Trinity: "That they may all be one; even as thou, Father, art in me, and I in thee, that they also may be in us, so that the world may believe that thou hast sent me" (John 17:21).

#C37-4

We should have special love for our fellow members in the Mystical Body of Christ, because in loving the members of His Body we are loving Christ.

Catechism of the Catholic Church
Q. 171. Paragraphs 738,774-**776**, **850-852**.

For cross-references with Vatican II, Papal documents & other resources, see Family Wisdom Library on page 734.
For commentaries on each question with Cardinal Arinze, Sr. John Vianney and Fr. Straub (in Spanish), see Appendix C.

We are one with Christ and with one another in the union of the Mystical Body of Christ here on earth. So close is this union that Jesus said, "Truly, I say to you, as you did it to one of the least of these my brethren, you did it to me" (Matthew 25:40).

We should have special love for our fellow members in the Mystical Body of Christ, because in loving the members of His Body we are loving Christ. We must treat all men as we would treat Christ Himself since Christ died for them.

2. The Catholic Church is an institution of Salvation since it has been given the mission of communicating the Good News of Salvation to all mankind.

#F6-2

The Catholic Church is an institution of Salvation since it has been given the mission of communicating the Good News of Salvation to all mankind.

The Church is also a structured institution. There are two kinds of authority in the Church: the ordinary authority which every society has to organize and direct its own affairs, and the special authority given by Jesus Christ to teach and act in His name. The Church exercises her ordinary authority by enacting laws to regulate her internal affairs, to promote the good of all, and to fulfill the purposes of the Church. The Church exercises the special authority that is given by Jesus through her teaching, worship, and all service done in the name of Jesus. His person and power are present in her when she acts under this authority.

The Pope and the bishops exercise authority for the Church. Priests and laity also share in the exercise of the Church's authority in different degrees.

The Church speaks the Good News of our Salvation in the world through her teaching and preaching, through her life and worship, through her Bible and the writings of her saints, and sometimes through the words of a single Christian expressing his hopes. The mission of the Church is to bring this message of Salvation to all men.

#L3-14-2

The Church "wishes to serve this single end: that each person may be able to find Christ, in order that Christ may walk with each person the path of life."
(Splendor of Truth, 7)

Sacred Scripture

And Jesus came and said to them, "All authority in heaven and on earth has been given to me. Go therefore and make disciples of all nations, baptizing them in the name of the Father and of the Son and of the Holy Spirit, teaching them to observe all that I have commanded you; and lo, I am with you always, to the close of the age." *Matthew 28:18-20*

Catechism of the Catholic Church

849 *The missionary mandate.* "Having been divinely sent to the nations that she might be 'the universal sacrament of salvation,' the Church, in obedience to the command of her founder and because it is demanded by her own essential universality, strives to preach the Gospel to all men":[1] "Go therefore and make disciples of all nations, baptizing them in the name of the Father and of the Son and of the Holy Spirit, teaching them to observe all that I have commanded you; and Lo, I am with you always, until the close of the age."[2]

#F6-4

Father, You will that Your Church be the sacrament of Salvation for all people. Make us feel more urgently the call to work for the Salvation of all men, until You have made us all one people.

Splendor of Truth

In order to make this "encounter" with Christ possible, God willed his Church. Indeed, the Church "wishes to serve this single end: that each person may be able to find Christ, in order that Christ may walk with each person the path of life." *(section 7)*

Christ reveals, first and foremost, that the frank and open acceptance of truth is the condition for authentic freedom: "You will know the truth, and the truth will set you free" (Jn 8:32)...Worship of God and a relationship with truth are revealed in Jesus Christ as the deepest foundation of freedom. *(section 87)*

Vatican Council II

That messianic people has as its head Christ, "who was delivered up for our sins and rose again for our justification" (Rom. 4:25), and now, having acquired the name which is above all names, reigns gloriously in heaven. The state of this people is that of the dignity and freedom of the sons of God, in whose hearts the

Holy Spirit dwells as in a temple. Its law is the new commandment to love as Christ loved us (cf. Jn. 13:34). Its destiny is the kingdom of God which has been begun by God himself on earth and which must be further extended until it is brought to perfection by him at the end of time when Christ our life (cf. Col. 3:4), will appear and "creation itself also will be delivered from its slavery to corruption into the freedom of the glory of the sons of God" (Rom. 8:21). Hence that messianic people, although it does not actually include all men, and at times may appear as a small flock, is, however, a most sure seed of unity, hope and salvation for the whole human race. Established by Christ as a communion of life, love and truth, it is taken up by him also as the instrument for the salvation of all; as the light of the world and the salt of the earth (cf. Mt. 5:13-16) it is sent forth into the whole world. *Lumen Gentium, 9*

Later, before he was assumed into heaven (cf. Acts 1:11), after he had fulfilled in himself the mysteries of our salvation and the renewal of all things by his death and resurrection, the Lord, who had received all power in heaven and on earth (cf. Mt. 28:18), founded his Church as the sacrament of salvation; and just as he had been sent by the Father (cf. Jn 20:21), so he sent the apostles into the whole world. *Missionary Activity, 5*

Doctrine • Moral • Worship Exercise

(See Appendix A for answer key, questions 169–171.)

1. Who belongs to the laity? What is the vocation of lay persons?
2. As members of the laity, how can you and your family proclaim the Gospel (in word and deed) to others in your school, office, workplace, neighborhood, or community?
3. During the Mass, offer yourself to God the Father, in union with Jesus and the Holy Spirit, as an instrument to help bring the message of Salvation to all people, beginning with those around you.

Chapter Summary Prayer

Father, You will that Your Church be the sacrament of Salvation for all people. Make us feel more urgently the call to work for the Salvation of all men, until You have made us all one people.

God of unchanging power and might, look with mercy and favor on Your entire Church. Bring lasting Salvation to mankind, so that the world may see the fallen lifted up, the old made new, and all things brought to perfection, through Him Who is their origin, our Lord Jesus Christ.

Lord God, guide us with Your love in Your Church. Keep us faithful that we may be helped through life and brought to Salvation through her teaching and sacraments.

When Jesus, Your Son, humbled Himself to come among us as man, He fulfilled the plan You had formed long ago, and so opened for us the way to Salvation, especially through the Church He founded. Now we watch for the day when we hope that the Salvation He promises us will be ours when He will come again in glory. Amen.

Thought Provokers

Please see Appendix B for the answers.

Q. 169: In 1302, Pope Boniface VIII, clearly taught in a document concerning the Catholic Church entitled Unam Sanctum, that "Outside this Church there is no salvation and no remission of sins...Further, We declare, say, define, and pronounce that it is absolutely necessary for the salvation of every human creature to be subject to the Roman Pontiff." This being true, how can non-Catholics be saved?

Q. 170: Please think for a moment. In your own family, in your neighborhood, in your school, in your work place, do you know people who are leading immoral lives, who are not regular Sunday church-goers, or who see no need for organized religion?

You can be certain that these people lack the fullness of Truth in their lives. And to the degree that this is so, they lack the peace and happiness that could otherwise be theirs as believing Catholics living according to the Church's teaching. They need God and His Church as much as we do. What steps, if any, have you taken to help give them only that which Christ can give in and through His Catholic Church?

Is it reasonable to say, without firm evidence to the contrary, that we should not try to evangelize these people since it will do no good? What does such an attitude say about our trust in God to help us, even in difficult situations? If he wants these people evangelized (and he does), isn't he sure to help us, if we ask Him?

Q. 171: The term "Salvation" may be rightly understood in a negative sense. That is, when a person receives the gift of Salvation at Baptism, for instance, he is said to be saved from sin and eternal punishment. But can Salvation also have a positive meaning?

#E4-86-2

God our Father, through the Gospel and the Eucharist, bring Your people together in the Holy Spirit and guide us in Your love.

CHAPTER FORTY-NINE

The Marks of the Church: The Church Is One

Q. 172. What are the marks that point out the true Church founded by Jesus?

There are four marks which point out the true Church founded by Jesus. They are four adjectives: one, holy, catholic and apostolic Church.

Having made His Church a means of our everlasting happiness, our Lord has stamped it plainly with the mark of its divine origin. In the Nicene Creed we say: "We believe in one, holy, catholic, and apostolic Church."

Catechism of the Catholic Church

865 The Church is ultimately *one, holy, catholic, and apostolic* in her deepest and ultimate identity, because it is in her that "the Kingdom of heaven," the "Reign of God,"[1] already exists and will be fulfilled at the end of time. The kingdom has come in the person of Christ and grows mysteriously in the hearts of those incorporated into him, until its full eschatological manifestation. Then all those he has redeemed and made "holy and blameless before him in love,"[2] will be gathered together as the one People of God, the "Bride of the Lamb,"[3] "the holy city Jerusalem coming down out of heaven from God, having the glory of God."[4] For "the wall of the city had twelve foundations, and on them the twelve names of the *twelve apostles of the Lamb*."[5]

Splendor of Truth

When people ask the Church the questions raised by their consciences, when the faithful in the Church turn to their bishops and pastors, the Church's reply contains the voice of Jesus Christ, the voice of the truth about good and evil. In the words spoken by the Church there resounds, in people's inmost being, the voice of God who "alone is good" (cf. Mt 19:17), who alone "is love" (1 Jn 4:8, 16). *(section 117)*

Vatican Council II

A diocese is a section of the People of God entrusted to a bishop to be guided by him with the assistance of his clergy so that, loyal to its pastor and formed by him into one community in the Holy Spirit through the Gospel and the Eucharist, it constitutes one particular church in which the one, holy, catholic and apostolic Church of Christ is truly present and active. *Bishops, 11*

Catechism of the Catholic Church
Q. 172. Paragraphs **811-870**.

For cross-references with Vatican II, Papal documents & other resources, see Family Wisdom Library on page 734.
For commentaries on each question with Cardinal Arinze, Sr. John Vianney and Fr. Straub (in Spanish), see Appendix C.

We believe that this one true religion continues to exist in the Catholic and Apostolic Church, to which the Lord Jesus entrusted the task of spreading it among all men when he said to the apostles: "Go therefore and make disciples of all nations baptizing them in the name of the Father and of the Son and of the Holy Spirit, teaching them to observe all that I have commanded you" (Mt. 18:19-20). *Liberty, 1*

Missionary activity extends the saving faith of the Church, it expands and perfects its catholic unity, it is sustained by its apostolicity, it activates the collegiate sense of its hierarchy, and bears witness to its sanctity which it both extends and promotes. *Missionary Activity, 6*

#C15-42

We believe in one, holy, catholic, and apostolic Church.

Summary Prayer

God our Father, through the Gospel and the Eucharist, bring Your people together in the Holy Spirit and guide us in Your love. Make us a sign of Your love for all people, and help us to be the living presence of Christ in the world. We ask this in His most Holy Name. Amen.

Q. 173. Why is the Catholic Church one?

The Church is one because it is unified in belief.

The truths which the members of the Catholic Church hold are the truths made known to us by Jesus Himself; they are truths which come to us directly from God. God is Truth. He knows all things and cannot be mistaken. He is infinitely truthful and cannot lie. Whatever God has said is true forever and for everybody. It is not for us to pick and choose and to adjust God's revelation to our own convenience. In the Catholic Church, all are obligated to believe the same truths. Thus, every Catholic must mean exactly the same thing when he recites the Apostles' and Nicene Creeds.

#C15-47

In the Catholic Church, all are obligated to believe the same truths. Thus, every Catholic must mean exactly the same thing when he recites the Apostles' and Nicene Creeds.

Catechism of the Catholic Church

815 What are these bonds of unity? Above all, charity "binds everything together in perfect harmony."[1] But the unity of the pilgrim Church is also assured by visible bonds of communion:

- profession of one faith received from the Apostles;

- common celebration of divine worship, especially of the sacraments;

- apostolic succession through the sacrament of Holy Orders, maintaining the fraternal concord of God's family.[2]

Catechism of the Catholic Church
Q. 173. Paragraphs **813-816**.

For cross-references with Vatican II, Papal documents & other resources, see Family Wisdom Library on page 734.
For commentaries on each question with Cardinal Arinze, Sr. John Vianney and Fr. Straub (in Spanish), see Appendix C.

Catechism by Diagram

#C15-77

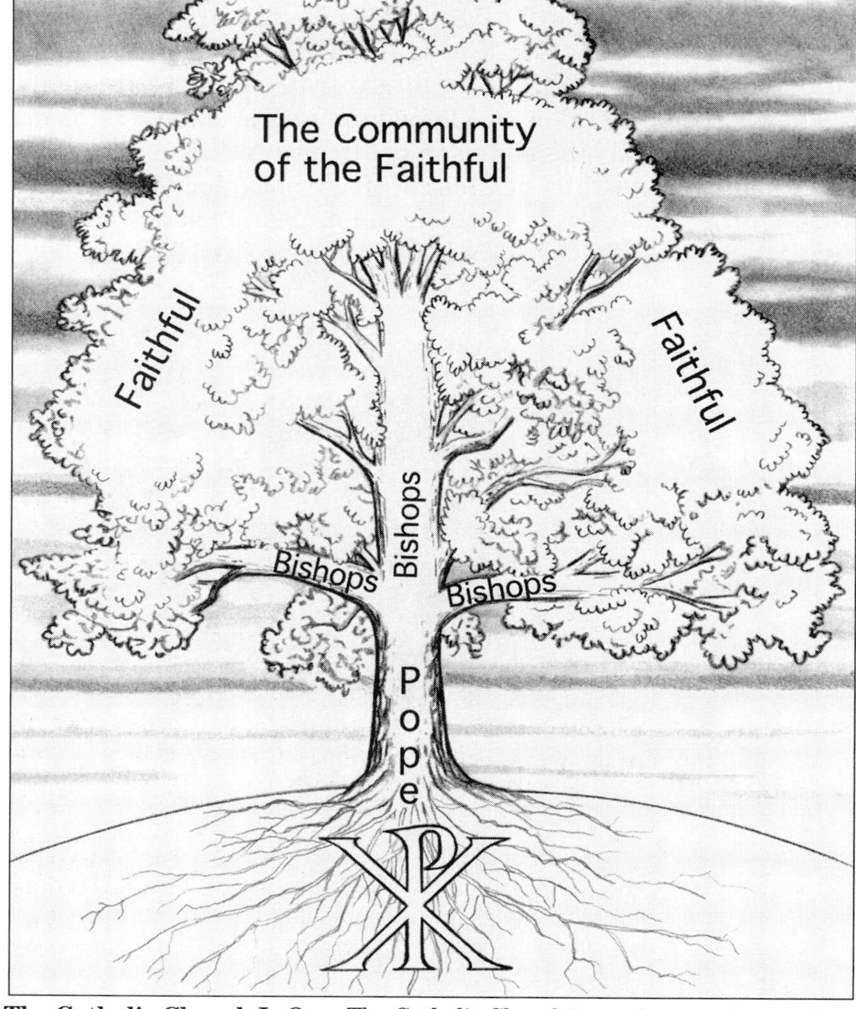

The Catholic Church Is One. The Catholic Church is one because its members have unity of belief; all are united under the same spiritual leadership and the same worship. They are united through the Seven Sacraments, especially the Eucharist. Jesus willed that the bishops, the successors of the Apostles, should be shepherds in His Church. He placed Peter over the other Apostles. The Church is like a great tree: it carries its life-giving sap through all the branches (bishops) to all the leaves (the community of the faithful). Jesus Christ (monogram) is the source of life for the Church. The Pope is a visible sign of Jesus and the symbol of unity for the Church. Together with the bishops, and as their head, the Pope is the universal teacher and governor of the Church. The bishops are visible signs of Jesus in each diocese and are the symbol of unity in them.

Splendor of Truth

From the Church's beginnings, the Apostles, by virtue of their pastoral responsibility to preach the Gospel, were vigilant over the right conduct of Christians, just as they were vigilant for the purity of the faith and the handing down of the divine gifts in the sacraments...And ever since Apostolic times the Church's Pastors have unambiguously condemned the behavior of those who fostered division by their teaching or by their actions. *(section 26)*

Vatican Council II

All those, who in faith look towards Jesus, the author of salvation and the principle of unity and peace, God has gathered together and established as the Church, that it may be for each and everyone the visible sacrament of this saving unity. *Lumen Gentium, 9*

174. How did Jesus indicate that His Church is one?

Jesus said, "And I have other sheep, that are not of this fold; I must bring them also, and they will heed my voice. So there shall be one flock, one shepherd" (John 10:16).

Jesus prayed to His Father: "That they may all be one; even as thou, Father, art in me, and I in thee, that they also may be in us, so that the world may believe that thou hast sent me" (John 17:21).

Sacred Scripture

If a kingdom is divided against itself, that kingdom cannot stand. *Mark 3:24*

Catechism of the Catholic Church

820 "Christ bestowed unity on his Church from the beginning. This unity, we believe, subsists in the Catholic Church as something she can never lose, and we hope that it will continue to increase until the end of time."1 Christ always gives his Church the gift of unity, but the Church must always pray and work to maintain, reinforce, and perfect the unity that Christ wills for her. This is why Jesus himself prayed at the hour of his Passion, and does not cease praying to his Father, for the unity of his disciples: "That they may all be one. As you, Father, are in me and I am in you, may they also be one in us,... so that the world may know that you have sent me."2 The desire to recover the unity of all Christians is a gift of Christ and a call of the Holy Spirit.[3]

Vatican Council II

The universal Church is seen to be "a people brought into unity from the unity of the Father, the Son and the Holy Spirit." *Lumen Gentium, 4*

Sacred Scripture
Q. 174. Jn 15:1-5.

Catechism of the Catholic Church
Q. 174. Paragraphs 552, 816.

For cross-references with Vatican II, Papal documents & other resources, see Family Wisdom Library on page 734.
For commentaries on each question with Cardinal Arinze, Sr. John Vianney and Fr. Straub (in Spanish), see Appendix C.

Q. 175. Why are we united by a spiritual leader?

All Catholics are united under the same spiritual leadership because Jesus Christ made Peter the chief shepherd of His flock, and provided that Peter's successors, the Bishops of Rome, would be the heads of His Church and guardians of His truths until the end of time.

Loyalty to the Bishop of Rome, the Pope, will ever be the binding center of our unity and the test of our membership in Christ's Church.

#C15-37

Loyalty to the Bishop of Rome, the Pope, will ever be the binding center of our unity and the test of our membership in Christ's Church.

Sacred Scripture

"And I tell you, you are Peter, and on this rock I will build my church, and the powers of death shall not prevail against it." *Matthew 16:18*

Catechism of the Catholic Church

553 Jesus entrusted a specific authority to Peter: "I will give you the keys of the kingdom of heaven, and whatever you bind on earth shall be bound in heaven, and whatever you loose on earth shall be loosed in heaven."[1] The "power of the keys" designates authority to govern the house of God, which is

Sacred Scripture
Q. 175. Jn 21:15-17.

Catechism of the Catholic Church
Q. 175. Paragraphs **880-882**, 892.

For cross-references with Vatican II, Papal documents & other resources, see Family Wisdom Library on page 734.
For commentaries on each question with Cardinal Arinze, Sr. John Vianney and Fr. Straub (in Spanish), see Appendix C.

the Church. Jesus, the Good Shepherd, confirmed this mandate after his Resurrection: "Feed my sheep."[2] The power to "bind and loose" connotes the authority to absolve sins, to pronounce doctrinal judgments, and to make disciplinary decisions in the Church. Jesus entrusted this authority to the Church through the ministry of the apostles[3] and in particular through the ministry of Peter, the only one to whom he specifically entrusted the keys of the kingdom.

Vatican Council II

The Roman Pontiff, as the successor of Peter, is the perpetual and visible source and foundation of the unity both of the bishops and of the whole company of the faithful. The individual bishops are the visible source and foundation of unity in their own particular Churches, which are constituted after the model of the universal Church; it is in these and formed out of them that the one and unique Catholic Church exists. And for that reason precisely each bishop represents his own Church, whereas all, together with the pope, represent the whole Church in a bond of peace, love and unity. *Lumen Gentium, 23*

Q. 176. Why are we united in worship?

We are united in worship because we have but one altar, upon which Jesus Christ daily renews the offering of Himself upon the Cross. Everywhere we have the same Mass and everywhere the same Seven Sacraments.

#E4.5-1

We are united in worship because we have but one altar, upon which Jesus Christ daily renews the offering of Himself upon the Cross.

Catechism of the Catholic Church
Q. 176. Paragraphs **1325, 1368-1372**.

For cross-references with Vatican II, Papal documents & other resources, see Family Wisdom Library on page 734.
For commentaries on each question with Cardinal Arinze, Sr. John Vianney and Fr. Straub (in Spanish), see Appendix C.

By means of the Eucharist, Christ re-offers Himself to the Father through the ministry of His priests in the Sacrifice of the Mass. At Mass, Jesus and the faithful daily adore the Father. With Him they give glory to God and praise Him for His kindness toward mankind. With Him they ask God for His forgiveness and beg His help. We are one with Jesus in His Sacrifice.

Sacred Scripture

Because there is one bread, we who are many are one body, for we all partake of the one bread. *1 Corinthians 10:17*

Catechism of the Catholic Church

1108 In every liturgical action the Holy Spirit is sent in order to bring us into communion with Christ and so to form his Body. The Holy Spirit is like the sap of the Father's vine which bears fruit on its branches.[1] The most intimate cooperation of the Holy Spirit and the Church is achieved in the liturgy. The Spirit, who is the Spirit of communion, abides indefectibly in the Church. For this reason the Church is the great sacrament of divine communion which gathers God's scattered children together. Communion with the Holy Trinity and fraternal communion are inseparably the fruit of the Spirit in the liturgy.[2]

1209 The criterion that assures unity amid the diversity of liturgical traditions is fidelity to apostolic Tradition, i.e., the communion in the faith and the sacraments received from the apostles, a communion that is both signified and guaranteed by apostolic succession.

Doctrine • Moral • Worship Exercise

(See Appendix A for answer key, questions 172–176.)

1. The Catholic Church is one because her members are united in belief and worship. How can you explain this in simple terms?
2. Do you believe all the truths of our faith and make a continuous effort to learn and understand them? How do you show your loyalty to the Pope, our spiritual leader?
3. Reflect on the Scripture verse, "If a kingdom is divided against itself, that kingdom cannot stand" (Mark 3:24). Reflect on the lyrics of the song "One Bread, One Body." Pray for Christian unity.

Chapter Summary Prayer

Father, through Christ You bring us to the knowledge of Your truth, that we may be united by one faith and one Baptism, and thus become His Body. Through Christ, You have given the Holy Spirit to all people. How wonderful are the works of the Spirit, revealed in so many gifts! How marvelous is the unity the Spirit creates from their diversity, as He dwells in the hearts of Your children, filling the whole Church with His presence and guiding it with His wisdom.

Lord, by the sacrament of the Eucharist, You make us one family in Christ Your Son, one in the sharing of His Body and Blood, and one in the communion of His Spirit. Help us to grow in love for one another and to come to full maturity in the Body of Christ.

God of wisdom and truth, without You, neither truth nor holiness can survive. Safeguard the Church You have made one and make us glad to proclaim Your glory, through Christ our Lord. Amen.

Thought Provokers

Please see Appendix B for the answers.

Q. 172: It is incorrectly taught by some theologians that Jesus did not intend to found a Church. In fact, they claim, it was founded by His followers and is, therefore, not of divine origin. Can you think of any Scripture passages which indicate that Jesus really did found the Catholic Church?

Q. 173: Where does the Catholic Church's unity of belief come from?

Q. 174: What is the basic visible sign of the unity of the Catholic Church?

Q. 175: How does being in communion with the Pope, the Successor of St. Peter, in the primacy of authority over the Church, assure her members that the Church possesses the totality of doctrinal truth?

Q. 176: The Holy Eucharist is sometimes called the Sacrament of Unity. Why?

#C15-48

The Holy Spirit preserves the Church as the Body of Christ and His Bride, so that in spite of the sins of its members it will never fail in faithfulness to Him and will meet Him in holiness at the end of the world.

CHAPTER FIFTY

The Marks of the Church: The Church Is Holy

Q. 177. Why is the Catholic Church holy?

The Catholic Church is holy because it was founded by Jesus Christ, Who is all-holy, and because it teaches holy doctrines according to the will of Christ. It provides the means of leading a holy life, thereby giving holy members to every age.

We can point to the saints as proof that the holiness of Christ is at work in the Catholic Church. But it would be an even greater proof of the holiness of the Church if all of us would live holy lives, if every Catholic were a person of outstanding Christian virtue.

#J2-555

The Catholic Church is holy because it was founded by Jesus Christ, Who is all-holy, and because it teaches holy doctrines according to the will of Christ.

Jesus prayed to His Father for His Church, "Sanctify them in the truth; thy word is truth... And for their sake I consecrate myself, that they also may be consecrated in truth" (John 17:17, 19).

St. Paul reminds us that Jesus Christ "gave himself for us to redeem us from all iniquity and to purify for himself a people of his own who are zealous for good deeds" (Titus 2:14).

Catechism of the Catholic Church
Q. 177. Paragraphs **823-829**.

For cross-references with Vatican II, Papal documents & other resources, see Family Wisdom Library on page 734.
For commentaries on each question with Cardinal Arinze, Sr. John Vianney and Fr. Straub (in Spanish), see Appendix C.

The Holy Spirit preserves the Church as the Body of Christ and His Bride, so that in spite of the sins of its members it will never fail in faithfulness to Him and will meet Him in holiness at the end of the world. The Holy Spirit also helps the Church constantly to purify and renew itself.

#C40-2

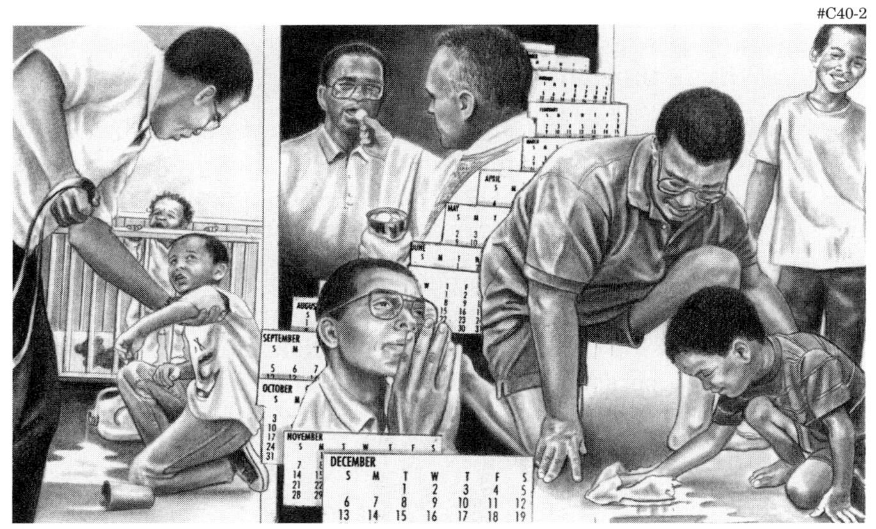

The Catholic Church provides the means of leading a holy life, thereby giving holy members to every age.

Catechism of the Catholic Church

824 United with Christ, the Church is sanctified by him; through him and with him she becomes sanctifying. "All the activities of the Church are directed, as toward their end, to the sanctification of men in Christ and the glorification of God."[1] It is in the Church that "the fullness of the means of salvation"[2] has been deposited. It is in her that "by the grace of God we acquire holiness."[3]

Splendor of Truth

Finally, martyrdom is an outstanding sign of the holiness of the Church. Fidelity to God's holy law, witnessed to by death, is a solemn proclamation and missionary commitment... so that the splendor of moral truth may be undimmed in the behavior and thinking of individuals and society... By their eloquent and attractive example of a life completely transfigured by the splendor of moral truth, the martyrs and, in general, all the Church's Saints, light up every period of history by reawakening its moral sense. By witnessing fully to the good, they are a living reproof to those who transgress the law (cf. Wis 2:12), and they make the words of the Prophet echo ever afresh: "Woe to those who call evil good and good evil, who put darkness for light and light for darkness, who put bitter for sweet and sweet for bitter!" (Is 5:20). *(section 93)*

Vatican Council II

Christ, "holy, innocent and undefiled" (Heb. 7:26) knew nothing of sin (2 Cor. 5:21), but came only to expiate the sins of the people (cf. Heb. 2:17). The Church, however, clasping sinners to her bosom, at once holy and always in need of purification, follows constantly the path of penance and renewal. *Lumen Gentium, 8*

The Church, whose mystery is set forth by this sacred Council, is held, as a matter of faith, to be unfailingly holy. This is because Christ, the Son of God, who with the Father and the Spirit is hailed as "alone holy," loved the Church as his Bride, giving himself up for her so as to sanctify her (cf. Eph. 5:25-26); he joined her to himself as his body and endowed her with the gift of the Holy Spirit for the glory of God. *Lumen Gentium, 39*

Likewise the Church's holiness is fostered in a special way by the manifold counsels which the Lord proposes to his disciples in the Gospel for them to observe. Towering among these counsels is that precious gift of divine grace given to some by the Father (cf. Mt. 19:11; 1 Cor. 7:7) to devote themselves to God alone more easily with an undivided heart (cf. 1 Cor. 7:32-34) in virginity or celibacy. *Lumen Gentium, 42*

The state of life, then, which is constituted by the profession of the evangelical counsels, while not entering into the hierarchical structure of the Church, belongs undeniably to her life and holiness. *Lumen Gentium, 44*

#F1-81

Jesus prayed to His Father for His Church, "Sanctify them in the truth; thy word is truth... And for their sake I consecrate myself, that they also may be consecrated in truth" *(John 17:17, 19).*

Catechism by Diagram

#C15-78

The Catholic Church Is Holy. The Catholic Church (St. Peter's Basilica) is holy because it was founded by Jesus Christ (monogram) Who is all-holy, and because it teaches holy doctrines (Gospel book), and virtues (lilies), according to His will, and gives us the means of leading a holy life through the sacraments (seven streams from the altar), especially the Holy Eucharist. The Holy Spirit (dove) preserves the Church as the Body of Christ and His bride, so that—in spite of the sins of its members—it will never fail in faithfulness to Him and will meet Him in holiness at the end of the world (hearts in Heaven, triangle). The Holy Spirit also helps the Church constantly to purify and renew itself and its members.

Martyrdom is an outstanding sign of the holiness of the Church. Fidelity to God's holy law, witnessed to by death, is a solemn proclamation and missionary commitment. *(Splendor of Truth, 93)*

Summary Prayer

Eternal God, Your Spirit guides the Church and makes it holy. Listen to our prayers and help each of us in Your Church, in his own vocation, to do Your work more faithfully, through Christ our Lord. Amen.

Doctrine • Moral • Worship Exercise

(See Appendix A for answer key, question 177.)

1. The Catholic Church is holy in spite of the sins of its members. Why?
2. How do you strive to live a holy life? Examine your conscience in the five areas of responsibility that we should make time for each day: sacramental life, prayer and formation, family and community, work, and evangelization. Write down the areas in your life where you need to improve in your pursuit of holiness.
3. Each day, renew your desire to become holy. Pray that the Church and her members may be constantly purified and renewed by the Holy Spirit.

Chapter Summary Prayer

Almighty God, only hope of the world, by the preaching of the prophets, You proclaimed the mysteries we celebrate in the Sacrifice of the Mass. Help us to be Your faithful people, for it is by Your Inspiration alone that we can grow in holiness.

Father, the Body of Your risen Son is the temple not made by human hands and the defending wall of the New Jerusalem. May this holy city, built of living stones, shine with spiritual radiance and so witness to Your greatness in the sight of all the nations.

God, You are the source of all holiness. Though no one can see You and live, You give life more generously, and, in an even greater way, You restore it. Sanctify Your priests through Your life-giving Word and consecrate Your people in His Blood until the day that our eyes may see Your face in heavenly bliss.

Words cannot measure the boundaries of love for those who are born to a new life in Christ Jesus. Raise men beyond the limits of this world, so that we may be free to love as Christ teaches us and to find our joy in Your glory.

Clothe Your priests in righteousness and make Your Chosen People joyful. Give Your people strength and holiness. Bless Your people with peace and love, through Jesus Christ our Lord. Amen.

Thought Provokers

Please see Appendix B for the answers.

Q. 177: Are the members of the Catholic Church holy?

CHAPTER FIFTY-ONE

The Marks of the Church: The Church Is Catholic

Q. 178. Why is the Church catholic or universal?

The Church is catholic or universal because Christ established it to proclaim all of His teaching to all men, at all times, and in all places.

#T3-38-2

The Church is catholic or universal because Christ established it to proclaim all of His teaching to all men, at all times, and in all places.

Jesus said, "Go into all the world and preach the gospel to the whole creation" (Mark 16:15). "But you shall receive power when the Holy Spirit has come upon you; and you shall be my witnesses in Jerusalem and in all Judea and Samaria and to the end of the earth" (Acts 1:8).

Jesus spoke of the growth of His Church when He gave us the parable of the mustard seed. "The kingdom of heaven is like a grain of mustard seed which a man took and sowed in his field; it is the smallest of all seeds, but when it has grown it is the greatest of shrubs and becomes a tree, so that the birds of the air come and make nests in its branches" (Matthew 13:31-32).

Sacred Scripture
Q. 178. Acts 2:38-39; Rom 1:1-6.

Catechism of the Catholic Church
Q. 178. Paragraph 830-831.

For cross-references with Vatican II, Papal documents & other resources, see Family Wisdom Library on page 734.
For commentaries on each question with Cardinal Arinze, Sr. John Vianney and Fr. Straub (in Spanish), see Appendix C.

#N1.4-56

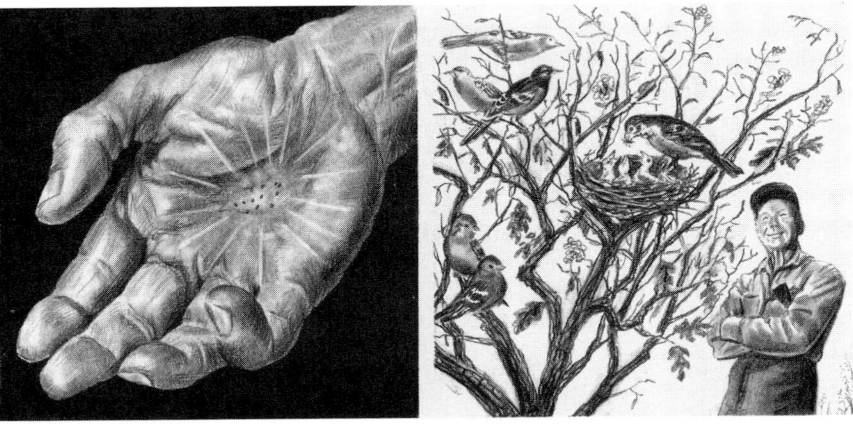

Jesus spoke of the growth of His Church when He gave us the parable of the mustard seed. "It is the smallest of all seeds, but when it has grown it is the greatest of shrubs and becomes a tree" *(Matthew 13:32).*

Sacred Scripture

"And this gospel of the kingdom will be preached throughout the whole world, as a testimony to all nations." *Matthew 24:14*

Catechism of the Catholic Church

1202 The diverse liturgical traditions have arisen by very reason of the Church's mission. Churches of the same geographical and cultural area came to celebrate the mystery of Christ through particular expressions characterized by the culture: in the tradition of the "deposit of faith,"[1] in liturgical symbolism, in the organization of fraternal communion, in the theological understanding of the mysteries, and in various forms of holiness. Through the liturgical life of a local church, Christ, the light and salvation of all peoples, is made manifest to the particular people and culture to which that Church is sent and in which she is rooted. The Church is catholic, capable of integrating into her unity, while purifying them, all the authentic riches of cultures.[2]

Splendor of Truth

It is the task of the Church's Magisterium to see that the dynamic process of following Christ develops in an organic manner, without the falsification or obscuring of its moral demands, with all their consequences. *(section 119)*

Vatican Council II

All men are called to belong to the new People of God. This People therefore, whilst remaining one and only one, is to be spread throughout the whole world and to all ages in order that the design of God's will may be fulfilled. *Lumen Gentium, 13*

The special undertakings in which preachers of the Gospel, sent by the Church, and going into the whole world, carry out the work of preaching the Gospel and implanting the Church among people who do not yet believe in Christ, are generally called "missions." Such undertakings are accomplished by missionary activity and are, for the most part, carried out in defined territories recognized by the Holy See. *Missionary Activity, 6*

The period, therefore, between the first and second coming of the Lord is the time of missionary activity, when, like the harvest, the Church will be gathered from the four winds into the kingdom of God. For the Gospel must be preached to all peoples before the Lord comes (cf. Mk. 13:10). Missionary activity is nothing else, and nothing less, than the manifestation of God's plan, its epiphany and realization in the world and in history; that by which God, through mission, clearly brings to its conclusion the history of salvation. *Missionary Activity, 9*

Q. 179. How long has the Catholic Church been in existence?

The Church has been in existence since the sacrificial Death and Resurrection of Jesus. This took place about 33 A.D.

The Catholic Church has had a continuous existence of more than two thousand years, and it is the only Christian institution of which this is true.

#O8-22

The origin and growth of the Church are symbolized by the blood and water which flowed from the open side of the crucified Jesus.
(Catechism of the Catholic Church, 766)

Sacred Scripture

And he went up into the hills, and called to him those whom he desired; and they came to him. And he appointed twelve, to be with him, and to be sent out

Sacred Scripture
Q. 179. Acts 1:1-9.

Catechism of the Catholic Church
Q. 179. Paragraphs 767-769.

For cross-references with Vatican II, Papal documents & other resources, see Family Wisdom Library on page 734.
For commentaries on each question with Cardinal Arinze, Sr. John Vianney and Fr. Straub (in Spanish), see Appendix C.

to preach and have authority to cast out demons: Simon whom he surnamed Peter; James the son of Zebedee and John the brother of James, whom he surnamed Boanerges, that is, sons of thunder; Andrew, and Philip, and Bartholomew, and Matthew, and Thomas, and James the son of Alphaeus, and Thaddaeus, and Simon the Cananaean, and Judas Iscariot, who betrayed him. *Mark 3:13-19*

#R4.1-29

The Church has been in existence since the sacrificial Death and Resurrection of Jesus. This took place about 33 A.D.

Catechism of the Catholic Church

766 The Church is born primarily of Christ's total self-giving for our salvation, anticipated in the institution of the Eucharist and fulfilled on the cross. "The origin and growth of the Church are symbolized by the blood and water which flowed from the open side of the crucified Jesus."[1] "For it was from the side of Christ as he slept the sleep of death upon the cross that there came forth the 'wondrous sacrament of the whole Church.'"[2] As Eve was formed from the sleeping Adam's side, so the Church was born from the pierced heart of Christ hanging dead on the cross.[3]

Summary Prayer

Heavenly Father, You will that all men be saved and come to the knowledge of Your truth. Send workers into Your great harvest, that the Gospel may be preached to every creature so that Your people may be gathered together by the Word of Life. Strengthened by the power of the sacraments, may all of mankind advance in the way of Salvation and love, through Jesus Christ our Lord and Savior. Amen.

Q. 180. Does the Catholic Church teach all the truths that Jesus Christ taught?

Yes. The Catholic Church is the only Church which teaches all the truths that Jesus Christ taught. Many other Christian communities have rejected the Sacraments of Penance and Anointing of the Sick, the Mass and the Real Presence of Jesus in the Eucharist, the spiritual supremacy of Peter and his successors, the popes, the efficacy of grace, and man's ability to merit grace and Heaven. Some even question whether Jesus Christ is truly God. There is not a single truth that Jesus Christ revealed (whether personally or through His Apostles) which the Catholic Church does not still faithfully declare and teach.

#C15-45

There is not a single truth that Jesus Christ revealed (whether personally or through His Apostles) which the Catholic Church does not still faithfully declare and teach.

Sacred Scripture
Q. 180. Mt 5:17-19; Jn 14:25-26, 16:12-15; 2 Tim 1:11-14.

Catechism of the Catholic Church
Q. 180. Paragraphs 74-79, 830-831, 838.

For cross-references with Vatican II, Papal documents & other resources, see Family Wisdom Library on page 734.
For commentaries on each question with Cardinal Arinze, Sr. John Vianney and Fr. Straub (in Spanish), see Appendix C.

#E5-8

Preach the word, be urgent in season and out of season, convince, rebuke, and exhort, be unfailing in patience and in teaching. *(2 Timothy 4:2)*

Sacred Scripture

Preach the word, be urgent in season and out of season, convince, rebuke, and exhort, be unfailing in patience and in teaching. For the time is coming when people will not endure sound teaching, but having itching ears they will accumulate for themselves teachers to suit their own likings, and will turn away from listening to the truth and wander into myths. *2 Timothy 4:2-4*

Catechism of the Catholic Church

77 "In order that the full and living Gospel might always be preserved in the Church the apostles left bishops as their successors. They gave them 'their own position of teaching authority.'"[1] Indeed, "the apostolic preaching, which is expressed in a special way in the inspired books, was to be preserved in a continuous line of succession until the end of time."[2]

Splendor of Truth

The Magisterium carries out an important work of vigilance, warning the faithful of the presence of possible errors, even merely implicit ones, when their consciences fail to acknowledge the correctness and the truth of the moral norms, which the Magisterium teaches. *(section 110)*

Opposition to the teaching of the Church's Pastors cannot be seen as a legitimate expression either of Christian freedom or of the diversity of the Spirit's gifts. When this happens, the Church's Pastors have the duty to act in conformity with their apostolic mission, insisting that the right of the faithful to receive Catholic doctrine in its purity and integrity must always be respected. *(section 113)*

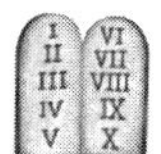

Doctrine • Moral • Worship Exercise

(See Appendix A for answer key, questions 178–180.)

1. In the Creed we pray, "I believe in…the holy catholic Church." Explain why the Church is catholic or universal.
2. As a member of the Catholic Church, how are you contributing to the proclamation of the Good News?
3. Make a deeper commitment to help the Church in its task of evangelization.

Chapter Summary Prayer

Lord, glorify Your Name by increasing Your Chosen People as You promised long ago. In reward for their trust, may we see in the Church the fulfillment of Your promise.

It is through Your Church, generously endowed with gifts of grace and fortified by the Holy Spirit, that You send out Your Word to all nations. Strengthen Your Church with the best of all food and make it dauntless in faith. Multiply its children to celebrate with one accord the mysteries of Your love at the altar on high.

God our Father, You sent Your Son into the world to be its true Light. Pour out the Spirit He promised us in order to sow truth in men's hearts and awaken in them obedience to the faith. May all men be born again to a new life in Baptism and so enter the fellowship of Your one holy people.

You command the seed to rise, Lord God, though the farmer is unaware. Grant that those who labor for You may trust not in their own work but in Your help. Remembering that the land is brought to flower not with human tears, but with those of Your Son, may the Church rely only upon Your gifts.

Strengthen the minds and hearts of missionaries with Your Spirit, and raise up a great company to help them from every nation. We ask this through Jesus Christ our only Savior. Amen.

Thought Provokers

Please see Appendix B for the answers.

Q. 178: A. The Church founded by Jesus Christ is not called the Catholic Church in the Bible. Where, then, does the term come from?

B. Is the fact that the term "Catholic" is not scriptural make it less valid than those scriptural terms which describe the Church, such as "the Body of Christ"?

Q. 179: How long will the Catholic Church remain on earth?

Q. 180: What one Catholic doctrine is rejected by every other Christian body?

CHAPTER FIFTY-TWO

The Marks of the Church: The Church Is Apostolic

Q. 181. Why is the Catholic Church apostolic?

The Catholic Church is apostolic because it is able to trace its lineage in unbroken continuity back to the Apostles.

#C15-53

Since the days of the Apostles, episcopal power, that power held by the bishops, has been passed on through the Sacrament of Holy Orders, from generation to generation, from bishop to bishop.

Jesus said to Peter, "And I tell you, you are Peter, and on this rock I will build my church, and the powers of death shall not prevail against it" (Matthew 16:18).

Speaking to all the Apostles, He said, "All authority in heaven and on earth has been given to me. Go therefore and make disciples of all nations, baptizing them in the name of the Father and of the Son

Sacred Scripture
Q. 181. 1 Cor 11:2; 2 Tim 1:6, 11-14.

Catechism of the Catholic Church
Q. 181. Paragraphs **857-865**, 869.

For cross-references with Vatican II, Papal documents & other resources, see Family Wisdom Library on page 734.
For commentaries on each question with Cardinal Arinze, Sr. John Vianney and Fr. Straub (in Spanish), see Appendix C.

and of the Holy Spirit, teaching them to observe all that I have commanded you; and lo, I am with you always, to the close of the age" (Matthew 28:18-20).

Among the Apostles, Christ chose St. Paul to spread His Church. Speaking of him, Jesus said, "He is a chosen instrument of mine to carry my name before the Gentiles and kings and the sons of Israel; for I will show him how much he must suffer for the sake of my name" (Acts 9:15-16). Paul became the greatest missionary of all time. He brought the Gospel of Christ to the pagan world at the cost of great sacrifices.

Paul became the greatest missionary of all time. He brought the Gospel of Christ to the pagan world at the cost of great sacrifices.

To the Ephesians Paul wrote: "So then you are no longer strangers and sojourners, but you are fellow citizens with the saints and members of the household of God, built upon the foundation of the apostles and prophets, Christ Jesus himself being the cornerstone" (Ephesians 2:19-20).

Since the days of the Apostles, episcopal power, that power held by the bishops, has been passed on through the Sacrament of Holy Orders, from generation to generation, from bishop to bishop. By the popes, bishops, priests, and deacons, the Gospel of Christ is preached in every part of the world, in fulfillment of the promise of Christ, "And I, when I am lifted up from the earth, will draw all men to myself" (John 12:32).

Sacred Scripture

"You then, my son, be strong in the grace that is in Christ Jesus, and what you have heard from me before many witnesses entrust to faithful men who will be able to teach others also." *2 Timothy 2:1-2*

#S2-272

The Catholic Church is apostolic because it is able to trace its lineage in unbroken continuity back to the Apostles.

Catechism of the Catholic Church

858 Jesus is the Father's Emissary. From the beginning of his ministry, he "called to him those whom he desired;.... And he appointed twelve, whom also he named apostles, to be with him, and to be sent out to preach."[1] From then on, they would also be his "emissaries" (Greek *apostoloi*). In them, Christ continues his own mission: "As the Father has sent me, even so I send you."[2] The apostles' ministry is the continuation of his mission; Jesus said to the Twelve: "he who receives you receives me."[3]

Splendor of Truth

Within the unity of the Church, promoting and preserving the faith and the moral life is the task entrusted by Jesus to the Apostles (cf. Mt 28:19-20), a task which continues in the ministry of their successors. This is apparent from the living Tradition, whereby—as the Second Vatican Council teaches—"the Church, in her teaching, life and worship, perpetuates and hands on to every generation all that she is and all that she believes. This Tradition which comes from the Apostles, progresses in the Church under the assistance of the Holy Spirit." *(section 27)*

The Church has faithfully preserved what the word of God teaches, not only about truths which must be believed but also about moral action, action pleasing to God (cf. 1 Th 4:1); she has achieved a doctrinal development analogous to that which has taken place in the realm of the truths of faith. Assisted by the Holy Spirit who leads her into all the truth (cf. Jn 16:13), the Church has not ceased, nor can she ever cease, to contemplate the "mystery of the Word Incarnate," in whom "light is shed on the mystery of man." *(section 28)*

Vatican Council II

The Lord Jesus, having prayed at length to the Father, called to himself those whom he willed and appointed twelve to be with him, whom he might send to preach the kingdom of God (cf. Mk. 3:13-19; Mt. 10:1-42). These apostles (cf. Lk. 6:13) he constituted in the form of a college or permanent assembly, at the head of which he placed Peter, chosen from amongst them (cf. Jn. 21:15-17). He sent them first of all to the children of Israel and then to all peoples (cf. Rom. 1:16), so that, sharing in his power, they might make all peoples his disciples and sanctify and govern them (cf. Mt. 28:16-20; Mk. 16:15; Lk. 24:45-48; Jn. 20:21-23) and thus spread the Church and, administering it under the guidance of the Lord, shepherd it all days until the end of the world (cf. Mt. 28:20). They were fully confirmed in this mission on the day of Pentecost (cf. Acts 2:1-26) according to the promise of the Lord: "You shall receive power when the Holy Ghost descends upon you; and you shall be my witnesses both in Jerusalem and in all Judea and Samaria, and to the remotest part of the earth" (Acts 1:8). By preaching everywhere the Gospel (cf. Mk. 16:20), welcomed and received under the influence of the Holy Spirit by those who hear it, the apostles gather together the universal Church, which the Lord founded upon the apostles and built upon blessed Peter their leader, the chief corner-stone being Christ Jesus himself (cf. Apoc. 21:14; Mt. 16:18; Eph. 2:20). *Lumen Gentium, 19*

Catechism by Diagram

#C15-81

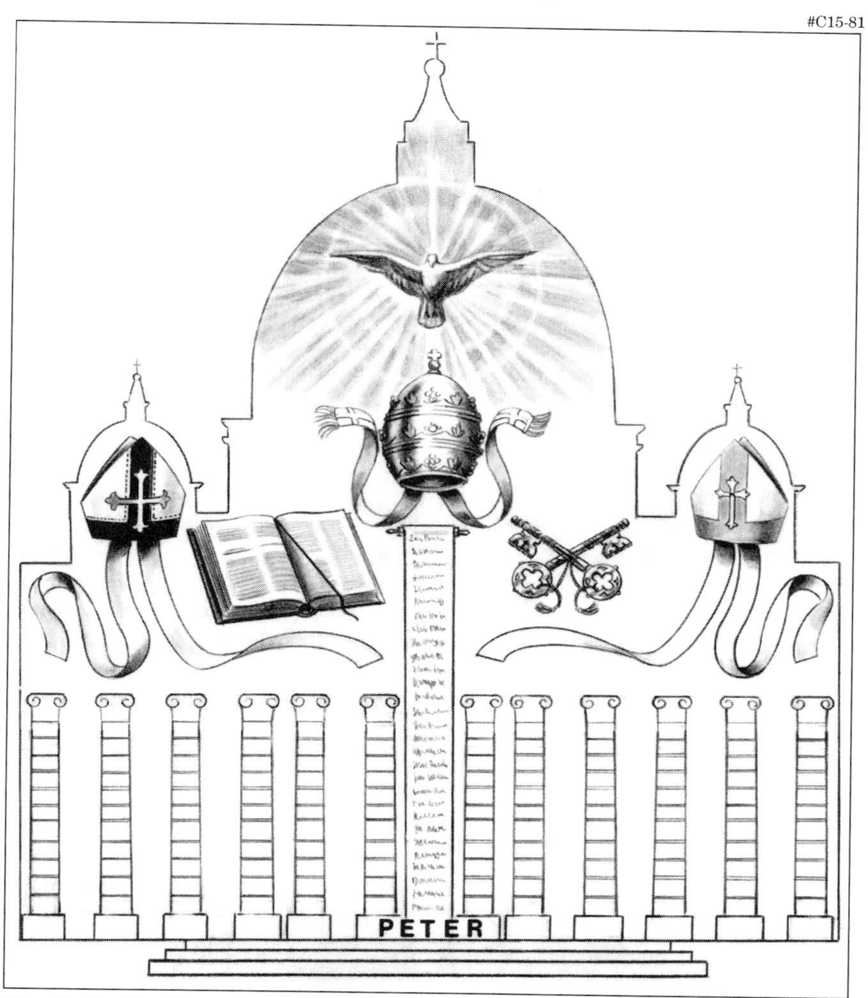

The Catholic Church Is Apostolic. The Catholic Church is able to prove its legitimate descent from the Apostles, upon whom as a foundation (twelve white blocks) Jesus established His Church (St. Peter's Basilica). We have the list of the Bishops of Rome (tiara), going back from the Holy Father of our own day in a continuous line to St. Peter. The other bishops (miters, twelve columns) are today's links in an unbroken chain back over more than nineteen hundred years. Since the days of the Apostles, the bishops have had the episcopal power to teach, sanctify (Gospel book) and rule (keys) the faithful as shepherds of the flock of Christ. The Holy Spirit (dove) carries out Christ's work in the world.

#R4.1-9a

That divine mission, which was committed by Christ to the apostles, is destined to last until the end of the world. For that very reason the apostles were careful to appoint successors in this hierarchically constituted society.
(Lumen Gentium, 20)

That divine mission, which was committed by Christ to the apostles, is destined to last until the end of the world (cf. Mt. 28:20), since the Gospel, which they were charged to hand on, is, for the Church, the principle of all its life for all time. For that very reason the apostles were careful to appoint successors in this hierarchically constituted society. *Lumen Gentium, 20*

God graciously arranged that the things he had once revealed for the salvation of all peoples should remain in their entirety, throughout the ages, and be transmitted to all generations. Therefore, Christ the Lord, in whom the entire Revelation of the most high God is summed up (cf. 2 Cor. 1:20; 3:16-4, 6) commanded the apostles to preach the Gospel, which had been promised beforehand by the prophets, and which he fulfilled in his own person and promulgated with his own lips. In preaching the Gospel they were to communicate the gifts of God to all men. This Gospel was to be the source of all saving truth and moral discipline. This was faithfully done: it was done by the apostles who handed on, by the spoken word of their preaching, by the example they gave, by the institutions they established, what they themselves had received—whether from the lips of Christ, from his way of life and his works, or whether they had learned it at the prompting of the Holy Spirit; it was done by those apostles and other men associated with the apostles who, under the inspiration of the same Holy Spirit, committed the message of salvation to writing. *Dei Verbum, 7*

The apostolic preaching, which is expressed in a special way in the inspired books, was to be preserved in a continuous line of succession until the end of time. Hence the apostles, in handing on what they themselves had received, warn the faithful to maintain the traditions which they had learned either by word of mouth or by letter (cf. 2 Th. 2:15); and they warn them to fight hard for the faith that had been handed on to them once and for all (cf. Jude 3). What was handed on by the apostles comprises everything that serves to make the People of God live their lives in holiness and increase their faith. In this way the Church, in her doctrine, life and worship, perpetuates and transmits to every generation all that she herself is, all that she believes.

The Tradition that comes from the apostles makes progress in the Church, with the help of the Holy Spirit. There is a growth in insight into the realities and words that are being passed on. This comes about in various ways. It comes through the contemplation and study of believers who ponder these things in their hearts (cf. Lk. 2:19 and 51). It comes from the intimate sense of spiritual realities which they experience. And it comes from the preaching of those who have received, along with their right of succession in the episcopate, the sure charism of truth. Thus, as the centuries go by, the Church is always advancing towards the plenitude of divine truth, until eventually the words of God are fulfilled in her. *Dei Verbum, 8*

#R4.1-9b

By the popes, bishops, priests, and deacons, the Gospel of Christ is preached in every part of the world.

#R4.2-12

Speaking to all the Apostles, Jesus said, "All authority in heaven and on earth has been given to me. Go therefore and make disciples of all nations, baptizing them in the name of the Father and of the Son and of the Holy Spirit, teaching them to observe all that I have commanded you; and lo, I am with you always, to the close of the age" *(Matthew 28:18-20).*

Summary Prayer

Father, through the Apostles, Your Church first received the faith; keep us true to their teaching. Through the prayers of the Apostles, may we who received this faith through their preaching share their joy in following the Lord to the unfading inheritance which is reserved for us in Heaven. We ask this in the powerful name of Jesus Christ our Lord. Amen.

Doctrine • Moral • Worship Exercise

(See Appendix A for answer key, question 181.)

1. Which passage in Sacred Scripture shows Jesus founding the Catholic Church on the Apostles? Try to find a list of the popes from St. Peter to the present day. Show this list to your family and friends as you explain why the Catholic Church is called apostolic.
2. Jesus willed that the authority and ministry which He gave to the Apostles be passed on to the Pope and the bishops. If you have a chance to meet a bishop, how will you treat him? What will you tell him?
3. Using the Chapter Summary Prayer, reflect on the authority of the Pope and the bishops. Pray that the Holy Spirit will help them to be holy and dedicated shepherds of the flock entrusted to them.

Chapter Summary Prayer

Father in Heaven, You founded Your Church on the Apostles so that she might stand firm forever as the sign on earth of Your infinite holiness and as the living Gospel for all men to hear.

You are the eternal Shepherd Who never leaves His flock untended. Through the Apostles, You watched over and protected the Church.

You made them shepherds of the flock to share in the work of Your Son; from their place in Heaven, they guide us still.

Lord our God, encourage us through the prayers of Saints Peter and Paul. May the Apostles, who strengthened the faith of the infant Church, help us on our way of Salvation.

The light of Your revelation brought Peter and Paul the gift of faith in Jesus, Your Son. Through their prayers, may we always give thanks for Your life, which is given to us in Christ Jesus, and for the knowledge and love with which He has enriched us.

You have set us firmly within Your Church, which You built upon the rock of Peter, our first Pope. May You bless us with a faith that never falters. You have given us knowledge of the faith through the labor and preaching of St. Paul. May his example inspire us to lead others to Christ by the manner of our lives.

May Peter and Paul, by their undying witness and their prayers, lead us to the joy of that eternal home which Peter gained by his cross, and Paul by the sword.

Pour on us the Holy Spirit, Who filled Your Apostles, that we may acknowledge the gifts we have received through them. Keep us faithful to the teaching of the Apostles, united in prayer and in the Breaking of Bread in the Eucharist, and in joy and simplicity of heart.

Lord God, You appointed Paul, Your Apostle, to preach the Good News of Salvation. Fill the entire world with the faith he carried to so many peoples and nations, that Your Church may continue to grow. May Your Spirit fill us with the light which led St. Paul to make Your glory known. May Christ be our life and let nothing separate us from His love. Following the teachings of St. Paul, may we live in love with our brothers and sisters in Christ.

Teach us, Father, to lift up our hands and our hearts reverently in prayer and to hold to the pattern of sound teaching which You delivered to the holy Apostles. To You be glory now and all honor forever. Amen.

Thought Provokers

Please see Appendix B for the answers.

Q. 181: Do all bishops, who are successors of the Apostles, belong to the Catholic Church?

By Heart Catechism and Scripture Review™

The "By Heart Catechism and Scripture Review" lists a selected number of questions and Scripture references from "The Apostolate's Family Catechism" to make memorization easier. Q = Question, SR = Scripture Reference

Q. 138. What is the Catholic Church? The Catholic Church is the community of all baptized persons who share the same Faith and who obey the Pope and the bishops loyal to him.

Q. 139. When did Jesus start the Catholic Church? Jesus started the Catholic Church at the time of His Death and Resurrection, more than two thousand years ago.

Q. 141. What are the two sources of Divine Truth? The two sources of Divine Truth are (1) Sacred Scripture and (2) Sacred Tradition.

SR 141 2 Thessalonians 2:15

So then, brethren, stand firm and hold to the traditions which you were taught by us, either by word of mouth or by letter.

SR 144 1 Timothy 3:14-15

I hope to come to you soon, but I am writing these instructions to you so that, if I am delayed, you may know how one ought to behave in the household of God, which is the church of the living God, the pillar and bulwark of the truth.

Q. 148. Why is the Catholic Church called the Sacrament of Christ? The Catholic Church is called the Sacrament of Christ because it is a visible sign of Christ's presence through which God gives His grace to the world.

Q. 150. Does the Catholic Church have leaders? The Catholic Church has leaders in ranks called a hierarchy. Catholics obey the Pope and the bishops who follow him.

Q. 151. Who is the Pope? The Pope is the Bishop of Rome and the Vicar of Christ. He is the supreme teacher and ruler of the Catholic Church.

SR 151 Matthew 16:18

And I tell you, you are Peter, and on this rock I will build my church, and the powers of death shall not prevail against it.

By Heart Catechism and Scripture Review™

The "By Heart Catechism and Scripture Review" lists a selected number of questions and Scripture references from "The Apostolate's Family Catechism" to make memorization easier. Q = Question, SR = Scripture Reference

Q. 152. Who are the bishops of the Church? The bishops are the successors of the Apostles.

Q. 155. What do Catholics owe the Pope and the bishops? To the Pope and the bishops, Catholics owe honor, respect, obedience, and love.

SR 156 Romans 8:15–17

When we cry "Abba! Father!" it is the Spirit himself bearing witness with our spirit that we are children of God, and if children, then heirs, heirs of God and fellow heirs with Christ, provided we suffer with him in order that we may also be glorified with him.

Q. 158. Is everyone in the Church equal? All persons are equal, but they have different duties and roles in the Church.

Q. 159. Who in the Church is called to holiness? Every member of the Church is called to be holy. We must will to be holy, and we must ask God for the grace to be holy.

Q. 160. Why is the Catholic Church missionary? The Catholic Church is missionary because every member shares the command from Christ to carry the Good News of His teaching to all mankind by word and example.

SR 160 Matthew 28:18–20

All authority in heaven and on earth has been given to me. Go therefore, and make disciples of all nations, baptizing them in the name of the Father, and of the Son, and of the Holy Spirit, teaching them to observe all that I have commanded you; and lo, I am with you always, to the close of the age.

Q. 161. What is the role of the Church in the world? The role of the Church in the world is to make Jesus known and loved. The Church prays, works, and suffers for the Salvation of souls.

Q. 164. How can we help unbelievers find God? We can help unbelievers find God by our example of love for God and by our goodness toward unbelievers.

By Heart Catechism and Scripture Review™

The "By Heart Catechism and Scripture Review" lists a selected number of questions and Scripture references from "The Apostolate's Family Catechism" to make memorization easier. Q = Question, SR = Scripture Reference

Q. 165. What is our duty toward the world? Our duty toward the world is to love our neighbors unselfishly, to help people solve their problems, and to help all people get to Heaven.

Q. 172. What are the four marks of the true Church? The four marks of the true Church founded by Jesus are: One, Holy, Catholic, and Apostolic.

Q. 173. Why is the Catholic Church one? The Catholic Church is one because it is unified in belief.

Q. 176. Why are we united in worship? We are united in worship because we share in the same Holy Sacrifice of the Mass and in the same Seven Sacraments.

Q. 177. Why is the Catholic Church holy? The Catholic Church is holy because it was founded by Jesus, Who is all-holy. Jesus gives His followers holy teachings and the power of the Holy Spirit to become holy.

Q. 178. Why is the Church catholic? The Church is catholic because Christ established it to proclaim all of His teaching to all men, at all times, and in all places.

Q. 180. Does the Catholic Church teach all of the truths that Jesus taught? Yes, the Catholic Church is the only church that teaches all of the truths that Jesus taught.

Q. 181. Why is the Catholic Church apostolic? The Catholic Church is apostolic because it can trace its leaders, in an unbroken line, back to the Apostles.

SR 181 Ephesians 2:19-20

So then you are no longer strangers and sojourners, but you are fellow citizens with the saints and members of the household of God, built upon the foundation of the apostles and prophets, Christ Jesus Himself being the cornerstone.

#S2-276

St. Joseph and the Child Jesus

The Communion of Saints

#P26-37

The Communion of Saints is the unity and cooperation of the members of the Church on earth with those in Heaven and those in Purgatory, all of whom are united in the one Mystical Body of Christ.

CHAPTER FIFTY-THREE

The Communion of Saints

Q. 182. What do we mean when we say, "I believe in the Communion of Saints"?

When we say, "I believe in the Communion of Saints," we mean that we believe that there is a union, a fellowship, of all souls in whom the Holy Spirit, the Spirit of Christ, dwells. This communion is the union of the members of the Church on earth, in Heaven, and in Purgatory.

The word "communion" means "union with." The word "saint" means "holy." Every Christian soul, incorporated with Christ by Baptism and having within himself the Holy Spirit, is holy so long as he remains in the state of sanctifying grace. In the early Church, all faithful members of the Mystical Body of Christ were called saints.

The Communion of Saints is the unity and cooperation of the members of the Church on earth with those in Heaven and those in Purgatory, all of whom are united in the one Mystical Body of Christ.

The faithful on earth are in communion with each other by professing the same faith, by obeying the same authority, and by assisting each other with prayers and good works. They have communion with the saints in Heaven by honoring them as glorified members of the Church, by invoking their prayers and aid, and by striving to imitate their virtues. They are in communion with the souls in Purgatory by helping them through prayers and good works, especially through the Holy Sacrifice of the Mass.

The Church is not only the family of those living in faith here on earth. It is a Communion of Saints. It reaches into eternity, embracing also all who are being purified to enter the Beatific Vision and all who are already rejoicing in the beholding of God's glory. Our union with those we love who have gone to sleep in the peace of Christ is not in the least interrupted. Their entrance into life has not ended their union with us. Through their entrance into life, we too are brought nearer to God.

Sacred Scripture
Q. 182. 2 Mac 12:44-45; Eph 2:19-22.

Catechism of the Catholic Church
Q. 182. Paragraphs **946-948**, 1474-1477.

For cross-references with Vatican II, Papal documents & other resources, see Family Wisdom Library on page 734.
For commentaries on each question with Cardinal Arinze, Sr. John Vianney and Fr. Straub (in Spanish), see Appendix C.

#S2-262

The faithful on earth have communion with the saints in Heaven by honoring them as glorified members of the Church, by invoking their prayers and aid, and by striving to imitate their virtues.

Their blessedness is not yet totally fulfilled, for they await the final resurrection and the sharing of that flesh which is part of their being in the joy of eternal life. They await the Last Judgment with the gathering into total newness of life the full number of all the redeemed. But the source of their beatitude is already theirs. They have come to see and to possess their God in the Beatific Vision.

The blessed not only enjoy the blessedness of God's immediate presence, the indescribable happiness of knowing and loving God as He knows and loves Himself, but they also contribute to the building of the Kingdom by praying for their brothers and sisters in Christ who are still here on earth. Their happiness is intensified by the realization that they can influence the Salvation of those whom they know and love. They look upon the goodness and share the perfect peace of Christ as they await with joyful longing the final resurrection and final judgment when all will be made perfect in God.

Sacred Scripture

If one member suffers, all suffer together; if one member is honored, all rejoice together. Now you are the body of Christ and individually members of it. *1 Corinthians 12:26-27*

Catechism of the Catholic Church

946 After confessing "the holy catholic Church," the Apostles' Creed adds "the communion of saints." In a certain sense this article is a further explanation of the preceding: "What is the Church if not the assembly of all the saints?"[1] The communion of saints is the Church.

Splendor of Truth

The Church, as a wise teacher of morality, has always invited believers to seek and to find in the saints, and above all in the Virgin Mother of God 'full of grace' and 'all-holy,' the model, the strength and the joy needed to live a life in accordance with God's commandments and the Beatitudes of the Gospel. *(section 107)*

Vatican Council II

When the Lord will come in glory, and all his angels with him (cf. Mt. 25:31), death will be no more and all things will be subject to him (cf. 1 Cor. 15:26-27). But at the present time some of his disciples are pilgrims on earth. Others have died and are being purified, while still others are in glory, contemplating "in full light, God himself triune and one, exactly as he is." All of us, however, in varying degrees and in different ways share in the same charity towards God and our neighbors, and we all sing the one hymn of glory to our God. All, indeed, who are of Christ and who have his Spirit form one Church and in Christ cleave together (Eph. 4:16). *Lumen Gentium, 49*

#M3-58

The Church...has always invited believers to seek and to find in the saints, and above all in the Virgin Mother of God,...the model, the strength and the joy needed to live a life in accordance with God's commandments and the Beatitudes of the Gospel. *(Splendor of Truth, 107)*

Catechism by Diagram

#C15-68

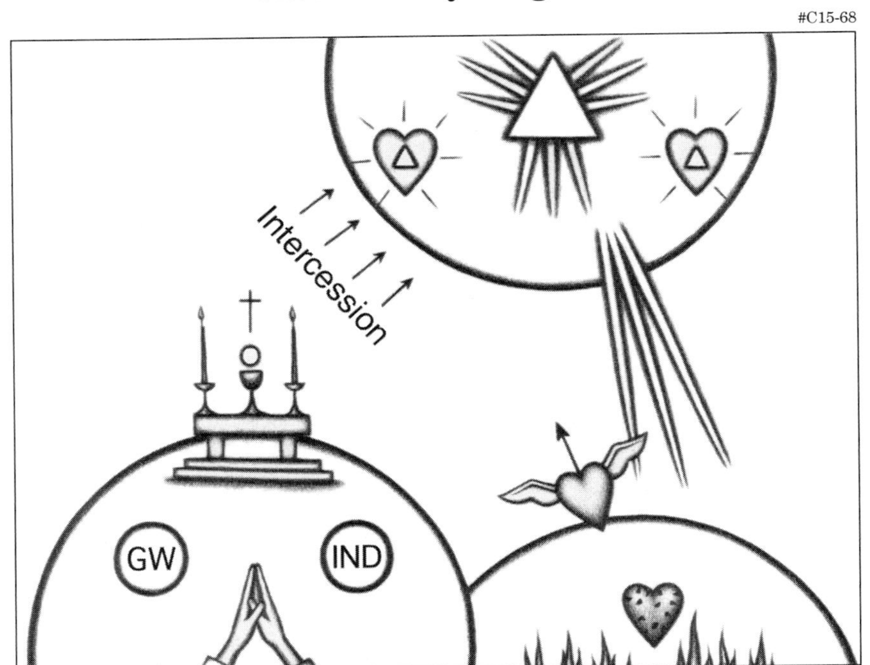

Members Helping Each Other. We pray (hands joined) for deceased relatives and friends and all the faithful departed in Purgatory (spotted heart and flames). We offer indulgences (IND) and good works (GW) for them, but the greatest means of helping them and of leading them to God (heart with wings) is the Sacrifice of the Mass (altar). Through the Communion of Saints, we are one with those who share in the life of the larger family of God. We honor the saints (hearts with triangle) who are already with the Lord in Heaven and who intercede for us.

Summary Prayer

Our Father, protect those whom You have united and look kindly on all who follow Jesus Your Son. We are consecrated to You by our Baptism; make us one in the fullness of our faith and keep us one in the fellowship of love through Jesus Christ our Lord. Amen.

Q. 183. Why is the Church called the Church Militant?

The Church is called the Church Militant because it is the Church here on earth which is still fighting against sin and error. It is also called the Pilgrim Church, since its ultimate goal is Heaven, rather than earth.

If we should fall into mortal sin, we do not cease to be members of the Communion of Saints, but we are cut off from all spiritual communion with our fellow Christians as long as we continue to exclude the Holy Spirit from our souls.

The Church is called the Church Militant because it is the Church here on earth which is still fighting against sin and error. It is also called the Pilgrim Church, since its ultimate goal is Heaven, rather than earth.

Sacred Scripture

"From the days of John the Baptist until now the kingdom of heaven has suffered violence, and men of violence take it by force." *Matthew 11:12*

Finally, be strong in the Lord and in the strength of his might. Put on the whole armor of God, that you may be able to stand against the wiles of the devil. For we are not contending against flesh and blood, but against the principalities, against the powers, against the world rulers of this present darkness, against the spiritual hosts of wickedness in the heavenly places. Therefore take the whole armor of God, that you may be able to withstand in the evil day, and having done all, to stand. Stand therefore, having girded your loins with truth, and having put on the breastplate of righteousness, and having shod your feet with the equipment of the gospel of peace; above all taking the shield of faith, with which you can quench all the flaming darts of the evil one. And take the helmet of salvation, and the sword of the Spirit, which is the word of God. *Ephesians 6:10-17*

Sacred Scripture
Q. 183. 2 Thess 1:4-5; Heb 3:12-14.

Catechism of the Catholic Church
Q. 183. Paragraphs 2725, 2848-**2849**.

For cross-references with Vatican II, Papal documents & other resources, see Family Wisdom Library on page 734.
For commentaries on each question with Cardinal Arinze, Sr. John Vianney and Fr. Straub (in Spanish), see Appendix C.

#S13-16-2

The Church is therefore holy, though having sinners in her midst, because she herself has no other life but the life of grace. If they live her life, her members are sanctified. *(Catechism of the Catholic Church, 827)*

Catechism of the Catholic Church

827 "Christ, 'holy, innocent, and undefiled,' knew nothing of sin, but came only to expiate the sins of the people. The Church, however, clasping sinners to her bosom, at once holy and always in need of purification, follows constantly the path of penance and renewal."[1] All members of the Church, including her ministers, must acknowledge that they are sinners.[2] In everyone, the weeds of sin will still be mixed with the good wheat of the Gospel until the end of time.[3] Hence the Church gathers sinners already caught up in Christ's salvation but still on the way to holiness: "The Church is therefore holy, though having sinners in her midst, because she herself has no other life but the life of grace. If they live her life, her members are sanctified; if they move away from her life, they fall into sins and disorders that prevent the radiation of her sanctity. This is why she suffers and does penance for those offenses, of which she has the power to free her children through the blood of Christ and the gift of the Holy Spirit."[4]

Splendor of Truth

It is the Gospel which reveals the full truth about man and his moral journey, and thus enlightens and admonishes sinners; it proclaims to them God's mercy, which is constantly at work to preserve them both from despair at their inability fully to know and keep God's law and from the presumption that they can be saved without merit. God also reminds sinners of the joy of forgiveness, which alone grants the strength to see in the moral law a liberating truth, a grace-filled source of hope, a path of life. *(section 112)*

Vatican Council II

The Church... which is called "that Jerusalem which is above" and "our mother" (Gal. 4:26; cf. Apoc. 12:17), is described as the spotless spouse of the spotless lamb (Apoc. 19:7; 21:2 and 9; 22:17). It is she whom Christ "loved and for whom he delivered himself up that he might sanctify her" (Eph. 5:26). It is she whom he unites to himself by an unbreakable alliance, and whom he constantly "nourishes and cherishes" (Eph. 5:29). It is she whom, once purified, he willed to be joined to himself, subject in love and fidelity (cf. Eph. 5:24), and whom, finally, he filled with heavenly gifts for all eternity, in order that we may know that love of God and of Christ for us, a love which surpasses all understanding (cf. Eph. 3:19). While on earth she journeys in a foreign land away from the Lord (cf. 2 Cor. 5:6), the Church sees herself as an exile. She seeks and is concerned about those things which are above, where Christ is seated at the right hand of God, where the life of the Church is hidden with Christ in God until she appears in glory with her Spouse (cf. Col. 3:1-4). *Lumen Gentium, 6*

Summary Prayer

Lord, unite Your Church in the Holy Spirit that we may serve You with all our hearts and work together with unselfish love. Teach us to value all the good You give us in the Catholic Church. Make us strong in faith, through Jesus Christ our Lord to Whom with You and the Holy Spirit be all honor and glory. Amen.

#C15-55

Therefore take the whole armor of God, that you may be able to withstand in the evil day, and having done all, to stand. *(Ephesians 6:13)*

Q. 184. How do we help each other?

We upon earth must pray for one another so we may all be faithful to our obligations as members of the Communion of Saints. We must also perform the spiritual and corporal works of mercy.

#P26-5-2

We upon earth must pray for one another so we may all be faithful to our obligations as members of the Communion of Saints.

Sacred Scripture

First of all, then, I urge that supplications, prayers, intercessions, and thanksgivings be made for all men. *1 Timothy 2:1*

Let us hold fast the confession of our hope without wavering, for he who promised is faithful; and let us consider how to stir up one another to love and good works, not neglecting to meet together, as is the habit of some, but encouraging one another. *Heb 10:23-25*

Therefore confess your sins to one another, and pray for one another, that you may be healed. The prayer of a righteous man has great power in its effects. *James 5:16*

Catechism of the Catholic Church

2634 Intercession is a prayer of petition which leads us to pray as Jesus did. He is the one intercessor with the Father on behalf of all men, especially sinners.[1] He is "able for all time to save those who draw near to God through him, since he always lives to make intercession for them."[2] The Holy Spirit "himself intercedes for us… and intercedes for the saints according to the will of God."[3]

Sacred Scripture
Q. 184. Rom 1:9-12, 15:30.

Catechism of the Catholic Church
Q. 184. Paragraphs 2447, **2635**-2636.

For cross-references with Vatican II, Papal documents & other resources, see Family Wisdom Library on page 734.
For commentaries on each question with Cardinal Arinze, Sr. John Vianney and Fr. Straub (in Spanish), see Appendix C.

Vatican Council II

The Council lays stress on respect for the human person: everyone should look upon his neighbor (without any exception) as another self, bearing in mind above all his life and the means necessary for living it in a dignified way. *Gaudium et Spes, 27*

Q. 185. What is the Church Suffering?

The Church Suffering, or the Church Expectant, consists of the souls in Purgatory. This is the Church of all the faithful departed who are saved but are still being purified in purgatorial suffering. They cannot see God, but the Holy Spirit is in them. Being made ready for Heaven, they will never again sin.

#P28-5

The Church Suffering is the Church of all the faithful departed who are saved but are still being purified in purgatorial suffering.

Sacred Scripture

And they turned to prayer, beseeching that the sin which had been committed might be wholly blotted out. And the noble Judas exhorted the people to keep themselves free from sin, for they had seen with their own eyes what had happened because of the sin of those who had fallen. He also took up a collection, man by man, to the amount of two thousand drachmas of silver, and sent it to Jerusalem to provide for a sin offering. In doing this he acted very well and honorably, taking account of the resurrection. For if he were not expecting that those who had fallen would rise again, it would have been superfluous and foolish to pray for the dead. But if he was looking to the

Catechism of the Catholic Church
Q. 185. Paragraphs **1030-1032**.

For cross-references with Vatican II, Papal documents & other resources, see Family Wisdom Library on page 734.
For commentaries on each question with Cardinal Arinze, Sr. John Vianney and Fr. Straub (in Spanish), see Appendix C.

splendid reward that is laid up for those who fall asleep in godliness, it was a holy and pious thought. Therefore he made atonement for the dead, that they might be delivered from their sin. *2 Maccabees 12:42-45*

Each man's work will become manifest; for the Day will disclose it, because it will be revealed with fire, and the fire will test what sort of work each one has done. If the work which any man has built on the foundation survives, he will receive a reward. If any man's work is burned up, he will suffer loss, though he himself will be saved, but only as through fire. *1 Corinthians 3:13-15*

#P26-38

It is a holy and a wholesome thought to pray for the dead that they may be loosed from their sins (2 Mac. 12:46). *(Lumen Gentium, 50)*

Catechism of the Catholic Church

1031 The Church gives the name *Purgatory* to this final purification of the elect, which is entirely different from the punishment of the damned.[1] The Church formulated her doctrine of faith on Purgatory especially at the Councils of Florence and Trent. The tradition of the Church, by reference to certain texts of Scripture, speaks of a cleansing fire:[2] "As for certain lesser faults, we must believe that, before the Final Judgment, there is a purifying fire. He who is truth says that whoever utters blasphemy against the Holy Spirit will be pardoned neither in this age nor in the age to come. From this sentence we understand that certain offenses can be forgiven in this age, but certain others in the age to come."[3]

Vatican Council II

In full consciousness of this communion of the whole Mystical Body of Jesus Christ, the Church in its pilgrim members, from the very earliest days of the Christian religion, has honored with great respect the memory of the dead;

and,"because it is a holy and a wholesome thought to pray for the dead that they may be loosed from their sins" (2 Mac. 12:46) she offers her suffrages for them. *Lumen Gentium, 50*

Summary Prayer

Most Providential Father, keep the Church faithful to its mission: may it be a leaven in the world that renews us in Christ and transforms us into Your family. May the Church continue to grow in holiness through the sacrifice of Christ which gave it life.

Lord God, You are the glory of believers and the life of the just. Your Son redeemed us by dying and rising to life again. Since our departed brothers and sisters believed in the mystery of Your Son's Resurrection, let them share in the joys and blessings of the life to come.

God our Creator, by Your power Christ conquered death and returned to You in glory. May all the people who have gone before us in faith share His victory and enjoy the vision of Your glory forever. May His perfect sacrifice free them from the power of death and give them eternal life; may it bring them peace and forgiveness. Bring the new life which You gave them in Baptism to the fullness of eternal joy. We ask this through Jesus Christ our Lord and Savior. Amen.

#R2.4-7

Lord God, since our departed brothers and sisters believed in the mystery of Your Son's Resurrection, let them share in the joys and blessings of the life to come.

Q. 186. What is our duty toward the deceased?

We must have reverence toward the bodies of those who have gone before us in death, and we must pray for the souls of our deceased relatives and friends, and all of the faithful departed. We show respect for the bodies of the deceased because they were temples of the Holy Spirit and are destined to rise gloriously.

#D2-21-2

The souls in Purgatory benefit from indulgences that are obtained for them. They can and do pray for us, even though they cannot help themselves.

We can help the suffering members of God's family whose souls are being purified in Purgatory by our prayers and sacrifices, especially by participation in the Holy Sacrifice of the Mass. The souls in Purgatory also benefit from indulgences that are obtained for them. They can and do pray for us, even though they cannot help themselves. Through the Communion of Saints, we are one with those loved ones and friends of ours who rest in Christ. Once they are numbered among the saints in Heaven, they will be our special intercessors with God.

Sacred Scripture

But we would not have you ignorant, brethren, concerning those who are asleep, that you may not grieve as others do who have no hope. For since we believe that Jesus died and rose again, even so, through Jesus, God will bring with him those who have fallen asleep. *1 Thessalonians 4:13-14*

Sacred Scripture
Q. 186. Tob 12:12-15; Sir 7:32-33.

Catechism of the Catholic Church
Q. 186. Paragraphs **364-366**.

For cross-references with Vatican II, Papal documents & other resources, see Family Wisdom Library on page 734.
For commentaries on each question with Cardinal Arinze, Sr. John Vianney and Fr. Straub (in Spanish), see Appendix C.

Catechism of the Catholic Church

1032 This teaching is also based on the practice of prayer for the dead, already mentioned in Sacred Scripture: "Therefore [Judas Maccabeus] made atonement for the dead, that they might be delivered from their sin."[1] From the beginning the Church has honored the memory of the dead and offered prayers in suffrage for them, above all the Eucharistic sacrifice, so that, thus purified, they may attain the beatific vision of God.[2] The Church also commends almsgiving, indulgences, and works of penance undertaken on behalf of the dead: "Let us help and commemorate them. If Job's sons were purified by their father's sacrifice, why would we doubt that our offerings for the dead bring them some consolation? Let us not hesitate to help those who have died and to offer our prayers for them."[3]

Vatican Council II

This sacred council accepts loyally the venerable faith of our ancestors in the living communion which exists between us and our brothers who are in the glory of heaven or who are yet being purified after their death. *Lumen Gentium, 51*

#E4-58

We can help the suffering members of God's family whose souls are being purified in Purgatory by our prayers and sacrifices, especially by participation in the Holy Sacrifice of the Mass.

Summary Prayer

God, our Father, may the Sacrifice of the Mass wash away our sins in the blood of Christ. You cleansed us in the waters of Baptism; in Your loving mercy, grant us pardon and peace. In the Sacrament of the Eucharist, You give us Your crucified and risen Son. Bring to the glory of the Resurrection the departed souls who have been purified by this holy mystery. We ask this in the most holy name of Jesus our Lord. Amen.

Doctrine • Moral • Worship Exercise

(See Appendix A for answer key, questions 182–186.)

1. Who are included in the Communion of Saints? How are they united to each other?
2. As a member of the Church Militant, or Pilgrim Church, how can you be united to the other members of the Church Militant, as well as to the members of the Church Suffering and the Church Triumphant?
3. Offer a prayer or sacrifice to Jesus, through Mary, in reparation for sin for the souls in Purgatory. Pray the Creed slowly and reflectively.

Q. 187. What is the Church Triumphant?

The Church Triumphant consists of all the souls of the blessed in Heaven. It is the Church of all those in heavenly glory who have triumphed over their evil inclinations, the seductions of the world, and the temptations of the evil spirit.

Sacred Scripture

But he who endures to the end will be saved. *Matthew 24:13*

Who are these, clothed in white robes, and whence have they come?... These are they who have come out of the great tribulation; they have washed their robes and made them white in the blood of the Lamb. Therefore are they before the throne of God, and serve him day and night within his temple; and he who sits upon the throne will shelter them with his presence. They shall hunger no more, neither thirst any more; the sun shall not strike them, nor any scorching heat. For the Lamb in the midst of the throne will be their shepherd, and he will guide them to springs of living water; and God will wipe away every tear from their eyes. *Revelation 7:13-17*

Sacred Scripture
Q. 187. Jn 14:1-3; 1 Cor 2:9.

Catechism of the Catholic Church
Q. 187. Paragraphs **1024**-1029.

For cross-references with Vatican II, Papal documents & other resources, see Family Wisdom Library on page 734.
For commentaries on each question with Cardinal Arinze, Sr. John Vianney and Fr. Straub (in Spanish), see Appendix C.

Those who die in God's grace and friendship and are perfectly purified live for ever with Christ. They are like God for ever, for they "see him as he is," face to face. *(Catechism of the Catholic Church, 1023)*

Catechism of the Catholic Church

1023 Those who die in God's grace and friendship and are perfectly purified live for ever with Christ. They are like God for ever, for they "see him as he is," face to face:[1]

"By virtue of our apostolic authority, we define the following: According to the general disposition of God, the souls of all the saints... and other faithful who died after receiving Christ's holy Baptism (provided they were not in need of purification when they died,... or, if they then did need or will need some purification, when they have been purified after death,...) already before they take up their bodies again and before the general judgment—and this since the Ascension of our Lord and Savior Jesus Christ into heaven—have been, are and will be in heaven, in the heavenly Kingdom and celestial paradise with Christ, joined to the company of the holy angels. Since the Passion and death of our Lord Jesus Christ, these souls have seen and do see the divine essence with an intuitive vision, and even face to face, without the mediation of any creature."[2]

Splendor of Truth

But temptations can be overcome, sins can be avoided, because together with the commandments the Lord gives us the possibility of keeping them... Keeping God's law in particular situations can be difficult, extremely difficult, but it is never impossible. *(section 102)*

Vatican Council II

Our communion with these in heaven, provided that it is understood in the full light of faith, in no way diminishes the worship of adoration given to God the Father, through Christ, in the Spirit; on the contrary, it greatly enriches it. *Lumen Gentium, 51*

Catechism by Diagram

#C15-67

The Communion of Saints. There exists a union, a fellowship, among souls in whom the Holy Spirit dwells through sanctifying grace. He is the Spirit of Christ (monogram). This fellowship (three circles) includes the Church Militant, the Church Suffering, and the Church Triumphant. The Church Militant: members of the Church on earth who must practice and defend their faith (cross, shield, spear) at the cost of self-sacrifice (thorns). The Church Suffering: the souls in Purgatory who are established in grace forever, even though minor sins and debts of penance (spots on hearts) still have to be cleansed away (flames). The Church Triumphant: the souls of the blessed in Heaven, the everlasting Church, now triumphantly enjoying (crown, palm of victory) the vision of God (triangle), into which, after the Last Judgment, will be absorbed the Church Militant and the Church Suffering (angel, heart in sanctifying grace).

188. Why does the Church honor the canonized saints?

The Church honors the canonized saints who are already with the Lord in Heaven because they inspire us by the good example of their lives, and because they can help us by their prayers.

We must honor the saints not just because they can and will pray for us, but also because our love for God demands it. The saints are masterpieces of God's grace; when we honor them, we are honoring their Maker, their Sanctifier, and their Redeemer. The saints inspire us by the heroic example of their lives. To them we pray, asking their intercession with God for us.

#S2-241

The Church honors the canonized saints because they inspire us by the good example of their lives, and because they can help us by their prayers.

Jesus, having entered into glory and as the eternal High Priest, continues to pray for us. Mary, ever associated with her Son, prays for us with Him. She is not alone in this; the whole community of the blessed in Heaven imitates Christ in their continual concern for us. As we pray for one another upon earth and for the souls in Purgatory, so our brothers and sisters in Heaven intercede for us. We are united with all of them by intimate bonds of Christian love. Mary, our spiritual mother, however, has an altogether exceptional role in this union. Among those who have been redeemed by her Son, her intercessory power is by far the most extensive and effective.

To invoke the intercession of the saints, including Mary, is really to pray that, together with them, we may grow in the love of the triune God, Who wills the Salvation of all; it is to express the longing that

Catechism of the Catholic Church
Q. 188. Paragraphs 957, 1173.

For cross-references with Vatican II, Papal documents & other resources, see Family Wisdom Library on page 734.
For commentaries on each question with Cardinal Arinze, Sr. John Vianney and Fr. Straub (in Spanish), see Appendix C.

the saints, living in personal love of God, will also embrace us in that personal God-given love, and will, by their prayers, assist us in obtaining benefits from God.

When we honor the canonized (and uncanonized) saints, we are honoring many of our own loved ones who now are with God in Heaven, because every soul in Heaven is a saint.

#H1-261

St. Joseph, Model for Husbands and Fathers
Virgin-father and Guardian of Jesus, Spouse of Mary

Sacred Scripture

And when he had taken the scroll, the four living creatures and the twenty-four elders fell down before the Lamb, each holding a harp, and with golden bowls full of incense, which are the prayers of the saints. *Revelation 5:8*

I looked, and behold, a great multitude which no man could number, from every nation, from all tribes and peoples and tongues, standing before the throne and before the Lamb, clothed in white robes, with palm branches in their hands, and crying out with a loud voice, "Salvation belongs to our God who sits upon the throne, and to the Lamb!" *Revelation 7:9-10*

And the smoke of the incense rose with the prayers of the saints from the hand of the angel before God. *Revelation 8:4*

Catechism of the Catholic Church

956 *The intercession of the saints.* "Being more closely united to Christ, those who dwell in heaven fix the whole Church more firmly in holiness.... [T]hey do not cease to intercede with the Father for us, as they proffer the merits which they acquired on earth through the one mediator between God and men, Christ Jesus.... So by their fraternal concern is our weakness greatly helped."[1]

Splendor of Truth

The Church proposes the example of numerous Saints who bore witness to and defended moral truth even to the point of enduring martyrdom, or who preferred death to a single mortal sin. In raising them to the honor of the altars, the Church has canonized their witness and declared the truth of their judgment, according to which the love of God entails the obligation to respect his commandments, even in the most dire of circumstances, and the refusal to betray those commandments, even for the sake of saving one's own life. *(section 91)*

Martyrdom... bears splendid witness both to the holiness of God's law and to the inviolability of the personal dignity of man, created in God's image and likeness. *(section 92)*

#S2-283

St. Therese, Patroness of the Little Way

St. Therese offered to Jesus the ordinary duties of her life with great love.

#S2-282

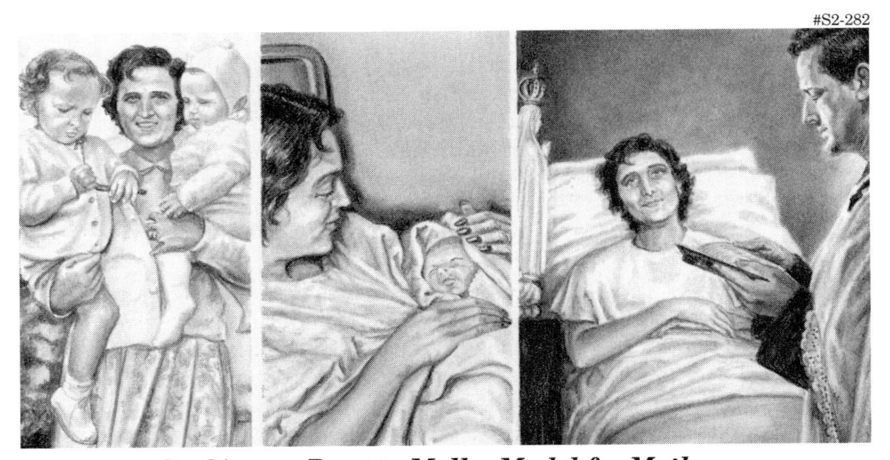

St. Gianna Beretta Molla, Model for Mothers
St. Gianna gave her life for her baby by refusing to have an abortion even though she was in danger of death.

Vatican Council II

The Church has always believed that the apostles and Christ's martyrs, who gave the supreme witness of faith and charity by the shedding of their blood, are closely united with us in Christ; she has always venerated them, together with the Blessed Virgin Mary and the holy angels, with a special love, and has asked piously for the help of their intercession. Soon there were added to these others who had chosen to imitate more closely the virginity and poverty of Christ, and still others whom the outstanding practice of the Christian virtues and the wonderful graces of God recommended to the pious devotion and imitation of the faithful. *Lumen Gentium, 50*

To look on the life of those who have faithfully followed Christ is to be inspired with a new reason for seeking the city which is to come (cf. Heb. 13:14 and 11:10), while at the same time we are taught to know a most safe path by which, despite the vicissitudes of the world, and in keeping with the state of life and condition proper to each of us, we will be able to arrive at perfect union with Christ, that is, holiness. God shows to men, in a vivid way, his presence and his face in the lives of those companions of ours in the human condition who are more perfectly transformed into the image of Christ (cf. 2 Cor. 3:18). He speaks to us in them and offers us a sign of this kingdom, to which we are powerfully attracted, so great a cloud of witnesses is there given (cf. Heb. 12:1) and such a witness to the truth of the Gospel.

It is not merely by the title of example that we cherish the memory of those in heaven; we seek, rather, that by this devotion to the exercise of fraternal charity the union of the whole Church in the Spirit may be strengthened (cf. Eph. 4:1-6). Exactly as Christian communion between men on their earthly pilgrimage brings us closer to Christ, so our community with the saints joins us to Christ, from whom as from its fountain and head issues all grace and the life of the People of God itself. It is most fitting, therefore, that we love those friends and co-heirs of Jesus Christ who are also our brothers and outstanding benefactors, and that we give due thanks to God for them, "humbly invoking them, and having recourse to their prayers, their aid and help in obtaining from God through his Son, Jesus Christ, Our Lord, our only Redeemer and

Savior, the benefits we need." Every authentic witness of love, indeed, offered by us to those who are in heaven tends to and terminates in Christ, "the crown of all the saints," and through him in God who is wonderful in his saints and is glorified in them. *Lumen Gentium, 50*

The authentic cult of the saints does not consist so much in a multiplicity of external acts, but rather in a more intense practice of our love, whereby, for our own greater good and that of the Church, we seek from the saints "example in their way of life, fellowship in their communion, and the help of their intercession." *Lumen Gentium, 51*

The Church has also included in the annual cycle memorial days of the martyrs and other saints. Raised up to perfection by the manifold grace of God and already in possession of eternal salvation, they sing God's perfect praise in heaven and pray for us. By celebrating their anniversaries the Church proclaims achievement of the paschal mystery in the saints who have suffered and have been glorified with Christ. She proposes them to the faithful as examples who draw all men to the Father through Christ, and through their merits she begs for God's favors. *Sacrosanctum Concilium, 104*

#G14-2

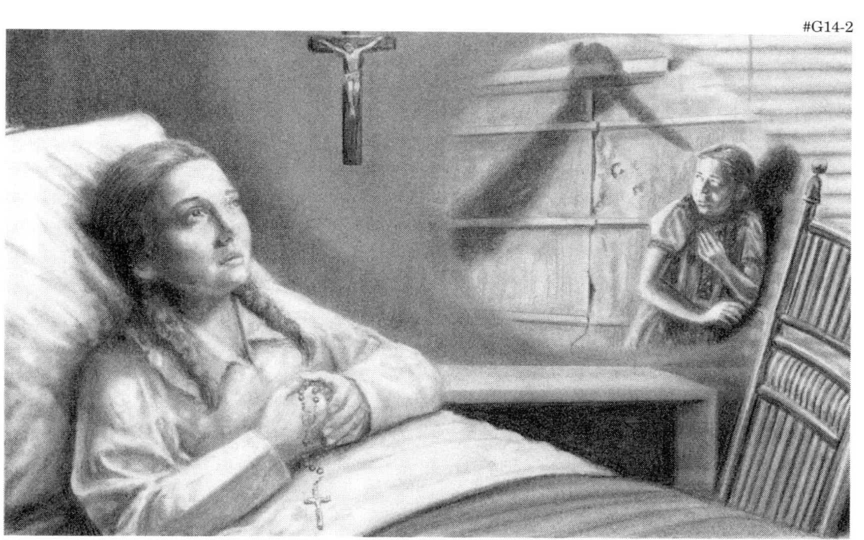

St. Maria Goretti, Patroness of Purity

She died after being stabbed for refusing to commit a mortal sin against purity.

Summary Prayer

Heavenly Father, we honor the saints who consecrated their lives to Christ for the sake of the Kingdom of Heaven. What love You show us as You recall mankind to its innocence and invite us to taste on earth the gifts of the world to come. With the saints and all the angels, we praise You forever, through Jesus Christ our Lord to Whom with You and God the Holy Spirit be all honor and glory. Amen.

#M3-245-2

St. Juan Diego, Model for Lay Evangelists
The saints are masterpieces of God's grace; when we honor them, we are honoring their Maker, their Sanctifier, and their Redeemer.

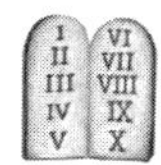

Doctrine • Moral • Worship Exercise

(See Appendix A for answer key, questions 187–188.)

1. Why do we honor the Blessed Virgin Mary and the canonized saints? What role should they play in our lives?
2. Do you have a favorite saint? How can you imitate your favorite saint's virtues in your daily life?
3. Start a novena to your favorite saint. Pray for the conversion of sinners and for world peace.

Chapter Summary Prayer

Good Shepherd, You made us, and we belong to You; You are our first beginning and our last end. In union with all Your saints, we praise and thank You for Your enduring love.

Preserve, O God, those who take refuge in You. By the power of Christ's Resurrection from the dead, may we attain to the fullness of joy in Your presence, in union with all Your saints.

Father, we ask You to give us victory and peace. In Jesus Christ, our Lord and King, we are already seated at Your right hand. We look forward to praising You in the fellowship of all Your saints in our heavenly homeland.

Lord God, You are glorified in Your saints, for their glory is the crowning of Your gifts. In their lives on earth, You give us an example; in our communion with them, You give us their friendship; in their prayer for the Church, You give us strength and protection. The great company of witnesses spurs us on to victory, so that we may share their prize of everlasting glory.

We honor the saints who live in Your holy city, the heavenly Jerusalem, our mother. Around Your throne the saints, our brothers and sisters, sing Your praises forever. Their glory fills us with joy, and their communion with us in Your Church gives us Inspiration and strength, as we hasten on our pilgrimage of faith eager to meet them. With their great company, and all the angels, we praise Your glory, now and forever. Amen.

#K27-1

Blessed Kateri Tekakwitha

When we honor the canonized (and uncanonized) saints, we are honoring many of our own loved ones who now are with God in Heaven, because every soul in Heaven is a saint.

Thought Provokers

Please see Appendix B for the answers.

Q. 182: Catholics are encouraged to seek the intercession of the saints in Heaven. Protestants are not. Why not?

Q. 183: As Soldiers of Christ in the Church Militant on earth, what are some of the ways in which we can fight sin and error?

Q. 184: On the level of marriage and the family, what is one of modern man's greatest needs?

Q. 185: Many today reject the Church's teaching on Purgatory in favor of the false doctrine of reincarnation. How would you defend the Church's teaching in this area?

Q. 186: It can be argued that Masses, prayers, indulgences, almsgiving and other good works for the Poor Souls in Purgatory are of greater worth than the spiritual good works which we perform on behalf of those still on earth. Why?

Q. 187: Do all canonized saints enter immediately into the Church Triumphant upon death and their particular judgment?

Q. 188: Why are there so few canonized saints among the laity ?

#S2-271

St. Maximilian Kolbe, Martyr and Model for Marian Devotion
The Church has also included in the annual cycle memorial days of the martyrs and other saints. By celebrating their anniversaries the Church proclaims achievement of the paschal mystery in the saints who have suffered and have been glorified with Christ. *(Sacrosanctum Concilium, 104)*

By Heart Catechism and Scripture Review™

The "By Heart Catechism and Scripture Review" lists a selected number of questions and Scripture references from "The Apostolate's Family Catechism" to make memorization easier. Q = Question, SR = Scripture Reference

Q. 182. What is the Communion of Saints? The Communion of Saints is the union of all souls who share the life of the Holy Spirit on earth, in Purgatory, and in Heaven.

Q. 183. Why is the Church on earth called the Church Militant? The Church on earth is called the Church Militant because it is still fighting against sin and error.

Q. 185. What is the Church Suffering? The Church Suffering consists of the souls in Purgatory, those who died with the Holy Spirit within them but who are still being purified.

SR 185 2 Maccabees 12:45

But if he was looking to the splendid reward that is laid up for those who fall asleep in godliness, it was a holy and pious thought. Therefore he made atonement for the dead, that they might be delivered from their sin.

Q. 186. What is our duty toward the dead? Our duty toward the dead is to respect their bodies and to pray for their souls.

Q. 187. What is the Church Triumphant? The Church Triumphant consists of the souls in Heaven, who have triumphed over sin and death.

Q. 188. Why does the Church honor canonized saints? The Church honors canonized saints because they inspire us by the good example of their lives, and they can help us with their prayers.

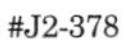
#J2-378

Zacchaeus, a wealthy chief tax collector, said to Jesus, "Behold, Lord, the half of my goods I give to the poor; and if I have defrauded any one of anything, I restore it fourfold." And Jesus said to him, "Today salvation has come to this house.... For the Son of man came to seek and to save the lost." *(Luke 19:1–10)*

The Forgiveness of Sins

#H1-238

Christ merited for us the benefits of His Redemption.

CHAPTER FIFTY-FOUR

The Forgiveness of Sins

Q. 189. What do we mean when we say, "I believe in the forgiveness of sins"?

When we say, "I believe in the forgiveness of sins," we mean that we believe in the pardon, not only of original sin, but of all personal sins, mortal and venial.

Christ died for all men. By the infinite value of His sacrifice, the sin of Adam, which we inherit, is erased.

#J2-340-2

When we say, "I believe in the forgiveness of sins," we mean that we believe in the pardon, not only of original sin, but of all personal sins, mortal and venial.

Jesus appeared to the Apostles on Easter Sunday evening and said, "Peace be with you" (John 20:19). "He showed them his hands and his side. Then the disciples were glad when they saw the Lord. Jesus said to them again, 'Peace be with you. As the Father sent me, even so I send you.' And when he had said this, he breathed on them, and said to them, 'Receive the Holy Spirit. If you forgive the sins of any, they are forgiven; if you retain the sins of any, they are

Catechism of the Catholic Church
Q. 189. Paragraphs **976-987**.

For cross-references with Vatican II, Papal documents & other resources, see Family Wisdom Library on page 734.
For commentaries on each question with Cardinal Arinze, Sr. John Vianney and Fr. Straub (in Spanish), see Appendix C.

retained'" (John 20:20-23). On this occasion Jesus instituted the Sacrament of Penance.

Then Jesus gave Peter and the other Apostles the power to forgive and retain sins. This power is given not only to the Apostles, but also to their lawful successors. When the Sacrament of Penance is administered, the very formula of absolution notes the role of the Holy Spirit in the forgiveness of sins.

Since the Apostles and their successors cannot acquire the necessary knowledge of sin unless the penitent himself gives it to them, Jesus demands a confession or an accusation of sins.

It is also true that a sinner can be restored to grace by perfect sorrow or perfect contrition. There are no sins, however serious, for which a repentant person cannot find forgiveness from God. A merciful Father has compassion on His children who want to love and serve Him.

#J2-358-2

Jesus appeared to the Apostles on Easter Sunday evening and said, "Receive the Holy Spirit. If you forgive the sins of any, they are forgiven; if you retain the sins of any, they are retained" *(John 20:22).*

"'Come now, let us reason together,' says the Lord: 'though your sins are like scarlet, they shall be as white as snow; though they are red like crimson, they shall become like wool'" (Isaiah 1:18).

"For the mountains may depart and the hills be removed, but my steadfast love shall not depart from you, and my covenant of peace shall not be removed, says the Lord, who has compassion on you" (Isaiah 54:10).

Since the Apostles and their successors cannot acquire the necessary knowledge of sin unless the penitent himself gives it to them, Jesus demands a confession of sins.

Jesus is the Lamb of God Who takes away the sins of the world. Our sins are washed away in His Blood: that Blood is offered to God in the Mass.

Certainly Christ did not take away the sins of future men unconditionally, but He provided the means by which our sins can be forgiven, as long as we cooperate with grace. We receive this particular grace through the Sacraments of Baptism and Penance.

Christ merited for us the benefits of His Redemption. He fully satisfied the justice of God for the infinite offense of sin; He freed mankind from its slavery; He made it possible for man to be united with God on earth by regaining for him the grace of divine life, that is, sanctifying grace. Thus man became an adopted son of God and an heir to Heaven.

The Catholic Church believes that sins forgiven are actually removed from the soul and not merely covered over by the merits of Christ. Only God can forgive sins, since He alone can restore sanctifying grace to a person who has sinned gravely and thereby lost the state of grace. God forgives the grave or mortal sins of the truly repentant sinner immediately through an act of perfect contrition or through a sacrament.

The sacraments primarily directed to the forgiveness of sins are Baptism and Penance, and secondarily, under certain conditions, the Sacrament of the Anointing of the Sick.

Catechism of the Catholic Church

987 "In the forgiveness of sins, both priests and sacraments are instruments which our Lord Jesus Christ, the only author and liberal giver of salvation, wills to use in order to efface our sins and give us the grace of justification."[1]

Catechism by Diagram

#C15-69

The Forgiveness of Sins. Christ provided the means by which our sins (black heart) can be forgiven, as long as we cooperate with grace (arrows to keys and to the Holy Spirit). This grace we receive through the Sacraments of Baptism (water, apple—original sin) and Penance (keys). Jesus gave His Apostles the Holy Spirit and the power to forgive sins through the Sacrament of Penance. A sinner who commits a mortal sin can also be restored to grace (white heart) by an act of perfect sorrow (tears) and penance (cross), but the Church demands that, after an act of perfect sorrow, all mortal sins be confessed in the Sacrament of Penance (keys in heart, arrows from black heart to white heart to Holy Spirit).

Splendor of Truth

Appropriate allowance is made both for God's mercy towards the sin of the man who experiences conversion and for the understanding of human weakness. Such understanding never means compromising and falsifying the standard of good and evil in order to adapt it to particular circumstances. It is quite human for the sinner to acknowledge his weakness and to ask mercy for his failings; what is unacceptable is the attitude of one who makes his own weakness the criterion of the truth about the good, so that he can feel self-justified, without even the need to have recourse to God and his mercy. *(section 104)*

Vatican Council II

Since human freedom has been weakened by sin it is only by the help of God's grace that man can give his actions their full and proper relationship to God. Before the judgment seat of God an account of his own life will be rendered to each one according as he has done either good or evil. *Gaudium et Spes, 17*

Summary Prayer

Father, we have wounded the Heart of Jesus Your Son, but He brings us forgiveness and grace. Help us to prove our grateful love and to make amends for our sins. Look on the Heart of Christ Your Son filled with love for us. Because of His love accept our contrition and forgive our sins.

You know our hearts, Lord, but You are slow to anger and merciful in judging. Come, examine Your Church; wash her clean of sin. Forgive the sins of our youth and stupidity, and remember us with Your love. May the fire of Your word consume our sins, and its brightness illumine our hearts. Let us feel the healing calm of Your forgiveness. We ask this through Jesus Christ our Lord. Amen.

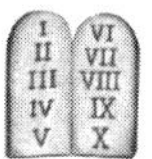

Doctrine • Moral • Worship Exercise

(See Appendix A for answer key, question 189.)

1. Jesus is the Lamb of God who takes away the sins of the world. What does this mean?
2. Think of the people, situations, or circumstances that usually lead you to sin. How can you avoid these occasions of sin so that you can remain in the state of sanctifying grace? (Do not discuss your answers with anyone except with a priest in Confession.)
3. Reflect on Isaiah 1:18 and 54:10. Examine your conscience to see whether you have committed any grave, or mortal, sin. If so, go to Confession as soon as possible to receive God's forgiveness. Make it a habit to

examine your conscience every night and conclude with a perfect Act of Contrition for the sins that you have committed during the day.

Chapter Summary Prayer

Almighty Father, apart from You there is nothing true, nothing holy on earth. Forgive our sins and give us strength in our weakness, so that we who believe in Your Son may rejoice in His glory.

Do not abandon us, Lord our God; You did not forget the broken body of Your Christ, nor the mockery His love received. We, Your children, are weighed down with sin; give us the fullness of Your mercy.

Almighty God, remember our lowliness and have mercy on us. Free us today from sin and give us a share in your inheritance. We ask this in the Name of our Merciful Lord and Savior, Jesus Christ. Amen.

Thought Provokers

Please see Appendix B for the answers.

Q. 189: What is "perfect sorrow" or "perfect contrition"?

By Heart Catechism and Scripture Review™

The "By Heart Catechism and Scripture Review" lists a selected number of questions and Scripture references from "The Apostolate's Family Catechism" to make memorization easier. Q = Question, SR = Scripture Reference

Q. 189. What do we mean when we say, "We believe in the forgiveness of sins"? We mean that we believe in the pardon of all sins, original sin and personal sins, both mortal and venial.

Family Wisdom Library™

Papal documents listed below can be viewed at www.vatican.va.
For new cross-references, visit www.familyland.org

Q. 138. What is the Catholic Church?

Church Documents

Compendium of the Catechism of the Catholic Church, sect. 147, 166-168
Dei Verbum (Dogmatic Constitution on Divine Revelation), Vatican II, sect. 7-8, 23
Gaudium et Spes (Pastoral Constitution on the Church in the Modern World), Vatican II, sect. 11, 21, 32, 40-41, 43, 45
God is Love, Benedict XVI, sect. 19-20
Lumen Gentium (Dogmatic Constitution on the Church), Vatican II, sect. 1, 6-9, 49
On Evangelization in the Modern World, Paul VI, sect. 75
On the Holy Spirit in the Life of the Church and the World, John Paul II, sect. 62-64
Redeemer of Man, John Paul II, sect. 18-19
Sacrament of Charity, Benedict XVI, sect. 15-16
Sacrosanctum Concilium (Constitution on the Sacred Liturgy), Vatican II, sect. 6
U. S. Catholic Catechism for Adults, [2006] pp. 112-123

Other Resources

Basics of the Faith: A Catholic Catechism, Schreck, pp. 177-178
The Catholic Catechism, Hardon, pp. 206-211, 234 237
The Church's Confession of Faith, Ignatius Press, pp. 223-230
Faith for Today, Hogan and LeVoir, [First Edition] pp. 117-123; [Second Edition] pp. 151-158
Fundamentals of Catholic Dogma, Ott, pp. 270-272
Fundamentals of Catholicism, Baker, Vol. 1, pp. 100-103; Vol. 3 pp. 90-91, 98-101, 143, 158
Modern Catholic Dictionary, Hardon, see "Church", "Mystical Body" and "People of God"
The Teaching of Christ, Lawler, Wuerl, and Lawler, [First Edition] pp. 187-196; [Second Edition] pp. 175-184; [Third Edition] pp. 152-161
Transformation in Christ, von Hildebrand, pp. 460-461

Q. 139. When did Jesus start the Catholic Church?

Church Documents

Compendium of the Catechism of the Catholic Church, sect. 149
Dei Verbum (Dogmatic Constitution on Divine Revelation), Vatican II, sect. 17
Lumen Gentium (Dogmatic Constitution on the Church), Vatican II, sect. 4, 5, 49
On the Holy Spirit in the Life of the Church and the World, John Paul II, sect. 25, 52, 66
Sacrament of Charity, Benedict XVI, sect. 14
Sacrosanctum Concilium (Constitution on the Sacred Liturgy), Vatican II, sect. 6
U. S. Catholic Catechism for Adults, [2006] p. 114

Other Resources

Basics of the Faith: A Catholic Catechism, Schreck, pp. 78-80
The Catholic Catechism, Hardon, pp. 206-208, 237
The Church's Confession of Faith, Ignatius Press, pp. 213-214
Fundamentals of Catholicism, Baker, Vol. 3, pp. 94, 125-126
Fundamentals of Catholic Dogma, Ott, p. 274
The Teaching of Christ, Lawler, Wuerl, and Lawler, [First Edition] p. 193; [Second Edition] p. 181 [Third Edition] p. 158

Q. 140. What are some of the basic gifts given by God to the Catholic Church?

Church Documents

Compendium of the Catechism of the Catholic Church, sect. 11-17, 179-187, 224-232
Gaudium et Spes (Pastoral Constitution on the Church in the Modern World), Vatican II, sect. 38, 42-43
God is Love, Benedict XVI, sect. 21-25
The Lay Members of Christ's Faithful People, John Paul II, sect. 24
Lumen Gentium (Dogmatic Constitution on the Church), Vatican II, sect. 5-9, 18
On the Dignity and Vocation of Women, John Paul II, sect. 28
Sacrament of Charity, Benedict XVI, sect. 15-16
Sacrosanctum Concilium (Constitution on the Sacred Liturgy), Vatican II, sect. 6
Splendor of Truth, John Paul II, sect. 2, 8
U. S. Catholic Catechism for Adults, [2006] pp. 115-119, 132-134

Other Resources

Basics of the Faith: A Catholic Catechism, Schreck, pp. 103-110
The Catholic Catechism, Hardon, pp. 211-213, 224-233, 236
The Church's Confession of Faith, Ignatius Press, pp. 219, 228-231, 256-257

Family Wisdom Library™

Papal documents listed below can be viewed at www.vatican.va.
For new cross-references, visit www.familyland.org

Faith for Today, Hogan and LeVoir, [First Edition] pp. 149-155; [Second Edition] pp. 186-193
Fundamentals of Catholicism, Baker, Vol. 3, pp. 98, 139, 148
Fundamentals of Catholic Dogma, Ott, p. 276
Modern Catholic Dictionary, Hardon, see "Revealed Law" and "Divine Revelation"
The Teaching of Christ, Lawler, Wuerl, and Lawler, [First Edition] pp. 199, 222-225, 413-414; [Second Edition] pp. 211-212, 403-404; [Third Edition] pp. 184-185, 357-358

Q. 141. What are the two sources of Divine Truth which constitute the truths of the faith?

Church Documents

Catechesis in Our Time, John Paul II, sect. 27
Compendium of the Catechism of the Catholic Church, sect. 11, 12, 14
Dei Verbum (Dogmatic Constitution on Divine Revelation), Vatican II, sect. 7-13
Gaudium et Spes (Pastoral Constitution on the Church in the Modern World), Vatican II, sect. 12, 24, 37, 58
The Gospel of Life, John Paul II, sect. 54, 57, 62, 65
Sacrament of Charity, Benedict XVI, sect. 37
Splendor of Truth, John Paul II, sect. 3, 4, 30, 95, 107, 109
U. S. Catholic Catechism for Adults, [2006] pp. 23-27, 132-134

Other Resources

Basics of the Faith: A Catholic Catechism, Schreck, pp. 121-125
The Catholic Catechism, Hardon, pp. 36-37, 41-52, 47
The Church's Confession of Faith, Ignatius Press, pp. 37-48, 263
Faith for Today, Hogan and LeVoir, [First Edition] pp. 155-173; [Second Edition] pp. 193-213
Fundamentals of Catholic Dogma, Ott, pp. 298-299
Modern Catholic Dictionary, Hardon, see "Tradition"
The Teaching of Christ, Lawler, Wuerl, and Lawler, [First Edition] pp. 216-222; [Second Edition] pp. 204-210; [Third Edition] pp. 178-184

Q. 142. What are some other gifts of the Catholic Church besides the truths of the faith?

Church Documents

Catechesis in Our Time, John Paul II, sect. 23
Compendium of the Catechism of the Catholic Church, sect. 224-232
Gaudium et Spes (Pastoral Constitution on the Church in the Modern World), Vatican II, sect. 38, 42
God is Love, Benedict XVI, sect. 21-26, 28-32
The Lay Members of Christ's Faithful People, John Paul II, sect. 24
Lumen Gentium (Dogmatic Constitution on the Church), Vatican II, sect. 5-9, 11, 49
On the Holy Spirit in the Life of the Church and the World, John Paul II, sect. 25, 66
On Reconciliation and Penance, John Paul II, sect. 24
Sacrosanctum Concilium (Constitution on the Sacred Liturgy), Vatican II, sect. 6
U. S. Catholic Catechism for Adults, [2006] pp. 168-170

Other Resources

Basics of the Faith: A Catholic Catechism, Schreck, pp. 147-155
The Catholic Catechism, Hardon, pp. 172, 446-447, 457-547
The Church's Confession of Faith, Ignatius Press, pp. 262-265
Fundamentals of Catholic Dogma, Ott, p. 337
Fundamentals of Catholicism, Baker, Vol. 3, pp. 181-184
Faith for Today, Hogan and LeVoir, [First Edition] pp. 177-199; [Second Edition] pp. 160-181
Modern Catholic Dictionary, Hardon, see "Sacrament"
The Teaching of Christ, Lawler, Wuerl, and Lawler, [First Edition] pp. 232-233,409-414; [Second Edition] pp. 220-221, 399-404; [Third Edition] pp. 192-193, 354-358

Q. 143. Are there other gifts of the Church besides the truths of the faith and the sacraments?

Church Documents

Compendium of the Catechism of the Catholic Church, sect. 162, 179-184
Gaudium et Spes (Pastoral Constitution on the Church in the Modern World), Vatican II, sect. 43
God is Love, Benedict XVI, sect. 21-26, 28-32

Family Wisdom Library™

Papal documents listed below can be viewed at www.vatican.va.
For new cross-references, visit www.familyland.org

Lumen Gentium (Dogmatic Constitution on the Church), Vatican II, sect. 5-9, 11, 18, 49
On the Dignity and Vocation of Women, John Paul II, sect. 26
On the Holy Spirit in the Life of the Church and the World, John Paul II, sect. 25
Sacrosanctum Concilium (Constitution on the Sacred Liturgy), Vatican II, sect. 6
U. S. Catholic Catechism for Adults, [2006] pp. 132-134

Other Resources

Basics of the Faith: A Catholic Catechism, Schreck, pp. 207-213
The Catholic Catechism, Hardon, pp. 219-223, 446, 449-451, 520-531
The Church's Confession of Faith, Ignatius Press, pp. 243-248
Faith for Today, Hogan and LeVoir, [First Edition] pp. 125-144; [Second Edition] pp. 160-181
Fundamentals of Catholic Dogma, Ott, pp. 276-279
Fundamentals of Catholicism, Baker, Vol. 3, pp. 101-104
Modern Catholic Dictionary, Hardon, see "Ministerial Priesthood," "Ministry," "Priesthood" and "Priesthood of the Faithful"
The Teaching of Christ, Lawler, Wuerl, and Lawler, [First Edition] pp. 231-232; [Second Edition] pp. 219-220; [Third Edition] pp. 191-192

Q. 144. By means of these gifts, what does the Catholic Church do for mankind?

Church Documents

Catechesis in Our Time, John Paul II, sect. 24
Compendium of the Catechism of the Catholic Church, sect. 154, 172-173, 190
Dei Verbum (Dogmatic Constitution on Divine Revelation), Vatican II, sect. 21-26
God is Love, Benedict XVI, sect. 21-26, 28-31
The Lay Members of Christ's Faithful People, John Paul II, sect. 18-20
Lumen Gentium (Dogmatic Constitution on the Church), Vatican II, sect. 5-9, 11, 14, 18, 49
On the Dignity and Vocation of Women, John Paul II, sect. 26
On Human Work, John Paul II, sect. 1
On the Hundredth Anniversary of Rerum Novarum, John Paul II, sect. 51, 55
On Social Concern, John Paul II, sect. 41
Sacrosanctum Concilium (Constitution on the Sacred Liturgy), Vatican II, sect. 6
Splendor of Truth, John Paul II, sect. 73, 144
To the Youth of the World, John Paul II, sect. 15
U. S. Catholic Catechism for Adults, [2006] pp. 115-119

Other Resources

Basics of the Faith: A Catholic Catechism, Schreck, pp. 108-109
The Catholic Catechism, Hardon, pp. 234-238
The Church's Confession of Faith, Ignatius Press, pp. 216-219
Faith for Today, Hogan and LeVoir, [First Edition] pp. 123-125, 209-210; [Second Edition] pp. 158-160, 253
Fundamentals of Catholic Dogma, Ott, pp. 274-275
Fundamentals of Catholicism, Baker, Vol. 1, pp. 107-108; Vol. 3, 95-96, 159-160
The Teaching of Christ, Lawler, Wuerl and Lawler, [First Edition] pp. 223, 232; [Second Edition] pp. 220, 221; [Third Edition] pp. 192-193

Q. 145. Why does the Catholic Church belong entirely to Christ?

Church Documents

Compendium of the Catechism of the Catholic Church, sect. 156-158
Dei Verbum (Dogmatic Constitution on Divine Revelation), Vatican II, sect. 21-26
Gaudium et Spes (Pastoral Constitution on the Church in the Modern World), Vatican II, sect. 18, 22, 41, 43, 48
God is Love, Benedict XVI, sect. 21-26, 28-31
Lumen Gentium (Dogmatic Constitution on the Church), Vatican II, sect. 3-9, 14
On the Dignity and Vocation of Women, John Paul II, sect. 25-27
On the Holy Spirit in the Life of the Church and the World, John Paul II, sect. 52
Redeemer of Man, John Paul II, sect. 7, 18
Sacrament of Charity, Benedict XVI, sect. 14-16
*Sacrosanctum Concilium (*Constitution on the Sacred Liturgy), Vatican II, sect. 6
Splendor of Truth, John Paul II, sect. 1, 2
U. S. Catholic Catechism for Adults, [2006] p. 122

Family Wisdom Library™

Papal documents listed below can be viewed at www.vatican.va.
For new cross-references, visit www.familyland.org

Other Resources

Basics of the Faith: A Catholic Catechism, Schreck, pp. 111-112
The Catholic Catechism, Hardon, pp. 206-211, 237-238
The Church's Confession of Faith, Ignatius Press, pp. 218, 226-228
Faith for Today, Hogan and LeVoir, [First Edition] pp. 118-121; [Second Edition] pp. 152-155
Fundamentals of Catholic Dogma, Ott, pp. 291-294
Fundamentals of Catholicism, Baker, Vol. 3, pp. 92-95, 99, 125-128
Modern Catholic Dictionary, Hardon, see "Church"
The Teaching of Christ, Lawler, Wuerl, and Lawler, [First Edition] p. 186; [Second Edition] p. 174; [Third Edition] p. 152

Q. 146. How does the Catholic see the Church?

Church Documents

Compendium of the Catechism of the Catholic Church, sect. 156-158
Gaudium et Spes (Pastoral Constitution on the Church in the Modern World), Vatican II, sect. 22
God is Love, Benedict XVI, sect. 21-26, 28-31, 33
Lumen Gentium (Dogmatic Constitution on the Church), Vatican II, sect. 14
On the Dignity and Vocation of Women, John Paul II, sect. 25-26
On the Holy Spirit in the Life of the Church and the World, John Paul II, sect. 52, 61-64
Sacrament of Charity, Benedict XVI, sect. 14-16
Sacrosanctum Concilium (Constitution on the Sacred Liturgy), Vatican II, sect. 6
U. S. Catholic Catechism for Adults, [2006] pp. 127-137

Other Resources

The Catholic Catechism, Hardon, pp. 210-211, 234-236
The Church's Confession of Faith, Ignatius Press, pp. 223-230, 233, 266-267
Faith for Today, Hogan and LeVoir, [First Edition] pp. 117-123; [Second Edition] pp. 151-158
Fundamentals of Catholic Dogma, Ott, pp. 270-272
Fundamentals of Catholicism, Baker, Vol. 1, pp. 99-102; Vol. 3, pp. 98, 127-128
Modern Catholic Dictionary, Hardon, see "Mystical Body"
The Teaching of Christ, Lawler, Wuerl, and Lawler, [First Edition] pp. 187, 208-209; [Second Edition] pp. 175, 196-197; [Third Edition] pp. 152, 173

Q. 147. Why is the Catholic Church a living continuation of Christ on earth?

Church Documents

Compendium of the Catechism of the Catholic Church, sect. 156
Gaudium et Spes (Pastoral Constitution on the Church in the Modern World), Vatican II, sect. 22, 38, 43, 45
God is Love, Benedict XVI, sect. 21-26, 28-31, 33
The Lay Members of Christ's Faithful People, John Paul II, sect. 7, 15, 42
Lumen Gentium (Dogmatic Constitution on the Church), Vatican II, sect. 3-9, 13
On the Holy Spirit in the Life of the Church and the World, John Paul II, sect. 5, 25, 63
On the Hundredth Anniversary of Rerum Novarum, John Paul II, sect. 5, 43
On Social Concern, John Paul II, sect. 41
Redeemer of Man, John Paul II, sect. 19
Sacrament of Charity, Benedict XVI, sect. 14-15
Sacrosanctum Concilium (Constitution on the Sacred Liturgy), Vatican II, sect. 6
U. S. Catholic Catechism for Adults, [2006] pp. 115-116

Other Resources

The Catholic Catechism, Hardon, pp. 206-208, 236-238
The Church's Confession of Faith, Ignatius Press, pp. 211-212, 218, 223, 233
Faith for Today, Hogan and LeVoir, [First Edition] pp. 117-123; [Second Edition] pp. 151-158
Fundamentals of Catholicism, Baker, Vol. 3, pp. 95-96, 105
Fundamentals of Catholic Dogma, Ott, pp. 274-275
Modern Catholic Dictionary, Hardon, see "Church" and "Mystical Body"
The Teaching of Christ, Lawler, Wuerl and Lawler, [First Edition] pp. 188-189; [Second Edition] pp. 176-177; [Third Edition] pp. 154-155

Family Wisdom Library™

Papal documents listed below can be viewed at www.vatican.va.
For new cross-references, visit www.familyland.org

Q. 148. Why is the Catholic Church called the sacrament of Christ?

Church Documents

Compendium of the Catechism of the Catholic Church, sect. 152
Gaudium et Spes (Pastoral Constitution on the Church in the Modern World), Vatican II, sect. 42, 45
God is Love, Benedict XVI, sect. 21-26, 28-31
*Lumen Gentium (*Dogmatic Constitution on the Church), Vatican II, sect. 1, 3-9, 11-14, 48-49
On the Dignity and Vocation of Women, John Paul II, sect. 2
On the Holy Spirit in the Life of the Church and the World, John Paul II, sect. 63
Redeemer of Man, John Paul II, sect. 18
Sacrament of Charity, Benedict XVI, sect. 14-16
Sacrosanctum Concilium (Constitution on the Sacred Liturgy), Vatican II, sect. 6, 61
U. S. Catholic Catechism for Adults, [2006] pp. 115-116

Other Resources

Basics of the Faith: A Catholic Catechism, Schreck, p. 151
The Catholic Catechism, Hardon, pp. 234-238
The Church's Confession of Faith, Ignatius Press, pp. 211-212, 218-219
Faith for Today, Hogan and LeVoir, [First Edition] pp. 117-123; [Second Edition] pp. 151-158
Fundamentals of Catholic Dogma, Ott, pp. 301-302
Modern Catholic Dictionary, Hardon, see "Mystical Body"
The Teaching of Christ, Lawler, Wuerl, and Lawler, [First Edition] pp. 187-188, 197; [Second Edition] pp. 175-176, 185; [Third Edition] pp. 153-154, 161

Q. 149. What do we mean when we speak of the Church in Heaven?

Church Documents

Compendium of the Catechism of the Catholic Church, sect. 209
Gaudium et Spes (Pastoral Constitution on the Church in the Modern World), Vatican II, sect. 38, 40, 57, 93
*Lumen Gentium (*Dogmatic Constitution on the Church), Vatican II, sect. 49
Sacrament of Charity, Benedict XVI, sect. 31
Sacrosanctum Concilium (Constitution on the Sacred Liturgy), Vatican II, sect. 8
U. S. Catholic Catechism for Adults, [2006] pp. 153-154, 160-161

Other Resources

Basics of the Faith: A Catholic Catechism, Schreck, pp. 80-84
The Catholic Catechism, Hardon, pp. 266-267
The Church's Confession of Faith, Ignatius Press, pp. 253-254
Faith for Today, Hogan and LeVoir, [First Edition] pp. 210-211; [Second Edition] pp. 253-255
Fundamentals of Catholicism, Baker, Vol. 3, p. 150
Fundamentals of Catholic Dogma, Ott, pp. 476-479
Modern Catholic Dictionary, Hardon, see "Church Triumphant" and "Heaven"
The Teaching of Christ, Lawler, Wuerl, and Lawler, [First Edition] p. 187; [Second Edition] p. 175; [Third Edition] p. 152

Q. 150. Does the Catholic Church have leaders?

Church Documents

Compendium of the Catechism of the Catholic Church, sect. 178-180
Dei Verbum (Dogmatic Constitution on Divine Revelation), Vatican II, sect. 7-8, 10
Gaudium et Spes (Pastoral Constitution on the Church in the Modern World), Vatican II, sect. 43
God is Love, Benedict XVI, sect. 21-26, 28-32
Lumen Gentium (Dogmatic Constitution on the Church), Vatican II, sect. 8, 12-13, 18-19
On the Holy Spirit in the Life of the Church and the World, John Paul II, sect. 25
Sacrament of Charity, Benedict XVI, sect. 39
*Sacrosanctum Concilium (*Constitution on the Sacred Liturgy), Vatican II, sect. 42
Splendor of Truth, John Paul II, sect. 2, 115
The Relationship Between Faith and Reason, John Paul II, sect. 49-63
U. S. Catholic Catechism for Adults, [2006] pp. 118, 133, 264-265

Other Resources

Basics of the Faith: A Catholic Catechism, Schreck, pp. 93-95
The Catholic Catechism, Hardon, pp. 219-223
The Church's Confession of Faith, Ignatius Press, pp. 222-223, 245-246, 248, 251
Faith for Today, Hogan and LeVoir, [First Edition] pp. 125-129; [Second Edition] pp. 160-165

Family Wisdom Library™

Papal documents listed below can be viewed at www.vatican.va.
For new cross-references, visit www.familyland.org

Fundamentals of Catholic Dogma, Ott, pp. 276-279, 308-309
Fundamentals of Catholicism, Baker, Vol. 3, p. 101
Modern Catholic Dictionary, Hardon, see "Episcopacy", "Hierarchy", "Mystical Body" and "People of God"
The Teaching of Christ, Lawler, Wuerl, and Lawler, [First Edition] pp. 200-210; [Second Edition] pp. 188-198; [Third Edition] pp. 164-173

Q. 151. Who is the Pope?

Church Documents

Compendium of the Catechism of the Catholic Church, sect. 182
Dei Verbum (Dogmatic Constitution on Divine Revelation), Vatican II, sect. 7-8, 10
Gaudium et Spes (Pastoral Constitution on the Church in the Modern World), Vatican II, sect. 43
God is Love, Benedict XVI, sect. 21-26, 28-32
Lumen Gentium (Dogmatic Constitution on the Church), Vatican II, sect. 8, 12-13, 18-27
The Relationship Between Faith and Reason, John Paul II, sect. 49-63
U. S. Catholic Catechism for Adults, [2006] pp. 113, 128, 130, 133-134

Other Resources

The Catholic Catechism, Hardon, pp. 221-223
The Church's Confession of Faith, Ignatius Press, pp. 248-252
Faith for Today, Hogan and LeVoir, [First Edition] pp. 131, 136; [Second Edition] pp. 167, 173
Fundamentals of Catholic Dogma, Ott, pp. 282-289
Fundamentals of Catholicism, Baker, Vol. 3, pp. 101, 110-116
Modern Catholic Dictionary, Hardon, see "Pope"
The Teaching of Christ, Lawler, Wuerl, and Lawler, [First Edition] pp. 205-206; [Second Edition] pp. 193-194; [Third Edition] pp. 168-169

Q. 152. Who are the bishops of the Church?

Church Documents

Catechesis in Our Time, John Paul II, sect. 10-12
Compendium of the Catechism of the Catholic Church, sect. 176
Dei Verbum (Dogmatic Constitution on Divine Revelation), Vatican II, sect. 7-8, 10
Gaudium et Spes (Pastoral Constitution on the Church in the Modern World), Vatican II, sect. 43
God is Love, Benedict XVI, sect. 21-26, 28-32
Lumen Gentium (Dogmatic Constitution on the Church), Vatican II, sect. 8, 12, 18-28
On the Holy Spirit in the Life of the Church and the World, John Paul II, sect. 25
The Relationship Between Faith and Reason, John Paul II, sect. 49-63
Sacrament of Charity, Benedict XVI, sect. 39
Sacrosanctum Concilium (Constitution on the Sacred Liturgy), Vatican II, sect. 41
Splendor of Truth, John Paul II, sect. 3, 115
U. S. Catholic Catechism for Adults, [2006] pp. 265-266

Other Resources

Basics of the Faith: A Catholic Catechism, Schreck, pp. 95-97
The Catholic Catechism, Hardon, pp. 42, 220-223, 232-233
The Church's Confession of Faith, Ignatius Press, pp. 239-240, 244
Faith for Today, Hogan and LeVoir, [First Edition] pp. 127, 129, 136-138, 193, 195-196; [Second Edition] pp. 162, 164, 172-174, 235, 237-238
Fundamentals of Catholic Dogma, Ott, pp. 289-290
Fundamentals of Catholicism, Baker, Vol. 3, pp. 101, 104-107, 119-122
Modern Catholic Dictionary, Hardon, see "Bishop" and "Episcopacy"
The Teaching of Christ, Lawler, Wuerl, and Lawler, [First Edition] pp. 203-204, 206-208; [Second Edition] pp. 191-192, 194-196; [Third Edition] pp. 166-167, 170-172

Q. 153. What are the chief responsibilities of the Pope and bishops of the Catholic Church?

Church Documents

Catechesis in Our Time, John Paul II, sect. 10-11
Compendium of the Catechism of the Catholic Church, sect. 182-184
Dei Verbum (Dogmatic Constitution on Divine Revelation), Vatican II, sect. 7-8, 10
Gaudium et Spes (Pastoral Constitution on the Church in the Modern World), Vatican II, sect. 43
God is Love, Benedict XVI, sect. 21-26, 28-32

Family Wisdom Library™

Papal documents listed below can be viewed at www.vatican.va.
For new cross-references, visit www.familyland.org

Lumen Gentium (Dogmatic Constitution on the Church), Vatican II, sect. 8, 12-13, 18-28
On the Holy Spirit in the Life of the Church and the World, John Paul II, sect. 25
On the Hundredth Anniversary of Rerum Novarum, John Paul II, sect. 54-55
On Social Concern, John Paul II, sect. 1, 8-9, 41
The Relationship Between Faith and Reason, John Paul II, sect. 6, 49–63
Sacrament of Charity, Benedict XVI, sect. 39
*Sacrosanctum Concilium (*Constitution on the Sacred Liturgy), Vatican II, sect. 41
Splendor of Truth, John Paul II, sect. 3
U. S. Catholic Catechism for Adults, [2006] pp. 132-134

Other Resources

Basics of the Faith: A Catholic Catechism, Schreck, pp. 95-106
The Catholic Catechism, Hardon, pp. 219-220
The Church's Confession of Faith, Ignatius Press, pp. 244-245, 248-252
Faith for Today, Hogan and LeVoir, [First Edition] pp. 125-129, 135, 136, 195-196; [Second Edition] pp. 160-165, 171, 172, 237-238
Fundamentals of Catholic Dogma, Ott, pp. 276-279
Fundamentals of Catholicism, Baker, Vol. 3, pp. 101-103
Modern Catholic Dictionary, Hardon, see "Catholic", "Episcopacy", "Hierarchy", "Magisterium" and "Priest"
The Teaching of Christ, Lawler, Wuerl, and Lawler, [First Edition] pp. 211-233; [Second Edition] pp. 199-221; [Third Edition] pp. 175-193

Q. 154. Who directs Christ's work in the Catholic Church?

Church Documents

Catechesis in Our Time, John Paul II, sect. 11-12
Compendium of the Catechism of the Catholic Church, sect. 187
Dei Verbum (Dogmatic Constitution on Divine Revelation), Vatican II, sect. 7-8, 10
Gaudium et Spes (Pastoral Constitution on the Church in the Modern World), Vatican II, sect. 43
God is Love, Benedict XVI, sect. 21-26, 28-32
Lay Members of Christ's Faithful People, John Paul II, sect. 25-27
Lumen Gentium (Dogmatic Constitution on the Church), Vatican II, sect. 8, 12-13, 18-28
On the Holy Spirit in the Life of the Church and the World, John Paul II, sect. 25
Sacrament of Charity, Benedict XVI, sect. 39
*Sacrosanctum Concilium (*Constitution on the Sacred Liturgy), Vatican II, sect. 41
Splendor of Truth, John Paul II, sect. 3, 114
U. S. Catholic Catechism for Adults, [2006] pp. 128-129, 132-134

Other Resources

The Catholic Catechism, Hardon, pp. 42-43, 219-223, 449-451
The Church's Confession of Faith, Ignatius Press, pp. 245-246
Faith for Today, Hogan and LeVoir, [First Edition] pp. 128-129, 137-142; [Second Edition] pp.163-164, 173-179
Fundamentals of Catholic Dogma, Ott, pp. 285-290
Fundamentals of Catholicism, Baker, Vol. 3, pp. 101-103
Modern Catholic Dictionary, Hardon, see "Catholic", "Episcopacy", "Hierarchy" and "Pope"
The Teaching of Christ, Lawler, Wuerl, and Lawler, [First Edition] pp. 205-208; [Second Edition] pp. 193-196; [Third Edition] pp. 168-172

Q. 155. What is owed the Pope and bishops by the faithful?

Church Documents

Compendium of the Catechism of the Catholic Church, sect. 15-16, 184-185, 187
Dei Verbum (Dogmatic Constitution on Divine Revelation), Vatican II, sect. 7-8, 10
Gaudium et Spes (Pastoral Constitution on the Church in the Modern World), Vatican II, sect. 43
God is Love, Benedict XVI, sect. 21-26, 28-32
The Lay Members of Christ's Faithful People, John Paul II, sect. 9, 30
Lumen Gentium (Dogmatic Constitution on the Church), Vatican II, sect. 8, 12, 18-28
The Relationship Between Faith and Reason, John Paul II, sect. 49-63
Sacrament of Charity, Benedict XVI, sect. 39
*Sacrosanctum Concilium (*Constitution on the Sacred Liturgy), Vatican II, sect. 41
Splendor of Truth, John Paul II, sect. 3-4, 30, 37, 65, 109, 114
U. S. Catholic Catechism for Adults, [2006] pp. 133-134

Family Wisdom Library™

Papal documents listed below can be viewed at www.vatican.va.
For new cross-references, visit www.familyland.org

Other Resources

Basics of the Faith: A Catholic Catechism, Schreck, pp. 96-97, 105
The Catholic Catechism, Hardon, p. 212
The Church's Confession of Faith, Ignatius Press, p. 243
Faith for Today, Hogan and LeVoir, [First Edition] pp. 131-134; [Second Edition] pp. 166-170
Modern Catholic Dictionary, Hardon, see "Evangelical Obedience" and "Obedience"
The Teaching of Christ, Lawler, Wuerl, and Lawler, [First Edition] pp. 219-232; [Second Edition] pp. 207-220; [Third Edition] pp. 181-192

Q. 156. Why is respect owed to everyone in the Church?

Church Documents

Compendium of the Catechism of the Catholic Church, sect. 177
Gaudium et Spes (Pastoral Constitution on the Church in the Modern World), Vatican II, sect. 3, 22-23
God is Love, Benedict XVI, sect. 18, 20
The Lay Members of Christ's Faithful People, John Paul II, sect. 12, 28-29, 37
Lumen Gentium (Dogmatic Constitution on the Church), Vatican II, sect. 7, 9, 11-13, 30-33
On the Dignity and Vocation of Women, John Paul II, sect. 13, 25, 27, 29, 30
Redeemer of Man, John Paul II, sect. 14, 18
Sacrament of Charity, Benedict XVI, sect. 7-8
U. S. Catholic Catechism for Adults, [2006] pp. 67-68

Other Resources

Basics of the Faith: A Catholic Catechism, Schreck, p. 108
The Catholic Catechism, Hardon, pp. 210-211, 214-217, 419, 509-510
The Church's Confession of Faith, Ignatius Press, pp. 219, 225, 227-228, 24
Faith for Today, Hogan and LeVoir, [First Edition] pp. 120, 125, 128; [Second Edition] pp. 154, 160, 163
Fundamentals of Catholic Dogma, Ott, pp. 270-271, 294, 309-310
Fundamentals of Catholicism, Baker, Vol. 3, p. 128
Modern Catholic Dictionary, Hardon, see "Church", "Mystical Body", "People of God" and "Priesthood of the Faithful"
The Teaching of Christ, Lawler, Wuerl, and Lawler, [First Edition] pp. 68-77; [Second Edition] pp. 56-65; [Third Edition] pp. 49-57

Q. 157. Why is the Catholic Church a community?

Church Documents

Catechesis in Our Time, John Paul II, sect. 24
Compendium of the Catechism of the Catholic Church, sect. 161
Gaudium et Spes (Pastoral Constitution on the Church in the Modern World), Vatican II, sect. 11, 24, 28, 32, 45, 88, 92
God is Love, Benedict XVI, sect. 21-26, 28-31
The Lay Members of Christ's Faithful People, John Paul II, sect. 18-20
Lumen Gentium (Dogmatic Constitution on the Church), Vatican II, sect. 2, 7-9, 11, 13-14, 27, 30-33
On the Dignity and Vocation of Women, John Paul II, sect. 25, 27
On the Holy Spirit in the Life of the Church and the World, John Paul II, sect. 25-26
Redeemer of Man, John Paul II, sect. 18
The Relationship Between Faith and Reason, John Paul II, sect. 70, 73
Sacrament of Charity, Benedict XVI, sect. 15
Splendor of Truth, John Paul II, sect. 26, 35, 107, 118
U. S. Catholic Catechism for Adults, [2006] pp. 118-119

Other Resources

Basics of the Faith: A Catholic Catechism, Schreck, pp. 77-78
The Catholic Catechism, Hardon, pp. 211-213
The Church's Confession of Faith, Ignatius Press, pp. 224-225
Faith for Today, Hogan and LeVoir, [First Edition] pp. 121-123; [Second Edition] pp. 155-158
Fundamentals of Catholic Dogma, Ott, pp. 270-276
Fundamentals of Catholicism, Baker, Vol. 3, pp. 96-101, 158
Modern Catholic Dictionary, Hardon, see "Community" and "People of God"
The Teaching of Christ, Lawler, Wuerl, and Lawler, [First Edition] p. 191; [Second Edition] p. 179; [Third Edition] p. 156

Q. 158. Is everyone in the Church equal?

Church Documents

Compendium of the Catechism of the Catholic Church, sect. 177
Gaudium et Spes (Pastoral Constitution on the Church in the Modern World), Vatican II, sect. 3, 11, 22-24, 32, 45, 92

Family Wisdom Library™

Papal documents listed below can be viewed at www.vatican.va.
For new cross-references, visit www.familyland.org

God is Love, Benedict XVI, sect. 21-26, 28-31
The Lay Members of Christ's Faithful People, John Paul II, sect. 15, 28
Lumen Gentium (Dogmatic Constitution on the Church), Vatican II, sect. 30-33
On the Dignity and Vocation of Women, John Paul II, sect. 27, 30
On the Holy Spirit in the Life of the Church and the World, John Paul II, sect. 25
Redeemer of Man, John Paul II, sect. 14
Sacrament of Charity, Benedict XVI, sect. 17
Splendor of Truth, John Paul II, sect. 1, 107
U. S. Catholic Catechism for Adults, [2006] pp. 193-197

Other Resources

Basics of the Faith: A Catholic Catechism, Schreck, p. 109
The Catholic Catechism, Hardon, pp. 419-420, 437, 468-470
The Church's Confession of Faith, Ignatius Press, pp. 240-243, 245-246
Faith for Today, Hogan and LeVoir, [First Edition] pp. 125, 126, 128, 193, 195, 228, 231, 232; [Second Edition] pp. 160, 161, 163, 235, 237, 273-274, 277-278
Modern Catholic Dictionary, Hardon, see "Catholic Action", "Mystical Body", "People of God" and "Priesthood of the Faithful"
The Teaching of Christ, Lawler, Wuerl, and Lawler, [First Edition] p. 190; [Second Edition] p. 178; [Third Edition] p. 156

Q. 159. Who in the Church is called to a life of holiness?

Church Documents

Compendium of the Catechism of the Catholic Church, sect. 428
Gaudium et Spes (Pastoral Constitution on the Church in the Modern World), Vatican II, sect. 32
God is Love, Benedict XVI, sect. 21-26, 28-31
The Lay Members of Christ's Faithful People, John Paul II, sect. 16-17, 30, 55
Lumen Gentium (Dogmatic Constitution on the Church), Vatican II, sect. 7, 9, 11-14, 30-33, 39-47
On the Dignity and Vocation of Women, John Paul II, sect. 25, 27, 30
Sacrament of Charity, Benedict XVI, sect. 70-71
Sacrosanctum Concilium (Constitution on the Sacred Liturgy), Vatican II, sect. 10
To the Youth of the World, John Paul II, sect. 9
U. S. Catholic Catechism for Adults, [2006] pp. 113, 121, 138-139, 195-197

Other Resources

Basics of the Faith: A Catholic Catechism, Schreck, p. 109
The Catholic Catechism, Hardon, pp. 419-420
The Church's Confession of Faith, Ignatius Press, pp. 234, 245-246
Faith for Today, Hogan and LeVoir, [First Edition] pp. 235-236; [Second Edition] pp. 282-283
Fundamentals of Catholic Dogma, Ott, p. 305
Modern Catholic Dictionary, Hardon, see "Holiness" and "Vocation"
The Teaching of Christ, Lawler, Wuerl, and Lawler, [First Edition] pp. 355-369, 198-199; [Second Edition] pp. 186-187, 345-359; [Third Edition] pp. 162-163, 306-319
Transformation in Christ, von Hildebrand, pp. 192-193

Q. 160. Why is the Catholic Church essentially missionary?

Church Documents

Catechesis in Our Time, John Paul II, sect. 18
Compendium of the Catechism of the Catholic Church, sect. 172-174
Dei Verbum (Dogmatic Constitution on Divine Revelation), Vatican II, sect. 7, 21-26
Gaudium et Spes (Pastoral Constitution on the Church in the Modern World), Vatican II, sect. 32, 42, 58, 76, 89, 92
God is Love, Benedict XVI, sect. 21-26, 28-31
The Lay Members of Christ's Faithful People, John Paul II, sect. 15, 23, 32-36, 51
Lumen Gentium (Dogmatic Constitution on the Church), Vatican II, sect. 5-9, 12-13, 16-17, 20-23, 27-33
On the Eucharist in Its Relationship to the Church, John Paul II, sect. 22
On Evangelization in the Modern World, Paul VI, sect. 3, 5, 57
On the Holy Spirit in the Life of the Church and the World, John Paul II, sect. 26
On Reconciliation and Penance, John Paul II, sect. 10, 11
Sacrament of Charity, Benedict XVI, sect. 78-79
Sacrosanctum Concilium (Constitution on the Sacred Liturgy), Vatican II, sect. 6, 9
Splendor of Truth, John Paul II, sect. 26
U. S. Catholic Catechism for Adults, [2006] pp. 117-118, 125-126, 131, 138, 207

Family Wisdom Library™

Papal documents listed below can be viewed at www.vatican.va.
For new cross-references, visit www.familyland.org

Other Resources

Basics of the Faith: A Catholic Catechism, Schreck, p. 108
The Catholic Catechism, Hardon, pp. 234-240
The Church's Confession of Faith, Ignatius Press, pp. 220-221, 236-237
Faith for Today, Hogan and LeVoir, [First Edition] pp. 118, 124; [Second Edition] pp. 152, 159
Fundamentals of Catholicism, Baker, Vol. 1, p. 107; Vol. 3, pp. 159-160
Fundamentals of Catholic Dogma, Ott, pp. 274-275, 306-308
Modern Catholic Dictionary, Hardon, see "Apostolic See", "Catholic Action", "Catholicity" and "Mission";
The Teaching of Christ, Lawler, Wuerl, and Lawler, [First Edition] pp. 247, 260; [Second Edition] pp. 235, 248-249; [Third Edition] pp. 206, 217-218

Q. 161. What is the role of the Church in the world?

Church Documents

Compendium of the Catechism of the Catholic Church, sect. 150, 152, 172, 433
Dei Verbum (Dogmatic Constitution on Divine Revelation), Vatican II, sect. 21-26
Gaudium et Spes (Pastoral Constitution on the Church in the Modern World), Vatican II, sect. 32, 40, 42, 44, 58, 76, 89, 92
God is Love, Benedict XVI, sect. 21-26, 28-31
The Lay Members of Christ's Faithful People, John Paul II, sect. 2-3, 14, 34-35
Lumen Gentium (Dogmatic Constitution on the Church), Vatican II, sect. 5-9, 12-21, 23-24, 27-33
On the Eucharist in Its Relationship to the Church, John Paul II, sect. 22
On Evangelization in the Modern World, Paul VI, sect. 49
On the Holy Spirit in the Life of the Church and the World, John Paul II, sect. 53
On the Hundredth Anniversary of Rerum Novarum, John Paul II, sect. 5, 43
On Reconciliation and Penance, John Paul II, sect. 11
On Social Concern, John Paul II, sect. 41
Sacrament of Charity, Benedict XVI, sect. 78-79
*Sacrosanctum Concilium (*Constitution on the Sacred Liturgy), Vatican II, sect. 6, 9
Splendor of Truth, John Paul II, sect. 2, 99, 118
U. S. Catholic Catechism for Adults, [2006] pp. 117-118, 131, 420-421

Other Resources

Basics of the Faith: A Catholic Catechism, Schreck, pp. 110-111
The Catholic Catechism, Hardon, pp. 236-240
The Church's Confession of Faith, Ignatius Press, pp. 215-218
Fundamentals of Catholic Dogma, Ott, pp. 275-276
Fundamentals of Catholicism, Baker, Vol. 3, pp. 158-160
Modern Catholic Dictionary, Hardon, see "Catholic Action"
The Teaching of Christ, Lawler, Wuerl, and Lawler, [First Edition] pp. 247-261; [Second Edition] pp. 235-250; [Third Edition] pp. 206-219

Q. 162. How does the Catholic Church minister to our spiritual needs?

Church Documents

Catechesis in Our Time, John Paul II, sect. 24
Compendium of the Catechism of the Catholic Church, sect. 172-173, 190
Dei Verbum (Dogmatic Constitution on Divine Revelation), Vatican II, sect. 21-26
Gaudium et Spes (Pastoral Constitution on the Church in the Modern World), Vatican II, sect. 22, 38
God is Love, Benedict XVI, sect. 21-26, 28-31
Lumen Gentium (Dogmatic Constitution on the Church), Vatican II, sect. 5-7, 9, 11-14, 26-28, 33-35
On the Holy Spirit in the Life of the Church and the World, John Paul II, sect. 62-64
Sacrament of Charity, Benedict XVI, sect. 30-31, 70-71
Sacrosanctum Concilium (Constitution on the Sacred Liturgy), Vatican II, sect. 6
U. S. Catholic Catechism for Adults, [2006] pp. 115-119

Other Resources

Basics of the Faith: A Catholic Catechism, Schreck, p. 111
The Catholic Catechism, Hardon, p. 214
The Church's Confession of Faith, Ignatius Press, pp. 212-213, 227
Faith for Today, Hogan and LeVoir, [First Edition] pp. 177-181; [Second Edition] pp. 217-221
Fundamentals of Catholic Dogma, Ott, pp. 275-276

Family Wisdom Library™

Papal documents listed below can be viewed at www.vatican.va.
For new cross-references, visit www.familyland.org

Fundamentals of Catholicism, Baker, Vol. 3, pp. 95-97
The Teaching of Christ, Lawler, Wuerl, and Lawler, [First Edition] pp. 194-199; [Second Edition] pp. 182-187; [Third Edition] pp. 159-163

Q. 163. How does the Catholic Church minister to the bodily needs of people?

Church Documents

Compendium of the Catechism of the Catholic Church, sect. 155, 315, 411-414
Gaudium et Spes (Pastoral Constitution on the Church in the Modern World), Vatican II, sect. 27, 69, 70, 72
God is Love, Benedict XVI, sect. 21-26, 28-31
The Lay Members of Christ's Faithful People, John Paul II, sect. 53
Lumen Gentium (Dogmatic Constitution on the Church), Vatican II, sect. 30-36
On Human Work, John Paul II, sect. 1
On the Hundredth Anniversary of Rerum Novarum, John Paul II, sect. 53, 57-58
On Social Concern, John Paul II, sect. 42
The Role of the Christian Family in the Modern World, John Paul II, sect. 41-44
Sacrament of Charity, Benedict XVI, sect. 90-91
Sacrosanctum Concilium (Constitution on the Sacred Liturgy), Vatican II, sect. 105
Splendor of Truth, John Paul II, sect. 66
U. S. Catholic Catechism for Adults, [2006] pp. 420-425

Other Resources

The Church's Confession of Faith, Ignatius Press, pp. 216-217, 220, 227-228
Faith for Today, Hogan and LeVoir, [First Edition] pp. 124-125, 142, 229-230, 233; [Second Edition] pp. 159-160, 179, 275-276, 279
Fundamentals of Catholicism, Baker, Vol. 3, p. 159
The Teaching of Christ, Lawler, Wuerl, and Lawler, [First Edition] pp. 359-360; [Second Edition] pp. 349-350; [Third Edition] pp. 310-311

Q. 164. How can we help unbelievers find God?

Church Documents

Compendium of the Catechism of the Catholic Church, sect. 150, 172, 190
Dei Verbum (Dogmatic Constitution on Divine Revelation), Vatican II, sect. 21-26
Gaudium et Spes (Pastoral Constitution on the Church in the Modern World), Vatican II, sect. 19-22, 24, 28
God is Love, Benedict XVI, sect. 21-26, 28-31
Lumen Gentium (Dogmatic Constitution on the Church), Vatican II, sect. 15-17, 30-38
On Evangelization in the Modern World, Paul VI, sect. 21-26, 41, 55
On the Holy Spirit in the Life of the Church and the World, John Paul II, sect. 53
On Reconciliation and Penance, John Paul II, sect. 12, 26
Sacrament of Charity, Benedict XVI, sect. 78-79, 84-85
Sacrosanctum Concilium (Constitution on the Sacred Liturgy), Vatican II, sect. 9
Splendor of Truth, John Paul II, sect. 26, 107
U. S. Catholic Catechism for Adults, [2006] pp. 117-118, 134-137

Other Resources

The Catholic Catechism, Hardon, pp. 238-240
The Church's Confession of Faith, Ignatius Press, pp. 216-217, 241-243
Faith for Today, Hogan and LeVoir, [First Edition] pp. 229-230; [Second Edition] pp. 275-276
Modern Catholic Dictionary, Hardon, see "Evangelization"
The Teaching of Christ, Lawler, Wuerl, and Lawler, [First Edition] pp. 361-362; [Second Edition] pp. 351-352; [Third Edition] pp. 311-312
Transformation in Christ, von Hildebrand, pp. 330-332

Q. 165. What is our duty towards the world?

Church Documents

Compendium of the Catechism of the Catholic Church, sect. 411-414
Dei Verbum (Dogmatic Constitution on Divine Revelation), Vatican II, sect. 21-26
Gaudium et Spes (Pastoral Constitution on the Church in the Modern World), Vatican II, sect. 24, 28
God is Love, Benedict XVI, sect. 16, 18, 20-25, 28-33, 34
The Lay Members of Christ's Faithful People, John Paul II, sect. 15
Lumen Gentium (Dogmatic Constitution on the Church), Vatican II, sect. 15-17, 30-38
On Evangelization in the Modern World, Paul VI, sect. 30-32, 49
On the Holy Spirit in the Life of the Church and the World, John Paul II, sect. 53

Family Wisdom Library™

Papal documents listed below can be viewed at www.vatican.va.
For new cross-references, visit www.familyland.org

On the Hundredth Anniversary of Rerum Novarum, John Paul II, sect. 22, 25, 57
On Social Concern, John Paul II, sect. 31-32, 47
Redeemer of Man, John Paul II, sect. 14-16
Sacrament of Charity, Benedict XVI, sect. 88-91
Sacrosanctum Concilium (Constitution on the Sacred Liturgy), Vatican II, sect. 9
Splendor of Truth, John Paul II, sect. 14, 26
U. S. Catholic Catechism for Adults, [2006] pp. 420-425

Other Resources

Basics of the Faith: A Catholic Catechism, Schreck, pp. 107-108
The Catholic Catechism, Hardon, pp. 238-240
The Church's Confession of Faith, Ignatius Press, pp. 216-217, 221, 225, 227, 236, 241-242
Faith for Today, Hogan and LeVoir, [First Edition] pp. 124-125, 229-230; [Second Edition] pp. 159-160, 275-276
Fundamentals of Catholicism, Baker, Vol. 3, p. 133
The Teaching of Christ, Lawler, Wuerl, and Lawler, [First Edition] pp. 359-360; [Second Edition] pp. 349-350; [Third Edition] pp. 309-310

Q. 166. Why is the unity of Christians in faith and love God's will?

Church Documents

Compendium of the Catechism of the Catholic Church, sect. 163, 170, 172
Gaudium et Spes (Pastoral Constitution on the Church in the Modern World), Vatican II, sect. 24, 32, 42, 78
God is Love, Benedict XVI, sect. 21-26, 28-31
Lumen Gentium (Dogmatic Constitution on the Church), Vatican II, sect. 3, 8-9, 13, 15, 16
On the Dignity and Vocation of Women, John Paul II, sect. 25
On the Eucharist in Its Relationship to the Church, John Paul II, sect. 22-24
On Evangelization in the Modern World, Paul VI, sect. 77
On the Holy Spirit in the Life of the Church and the World, John Paul II, sect. 62-64
Redeemer of Man, John Paul II, sect. 6
The Relationship Between Faith and Reason, John Paul II, sect. 70
Sacrament of Charity, Benedict XVI, sect. 14-16
Sacrosanctum Concilium (Constitution on the Sacred Liturgy), Vatican II, sect. 2, 10
U. S. Catholic Catechism for Adults, [2006] pp. 22, 127-128

Other Resources

Basics of the Faith: A Catholic Catechism, Schreck, pp. 85-86
The Catholic Catechism, Hardon, pp. 213, 240-241
The Church's Confession of Faith, Ignatius Press, pp. 221, 224, 226, 230-231
Fundamentals of Catholic Dogma, Ott, pp. 302-303
Fundamentals of Catholicism, Baker, Vol. 1, pp. 103-104
Modern Catholic Dictionary, Hardon, see "Catholicity"
The Teaching of Christ, Lawler, Wuerl, and Lawler, [First Edition] pp. 251-258; [Second Edition] pp. 239-246; [Third Edition] pp. 209-215

Q. 167. How is Christian unity promoted by Catholics?

Church Documents

Catechesis in Our Time, John Paul II, sect. 32
Compendium of the Catechism of the Catholic Church, sect. 164
Dei Verbum (Dogmatic Constitution on Divine Revelation), Vatican II, sect. 22
Gaudium et Spes (Pastoral Constitution on the Church in the Modern World), Vatican II, sect. 21, 38, 72, 78
Lumen Gentium (Dogmatic Constitution on the Church), Vatican II, sect. 8-9, 13, 15-16
On the Eucharist in Its Relationship to the Church, John Paul II, sect. 22-24
On the Holy Spirit in the Life of the Church and the World, John Paul II, sect. 60
On Reconciliation and Penance, John Paul II, sect. 2
Redeemer of Man, John Paul II, sect. 6
The Relationship Between Faith and Reason, John Paul II, sect. 70
Sacrament of Charity, Benedict XVI, sect. 14-16
Sacrosanctum Concilium (Constitution on the Sacred Liturgy), Vatican II, sect. 2
Splendor of Truth, sect. 102, 103
U. S. Catholic Catechism for Adults, [2006] pp. 128, 133-134

Other Resources

Basics of the Faith: A Catholic Catechism, Schreck, pp. 86-89
The Catholic Catechism, Hardon, p. 243

Family Wisdom Library™

Papal documents listed below can be viewed at www.vatican.va.
For new cross-references, visit www.familyland.org

The Church's Confession of Faith, Ignatius Press, pp. 231-233, 237
Fundamentals of Catholicism, Baker, Vol. 1, p. 104; Vol. 3, p. 160
Modern Catholic Dictionary, Hardon, see "Ecumenism"and "Unitatis Redintegratio"
The Teaching of Christ, Lawler, Wuerl, and Lawler, [First Edition] pp. 255-258; [Second Edition] pp. 243-246 ; [Third Edition] pp. 213-215

Q. 168. Why should we respect all men of good will?

Church Documents

Compendium of the Catechism of the Catholic Church, sect. 170, 412
Gaudium et Spes (Pastoral Constitution on the Church in the Modern World), Vatican II, sect. 3, 22-23, 32
God is Love, Benedict XVI, sect. 21-26, 28-31
Lumen Gentium (Dogmatic Constitution on the Church), Vatican II, sect. 8-9, 13, 16, 30-31
The Lay Members of Christ's Faithful People, John Paul II, sect. 5, 37-39
On the Hundredth Anniversary of Rerum Novarum, John Paul II, sect. 51
Redeemer of Man, John Paul II, sect. 6, 12
Sacrament of Charity, Benedict XVI, sect. 88-89
U. S. Catholic Catechism for Adults, [2006] pp. 131-132

Other Resources

Basics of the Faith: A Catholic Catechism, Schreck, p. 112
The Catholic Catechism, Hardon, pp. 102-107
The Church's Confession of Faith, Ignatius Press, pp. 216-220
Faith for Today, Hogan and LeVoir, [First Edition] pp. 42-43; [Second Edition] pp. 68-69
Modern Catholic Dictionary, Hardon, see "Dignitatis Humanae" and "Human Nature"
The Teaching of Christ, Lawler, Wuerl, and Lawler, [First Edition] pp. 247-261; [Second Edition] pp. 235-250; [Third Edition] pp. 306-319

Q. 169. What do we believe about the Catholic Church and Salvation?

Church Documents

Compendium of the Catechism of the Catholic Church, sect. 168-171
Dei Verbum (Dogmatic Constitution on Divine Revelation), Vatican II, sect. 17
Gaudium et Spes (Pastoral Constitution on the Church in the Modern World), Vatican II, sect. 45
God is Love, Benedict XVI, sect. 21-26, 28-31
Lumen Gentium (Dogmatic Constitution on the Church), Vatican II, sect. 5, 8-9, 13-14
On the Holy Spirit in the Life of the Church and the World, John Paul II, sect. 25-26, 64
On the Hundredth Anniversary of Rerum Novarum, John Paul II, sect. 51
Redeemer of Man, John Paul II, sect. 18
The Relationship Between Faith and Reason, John Paul II, sect. 11
Sacrament of Charity, Benedict XVI, sect. 14-16
Sacrosanctum Concilium (Constitution on the Sacred Liturgy), Vatican II, sect. 5-6
Splendor of Truth, John Paul II, sect. 2, 3
U. S. Catholic Catechism for Adults, [2006] pp. 127-135

Other Resources

Basics of the Faith: A Catholic Catechism, Schreck, p. 111
The Catholic Catechism, Hardon, pp. 234-236
The Church's Confession of Faith, Ignatius Press, pp. 211-213
Faith for Today, Hogan and LeVoir, [First Edition] p. 118; [Second Edition] p. 152
Fundamentals of Catholic Dogma, Ott, pp. 312-313
Fundamentals of Catholicism, Baker, Vol. 1, pp. 99-111; Vol. 3. pp. 92-93, 96-97, 110, 130, 133, 142, 144-148, 160
Modern Catholic Dictionary, Hardon, see "Catholic", "Catholicism" and "Unam Sanctam"
The Teaching of Christ, Lawler, Wuerl, and Lawler, [First Edition] pp. 208-210; [Second Edition] pp. 196-198; [Third Edition] pp. 172-173

Q. 170. How do the laity share in Christ's mission?

Church Documents

Catechesis in Our Time, John Paul II, sect. 10, 14, 18
Compendium of the Catechism of the Catholic Church, sect. 188-191
Gaudium et Spes (Pastoral Constitution on the Church in the Modern World), Vatican II, sect. 27, 43, 47-52
God is Love, Benedict XVI, sect. 21-26, 28-31
The Lay Members of Christ's Faithful People, John Paul II, sect. 2-3, 15, 34-36, 45-52

Family Wisdom Library™

Papal documents listed below can be viewed at www.vatican.va.
For new cross-references, visit www.familyland.org

Lumen Gentium (Dogmatic Constitution on the Church), Vatican II, sect. 10-12, 30-38
On the Dignity and Vocation of Women, John Paul II, sect. 27, 30
On Evangelization in the Modern World, Paul VI, sect. 2, 3, 14, 21, 27, 41, 70
On Reconciliation and Penance, John Paul II, sect. 12
The Role of Christian Family in the Modern World, John Paul II, sect. 44, 47, 49-53
Sacrament of Charity, Benedict XVI, sect. 79, 82-85
Splendor of Truth, John Paul II, sect. 26, 101, 109
U. S. Catholic Catechism for Adults, [2006] pp. 134-135

Other Resources

Basics of the Faith: A Catholic Catechism, Schreck, pp. 107-110
The Catholic Catechism, Hardon, p. 437
The Church's Confession of Faith, Ignatius Press, pp. 217, 241-243
Faith for Today, Hogan and LeVoir, [First Edition] pp. 125, 126, 193, 227, 228, 231, 232, 236; [Second Edition] pp. 160-161, 235, 257-258, 277-278, 282-283
Modern Catholic Dictionary, Hardon, see "Apostolicam Actuositatem", "Catholic Action" and "Priesthood of the Faithful"
The Teaching of Christ, Lawler, Wuerl, and Lawler, [First Edition] pp. 336-354; [Second Edition] pp. 325-344; [Third Edition] pp. 288-305

Q. 171. How is the Catholic Church an institution of Salvation?

Church Documents

Catechesis in Our Time, John Paul II, sect. 18, 24
Compendium of the Catechism of the Catholic Church, sect. 172-173
Dei Verbum (Dogmatic Constitution on Divine Revelation), Vatican II, sect. 7, 17, 21-26
Gaudium et Spes (Pastoral Constitution on the Church in the Modern World), Vatican II, sect. 45
God is Love, Benedict XVI, sect. 21-26, 28-31
Lay Members of Christ's Faithful People, John Paul II, sect. 32-36, 44
Lumen Gentium (Dogmatic Constitution on the Church), Vatican II, sect. 5, 7-9, 11-14, 18-21, 33-38, 49
On the Dignity and Vocation of Women, John Paul II, sect. 27
On the Eucharist in Its Relationship to the Church, John Paul II, sect. 22-23
On Evangelization in the Modern World, Paul VI, sect. 9, 13-14
On the Holy Spirit in the Life of the Church and the World, John Paul II, sect. 25-26, 63-64
On the Hundredth Anniversary of Rerum Novarum, John Paul II, sect. 51
Redeemer of Man, John Paul II, sect. 18
The Relationship Between Faith and Reason, John Paul II, sect. 11
Sacrament of Charity, Benedict XVI, sect. 16
Sacrosanctum Concilium (Constitution on the Sacred Liturgy), Vatican II, sect. 5-6
Splendor of Truth, John Paul II, sect. 2
U. S. Catholic Catechism for Adults, [2006] pp. 115-119

Other Resources

Basics of the Faith: A Catholic Catechism, Schreck, p. 115
The Catholic Catechism, Hardon, pp. 234-236
The Church's Confession of Faith, Ignatius Press, pp. 212-213, 218-220, 223-224
Faith for Today, Hogan and LeVoir, [First Edition] pp. 118, 123-124; [Second Edition] pp. 152, 158-159
Fundamentals of Catholic Dogma, Ott, pp. 274-275
Fundamentals of Catholicism, Baker, Vol. 1, p. 107; Vol. 3, pp. 92-97
Modern Catholic Dictionary, Hardon, see "Catholicism" and "Unam Sanctam"
The Teaching of Christ, Lawler, Wuerl, and Lawler, [First Edition] pp. 208-209; [Second Edition] pp. 196-197; [Third Edition] p. 172

Q. 172. What are the marks that point out the true Church founded by Jesus?

Church Documents

Compendium of the Catechism of the Catholic Church, sect. 161, 165, 166, 174
Lumen Gentium (Dogmatic Constitution on the Church), Vatican II, sect. 8
Splendor of Truth, John Paul II, sect. 8, 107
U. S. Catholic Catechism for Adults, [2006] pp. 126-134

Other Resources

Basics of the Faith: A Catholic Catechism, Schreck, pp. 85-95
The Catholic Catechism, Hardon, pp. 211-223
The Church's Confession of Faith, Ignatius Press, p. 230
Fundamentals of Catholic Dogma, Ott, p. 309

Family Wisdom Library™

Papal documents listed below can be viewed at www.vatican.va.
For new cross-references, visit www.familyland.org

Fundamentals of Catholicism, Baker, Vol. 1, pp. 110-111; Vol. 3, pp. 140-142
Modern Catholic Dictionary, Hardon, see "Apostolicity", "Catholic", "Catholicity" and "Church"
The Teaching of Christ, Lawler, Wuerl, and Lawler, [First Edition] pp. 196-199; [Second Edition] pp. 184-187; [Third Edition] pp. 161-163

Q. 173. Why is the Catholic Church one?

Church Documents

Compendium of the Catechism of the Catholic Church, sect. 161
Gaudium et Spes (Pastoral Constitution on the Church in the Modern World), Vatican II, sect. 24
Lumen Gentium (Dogmatic Constitution on the Church), Vatican II, sect. 3-4, 8-9, 13, 15, 23, 26, 32, 49, 50
On the Dignity and Vocation of Women, John Paul II, sect. 27
On the Eucharist in Its Relationship to the Church, John Paul II, sect. 21, 23, 26-27, 39, 51
On the Holy Spirit in the Life of the Church and the World, John Paul II, sect. 25-26, 62
The Relationship Between Faith and Reason, John Paul II, sect. 70
Sacrament of Charity, Benedict XVI, sect. 15
U. S. Catholic Catechism for Adults, [2006] pp. 127-129

Other Resources

Basics of the Faith: A Catholic Catechism, Schreck, pp. 86-89
The Catholic Catechism, Hardon, pp. 211-213
The Church's Confession of Faith, Ignatius Press, pp. 230-231
Faith for Today, Hogan and LeVoir, [First Edition] pp. 117-123; [Second Edition] pp. 151-158
Fundamentals of Catholic Dogma, Ott, pp. 302-304
Fundamentals of Catholicism, Baker, Vol. 1, pp. 102-104; Vol. 3, pp. 100, 141
Modern Catholic Dictionary, Hardon, see "Catholic", "Catholicism", "Catholicity", "Church" and "University of the Faithful"
The Teaching of Christ, Lawler, Wuerl and Lawler, [First Edition] p. 198; [Second Edition] p. 186; [Third Edition] p. 162

Q. 174. How did Jesus indicate that His Church is one?

Church Documents

Compendium of the Catechism of the Catholic Church, sect. 164
Lumen Gentium (Dogmatic Constitution on the Church), Vatican II, sect. 8, 15
On the Eucharist in Its Relationship to the Church, John Paul II, sect. 21, 23-24, 43
On the Holy Spirit in the Life of the Church and the World, John Paul II, sect. 62
Sacrament of Charity, Benedict XVI, sect. 15
U. S. Catholic Catechism for Adults, [2006] pp. 127-129, 485

Other Resources

Basics of the Faith: A Catholic Catechism, Schreck, p. 85
The Church's Confession of Faith, Ignatius Press, pp. 230-231
Fundamentals of Catholic Dogma, Ott, p. 303
Fundamentals of Catholicism, Baker, Vol. 1, p. 103

Q. 175. Why are we united by a spiritual leader?

Church Documents

Compendium of the Catechism of the Catholic Church, sect. 109
Gaudium et Spes (Pastoral Constitution on the Church in the Modern World), Vatican II, sect. 43
Lumen Gentium (Dogmatic Constitution on the Church), Vatican II, sect. 8, 9, 18-21
On the Dignity and Vocation of Women, John Paul II, sect. 26
On the Eucharist in Its Relationship to the Church, John Paul II, sect. 38-39
U. S. Catholic Catechism for Adults, [2006] pp. 133-134

Other Resources

Basics of the Faith: A Catholic Catechism, Schreck, p. 96
The Catholic Catechism, Hardon, pp. 219-223
The Church's Confession of Faith, Ignatius Press, pp. 248-252
Faith for Today, Hogan and LeVoir, [First Edition] pp.125-129; [Second Edition] pp. 160-165
Fundamentals of Catholic Dogma, Ott, pp. 303-304
Fundamentals of Catholicism, Baker, Vol. 3, pp. 107-113
Modern Catholic Dictionary, Hardon, see "Apostolicity", "Apostolic Succession", "Catholic" and "Church"

Family Wisdom Library™

Papal documents listed below can be viewed at www.vatican.va.
For new cross-references, visit www.familyland.org

The Teaching of Christ, Lawler, Wuerl, and Lawler, [First Edition] p. 200; [Second Edition] p. 188; [Third Edition] p. 164

Q. 176. Why are we united in worship?

Church Documents

Compendium of the Catechism of the Catholic Church, sect. 223
Gaudium et Spes (Pastoral Constitution on the Church in the Modern World), Vatican II, sect. 38
God is Love, Benedict XVI, sect. 14
Lumen Gentium (Dogmatic Constitution on the Church), Vatican II, sect. 9-11
On the Dignity and Vocation of Women, John Paul II, sect. 26
On the Eucharist in Its Relationship to the Church, John Paul II, sect. 21-25
On the Holy Spirit in the Life of the Church and the World, John Paul II, sect. 62-64
On the Mystery and Worship of the Eucharist, John Paul II, sect. 3, 5, 12
On Social Concern, John Paul II, sect. 48
Sacrament of Charity, Benedict XVI, sect. 15
U. S. Catholic Catechism for Adults, [2006] pp. 167-168

Other Resources

Basics of the Faith: A Catholic Catechism, Schreck, pp. 90-91
The Catholic Catechism, Hardon, pp. 443-448
The Church's Confession of Faith, Ignatius Press, pp. 227, 253, 263-265, 291, 294, 295
Faith for Today, Hogan and LeVoir, [First Edition pp. 177-180; [Second Edition] pp. 217-220
Fundamentals of Catholic Dogma, Ott, p. 303
Modern Catholic Dictionary, Hardon, see "Catholic", "Church", "Liturgy" and "Mass"
The Teaching of Christ, Lawler, Wuerl, and Lawler, [First Edition] pp. 195-196, 432-433; [Second Edition] pp. 183-184, 423; [Third Edition] pp. 159-161, 374-375

Q. 177. Why is the Catholic Church holy?

Church Documents

Compendium of the Catechism of the Catholic Church, sect. 165
Gaudium et Spes (Pastoral Constitution on the Church in the Modern World), Vatican II, sect. 21, 37, 43
The Lay Members of Christ's Faithful People, John Paul II, sect. 16-17
Lumen Gentium (Dogmatic Constitution on the Church), Vatican II, sect. 8, 9, 12, 39-40
On the Dignity and Vocation of Women, John Paul II, sect. 27
On the Eucharist in Its Relationship to the Church, John Paul II, sect. 23-24
On the Holy Spirit in the Life of the Church and the World, John Paul II, sect. 25-26, 62-64
Sacrament of Charity, Benedict XVI, sect. 14-16
U. S. Catholic Catechism for Adults, [2006] pp. 129

Other Resources

Basics of the Faith: A Catholic Catechism, Schreck, pp. 91-93
The Catholic Catechism, Hardon, pp. 214-217
The Church's Confession of Faith, Ignatius Press, pp. 233-236
Faith for Today, Hogan and LeVoir, [First Edition] pp. 118-124, 177-181; [Second Edition] pp. 152-160, 217-221
Fundamentals of Catholic Dogma, Ott, pp. 304-305
Fundamentals of Catholicism, Baker, Vol. 1, pp. 104-106; Vol. 3, p. 141
Modern Catholic Dictionary, Hardon, see "Church", "Mystical Body" and "People of God"
The Teaching of Christ, Lawler, Wuerl, and Lawler, [First Edition] pp. 198-199; [Second Edition] pp. 186-187; [Third Edition] pp. 162-163

Q. 178. Why is the Church catholic or universal?

Church Documents

Compendium of the Catechism of the Catholic Church, sect. 166
Dei Verbum (Dogmatic Constitution on Divine Revelation), Vatican II, sect. 7
Gaudium et Spes (Pastoral Constitution on the Church in the Modern World), Vatican II, sect. 45
Lumen Gentium (Dogmatic Constitution on the Church), Vatican II, sect. 1-2, 8-9, 13, 19, 22
On the Dignity and Vocation of Women, John Paul II, sect. 27, 28
On the Eucharist in Its Relationship to the Church, John Paul II, sect. 8, 26, 39, 61
On the Holy Spirit in the Life of the Church and the World, John Paul II, sect. 25-26, 62-64

Family Wisdom Library™

Papal documents listed below can be viewed at www.vatican.va.
For new cross-references, visit www.familyland.org

The Relationship Between Faith and Reason, John Paul II, sect. 70-71
Sacrament of Charity, Benedict XVI, sect. 54
U. S. Catholic Catechism for Adults, [2006] pp. 129-131

Other Resources

Basics of the Faith: A Catholic Catechism, Schreck, pp. 89-91
The Catholic Catechism, Hardon, pp. 217-219
The Church's Confession of Faith, Ignatius Press, pp. 236-237
Fundamentals of Catholic Dogma, Ott, pp. 306-308
Fundamentals of Catholicism, Baker, Vol. 1, pp. 107-109; Vol. 3, pp. 90-91,141-142
Modern Catholic Dictionary, Hardon, see "University of the Faithful","Catholicism" and "Catholicity"
The Teaching of Christ, Lawler, Wuerl, and Lawler, [First Edition] p. 199; [Second Edition] p. 187; [Third Edition] p. 163

Q. 179. How long has the Catholic Church been in existence?

Church Documents

Compendium of the Catechism of the Catholic Church, sect. 149
Lumen Gentium (Dogmatic Constitution on the Church), Vatican II, sect. 5
On the Dignity and Vocation of Women, John Paul II, sect. 28
On the Holy Spirit in the Life of the Church and the World, John Paul II, sect. 25, 61
Sacrament of Charity, Benedict XVI, sect. 14
U. S. Catholic Catechism for Adults, [2006] pp. 114

Other Resources

The Catholic Catechism, Hardon, pp. 206-208, 218
The Church's Confession of Faith, Ignatius Press, pp. 212-214
Faith for Today, Hogan and LeVoir, [First Edition] pp. 118, 177-178; [Second Edition] pp. 152, 217-218
Fundamentals of Catholic Dogma, Ott, pp. 296-297, 308-309
Fundamentals of Catholicism, Baker, Vol. 1, p. 109; Vol. 3, pp. 92-93, 95-96, 142
Modern Catholic Dictionary, Hardon, see "Catholic", "Catholicism" and "Catholicity"
The Teaching of Christ, Lawler, Wuerl, and Lawler, [First Edition] pp. 167-168; [Second Edition] pp. 156-157; [Third Edition] pp. 136-137

Q. 180. Does the Catholic Church teach all the truths that Jesus Christ taught?

Church Documents

Compendium of the Catechism of the Catholic Church, sect. 11, 12
Lumen Gentium (Dogmatic Constitution on the Church), Vatican II, sect. 8
U. S. Catholic Catechism for Adults, [2006] pp. 132-134

Other Resources

Basics of the Faith: A Catholic Catechism, Schreck, p. 103
The Catholic Catechism, Hardon, pp. 224-233
The Church's Confession of Faith, Ignatius Press, pp. 258-261
Faith for Today, Hogan and LeVoir, [First Edition] pp. 129-134; [Second Edition] pp. 165-170
Fundamentals of Catholic Dogma, Ott, pp. 297-298, 308
Fundamentals of Catholicism, Baker, Vol. 1, p. 108; Vol. 3, pp. 135, 142
Modern Catholic Dictionary, Hardon, see "Catholic", "Catholicism" and "University of the Faithful"
The Teaching of Christ, Lawler, Wuerl, and Lawler, [First Edition] pp. 187, 215-216, 222-223; [Second Edition] pp. 199, 203-204, 210-211; [Third Edition] pp. 152, 178, 184

Q. 181. Why is the Catholic Church apostolic?

Church Documents

Compendium of the Catechism of the Catholic Church, sect. 174-176
Dei Verbum (Dogmatic Constitution on Divine Revelation), Vatican II, sect. 7-8, 25
Gaudium et Spes (Pastoral Constitution on the Church in the Modern World), Vatican II, sect. 76
God is Love, Benedict XVI, sect. 32
Lumen Gentium (Dogmatic Constitution on the Church), Vatican II, sect. 8, 18-28, 41
On the Dignity and Vocation of Women, John Paul II, sect. 26
On the Eucharist in Its Relationship to the Church, John Paul II, sect. 26-33
Sacrament of Charity, Benedict XVI, sect. 39
Splendor of Truth, John Paul II, sect. 107

Family Wisdom Library™

Papal documents listed below can be viewed at www.vatican.va.
For new cross-references, visit www.familyland.org

U. S. Catholic Catechism for Adults, [2006] pp. 132-134

Other Resources

Basics of the Faith: A Catholic Catechism, Schreck, pp. 93-95
The Catholic Catechism, Hardon, pp. 219-223
The Church's Confession of Faith, Ignatius Press, pp. 237-240, 243-248
Fundamentals of Catholic Dogma, Ott, pp. 282-285, 308
Fundamentals of Catholicism, Baker, Vol. 1, pp. 109-111; Vol. 3, pp. 101-102, 142
Modern Catholic Dictionary, Hardon, see "Apostolicity" and "Apostolic Succession"
The Teaching of Christ, Lawler, Wuerl, and Lawler, [First Edition] p. 199; [Second Edition] p. 187; [Third Edition] p. 163

Q. 182. What do we mean when we say, "I believe in the Communion of Saints"?

Church Documents

Compendium of the Catechism of the Catholic Church, sect. 194-195
God is Love, Benedict XVI, sect. 40, 42
The Lay Members of Christ's Faithful People, John Paul II, sect. 18-20, 32
Lumen Gentium (Dogmatic Constitution on the Church), Vatican II, sect. 13, 49, 50
On the Eucharist in Its Relationship to the Church, John Paul II, sect. 19
Sacrament of Charity, Benedict XVI, sect. 21, 76
Sacrosanctum Concilium (Constitution on the Sacred Liturgy), Vatican II, sect. 8, 104
U. S. Catholic Catechism for Adults, [2006] pp. 160-161

Other Resources

Basics of the Faith: A Catholic Catechism, Schreck, p. 81
The Catholic Catechism, Hardon, pp. 214-216, 267-268
The Church's Confession of Faith, Ignatius Press, pp. 253-254
Faith for Today, Hogan and LeVoir, [First Edition] p. 211; [Second Edition] p. 255
Fundamentals of Catholic Dogma, Ott, pp. 314-315
Fundamentals of Catholicism, Baker, Vol. 3, pp. 149-150
Modern Catholic Dictionary, Hardon, see "Communion of Saints"
The Teaching of Christ, Lawler, Wuerl, and Lawler, [First Edition] pp. 240-241; [Second Edition] pp. 228-229; [Third Edition] pp. 199-200

Q. 183. Why is the Church called the Church Militant?

Church Documents

Compendium of the Catechism of the Catholic Church, sect. 165
God is Love, Benedict XVI, sect. 40, 42
Lumen Gentium (Dogmatic Constitution on the Church), Vatican II, sect. 13, 49, 51
Splendor of Truth, John Paul II, sect. 68, 70

Other Resources

Basics of the Faith: A Catholic Catechism, Schreck, p. 81
The Catholic Catechism, Hardon, p. 267
The Church's Confession of Faith, Ignatius Press, pp. 214, 226
Fundamentals of Catholic Dogma, Ott, p. 271
Fundamentals of Catholicism, Baker, Vol. 3, p. 150
Modern Catholic Dictionary, Hardon, see "Church Militant"
Transformation in Christ, von Hildebrand, pp. 202-204

Q. 184. How do we help each other?

Church Documents

Compendium of the Catechism of the Catholic Church, sect. 211, 554
Gaudium et Spes (Pastoral Constitution on the Church in the Modern World), Vatican II, sect. 28
God is Love, Benedict XVI, sect. 40, 42
The Lay Members of Christ's Faithful People, John Paul II, sect. 32, 40
Lumen Gentium (Dogmatic Constitution on the Church), Vatican II, sect. 12-13, 49, 51
On the Dignity and Vocation of Women, John Paul II, sect. 7
Sacrament of Charity, Benedict XVI, sect. 76
U. S. Catholic Catechism for Adults, [2006] pp. 118-121

Other Resources

Basics of the Faith: A Catholic Catechism, Schreck, pp. 82-83
The Catholic Catechism, Hardon, p. 267
The Church's Confession of Faith, Ignatius Press, p. 254
Faith for Today, Hogan and LeVoir, [First Edition] pp. 210-216; [Second Edition] pp. 254-260
Fundamentals of Catholicism, Baker, Vol. 3, pp. 150-151
Fundamentals of Catholic Dogma, Ott, pp. 315-318
Modern Catholic Dictionary, Hardon, see "Communion of Saints"

Family Wisdom Library™

Papal documents listed below can be viewed at www.vatican.va.
For new cross-references, visit www.familyland.org

The Teaching of Christ, Lawler, Wuerl, and Lawler, [First Edition] pp. 240-241; [Second Edition] pp. 228-229; [Third Edition] pp. 199-200

Q. 185. What is the Church Suffering?

Church Documents

Compendium of the Catechism of the Catholic Church, sect. 210-211
God is Love, Benedict XVI, sect. 40, 42
Lumen Gentium (Dogmatic Constitution on the Church), Vatican II, sect. 49, 51
Sacrament of Charity, Benedict XVI, sect. 21, 32
U. S. Catholic Catechism for Adults, [2006] p. 154

Other Resources

Basics of the Faith: A Catholic Catechism, Schreck, p. 81
The Catholic Catechism, Hardon, pp. 267, 273-275
The Church's Confession of Faith, Ignatius Press, p. 254
Faith for Today, Hogan and LeVoir, [First Edition] pp. 210-211; [Second Edition] pp. 254-255
Fundamentals of Catholicism, Baker, Vol. 3, p. 150
Fundamentals of Catholic Dogma, Ott, p. 271
Modern Catholic Dictionary, Hardon, see "Communion of Saints", "Church Suffering" and "Purgatory"
The Teaching of Christ, Lawler, Wuerl, and Lawler, [First Edition] pp. 527-529; [Second Edition] pp. 517-519; [Third Edition] pp. 456-458

Q. 186. What is our duty toward the deceased?

Church Documents

Compendium of the Catechism of the Catholic Church, sect. 211
God is Love, Benedict XVI, sect. 40, 42
Lumen Gentium (Dogmatic Constitution on the Church), Vatican II, sect. 49, 51
Sacrament of Charity, Benedict XVI, sect. 21, 32
U. S. Catholic Catechism for Adults, [2006] pp. 154, 159-161

Other Resources

Basics of the Faith: A Catholic Catechism, Schreck, p. 83
The Catholic Catechism, Hardon, pp. 275, 277
The Church's Confession of Faith, Ignatius Press, p. 254
Faith for Today, Hogan and LeVoir, [First Edition] p. 211; [Second Edition] p. 255
Fundamentals of Catholicism, Baker, Vol. 3, pp. 155-157
Fundamentals of Catholic Dogma, Ott, pp. 321-322
Modern Catholic Dictionary, Hardon, see "Communion of Saints", "Indulgence" and "Purgatory"
The Teaching of Christ, Lawler, Wuerl, and Lawler, [First Edition] p. 528; [Second Edition] p. 518; [Third Edition] p. 457

Q. 187. What is the Church Triumphant?

Church Documents

Compendium of the Catechism of the Catholic Church, sect. 209
God is Love, Benedict XVI, sect. 40, 42
Lumen Gentium (Dogmatic Constitution on the Church), Vatican II, sect. 49-51
U. S. Catholic Catechism for Adults, [2006] pp. 153-154

Other Resources

Basics of the Faith: A Catholic Catechism, Schreck, p. 81
The Catholic Catechism, Hardon, pp. 266-267
The Church's Confession of Faith, Ignatius Press, p. 254
Faith for Today, Hogan and LeVoir, [First Edition] pp. 210-211; [Second Edition] pp. 254-255
Fundamentals of Catholicism, Baker, Vol. 3, p. 150
Fundamentals of Catholic Dogma, Ott, p. 271
Modern Catholic Dictionary, Hardon, see "Communion of Saints", "Church Triumphant" and "Heaven"

Q. 188. Why does the Church honor the canonized saints?

Church Documents

Compendium of the Catechism of the Catholic Church, sect. 564
God is Love, Benedict XVI, sect. 40, 42
Lumen Gentium (Dogmatic Constitution on the Church), Vatican II, sect. 49-50
Sacrament of Charity, Benedict XVI, sect. 94-95
Sacrosanctum Concilium (Constitution on the Sacred Liturgy), Vatican II, sect. 8, 104

Family Wisdom Library™

Papal documents listed below can be viewed at www.vatican.va.
For new cross-references, visit www.familyland.org

Splendor of Truth, John Paul II, sect. 89-90, 92-94, 102, 119
U. S. Catholic Catechism for Adults, [2006] p. 173

Other Resources

The Catholic Catechism, Hardon, pp. 215-216, 267, 424, 442
Basics of the Faith: A Catholic Catechism, Schreck, p. 82
The Church's Confession of Faith, Ignatius Press, p. 254
Faith for Today, Hogan and LeVoir, [First Edition] p. 256; [Second Edition] p. 305
Fundamentals of Catholicism, Baker, Vol. 3, pp. 152-154
Fundamentals of Catholic Dogma, Ott, pp. 318-321
Modern Catholic Dictionary, Hardon, see "Veneration of Saints"
The Teaching of Christ, Lawler, Wuerl, and Lawler, [First Edition] p. 389; [Second Edition] p. 379; [Third Edition] p. 336

Q. 189. What do we mean when we say, "I believe in the forgiveness of sins"?

Church Documents

Compendium of the Catechism of the Catholic Church, sect. 200-201
Lumen Gentium (Dogmatic Constitution on the Church), Vatican II, sect. 11
On the Dignity and Vocation of Women, John Paul II, sect. 13, 26
On the Holy Spirit in the Life of the Church and the World, John Paul II, sect. 42, 46
On Reconciliation and Penance, John Paul II, sect. 27
Sacrament of Charity, Benedict XVI, sect. 20-21
Splendor of Truth, John Paul II, sect. 31, 86, 103–105
U. S. Catholic Catechism for Adults, [2006] pp. 234-237

Other Resources

Basics of the Faith: A Catholic Catechism, Schreck, p. 218
The Catholic Catechism, Hardon, pp. 506-507
The Church's Confession of Faith, Ignatius Press, pp. 111, 114-117, 193-194, 198-199, 298-299, 301-302
Faith for Today, Hogan and LeVoir, [First Edition] pp. 123-124; [Second Edition] pp. 158-159
Fundamentals of Catholicism, Baker, Vol. 1, pp. 111-113; Vol. 3 pp. 57-59, 274, 274-282
Fundamentals of Catholic Dogma, Ott, pp. 219, 250-252
Modern Catholic Dictionary, Hardon, see "Baptism", "Baptismal Graces", "Forgiveness", "Justification, Theology of" and "Justifying Grace"
The Teaching of Christ, Lawler, Wuerl, and Lawler, [First Edition] pp. 169, 371; [Second Edition] pp. 158, 361; [Third Edition] pp. 321, 137-138

APPENDICES

#E4-9-2

APPENDIX A

Doctrine, Moral, Worship Exercises Answer Key

Questions 1-5

1. *What does "God is the Supreme Being" mean?* It means that God is the highest or greatest being. He is above all others. He is the source of all being.

2. *How can you show your friends and family each day that God is the Supreme Being of your life?* Answers will vary. We must express our desire to please God first, by all of our thoughts, words, and actions.

3. *Since God is the Supreme Being, He deserves all of our adoration and worship. How can you give God the adoration and worship He deserves?* We can give God the adoration and worship that He deserves by recognizing our total dependence upon Him and by fulfilling the responsibility of the present moment.

Questions 6-11

1. *God is the Supreme Being. He possesses many qualities. List six of these qualities.* Some of the outstanding qualities of God include His goodness, truth, beauty, mercy, love, peace, justice, wisdom, and power.

2. *In what ways have you experienced God's goodness? His truthfulness? His justice?* Answers will vary.

3. *How can you recognize God's presence wherever you go?* Some of the ways that we can recognize God's presence are through the beauty of nature, the teachings of the Church, the Scriptures, the goodness of our fellow human beings, God's still, small voice in our hearts when we pray, the liturgy of the Church, and through all expressions of beauty or other divine attributes.

Questions 12-15

1. *In what ways has God shown His mercy to you?* Answers will vary. Jesus has shown us His mercy through His suffering and Death for our sakes and by instituting the sacraments of Baptism, Penance, and Anointing of the Sick for the forgiveness of sins.

2. *We also possess God's justice and mercy. Think of some experiences in your life when you have been merciful and just to others.* Answers may include: offering little acts of service for others, even if you are inconvenienced or are not thanked for what you have done; being kind to somebody who is not kind to you; forgiving somebody who has hurt you.

3. *In your daily life, what are some ways that you can imitate God's mercy?* One should recognize that his first and most important responsibility is to love and forgive his own family members and relatives.

Questions 16-21

1. *How did God prove His love for man despite Adam and Eve's sin?* God proved His love for man by promising to send a Redeemer, by revealing Himself to Abraham and his descendants, and by preparing the Jewish nation to receive the Messiah, Jesus.

2. *When we look at the world around us and see poverty, wars, natural disasters, abuse, etc., how can we be sure that God really loves us? How does God show that He keeps His promises?* Most of the evils in the world are the result of sin. Even many illnesses, accidents, and natural disasters are the result of the lack of harmony between the human will and the divine Will. We can be sure that Jesus loves us, even in the midst of evil, because He willingly took upon Himself the punishment for all of our sins and endured every kind of physical and spiritual suffering for our sakes. Moreover, if we keep ourselves free from sin and apply ourselves to prayer, the sacraments, the study of our faith, and works of charity, each of us can experience God's peaceful and loving presence, even in the midst of trials. We can trust God to keep His Word because the Bible contains a faithful record of His past promises and their fulfillment.

3. *What can you do to show that you love and worship God, even amidst the challenges and trials of daily life?* We can show our love for God through regular prayer, frequent and fervent reception of the sacraments, study of the truth, and obedience to the will of God.

Questions 22-24

1. *What distinct quality of God is revealed in the history of salvation?* The Family Catechism emphasizes the distinctive role of God's mercy in the History of Salvation.

2. *Cite instances in your life when you have experienced God as a saving God.* Answers may include: receiving God's forgiveness in the sacrament of Reconciliation, receiving His Body and Blood at the Holy Sacrifice of the Mass, or overcoming temptation through the help of His grace.

3. *How can you respond to what God has revealed?* It may be by accepting it wholeheartedly and living it in your daily life.

Questions 25-30

1. *Describe the mystery of the Holy Trinity in your own words.* The mystery of the Holy Trinity is that there is one God in three divine Persons. The Father loves the Son; the Son loves the Father; and Their love is the Holy Spirit. The three divine Persons have one divine will.

2. *In your daily life, how can you show to those around you that you believe in the Holy Trinity?* Answers may include: through thoughts, words, and deeds of love since love is the essence of the Holy Trinity, by praying to the three divine Persons, and by making the Sign of the Cross with love.

3. *Look for ways to help others to know and love the Holy Trinity.*

Questions 31-35

1. *Describe the distinct roles of the Father, the Son, and the Holy Spirit.* The Father is the eternal Origin of the Son and, together with Him, of the Holy Spirit. The Son is the perfect Image, or Word, of the Father. The Holy Spirit is the Eternal Love of the Father and the Son.

2. *In what way can you honor the presence of the Trinity in every person you meet each day (i.e., your parents, friends, teachers, and others)?* We can honor the presence of the Trinity in every person through reverence, courtesy, respectfulness, and humble service.

3. *Write a prayer asking the Holy Trinity to help your family to become a more perfect model of Their unity.*

Questions 36-37

1. *What does Creation tell us about our God?* The beauty, intelligence, power, and other qualities of Creation tell us that there must be a Creator who possesses those same qualities to an unlimited degree.

2. *How can you help our society to preserve God's Creation?* We can help society to preserve God's Creation by: respecting human life from conception to natural death, working for a fair distribution of the earth's resources, and living a simple lifestyle that neither wastes nor abuses the goods of the earth.

3. *Read Psalm 8 and express your heartfelt gratitude to our Creator.*

Questions 38-41

1. *What characteristics of angels can we also find in human beings?* Angels and human beings both have intellect and free will.

2. *Think of instances in your life in which your guardian angel can help you.* Answers will vary. Our guardian angels can help us at all times, but especially when we ask for their help in the fulfillment of our duties and in times of temptation, danger, or suffering.

3. *Write a prayer to your guardian angel, asking him to help you to overcome the devil's temptations in your daily life.*

Questions 42-44

1. *How can your choices and decisions in life exemplify or mirror your dignity as God's greatest Creation?* Your choices in life exemplify your dignity as God's greatest creation when you freely choose to do God's will.

2. *Which particular attribute of God can you see in each of the members of your family?* Answers will vary.

3. *Look for ways to respect the image of God in those with whom you live and interact.*

Questions 45-46

1. *What benefits do we receive if we are obedient to God?* If we are truly obedient to God, we receive the blessings of peace, joy, love, and the other fruits of the Holy Spirit.

2. *Explain how your obedience to those in authority shows your love for God.* When we wholeheartedly obey our superiors and other legitimate authority, in spite of their faults and weaknesses, we are actually obeying God. God then knows that we are obeying for His sake.

3. *Make at least three resolutions that will help you to do God's will.*

Question 47

1. *What was God's response to the disobedience of our first parents and our own disobedience?* God responded to the disobedience of our first parents by punishing them, but He tempered the punishment by promising to send a Redeemer to restore them to His friendship.

2. *In your daily life, how do you show, in word and in deed, that Jesus Christ is your Savior?* Answers will vary. Each of us acknowledges Jesus as Savior whenever we forgive those who hurt us, when we trust in Him, when we reverence His name, when we meditate on His Passion, and when we obey His commandments.

3. *Think of instances from the past week in which Jesus strengthened you in times of temptations and saved you from sinful situations. Thank Jesus for those saving actions.*

Questions 48-52

1. *In what event in history did God's all-powerful action free man from the slavery of sin?* God's all-powerful action to free man from the slavery of sin is seen, especially, in Jesus' Resurrection from the dead.

2. *God is present among us in many ways. Think of instances from the past month in which you experienced God's presence.* God makes Himself present to us at Mass, in the Blessed Sacrament, in the sacraments, in the Catholic Church, in His Word, through prayer, in the Pope, bishops and priests, in our parents, in the souls of those in grace, in the beauty of Creation, etc.

3. *How can you be an instrument of God's presence to the people around you?* Only by practicing mental prayer and by entering into communion with God will we be able to reflect His presence to others. If our hearts and minds are fixed upon Jesus, we will reflect Him to those around us.

Questions 53-56

1. *What are some of the effects of original sin on all mankind?* Some of the consequences of original sin include the loss of perfect health of body, mind, and soul and vulnerability to death, diseases, weakness, and demonic influence.

2. *What graces do we receive at Baptism which enable us to live as God's own children?* We receive the great gift of sanctifying grace—a share in God's own life of Father, Son, and Holy Spirit dwelling in our souls, along with the theological virtues of faith, hope, and love. Baptism permits a person to enter into the life of God.

3. *Think of ways in which you can imitate the Blessed Virgin Mary in her faithfulness to God.* The great mark of a true imitator of Mary will be total obedience to the will of God as expressed in the teachings of the Church, the commands of lawful superiors (parents, teachers, supervisors), and the inspirations of the Holy Spirit.

Questions 57-58

1. *Why do we say that to sin is a personal decision to say "no" to God?* To sin is to decide to say "no" to God, because every sin is a deliberate choice to think, say, or do something which is contrary to God's will.

2. *Recall the last instance in which you chose to do your will rather than God's will. How did this affect you?* Answers will vary. To a greater or lesser degree, a decision to deviate from God's will results in unhappiness, restlessness, guilt, and a desire to escape from one's inner distress.

3. *In what concrete ways can you cooperate with the will of God?* Answers will vary. The person who fully embraces the will of God can be known by his spirit of love, obedience, and peace.

Questions 59-63

1. *Explain why committing both mortal and venial sins are ways of saying "no" to God.* To commit mortal and venial sins are saying "no" to God because both of them involve free choices to think, say, or do something displeasing to Him.

2. *What are the effects of mortal sin and venial sin?* A mortal sin is a serious offense against God which causes: the loss of sanctifying grace, the infused virtues, and the gifts of the Holy Spirit; the loss of the indwelling of the Holy Trinity in the soul; the loss of all merits acquired in one's past life; an ugly stain on the soul, leaving it dark and horrible; slavery to Satan; an increase of evil inclinations; a numbing of conscience; and the guilt of eternal punishment.

A venial sin is a less serious offense which does not rob the soul of sanctifying grace. However, venial sin deprives us of many actual graces which God would otherwise have given us. It lessens our charity and generosity in serving God and neighbor, makes the practice of virtue more difficult, and predisposes us to commit mortal sin.

3. *Schedule a nightly examination of conscience. If you have committed a mortal sin, how can the sacrament of Penance restore your relationship with God?* The sacrament of Penance removes the guilt of mortal sin and restores sanctifying grace to the soul of the penitent.

Questions 64-67

1. *Read Luke 15 and 19:1-10 and explain how God's mercy is greater than His justice.* God is love, and mercy is an expression of God's love. Therefore, God's mercy triumphs over justice. As creatures, we have no just claim on God's benefits. All of His blessings are free and unmerited gifts, but as God's children, we have a claim on His mercy so long as we, in turn, practice mercy toward others.

2. *God forgives those who are truly sorry for their sins. On our part, what can we do in order to be forgiven?* To be forgiven of our sins, we must ask God for the gift of true contrition. We must be sorry for our sins, resolve not to repeat them, confess them honestly, and perform the penance imposed on us by our confessor.

3. *When was the last time you received the sacrament of Reconciliation? Resolve to go to confession regularly (at least once a month).*

Questions 68-69

1. *What are the seven Capital Sins?* The seven Capital Sins are envy, pride, avarice, sloth, anger, lust, and gluttony.

2. *Think of the virtue which will best help you to overcome the sin you commit most often.* Answers will vary. Humility overcomes pride; meekness overcomes anger; moderation overcomes gluttony; purity overcomes lust; gratitude overcomes envy; generosity overcomes avarice or greed; diligence or discipline overcomes sloth or laziness.

3. *Write a short personal prayer which you can repeat each time you are tempted to commit any of the seven Capital Sins.*

Questions 70-71

1. *God has given us the strength to conquer temptation. How should we cooperate with God so that we can overcome temptations in our daily life?* All Christians can cooperate with God and conquer temptation through deep personal prayer (especially daily mental prayer), frequent reception of the sacraments, study of the truth, and obedience to the will of God (as expressed by the Magisterium, by our lawful superiors, and by the inspirations of the Holy Spirit).

2. *Identify the temptations that you encounter often and think of specific ways to triumph over these temptations.* Answers will vary. Some ways may include praying and asking for the help of one's guardian angel and Our Blessed Mother and avoiding occasions of sin.

3. *Try to participate in the Holy Mass and receive Holy Communion as often as possible and to go to confession regularly (at least once a month) to obtain God's graces to strengthen your will.*

Questions 72–73

1. *What does "Incarnation" mean?* Incarnation means that the second Person of the Holy Trinity became man.

2. *Jesus lived among us to reveal to us what it means to be man. What transformation in your life do you think you have to make to pattern your life after Jesus' life as a human being?* Answers will vary.

3. *The Angelus reminds us of the Incarnation, the greatest of God's works. Take a moment now to pray the Angelus with gratitude and reverence. Try to pray it three times daily.*

Question 74

1. *In what way does Jesus renew the world?* Jesus renews the world by giving us sanctifying grace; He is our source of eternal life and salvation.

2. *One of the fruits of the coming of Jesus to the earth is the life of grace in our souls. On your part, how can you keep the life of grace in your soul?* A good answer should mention the importance of prayer, keeping the commandments, following God's inspirations, and frequenting the sacraments, especially the Sacraments of Penance and the Holy Eucharist.

3. *Read and memorize John 3:16. What does this verse inspire you to do?* Answers will vary.

Questions 75–77

1. *Read John 1:1-4. What significant truth about Jesus is revealed through these verses?* A good answer should note that these verses clearly proclaim the divinity of Jesus, the Eternal Word.

2. *Cite an instance in your life in which you manifested your faith in Jesus as Lord and God.* Answers will vary.

3. *In silence, express your trust in Jesus' word that He is God.*

Question 78

1. *The prayer of Jesus before His Passion shows that He is truly God. Write two verses from John 17 which help us to know that Jesus is God.* Answers will vary and may include verses 2–4, 11, or 22–24.

2. *How can you show by your example that the death of Jesus on the Cross has borne redemptive fruit in your life?* A good answer should mention at least one or two of the following signs: (1) charity in dealing with others; (2) willingness to stand up for the truth; (3) obedience to the law of God and to lawful authority; (4) a spirit of prayer; (5) simplicity of life; and (6) cheerful acceptance of unavoidable sufferings.

3. *Meditate on this faith affirmation: Lord, by Your Cross and Resurrection, You have set us free, You are the Savior of the world.*

Questions 79–81

1. *Cite two passages from the New Testament which show that Jesus is God.* Some of the suitable passages quoted in the Family Catechism include: John 1:1-4; 8:42, 55, 58; 10:30; and 17:1–2.

2. *In the Angelus we pray, "The Word was made flesh and dwelt among us." What has our Faith taught us about the meaning of these words, and what do they mean for you personally?* Answers should mention that Jesus, the second Person of the Blessed Trinity, took flesh and became man so that He could save us from sin and death, restore us to God's friendship, and lead us to everlasting life.

3. *If you have a friend who does not believe that Jesus is God, which of your actions in your daily life help him to know that you are a Christian?* Possible answers might include saying grace at meals, attending Mass on Sundays and weekdays, making time to pray together, telling others about Jesus and the Catholic faith, and acting in a Christlike manner at work and in one's dealings with other people.

Question 82

1. *How is Jesus a true man?* Jesus was born, and He experienced the full range of human emotions and temptations. He was sad, angry, lonely, weary, etc. But, unlike us, he never gave in to temptation, and He always remained in control of His emotions.

2. *By becoming man, Jesus proved His love for us. Think of situations in your life in which you can love Jesus in return.* Answers will vary. One of the best ways to prove our love for Jesus is by remaining faithful to Him in sufferings, disappointments, and persecutions.

3. *Express in prayer your faith that Jesus enlightens and strengthens us so that we may resist every temptation that comes our way.*

Question 83

1. *As a true human being, Jesus has shown His concern for us in many ways. What are some of the ways?* Answers should include some of the following points: (1) Jesus suffered and died for us; (2) He revealed the truth to us; (3) He gives us a share in God's life through the sacraments, especially the Holy Eucharist; (4) He is always with us to hear and answer our prayers.

2. *Have you experienced Jesus' concern in your life? List the things that He has done for you.* Answers will vary.

3. *Through your actions, how can you thank Jesus for His concern for you?* Answers should include at least one or two of the following points: (1) offering Him frequent prayers of praise and thanksgiving; (2) attending the Holy Sacrifice of the Mass and receiving Him in Holy Communion; (3) treating others with charity and forgiving those who hurt me; (4) being obedient to God's will as expressed to me by the Magisterium of the Church and other lawful authority.

Questions 84-87

1. *By becoming man and offering His sacrificial death on the Cross, Jesus became our Savior. From what did Jesus save us? For what did He save us?* Jesus saved us from sin and death. He saved us for eternal life with God in Heaven.

2. *How can you cooperate with the saving act of Jesus' death and Resurrection? Write out two specific things that you will do to cooperate with Him in your daily life.* Answers should include one or more of the following points: (1) I will keep

Jesus in my thoughts throughout the day; (2) I will make frequent and fervent use of the sacraments, especially the sacraments of Penance and Holy Eucharist; (3) I will try to see Jesus in everyone I meet; (4) I will try to do what Jesus wants me to do in every situation, especially by being obedient to lawful authority.

3. *Thank Jesus for freeing you from the slavery of sin. Express your gratitude by continually cooperating with His saving act.*

Questions 88-89

1. *Jesus prayed in the Garden at the beginning of His Passion. What did He pray for?* Jesus prayed that the Father would remove the cup of suffering if it was in accord with His will. But most of all, Jesus prayed to do the will of the Father.

2. *Recall the last time that you risked hardship or persecution to do God's will.* Answers will vary.

3. *Think of situations in your role as a daughter, son, parent, friend, worker, or citizen in which you encounter challenges in fulfilling God's will. List the things that you can do as a Christian to meet these challenges.* Answers will vary.

Questions 90-93

1. *Jesus had to suffer to bring us eternal life. What did Jesus prove by doing this?* By suffering so much, spiritually and physically, Jesus proved His infinite love for each of us.

2. *Meditate on the Scripture verse, "By this we know love, that he laid down his life for us; and we ought to lay down our lives for the brethren" (1 John 3:16). Write down your reflections.* Answers should note that each of us must be willing to sacrifice—in big or little ways—for the sake of his fellow men.

3. *What actions will you take to be able to lay down your life for Jesus and for your brothers and sisters?* Answers should include one or more of the following: (1) I will pray often; (2) I will deny myself, for example, by fasting, serving the needy, and giving money to the poor; (3) I will meditate on the Passion and death of Jesus; (4) I will frequent the sacraments, especially the sacraments of Penance and the Holy Eucharist; (5) I will see Jesus in everyone I meet.

Questions 94-97

1. *Upon the Cross, Jesus suffered not only extreme physical pain, but also the indescribable pain of rejected love. Who rejected the love of Jesus?* Every one who has sinned has rejected the love of Jesus.

2. *In what ways have you rejected Jesus' love?* Answers will vary.

3. *How can you respond more generously to the love of Jesus?* Answers will vary.

Questions 98-101

1. *What truths did Jesus reveal through His Resurrection?* Jesus revealed the truth of His divinity through His Resurrection from the dead.

2. *What should we hope for from the Resurrection of Jesus? How do you manifest this hope in your everyday actions?* We should hope for a share in the glory of the risen Jesus.

3. *How does the Resurrection of Jesus influence your daily decisions?* Answers should mention that the Resurrection enables one to remain hopeful, loving, and peaceful in the midst of the crosses, trials, and disappointments of life.

Questions 102-103

1. *What did Jesus do after His Resurrection to strengthen His disciples' faith?* Jesus showed Himself to His disciples on many occasions, taught them about the Kingdom of God, and even allowed them to touch His risen Body so as to convince them of the truth of His Resurrection.

2. *Meditate on the Scripture verse, "Blessed are those who have not seen and yet believe" (John 20:29).*

3. *What specific steps can you take to strengthen your faith in the Resurrection?* Answers should include one or more of the following ideas: (1) I can meditate on the Gospel accounts of the Resurrection; (2) I can pray the Glorious Mysteries of the Rosary; (3) I can frequent the sacraments, especially the Holy Eucharist; (4) I can spend time in adoration before the risen Lord in the Blessed Sacrament; (5) I can avoid books, conversations, and other influences that may weaken my faith in the Resurrection.

Questions 104-105

1. *What did Jesus conquer by His Resurrection?* Jesus conquered death.

2. *How can this triumph of Jesus at His Resurrection help you in facing life's trials and struggles?* Answers will vary.

3. *Ask Jesus to give you the strength to conquer sin and death through His Resurrection.*

Questions 106-107

1. *After His Resurrection, Jesus continues to help us. In what ways?* Answers will vary.

2. *How can you cooperate with the grace of the Resurrection?* Answers should mention one or more of the following points: (1) I can keep His commandments; (2) I can accept my crosses patiently; (3) I can face death courageously.

3. *How can you show your gratitude to Jesus by word and action for His victorious and continuous presence in us today?* Answers will vary.

Questions 108-111

1. *Although Jesus ascended into heaven, He has not abandoned us. Where on earth is He especially present now?* Jesus is especially present in the Holy Eucharist. In the Blessed Sacrament, Jesus lives Body, Blood, Soul, and Divinity under the appearance of bread.

2. *Jesus is also present in the souls of those who love Him. How can you make Him more present in your life? Think of specific things that you can do.* Answers will vary.

3. *Through His Ascension, Jesus has prepared a place for us in heaven. Let the thought of this inspire you to carry out faithfully the things that you listed in your previous answer.*

Questions 112-113

1. *Think about times you have allowed Jesus to be King of your life.* Answers will vary.

2. *In what ways can you cooperate with God in carrying out His plan for us so that Jesus will truly become the King and center of your Christian life?* Answers will vary.

3. *Pray to Jesus that mankind will cooperate fully with God in the accomplishment of His plan.*

Questions 114-115

1. *Who is the Holy Spirit?* The Holy Spirit is the living love that flows between the Father and the Son. He is God just as the Father and the Son are God. The Holy Spirit is worthy of the same love and adoration that we owe to the Father and to the Son.

2. *In what way can you worship and glorify the Father, Son and Holy Spirit in your daily life?* Holiness is doing God's will. It is fulfilling the responsibility of the present moment (as parent, child, teacher, student, etc.) as perfectly as we can for pure love of God. Whenever we fulfill our responsibilities out of love for God, offering it to Jesus through Mary, we glorify the Holy Trinity. We glorify God by finishing the work He has given us to do (cf. Jn 17:4).

3. *Name a prayer that mentions the Father, Son and Holy Spirit. Slowly read the Summary Prayer after question 115, and make it your own prayer.* The most common form of prayer to the Holy Trinity is the Glory Be: "Glory be to the Father and to the Son and to the Holy Spirit, as it was in the beginning, is now, and ever shall be, world without end. Amen."

Question 116

1. *In the Scripture verses John 14:16-17 and 25-26, what does our Lord Jesus say about the Holy Spirit?* Jesus reveals that the Holy Spirit is our helper Who will guide us into all truth.

2. *"Paraclete" means "He who is called to help." Recall occasions when you experienced the help of the Holy Spirit. Describe one of your experiences in writing.* Answers will vary.

3. *Read John 14:16-17 again. Thank the Father and Jesus for the gift of the Holy Spirit. Ask the Holy Spirit to remain with you always and to inspire, strengthen, and guide you to greater intimacy with Jesus.*

Questions 117–118

1. *What does our Catholic faith tell us about Pentecost? Why is the feast of Pentecost very significant for us as Christians?* Our Catholic faith tells us that Pentecost was the birthday of the Church, when the Holy Spirit was given to the first Christian community. The feast of Pentecost is very significant for the Church because it reminds us that we are called to share in the life of the Holy Spirit. If we surrender ourselves completely to the Holy Spirit, He will help us to keep the commandments of God and of the Church and to fulfill the responsibility of the present moment ever more perfectly and with great love.

2. *How can you and your family answer God's invitation to love Him and one another? Be specific.* Answers will vary.

3. *Slowly read the Summary Prayer after question 117. Then close your eyes and pray to the Holy Spirit in your own words.*

Question 119

1. *The Holy Spirit is present in the Catholic Church through His divine life of grace. What does this grace enable us to do?* The grace of the Holy Spirit enables us to live as Jesus lived and to love as Jesus loved. In short, it enables us to obey the new commandment, "Love others as I have loved you" (Jn 15:12).

2. *The Holy Spirit is also present outside the Catholic Church. What can you do to promote the unity of all Christians?* We can promote unity by helping to make the members of the Catholic Church more faithful to the Gospel, by being a good example, by taking initiative in meeting and praying with non-Catholic Christians, and by praying for unity among all Christians. We can also invite our non-Catholic brethren to our formation programs in our homes and churches.

3. *Read John 17:11-12. Pray for the unity of all Christians. If possible, invite your family to join you.*

Questions 120-121

1. *How does the Holy Spirit animate and nourish the Church in her life of grace so that she can continue the work of salvation begun by Christ?* The Holy Spirit guides the leaders of the Church in their work of teaching, ruling, and making holy the People of God. The Holy Spirit guides the People of God in knowing the truth, teaches them to pray, and helps them to do God's will. Each of us, as a member of the Church, has the basic duty to share the Catholic faith. The Holy Spirit helps us to do this.

2. *In what concrete ways can you and your family take part in the work of the Church to bring the good news of God's love to others?* Answers will vary.

3. *Pray the Summary Prayer after question 121. Thank the Holy Spirit for His work in the Church.*

Question 122

1. *Why is the Catholic Church called the Body of Christ? What is the role of the Holy Spirit in the Body of Christ?* The Catholic Church is called the Body of Christ because, through the Holy Spirit, all Christians are united to each other and to Jesus as their Head. Just as each of the members of the human body serves a specific and unique purpose, so each member of the Church serves a specific and unique purpose in the Body of Christ.

2. *As a member of the Body of Christ, in what specific ways do you strive to become a worthy member of the Body of Christ?* Answers will vary.

3. *Each day, ask the Holy Spirit to help you and your family in your efforts to become holy, worthy members of the Body of Christ.*

Question 123

1. *Describe some of the ways in which you can honor the Holy Spirit.* We honor the Holy Spirit by remembering His presence and by praying to Him. We honor Him by being obedient to the inspirations we receive in prayer.

2. *When making decisions, how do you discern what will be most pleasing to God?* To make a decision that pleases God, we must pray deeply and follow the guidance that we receive from the Holy Spirit, making sure that the guidance that we receive is in keeping with the Commandments, the duties of our state in life, and with the just orders of those in lawful authority over us.

3. *Be aware of God's presence in your heart right now. Thank Him for the many times when you have experienced His protection, guidance, and strength. If you know the following song, "Come Holy Spirit, I Need You," sing it softly. If not, read it slowly and say the words from your heart. You may add additional verses.*

Come, Holy Spirit, I need You
Come, Holy Spirit, I pray.
Come with Your strength and Your power
Come in Your own special way.

Come, Holy Spirit, I need You
Come, Holy Spirit, I pray.
Come with Your light and Your guidance
Come in Your own special way.

Question 124

1. *Which sacrament gives us the Spirit of Christ?* All of the sacraments increase the life of the Holy Spirit in those who receive them worthily, but Baptism and Confirmation confer the gift of the Holy Spirit in a special way. When we receive and accept the Holy Spirit, God leads us into a new way of life in which we allow the Holy Spirit to lead and empower us in all that we think, say, and do.

2. *How can you show the people in your family, school, workplace, or community that you live "according to the Spirit of Christ"?* A life which faithfully fulfills the responsibility of the present moment is the best evidence that the Holy Spirit is fully alive in a soul. We should ask the Holy Spirit for the grace to plan our lives so that we maintain a healthy balance between the five basic dimensions of the Christian life: our sacramental life, our life of prayer and religious formation, our family and community life, our work life (in the home, school, factory, office, or field), and our apostolic life of making known the Good News of the Gospel (evangelization). Then we should ask the Holy Spirit to give us the grace to faithfully fulfill the responsibility of each present moment as we strive to carry out His plan for each of the five dimensions of our lives. Anyone who lives in this way will become a saint!

3. *Light a candle; then renew your Baptismal vows and ask the Holy Spirit to guide and strengthen you to live a truly Christian life.*

Baptismal vows:

Do you reject Satan and all his works and all his empty promises?

Do you believe in God, the Father Almighty, creator of heaven and earth?

Do you believe in Jesus Christ, his only Son our Lord, who was born of the Virgin Mary, was crucified, died, and was buried, rose from the dead, and is now seated at the right hand of the Father?

Do you believe in the Holy Spirit, the holy catholic Church, the communion of saints, the forgiveness of sins, the resurrection of the body, and life everlasting?

(Taken from "The Rites of the Catholic Church," Pueblo Publishing Company, New York, 1976).

Question 125

1. *How can you explain sanctifying grace to a friend?* Sanctifying grace is God's life which He gives to us in Baptism and which He increases in us through the other sacraments, through good works, and through prayers.

2. *In what ways can you grow in holiness so that you can better live as God's child?* Answers may include: fervent prayer, frequent reception of the sacraments, and obedience to the will of God through the heroic fulfillment of our responsibilities.

3. *Read Ephesians 1:7 and 2:7. Thank God for sharing His divine life with you and with all people.*

Question 126

1. *What does it mean to say that a person is in the "state of sanctifying grace" or in the "state of grace"? When can one say that he or she is not in the state of grace?* A person is in the state of grace (or sanctifying grace) if he has God's life in his soul. A person receives God's life into his soul through the sacrament of Baptism. A person who is in the state of grace will remain in that state unless he commits a mortal sin.

2. *How do you strive to remain in the state of grace?* The best way to remain in the state of grace is to pray always, to remember that we live in God's Presence, to fulfill the responsibility of the present moment, and to frequently receive the Sacraments of Penance and Holy Eucharist.

3. *Pray the Summary Prayer after question 126.*

Question 127

1. *What does Holy Mother Church teach us about sin? How does the Holy Spirit help us to die to sin and to live with God?* The Church teaches that sin is failure in genuine love of God and neighbor and the cause of all evil and unhappiness in the world (cf. "Catechism of the Catholic Church," 1849). The Holy Spirit helps us to die to sin by filling us with God's life and by giving us the power to do God's will and to avoid everything that leads to sin.

2. *Recall the occasions in the past month (or since your last confession) when you sinned against God by doing something that displeased Him or by failing to do something that He wanted you to do.* (All Christians should understand that sins of omission are just as serious as sins of commission.)

3. *Ask God's forgiveness for the times when you did not cooperate with His grace. Promise God that you will go to confession as soon as you can. Ask the Holy Spirit to give you the strength to overcome temptation and to practice the virtue that will overcome your primary fault.* (It is important for all Christians to understand that merely doing good acts is not enough to insure growth in holiness. One must truly desire holiness and trust in God's help. If we do not yet desire holiness by seeking to do God's will at each present moment, we can ask the Holy Spirit to give us that holy desire.)

Question 128

1. *Picture this situation in your mind. You are inside a locked room. Jesus is outside and wishes to enter. Only you can open the door because it has no knob on the outside. How does this situation relate to actual grace?* The scene in the locked room with Jesus outside could be used to describe any offer of grace. Jesus will never force Himself on anyone. Therefore, we must always open the door of our soul to receive grace from God.

2. *What are some signs that you have let Jesus into your life?* The best indication that a person has let Jesus into his life is the presence of the virtues, gifts, and fruits of the Holy Spirit in that person's life.

3. *If you know the following song, sing it softly. If not, read it slowly and say the words from your heart.*

Day by day,
Day by day,
Oh, dear Lord, three things I pray:
To see You more clearly,
Love You more dearly,
Follow You more nearly,
Day by day.

Question 129

1. *How does the Holy Spirit help us to lead good Christian lives?* The Holy Spirit helps us to lead good Christian lives by filling us with God's life, by inspiring us to know God's will, and by giving us the power to obey His inspirations and to practice virtues.

2.*Do you allow the Holy Spirit to guide you in your daily life? List the things that you will do to become more receptive to the grace of the Holy Spirit.* A good answer should include all or most of the following ideas: frequent confession and Holy Communion, constancy in prayer, obedience to all the Commandments and legitimate authority, service to others.

3. *Compose a personal prayer to the Holy Spirit. Make at least two copies. Keep one in your room so that you can use it, especially when you are feeling spiritually weak or discouraged. Insert one in your calendar, planner / organizer, or schedule / school notebook so that you can pray it whenever you make your plans.*

Question 130

1. *When did we become children of God? What are the implications of our being children of God—for our relationship to Him, to others, and to the earth on which we live?* We become children of God at Baptism. As God's children, we have a special responsibility to love and honor God as our Creator, Redeemer, and Sanctifier, to love other human beings as our brothers and sisters in Christ, and to care for the creation which has been entrusted to us by God.

2. *List some specific things that you will do in order to live according to your great dignity as a child of God.* Answers will vary. One good way we can live as a child of God is to love God in all the people that He brings into our lives, particularly those who do not like us or who irritate us.

3. *Be aware of God's presence and thank God the Father for the great dignity of being His child. Ask the Holy Spirit for the grace to think, feel, and act according to the values and teachings of Christ, your Brother, as set forth in Sacred Scripture and the "Catechism of the Catholic Church."*

Question 131

1. *Name the three theological virtues. Why are they called theological virtues? How do they help us in our daily lives?* The three theological virtues are faith, hope, and love. They are called theological virtues because they pertain to our relationship with God. They are our constant weapons in the battle against evil and our protection against the wiles of the devil.

2. *Recall occasions in your life when you acted as a person who believes in God, who hopes in God, and who loves God and other people for His sake.*

3. *Pray the Apostles' Creed, one Our Father, and three Hail Marys for an increase of faith, hope and charity, and pray one Glory Be in honor of the Most Holy Trinity.*

Question 132

1. *When did you receive the virtue of faith for the first time? What is the meaning of faith?* We receive the virtue of faith for the first time in Baptism. Faith is the power to believe in all that God has revealed about Himself through the Church. Faith includes a willingness to submit oneself to God's truth as it is revealed by the Church.

2. *List specific steps that you can take to deepen your knowledge of the truths of our Catholic faith.* A good answer should include some or all of the following ideas: Read the Bible daily, attend daily Mass, study the "Catechism of the Catholic Church" and "The Apostolate's Family Catechism," pay attention to homilies during Mass, discuss the teachings of the Church with friends and family, read the encyclicals of Pope John Paul II, particularly "Veritatis Splendor," and read Vatican Council II documents and the writings of the fathers, doctors, and saints of the Church.

3. *Read and meditate on a Scripture passage for ten minutes. For another ten minutes, read a sound Catholic formation book such as the "Catechism of the Catholic Church," "The Apostolate's Family Catechism" or Church documents and writings. Try to set aside time each day for this type of spiritual reading.*

Question 133

1. *If we have the virtue of hope, what do we desire, and what do we receive through this desire? What is the basis of our hope?* If we have hope, we desire eternal life with God in heaven. Hope gives us the strength to endure the crosses, trials, and disappointments of life and to trust that God will give us the graces we need to reach heaven. We base our hope on the power of God, on the mercy of God, and on the faithfulness of God to the promises that He has made to us.

2. *What are some signs that one is indeed a person full of hope?* In particular, the hope-filled person displays patience in suffering, cheerfulness, delight in speaking of God and spiritual things, courage in the face of death, disease, and disaster, trust in God, resignation to the will of God, peace of heart, and a constant desire to fulfill the responsibility of the present moment. A hope-filled person possesses Scriptures Four C's of confidence, conscience, charity, and constancy (see the "Family Consecration Prayer and Meditation Book," #53a).

3. *Copy the following prayer and try to memorize it so you can pray it often, especially in times of suffering or discouragement.*

> My God, I hope in You, for grace and for glory, because of Your promises, Your mercy and Your power. Amen.

Question 134

1. *What is the greatest commandment and what does it mean? What does it mean to love your neighbor as yourself or to love your neighbor as God has loved you?* The greatest commandment is to love God with your whole heart, with your whole soul, and with your whole mind, and your neighbor as yourself. This means that we are willing to give up anything—including our lives—rather than offend God through mortal sin. A genuine love for neighbor means that we love him for God's sake, we pray for him and always stand ready to help him, even when we experience negative feelings towards him, and we try to lead him to Christ.

2. *Read 1 John 4:20-21. Spend five minutes or more in silence reflecting on the times in your life when you experienced God's love and the love of the people around you.*

Thank God for those experiences. Ask the Holy Spirit to inspire you to think of concrete ways by which you can show your love for others—especially for those who are difficult to love. Write down your inspirations. Possible answers may include some or all of the following points: be constant in prayer, be mindful of the sufferings that Jesus endured for our sake, pay attention to the needs of other people, receive the sacraments of Holy Eucharist and Penance devoutly and frequently, meditate on the example of Jesus in the Gospels.

2. *Next time that you go to Mass, be aware of the special moments in the liturgy that show and celebrate God's love for you.*

Question 135

1. *Name the four cardinal virtues. How do each of these virtues help us in our lives?* The four cardinal virtues are prudence, justice, temperance, and fortitude. Prudence is the power to make good choices. Justice is the power to be fair to everyone. Temperance is the power to control the senses. Fortitude is the power to do God's will when it is hard.

2. *Think of specific times in your daily life when you will need to practice the cardinal virtues.* Answers will vary.

3. *Pray the Summary Prayer after question 135, with a deep desire that you and your family practice the cardinal virtues.*

Question 136

1. *What is a virtue? How might you explain in simple terms the meaning of the theological and cardinal virtues? What are some other moral virtues?* A virtue is a good habit. The theological and cardinal virtues are good habits which God infuses or places into our souls to help us to do His will. The theological virtues of faith, hope, and love help us to form a right relationship with God. Faith is the power to believe in God; hope is the power to trust in God; and love is the power to love God and neighbor for God's sake. The cardinal virtues help us to form a right relationship with our neighbor. Chastity, religion, obedience, honesty, and loyalty are some of the other moral virtues. In reality, however, all of these virtues can be traced back to one of the cardinal virtues. For example, chastity is related to temperance; religion is related to faith; obedience, honesty, and loyalty are related to justice.

2. *Which virtue is the most difficult for you to practice? Think of concrete steps by which you can develop this virtue.* Answers will vary. We should remember to pray for the grace to grow in the virtues which we lack. But, more importantly, we should keep in mind that the Holy Spirit is the source of all virtues and that our union with the Holy Spirit depends upon our fulfillment of the responsibilities of our state in life.

3. *Write down on a piece of paper the virtue you wish to focus on for a month. Include a Scripture passage that will help you practice that virtue. Post it in your room and pray to the Holy Spirit to inspire and strengthen you in developing that virtue. Try to make it a habit to write a different virtue and Scripture passage each month on which to focus.*

Question 137

1. *Name the seven gifts of the Holy Spirit. What does each gift do for us?* The gifts of the Holy Spirit are wisdom, understanding, knowledge, counsel, piety, fortitude, and fear of the Lord. Wisdom gives us the ability to see all things in relation to God;

understanding helps us to grasp the meaning of the truths of our Faith; knowledge gives us the ability to evaluate things at their true value, in relation to God; counsel gives us the ability to make or to advise good choices; piety helps us to love God as Father and to love and respect people and things consecrated to Him; fortitude gives us the ability to do God's will in difficult circumstances; and fear of the Lord makes us dread the loss of God's presence though sin.

2. *Recall some occasions in your life when you concretely experienced the gifts of the Holy Spirit. Write these down in a reflection notebook or spiritual journal.*

3. *Slowly pray the Summary Prayer after question 137. Invite your family to pray it with you. Pray also for your religious and civil leaders, that they may receive the seven gifts of the Holy Spirit.*

Question 138

1. *Why is the Catholic Church called the "new People of God"? What sets the Catholic Church apart from other religious bodies?* The Catholic Church is called the "new People of God" because Jesus formed the core of His Church from the faithful remnant of the original People of God, the Jewish people. What sets the Catholic Church apart from other religious bodies is that it was established by God Himself to reveal the fullness of God's truth through the Bible and the Magisterium, and the fullness of God's life through the sacraments. Other religious bodies were either established by men or—as in the case of the Hebrews—they were not given the fullness of God's truth and life.

2. *How can you concretely show your gratitude to God for having made you a member of the Catholic Church?* Answers will vary. The best way to show our gratitude to God for the gift of our Catholic faith is to evangelize other people so that they, too, can enjoy the same gift.

3. *Thank Jesus from the depths of your heart for His gift of the Catholic Church.*

Question 139

1. *When and how did Christ lay the foundations of the Catholic Church? How does one become a member of the Catholic Church, the Mystical Body of Christ?* By his death and Resurrection, Jesus laid the foundations of the Catholic Church. By the power of Baptism, we become members of the Church, the Mystical Body of Christ.

2. *What should our attitude be towards all members of the Church? How can we remain united with Christ and with one another?* We should love all members of the Church as our brothers and sisters. We can remain united with Christ and with one another by remaining in the state of sanctifying grace. We grow in sanctifying grace through prayer, good works, and the sacraments.

3. *Renew the promises which were made at your Baptism. Thank the Lord for making you part of His family and ask Him for the grace to remain faithful to your baptismal promises.*

Question 140

1. *God has given us gifts in the Catholic Church. What are these gifts? How does each of these gifts help us in our daily life?* The main gifts that God has given us in the Catholic Church are (1) the apostolic ministries of bishops, priests, and deacons, inherited from the Apostles, (2) the truths of the faith, and (3) the sacraments. In our daily lives, through the apostolic ministries of bishops, priests, and deacons, we receive instruction in the truths of the faith, spiritual direction, and grace through the sacraments. The truths of the faith help us to know, love,

and serve God from moment to moment, while the sacraments introduce, maintain, and strengthen God's life within us.

2. *Resolve to receive the sacraments more frequently and with greater devotion. Think of ways to help your family members do the same.*

3. *Pray that more families will receive the sacraments with fervor and devotion. Reflect on the goodness of God in giving us His gifts in the Catholic Church.*

Question 141

1. *Why must Sacred Scripture and Sacred Tradition be accepted and honored with equal devotion and reverence?* Sacred Scripture and Sacred Tradition must be accepted with equal devotion and reverence because both of them transmit the Word of God entrusted to the Apostles by Jesus and the Holy Spirit. The Sacred Scriptures contain the written Word of God. Sacred Tradition contains the entire Word of God in such a way that the successors of the Apostles may faithfully preserve, expound, and spread it abroad by their preaching.

2. *Make a concrete action plan which will enable you and your family to meditate on the Bible frequently and deepen your understanding of Sacred Tradition by reading books endorsed by the Magisterium, the teaching office of the Church. Write down your action plan for your family and put it in a place where you will see it every day. Ask God for the grace to faithfully carry out your action plan.* Example action plan: to gather the members of my family every night for at least fifteen minutes for a discussion of the truths of our faith using the Bible and a sound Catholic book, such as the "Catechism of the Catholic Church," as references.

3. *Read 2 Timothy 3:16, 2 Thess. 2:15, and Divine Revelation, section 26 (see the references after question 141). Thank God for revealing Himself and His plan for our salvation through Sacred Scripture and Sacred Tradition.*

Questions 142–144

1. W*hat does the Catholic Church do for mankind through the truths, ministries, and sacraments entrusted to her by God?* Through these gifts of God, the Catholic Church is able to grow as a community in Christ by serving mankind and giving it His saving word and activity.

2. *Do you try to get to know the bishop of your diocese and the priest(s) in your parish? How can you and your family show support for your parish priest in word and deed?* Catholic families can show support for their parish priests by praying for them, by assisting them as much as possible in every good work, and by expressing appreciation for them in word and action.

3. *Reflect on the important role of the Pope, bishops and priests in our Christian lives. Try to pray for their protection and guidance every day.*

Questions 145–149

1. *How does the Catholic Church finish the work begun by Christ?* Jesus Christ entrusted the Church to carry on His mission of teaching the Truth to all people and of serving mankind by administering the sacraments, through which graces are given to us.

2. *How can you be a sacrament of Christ's presence in your family, school, and workplace?* Answers may include: by being a "person for others," through our willingness to generously give of our time and talents in the service of others.

3. *Using the Chapter Summary Prayer, praise Jesus for His sacred presence in the Church.*

Questions 150–152

1. *What is the role of the Pope in the Church? Who gives him his authority?* As Vicar of Christ, the role of the Pope is to guide and care for the whole Church. He is in charge of all of the Church's efforts to teach, rule, and sanctify the People of God. The Pope receives his authority from Jesus Christ, Who gave supreme authority in the Church to St. Peter and his successors.

2. *How can you show your loyalty and obedience to the Pope in your family, school, workplace, and parish community?* Answers may vary. We can show our loyalty and obedience to the Pope by (1) praying for him; (2) reading, studying, and listening to his teachings; (3) obeying him and heeding his wishes; and (4) defending him against criticism.

3. *Thank Jesus for giving us a Pope to lead us to unity with Him and with each other. Pray every day for the intentions of our Holy Father and for his spiritual and physical well being.*

Questions 153–154

1. *What does it mean to say that the Church and the Pope are infallible in their teachings? In what instances are the Church and the Pope infallible?* Infallibility is a gift of the Holy Spirit by which the Church's faith is protected from error. When the Church teaches solemnly in the name of God, the teaching is infallible; that is, it cannot be mistaken in matters of faith and morals. When the Pope teaches solemnly in his official capacity as head of the Church, or when bishops assembled with the Pope in council solemnly pronounce upon a matter of faith or morals, that doctrine is the infallible teaching of the Church. Moreover, when the Pope and the body of bishops dispersed throughout the world teach that a certain doctrine has been revealed by God, that teaching is infallible, even though it has not been solemnly defined, for it is still Christ teaching through His universal Church.

2. *Do you strive to know and remain loyal to the teachings of the Church regarding moral issues? How can you keep informed of the Pope's stand on contemporary moral issues?* We can know the Pope's teachings on contemporary moral issues by reading his apostolic letters and other writings that present a synthesis of Scripture and the Magisterial teachings focused on current moral issues.

3. *Allot 5-10 minutes a day to reflect on one of the Holy Father's encyclicals or apostolic letters (e.g., "Letter to Children," "Guardian of the Redeemer" or "Lay Members of Christ's Faithful").*

Questions 155–157

1. *How is the Church a community?* The Catholic Church is a community in that it allows its members to share the life of Christ; it is a people assembled by God.

2. *How can you and your family use your time, talents, and possessions to build up your parish community?* Answers will vary. Catholics should help other families to know the truths of our faith and should be caring neighbors who are always willing to help—to be a family for others.

3. *Pray for all the members of the Catholic Church, that all may contribute to the strengthening of the Christian community.*

Questions 158–159

1. *In what sense are the members of the Church equal?* By Baptism, all Catholics are made one body with Christ and members of the People of God. But, while there is a basic equity among all the members of the Church, there are diverse functions and responsibilities.

2. *As a lay person, what is your distinct role and responsibility in the Church? Describe specific ways in which you can fulfill these responsibilities.* Living in the world, the laity are called by God to work for the sanctification of the neighborhood and the world like a leaven, from within, by carrying out their proper tasks according to the spirit of the Gospel. Some important ways in which lay people can fulfill their distinct mission in the Church are by learning the faith, developing a prayer and sacramental life, investing in family and community life, and doing all their work as best as they can for God's sake, while making sacrifices to evangelize their neighborhoods and the world.

3. *Foster a fervent and constant desire for holiness in the fulfillment of your daily duties.*

Questions 160–165

1. *What does it mean to be a missionary? How does a Catholic fulfill his or her task of being a missionary?* A missionary is one who helps to carry the Good News of Christ's teaching to all mankind by word and example. A Catholic fulfills his missionary task by practicing brotherly love, by sharing the Gospel message, and by serving his neighbor.

2. *In the ordinary circumstances of your life, how can you be a missionary to the people around you? Write down concrete things that you and your family can do to bring Christ to others (in your neighborhood, parish community, school, or workplace).* Answers will vary. A Catholic can be a missionary by making sure that he/she allots time to family, community, and apostolic life, especially in the area of evangelization. One way to evangelize is to invite others to formation and devotional programs in the home or parish.

3. *Frequently pray that all Christians respond generously to the call to make Christ known by spreading the knowledge of salvation everywhere and by praying and offering our daily trials for the salvation of souls.*

Questions 166–168

1. *Cite two passages in Sacred Scripture which show that Jesus wants all people to be united in faith in the one true Catholic Church which He founded? What does ecumenism mean?* Two possible Scripture passages are: "That they may all be one; even as thou, Father, art in me, and I in Thee; that they also may be in us; so that the world may believe that thou hast sent me." (John 17:20-21), and "I have other sheep, that are not of this fold; I must bring them also, and they will heed my voice. So there shall be one flock, one shepherd" (John 10:16). Ecumenism is the acceptance of the basic unity of the Church and the effort to make this unity present and visible in the whole life of the Church.

2. *One way to promote Christian unity is to lead others to the knowledge of the one true faith. What can you and your family do to teach or lead others to the truths of our Catholic Church?* Answers will vary. Catholics can teach religious education in their parishes, distribute good Catholic books, pamphlets, and tapes, and support television and radio ministries that are loyal to the Holy Father and the Teaching Magisterium of the Church.

3. *Pray for Christian unity and that all may come to the knowledge of the one true Catholic faith.*

Questions 169–171

1. *Who belongs to the laity? What is the vocation of lay persons?* The laity are all of the baptized members of the Church except for those specially consecrated to God as bishops, priests, deacons, or religious. The Catholic layman's vocation is to consecrate the world for Christ by seeking to transform the kingdom of the world into the Kingdom of God.

2. *As members of the laity, how can you and your family proclaim the Gospel (in word and deed) to others in your school, office, workplace, neighborhood, or community?* Answers will vary. The Gospel can be proclaimed by living a virtuous life, becoming active in community projects, especially works for the poor, and working to make just laws.

3. *During the Mass, offer yourself to God the Father, in union with Jesus and the Holy Spirit, as an instrument to help bring the message of salvation to all people, beginning with those around you.*

Questions 172–176

1. *The Catholic Church is one because her members are united in belief and worship. How can you explain this in simple terms?* The Truth is one. Therefore, those who know, accept, and worship the Source of that Truth—God—are also one.

2. *Do you believe all the truths of our faith and make a continuous effort to learn and understand them? How do you show your loyalty to the Pope, our spiritual leader?* Answers will vary. The best way to show loyalty to the Pope is to read, study, obey, and defend his teachings.

3.*Reflect on the Scripture verse, "If a kingdom is divided against itself, that kingdom cannot stand" (Mark 3:24). Reflect on the lyrics of the song "One Bread, One Body." Pray for Christian unity.*

Question 177

1. *The Catholic Church is holy in spite of the sins of its members. Why?* The Catholic Church is holy in spite of the sins of its members because its founder, Jesus Christ, is holy, and the One who animates the Church, the Holy Spirit, is also holy. Thanks to the work of the Holy Spirit in the Church, through the sacraments, teachings, and other graces which He pours out upon its members, the Church will never fail in faithfulness to Jesus and will meet Him in holiness at the end of the world.

2. *How do you strive to live a holy life? Examine your conscience in the five areas of responsibility that we should make time for each day: sacramental life, prayer and formation, family and community, work, and evangelization. Write down the areas in your life where you need to improve in your pursuit of holiness.* Answers will vary.

3. *Each day, renew your desire to become holy. Pray that the Church and her members may be constantly purified and renewed by the Holy Spirit.*

Questions 178–180

1. *In the Creed we pray, "I believe in...the holy catholic Church." Explain why the Church is catholic or universal.* The Church is catholic or universal because it teaches all of the teachings of Jesus, to all men, at all times, and in all places.

2. *As a member of the Catholic Church, how are you contributing to the proclamation of the Good News?* Answers may include some of the following ideas: gather together the members of your family, neighborhood, or community for daily spiritual formation; read part of a solid Catholic book every day for your own spiritual formation; join an approved Church organization in your parish and help in the work of spreading the truths of our faith; share your faith with your classmates, fellow workers, neighbors, and parishioners in your daily conversations with them.

3. *Make a deeper commitment to help the Church in its task of evangelization.*

Question 181

1. *Which passage in Sacred Scripture shows Jesus founding the Catholic Church on the Apostles? Try to find a list of the popes from St. Peter to the present day. Show this list to your family and friends as you explain why the Catholic Church is called apostolic.* Matthew 28:18-20 shows that Jesus founded the Catholic Church on the Apostles.

2. *Jesus willed that the authority and ministry which He gave to the Apostles be passed on to the Pope and the bishops. If you have a chance to meet a bishop, how will you treat him? What will you tell him?* Answers will vary. Catholics should treat all bishops with great reverence and respect as successors of the Apostles. As much as possible, they should assure their bishops of their prayers and support and should obey them.

3. *Using the Chapter Summary Prayer, reflect on the authority of the Pope and the bishops. Pray that the Holy Spirit will help them to be holy and dedicated shepherds of the flock entrusted to them.*

Questions 182–186

1. *Who are included in the Communion of Saints? How are they united to each other?* The Communion of Saints includes all of the members of the Church on earth, in heaven, and in Purgatory. The members of the Communion of Saints are united by the Holy Spirit, who fills their souls with sanctifying grace.

2. *As a member of the Church Militant, or Pilgrim Church, how can you be united to the other members of the Church Militant, as well as to the members of the Church Suffering and the Church Triumphant?* The members of the Church Militant are united with each other by professing the same faith, obeying the same authority, and helping each other through prayers and good works. They are united with the Church Suffering by helping them through prayer and good works. They are united with the Church Triumphant by honoring them, asking for their prayers, and imitating their virtues.

3. *Offer a prayer or sacrifice to Jesus, through Mary, in reparation for sin for the souls in Purgatory. Pray the Creed slowly and reflectively.*

Questions 187–188

1. *Why do we honor the Blessed Virgin Mary and the canonized saints? What role should they play in our lives?* We honor the Blessed Virgin Mary and the canonized saints because they can and will pray for us, and because they are masterpieces of God's grace. By honoring Our Lady and the saints, we honor God their Maker, Redeemer, and Sanctifier. We should keep Our Lady and the saints in mind continually so that we can begin to cultivate their friendship on earth—the same fellowship that we hope to enjoy forever in Heaven.

2. *Do you have a favorite saint? How can you imitate your favorite saint's virtues in your daily life?* Answers will vary. We should read and meditate on the lives of the saints and ask for their prayers, especially for growth in the virtues and the gifts of the Holy Spirit.

3. *Start a novena to your favorite saint. Pray for the conversion of sinners and for world peace.*

Question 189

1. *Jesus is the Lamb of God who takes away the sins of the world. What does this mean?* When we say that Jesus is the Lamb of God who takes away the sins of the world, we mean that by His suffering and death, Jesus bore the just punishment for all the sins of mankind and merited the grace of a share in God's life for all who believe and obey Him.

2. *Think of the people, situations, or circumstances that usually lead you to sin. How can you avoid these occasions of sin so that you can remain in the state of sanctifying grace? (Do not discuss your answers with anyone except with a priest in confession.)*

3. *Reflect on Isaiah 1:18 and 54:10. Examine your conscience to see whether you have committed any grave, or mortal, sin. If so, go to confession as soon as possible to receive God's forgiveness. Make it a habit to examine your conscience every night and conclude with a perfect Act of Contrition for the sins that you have committed during the day.*

#J2-346-2

APPENDIX B

Thought Provokers Answer Key

by Fr. Burns K. Seeley, Ph.D.

Question 1

A. Where in the Bible is it taught that God is the supreme Being?

See, for example, Psalm 95:3—"For the Lord is a great God, and a great King above all gods"; Psalm 135:5—"For I know that the Lord is great; and that our Lord is above all gods;" and Revelation 21:6—"And he said to me, 'It is done! I am the Alpha and Omega, the Beginning and the End....'"

B. By the use of reason alone, how can we conclude that God is the Supreme Being in the universe?

One of the most convincing reasons for concluding that God is the Supreme Being in the universe is as follows: Everything in the universe, whether in the outer reaches of space, or visible to the naked eye on earth, or visible only through the lens of an electron microscope, makes up an orderly whole. This amazing unity among such diversity can only be reasonably explained by the existence of a Supreme Intelligent Being, Whom we call God. This argument for the existence of a Supreme Being has been given by individuals of great intelligence since ancient times (cf. Address of Pope Pius XII to the Pontifical Academy of Science, November 22, 1951).

Question 2

A. Where in Sacred Scriptures can we learn that God is uncreated?

See, for example, Psalm 90:2 — "Before the mountains were brought forth, or ever thou hadst formed the earth and the world, from everlasting to everlasting thou art God."

B. How can reason alone demonstrate that God is uncreated?

We can note that everything in the universe comes from something else. We can argue in this manner, from effect to cause, until we come to the very first particles of matter and energy that came into existence. But where did these changing and changeable first things come from? Of necessity, they came from something uncreated and outside the chain of effect and cause [and cause and effect] found in the created universe. This Something we call God. To maintain that the most primitive particles in the universe had no beginning is not a scientific conclusion; rather, it is an arbitrary one without scientific support. The fact that these particles are changing and changeable indicates that they are derived from something else. Only something unchanging and unchangeable can be said to have always existed. To argue that all changing and changeable matter and energy have been eternally coming into existence in an unending chain of cause and effect, especially an intelligent and orderly chain of cause and effect, is unreasonable. And it is most certainly an unscientific conclusion.

Question 3

A. Where in the Bible does it say that there is only one God?

See Deuteronomy 4:39 — "Know therefore this day, and lay it to your heart, that the Lord is God in heaven above and on the earth beneath; there is no other."

B. Is it reasonable to say that there is only one God?

Yes. As was shown above, the universe indicates that there is an ultimate First Cause to explain its existence and unity. Experience shows that where disunity does exist (in the moral order, for example), it is due not to the existence of another Supreme Being (which is a contradiction in terms), but to the abuse of created, not uncreated, freedom.

Where apparent disunity exists in the physical order (earthquakes, for instance), we can reasonably conclude that they are not disruptive of the unity in the universe as a whole. Moreover, the forces that cause such apparent disunity are quite often (and perhaps most often) derived from the ultimate unifying force of the universe, namely God. Consequently, in these latter instances, what is perceived as disunity by us is not so in the eyes of the Creator.

On a purely human level, a snow storm, for example, is viewed differently by a trucker and by a skier. And prolonged hot, dry weather is viewed differently by a farmer and by a seaside resorter. In other words, what appears to be an "evil" to one person, on the purely physical plane, is not necessarily viewed as such by another. And in some instances, (for example, soil erosion, and certain illnesses), the improper use of created human freedom is directly to blame. — It can be seen that the above examples support the reasonableness of the existence of only one God.

Question 4

How can you explain that there must be a God who "started it all"?

If you had never heard of computers before, and someone showed you one (and explained how it worked, demonstrated some of the many intricate problems it could solve) and then showed you a detailed diagram of its inner workings, would you conclude that no one had designed it and made it, or that it just happened to come together by chance? If so, you would be very unreasonable in your conclusions.

By the same token, what sort of conclusion might you reach about the origin of the human body, if someone pointed out to you its vast complexity and at the same time demonstrated the harmonious working of its parts? Could you reasonably conclude that nothing intelligent had designed and created it?

Now for the sake of argument, what if you insisted that God did not exist; how would you then explain the vast complexity and harmonious workings of the human being?

Question 5

What is a spirit?

A spirit means something which has no body (incorporeal). There is nothing subject to corruption or decay. A spirit is immortal by nature.

Question 6

What do we mean when we speak of God's perfections?

God's perfections are those qualities or attributes which He possesses to the infinite degree. These attributes are infinite since each is identical to the very infinite and unchangeable essence of God. (God *is* love, truth, goodness, wisdom, etc.) Since God alone is infinite, infinite perfections are not found in creatures.

Catechism of the Catholic Church: 213–215, 220–221, 271

Question 7

God is infinitely good as noted above. Based upon your own experience, and from the use of your reason, note instances of God's goodness shown in your own life, in the lives of others, and in the world. (Answers will vary.)

Catechism of the Catholic Church: 41, 310, 339

Question 8

A. What is the difference between God's eternity and His infinity?

God is eternal, meaning that He never had a beginning, nor will He have an ending. He always was and always will be.

God is infinite; that is, He has no limits or bounds to His being and perfections.

B. Our own experience tells us that every creature has a beginning. But if God were to have a beginning (which He does not have), what else would that tell us about Him which would be contrary to the Catholic Faith?

It would tell us that God is in some sense created and that, therefore, He is not really the Ultimate Being. It would also tell us that God is in some sense finite or limited (and therefore not infinite).

Catechism of the Catholic Church: 34, 41, 43, 101, 245, 300, 395

Question 9

What does God know?

God knows everything that is, everything that was, everything that will be, and everything that could be but never will be. He knows intimately every angel, every human being, every animal, every plant, every insect, every virus, every bacterium, every star, every rock, every pebble, every planet, every atom, every electron, every particle, and every other created thing.

Catechism of the Catholic Church: 54, 258, 302–303

Question 10

Where is God present?

God, Who knows all things, is also present in all things. There is no place where He is not. But He is not limited to His presence in Creation. He is also beyond Creation and is completely other than Creation.

Catechism of the Catholic Church: 268, 300

Question 11

If God is almighty, is there anything that He cannot do?

When God is said to be almighty, it does not mean that God can do anything or everything. While He can do everything that is good, he cannot do anything that is evil, since that would be contrary to His infinite goodness. Nor can He violate the principle of non-contradiction which states that a thing cannot both be and not be at the same time.

Catechism of the Catholic Church: 271

Question 12

In what is God's wisdom especially seen?

God is Wisdom personified. He is sometimes referred to as Holy Wisdom. His wisdom is seen especially in His work of Creation and in His Providence.

Catechism of the Catholic Church: 292, 473

Question 13

A. Can man become holy?

Yes, man can become holy by sharing or participating in God's holiness (see 2 Peter 1:4). This is accomplished through receiving God's gift of sanctifying grace.

Sanctifying grace is received through the proper reception of the Church's sacraments and by prayer and good works performed in the state of grace.

The state of grace is that state in which one already possesses a certain degree of sanctifying grace. The more sanctifying grace one receives, the more holy or Godlike one becomes. The canonized saints are among those in Heaven who became extraordinarily holy while living on earth.

B. How do we cease to be holy?

We cease to be holy if we commit a mortal or grave sin. At that point we would no longer be in God's friendship.

We would be deprived of all sanctifying grace. We would no longer be in the state of grace. If we were to die in this state, we would be eternally cut off from God's friendship. We would be confined to hell.

Thankfully, mortal sins can be forgiven by the proper reception of the Sacrament of Penance.

Catechism of the Catholic Church: 198, 208, 233, 695, 828–829, 867, 1033, 1266, 1458, 1999–2003, 2023–2025

Question 14

If God were not merciful, we sinners could never receive His forgiveness and sanctifying grace. We could not become just or righteous in the eyes of God. In addition to avoiding divine punishment, why should we be merciful towards those who have wronged us?

We should be merciful towards those who have wronged us because we, being created in God's image and likeness, are to act as God acts. Since He is merciful, we also are to be merciful. "Forgive us our trespasses as we forgive those who trespass against us."

Catechism of the Catholic Church: 1033, 1397, 1424, 1465, 1716, 2840–2843

Question 15

God, being holy, is necessarily just (or righteous) as well. Moreover, we humans, created in God's image and likeness, are expected to be just (or righteous) also. But the fact that we sin clearly shows that we are not always just. What, if anything, can be done to remedy this situation?

Thankfully, there is a remedy for overcoming our failings in this regard. It lies in our cooperation with God's generous offer of help through means of His grace. We cannot become just or righteous by our own actions alone. Simply willing to be just in all our thoughts and in all our words and in all our actions is not enough. We must also seek and make use of God's grace won for us on the Cross and provided through the Church.

Catechism of the Catholic Church: 211, 410–411, 517, 614–615, 1265–1266

Question 16

Reflect on the following words of St. Paul: "Why, one will hardly die for a righteous man—though perhaps for a good man one will dare even to die. But God shows his love for us in that while we were yet sinners Christ died for us" (Romans 5:7–8). (Answers will vary.)

We are called to imitate Christ. Are we prepared to lay down our lives, if necessary, to bring about the conversion of those who have hurt us in any way?

"Be imitators of me, as I am of Christ" (1 Corinthians 11:1).

"If any man would come after me, let him deny himself and take up his cross and follow me" (Matthew 16:24).

Catechism of the Catholic Church: 618, 2473

Question 17

A. When we reflect on the great goodness of God, especially as experienced in our own lives, it is only right and just that we should thank Him. What is the best way to thank God?

The best, but certainly not the only, means of thanking God is by the active participation in the Church's great act of thanksgiving, which is the Holy Eucharist. (As is generally known, the very word "Eucharist" means thanksgiving.)

B. In addition to thanksgiving, what should the thought of God's goodness lead us to think or do?

Among other things, we should express sorrow for our sins and a have a strong desire to do only what is pleasing to God.

Catechism of the Catholic Church: 51–53, 235

Question 18

We worship God when we surrender to Him our entire selves, everything we are and have, to use as He wishes. Why is full participation in the celebration of the Holy Eucharist the most perfect form of worship we can offer God during our stay on earth?

In the celebration of the Holy Eucharist, we unite our own self-sacrifice to God the Father with Jesus' own perfect self-sacrifice made on the Cross. It is in the Holy Eucharist that this perfect act of self-immolation is perpetuated and made accessible to the faithful in an unbloody manner.

Catechism of the Catholic Church: 1070–1075

Question 19

What is the basis of people's hope for the grace necessary to do God's will and to obtain eternal happiness in Heaven?

It is based upon divine promises. Note, for example, "He who abides in Me, and I in him, he it is that bears much fruit, for apart from me you can do nothing" (John 15:5).

Note also, "He who believes and is baptized will be saved" (Mark 16:16).

Consider as well, "He who eats my flesh and drinks my blood has eternal life, and I will raise him up at the last day" (John 6:54).

Moreover, St. Paul, echoing Our Lord's words noted above, writes that without divine assistance we cannot do God's will. "For God is at work in you, both to will and to work for his good pleasure" (Philippians 2:13).

Catechism of the Catholic Church: 212, 215, 702–716, 1063

Question 20

When men do not place God and His will for them first in their lives, what ultimately becomes their chief concern?

Their chief concern becomes themselves as individuals, a concern which is basically selfish. In other words, they have made the choice that what they desire is more important than what God requires of them.

Catechism of the Catholic Church: 56–58, 1849–1850, 1931, 2094, 2514–2516, 2547–2549

Question 21

By using your reason, can you demonstrate the truth that every person has some desire for God in his heart?

Everyone wants to be happy. Yet true and lasting happiness cannot be found apart from being in communion with God. Therefore, no matter how remote, hidden, weak or qualified, everyone desires to be in communion with God since He alone can grant what the heart earnestly desires.

"Blessed is the man who walks not in the counsel of the wicked, nor stands in the way of sinners, nor sits in the seat of scoffers." (Psalm 1:1)

"Blessed is he whose transgression is forgiven, whose sin is covered" (Psalm 32:1).

"O Lord of hosts, blessed is the man who trusts in thee" (Psalm 84:12).

"Blessed are those who keep his testimonies, who seek him with their whole heart..." (Psalm 119:2).

Catechism of the Catholic Church: 27–30, 1701–1704, 1718

Question 22

Can you trace, in outline form, the history of man's salvation, beginning with the period immediately after the Fall and continuing up to our own day?

A. Immediately after the Fall, God promised our First Parents a Savior who would crush the head of Satan (cf. Genesis 3:15).

B. God gathered to Himself a people, the Israelites, who would experience Him in their lives and discover His will for them.

C. A Jew in His humanity, born of the Blessed Virgin Mary, Jesus came to be the long-promised Savior of the world.

D. By His Passion and Death on the Cross, Jesus merited our redemption, salvation and sanctification.

E. Jesus established His Catholic Church on the foundation of the Apostles, making Peter its head.

F. The Catholic Church, the Mystical Body of Christ, was brought into existence by Christ through the Holy Spirit to be the means through which mankind would have access to salvation and be brought into communion with God.

G. Over the centuries, by the will of God, the Catholic Church has been governed by the Pope, the Successor of Peter and Vicar of Christ. It has also been governed by the College of Bishops with the Pope as its head.

H. Today, the Catholic Church continues to bring Christ, the Savior, to those who do not know Him, through the work of the clergy, the religious and the laity.

Catechism of the Catholic Church: 234, 257, 332–333, 395, 408–410, 430–431, 450, 490, 593, 647–648, 737-741, 760–769

Question 23

Jesus is the Savior of all mankind. Therefore, He must also be the Savior of those who lived before He became our Savior; for example, Moses, Abraham, Sarah, Miriam, David, etc. How can this be possible?

The grace of salvation was made available to those living before the time of Christ in anticipation of its being merited for them by Our Lord's Passion and Crucifixion. God's grace was made available to them because their desire to know and love the Truth which is God. "I am the way, and the truth, and the life" (John 14:6).

(For more information on this topic, see Question 169.)

Catechism of the Catholic Church: 64, 389, 674

Question 24

A. In the Old Testament, God is clearly revealed as being the one and only true God. Find passages in the Old Testament that are capable of being interpreted as referring not only to God the Father, but also to God the Holy Spirit and God the Son.

For example, 1 Samuel 16:14; Joel 2:28–29; Isaiah 44:3; Ezekiel 36:26–27; Wisdom 7:25–26; and Proverbs 8:22–23.

B. How is it possible for something to be both one and three at the same time?

Consider a clover or a triangle.

Catechism of the Catholic Church: 200–202, 214–227

Question 25

How can the mystery of the Holy Trinity be explained in understandable (yet incomplete) terms to a child?

There is only one God or Godhead, yet there are three divine Persons: Father, Son, and Holy Spirit. In a similar way, a fountain having three streams of water can be said to be only one fountain or fountainhead, and yet have three distinct streams of water.

Catechism of the Catholic Church: 254–255, 261–264

Question 26

Find passages in the New Testament that demonstrate the teaching of the divinity of the Father, the Son, and the Holy Spirit, and that God is one.

The existence of God the Father, God the Son, and God the Holy Spirit is clearly taught in Matthew 28:19.

The divinity of the Father is also taught in John 17:1, 3; the divinity of the Son is seen in John 1:1, 14; and the divinity of the Holy Spirit is taught in Acts 5:3–4.

That God is only one God and not three is taught in 1 Corinthians 8:4.

Question 27

The word "Trinity" is not a biblical term. Nevertheless, it appropriately describes God as revealed in the New Testament. Why?

"Trinity" means three or threefold. When applied to God, it refers to three divine Persons, yet only one God. Similarly, the word "tricycle" refers to three wheels, but only one vehicle.

Catechism of the Catholic Church: 232–237, 249–256

Question 28

Who did Jesus say He was?

Jesus said He was God when He stated that He is equal to God the Father (see, for example, John 5:18; 10:30, 33).

Catechism of the Catholic Church: 442, 447, 459

Question 29

How would you explain that Jesus speaks of the Father as other than Himself, yet at the same time says that He and the Father are one?

The fact that Jesus prayed to God the Father and said that He came to do the will of the Father Who sent Him, indicates that He is other than the Father (see John 5:18–30).

There are various ways in which Jesus can be said to be one with the Father. He is, for instance, of one will and mind with Him. But more importantly, He is also one with the Father in that He shares with Him the very same divine substance. Thus the Father and the Son, along with the Holy Spirit, are only one God.

Catechism of the Catholic Church: 240, 2780

Question 30

Recall at least one passage from the New Testament which shows that Jesus refers at least indirectly to the divinity of the Holy Spirit.

Recall first, for example, Acts 5:3–4 where Peter said to Ananias, "Ananias, why has Satan filled your heart to lie to the Holy Spirit and to keep back part of the proceeds of the land? ...You have not lied to men but to God."

Here we see that St. Peter equates the Holy Spirit with God. But He is neither God the Father nor God the Son (see Matthew 28:19).

Now read John 14:16–17, 26. These two passages, in conjunction with Matthew 28:19, at least indirectly reveal that Jesus taught that the Holy Spirit is also God.

Catechism of the Catholic Church: 685, 689, 731

Question 31

Note the simple language Jesus used to teach us about the Most Holy Trinity, the greatest of all mysteries. What can parents and other teachers learn from this approach to teaching?

Among other things parents and teachers can learn from Jesus' teaching that difficult concepts can be taught in simple language so that even young children can quite often get at least a basic understanding of what is being taught. Jesus conveyed abstract ideas by using comparisons of objects and situations familiar to His listeners. Moreover, he used easy-to-understand stories (or parables) to teach about God and man.

Small children should not be underestimated when it comes to their ability to grasp truths about God and human nature. We should remember that some of their very first questions deal with who God is, where they came from, and the meanings of life and death. For the most part, they would not ask such questions if they did not have at least some ability to understand the correct answers to them. This is why using Jesus' method of teaching is extremely helpful.

Catechism of the Catholic Church: 4–10, 426, 1074–1075, 2226, 1697–1698, 2688

Question 32

A. God the Father begot God the Son, but He did not create Him. What is the difference between begetting and creating?

They can mean the same thing, but in the case of the Holy Trinity, God the Son is eternally generated, or born, or begotten from God the Father, but not made or created by Him. As we say in the Nicene Creed of God the Son, "begotten, not made."

B. If, contrary to fact, the Father created the Son, would the Son be divine?

Definitely not. He would be only a creature. On the other hand, when God the Son became incarnate in the womb of the Blessed Virgin Mary, His human nature, like ours, was created, but without His losing His uncreated and eternal divine nature.

Catechism of the Catholic Church: 242, 246, 254, 437, 461–465, 467

Question 33

With respect to mankind, what did God the Son do that was not done by either God the Father or God the Holy Spirit?

Only God the Son became incarnate. That is, He alone became man, while at the same time remaining fully God.

Catechism of the Catholic Church: 461–464

Question 34

We should refer to God the Holy Spirit as "He" and not "it." Why?

We should never refer to God the Holy Spirit as "it" since He is God, a divine Person and not an impersonal force.

Catechism of the Catholic Church: 253–256, 689–690

Question 35

A. Think of three or four ways in which we can honor the Holy Trinity.

(1) Striving always to do God's will in the course of our daily living.

(2) Respectfully praying, "Glory be to the Father, and to the Son, and to the Holy Spirit."

(3) Sharing with others the Trinitarian Faith as taught by the Catholic Church.

(4) Making acts of reparation on behalf of those who blaspheme or deny the Holy Trinity.

B. Of all the things we are capable of doing with divine help, what do you think would be most pleasing to the Holy Trinity?

Consciously striving to do God's will at all times for His honor and glory.

Catechism of the Catholic Church: 904–907, 1701–1715

Question 36

God has created all things, visible and invisible; seen and unseen. This being true, in what sense can we say that God creates a baby or a giraffe or an oak tree?

At the first moment of Creation, God brought into existence, "out of nothing," the entire universe, and everything within it, directly and immediately. In other words, He was the direct cause of all that existed outside of Himself. Now, however, God brings a vast variety of things into existence through what are called secondary causes; that is, through the laws of nature; laws which He also created. Thus new trees come into existence not directly by the hand of God, but indirectly, from the seeds of parent trees. And God indirectly brings mammals into existence by means of sexual reproduction. Here, God, while remaining the primary cause of existence, is not the immediate or direct cause but the mediate or indirect cause of existence.

The intellectual or rational souls of human beings, on the other hand, are directly and immediately created by God, while their bodies are indirectly created by Him through His secondary causality of sexual reproduction.

God creates and infuses ("pours in") an individual soul into its body at the very moment the body is created.

Catechism of the Catholic Church: 306–308, 366

Question 37

When we see the beautiful order and harmony in Creation, we naturally see reflected in it something of the mind of the Maker. On the other hand, we are accustomed to hearing today that such and such a thing is a product of evolution. Doesn't this explanation simply by-pass the question of who made the process of evolution, assuming that there may well be elements of truth in some of the various evolutionary theories?

Saying that creatures are the result of evolution is like saying cars are the product of an assembly line. It tells us absolutely nothing about the maker, manufacturer, designers and engineers of both the cars and the assembly lines.

Catechism of the Catholic Church: 306–308

Question 38

We fallen creatures quite often think of salvation only in terms of being saved from sin and hell; more importantly, we are saved for something. What?

We are saved, namely, for God, and for sharing in His happiness for all eternity. This is the end for which mankind and the angels were first created.

God's plan for our salvation was at work in the universe from the first moment of its creation. Creation itself, for instance, points to God its Maker. This fact, known by God from all eternity, would later help many fallen humans recognize the One to whom they owe their primary allegiance (cf. Romans 1:18–20).

Catechism of the Catholic Church: 289, 332, 349

Question 39

A. Angels, since they can't be seen, are often said not to exist. Does the mere fact that something can't be seen mean that it does not exist?

Of course not.

B. What are some invisible things which scientists say exist?

Some examples of invisible things are air, electricity, sound waves, and the created processes which ultimately govern plant and animal growth.

C. Can scientists, using scientific methods, demonstrate the existence of the human will and the human intellect?

No, they cannot, since scientists (as we normally think of them) deal only with the material world. The human will and intellect, on the other hand, are not only invisible but are spiritual, and are therefore not part of the material universe.

D. Could scientists prove that angels exist?

No. Using the scientific method, scientists could only conclude that there is no scientific evidence that angels exist, since angels are spiritual and not material.

Catechism of the Catholic Church: 32, 42, 142, 325, 331

Question 40

A. What advantages and gifts do the good angels have which are not present in the evil angels?

Unlike the demons (or fallen angels), good angels enjoy God's presence and love. Good angels, who are always in the state of supernatural grace, constantly exercise the gift of charity and are immensely and perfectly happy.

B. What advantages are there in establishing a friendship with your God-given guardian angel?

The more familiar (i.e., the more friendly) a person becomes with his or her guardian angel, the more that person will be helped on the road to increased sanctity. "Have confidence in your guardian angel. Treat him as a lifelong friend — that is what he is — and he will render you a thousand services in ordinary affairs each day" (St. Josemaria Escriva, *The Way*, no. 562).

In his book, *Rise, Let us be on our Way*, Pope John Paul II speaks of his devotion to his guardian angel. He says: "I have a special devotion to my Guardian Angel. Probably like all children, during my childhood I would often pray: 'Angel of God, my guardian, be always with me...always stand ready to help me, guard my soul and my body...' My Guardian Angel knows what I am doing. My faith in him, in his protective presence, continues to grow deeper and deeper."

In his general audience of August 6th,1986, Pope John Paul II confirmed the importance of our Guardian Angels by stating: "the Church *confesses her faith* in the guardian angels, venerating them in the liturgy with an appropriate feast and recommending recourse to their protection by frequent prayer, as in the invocation 'Angel of God.' This prayer seems to draw on the treasure of the beautiful words of St. Basil: 'Every one of the faithful has beside him an angel as tutor and pastor, to lead him to life' (cf. St. Basil, Adv. Eunonium, III, 1; cf. also St. Thomas, Summa Theol. I, q.11, a.3)."

Catechism of the Catholic Church: 331, 335–336

Question 41

Can you think of any reason or reasons why Jesus is not the Savior of the good angels?

He is not their Savior, basically, because the good angels never sinned; confirmed, or preserved, in the state of sanctifying grace after freely surrendering themselves to God, the good angels entered Heaven. Consequently, they never had the need of a savior. On the other hand, Jesus is their Lord and King, Whom they constantly adore and obey.

Catechism of the Catholic Church: 392–393

Question 42

A. Compare the two Creation accounts found in the first two chapters of Genesis. With respect to the creation of man, how are the two accounts similar and how do they differ?

They are similar in that both teach that God is man's Creator. They basically differ in that the first account states that man was made after the rest of the visible creation came into existence, whereas the second account portrays man being created prior to the plants and animals.

B. Even though these two accounts seem to contradict one another from a strictly scientific point of view, they both teach basic truths about God and man. What are some of the more important truths?

God created the universe, which reflects His goodness. Man is created in God's image and likeness in the sense that he has the powers of rational thought and a free will. Man can enjoy God's blessing and friendship. God instituted marriage.

C. Stories such as *Moby Dick* and *Tom Sawyer* are labeled as fiction, yet they contain basic truths about human nature. How do Jesus' parables compare to these stories?

Jesus' parables are also stories which convey basic truths about human nature, in addition to truths about God.

D. Can there possibly be a similarity between the two Genesis Creation accounts and Jesus' parables? If so, what do you think it might be?

The two Genesis accounts of Creation, like Jesus' parables, need not be taken as literally true, but they both illustrate truths that we need to know about God and our relationship with Him, both in this life and in the next.

The Creation accounts in Genesis are theological accounts of Creation. They are not scientific accounts or explanations; nor are they metaphysical or philosophical accounts or explanations. The two Creation accounts or stories simply tell us the basic facts that God made the universe, including man—who subsequently rebelled against his Maker and departed from His friendship. We are neither given a historical account of these occurrences in the sense that they were given to us by eye-witnesses, nor are we given scientific or philosophical explanations of how Creation occurred. As a matter of fact, the empirical sciences, by their very nature, cannot tell us how the universe was created. They can only properly deal with the universe as an existing reality. Once an empirical scientist, such as a physicist or biologist, starts speculating about the origins of the universe, he is doing so outside of the competency of his field of scientific inquiry.

Similarly, once a theologian begins to speculate about the physical nature of the universe; about how it was formed, and the chronological aspects of that formation, he is no longer speculating as a theologian. Such speculation does not belong to the field of theology.

With the above in mind, we should not be surprised that the two theological accounts of Creation found in Genesis are not scientific accounts.

Catechism of the Catholic Church: 342–343, 355–357, 362, 369–373

Question 43

A. In what ways can our bodily acts reflect the image and likeness of God?

Our bodily acts reflect the image and likeness of God when, for instance, we perform honest work, when we pray, and when we help those in need who cannot help themselves.

B. In what ways can our bodily acts reflect Satan?

Our bodily acts reflect Satan when, for instance, we perform dishonest or immoral work, when we lie or speak maliciously about others, and when we refuse to help those in need when we can easily do so.

Catechism of the Catholic Church: 1032, 1430, 1438, 1458–1460, 1473, 1478, 1626, 1697, 1815, 1821, 1852–1853, 1964, 2008, 2044, 2186, 2447, 2516, 2745

Question 44

A. What are some of the principal differences between the soul and the body in human beings?

The soul, often called the "substantial form" of the body by philosophers and theologians, is that which makes human beings distinctively human. Unlike the body, the soul is directly created by God. It is entirely spiritual, and therefore is not subject to corruption; thus it is immortal by nature. The intellect and free will, not found in other creatures with bodies, are the highest faculties of the soul.

B. How are humans radically different from all other animals in terms of what we can do?

Unlike other mammals, human beings are not governed solely by instinct. The so-called intelligent mammals, such as various species of apes and porpoises, are like very sophisticated computers which react rather predictably to given input data or stimuli. Human beings, on the other hand, have the capacity to make rational decisions; they have the ability to solve intricate problems; they can reflect on the past and contemplate the future; they have the capacity for abstract reasoning; and they can plan and be imaginative.

Being moral beings, humans are capable of distinguishing between that which is objectively good and that which is not, and through the use of their free will, they are usually responsible for their decisions and their actions. Humans have the freedom to choose their response to stimuli, situations, etc. "Angels and men, as intelligent and free creatures, have to journey toward their ultimate destinies by their free choice and preferential love" (*Catechism of the Catholic Church*, 311).

All of the above attributes of human beings cannot be attributed to chemical reactions, electrical energy, or genetic programming. Rather, they are indicative of independent reasoning (not the function of an organic brain) and a free will. Intellectual and volitional (i.e., willed) activities are spiritual functions, not material or organic. They transcend the body and are faculties or functions of a spiritual and immortal soul.

Catechism of the Catholic Church: 362–368, 1702–1706

Question 45

What effects do the loss of the special gifts given to our First Parents have on our everyday lives (i.e., the loss of the gifts of integrity, infused knowledge, and bodily immortality)?

For most of us, the difficulty of easily controlling our bodily appetites is experienced frequently in the course of daily living. This is due to the loss of the gift of integrity. Moreover, we do not have the gift of infused knowledge, which means that we now have to acquire all of our knowledge through study, experience, conversation, etc. Also it might be argued that the loss of the gift of bodily immortality does not affect our everyday lives as such, but it certainly makes bodily death inevitable.

Thankfully, the aging process and various diseases experienced by humans are providential reminders of the inevitability of death and of the need to constantly seek God's help in order to remain in the state of grace, especially at the hour of death.

Catechism of the Catholic Church: 377, 402–406, 1008, 2514–2516

Question 46

How do you think temptations to sin affected the minds and wills of our First Parents before they fell from grace, as opposed to afterwards? Or put another way, how do you think temptations would affect us if we had not been conceived in the state of original sin and had not fallen?

Before the Fall of our First Parents, temptations to sin did not occur from within their beings. In other words, there were no temptations of the flesh. Also, there were no temptations of the world, meaning those initiated by other humans. But there were, of course, the temptations of Satan, which appealed to the mind and will of Adam and Eve. Unlike after the Fall, these temptations did not tempt clouded minds or weakened wills. With relatively little effort, they could have realized that they were being tempted to think and act against God's will. Also, with relatively little effort, they could have successfully resisted these temptations.

Catechism of the Catholic Church: 374–377

Question 47

How would you explain that the creation of man is the first gift of God that leads to Christ?

If God did not create our First Parents, there would have been no need for God to become man.

Why not?...Because there would have been no humans to be saved from sin and eternal death, and there would have been no humans to whom God could reveal the fullness of divine love.

Catechism of the Catholic Church: 55, 356–360

Question 48

The Church teaches that God is providential. He, foreseeing our needs, provides for them. What are some of the ways that God, taking into account our capabilities and circumstances, provides for our needs (not necessarily our desires or wants)?

God generously provides for our physical and spiritual needs by giving us, for instance, soil and water to raise food and to obtain the raw materials for clothing and shelter. Other God-given natural resources are the basic sources for scientific and technological achievements, such as minerals, plants, and animals. God provides for us spiritually by supplying us with the Catholic Church, the Catholic faith, the sacraments, vocations to the priestly, religious and lay celibate life, and with examples of holiness on which to pattern our lives. He also permits many crosses to help us on our way to sanctity.

Catechism of the Catholic Church: 302–308

Question 49

It is comforting to know that very reliable historical evidence supports the Christian belief in the bodily Resurrection of Jesus from the dead. In spite of this, however, there are those who deny it. What would be some of the implications for Christianity, if contrary to fact, those who deny the Resurrection were correct?

Jesus, Himself, would not have conquered death. And if He did not conquer death, neither could we. Therefore, there could be no life for us after death in the sense of being with God in Heaven for all eternity. Moreover, since Jesus taught that He would be "raised up on the third day" (cf. Matthew 16:21; 17:23; and 20:19), He would either have been mistaken or have lied. Consequently, He could not have been our Savior.

Catechism of the Catholic Church: 638–658

Question 50

Think for a few moments of several ways in which God continuously cares and provides for His Creation directly, especially for each of us humans!

God directly cares and provides for His Creation by keeping it in existence. It is He Who is found everywhere, in everything, and through everything, upholding and maintaining all that exists. As noted above, God especially cares and provides for us humans on the spiritual level through His Holy Catholic Church. He comes to our aid directly in response to prayer and the sacraments.

Catechism of the Catholic Church: 300–305, 1076–1134

Question 51

God, being providential, is constantly acting in human history. How does history viewed in this manner differ from the histories presented in so many contemporary textbooks?

Most history textbooks written today center entirely on humans and their interrelationships, especially political interrelationships on the local, national, and international levels. Also, many history textbooks focus on natural events in the universe, such as the weather and natural calamities, which affect human beings. While histories of mankind should obviously concentrate on human beings, to neglect the crucial and necessary presence and influence of God in human affairs is like writing about dairy cows and milk production without any reference to dairy farmers. Purely secular histories deal with relatively unimportant causes and events, since scant attention, if any, is paid to God, Who is the very reason for and the purpose of man's existence and the most important personage on the stage of human history.

Catechism of the Catholic Church: 303–304, 758–759

Question 52

While God is always present in the physical universe, beginning with the descent of the Holy Spirit on the first Christians at Pentecost, He has been present in the world in a special way through His Catholic Church. What are some of the advantages for mankind in having this particular presence of God in the world?

Quite simply, without the Catholic Church salvation would not be available to mankind. Beginning in and with the Catholic Church, and operating through it, Jesus Christ, Our Savior, makes Himself and His saving graces available to us.

Even though non-Catholics may be saved and never become formal Catholics in this life, they may not be saved except by Christ acting through His Holy Catholic Church. (See the Vatican II document, *The Dogmatic Constitution on the Church [Lumen Gentium]*, 14–17).

Catechism of the Catholic Church: 432, 774–776, 846–848

Question 53

A. What similarities exist between the original sin committed by our First Parents and the sins we commit?

Every sin committed is offensive to God. Every sin is also harmful to the person committing the sin, as well as to all others living on earth. Moreover, each sin makes a negative impact on the entire world.

Each sin is an abuse of the gift of free will, an act of disobedience to God that shows a lack of trust in His goodness. Sin is a morally evil act which goes against God's design for our proper conduct.

B. Can you think of any dissimilarities?

The original or originating sin committed by Adam, the head of the human race, was different than the sins committed by us, his offspring, in the sense that it was indeed the original or very first sin committed by human beings. But far more worthy of note is the fact that it was responsible for the fall of all mankind from the state of grace.

This original sin or originating sin, unlike the sins we commit, was not due to human weakness. Before his fall from grace, Adam enjoyed an ability to resist sin with an ease that fallen human nature does not have.

Question 54

What is meant by the term "fallen" when applied to the human race? That is, from what has mankind fallen?

Our First Parents were created not only on the level of human nature, but at the moment of their creation, they were also elevated to a supernatural state in which they shared in God's very own life. Basically, this elevation consisted in the granting of sanctifying grace, the theological virtues, the seven gifts of the Holy Spirit, the supernatural Cardinal Virtues, and certain gifts called preternatural gifts.

When our First Parents "fell," they fell from the supernatural state to the natural state, accompanied by a weakened will and an occluded or clouded mind.

Catechism of the Catholic Church: 375, 399–401

Question 55

Why is water an especially appropriate outward sign for the Sacrament of Baptism?

Since water is used universally for washing or cleansing, it very appropriately symbolizes the washing away of our sins through the Sacrament of Baptism.

Catechism of the Catholic Church: 694, 1217–1222

Question 56

What similarities can be found between the Blessed Virgin Mary and Eve (i.e., Eve prior to her falling from divine grace)?

Mary and Eve were both created for supernatural life, as were all God's children. However, Eve, before her fall, and Mary, from her conception, were in a state of perfect grace to accomplish this end. They both were, therefore, free from sin and from the effects of sin. They also both enjoyed God's special friendship.

Catechism of the Catholic Church: 375, 493–494

Question 57

What are some of the basic reasons for the sins we commit?

We have weakened wills and a tendency towards self-centeredness (as opposed to God-centeredness) which we inherited from the fall of our First Parents. Also, the bad examples of others often tempt us to sin, as well as the temptations of the evil spirits.

Catechism of the Catholic Church: 398, 1850, 2846–2849

Question 58

When we commit one or more sins, what happens to us as far as our relationship with God is concerned and how should we react to the fact that we have sinned?

If a mortal sin is committed while in the state of grace, God's friendship is forfeited. The more numerous the mortal sins, the greater the barrier (created by the sinner) between the sinner and God. If one dies in the state of mortal sin, God's friendship is lost forever.

While venial sins do not in themselves separate us from God's friendship, the more they are deliberately and carelessly committed, the greater the danger of falling into mortal sin.

The only proper way to react to our sins is to acknowledge them immediately with sorrow in our hearts and to seek God's forgiveness while promising not to commit them again.

Catechism of the Catholic Church: 1854–1864

Question 59

Mortal sin is rightly said to result in the "death of the soul." What does this mean, especially when one considers the fact that the soul is immortal by nature?

The "death of the soul" that results from mortal sin refers to the absence of the "supernatural life of the soul," i.e., sanctifying grace, which the soul does not have by nature. While a soul in the state of mortal sin remains immortal by nature, it is said to be spiritually dead because without sanctifying grace it will not enjoy eternal life in Heaven.

Catechism of the Catholic Church: 1264–1265, 1446, 1789–1792, 1855, 1857, 1861, 1996–2000

Question 60

What concrete steps can be taken in our lives to avoid committing mortal sins?

In order to avoid committing mortal sins, the Church urges us to go to the Sacrament of Penance frequently and to receive Holy Communion often. We are also told to avoid occasions of sin, i.e, avoiding those people, places, or things which are apt to tempt us to commit mortal sins. Nor should we neglect frequent prayer to overcome temptations to commit mortal sins. Our guardian angels and the saints, especially the Blessed Virgin Mary and St. Joseph, are powerful intercessors before the throne of God to obtain help against temptations to sin. Therefore, we would be foolish not to seek their assistance.

Catechism of the Catholic Church: 1384–1390, 1395, 1440–1463, 1803–1829, 2623–2649

Question 61

If venial sins do not separate us from the state of grace, why should we be concerned about avoiding them and confessing them?

Venial sins, as noted above, are always offensive to God, and if we commit them with little or no intention to rid ourselves of them, our desire and ability to resist mortal sins becomes increasingly diminished.

Catechism of the Catholic Church: 1849–1850, 1855

Question 62

A. What effects do our mortal sins have on us?

Mortal sins are, literally, deadly sins since they rob us of life with God in this world and in the next. If we were to die with even one mortal sin on our soul, we will have condemned ourselves to hell forever. Therefore, the Church, as our loving Mother, constantly urges us to examine our consciences frequently, and with a repentant heart to confess our sins in the Sacrament of Penance, thereby receiving God's forgiveness and the grace to overcome our sins.

B. In what ways can our mortal sins affect others?

Sin not only inflicts a wound on each individual who commits it, but on each and every person.

In paragraphs 15 and 16 of his encyclical *Reconciliation and Penance,* Pope John Paul II discusses how each sin affects others. He states: "From one point of view, every sin is personal; from another point of view, every sin is social insofar as and because it also has social repercussions... by virtue of human solidarity which is as mysterious and intangible as it is real and concrete, each individual's sin in some way affects others. This is the other aspect of that solidarity which on the religious level is developed in the profound and magnificent mystery of the Communion of Saints, thanks to which it has been possible to say that 'every soul that rises above itself, raises up the world.' To this law of ascent there unfortunately corresponds the law of descent.

"Consequently one can speak of a communion of sin, whereby a soul that lowers itself through sin drags down with itself the church and, in some way, the whole world. In other words, there is no sin, not even the most intimate and secret one, the most strictly individual one, that exclusively concerns the person committing it. With greater or lesser violence, with greater or lesser harm, every sin has repercussions on the entire ecclesial body and the whole human family. According to this first meaning of the term, every sin can undoubtedly be considered as social sin.

"Some sins, however, by their very matter constitute a direct attack on one's neighbor and more exactly, in the language of the Gospel, against one's brother or sister. They are an offense against God because they are offenses against one's neighbor."

Those who commit mortal sin are often bad examples for others, tempting them also to commit mortal sins. The widespread existence of mortal sin contributes to a morally debased environment, making resistance to mortal sins much more difficult by members of society in general.

Teachers, writers, clerics, actors, etc., who portray mortal sins as morally good or neutral are particularly dangerous since they usually influence large numbers of people.

Catechism of the Catholic Church: 402–409, 953, 817, 1855–1857, 1861, 1865

Question 63

Where is the ultimate, unchangeable, and eternal norm or standard for morally good acts to be found?

In the mind of the unchanging and unchangeable God, Creator of the universe and all that is in it. It can also be found "inscribed" on the consciences of human beings (cf. Romans 2:14–15).

Catechism of the Catholic Church: 1950–1952

Question 64

Are our consciences always right?

Not necessarily. To be right, our consciences must be correctly formed by right reasoning, by divine revelation (Scripture and Tradition), and by the Church's Magisterium.

Catechism of the Catholic Church: 1776–1802, 1950–1986, 2032–2043

Question 65

A. Do we deserve to have our sins forgiven?

No. Nothing, absolutely nothing that we do on our own, or all of the good that we will ever do on our own put together, will ever merit God's forgiveness of our sins, since each sin we commit is an infinite offense against God and His goodness. This is true because we are both finite creatures and unworthy sinners.

B. Why is God willing to forgive our sins?

Though we do not deserve to have our sins forgiven by God, He loves us with an infinite love and wants us to be happy with Him forever. If He were not to forgive us our sins, we could not be received into His friendship either in this life or in Heaven. But in order to have our sins forgiven, the infinite injustice against God's infinite goodness and righteousness caused by our sins must be done away with. Yet as noted above, there is no way, because of our unworthiness, that we could accomplish this righting of the wrongs we have committed against God. Therefore, the Father sent His only-begotten divine Son to become one of us, yet without sin and without forfeiting His divinity.

The self-offering of Jesus to the Father for our sakes, throughout His entire life on earth but especially during His Passion and Crucifixion, accomplished what we could not do for ourselves. Why?

Because Jesus was not only a sinless man, but a sinless man Who performed infinitely meritorious acts capable of undoing all the damage caused by our sins.

Why were these infinitely meritorious acts?

Because Jesus was, and is, also God who is of infinite worth.

Therefore, since Jesus paid the penalty for our sins, which we could not pay, God can forgive us our sins without doing violence to His infinite justice.

Catechism of the Catholic Church: 410–411, 2007, 2010–2011

Question 66

Think of several ways that God leads people to salvation through the grace merited for them by the Passion and Death of Jesus.

God leads people to salvation through those who teach the Faith to them; by the examples of the holy lives of family members, friends and acquaintances; through the prayers of others; through reading holy books; through viewing movies on the lives of the saints; through hearing good sermons; through tragedies, difficulties, and trials, etc.

Catechism of the Catholic Church: 901, 905, 1473, 2634–2636

Question 67

What advantages are there to confessing venial sins in the Sacrament of Penance?

When we properly confess our sins in the Sacrament of Penance, whether they are venial or mortal, we receive grace through the sacrament to lead a more holy life. Another advantage to confessing our venial sins in the Sacrament of Penance is the advice and counsel we might receive from the administering priest to lead a holier life.

Catechism of the Catholic Church: 1457–1458, 1493

Question 68

Is every capital sin necessarily a mortal sin?

No, because for a sin to be a mortal sin, there must be three things present. First of all, the sin must be of a serious nature (serious or grave matter). Secondly, there must be the knowledge that the sin committed was grave or serious. Thirdly, the sin must have been freely committed.

A capital sin may be either venial or mortal. Thus a small boy greedily refused to give his little sister some of his candy. While he committed an act of greed, a gravely serious matter was not involved.

On the other hand, an investor hid $75,000.00 in profits from his business associates with the intention of taking it for himself. As is evident, the greed involved in this instance is grave. For the sake of argument, we will say that the investor also knew that what he did was wrong and that he did so without any coercion. Consequently, he committed a mortal sin, which denied him sanctifying grace and God's friendship.

Catechism of the Catholic Church: 1866, 1875–1876

Question 69

Why do you think pride, or the unreasonable love of self, is a capital sin?

Because pride, to one degree or another, underlies every sin which is committed deliberately and with full knowledge that it is sinful. Every deliberate sin we commit is a saying "no" to God and a "yes" to the sin we want to commit, which is really selfishness.

Catechism of the Catholic Church: 2094, 2303, 2540

Question 70

Jesus was tempted to sin by the devil, yet He did not yield to the temptations, so He did not sin. Temptation, therefore, is not sin with respect to the person being tempted. What is the difference between temptation and sin?

Temptation and sin are often confused, but they are really distinct. A person sins only when he yields, or gives in, or consents to a temptation to sin. The consent may only be within the mind, but nevertheless, this internal consent is as much a sin as a sin committed outside the mind.

Willful consent to temptation, then, is where one's personal sinfulness lies, not in the attraction or temptation that the world (other humans, places or things), the flesh (our interior temptations), or the demonic may present to us. This attraction is only the temptation, not the sin.

Catechism of the Catholic Church: 2847, 2849

Question 71

Name some means of avoiding and overcoming temptations.

We should make every reasonable effort to avoid those persons, places, and things which we know will tempt us to sin. We should receive the sacraments of Penance and the Eucharist frequently. We should keep in close touch with God through frequent prayer and meditation on holy things. We should keep ourselves occupied with doing good works and shun idleness. We should acquire holy friends, including the saints, especially the Blessed Virgin Mary and Saint Joseph.

Catechism of the Catholic Church: 1394, 1395, 2849

Question 72

Why is the Incarnation regarded as the greatest of God's works?

God the Father, Son and Holy Spirit created the universe out of nothing. Yet, the creation of the universe, as vast and intricate as it is, with untold mysteries still to be discovered, is insignificant in comparison to the mystery of the Incarnation. By the Incarnation, God the Son became a part of creation while not ceasing to be God. All the rest of creation can be said to be outside of God, but not the human nature assumed by Our Lord. Here, human flesh is also God's own flesh. God became one of us while remaining God. He who is infinite also became finite. He Who is uncreated became created. What an act of creation! What a mystery!

"[Christ] is the image of the invisible God, the firstborn of all creation; for in him all things were created, in heaven and on earth, visible and invisible, whether thrones or dominions or principalities or authorities—all things were created through him and for him. He is before all things, and in him all things hold together." (Colossians 1:15–17)

Catechism of the Catholic Church: 463, 470

Question 73

As God made man, Jesus had a beginning and was given the name of Jesus. As God, He always was and is. Jesus is known by many titles. What are some of these titles?

He is known as the Word, the Second Person of the Holy Trinity, the Son of God. "In the beginning was the Word, and the Word was with God, and the Word was God. He was in the beginning with God ...And the Word became flesh and dwelt among us" (John 1:1-2, 14).

At the Annunciation, the Archangel Gabriel told Mary what the Son of God's Name would be when He became incarnate. Gabriel said, "...And behold, you will conceive in your womb and bear a son, and you shall call his name Jesus..." (Luke 1:31). In taking on our human nature and being born into a family, the Son of God also took on a human name, Jesus, a name which means "God saves."

Catechism of the Catholic Church: 240–241, 461

Question 74

What do we mean when we say Jesus is the New Adam?

We human beings are made for God and to share forever in His perfect and infinite happiness. But because of sin entering into the entire human race, this became impossible. However, when God the Son became man, He, Jesus of Nazareth, being perfectly sinless, became the New Adam. As such, He became the new head of the human race, Who, unlike the Old Adam, conquered sin and also death, which was the penalty for sin. Thankfully, He shares this victory over sin and death with all who accept His gift of salvation by placing Him, and His will for them, first in their lives. Thus, the Incarnate Son of God came to earth in order to raise us eventually to Heaven, that is, to everlasting happiness with the Blessed Trinity, with the angels, and with one another.

Catechism of the Catholic Church: 359, 396–409, 426–428, 456–460

Question 75

Was there ever a time that Jesus was not fully divine? Explain your answer.

In Jesus there was never a time in which He was not fully divine. In other words, He has always been the Second Person of the Most Holy Trinity, and He always will be. He has existed as God from all eternity. His humanity, on the other hand, did not exist prior to its conception in the womb of the Blessed Virgin Mary.

Catechism of the Catholic Church: 240–242, 464–469

Question 76

"God from God, Light from Light, true God from true God, begotten not made, of one substance with the Father." What basic truth is the Nicene Creed conveying by these words?

The divinity of Christ is substantially and numerically the same as that of God the Father (and of God the Holy Spirit). All of the divinity of the Father is in the Son. All of the divinity of the Son is in the Father. All of the divinity of the Father and the Son is in the Holy Spirit. And all of the divinity of the Holy Spirit is in the Father and in the Son.

There are not three Gods but one God. There are, however, three distinct divine Persons in the Trinity, not only one. Catholics and other Christians are therefore monotheistic, not polytheistic.

Theologians note that there is a relational distinction between the Persons of the Trinity, but not a substantial difference. That is, while possessing the same identical divine substance, the Father is not the Son or the Holy Spirit, and the Son is not the Father or the Holy Spirit, and the Holy Spirit is not the Father or the Son.

An ancient creed or confession of faith called the Athanasian Creed or the *Quicumque* contains the following words with respect to the Most Holy Trinity.

"Whoever wishes to be saved, needs above all to hold to the Catholic Faith; unless one preserves this whole and inviolate, he will without a doubt perish in eternity. But the Catholic Faith is this, that we venerate one God in the Trinity, and the Trinity in oneness; neither confounding the Persons, nor dividing the substance, for there is one Person of the Father, another of the Son [and], another of the Holy Spirit; but the divine nature of the Father and the Son and of the Holy Spirit is one, their glory is equal, their majesty is coeternal. Of such a nature as the Father is, so is the Son [and] so is the Holy Spirit..."

Catechism of the Catholic Church: 253–256

Question 77

What evidence is there that Jesus is God?

There are His claims to be God (cf. John 5:18; 8:58; 10:30, 33). These, however, are not conclusive in themselves, since others have also claimed to be divine.

There are the many miracles Jesus worked which supported His claims to be God. There is above all the miracle of Jesus' bodily Resurrection from the dead. This, together with His bodily Ascension into Heaven and the gift of the theological virtue of faith, convinced His followers that He had conquered death forever.

The Old Testament Jews believed death, the penalty for sin, was eternal. But Jesus, the man from Nazareth, had overcome death and its consequences. Therefore, His followers logically concluded that this unique victory indicated that Jesus must never have sinned. Convinced that this was so, they also reasoned that He, Who was so obviously a man, must have been telling the truth when he claimed also to be God.

Catechism of the Catholic Church: 547–548, 638, 653, 1441

Question 78

If, contrary to fact, Jesus were only a man, what effect would His Passion have on mankind?

It would have been a great example for us of love and sacrifice, but tragic because Jesus could not have redeemed us.

Assuming that Jesus was only a holy man, even the most holy of men, His Passion (and Death) could not, in and of themselves, have purchased our redemption, nor even His own. Only God can save us from our sinfulness.

Heaven and eternal salvation are gifts from our infinitely holy God, and they are of infinite worth. Therefore, there is no sacrifice which a finite human person could make which could merit or purchase such infinite gifts.

Only the sacrifice of Jesus, a divine Person, was worthy to merit our salvation. (Please note that Jesus is not a human person, but a divine person, possessing both a full divine nature and a full human nature.)

Catechism of the Catholic Church: 466

Question 79

In the New Testament, Jesus is referred to as "Our Lord Jesus Christ" (cf. Galatians 6:18), and we also find the expression, "Jesus Christ is Lord" (Philippians 2:11). What precisely does the title "Lord" mean in these passages?

It refers to Jesus' divinity. The term "Lord" is frequently used as a synonym for God in both the Old and New Testaments. Therefore, "Lord" is the same thing as saying "God." Thus to say, for example, "Christ, Our Lord" means "Christ, our God" (cf. Judges 10:10 and Acts 7:33).

Catechism of the Catholic Church: 209

Question 80

One of the clearest passages in the Bible indicating Jesus the man is also God is found in John 20:28. In this passage, St. Thomas the Apostle exclaims to the Risen Jesus, "My Lord and my God." But, in fact, Thomas, having just been invited by Our Lord to probe His Wounds, became convinced only of the fact that Jesus was no phantom. How did this incident lead him to further believe in Jesus' divinity?

He had no doubt that Jesus, Who claimed to be divine, was put to death. It would seem that any belief he might have had before the Crucifixion to the effect that Jesus was God was dampened by His death, which had occurred three days earlier (cf. Luke 24:13–53). But Jesus also told the Apostles that He would rise from the dead "on the third day" (Luke 9:22). Being, then, convinced that Jesus was risen from the dead, Thomas, exercising the theological virtue of faith, readily acknowledged His divinity.

"And no one can say 'Jesus is Lord' except by the Holy Spirit" (1 Corinthians 12:3).

"By means of touch and the sharing of a meal, the risen Jesus establishes direct contact with his disciples. He invites them in this way to recognize that he is not a ghost and above all to verify that the risen body in which he appears to them is the same body that had been tortured and crucified, for it still bears the traces of his Passion. Yet at the same time this authentic, real body possesses the new properties of a glorious body: not limited by space and time but able to be present how and when he wills; for Christ's humanity can no longer be confined to earth, and belongs henceforth only to the Father's divine realm. For this reason too the risen Jesus enjoys the sovereign freedom of appearing as he wishes: in the guise of a gardener or in other forms familiar to his disciples, precisely to awaken their faith." (*Catechism of the Catholic Church*, 645)

Catechism of the Catholic Church: cf. 448

Question 81

Some claim Jesus was only a moral teacher, that is, a teacher much like Confucius or the Buddha who taught their followers how to lead good lives. But what, in fact, does the New Testament teach us about Jesus to indicate that He was much more than a moral teacher?

As noted above, the New Testament tells us Jesus claimed to be God. His miracles, especially the Resurrection, supported these claims. He also forgave sins, which is a divine prerogative (cf. Matthew 9:4–7; John

20:20–23), and altered the Law of Moses which had been sanctioned by God. For instance, He forbade divorce and remarriage which Moses had permitted (cf. Matthew 5:31). Therefore, unlike other great teachers, Jesus taught that He, being God, was more important than His teachings.

Catechism of the Catholic Church: 574, 589

Question 82

Today many people have difficulty believing Jesus is divine. On the other hand, during the first centuries of the Church's existence, there were many who had difficulty believing Jesus was a true man. Why, during this period, was His humanity questioned and denied?

In part it was because there were philosophical beliefs present in the Roman Empire to the effect that the human body, being composed of matter, was either evil or was so inferior to God that He would not associate with it. Christians who held these beliefs often concluded that God the Son acquired at most only the appearance of being a "flesh and blood" human being.

Others had difficulty believing that God could assume an entire human nature (body and soul) without the result being two persons, one divine and the other human. If there were in fact two persons, then God the Son would not really have become man. Jesus of Nazareth would have become a human person, but not divine. So to avoid this conclusion, they reasoned, contrary to Scripture, that God the Son did not assume a full human nature; therefore, He was not a true man.

Catechism of the Catholic Church: 464–470

Question 83

Our deliberate sins, especially our mortal sins, indicate our rejection of God's will. Yet, in spite of Jesus' full knowledge of this rejection, He assumed human nature so that we could enjoy true happiness both in this life and in the next. Why, in spite of our repeated rejections of His will, do you think He voluntarily suffered for us by accepting cruel scourging and an agonizing crucifixion?

In a certain sense this is a great mystery. If God treated us with strict justice, as we deserve, He would not have become man for us and would not have suffered and died for our salvation. But in fact He continually treats us with merciful, or undeserved, love. But again, the question—why?

In large measure, the answer lies in the fact that God sees in each and every one of us the potential for sanctity. That is, He sees in each of us the potential of becoming like He is; He sees us as capable of becoming perfectly happy in Heaven. However, this cannot be accomplished only by our own efforts. Only God could pay the price of our redemption, and only God could earn for us the graces we need to turn away from our selfishness, to overcome our sinfulness, and to grow in sanctity.

An analogy to this can be found in the family. Good Christian parents do not give up on their children, no matter how bad or rebellious they might be at times. The parents will continue to love, discipline and encourage them so that they might become holy. If this is true of parents, how much more so must this be true of God.

Catechism of the Catholic Church: 456–460

Question 84

What does Jesus' obedience to his earthly parents teach us?

"Jesus' obedience to his mother and legal father fulfills the fourth commandment perfectly and was the temporal image of his filial obedience to his Father in heaven. The everyday obedience of Jesus to Joseph and Mary both announced and anticipated the obedience of Holy Thursday: 'Not my will'... The obedience of Christ in the daily routine of his hidden life was already inaugurating his work of restoring what the disobedience of Adam had destroyed" (*Catechism of the Catholic Church*, 532).

Catechism of the Catholic Church: 475, 478

Question 85

Reflect on the following words of St. Paul: "Why, one will hardly die for a righteous man—though perhaps for a good man one will dare even to die. But God shows his love for us in that while we were yet sinners Christ died for us" (Romans 5:7–8).

Clearly, these words challenge Christians to imitate Christ's example of self-sacrificing love for others—especially for their enemies. How difficult this is, since enemies are those who are not liked; often they are intensely disliked. Yet, Jesus Himself taught us, "Love your enemies, do good to those who hate you, bless those who curse you, pray for those who abuse you" (Luke 6:27–28).

Are we, in imitation of Jesus, prepared to lay down our lives, if necessary, to bring about the conversion of those who have hurt us in any way? Or are we even willing to go out of our way in some less severe way to obtain their conversion?

Actually God is not calling most of us to lay down our lives for others, but He is certainly calling us to sacrifice ourselves for them. In what ways can we make sacrifices to help bring about the conversion of both those whom we like and dislike? Would we even do such a small thing, in obedience to Christ, as to pray for their conversion?

There can be no doubt that a clear test of a faithful follower of Christ is the love he has for his enemies.

Catechism of the Catholic Church: 520, 604–605, 932, 1345

Question 86

A. Is there any other Savior than Jesus Christ?

No, St. Peter clearly teaches with reference to Jesus Christ: "There is salvation in no one else, for there is no other name under heaven given among men by which we must be saved" (Acts 4:12).

B. What does the Catholic Church mean when it refers to being saved?

It means to be saved from our sins and from their consequences and to be saved for Heaven, the dwelling place of God.

We cannot obtain forgiveness and avoid sin, however, without the help of God's grace which was originally denied us when our First Parents fell from grace. We, being mere creatures, and sinful ones at that, cannot merit the grace we need to enjoy God's friendship here and in Heaven, and to be saved from our sinful condition. Only God, our Creator and the creator of grace, can merit grace for us. Therefore, only God can be our Savior.

A Buddha, a Mohammed, a Confucius, being mere mortal humans, cannot merit our salvation for us. But Jesus can because He is God, as well as perfect man.

Catechism of the Catholic Church: 432, 616–617, 2006–2011

Question 87

What is meant when it is said that Jesus redeemed us?

Basically, it means that by His whole life on earth, but especially by His Passion and Death on the Cross, Jesus freed us from the forces of sin and death which kept us from achieving the destiny intended for us by God. That is, we were, because of sin, prevented from obtaining eternal happiness in Heaven with God and with the angels and saints. Put another way, Jesus redeemed or "purchased" us back from the powers of evil, especially from the hold Satan had on us humans since the time of the Fall.

In ancient times, if pirates or other outlaws (such as those who exist also in our own day) captured a man of wealth, they would demand that his relatives and friends pay a certain "ransom" in order to "redeem" his life and freedom. Because Adam rejected God's friendship and chose to follow the devil's promises, God not only withdrew His promise of eternal life, but also left us humans in the power of the devil and our own sinful tendencies. Jesus, by His life and especially His Passion and Death, paid the debt we owed to God, thereby "redeeming" us from the devil's dominion. We can see clearly today how Western society, having rejected God, remains in the devil's grasp. How badly we need to accept Christ's redemption!

Catechism of the Catholic Church: 517, 802, 1741

Question 88

In the Garden of Gethsemane, Jesus expressed His natural fear of the tremendous physical and emotional suffering he was about to undergo (cf. Matthew 26:36–46). God the Father willed that Jesus' suffering be so intense in order to make clear how evil sin really is. But the Father also wanted to redeem suffering and turned Jesus' intense torment into a supreme good, for it became, together with His death, the means of our Redemption.

But what about our suffering? Does it have any positive value, morally speaking?

Yes, when we are in the state of grace and join our suffering to that which Jesus bore, we help repair for the damage to the world caused by our own sins and by those of others.

Pope John Paul II wrote: "The Redeemer suffered in place of man and for man. Every man has his own share in the redemption. Each one is also called to share in that suffering through which the Redemption was accomplished. He is called to share in that suffering through which all human suffering has also been redeemed. In bringing about the Redemption through suffering, Christ has also raised human suffering to the level of the Redemption" (*On the Christian Meaning of Human Suffering,* 19)

Catechism of the Catholic Church: 307, 618, 793, 1368, 1506–1508, 1521

Question 89

Who among the Christians have demonstrated the greatest love for God and for mankind?

Those Christians who have demonstrated the greatest love for God and mankind are those who, in imitation of Christ, have suffered the most for God and for mankind. Among these are Our Lady, St. Joseph, the martyrs, and the canonized saints.

It should be noted that one of the tests of a canonized saint is that he or she practiced the virtues to the heroic degree which could not be accomplished without extraordinary suffering.

Catechism of the Catholic Church: 825–829, 1942

Question 90

What sort of sufferings can we offer to the Father in union with Jesus' self-sacrifice in order to help repair for the sins of the world?

The acceptable sufferings we can offer to the Father in union with the Sacrifice of the Cross include those encountered in fulfilling our responsibilities as Christians. They do not have to be spectacular. For example, they can include our suffering encountered in resisting temptations and the suffering we experience at work and at home. Acceptable sufferings can also be the pains and frustrations of an illness, a handicap, or embarrassments. Such offerings are pleasing to God and help make this world a better place to live in. When we offer these up, they become spiritual sacrifices and help draw us closer to God and more like His divine Son.

Catechism of the Catholic Church: 618, 901–903, 1521

Question 91

We have learned that Christ's mission to earth was to save us from sin, death and hell, and also to save us for eternal life with God and with the angels and saints. Why couldn't God have appointed someone like Moses to accomplish this for us instead of sending His own divine Son?

No mere mortal human being could have saved us, not even the Blessed Virgin Mary. Only God could have made adequate satisfaction for the infinite offenses committed against Him by our sins. Furthermore, Heaven is God's home, so to speak. Only He could open its doors to us after they had been closed because of the fall of our First Parents.

Catechism of the Catholic Church: 599–618

Question 92

Although Jesus could have redeemed and saved us in a manner other than undergoing His Passion and Death, why do you think this way was taken?

In addition to showing His infinite love for both His Heavenly Father and for us, Jesus, by His Passion and Death, fulfilled what neither the Old Testament sacrifices, nor the sacrifices of any other religion, could accomplish. Since these were merely sacrifices of animals and other finite creatures offered by sinful men, they could not really make adequate satisfaction for sin.

Jesus, as the sinless God-man, was both perfect Victim and perfect Priest. Therefore, His sacrifice of Himself in loving obedience to the Father more than made up for all the sins of mankind throughout history.

Catechism of the Catholic Church: 604, 612–623, 1540, 1544–1545

Question 93

Jesus told all who would be His followers that they must deny themselves, take up their crosses and follow Him. (cf. Matthew 16:24). In other words, Jesus said that His true followers would suffer simply by leading a Christian life. Why?

Essentially, the crosses or sufferings Christians are expected to shoulder are those resulting from saying "yes" to God and "no" to the three-fold temptations to sin deriving from the world, the flesh, and the devil. But Jesus also taught, "My yoke is easy, and my burden is light" (Matthew 11:30), meaning that practicing Christians can also expect the sweetness of His friendship and experience the purity of their consciences. Moreover, we have the assurance of His constant help in overcoming temptation and doing good (cf. 1 Corinthians 10:13). Nor should we forget that the reward for faithfully carrying our crosses is eternal bliss.

Catechism of the Catholic Church: 2846–2849

Question 94

Jesus suffered with extreme intensity on the Cross, but did He experience it in His divine nature?

No, since divinity is incapable of suffering and death. Nonetheless, it is paradoxically correct to say that God suffered and was put to death upon the Cross.

How can this be so? Because Jesus as a divine Person suffered in His human nature. Thus in His human nature, God experienced suffering and death.

"Jesus' cry on the Cross, dear Brothers and Sisters, is not the cry of anguish of a man without hope, but the prayer of the Son who offers his life to the Father in love, for the salvation of all. At the very moment when he identifies with our sin, 'abandoned' by the Father, he 'abandons' himself into the hands of the Father. His eyes remain fixed on the Father. Precisely because of the knowledge and experience of the Father which he alone has, even at this moment of darkness he sees clearly the gravity of sin and suffers because of it. He alone, who sees the Father and rejoices fully in him, can understand completely what it means to resist the Father's love by sin. More than an experience of physical pain, his Passion is an agonizing suffering of the soul. Theological tradition has not failed to ask how Jesus could possibly experience at one and the same time his profound unity with the Father, by its very nature a source of joy and happiness, and an agony that goes all the way to his final cry of abandonment. The simultaneous presence of these two seemingly irreconcilable aspects is rooted in the fathomless depths of the hypostatic union...

"Not infrequently the saints have undergone something akin to Jesus' experience on the Cross in the paradoxical blending of bliss and pain. In the *Dialogue of Divine Providence*, God the Father shows Catherine of Siena how joy and suffering can be present together in holy souls: 'Thus the soul is blissful and afflicted: afflicted on account of the sins of its neighbor, blissful on account of the union and the affection of charity which it has inwardly received. These souls imitate the spotless Lamb, my Only-begotten Son, who on the Cross was both blissful and afflicted.'

"...Moreover, the accounts given by the Evangelists themselves provide a basis for this intuition on the part of the Church of Christ's consciousness when they record that, even in the depths of his pain, he died imploring forgiveness for his executioners (cf. Lk 23:34) and expressing to the Father his ultimate filial abandonment: 'Father, into your hands I commend my spirit' (Lk 23:46)." (*Novo Millennio Ineunte*, by Pope John Paul II, 26-27)

Catechism of the Catholic Church: 461–470

Question 95

Quoting Psalm 22, Jesus cried out from the Cross, "My God, my God, why hast thou forsaken me?" Doesn't this suggest that Jesus believed He has been abandoned by His Father?

Not when we consider the context of Jesus' words. Psalm 22 reflects perfect hope and trust in God in the midst of what appeared to be divine abandonment. Consider, for example, the hope expressed in the following verse. "...stand in awe of him, all you sons of Israel! For he has not despised or abhorred the affliction of the afflicted; and he has not hid his face from him, but has heard, when he cried to him" (verses 23–24). Since Jesus paid the price for our sins, it should not be surprising that He *felt* abandoned by His Father. But being God-Man, Jesus always enjoyed the Beatific Vision; therefore, even during the worst moments of His Passion, He knew (not felt) that He was not abandoned by His Heavenly Father.

Catechism of the Catholic Church: 603, 2605

Question 96

Why did Jesus die on a cross?

The leaders of the Jews, out of envy and in order to thoroughly discredit Jesus, plotted to have Jesus put to death by crucifixion, falsely alleging that Jesus was challenging the authority of the Roman emperor by seeking to make Himself a worldly ruler over the Jews.

[Crucifixion is such a horrible instrument of death, that even the worst criminals among the Roman citizens were forbidden by law to be put to death in this manner. Jesus, on the other hand, was not a Roman citizen.]

Pontius Pilate, the Roman governor of Judea, hearing the accusations against Jesus, believed they were false. But being weak, he caved in to the accusers' demands, and he sentenced Jesus to die on a cross, after being lashed with whips.

Catechism of the Catholic Church: 596

Question 97

Is Jesus' Redemption available for everyone?

Yes, Jesus died for all of mankind (cf. 2 Corinthians 5:15; 1 Timothy 2:4). But it is up to each individual to appropriate this redemption for himself. The normal way to accomplish this is through the Sacrament of Baptism and then to remain in the state of sanctifying grace.

Catechism of the Catholic Church: 601–603, 605

Question 98

A. What historical evidence is there for Jesus' bodily Resurrection from the dead?

The best historical evidence for Jesus' Resurrection is the testimony of the Apostles. They insisted that they experienced Christ risen bodily from the dead over a forty day period, which ended with His bodily Ascension into Heaven. They continuously maintained this testimony in spite of threats, imprisonment, and persecution (cf. Acts 4).

B. What was their earthly reward for insisting on the truth of the Resurrection?

All of them, with the exception of St. John, were put to death. Would they have been willing to experience these great trials if they were merely fabricating a hoax?

Catechism of the Catholic Church: 638–645

Question 99

The bodily resurrection of Jesus from the dead is a central dogma of the Catholic Faith, attested to, as we noted above, by the heroic witness of the Apostles. If, contrary to fact, the Resurrection proclaimed by the Catholic Church were not true, what would be some of the consequences?

St. Paul tells us vividly in his First Letter to the Corinthians.

"Now if Christ is preached as raised from the dead, how can some of you say that there is no resurrection of the dead? But if there is no resurrection of the dead, then Christ has not been raised; if Christ has not been raised, then our preaching is in vain and your faith is in vain. We are even found to be misrepresenting God, because we testified of God that he raised Christ, whom he did not raise if it is true that the dead are not raised. For if the dead are not raised, then Christ has not been raised. If Christ has not been raised, your faith is futile and you are still in your sins. Then those also who have fallen asleep in Christ have perished. If for this life only we have hoped in Christ, we are of all men most to be pitied. But in fact Christ has been raised from the dead, the first fruits of those who have fallen asleep" (1 Corinthians 15:12–20).

Catechism of the Catholic Church: 651, 991

Question 100

Think for a few moments of some of the implications for you and your family, if Jesus had not been raised from the dead and ascended bodily into Heaven.

You might well think that Jesus, Who was put to death on the Cross, was at best only a moral teacher Who died for what He mistakenly believed in. At worst, you might think He was a charlatan, since He had predicted His Resurrection, which would have never taken place (cf. Matthew 16:21).

If Jesus were not raised bodily from the dead, you would have no reasonable basis for belief in a bodily resurrection for either yourself or anyone else. And there would be no solid basis for the belief that sin and death had been conquered resulting in the reopening of the gates of Heaven.

There would be no Mass celebrated by the Catholic Church, since there would be no Body, Blood, Soul and Divinity of Christ to become transubstantiated.

Catechism of the Catholic Church: 655, 658

Question 101

Why is Easter the most important feast in the Church's calendar?

Easter commemorates Jesus' decisive victory over sin and death. His bodily Resurrection on that first Easter also confirmed that He was the divine Messiah and that all He had previously taught was true. Easter is celebrated by the Church for fifty days, while Christmas, for example, which commemorates Jesus' birth, is celebrated for a much shorter period.

Catechism of the Catholic Church: 1067, 2174

Question 102

Why do you suppose that the Apostles at first doubted Jesus' bodily Resurrection from the dead, even though He had foretold it?

It would seem that Jesus' excruciating death on the Cross, preceded by His agonizing Passion, led many, if not all, of the Apostles to doubt that Jesus could really be the Messiah. "Certainly," they might have thought, "God would not have allowed these things to have happened to the real Messiah."

The following account of the two disciples meeting the unrecognized and risen Jesus on the way to Emmaus would support this view.

"Then one of them, named Cleopas, answered him, 'Are you the only visitor to Jerusalem who does not know the things that have happened there in these days?' And he said to them, 'What things?' And they said to him, 'Concerning Jesus of Nazareth, who was a prophet mighty in deed and word before God and all the people, and how our chief priests and rulers delivered him up to be condemned to death, and crucified him. But we had hoped that he was the one to redeem Israel. Yes, and besides all this, it is now the third day since this happened' " (Luke 24:18–21).

Catechism of the Catholic Church: 643–644

Question 103

The Holy Spirit, through the gift of faith, enabled the Apostles to believe that the resurrected Jesus was the Messiah Who had conquered sin and death. But couldn't their senses and unaided reason alone also have led them to the same firm and certain conviction?

No, only the gift of faith, given by the Holy Spirit, enabled the Apostles to believe with unwavering certitude what had been divinely revealed to them, namely, that Jesus was the Messiah and that He had conquered sin and death. The evidence of their senses and reasoning powers supported their certitude but was not its source.

" '...And they will kill him, and he will be raised on the third day.' And they were greatly distressed" (Matthew 17:23).

"Jesus said to her, 'I am the resurrection and the life; he who believes in me, though he die, yet shall he live, and whoever lives and believes in me shall never die' " (John 11:25–26).

"For we know that Christ being raised from the dead will never die again; death no longer has dominion over him. The death he died he died to sin, once for all, but the life he lives he lives to God" (Romans 6:9–10).

Catechism of the Catholic Church: 644, 647

Question 104

The Second Ecumenical Council of Lyons in 1274, for instance, definitively taught: "The third day He rose from the dead by a true resurrection of the body. With the body of His resurrection and with His soul, He ascended into Heaven on the fortieth day after the Resurrection."

Catechism of the Catholic Church: 999

Question 105

What connection is there between Jesus' Resurrection and our resurrection which will take place at the time of the Final Judgment?

Jesus' glorious bodily Resurrection from the dead is evidence that He had overcome in His body what no other human being prior to His coming upon earth had been able to do. His Resurrection from the dead means that He never sinned. Jesus, the Second Adam, overcame the penalty of sin which is death.

Jesus' Resurrection, therefore, gives us, His followers, hope—hope that with His help we can die to our sinfulness and live solely to do His will; hope that with the grace He merited for us, we can die in His friendship and in the state of sanctifying grace. To do so means that we shall inherit eternal glory with Him, and at the time of the Final Judgment, our souls shall be united forever in Heaven to our glorified bodies, which will be like His glorified body. Failure to achieve this end means our souls shall be united forever to our inglorious bodies, which will be condemned to hell.

Catechism of the Catholic Church: 1001, 1004

Question 106

Through Jesus' Resurrection, what is made available to us?

Through Jesus' Resurrection the fruits of His victory over sin and death are made available to all.

Through Jesus' Resurrection, the gifts of eternal life and happiness with Him are made available to us who belong to His Church. Prayer, the sacraments, and good works performed in the state of grace are the means given us by Jesus to acquire these gifts.

Catechism of the Catholic Church: 168, 1020, 1024–1029

Question 107

What does the risen Lord help us become?

In a word, the risen Lord helps us become and remain what we were created to be, namely, saints. We were not created primarily for life on earth but for life in Heaven. Therefore, He created the Catholic Church on earth, the Pilgrim Church, through which He prepares us for eternal life in Heaven. It is through the Pilgrim Church that Jesus' victory over sin and death is made available to us.

Catechism of the Catholic Church: 460, 671, 769, 962, 1020, 1023–1025, 1474, 1999, 2012–2016

Question 108

What relationship does the Ascension have with the Resurrection?

Jesus' bodily Ascension into Heaven, which He referred to on Easter Sunday (cf. John 20:17 and John 6:62), pointed to the permanence of the Resurrection. Unlike the resurrection from the dead of Lazarus, Jesus' Resurrection signaled an eternal victory over death and over sin (which was the cause of man's death).

Catechism of the Catholic Church: 640, 646–647, 659–660

Question 109

What does Jesus' Ascension (body and soul) into Heaven tell us about human destiny?

Prior to Jesus' Ascension, no human being had entered Heaven. Jesus, as the victorious Messiah, opened Heaven's gates, entered there Himself, and made a place for us.

"In my Father's house are many rooms; if it were not so, would I have told you that I go to prepare a place for you?" (John 14:2).

Catechism of the Catholic Church: 660–662

Question 110

Weren't the Apostles and other disciples of Jesus privileged since they knew Him while he was on earth?

Yes, they were indeed privileged. But so are we who are His present day disciples and apostles. It is true that, unlike His first followers, we are not able to see and touch Him. On the other hand, if we are in the state of grace, He pours His love into our hearts, and we are privileged to receive Him, Body, Blood, Soul, and Divinity within us when we receive Holy Communion. In a real sense, we can have a more intimate union with Jesus than His Apostles had prior to their receiving the sacraments.

Catechism of the Catholic Church: 1076, 1996–2005

Question 111

In addition to the Holy Eucharist, what are some other ways in which Christ is present in His Church?

While Christ is with us most intimately and completely in the Holy Eucharist, He dwells in the souls of all who are in the state of grace, wherever we may be or whatever we may be doing. Therefore, He is always open to our prayers and is always ready to guide and strengthen us as we seek and strive to do His will. He is especially present in all the sacraments, and we can find Him in those who are in need and in those who help others for His Name's sake. Furthermore, we can truly say that He is present in His Church when He is teaching us through the words of Scripture and Tradition. We know His will for us also in the portions of canon law that apply to us and in other pertinent directives issued by the Holy Father, the Roman Curia, and the bishops who are in hierarchical communion with the Holy Father.

Catechism of the Catholic Church: 80, 101–104, 135, 141, 678, 1076, 1932, 1996–2000

Question 112

How can we discover God's particular plan for us as individuals?

It is God's plan that all human beings keep the moral (natural) law, keep the two great commandments of love of God and love of neighbor, become Catholic and obtain eternal salvation. In order to correctly determine God's will in our particular circumstances, we must spend time in study and prayer trying to understand the words of Scripture and the teachings of the Church. Through the Holy Spirit, we will then be able to apply God's word to the needs of those around us, and to the gifts and opportunities we have been given. When it comes to making important or big decisions regarding God's plan or plans for us, we should always resort to prayer, asking for divine guidance, and if possible, seek the counsel of wise and holy people.

Catechism of the Catholic Church: 1934–1937, 2030, 2823, 2826

Question 113

How should we regard Jesus?

We should look upon Jesus as our God, our Savior, our King, our Teacher, our Brother, and our best Friend. Without Him we would be literally nothing. And if we ignore Him, we do so to our own detriment. He is the Way, the Truth and the Life. Apart from Him, there can be no lasting happiness.

Catechism of the Catholic Church: 422–424, 426, 441–442, 446–447, 459, 464, 487–488, 678–679

Question 114

Where in the Bible is the divinity of God the Holy Spirit clearly taught?

The divinity of God the Holy Spirit is clearly taught in Acts. St. Peter, referring to the greed and untruthfulness of Ananias, said: "Ananias, why has Satan filled your heart to lie to the Holy Spirit and to keep back part of the proceeds of the land? ...You have not lied to men but to God" (Acts 5:3–4). (cf. 1 Corinthians 2:11, 3:16, and 6:19)

Catechism of the Catholic Church: 684–687

Question 115

What are the basic similarities and differences between the love exchanged between a Christian husband and wife in the state of grace and that exchanged between God the Father and God the Son?

The love exchanged between a husband and wife in the state of grace is a human quality resembling God's love in that it is personal, generous or self-giving, and fruitful. The spouses' love is fruitful in the sense that being open to human conception, and there being present no physiological or medical difficulties, it results in the creation of a third person.

The love which flows between God the Father and God the Son is not only personal, generous, and fruitful but, unlike human espousal love, is identical to the divine nature. St. John teaches us that "God is love" (1 John 4:8, 16). In fact, this personal love proceeding from the Father and the Son is God the Holy Spirit, the third Person of the Holy Trinity. He is the personal fruit of the Father and the Son's love for one another.

Catechism of the Catholic Church: 1602, 1604–1605

Question 116

How do we know when God the Holy Spirit is dwelling in us helping us to become holy?

We know that God the Holy Spirit is present within us and helping us to become holy when we do those things pleasing to God which we cannot do by our efforts alone. Thus we possess the Holy Spirit of God when we place His Will first in our lives by totally surrendering our wills to His.

Put another way, we can say that we have the Holy Spirit with us when we accept the Catholic Faith in its entirety, including Catholic moral doctrine, and then live in accordance with it by avoiding at least mortal sin.

Catechism of the Catholic Church: 683, 2615, 2650, 2652

Question 117

When does God the Holy Spirit first dwell intimately in the lives of most Christians?

God the Holy Spirit dwells intimately in the lives of most Christians, for the first time, when they receive the Sacrament of Baptism. Thus they are said to be born again as children of God, gaining access to the Kingdom of God and to everlasting happiness (cf. John 3:3–5).

Catechism of the Catholic Church: 1213, 1226–1227

Question 118

On the level of everyday living, how does God the Holy Spirit help us?

God the Holy Spirit is always ready to help us fulfill our daily God-given responsibilities. Through the Church's sacraments, through our prayers, and through our good works performed in the state of sanctifying grace, He gives us the grace to grow in love of Him and to fulfill our God-given responsibilities.

Catechism of the Catholic Church: 739–741

Question 119

In a general sense, where can the Holy Spirit be found?

God the Holy Spirit, along with God the Father and God the Son, is found everywhere in creation upholding its existence. The Holy Trinity is found not only throughout Creation, but first and foremost outside of Creation. This is important to know since God, Father, Son, and Holy Spirit, are not identical with Creation, but prior to it from all eternity, and completely other than Creation.

(Note: also see Question 129)

Catechism of the Catholic Church: 42, 202, 302–305

Question 120

What is sanctifying grace?

When the Church speaks of sanctifying grace, it is speaking of a supernatural gift freely given by God the Holy Spirit to rational creatures (i.e., to angels and men), by which they participate in God's own life and become holy (cf. 2 Peter 1:4). Sometimes sanctifying grace is called deifying grace because it elevates us above the level of our nature to what is called the supernatural level of human existence.

Catechism of the Catholic Church: 1999–2000

Question 121

As the "Soul of the Church," God the Holy Spirit gives it life. What does this mean?

The human soul gives life to a body, and makes it human through its very presence in the body. Similarly, the Holy Spirit gives life to the Church. By His presence in it through sanctifying grace, He enables all the members of Christ's Body to participate in God's own life. He also causes in us the activities of supernatural life—faith, hope, and love.

The life the Holy Spirit gives to the Church, the Body of Christ, is "supernatural life." That is to say, it is the life of grace, or sanctifying grace, which elevates souls (which make up the Body of Christ) to participate in God's very own life. This supernatural life is ordinarily conferred first when the Sacrament of Baptism is received, and it remains in a soul as long as mortal sin is absent.

Catechism of the Catholic Church: 759, 1266, 1988, 1999–2000

Question 122

How can individual Christians help the Holy Spirit in His work of purifying and renewing the Church?

It should be remembered that God always respects our free will. If we want to be disobedient and sinful, He will not force us to be otherwise. On the other hand, if we, the members of the Church, want to be purified of our sinfulness by the Holy Spirit and to become increasingly holy, we can do so to the degree that we surrender ourselves to Him and to the actual graces He offers us.

Catechism of the Catholic Church: 1999–2005

Question 123

Why should we honor the Holy Spirit?

We should honor Him because He is God, a Divine Person, equal to the Father and the Son. Sometimes we have to remind ourselves of this since it is often easier to think of the Father and the Son as Persons than the Spirit, since the English term "Spirit" may sometimes give us the impression of a being who is neither fully personal nor divine. It may also be helpful, in thinking of the Holy Spirit as a Divine Person, to refer to Him as "God the Holy Spirit" instead of simply as "the Holy Spirit" or "the Spirit."

The thought that God the Holy Spirit dwells in our souls makes us aware of the intimacy of God's love for us and should fill us with awe, gratitude, love, and complete confidence.

Catechism of the Catholic Church: 685–690

Question 124

St. Paul says that Christians are "temples of God the Holy Spirit" (cf. 1 Corinthians 6:19). What does this mean?

When we were baptized, God the Holy Spirit came and dwelt in us in a special way to help us to remain holy, that is, to stay in the state of sanctifying grace. Thus each of us became a temple for Him to dwell in. How important it is then that we not defile our bodies with sins. Mortal sin, in particular, will prevent His special dwelling within us, so that we will be denied His gifts of sanctifying grace and charity.

Catechism of the Catholic Church: 460, 1265, 1391, 1988, 1999

Question 125

A. After we are baptized, is it possible to receive more sanctifying grace?

Yes, we can receive increases of sanctifying grace through the proper reception of the sacraments, through our prayers, and through our good works performed in the state of sanctifying grace. The amount of sanctifying grace we obtain depends to a large extent on how well disposed we are for receiving such a precious gift.

B. What are the benefits of receiving additional sanctifying grace?

The more sanctifying grace we receive the more holy we become. Thus, the more we resemble Jesus, Our Lady and all the saints.

Catechism of the Catholic Church: 1297, 1384, 1391–1395

Question 126

Once lost through mortal sin, can sanctifying grace be recovered?

Yes, sanctifying grace can be recovered through the sacrament of Penance.

"The whole power of the sacrament of Penance consists in restoring us to God's grace and joining us with him in an intimate friendship. Reconciliation with God is thus the purpose and effect of this sacrament. For those who receive the sacrament of Penance with contrite heart and religious disposition, reconciliation 'is usually followed by peace and serenity of conscience with strong spiritual consolation.' Indeed the sacrament of Reconciliation with God brings about a true 'spiritual resurrection,' restoration of the dignity and blessings of the life of the children of God, of which the most precious is friendship with God" (*Catechism of the Catholic Church*, 1468).

Catechism of the Catholic Church: 1468–1470, 1496

Question 127

How does being in the state of grace, or sanctifying grace, affect our view of reality?

When we are in the state of sanctifying grace, we are able to see reality from God's point of view. We are able to have a God-centered, as opposed to a self-centered, outlook on life. This frees our minds and hearts so that without fear we can see the truth about ourselves and our responsibilities and be able to love the good wherever we see it.

Catechism of the Catholic Church: 386, 1036, 1997

Question 128

Is actual grace necessary for every good act we perform?

It is necessary for every good act we perform in the state of grace, that is, for every salutary act. As a matter of fact, we can perform no salutary act unless it is preceded by an infusion of actual grace, accompanied by it, and followed through to completion by it. "For God is at work in you, both to will and to work for his good pleasure" (Philippians 2:13).

Catechism of the Catholic Church: 2007–2011

Question 129

A. What does "indwelling of the Holy Spirit" mean?

Strictly speaking, the "Indwelling Holy Spirit" refers to the presence or indwelling of the Holy Spirit in the souls of those who have been affected by Him in a special way, enabling them to enter into the state of sanctifying grace.

B. Is God the Holy Spirit present even in great sinners?

The Holy Spirit, along with the Father and the Son, is found everywhere, even in those who have committed mortal sin and are unrepentant. But in the case of these people, sanctifying grace, the supernatural life of the soul is absent. How is God present? By His power which keeps these souls in existence (cf. *Catechism of the Catholic Church*, 300-301).

Catechism of the Catholic Church: 268, 291, 702

Question 130

In addition to the existence of the state of original sin and the existence of actual sins, what other condition makes men unworthy of sharing in God's own life?

Human nature itself—even if we had never sinned, we still would be unworthy of sharing in God's own life. We humans, though created in the image and likeness of God, are mere creatures. As such we have no inherent right or claim to share in the perfect life, happiness, and love of our Creator. It is solely due to God's infinite mercy and love that we are invited to share in His life. This is a stupendous mystery, especially when we consider to what lengths God has gone to redeem, save, and sanctify us.

Catechism of the Catholic Church: 1996, 1998–1999

Question 131

A person in the state of mortal sin is deprived of the theological virtue of charity. Is this also true of faith and hope?

Not necessarily. Depending upon the circumstances, a person in the state of mortal sin may still have faith and hope. Consider how much more tragic it would be if a such a person did not have these infused virtues, how much more difficult true repentance would be.

Catechism of the Catholic Church: 1815, 1855–1856

Question 132

What can lead people to lose their gift of faith?

Many things could bring about this extremely sad condition, including an indulgent life-style and the pervasive influence of non-Catholic and anti-Catholic ideas conveyed by the secular and non-Catholic communications media. For our part, however, we should take great care not to offend others by sinful actions or by misrepresenting authentic Catholic doctrine.

The late Archbishop Fulton J. Sheen told a story about a woman who came to argue with him that a person need not go to a priest to receive forgiveness for a serious sin. She was so angry with the Catholic Church for teaching this that Archbishop Sheen suspected that she herself was afraid to confess something. He asked her whether she had ever had an abortion. She broke down in tears because she had.

How many people who rail against the teachings of the Church on the permanence of marriage and on abortion, contraception, and other related issues have evil desires at the root of their dissensions?

Catechism of the Catholic Church: 1815, 1827, 1834

Question 133

How can a person lose the theological virtue of hope?

When a person loses the virtue of faith, or fails to exercise this virtue, he also loses the virtue of hope, since St. Paul teaches us that "faith is the assurance of things hoped for" (Hebrews 11:1).

Catechism of the Catholic Church: 146

Question 134

How does a person lose the theological virtue of charity?

Charity is lost through deliberate mortal sin, but also through neglect. A person who does not take some care about his friendship with God and the needs of God's children is in great danger of losing this most precious friendship.

As noted above, when a person commits a mortal sin, he loses the virtue of charity and access to Heaven. Charity is restored through the proper reception of the Sacrament of Penance.

Catechism of the Catholic Church: 1855–1856, 1874

Question 135

How are moral virtues received?

Moral virtues are acquired by repeatedly performing good acts such as honesty or patience. God can also directly infuse moral virtues into a person. In any event, merit in God's eyes is derived from the exercise of a virtue and not by its mere possession.

Catechism of the Catholic Church: 1804, 2006–2011

Question 136

What does each of the four cardinal virtues mean?

Prudence as a virtue refers to the ability to know consistently what is to be done and what is to be avoided under various sets of circumstances. The key to this virtue is taking the time to make sure that all pertinent facts are considered and weighed.

Justice as a virtue refers to constantly discerning what is justly owed to others and also the desire to provide what is owed.

Fortitude as a virtue refers to consistency in doing what is right in the performance of one's duties despite the presence of obstacles and oppositions which make one afraid or rash in his judgment.

Temperance as a virtue refers to the constant moderation of the desire for pleasure.

Catechism of the Catholic Church: 1806–1809

Question 137

The consistent use of the Gifts of the Holy Spirit is said to produce in the soul the desirable trait of docility. Precisely what is docility?

Docility in this context means that being open to the Gifts of the Holy Spirit, a person is rendered submissive to the inspirations of grace. These lead us to deepen our union with God in prayer, and to attempt the more demanding of the commands and counsels of God.

Catechism of the Catholic Church: 1830–1832

Question 138

Is the Church, the new People of God, a continuation of the old People of God, that is, the Jews of the Old Testament period?

Yes and no. Yes, in the sense that a "saving remnant" of the Old Testament Jews, who, as a people, had been prepared for centuries for the coming of Christ, accepted Jesus as their Savior and Messiah. In fact, Jews were the very first members of the new People of God which included Our Lady and the Apostles.

No, in the sense that the new People of God, the Mystical Body of Christ, is an entirely new entity, built upon the crucified and risen Christ and also upon the Apostles, and is open to both Jews and Gentile.

Catechism of the Catholic Church: 761–762, 781

Question 139

Sometimes the Church is said to have begun at Pentecost; and sometimes, with Jesus' death upon the Cross. Why is this?

When Jesus, the perfect sacrificial Lamb of God, died and shed His Precious Blood for us, the One, Holy, Catholic, and Apostolic Church was born, since this was the beginning of the New Testament (or New Covenant). On the Feast of Pentecost, the Church, in her first members, was strengthened by an extraordinary outpouring of the Holy Spirit. This marked the beginning of the Church's public activity.

Catechism of the Catholic Church: 766–767

Question 140

What is the most basic and important gift of God to His Church?

Jesus Christ, Who is the Source of all the other gifts.

Catechism of the Catholic Church: 426–429

Question 141

Does the Bible give us any hint of the existence of Holy Tradition?

Yes. In St. John's Gospel we read, "This is the disciple who is bearing witness to these things, and who has written these things; and we know that his testimony is true. But there are also many other things which Jesus did; were every one of them to be written, I suppose that the world itself could not contain the books that would be written." (John 21:24–25) Also, in St. Paul's writings we find: "So then, brethren, stand firm and hold to the traditions which you were taught by us, either by word of mouth or by letter." 2 Thessalonians 2:15

Catechism of the Catholic Church: 120, 1276

Question 142

What constitutes a valid sacrament?

In order for a sacrament to be valid, four things are necessary: (1) a valid minister; (2) essential matter; (3) essential form; and (4) proper intention. Thus a valid Mass requires a validly ordained priest, pure wheat bread and natural grape wine (essential matter), the recitation, by the ministerial priest of Christ's words of institution during the prayer of consecration ["This is My Body", and "This is My Blood."] (essential form), and the general intention by the priest to do what the Church does with respect to celebrating the sacrament. It is not necessary, though obviously highly desirable, that the priest be in the state of grace or that he believe in transubstantiation.

Catechism of the Catholic Church: 1278, 1284, 1318–1320, 1411–1412, 1491, 1530–1531, 1597–1600, 1660, 1662

Question 143

With the exception of the auxiliary bishops of the Diocese of Rome, and those who serve in the Roman Curia, are the Bishops of the Catholic Church representatives of the Bishop of Rome, the Pope?

No, each diocesan bishop, or Ordinary, is fully in charge of his diocese or particular Church. Unlike parish priests who represent their Ordinary in governing their parishes, Ordinaries, as successors of the Apostles, do not govern their dioceses as representatives of the Pope.

The Pope, however, as the Successor of St. Peter, the Prince of the Apostles, does have authority, granted to him by Christ, to govern the universal Church without the consent of the Church's bishops. The First Vatican Ecumenical Council (1869–1870) taught:

"And so if anyone says that the Roman Pontiff has only the office of inspection or direction, but not the full and supreme power of jurisdiction over the whole Church, not only in matters that pertain to faith and morals, but also in matters that pertain to the discipline and government of the Church throughout the whole world; or if anyone says that he has only a more important part and not the complete fullness of this supreme power; or if anyone says that this power is not ordinary and immediate either over each and every church or over each and every shepherd and faithful member: let him be anathema" (*The First Dogmatic Constitution on the Church of Christ*, Canon, chapter 3).

Auxiliary or suffragan bishops assist their Ordinaries in the governing of their dioceses or particular Churches.

Catechism of the Catholic Church: 3, 77, 861–862

Question 144

How should we receive Our Lord's divine gifts to us?

The Church's Faith, her sacraments, and her apostolic ministry are divine gifts; that is, they are freely given to us by Our Lord for our salvation and sanctification. How often they are ignored by Church members, or receive very little notice or attention. This not only reflects a lack of gratitude but foolhardiness.

What if someone were shipwrecked and he refused to accept a lifesaver freely offered him? We would probably shake our heads in dismay. With this in mind, how much more foolish it would be to refuse Our Lord's gifts which His Church offers us for our salvation and sanctification.

There are also others who want to receive God's gifts but only on their own terms. This attitude is ungrateful and insulting to God.

Catechism of the Catholic Church: 1033–1037

Question 145

If the Catholic Church belongs entirely to Christ, what about her members?

All Catholics, being members of the Church, belong entirely to Christ. To belong to Him means that we are owned by Him. He has made us and has purchased us with His own Most Precious Blood. How much He loves us! How much He desires our happiness with Him in this life and in the next! How much He wants us to return His love by believing all He teaches and by doing what He commands in and through His Catholic Church. Our happiness depends on it.

Catechism of the Catholic Church: 751, 787–789, 1265

Question 146

How should Catholics respect the Church?

Catholics should respect the Church with a very deep reverence and love, since it is Christ's Mystical Body and His Bride. The Church is of divine origin, not human. Since God has made the Church the channel of His truth and grace, she is rightfully called Holy Mother Church. Catholics should strive to imitate Jesus in His respect for His Church (cf. Ephesians 5:25–30).

Catechism of the Catholic Church: 757. 771–772, 808

Question 147

A. The Catholic Church is a living continuation of Christ in space and time. What does this truth imply for us her living members?

Christ wants to work with and through each one of us for the salvation and sanctification of the entire world. We are called to be both His representatives and His instruments. Most of us, however, are not called to reach out beyond our own families, neighborhoods, places of employment, and schools. This is, however, no small task. For many of our non-Catholic and non-practicing Catholic acquaintances, we are the only representatives of the Church they ever see. If our lives radiate our Faith, they will think well of the Church. But if our daily lives do not reflect our Faith, should we be surprised if they should think the Church is spiritually dead?

B. Can you think of several things that Jesus expects of us to reach out to others?

These things would include prayer for ourselves and for those whom God has placed in our lives so that they may come into the Church. We should possess a genuine desire to help these people, as much as we reasonably can, on both the spiritual and material levels. We should always keep in mind, however, that their spiritual needs are more important than their material needs. Active membership in a chapter of the Apostolate for Family Consecration would be an excellent way to help effectively transform families, parishes and neighborhoods into God-centered communities.

Catechism of the Catholic Church: 863–864

Question 148

Can we Catholics be regarded as sacraments of Christ?

Yes, but only in an imperfect sense. Nonetheless, as members of the Church, instituted as such by Christ Himself through Baptism, we are called to be visible signs of Christ's presence in the world. We actually become so to the degree that we become holy. Holy people not only represent Christ, but they radiate His presence through their unaffected piety, and through their charity, humility, and solicitude for the needs of others. Like the sacramentals of the Church, such people provide many occasions for God's grace to work in men's hearts.

Catechism of the Catholic Church: 766, 774, 776

Question 149

In what does the happiness of Heaven chiefly consist?

The happiness of Heaven consists principally in knowing and loving God "face to face." The degree of one's happiness in Heaven depends directly upon the degree of love for God one has acquired in this life, especially at the moment of one's death. An inhabitant of Heaven will also derive happiness from being in the company of the angels and saints, but the degree of this happiness will also depend upon the degree of love one has for God.

It has been said that Heaven would be a hell for those who don't love God. How true this is! Think about it. How merciful God is not to force people into Heaven who do not place Him and His will for them first in their lives.

Catechism of the Catholic Church: 1023–1024, 1729

Question 150

Members of the Catholic Church belong also to civil or temporal societies. Doesn't this fact tend to cause divided and conflicting loyalties?

Not necessarily. It is part of the eternal plan of God, the Creator of all things, that harmony should always exist between the Church and the State, that is, between the Church and the temporal order. Each is ordained by God for the common good. In practice, however, the laws, customs, mores, etc. of the temporal order often conflict with those of the Church. In such situations a Catholic is bound to follow the teaching and discipline of the Church, regardless of the consequences. As St. Peter teaches us, "We must obey God rather than men" (Acts 5:29). Where such conflicts exist, Catholics are called by God to do what they can to bring the temporal order into harmony with the teaching of the Church.

Catechism of the Catholic Church: 1877–1927

Question 151

It is sometimes said that the Pope teaches without error in matters pertaining to faith and morals only when he exercises his extraordinary or *ex cathedra* teaching authority or magisterium. Is this correct?

No. The Pope also teaches without error in matters of faith and morals when he exercises his ordinary and universal teaching authority. That is, the Pope teaches without error when, in the exercise his ordinary day to day teaching authority over the Church, he reiterates the constant teaching of the Church in matters of faith or morals (see section 25 of the Vatican Council II document entitled *Dogmatic Constitution on the Church*). An example of this immutable teaching would be Pope John Paul II's condemnation of contraception.

Exercising his ordinary magisterium in March, 1988, Pope John Paul II said that the condemnation of contraception is "a teaching which belongs to the permanent patrimony of the moral doctrine of the Church...The uninterrupted continuity with which the Church has proposed (this teaching) is born from its responsibility for the true good of the human person" (March 14, 1988, an address given to the Fourth International Congress for the family in Africa and Europe).

The Pope, then, taught that the Church's condemnation of contraception is, like her consistent condemnation of adultery, a part of "the permanent patrimony of the moral doctrine of the Church," which is infallible or irreformable.

The Pope also teaches without error when, in exercising his ordinary magisterium, he canonizes saints and declares certain gatherings of bishops to be ecumenical or general councils.

Canon 750 of the "Code of Canon Law" states: "All that is contained in the written word of God or in Tradition, that is, in the one deposit of Faith entrusted to the Church and also proposed as divinely revealed either by the solemn magisterium of the Church or by its ordinary and universal magisterium, must be believed with divine and Catholic Faith; it is manifested by the common adherence of the Christian faithful under the leadership of the sacred magisterium, therefore, all are bound to avoid all doctrines whatever which are contrary to these truths.

Catechism of the Catholic Church: 880–892, 1576

Question 152

The Church teaches that Catholic bishops enjoy the fullness of the sacrament of Holy Orders. What does this mean?

It means that the full power (potestas) of the sacrament of Holy Orders is given only to bishops. This means that only bishops can ordain a man as a deacon, priest or bishop.

Catechism of the Catholic Church: 1555–1561, 1569, 1573, 1576

Question 153

The Pope, as the Successor of St. Peter and the Vicar of Christ, enjoys full, supreme, and universal power over the entire Church. Among other things, this means that the Pope may govern the Church without the consent of the other bishops. Do the other bishops, in any sense, as successors of the Apostles, share with the Pope in the government of the whole Church?

Yes. The bishops of the Catholic world collectively constitute what is called the Episcopal College, with the Pope, the Successor of St. Peter, as their head. As such, they also may exercise full and supreme power over the entire Church, but never without the consent of their head (cf. Vatican II's *Dogmatic Constitution on the Church*, 22).

The College of Bishops exercises this full and supreme power especially in Ecumenical Councils (such as

Vatican II), in which the bishops are called by the Pope to deal with matters concerning faith, morals, worship and discipline. Each bishop, therefore, has the duty to be concerned about the welfare of the whole Church, and not only that of his own diocese.

Catechism of the Catholic Church: 882–884

Question 154

Who directs all work in the cause of Christ in the Catholic home?

The parents have the responsibility for directing all work in the cause of Christ in the Catholic home. How necessary it is, then, that parents be well-formed in the Faith. It is equally important that those charged with forming parents in the Faith, such as pastors and directors of religious education, take this responsibility seriously.

The most effective place to teach children the Faith is in the home. Many parents, however, are not aware of this. The Second Vatican Council could not have been more to the point when it taught: "As it is the parents who have given life to their children, on them lies the gravest obligation of educating their family. They must therefore be recognized as being primarily and principally responsible for their education. The role of parents in education is of such importance that it is almost impossible to provide an adequate substitute." (*Christian Education*, section 3)

Catechism of the Catholic Church: 1656, 2214, 2221–2231

Question 155

In addition to respect and obedience, how else should we provide help for the Pope and for our bishops, priests, and deacons?

These specially God-chosen men need our prayers. The responsibility they have for the salvation of those whom they serve is very great. It is a responsibility which they cannot fulfill without God's help, and for which they themselves must continually seek. But we, too, should seek God's help for them through our prayers: that they may become models of sanctity for us; that they may be faithful to the Church's teaching authority, fearlessly feeding us with the fullness of the Catholic faith; and that they may faithfully administer the sacraments.

We should not regard our prayers for these men as something optional. They are our spiritual leaders, and we can be sure that the forces of evil are especially intent on destroying their effectiveness. Our prayers will help strengthen them and may well prevent the loss of the souls of some of them.

Catechism of the Catholic Church: 2636

Question 156

Every human person deserves our respect. Why?

Every human person deserves our respect because each one is created in God's image and likeness and is called to live forever with God in Heaven. In other words, every human being has a vocation to be a saint. We should deeply respect this vocation and help as many as we can to fulfill it, beginning with the members of our own families. We can show our respect for them by setting a good example in our words and deeds and by praying for them. We need not especially like them, particularly if they have no respect for God or their fellow humans. We might even rightfully fear them, but our respect for them, because they are made in God's image and likeness, can be a very effective means of leading them to salvation and sanctity.

Catechism of the Catholic Church: 1702–1703

Question 157

In what sense is the Christian family a community?

The Christian family, consisting of father, mother and children resembles the community of the Holy Trinity of Father, Son and Holy Spirit. It also resembles the community of the Holy Family of Jesus, Mary and Joseph.

Each Christian family, like the communities it resembles, has a vocation to be holy. Strengthened by the sacraments, by prayer and by good works, each is called upon to make itself holy, thereby, deepening its communion with the Holy Trinity and with its own members.

Reflecting the love between Jesus, Mary and Joseph, Christian family members have the responsibility of sacrificing themselves continuously with a holy love for one another. The example of parents in this regard is paramount for the good of the entire family.

Catechism of the Catholic Church: 2201–2233

Question 158

What did St. Paul mean when he wrote: "For in Christ Jesus you are all sons of God, through faith. For as many of you as were baptized into Christ have put on Christ. There is neither Jew nor Greek, there is neither slave nor free, there is neither male nor female; for you are all one in Christ Jesus."? (Galatians 3:26–28)

St. Paul meant that Christians being one in Christ, by virtue of the Sacrament of Baptism, are all God's children and are of equal concern to Him. He has no preference for one person over another based upon one's age, gender, ethnic background, social status, wealth, or education, etc. As we learn from St. Peter, God is no respecter of persons (cf. Acts 10:34). On the other hand, important differences in holiness among Christians do exist, and it is these in which God is very much interested.

A street vendor, for example, might be far more holy than a king, and a parish priest could be much holier than a bishop. This could be true because the street vendor and the parish priest are more open to divine grace and they practice more virtuous lives.

The world places a high value on wealth, position, a prestigious education, good looks, etc. God does not. On the Day of Judgment, how much one loves God and how much he has helped his neighbor spiritually and materially will determine his eternal destiny and the degree of glory he will or will not receive.

Catechism of the Catholic Church: 791, 1227–1228

Question 159

Why is growth in holiness, or sanctity, so hard to achieve?

Basically, we find growth in holiness hard to achieve because it involves a continuous struggle against temptations to sin. But God provides everyone who really wants to be holy with helps, or graces, to do His will. St. Paul wrote, "No temptation has overtaken you that is not common to man. God is faithful, and he will not let you be tempted beyond your strength, but with the temptation will also provide the way of escape, that you may be able to endure it" (1 Corinthians 10:13).

Thankfully, the more we struggle, with God's grace, against temptation, the less powerful the temptations become. As we grow in sanctity, God gives us an inner peace that makes all the struggles seem as nothing in comparison.

"Have no anxiety about anything, but in everything by prayer and supplication with thanksgiving let your requests be made known to God. And the peace of God, which passes all understanding, will keep your hearts and your minds in Christ Jesus" (Philippians 4:6–7). To the degree that we grow in sanctity in this life shall we find happiness in Heaven. "I consider that the sufferings of this present time are not worth comparing with the glory that is to be revealed to us" (Romans 8:18).

Catechism of the Catholic Church: 407, 2015, 2725

Question 160

How do we receive the Catholic Faith?

Every Catholic receives the Catholic Faith from at least one missionary. In many instances, several missionaries are involved such as parents, relatives, godparents, friends, teachers, and priests. For most Catholics, at least one of their parents is their first missionary. Did you ever stop to think that the Church would not exist today if she were not missionary from the very beginning?

The Catholic faith is a freely given treasure which God expects us to share with others. We could think of it as a freely given talent which is not to be hidden or "buried in the ground." (cf. Matthew 14:25–30) Many think of missionaries as being mostly priests and religious. But if this were the case, the Church would be able to evangelize relatively few people. Parish priests, for instance, find it difficult to keep in touch with all of their parishioners, let alone to find the time to evangelize non-Catholics, whom they seldom see or have contact with. The laity are those who live in the world. They are, by far, the most numerous Catholics, and they have the most opportunities to evangelize non-Catholics and nominal Catholics, as well as to reach out to those who have fallen away from the Faith.

Catechism of the Catholic Church: 239, 1656, 2205

Question 161

Why did Jesus refer to the devil as the prince of this world? (cf. John 12:31)

Ever since the Fall of our First Parents, those who choose to live without God are, in fact, following the devil's example and plan for humanity, even though most do not consciously do so. In this way, he is their leader and "prince," even as Jesus is the King of those who follow Him. It is these followers of the devil who collectively make up a rebellious world. And it is these to whom we, the active members of the Church, are sent by Christ to win over to Him and to His kingdom of goodness, righteousness and love.

Catechism of the Catholic Church: 385, 550, 2853, 2855

Question 162

How can parents minister to the spiritual needs of their children?

Parents can minister to the spiritual needs of their children by seeing to it that they are baptized, confirmed, go to Confession and receive Holy Communion frequently. Parents also minister to the spiritual needs of their children by teaching them how to pray, by praying with them, and by praying for them. It has been noted elsewhere that parents are the ones primarily responsible for teaching their children the Church's Faith (see *Catechism of the Catholic Church:* 1653, 2221–2226). By their example, advice and exhortations, parents are the ones who make the Faith "come alive" for their children; that is, they show children how Christ can and should be the primary means for guiding all their decisions and activities.

Catechism of the Catholic Church: 901–902, 1250–1251, 1255, 1632, 1653, 1656, 2221–2223, 2252

Question 163

In what concrete ways has the Church shown concern for the bodily needs of people?

Although the Catholic Church is primarily concerned with the spiritual needs of people, she is very much concerned about their bodily needs as well. For centuries she has educated health personnel and has built and operated hospitals and orphanages. She has also been actively engaged in providing food, clothing and vocational training for the needy. For her members the Church encourages the practice of the seven corporal or bodily works of mercy. They are: (1) feeding the hungry, (2) providing drink for the thirsty, (3) clothing the naked, (4) sheltering the homeless, (5) visiting the sick, (6) visiting prisoners, and (7) burying the dead.

Catechism of the Catholic Church: 2447, 2419–2426, 2443–2449

Question 164

How can we speak to unbelievers about God?

Since each person is different, different approaches are often necessary. But our love for our neighbors should include a deep desire to share our faith with all unbelievers, especially those who are our friends and acquaintances. We can begin by praying frequently for their conversion, by name if possible. And when we learn from time to time of difficulties they are experiencing, we can express our sorrow and concern with a promise to pray for them. Rarely will they reject such an act of kindness, even though they may not themselves believe in the power of prayer. When we promise to pray for them, we might also witness to them the power of prayer in our own lives, how much our faith and the Catholic Church mean to us, and what God has done for us, especially during trials and difficulties.

From time to time, we can ask these friends and acquaintances of ours how they are getting along with their problems. If they still exist, we could renew our promise to pray for them, and express a desire to help them further. A time may come when some of these people will not only express gratitude for our prayers, but also a desire to know more about God and the Church. Then we can answer their questions to the best of our ability.

Catechism of the Catholic Church: 899, 905–907, 2472

Question 165

How can the laity help bring the world back under the loving and merciful dominion of God?

In addition to prayer and the evangelization of our families and neighborhoods, for example, the Church calls upon Catholic laity to get involved in the legitimate affairs of the world in order to influence them with Christ's teaching. Politics, civil affairs, businesses, secular schools, the arts and sciences, the social communications media, etc. are all areas which can and should be permeated with Christian principles and values. This must be done so that the world can be won back for Christ, Who is its rightful Ruler.

Catechism of the Catholic Church: 1887–1889, 1913–1917, 2242, 2244–2246

Question 166

Where should Christian unity in faith and love begin?

It must begin with ourselves. Not only should we accept all the truths of Catholic doctrine, but we should strive, with God's help, to live according to what we believe. To the degree that we do so, we become united with Christ. Next we should contribute to uniting our immediate families in Faith and love.

Catechism of the Catholic Church: 1794, 1815–1816, 1826–1827

Question 167

In addition to showing a deep love for our Christian, but non-Catholic, family members, friends, and acquaintances, how else can we Catholics promote Christian unity with them, as well as with other non-Catholic Christians?

Prayer for Christian unity is essential, since ultimately only Our Lord can unite all Christians into His Catholic Church. On the other hand, he expects us to help Him in this undertaking. Besides praying, it is important that we know, understand and are able to defend our Faith as best we can. Non-Catholics, by and large, have lots of serious misunderstandings about what our Church teaches. Not only that, but the authentic teachings of the Catholic Church are often ridiculed by non-Catholic Christian leaders.

It is also very important that we understand what our non-Catholic relatives, friends, acquaintances, etc. believe with respect to Christianity. We certainly should not ridicule their beliefs. Instead, in a charitable manner, we should share our beliefs with one another, and note differences and similarities. If we really know and understand our Faith, we shouldn't be surprised that at least some of those with whom we discuss Christianity, will want to learn more about Catholicism.

Catechism of the Catholic Church: 818–819, 821, 855–856, 1271, 1399

Question 168

Why should we show respect to those who profess good will but who, nonetheless, hold views which are contrary to Christianity?

Those who profess genuine good will towards others, including ourselves, intend no harm. They possess a sense of justice. They want to do what is right, which implies that they are generally open to the truth.

We should never forget Our Lord's words uttered on the Cross, "Father, forgive them, for they don't know what they are doing." The soldiers who were involved in the Crucifixion, for example, were simply doing their job. Apparently, most, if not all of them, thought Jesus was a criminal deserving of the death penalty. They intended no more harm to Jesus than that which they honestly thought he deserved. On the other hand, if they possessed all of the facts in the matter, it is quite likely that at least some of them would have had grave misgivings about putting Him to death. Some might even have refused to do so.

Non-Christians, or non-Catholic Christians, for that matter, who possess general good will should be respected for their openness to the truth. This implies that they are also open to the Truth Who is Jesus Christ, even though some may have false and misguided views in this regard. We should hope that under the proper circumstances, they will accept the Catholic Faith. We should pray for them and do all that we reasonably can to bring them to the fullness of the truth.

Catechism of the Catholic Church: 1930–1931

Question 169

In 1302, Pope Boniface VIII, clearly taught in a document concerning the Catholic Church entitled *Unam Sanctum*, that "Outside this Church there is no salvation and no remission of sins…Further, We declare, say, define, and pronounce that it is absolutely necessary for the salvation of every human creature to be subject to the Roman Pontiff." This being true, how can non-Catholics be saved?

With respect to the Catholic Church being necessary for salvation, The Second Vatican Council taught:

"This holy Council first of all turns its attention to the Catholic faithful. Basing itself on scripture and tradition, it teaches that the Church, a pilgrim now on earth, is necessary for salvation: the one Christ is mediator and the way of salvation: he is present to us in his body which is the Church. He himself explicitly asserted the necessity of faith and baptism (cf. Mark 16:16; John 3:5), and thereby affirmed at the same time the necessity of the Church which men enter through baptism as through a door. Hence they could not be saved who, knowing that the Catholic Church was founded as necessary by God through Christ, would refuse either to enter it, or to remain in it" (*Lumen Gentium*, 14).

With respect to non-Catholic Christians, the Council said:

"The Church knows that she is joined in many ways to the baptized who are honored by the name of Christian, but who do not however profess the Catholic faith in its entirety or have not preserved unity or communion under the successor of Peter. For there are many who hold sacred scripture in honor as a rule of faith and of life, who have a sincere religious zeal, who lovingly believe in God the Father Almighty and in Christ, the Son of God and the Savior, who are sealed by baptism which unites them to Christ, and who indeed recognize and receive other sacraments in their own Churches or ecclesiastical communities (*Lumen Gentium*, 15).

Regarding non-Christians, the Second Vatican Council stated:

"Those who, through no fault of their own, do not know the Gospel of Christ or his Church, but who nevertheless seek God with a sincere heart, and moved by grace, try in their actions to do his will as they know it through the dictates of their conscience—those too may achieve eternal salvation. Nor shall divine providence deny the assistance necessary for salvation to those who, without any fault of theirs, have not yet arrived at an explicit knowledge of God, and who, not without grace, strive to lead a good life. Whatever good or truth is found amongst them is considered by the Church to be a preparation for the Gospel and given by him who enlightens all men that they may at length have life" (*Lumen Gentium*, 16).

Concerning catechumens, who have yet to receive the Sacrament of Baptism, the Council affirmed:

"Catechumens who, moved by the Holy Spirit, desire with an explicit intention to be incorporated into the Church, are by that very intention joined to her. With love and solicitude mother Church already embraces them as her own" (*Lumen Gentium*, 14).

Thus, those who are not Catholics can be saved. But they cannot be saved apart from Christ and the saving graces he offers them through His Catholic Church.

It is our responsibility as Catholics, however, and as the Council stipulates, to evangelize all non-Catholics to bring them to the fullness of the Faith.

"Very often, deceived by the Evil One, men have become vain in their reasonings, have exchanged the truth of God for a lie and served the world rather than the Creator (cf. Romans 1:21). Or else, living and dying in this world without God, they are exposed to ultimate despair. Hence to procure the glory of God and the salvation of all these, the Church, mindful of the Lord's command, 'preach the Gospel to every creature' (Mark 16:16) takes zealous care to foster the missions" (*Lumen Gentium*, 16).

Catechism of the Catholic Church: 839–848, 1259–1260

Question 170

Please think for a moment. In your own family, in your neighborhood, in your school, in your work place, do you know people who are leading immoral lives, who are not regular Sunday church-goers, or who see no need for organized religion?

You can be certain that these people lack the fullness of Truth in their lives. And to the degree that this is so, they lack the peace and happiness that could otherwise be theirs as believing Catholics living according to the Church's teaching. They need God and His Church as much as we do. What steps, if any, have you taken to help give them only that which Christ can give in and through His Catholic Church?

Is it reasonable to say, without firm evidence to the contrary, that we should not try to evangelize these people since it will do no good? What does such an attitude say about our trust in God to help us, even in difficult situations? If he wants these people evangelized (and he does), isn't he sure to help us, if we ask Him?

With respect to lay evangelization, the Second Vatican Council taught the following:

"Laymen have countless opportunities for exercising the apostolate of evangelization and sanctification. The very witness of a Christian life, and good works done in a supernatural spirit, are effective in drawing men to the faith and to God; and that is what the Lord has said: "Your light must shine so brightly before men that they may see your good works and give glory to your Father who is in Heaven" (Matthew 5:16).

This witness of life, however, is not the sole element in the apostolate; the true apostle is on the lookout for occasions of announcing Christ by word, either to unbelievers to draw them towards the faith, or to the faithful to instruct them, strengthen them, incite them to a more fervent life; "for Christ's love urges us on" (2 Corinthians 5:14), and in the hearts of all should the Apostle's words find echo: "Woe to me if I do not preach the Gospel" (1 Corinthians 9:16). (*Decree on the Apostolate of Lay People*, 6.)

Catechism of the Catholic Church: 849–856, 863–864, 2044–2046, 2472

Question 171

The term "salvation" may be rightly understood in a negative sense. That is, when a person receives the gift of salvation at Baptism, for instance, he is said to be saved from sin and eternal punishment. But can salvation also have a positive meaning?

Yes. When a person is saved from sin and eternal punishment, he is also saved for friendship with God in this life and in eternity. And it is for these that he was created.

Catechism of the Catholic Church: 55, 161, 163, 402, 425, 460

Question 172

It is incorrectly taught by some theologians that Jesus did not intend to found a Church. In fact, they claim, it was founded by His followers and is, therefore, not of divine origin. Can you think of any Scripture passages which indicate that Jesus really did found the Catholic Church?

"You are Peter, and on this rock, I will build my Church" (Matthew 16:18). "And he [the Father] has put all things under his [Jesus'] feet and has made him the head over all things for the Church, which is his Body" (Ephesians 1:22). "He [Christ] is the head of the body, the church" (Colossians 1:18). "So then you are no longer strangers and sojourners, but you are fellow citizens with the saints and members of the household of God, built upon the foundation of the apostles and prophets, Christ Jesus himself being the cornerstone, in whom the whole structure is joined together and grows into a holy temple in the Lord" (Ephesians 2:19–21).

That Jesus founded the Catholic Church is part of the Catholic faith. It is true. We can see this irreformable teaching in the following magisterial statements.

The Eternal Shepherd and Bishop of our souls [that is, Jesus] resolved, in order to give permanent duration to the saving work of the Redemption, to establish the Holy Church, in which the faithful would be welded together as in the house of the Living God, by the bond of the one Faith and of the one charity. (*Dogmatic Constitution on the Church of Christ*, Vatican I.)

To carry out the will of the Father, Christ inaugurated the kingdom of Heaven on earth and revealed to us his mystery; by his obedience he brought about our redemption. The Church—that is, the kingdom of Christ already present in mystery—grows visibly through the power of God in the world. (*Dogmatic Constitution on the Church*, Vatican II.)

The Church was founded immediately and personally by the true and historical Christ during the time of His earthly life. (*Oath Against the Errors of Modernism*, Pope St. Pius X.)

We believe in One, Holy, Catholic and Apostolic Church, built by Jesus Christ on that rock which is Peter. (*Credo of the People of God*, Pope Paul VI.)

Catechism of the Catholic Church: 442, 552, 763–766

Question 173

Where does the Catholic Church's unity of belief come from?

The Catholic Church's unity of belief comes entirely from Jesus Christ, Who is the Truth (cf. John 14:6). Other Christian bodies might have a unity of belief as well, but, in every instance, this unity does not fully reflect Jesus' teaching.

Catechism of the Catholic Church: 51, 65, 73, 173

Question 174

What is the basic visible sign of the unity of the Catholic Church?

The Pope, the Successor of St. Peter in the primacy of authority over the Catholic Church, is the basic visible sign of the Church's unity. "You are Peter [Peter means rock], and on this rock I will build my church" (Matthew 16:18).

Catechism of the Catholic Church: 880–882

Question 175

How does being in communion with the Pope, the Successor of St. Peter, in the primacy of authority over the Church, assure her members that the Church possesses the totality of doctrinal truth?

Jesus gave St. Peter an unfailing faith by which he would be able to strengthen the Church's members. Our Lord said, "Simon, Simon, behold, Satan demanded to have you, that he might sift you like wheat, but I have prayed for you [Simon] that your faith may not fail; and when you have turned again, strengthen your brethren" (Luke 22:31–32).

Catechism of the Catholic Church: 880–882

Question 176

The Holy Eucharist is sometimes called the Sacrament of Unity. Why?

Christian unity comes from our belief in and love of one Person, Jesus, our Savior. The Holy Eucharist makes our Savior, in both His divine and human natures, really present on earth again, and allows us to receive Him into the depths of our hearts. By strengthening our faith and by inflaming our love for Jesus, this sacrament draws us closer to our fellow Catholics. Because Jesus desires that all His followers be one in mind and heart, he gives us special graces in the Eucharist so that we may love one another.

This is especially important for strengthening the union that exists between the Pope and the Church's bishops, between the bishops and their priests and deacons, and between spouses and their children.

Catechism of the Catholic Church: 1331, 1396

Question 177

Are the members of the Catholic Church holy?

The members of the Catholic Church are holy if they are in the state of sanctifying grace. In this sense they

also can be called saints, which means "the holy or sanctified ones." This term, however, is usually reserved for those who are in Heaven. We see it used in the former sense, however, by St. Paul when he wrote the following: "Paul, an Apostle of Christ Jesus by the will of God, and Timothy our brother. To the church of God which is at Corinth, with all the saints who are in the whole of Achaia" (2 Corinthians 1:1), and "Paul, an Apostle of Christ Jesus, by the will of God, to the saints who are also faithful in Christ Jesus" (Ephesians 1:1).
Catechism of the Catholic Church: 823–829

Question 178

A. The Church founded by Jesus Christ is not called the Catholic Church in the Bible. Where, then, does the term come from?

Scholars believe that St. Ignatius of Antioch (c. 35–107 A.D.) was the first to describe the Church founded by our Lord as "catholic." In his letter to the Smyrnaeans he wrote :

"See that you all follow the bishop, as Jesus Christ follows the Father, and the presbyters [priests] as you would the Apostles. And respect the deacons as the command of God. Let no one do any of the things appertaining to the Church without the bishop. Let that be considered a valid Eucharist which is celebrated by the bishop, or by one whom he appoints. Wherever the bishop appears, let the congregation be present, just as wherever Jesus Christ is present, there is the Catholic Church" (*Epistula ad Smyrnaeos* 8,1).

B. Is the fact that the term "Catholic" is not scriptural make it less valid than those scriptural terms which describe the Church, such as "the Body of Christ"?

Not at all. Terms such as "Trinity" and "Mass" are not found in Scripture either, yet these also are valid words for us to use, since, like "catholic," they faithfully convey ideas contained in Scripture as well as in Sacred Tradition.
Catechism of the Catholic Church: 830, 831

Question 179

How long will the Catholic Church remain on earth?

The Catholic Church will remain on earth till the end of time. Speaking to St. Peter, Our Lord said, "And I tell you, you are Peter, and on this rock I will build my church and the powers of death shall not prevail against it." (Matthew 16:18) Shortly before His Ascension, Our Lord said to the Church he had founded upon St. Peter, "And lo, I am with you always, to the close of the age" (Matthew 28:20).

The historical continuity of the Catholic Church, based upon these words of Our Lord to Peter, is one of the Church's strongest arguments in favor of its claim to having divine origins.
Catechism of the Catholic Church: 675, 677, 865

Question 180

What one Catholic doctrine is rejected by every other Christian body?

The primacy of jurisdiction or authority over the Church given by Jesus to St. Peter and His successors, the Roman Pontiffs. Can this doctrine be accurately and unambiguously demonstrated? Yes. Careful, objective scholarship has concluded that St. Peter was given a primacy of jurisdiction over the Church by Christ. Even some Protestant scholars acknowledge this, for example, Oscar Cullmann.

The teaching of both the Greek and Latin Fathers of the early Church state that St. Peter bestowed his primacy of authority over the Church on his successors in this primacy, namely the Bishops of Rome. In the early undivided Catholic Church this teaching was found as well in the Ecumenical Council of Chalcedon held in 451.

Assuming that the Roman Catholic Church is correct about her teaching on papal primacy, what conclusion must be reached about every other Christian body?

The conclusion must be reached that none of these bodies has kept intact all of Jesus' teaching.

Catechism of the Catholic Church: 880–882

Question 181

Do all bishops, who are successors of the Apostles, belong to the Catholic Church?

No. There is a large number of bishops who are successors of the Apostles, yet belong to non-Catholic Churches; the most prominent being the Eastern Orthodox Church. Since these bishops are not in union with the Roman Pontiff they do not belong to the Episcopal College. The Episcopal College, in turn, succeeds the Apostolic College which had St. Peter as its head. (See question 153 and Vatican Council II document, *Lumen Gentium*, 23.)

Catechism of the Catholic Church: 838, 1399

Question 182

Catholics are encouraged to seek the intercession of the saints in Heaven. Protestants are not. Why not?

Protestant bodies do not teach with certainty that those who dwell in Heaven can hear our prayers, whereas Catholics are assured of this truth in conjunction with the doctrine of the Communion of Saints which states that the saints in Heaven are able to hear our prayers. That the faithful on earth are in communion with the saints in Heaven is an article of Faith taught by the Ecumenical Council of Trent in the sixteenth century. (Council of Trent 1562, Canon 5 on the Most Holy Sacrifice of the Mass.)

Catechism of the Catholic Church: 956, 2683–2684

Question 183

As Soldiers of Christ in the Church Militant on earth, what are some of the ways in which we can fight sin and error?

We can fight sin and error by knowing our Catholic doctrine well. Those who use this catechism continually and who consult the "Catechism of the Catholic Church", cross-referenced within the body of each question, and any of the books listed at the end of each chapter, will be well on their way to knowing the doctrine of the Catholic Church very well. On the level of living our Catholic Faith, we must be ever-vigilant in combating the temptations of the world, the flesh, and the devil. In order to do this, we must strengthen our wills by daily prayer and frequent reception of the sacraments of Penance and the Eucharist.

By way of direct attack on our souls, however, St. Paul singles out the evil one and his fellow demons. In order to defend ourselves from the attacks, he advised:

"Finally, be strong in the Lord and in the strength of his might. Put on the whole armor of God, that you may be able to stand against the wiles of the devil. For we are not contending against flesh and blood, but against the principalities, against the powers, against the world rulers of this present darkness, against the spiritual hosts of wickedness in the heavenly places. Therefore take the whole armor of God, that you may be able to withstand in the evil day, and having done all, to stand. Stand therefore, having girded your loins with truth, and having put on the breastplate of righteousness, and having shod your feet with the equipment of the gospel of peace; above all taking the shield of faith, with which you can quench all the flaming darts of the evil one. And take the helmet of salvation, and the sword of the Spirit, which is the word of God. Pray at all times in the Spirit, with all prayer and supplication. To that end keep alert with all perseverance, making supplication for all the saints" (Ephesians 6:10–18).

Catechism of the Catholic Church: 1248, 2697, 2699, 2846–2849

Question 184

On the level of marriage and the family, what is one of modern man's greatest needs?

One of modern man's greatest needs is knowledge of what the Sacrament of Marriage is and how it is to be lived. Widespread ignorance in this area has been a principal contributor to divorce and other manifestations of family breakdown, touching millions of families in the United States alone. Certainly, receiving correct knowledge about marriage and family life is not a cure-all. It is one thing to know what is right; but it is quite another to believe it and to desire to live out its implications. It is a beginning, however, a very essential beginning.

In the early years of this century, Western civilization was predominantly Christian and, therefore, strongly pro-family and strongly supportive of lifetime marriages. Divorce and its many accompanying evils were a rarity. Nevertheless, ideas contrary to Christian marriage and family life had gained acceptance in certain circles long before this century began. Only with the communications explosion of our present era, however, did these ideas gain widespread acceptance.

The Popes, in particular, have not remained silent in matters of marriage and family life during this period; but their teaching has often been attacked or simply not made available to the millions who need to receive it.

Pope John Paul II, addressing himself to the present crisis, wrote "Familiaris Consortio," an in-depth document on marriage and family life. Moreover, the Apostolate for Family Consecration has several series of video programs based on "Familiaris Consortio" which are available to the public at a modest cost. These programs are ideal for family and classroom viewing. Viewing these programs and reading "Familiaris Consortio" will be extremely helpful to those who want to learn what Christ actually taught about marriage and family life and how they can be successful at both.

Catechism of the Catholic Church: 1601–1658

Question 185

Many today reject the Church's teaching on Purgatory in favor of the false doctrine of reincarnation. How would you defend the Church's teaching in this area?

In the first place, you might point out that as attractive as the idea of reincarnation might be, it is the result of speculation, not divine revelation.

References to Purgatory, on the other hand, are found in Scripture (see, for example, 2 Maccabees 12:42–46). Reincarnation itself is ruled out in Hebrews 9:27, "And...it is appointed for men to die once, and after that comes judgment." Unlike the doctrine of reincarnation, there is no hint in Scripture or Sacred Tradition of a second chance on earth after death.

"It is the historical and hope-inspiring truth of Jesus Christ's Resurrection that reveals the ultimate end of man. We cannot deny the indisputable evidence that some time or another death is placed before our eyes: it catches up with every man as the final outcome of his existence. Returning to this life is impossible and does not occur. After this life there is a total, eternal transformation of each individual, not an endless, meaningless succession of lives and deaths. Christ conquered death once and for all and we share in his triumph" ("A Call to Vigilance" by Archbishop Norberto Rivera Carrera, sect. 30).

"For the trumpet will sound, the dead will be raised incorruptible and we shall be changed. For that which is corruptible must clothe itself with incorruptibility, and that which is mortal must clothe itself with immortality, then the word that is written shall come about—'Death is swallowed up in victory'" (1 Cor 15:52-54).

In his document *Tertio Millennio Adveniente*, Pope John Paul II explains, "Christian revelation excludes reincarnation, and speaks of a fulfilment which man is called to achieve in the course of a single earthly existence. Man achieves this fulfilment of his destiny through the sincere gift of self, a gift which is made possible only through his encounter with God. It is in God that man finds full self-realization: this is the truth revealed by Christ. Man fulfills himself in God, who comes to meet him through his Eternal Son. Thanks to God's coming on earth, human time, which began at Creation, has reached its fullness. 'The fullness of time' is in fact eternity, indeed, it is the One who is eternal, God himself. Thus, to enter into 'the fullness of time' means to reach the end of time and to transcend its limits, in order to find time's fulfilment in the eternity of God.

"In Christianity time has a fundamental importance. Within the dimension of time the world was created; within it the history of salvation unfolds, finding its culmination in the 'fullness of time' of the Incarnation, and its goal in the glorious return of the Son of God at the end of time. In Jesus Christ, the Word made flesh, time becomes a dimension of God, who is himself eternal. With the coming of Christ there begin 'the last days' (cf. Heb 1:2), the 'last hour'(cf. 1 Jn 2:18), and the time of the Church, which will last until the Parousia" (*Tertio Millennio Adveniente*, sect. 9-10).

Catechism of the Catholic Church: 366, 1013,1021–1022, 1032, 1038

Question 186

It can be argued that Masses, prayers, indulgences, almsgiving and other good works for the Poor Souls in Purgatory are of greater worth than the spiritual good works which we perform on behalf of those still on earth. Why?

Those in Purgatory cannot help themselves by way of relieving their just punishments. Thus, for this purpose, they are completely dependent on the prayers, good works, Masses and indulgences of those still living on earth.

Unlike the Poor Souls in Purgatory, those still living on earth and who are in the state of grace (and who die in that state), can reduce the amount of suffering they themselves would otherwise endure in Purgatory by leading holy lives. Not only is this so, but they can also benefit spiritually from the prayers and other sacrifices that others choose to make for them.

This being so, the need of the Poor Souls for outside help is considerably greater. And the help we render them is more valuable.

Catechism of the Catholic Church: 1471–1479

Question 187

Do all canonized saints enter immediately into the Church Triumphant upon death and their particular judgment?

Not necessarily. In the canonization formula, the Pope states only that the saint is in Heaven. He does not say that he or she passed immediately into Heaven. Theoretically, some candidate for canonization, while having led a life of heroic virtue for an extended period of time, still might have been afflicted with some nagging minor venial sin or sins for which he or she needed to be purified in Purgatory.

Catechism of the Catholic Church: 828, 956, 1023, 1173, 2683

Question 188

Why are there so few canonized saints among the laity ?

The fact that there are very few canonized saints among the laity does not mean that there are necessarily very few laity worthy of canonization. There may, in fact, be thousands in Heaven who led not only exemplary lives while on earth, but who did so heroically, and for extended periods of time.

One of the chief reasons why there are so few canonized lay people is because someone or some group of people must have more than an initial desire to seek the canonization of a prospective lay saint. This desire must be followed through with a great amount of time and perseverance. This fact often discourages people who subsequently give up the pursuit. On the other hand, a holy religious candidate for canonization often enjoys the persistent support of his or her order or institute.

Perhaps more Catholic parishes, lay groups and family organizations should take an active interest in pursuing the canonization of some of their own deceased members. Those who are eventually raised to the Church's altars can serve not only as role models and heroes for the laity, but their intercessory power from Heaven, sought by us on earth, can bring about incalculable good for the Church Militant.

Catechism of the Catholic Church: 825, 901, 2012

Question 189

What is "perfect sorrow" or "perfect contrition"?

Perfect sorrow or contrition consists in a person's sorrow for his sin or sins primarily because he has offended his all-loving and all-merciful God. Perfect contrition remits venial sin. Mortal sins can also be forgiven through perfect contrition as long as the person firmly intends to go to the Sacrament of Confession as soon as possible.

On the other hand, with imperfect contrition, a person expresses sorrow for his sins primarily because he is afraid of God's wrath or of spending an eternity in hell. By itself, imperfect contrition does not obtain forgiveness of mortal sins, but it disposes a person to receive forgiveness in the sacrament of Confession.

Catechism of the Catholic Church: 1450–1454

Family Catechism Commentaries Chart

Francis Cardinal Arinze (in English),
Fr. Pablo Straub (in Spanish)
and Sr. John Vianney (for children, in English)
explain the questions and answers in
The Apostolate's Family Catechism.
Time lengths for each question are shown below.

DVD: #115-93DK
CD: #115-93CK

DVD: #115-B368DK
CD: #115-B368CK

DVD: #115-110DK
CD: #115-180CK

Family Catechism Question	Time Lengths		
	Arinze	Straub	Vianney
Q. 1. Who is God?	01:08	03:58	08:32
Q. 2. Who made God?	02:06	02:37	03:48
Q. 3. Can there be more than one God?	02:37	02:29	
Q. 4. Why must there be a God?	03:20	06:00	
Q. 5. Why is God an infinitely perfect being?	03:51	03:09	03:05
Q. 6. What are God's perfections?	00:30	03:40	02:08
Q. 7. Is God infinitely good?	01:54	11:17	08:49
Q. 8. Is God eternal?	03:22	02:23	02:15
Q. 9. Why is God all-knowing?	04:06	01:45	01:12
Q. 10. Is God present everywhere?	05:15	00:25	03:39
Q. 11. Is God almighty?	01:05	02:41	01:54
Q. 12. Is God all-wise?	00:41	01:07	07:40
Q. 13. Why is God all-holy?	06:15	00:57	02:39
Q. 14. Why is God all-merciful?	01:49	09:42	
Q. 15. Why is God all-just?	04:05	01:50	02:21
Q. 16. In what ways has God shown His love for us?	03:12	01:27	06:15
Q. 17. How should we respond to God's goodness?	01:11	04:45	
Q. 18. In what ways do we worship God?	05:45	01:45	
Q. 19. What should we hope to receive from the goodness of God?	04:05	02:56	02:11
Q. 20. Why is it that so few people pay attention to God?	03:44	01:04	
Q. 21. Does every man have some desire for God?	01:00	06:39	01:31
Q. 22. What is the history of salvation?	02:10	04:00	
Q. 23. How did God deal with mankind?	02:40	02:02	04:52
Q. 24. How did God choose to show himself to the people of the Old Testament?	03:01	02:43	04:05
Q. 25. What is the mystery of the Holy Trinity?	01:49	04:38	
Q. 26. Why do we believe in the mystery of the Holy Trinity?	01:19	01:29	
Q. 27. How is the mystery of the Holy Trinity revealed in the New Testament?	02:21	00:12	
Q. 28. What did Jesus reveal about Himself?	04:11	00:51	
Q. 29. How was God the Father revealed by Jesus?	04:42	02:10	
Q. 30. How did Jesus reveal the Holy Spirit?	02:51	01:52	

Download the Family Catechism Commentaries for free at www.familyland.org

Family Catechism Commentaries Chart
Francis Cardinal Arinze (in English),
Fr. Pablo Straub (in Spanish)
and Sr. John Vianney (for children, in English)
explain the questions and answers in
The Apostolate's Family Catechism.
Time lengths for each question are shown below.

DVD: #115-93DK
CD: #115-93CK

DVD: #115-B368DK
CD: #115-B368CK

DVD: #115-110DK
CD: #115-180CK

Family Catechism Question	Time Lengths		
	Arinze	Straub	Vianney
Q. 31. What did Jesus teach His disciples about God the Father, God the Son and God the Holy Spirit?	03:31	19:32	
Q. 32. Who is God the Father?	01:15	combined with Q.31	00:50
Q. 33. Who is God the Son?	02:49	combined with Q.31	00:50
Q. 34. Who is God the Holy Spirit?	02:35	combined with Q.31	02:28
Q. 35. In what ways can we honor the Holy Trinity?	03:08	01:38	06:25
Q. 36. What is creation?	05:26	06:43	01:34
Q. 37. Can we know God through created things?	06:01	05:24	03:29
Q. 38. When did the mystery of salvation begin?	00:42	01:06	
Q. 39. Who are the angels?	05:13	02:14	07:18
Q. 40. Who are the devils?	04:41	05:54	
Q. 41. Where are the angels who remained faithful to God?	04:09	01:00	02:38
Q. 42. How was man created?	01:45	03:10	
Q. 43. In what way was man created in the image and likeness of God?	02:22	02:08	06:41
Q. 44. Is the soul directly created by God?	04:49	05:31	01:59
Q. 45. What special gifts did God give to Adam and Eve?	00:44	00:59	04:08
Q. 46. What commandment did God give Adam and Eve?	03:49	06:32	06:13
Q. 47. What was God's first gift leading us to Christ?	03:27	00:22	
Q. 48. What did God's action in the Old Testament reveal and prove to us?	02:03	00:36	
Q. 49. In what event is God's all-powerful action for our salvation especially seen?	02:21	01:02	
Q. 50. How should we regard creation?	00:59	00:37	
Q. 51. How was God especially present in the history of man?	02:53	00:37	
Q. 52. How is God present to us in our own day?	03:37	02:18	01:25
Q. 53. What was the original sin?	01:33	03:24	01:14
Q. 54. Why are all men conceived and born in original sin?	01:00	07:08	06:42
Q. 55. What happens in Baptism?	03:57	03:58	02:33
Q. 56. Was anyone exempt from original sin?	05:22	08:25	01:54
Q. 57. What is actual or personal sin?	01:17	01:52	17:44
Q. 58. When someone commits a personal sin, what happens?	01:29	01:46	
Q. 59. What is mortal sin?	01:32	00:29	10:44
Q. 60. What are the effects of mortal sin?	12:27	09:58	
Q. 61. What is venial sin?	03:13	03:24	

Download the Family Catechism Commentaries for free at www.familyland.org

Family Catechism Commentaries Chart
Francis Cardinal Arinze (in English),
Fr. Pablo Straub (in Spanish)
and Sr. John Vianney (for children, in English)
explain the questions and answers in
The Apostolate's Family Catechism.
Time lengths for each question are shown below.

DVD: #115-93DK
CD: #115-93CK

DVD: #115-B368DK
CD: #115-B368CK

DVD: #115-1
CD: #115-180

Family Catechism Question	Time Lengths		
	Arinze	Straub	Vianney
Q. 62. Under what conditions does a Christian commit a mortal sin?	11:11	04:40	
Q. 63. When is an act right or wrong?	11:53	00:41	
Q. 64. How do we know God's will?	04:26	02:30	
Q. 65. Does God forgive our sins?	01:13	09:25	03:34
Q. 66. How does God draw the sinner to salvation?	05:42	02:17	09:05
Q. 67. How are venial sins forgiven?	04:50	combined with Q.66	
Q. 68. What is a capital sin?	00:23	00:31	
Q. 69. What are the capital sins?	11:33	09:23	
Q. 70. What is temptation?	00:33	05:25	09:01
Q. 71. Where do temptations come from?	06:05	06:10	
Q. 72. Of all of God's works, which is the greatest?	01:57	01:41	
Q. 73. What does the Incarnation mean?	04:20	00:37	06:35
Q. 74. Why did God the Son come into the world?	03:00	09:10	14:37
Q. 75. Is Jesus Christ true God?	07:18	04:49	01:52
Q. 76. How does the Nicene Creed express our faith in Christ's divinity?	03:46	03:08	
Q. 77. Did Jesus say He was God?	08:07	06:24	13:35
Q. 78. During His Passion, did Jesus say He was God?	04:43	01:04	
Q. 79. Does the Catholic Church teach that Jesus is truly God?	02:37	01:13	
Q. 80. Is there any further evidence in the New Testament pointing to Jesus as God?	03:57	04:34	
Q. 81. How does the New Testament portray Jesus?	00:53	01:42	
Q. 82. Is Jesus Christ true man?	02:48	06:44	21:04
Q. 83. In what ways did Jesus show His concern for us?	04:08	04:17	03:11
Q. 84. Why did Jesus Christ become man?	08:00	07:54	
Q. 85. What do we mean when we say that Jesus is our Savior?	01:15	00:47	09:54
Q. 86. Is there any other Savior besides Jesus?	09:01	01:07	07:06
Q. 87. How did Jesus Christ redeem us?	01:23	02:31	08:43
Q. 88. What did the agony and prayer in the garden express?	01:28	06:17	
Q. 89. Why were the sufferings Christ bore for us so severe?	02:47	01:46	22:21
Q. 90. Before His death, what trials did Jesus undergo?	03:48	01:13	
Q. 91. What was Christ's mission on earth?	06:47	01:45	
Q. 92. In what sense do we speak of the necessity of the Passion and death of Jesus?	01:03	04:32	

Download the Family Catechism Commentaries for free at www.familyland.org

Family Catechism Commentaries Chart
Francis Cardinal Arinze (in English),
Fr. Pablo Straub (in Spanish)
and Sr. John Vianney (for children, in English)
explain the questions and answers in
The Apostolate's Family Catechism.
Time lengths for each question are shown below.

DVD: #115-93DK
CD: #115-93CK

DVD: #115-B368DK
CD: #115-B368CK

DVD: #115-110DK
CD: #115-180CK

Family Catechism Question	Time Lengths		
	Arinze	Straub	Vianney
Q. 93. Did Jesus Himself declare that He had to suffer?	02:41	01:27	
Q. 94. What did Jesus suffer upon the Cross?	01:06	03:48	
Q. 95. What are the "seven last words" of Jesus as recorded in the Gospels?	15:10	03:09	
Q. 96. How did Jesus die?	00:31	00:35	
Q. 97. What effects did the Passion of Jesus have?	04:10	00:55	05:43
Q. 98. How did Jesus Christ show the power He has as the Son of God?	01:32	04:22	21:55
Q. 99. Why is the Resurrection of Our Lord so important?	04:21	01:54	
Q.100. Why does the Resurrection of Jesus play a central part in the life of faith?	05:00	06:59	
Q.101. What was the Easter Proclamation?	01:11	00:50	
Q.102. How did Jesus lead His Apostles to faith in His Resurrection?	01:26	04:23	
Q.103. How did the Holy Spirit lead the Apostles towards faith in the Resurrection of Jesus?	06:32	00:55	
Q.104. What does the Church teach about the Resurrection?	04:10	00:43	16:42
Q.105. What does it mean to believe in the bodily Resurrection of Jesus from the dead?	01:06	00:38	
Q.106. What has Jesus Christ done for us through His Resurrection?	06:26	01:27	
Q.107. How does the Risen Jesus help us now?	01:10	03:20	02:19
Q.108. What is the meaning of the Ascension of Christ?	03:11	04:27	06:10
Q.109. What are the two distinctive aspects of the mystery of the Ascension?	04:27	03:44	
Q.110. What has Christ done for us through His Ascension?	03:42	06:39	03:32
Q.111. How is Christ present with the Church?	05:25	02:24	05:54
Q.112. What plan does God have for mankind?	01:29	02:58	07:11
Q.113. Is Jesus Christ the center of all God's saving works?	00:36	02:39	07:04
Q.114. Who is God the Holy Spirit?	01:26	02:18	10:48
Q.115. The Holy Spirit proceeds from the Father and the Son. What is meant by this?	01:03	04:24	
Q.116. What did Jesus Christ say about the Holy Spirit?	01:24	00:55	01:10
Q.117. When did the Holy Spirit descend upon the Church?	02:27	02:18	02:56
Q.118. How does the Holy Spirit carry out Christ's work in the Church?	00:48	02:57	
Q.119. Where is God the Holy Spirit especially present?	07:28	04:24	
Q.120. What does the Holy Spirit accomplish for the Church?	00:46	01:30	00:55
Q.121. Why is the Holy Spirit called the Soul of the Church?	01:16	00:31	02:42

Download the Family Catechism Commentaries for free at www.familyland.org

Family Catechism Commentaries Chart
Francis Cardinal Arinze (in English),
Fr. Pablo Straub (in Spanish)
and Sr. John Vianney (for children, in English)
explain the questions and answers in
The Apostolate's Family Catechism.
Time lengths for each question are shown below.

DVD: #115-93DK
CD: #115-93CK

DVD: #115-B368DK
CD: #115-B368CK

DVD: #115-110DK
CD: #115-180CK

Family Catechism Question	Time Lengths		
	Arinze	Straub	Vianney
Q.122. What is the task of the Holy Spirit in the Church?	03:00	04:31	23:31
Q.123. How should the Holy Spirit be honored?	08:05	00:26	02:03
Q.124. What takes place when a person accepts the Spirit of Christ?	00:34	17:15	15:42
Q.125. What is sanctifying grace?	02:30	combined with Q.124	03:35
Q.126. What does this new life of sanctifying grace do for man?	01:09	combined with Q.124	
Q.127. What does God's gift of grace do for us?	00:54	combined with Q.124	
Q.128. What is actual grace?	04:51	06:54	04:11
Q.129. What does the indwelling of the Holy Spirit do for man?	03:56	02:58	03:25
Q.130. What is our greatest dignity?	01:34	02:06	
Q.131. What are the theological virtues?	01:20	01:29	26:03
Q.132. What is the theological virtue of faith?	01:24	01:53	
Q.133. What is the theological virtue of hope?	02:14	04:19	
Q.134. What is the theological virtue of charity?	06:19	07:38	
Q.135. What are the cardinal virtues?	00:23	02:30	
Q.136. Why are prudence, justice, fortitude, and temperance, called cardinal virtues?	13:07	00:46	09:41
Q.137. What are the seven gifts of the Holy Spirit?	17:07	06:21	12:58
Q.138. What is the Catholic Church?	05:15	01:17	02:21
Q.139. When did Jesus start the Catholic Church?	03:12	02:15	11:51
Q.140. What are some of the basic gifts given by God to the Catholic Church?	02:53	01:23	12:16
Q.141. What are the two sources of divine truth which constitue the truths of Faith?	19:05	03:43	20:39
Q.142. What are some other gifts of the Catholic Church besides the truths of the Faith?	01:12	01:00	
Q.143. Are there other gifts of the Church besides the truths of the faith and the sacraments?	01:29	combined with Q.142	11:02
Q.144. By means of these gifts, what does the Catholic Church do for mankind?	01:39	02:58	
Q.145. Why does the Catholic Church belong entirely to Christ?	04:03	03:02	
Q.146. How does the Catholic see the Church?	02:19	01:42	
Q.147. Why is the Catholic Church a living continuation of Christ on earth?	07:42	00:29	03:22

Download the Family Catechism Commentaries for free at www.familyland.org

Family Catechism Commentaries Chart
Francis Cardinal Arinze (in English),
Fr. Pablo Straub (in Spanish)
and Sr. John Vianney (for children, in English)
explain the questions and answers in
The Apostolate's Family Catechism.
Time lengths for each question are shown below.

DVD: #115-93DK
CD: #115-93CK

DVD: #115-B368DK
CD: #115-B368CK

DVD: #115-110DK
CD: #115-180CK

Family Catechism Question	Time Lengths		
	Arinze	Straub	Vianney
Q.148. Why is the Catholic Church called the sacrament of Christ?	01:19	5:16	01:56
Q.149. What do we mean when we speak of the Church in heaven?	12:51	01:31	
Q.150. Does the Catholic Church have leaders?	01:27	00:57	02:02
Q.151. Who is the Holy Father, the Pope?	06:18	03:56	01:56
Q.152. Who are the bishops of the Church?	02:40	03:09	01:37
Q.153. What are the chief responsibilities of the Pope and bishops of the Catholic Church?	02:08	00:59	02:46
Q.154. Who directs Christ's work in the Catholic Church?	02:41	01:30	
Q.155. What is owed to the Pope and bishops by the faithful?	01:30	03:55	02:27
Q.156. Why is respect owed to everyone in the Church?	02:51	03:36	11:45
Q.157. Why is the Catholic Church a community?	01:38	00:25	06:54
Q.158. Is everyone in the Church equal?	01:39	03:57	03:20
Q.159. Who in the Church is called to a life of holiness?	03:58	03:10	05:03
Q.160. Why is the Catholic Church essentially missionary?	04:05	04:40	01:51
Q.161. What is the role of the Church in the world?	03:46	02:00	00:51
Q.162. How does the Catholic Church minister to our spiritual needs?	00:50	02:39	
Q.163. How does the Catholic Church minister to the bodily needs of people?	03:26	02:54	
Q.164. How can we help unbelievers find God?	01:38	02:37	
Q.165. What is our duty towards the world?	00:38	02:09	
Q.166. Why is the unity of Christians in faith and love God's Will?	01:39	01:06	
Q.167. How is Christian unity promoted by Catholics?	04:01	05:22	
Q.168. Why should we respect all men of good will?	03:26	01:08	
Q.169. What do we believe about the Catholic Church and salvation?	02:23	02:04	
Q.170. How do the laity share in Christ's mission?	05:31	09:54	
Q.171. How is the Catholic Church an institution of salvation?	00:53	01:20	
Q.172. What are the marks that point out the true Church founded by Jesus?	08:24	01:15	06:46
Q.173. Why is the Catholic Church one?	00:13	01:33	
Q.174. How did Jesus indicate that His Church is one?	00:46	00:39	
Q.175. Why are we united by a spiritual leader?	01:02	00:19	01:44
Q.176. Why are we united in worship?	01:16	01:34	
Q.177. Why is the Catholic Church holy?	01:06	16:11	
Q.178. Why is the Church catholic or universal?	00:54	03:57	

Download the Family Catechism Commentaries for free at www.familyland.org

Family Catechism Commentaries Chart
Francis Cardinal Arinze (in English),
Fr. Pablo Straub (in Spanish)
and Sr. John Vianney (for children, in English)
explain the questions and answers in
The Apostolate's Family Catechism.
Time lengths for each question are shown below.

DVD: #115-93DK
CD: #115-93CK

DVD: #115-B368DK
CD: #115-B368CK

DVD: #115-110DK
CD: #115-180CK

Family Catechism Question	Time Lengths		
	Arinze	Straub	Vianney
Q.179. How long has the Catholic Church been in existence?	01:44	03:52	
Q.180. Does the Catholic Church teach all the truths that Jesus Christ taught?	01:31	05:39	05:05
Q.181. Why is the Catholic Church apostolic?	03:19	04:30	04:24
Q.182. What do we mean when we say, "I Believe in the Communion of Saints" ?	02:07	03:39	02:38
Q.183. Why is the Church called the Church Militant?	03:45	00:48	01:38
Q.184. How do we help each other?	01:16	01:14	01:16
Q.185. What is the Church Suffering?	01:17	02:40	08:00
Q.186. What is our duty toward the deceased?	06:13	02:23	04:43
Q.187. What is the Church Triumphant?	01:34	01:38	01:27
Q.188. Why does the Church honor the canonized saints?	00:34	03:27	12:52
Q.189. What do we mean when we say, "I believe in the forgiveness of sins"?	01:56	00:31	

#S2-258

APPENDIX D

Illustration Index

APPENDIX E

Catechism of the Catholic Church Endnotes

Chapter One

CCC 300
1. *Ps* 8:2; cf. *Sir* 43:28
2. *Ps* 145:3
3. *Acts* 17:28
4. St. Augustine, *Conf.* 3, 6, 11: PL 32, 688

CCC 34
1. St. Thomas Aquinas, *STh* I, 2, 3

Chapter Two

CCC 41
1. *Wis* 13:15

CCC 34
1. *Wis* 13:15

CCC 221
1. *1 Jn* 4:8,16
2. Cf. *1 Cor* 2:7-16; *Eph* 3:9-12

CCC 207
1. *Ex* 3:6, 12

CCC 216
1. Cf. *Wis* 13:19
2. Cf. *Ps* 115:15; *Wis* 7:17-21

CCC 268
1. Cf. *Gen* 1:1; *Jn* 1:3; *Mt* 6:9; 2 *Cor* 12:9; cf. 1 *Cor* 1:18

Chapter Three

CCC 295
1. Cf. *Wis* 9:9
2. *Rev* 4:11
3. *Ps* 104:24; 145:9

CCC 1608
1. Cf. *Gen* 3:21

CCC 1040
1. Cf. *Song* 8:6

Chapter Four

CCC 609
1. *Jn* 13:1; 15:13
2. Cf. *Heb* 2:10, 17-18; 4:15; 5:7-9
3. *Jn* 10:18
4. Cf. *Jn* 18:4-6; *Mt* 26:53

CCC 1378
1. Paul VI, *MF* 56

CCC 2113
1. *Mt* 6:24
2. Cf. *Rev* 13-14
3. Cf. *Gal* 5:20; *Eph* 5:5

CCC 27
1. Vatican Council II, *GS* 19 § 1

Chapter Five

CCC 763
1. Cf. *LG* 3; *AG* 3
2. *LG* 5
3. *LG* 3

CCC 50
1. Cf. *Dei Filius*: DS 3015

CCC 201
1. *Deut* 6:4-5
2. *Isa* 45:22-24; cf. *Phil* 2:10-11

Chapter Six

CCC 253
1. Council of Constantinople II (553): DS 421
2. Council of Toledo XI (675): DS 530:26
3. Lateran Council IV (1215) DS 804

CCC 234
1. *GCD 43*
2. *GCD 47*

CCC 243
1. Cf. *Gen* 1:2; Nicene Creed (DS 150); *Jn* 14:17, 26; 16:13

CCC 443
1. *Lk* 22:70; cf. *Mt* 26:64; *Mk* 14:61-62
2. *Mt* 11:27; 21:34-38; 24:36
3. *Mt* 5:48; 6:8-9; 7:21; *Lk* 11:13; *Jn* 20:17

CCC 240
1. *Mt* 11:27

CCC 728
1. Cf. *Jn* 6:27, 51, 62-63
2. Cf. *Jn* 3:5-8
3. Cf. *Jn* 4:10, 14, 23-24
4. Cf. *Jn* 7:37-39
5. Cf. *Lk* 11:13
6. Cf. *Mt* 10:19-20

Chapter Seven

CCC 270
1. *2 Cor* 6:18; cf. *Mt* 6:32

CCC 444
1. Cf. *Mt* 3:17; cf. *Mt* 17:5
2. *Jn* 3:16; cf. 10:36
3. *Jn* 3:18
4. *Mk* 15:39

CCC 689
1. Cf. *Gal* 4:6

Chapter Eight

CCC 320
1. *Heb* 1:3

Chapter Nine

CCC 288
1. Cf. *Gen* 15:5; Jer 33:19-26
2. Cf. *Isa* 44:24; *Ps* 104; *Prov* 8:22-31

CCC 336
1. Cf. *Mt* 18:10; *Lk* 16:22; *Ps* 34:7; 91:10-13; *Job* 33:23-24; *Zech* 1:12; *Tob* 12:12
2. St. Basil, *Adv. Eunomium* III, 1: PG 29, 656B

CCC 391
1. Cf. *Gen* 3:1-5; *Wis* 2:24
2. Cf. *Jn* 8:44; *Rev* 12:9
3. Lateran Council IV (1215):DS 800

CCC 329
1. St. Augustine, *En in Ps.* 103, 1, 15: PL 37, 1348
2. *Mt* 18:10; *Ps* 103:20

Chapter Ten

CCC 364
1. Cf. *1 Cor* 6:19-20; 15:44-45

CCC 356
1. *GS* 12 § 3
2. *GS* 24 § 3

CCC 366
1. Cf. Pius XII, *Humani Generis*: DS 3896; Paul VI, *CPG* § 8; Lateran Council V (1513): DS 1440

CCC 1703
1. *GS* 14 § 2.
2. *GS* 24 § 3.

CCC 2270
1. Cf. CDF, *Donum Vitae* I, 1.

Chapter Eleven

CCC 396
1. *Gen* 2:17
2. *Gen* 2:17

Chapter Twelve

CCC 62
1. Cf. *DV* 3

CCC 648
1. *Rom* 1:3-4; cf. *Acts* 2:24
2. Cf. *Rom* 6:4; 2 *Cor* 13:4; *Phil* 3:10; *Eph* 1:19-22; *Heb* 7:16

CCC 280
1. *GCD* 51
2. *Gen* 1:1; cf. *Rom* 8:18-23

CCC 219
1. *Jn* 3:16; cf. *Hos* 11:1; *Isa* 49:14-15; 62:4-5; *Ezek* 16; *Hos* 11

CCC 769
1. *LG* 48
2. St. Augustine, *De civ. Dei*, 18, 51: PL 41, 614; cf. *LG* 8
3. *LG* 5; cf. 6; *2 Cor* 5:6
4. *LG* 2

Chapter Thirteen

CCC 397
1. Cf. *Gen* 3:1-11; *Rom* 5:19

CCC 404
1. St. Thomas Aquinas, *De Malo* 4, 1
2. Cf. Council of Trent: DS 1511-1512

CCC 1263
1. Cf. Council of Florence (1439): DS 1316

CCC 491
1. *Lk* 1:28
2. Pius IX, *Ineffabilis Deus*, 1854: DS 2803

Chapter Fourteen

CCC 1850
1. *Ps* 51:4
2. *Gen* 3:5
3. St. Augustine, *De civ. Dei* 14, 28 : PL 41, 436
4. Cf. *Phil* 2:6-9

CCC 1440
1. Cf. *LG* 11

Chapter Fifteen

CCC 1858
1. *Mk* 10:19

Chapter Sixteen

CCC 208
1. Cf. *Ex* 3:5-6
2. *Isa* 6:5
3. *Lk* 5:8
4. *Hos* 11:9
5. *1 Jn* 3:19-20

CCC 605
1. *Mt* 18:14
2. *Mt* 20:28; cf. *Rom* 5:18-19
3. Council of Quiercy (853): DS 624; cf. *2 Cor* 5:15; *1 Jn* 2:2

CCC 1394
1. Cf. Council of Trent (1551): DS 1638

Chapter Seventeen
CCC 1866
1. Cf. St. Gregory the Great, *Moralia in Job*, 31, 45: PL 76, 621A

Chapter Eighteen
CCC 2847
1. Cf. *Lk* 8:13-15; *Acts* 14:22; *Rom* 5:3-5; *2 Tim* 3:12
2. Cf. *Jas* 1:14-15
3. Cf. *Gen* 3:6

Chapter Nineteen
CCC 461
1. *Jn* 1:14
2. *Phil* 2:5-8; cf *LH*, Saturday, Canticle at Evening Prayer

CCC 463
1. *1 Jn* 4:2
2. *1 Tim* 3:16

CCC 744
1. *Mt* 1:23.

CCC 458
1. *1 Jn* 4:9
2. *Jn* 3:16

Chapter Twenty
CCC 468
1. Council of Constantinople II (553): DS 424
2. Council of Constantinople II (553) DS 432; cf. DS 424; Council of Ephesus, DS 255

CCC 242
1. The English phrases "of one being" and "one in being" translate the Greek word *homoousios*, which was rendered in Latin by *consubstantialis*
2. Niceno-Constantinopolitan Creed; cf. DS 150

CCC 589
1. Cf. *Mt* 9:13; *Hos* 6:6
2. Cf. *Lk* 15:1-2, 22-32
3. *Mk* 2:7
4. Cf. *Jn* 5:18; 10:33; 17:6, 26

CCC 591
1. *Jn* 10:36-38
2. Cf. *Jn* 3:7; 6:44
3. Cf. *Isa* 53:1
4. Cf. *Mk* 3:6; *Mt* 26:64-66
5. Cf. *Lk* 23:34; *Acts* 3:17-18; *Mk* 3:5; *Rom* 11:25, 20

CCC 448
1. Cf. *Mt* 8:2; 14:30; 15:22; *et al*
2. Cf. *Lk* 1:43; 2:11
3. *Jn* 20:28; *Jn* 21:7

CCC 449
1. Cf. *Acts* 2:34-36; *Rom* 9:5; *Titus* 2:13; *Rev* 5:13; *Phil* 2:6 Cf. *Rom* 10:9; *1 Cor* 12:3; *Phil* 2:9-11

CCC 151
1. *Mk* 1:11; cf. 9:7
2. *Jn* 14:1
3. *Jn* 1:18
4. *Jn* 6:46; cf. *Mt* 11:27

Chapter Twenty-one
CCC 475
1. Council of Constantinople III (681): DS 556-559
2. Council of Constantinople III: DS 556

CCC 607
1. Cf. *Lk* 12:50; 22:15; *Mt* 16:21-23
2. *Jn* 12:27
3. *Jn* 18:11
4. *Jn* 19:30; 19:28

Chapter Twenty-two
CCC 608
1. *Jn* 1:29; cf. *Lk* 3:21; *Mt* 3:14-15; *Jn* 1:36
2. *Isa* 53:7, 12; cf. *Jer* 11:19; *Ex* 12:3-14; *Jn* 19:36; *1 Cor* 5:7
3. *Mk* 10:45

CCC 549
1. Cf. *Jn* 6:5-15; *Lk* 19:8; *Mt* 11:5
2. Cf. *Lk* 12:13-14; *Jn* 18:36
3. Cf. *Jn* 8:34-36

CCC 430
1. Cf. *Lk* 1:31
2. *Mt* 1:21; cf. 2:7

CCC 561
1. John Paul II, CT 9

Chapter Twenty-three
CCC 612
1. Cf. *Mt* 26:42; *Lk* 22:20
2. *Phil* 2:8; *Mt* 26:39; cf. *Heb* 5:7-8
3. Cf. *Rom* 5:12; *Heb* 4:15
4. Cf. *Acts* 3:15; *Rev* 1:17; *Jn* 1:4; 5:26
5. *1 Pet* 2:24; cf. *Mt* 26:42

CCC 1851
1. Cf. *Jn* 14:30

Chapter Twenty-four
CCC 574
1. Cf. *Mk* 3:6; 14:1
2. Cf. *Mt* 12:24; *Mk* 2:7, 14-17; 3:1-6; 7:14-23
3. Cf. *Mk* 3:22; *Jn* 8:48; 10:20
4. Cf. *Mk* 2:7; *Jn* 5:18; *Jn* 7:12; 7:52; 8:59; 10:31; 33

CCC 457
1. *1 Jn* 4:10; 4:14; 3:5
2. St. Gregory of Nyssa, *Orat catech.* 15: PG 45, 48B

CCC 599
1. *Acts* 2:23
2. Cf. *Acts* 3:13

CCC 606
1. *Jn* 6:38
2. *Heb* 10:5-10
3. *Jn* 4:34
4. *1 Jn* 2:2
5. *Jn* 10:17; 14:31

Chapter Twenty-five
CCC 603
1. Cf. *Jn* 8:46
2. *Mk* 15:34; *Ps* 22:2; cf. *Jn* 8:29
3. *Rom* 8:32, 5:10

CCC 618
1. *1 Tim* 2:5
2. *GS* 22 § 5; cf. § 2
3. *Mt* 16:24
4. *1 Pet* 2:21
5. Cf. *Mk* 10:39; *Jn* 21:18-19; *Col* 1:24
6. Cf. *Lk* 2:35
7. St. Rose of Lima, cf. P. Hansen, *Vita mirabilis* (Louvain, 1668)

Chapter Twenty-six
CCC 445
1. *Rom* 1:3; cf. *Acts* 13:33
2. *Jn* 1:14

CCC 653
1. *Jn* 8:28
2. *Acts* 13:32-34; cf. *Ps* 2:7

CCC 638
1. *Acts* 13:32-33
2. Byzantine Liturgy, Troparion of Easter

CCC 640
1. *Lk* 24:5-6
2. Cf. *Jn* 20:13; *Mt* 28:11-15
3. Cf. *Lk* 24:3, 12, 22-23
4. *Jn* 20:2, 6, 8
5. Cf. *Jn* 11:44; 20:5-7

Chapter Twenty-seven
CCC 642
1. *1 Cor* 15:4-8; cf. *Acts* 1:22

CCC 644
1. *1 Lk* 24:38-41
2. Cf. *Jn* 20:24-27; *Mt* 28:17

Chapter Twenty-eight
CCC 648
1. *Rom* 1:3-4; cf. *Acts* 2:24
2. Cf. *Rom* 6:4; *2 Cor* 13:4; *Phil* 3:10; *Eph* 1:19-22; *Heb* 7:16

CCC 654
1. *Rom* 6:4; cf. 4:25
2. Cf. *Eph* 2:45; *1 Pet* 1:3
3. *Mt* 28:10; *Jn* 20:17

Chapter Twenty-nine
CCC 995
1. *Acts* 1:22; 10:41; cf. 4:33

Chapter Thirty
CCC 659
1. *Mk* 16:19
2. Cf. *Lk* 24:31; *Jn* 20:19, 26
3. Cf. *Acts* 1:3; 10:41; *Mk* 16:12; *Lk* 24:15; *Jn* 20: 14-15; 21:4
4. Cf. *Acts* 1:9; 2:33; 7:56; *Lk* 9:34-35; 24:51; *Ex* 13:22; *Mk* 16:19; *Ps* 110:1
5. *1 Cor* 15:8; cf. 9:1; *Gal* 1:16

CCC 788
1. Cf. *Jn* 14:18; 20:22; *Mt* 28:20; *Acts* 2:33
2. *LG* 7

CCC 737
1. *Jn* 15:8, 16

Chapter Thirty-one
CCC 436
1. Cf. *Ex* 29:7; *Lev* 8:12; *1 Sam* 9:16; 10:1; 16:1,12-13; *1 Kings* 1:39; 19:16
2. Cf. *Ps* 2:2; *Acts* 4:26-27
3. Cf. *Isa* 11:2; 61:1; *Zech* 4:14; 6:13; *Lk* 4:16-21

CCC 1066
1. *Eph* 1:9
2. *Eph* 3:9; cf. 3:4

CCC 2074
1. *Jn* 15:5
2. *Jn* 15:12

Chapter Thirty-two
CCC 684
1. *Jn* 17:3
2. St. Gregory of Nazianzus, *Oratio theol.* 5, 26 (=*Oratio* 31, 26): PG 36, 161-163

CCC 248
1. *Jn* 15:26; cf. *AG* 2
2. Council of Florence (1439): DS 1302
3. Council of Florence (1442): DS 1331
4. Cf. Council of Lyons II (1274): DS 850

CCC 729
1. Cf. *Jn* 14:16-17, 26; 15:26; 16:7-15; 17:26

Chapter Thirty-three
CCC 731
1. Cf. *Acts* 2:33-36

CCC 243
1. Cf. *Gen* 1:2; Nicene Creed (DS 150); *Jn* 14:17, 26; 16:13

CCC 749
1. *Roman Catechism* I, 10, 1
2. St. Hippolytus, *Trad. Ap.* 35: SCh 11, 118

CCC 976
1. *Jn* 20:22-23

CCC 797
1. St. Augustine, *Sermo* 267, 4: PL 38, 1231D
2. Pius XII, encyclical, *Mystici Corporis*: DS 3808
3. *2 Cor* 6:16; cf. *1 Cor* 3:16-17; *Eph* 2:21
3. St. Irenaeus, *Adv. haeres.* 3, 24, 1: PG 7/1, 966

CCC 737
1. Jn 15:8, 16

CCC 1989
1. *Mt* 4:17
2. Council of Trent (1547): DS 1528

Chapter Thirty-four

CCC 685
1. Nicene Creed; see above, par 465

Chapter Thirty-five

CCC 1966
1. St. Augustine, *De serm. Dom.* 1, 1: PL 34, 1229-1230

CCC 2003
1. Cf. *LG* 12
2. Cf. *1 Cor* 12

Chapter Thirty-seven

CCC 736
1. *Gal* 5:22-23
2. *Gal* 5:25, cf. *Mt* 16:24-26
3. St. Basil, *De Spiritu Sancto*, 15, 36: PG 32, 132

CCC 1803
1. *Phil* 4:8
2. St. Gregory of Nyssa, *De beatitudinibus*, 1: PG 44, 1200D

CCC 1700
1. *Lk* 15:11-32

CCC 1711
1. GS 15 § 2

Chapter Thirty-eight

CCC 1813
1. Cf. *1 Cor* 13:3

CCC 1816
1. *LG* 42; cf. *DH* 14
2. *Mt* 10:32-33

CCC 181
1. St. Cyprian, *De unit.* 6: PL 4, 519

CCC 1817
1. *Heb* 10:23
2. *Titus* 3:6-7

CCC 1823
1. Cf. *Jn* 13:34
2. *Jn* 13:1
3. *Jn* 15:9, 12

CCC 1827
1. *Col* 3:14

Chapter Forty-one

CCC 751
1. Cf. *Acts* 19:39
2. Cf. *Ex* 19.

CCC 839
1. *LG* 16.
2. Cf. *NA* 4.
3. *Roman Missal*, Good Friday 13: General Intercessions, VI.
4. *Rom* 9:4-5.
5. *Rom* 11:29.

CCC 778
1. Cf. *Rev* 14:4.

Chapter Forty-two

CCC 81
1. *DV* 9.
2. *DV* 9.

Chapter Forty-three

CCC 864
1. *AA* 4; cf. *Jn* 15:5.
2. *AA* 3.

CCC 775
1. *LG* 1.
2. *Rev* 7:9.

Chapter Forty-four

CCC 876
1. Cf. *Rom* 1:1.
2. *Phil* 2:7.
3. Cf. *1 Cor* 9:19.

CCC 881
1. Cf. *Mt* 16:18-19; *Jn* 21:15-17.
2. *LG* 22 § 2

CCC 862
1. *LG* 20 § 2.
2. *LG* 20 § 2.

CCC 894
1. *LG* 27; cf. *Lk* 22:26-27.

Chapter Forty-five

CCC 1900
1. Cf. as early as *1 Tim* 2:1-2.
2. St. Clement of Rome, *Ad Cor.* 61: SCh 167, 198-200.

CCC 1935
1. *GS* 29 § 2.

CCC 2013
1. *LG* 40 § 2.
2. *Mt.* 5:48.
3 *LG* 40 § 2.

Chapter Forty-six

CCC 863
1. *AA* 2.

CCC 905
1. *LG* 35 § 1, § 2.
2. *AA* 6 § 3; cf. *AG* 15.

CCC 2044
1. *AA* 6 § 2.

CCC 798
1. Pius XII, encyclical, *Mystici Corporis*: DS 3808.
2. Cf. *Eph.* 4:16.
3. *Acts* 20:32.
4. Cf. *1 Cor* 12:13.
5. *LG* 7 § 2.
6. *LG* 12 § 2; cf. *AA* 3.

CCC 786
1. Cf. *Jn* 12:32
2. *Mt.* 20:28.
3. *LG* 8; cf. 36.
4. St. Leo the Great, *Sermo* 4, 1: PL 54, 149.

CCC 851
1. *2 Cor* 5:14; cf. *AA* 6; *RMiss* 11.
2. *1 Tim* 2:4.

CCC 2426
1. Cf. *GS* 64.

CCC 2427
1. Cf. *Gen* 1:28; *GS* 34; *CA* 31.
2. *2 Thess* 3:10; cf. *1 Thess* 4:11.
3. Cf. *Gen* 3:14-19.
4. Cf. *LE* 27.

Chapter Forty-seven

CCC 815
1. *Col* 3:14.
2. Cf. *UR* 2; *LG* 14; CIC, can. 205.

CCC 822
1. *UR* 5.
2. *UR* 24 § 2.

CCC 1930
1. Cf. John XXIII, *PT* 65.

Chapter Forty-eight

CCC 846
1. Cf. Cyprian, *Ep.* 73.21: PL 3, 1169; *De unit.*: PL 4, 509-536.
2. *LG* 14; cf. *Mk* 16:16; *Jn* 3:5.

CCC 847
1. *LG* 16; cf. DS 3866-3872.

CCC 900
1. Cf. *LG* 33.

CCC 849
1. *AG* 1; cf. *Mt* 16:15.
2. *Mt* 28:19-20

Chapter Forty-nine

CCC 865
1. *Rev* 19:6.
2. *Eph* 1:4.
3. *Rev* 21:9
4. *Rev* 21:10-11
5. *Rev* 21:14

CCC 815
1. *Col* 3:14.
2. Cf. *UR* 2; *LG* 14; CIC, can. 205.

CCC 820
1. *UR* 4 § 3.
2. *Jn* 17:21; cf. *Heb* 7:25.
3. Cf. *UR* 1.

CCC 553
1. *Mt* 16:19
2. *Jn* 21:15-17; cf. 10:11.
3. Cf. *Mt* 18:18.

CCC 1108
1. Cf. *Jn* 15:1-17; *Gal* 5:22.
2. Cf. *1 Jn* 1:3-7.

Chapter Fifty

CCC 824
1. *SC* 10.
2. *UR* 3 § 5.
3. *LG* 48.

Chapter Fifty-one

CCC 1202
1. *2 Tim* 1:14 (Vulg.).
2. Cf. *LG* 23; *UR* 4.

CCC 766
1. *LG* 3; cf. *Jn* 19:34.
2. *SC* 5.
3. Cf. St. Ambrose, *In Luc.* 2, 85-89: PL 15, 1666-1668.

CCC 77
1. *DV* 7 § 2; St. Irenaeus, *Adv. haeres.* 3, 3, 1: PG 7, 848; Harvey, 2, 9.
2. *DV* 8 § 1.

Chapter Fifty-two

CCC 858
1. *Mk* 3:13-14.
2. *Jn* 20:21; cf. 13:20; 17:18.
3. *Mt* 10:40; cf. *Lk* 10:16.

Chapter Fifty-three

CCC 946
1. Nicetas, *Expl. symb.* 10: PL: 52:871B.

CCC 827
1. *LG* 8 §3; cf. *UR* 3; 6; *Heb* 2:17; 7:26; *2 Cor* 5:21.
2. Cf. *1 Jn* 1:8-10.
3. Cf. *Mt* 13:24-30.
4. Paul VI, *CPG* § 19.

CCC 2634
1. Cf. *Rom* 8:34; *1 Jn* 2:1; *1 Tim* 2:5-8.
2. *Heb* 7:25.
3. *Rom* 8:26-27.

CCC 1031
1. Cf. Council of Florence (1439): DS 1304; Council of Trent (1563): DS 1820; (1547): 1580; see also Benedict XII, *Benedictus Deus* (1336): DS 1000.
2. Cf. *1 Cor* 3:15; *1 Pet* 1:7.

CCC 1032
1. *2 Macc* 12:46.
2. Cf. Council of Lyons II (1274): DS 856.
3. St. John Chrysostom, *Hom. in 1 Cor.* 41, 5: PG 61, 361; cf. *Job* 1:5.

CCC 1023
1. *1 Jn* 3:2; cf. *1 Cor* 13:12; *Rev* 22:4.
2. Benedict XII, *Benedictus Deus* (1336):
DS 1000; cf. LG 49.

CCC 956
1. *LG* 49; cf. *1 Tim* 2:5.

Chapter Fifty-four

CCC 987
1. *Roman Catechism*, I, 11, 6.

Abbreviations:

AA	*Apostolicam actuositatem*
AAS	*Acta Apostolicae Sedis*
AG	*Ad gentes*
CA	*Centesimus annus*
CCEO	Corpus Canonum Ecclesiarum Orientalium
CD	*Christus Dominus*
CIC	Codex Iuris Canonici
CPG	*Solemn Profession of Faith:* Credo of the People of God
CT	*Catechesi tradendae*
DH	*Dignitatis humanae*
DS	Denzinger-Schönmetzer, *Enchiridion Symbolorum, definitionum et declarationum de rebus fidei et morum* (1965)
DV	*Dei Verbum*
FC	*Familiaris consortio*
GCD	*General Catechetical Directory*
GS	*Gaudium et spes*
HV	*Humanae vitae*
LE	*Laborem exercens*
LG	*Lumen gentium*
LH	*Liturgy of the Hours*
MF	*Mysterium fidei*
NA	*Nostra aetate*
OC	*Ordo confirmationis*
OP	*Ordo paenitentiae*
PG	J.P. Migne, ed., Patrologia Graeca (Paris, 1857-1866)
PL	J.P. Migne, ed., Patrologia Latina (Paris: 1841-1855)
PO	*Presbyterorum ordinis*
PT	*Pacem in terris*
SC	*Sacrosanctum concilium*
SCh	Sources Chrétiennes (Paris:1942-)
STh	Summa Theologiae
UR	*Unitatis redintegratio*